HUMAN SOCIETIES

An Introduction to
Macrosociology

The cover of this book reflects the revolutionary transformation of human societies brought about by modern industrial technology, farmers plowing in a field beside a modern coke plant in Poland's coal and steel region at Katowice.

FIFTH EDITION

HUMAN SOCIETIES

An Introduction to
Macrosociology

Gerhard Lenski

Jean Lenski

McGraw-Hill Book Company

New York St. Louis San Francisco Auckland
Bogotá Hamburg Johannesburg London Madrid
Mexico Milan Montreal New Delhi Panama
Paris São Paulo Singapore Sydney Tokyo Toronto

ISBN 0-07-037181-4

This book was set in Optima by Better Graphics, (ECU). The editors were Barbara L. Raab and James R. Belser; the cover was designed by Anne Canevari Green; the production supervisor was Leroy A. Young. New drawings were done by Danmark & Michaels, Inc.
R. R. Donnelley & Sons Company was printer and binder.

Cover photo by James P. Blair © 1972 National Geographic Society.
See Picture Credits on pages 470–472.
Copyrights included on this page by reference.

Lenski, Gerhard Emmanuel.
    Human societies.

    Bibliography: p.
    Includes indexes.
    1. Sociology. 2. Social evolution. 3. Social systems—History. I. Lenski, Jean. Title.
HM51.L357 1987   301   86-10586
ISBN 0-07-037181-4

For Our Children—And Theirs

ABOUT THE AUTHORS

Gerhard Lenski is Alumni Distinguished Professor of Sociology at the University of North Carolina at Chapel Hill. He is also author of *The Religious Factor*, *Power and Privilege*, and numerous articles. He has served as vice president of the American Sociological Association and president and vice president of the Southern Sociological Society. He is a Fellow of the American Academy of Arts and Sciences and a former Guggenheim Fellow, IREX Senior Faculty Exchange Fellow, and Senior Faculty Fellow of the Social Science Research Council. Jean Lenski is a writer, poet, and mother of four who collaborated in the writing of *Power and Privilege* and has coauthored the five editions of *Human Societies*.

CONTENTS

PART II: PREINDUSTRIAL SOCIETIES

Inside Back Cover: Map of Industrial and Industrializing Societies Mentioned in Text

PREFACE

This volume differs from most other introductory texts in sociology. It is not an institutional survey of contemporary American society, nor is it an attempt to summarize in encyclopedic fashion all the various specialties that have developed in our discipline. Instead, it is a comparative and historical analysis of human societies, the largest, most powerful, and most important social systems humans have created. The basic structure of the analysis is simple enough to be grasped by any student, yet the multilayered nature of the theory that guides the analysis can challenge the best of students.

The theory that provides the organizing framework for this volume is both ecological and evolutionary in nature. In other words, it is concerned with the relations of societies to their environments and with the relations of the parts of these social systems to one another, and it is also concerned with the process of change in societies. The latter is especially important for students who can expect to live well into the twenty-first century.

This volume is the fifth edition of *Human Societies*. As authors, we have been extremely pleased with the reception accorded previous editions by both students and instructors. We have been especially pleased with the opportunity that each new edition has provided for refinements in both the underlying theory and its presentation. We hope that this new edition lives up to the standards of its predecessors.

Changes in the Fifth Edition

No chapter is entirely the same in the present edition as in the last. In some chapters, the changes are largely stylistic and not very important; in others, the changes are substantive and very important. The substantive changes are chiefly in Parts I and III. They are all mentioned in the *Instructor's Manual* (available from the publisher), but the more important of them are noted here as well.

The opening pages of Chapter 1 have been completely rewritten and we hope that this new introduction will orient students effectively to what lies ahead. Some changes have also been made in the discussion of evolution in the section on characteristics that humans share with all other species and in the discussion of our species' common genetic heritage.

Chapter 2 has been reorganized in part, with the discussion of systems moved from the beginning of the chapter to the end (where it more properly belongs). Also, the discussion of institutions and institutional systems has been integrated into the analysis in a more effective way.

Chapter 3 has been completely reorganized in a way that highlights more effectively the distinction between the evolutionary process as it operates in individual societies and as it operates at the level of the world system of societies. A key aspect of the change is our discussion of what we refer to as "the great paradox."

In Chapter 4, we have added two important new sections. The first deals with the relation between societal types and the environment while the second contains a discussion of the nature of societal types (what they are and what they are not).

The most important changes in Part II are both in Chapter 6. The opening pages have been rewritten to bring the explanation of the shift from hunting and gathering to horticulture more closely into line with the evidence from recent research. In addition, we have added an Excursus at the end of Chapter 6. This offers a critical look at racialist theory from an ecological and evolutionary perspective. In Chapter 7, we have added a brief diversion in our boxed insert entitled "Mother Goose Revisited." We hope that this will help students to discover something new and unsuspected in something old and familiar.

Chapter 9 has been partly reorganized and the discussion of the causes of the continuing Industrial Revolution has been largely rewritten. Chapter 10 has been substantially rewritten. The material on the new secular ideologies is especially important and instructors who have used previous editions of this book are urged to take special note of the changes here.

Chapter 11 has also been substantially rewritten. A number of the changes in this chapter provide a follow-up to the new materials on ideology introduced in Chapter 10. In the section on stratification, there is greater attention now to power and the control of the economic surplus, including a comparison of the western industrial democracies with the Marxist-Leninist societies of Eastern Europe. There is also more attention given to the distribution of income and wealth in industrial societies in this new edition.

There are two important changes in Chapter 12. The material on the mass media has been completely rewritten, and a new unit has been added at the end of the chapter appraising the relevance for sociological theory of the tremendously important social experiments conducted in Eastern Europe in recent decades by Marxist-Leninist elites.

All of the materials in Part III have been updated wherever possible. The updating involves not merely the use of newer statistical materials, but more importantly the incorporation into the analysis of new developments of many kinds. For example, in Chapter 13 we take note of the new pragmatism in China and discuss its implications for other Third World societies.

We hope that all the many changes prove to be improvements, and we eagerly await the reactions and judgments of instructors who have worked with previous editions and can compare the present edition with them. As we have said before, we welcome all reactions, suggestions, and criticisms from students and instructors alike. We have benefited greatly from them in the past and will, we feel sure, continue to benefit from them.

We remind those of you who have used previous editions of *Human Societies* that an instructor's manual is available for the asking from the McGraw-Hill Book Company. This manual has been revised with each new edition of the text. We especially encourage those who are using the book for the first time to obtain a copy, since it provides numerous suggestions for class discussions, projects, films, and exams.

Acknowledgments

It is not possible to acknowledge adequately all our many intellectual debts in the brief space available here. But many who read this volume will recognize our debt to Thomas Malthus, Charles Darwin, Herbert Spencer, Karl Marx, Max Weber, Thorstein Veblen, Albert Keller, William Ogburn, V. Gordon Childe, George Peter Murdock, R. H. Tawney, Sir Julian Huxley, George Gaylord Simpson, Leslie White, Julian Steward, Amos Hawley, Marvin Harris, and William H. McNeill, among others. The citations that appear at the end of this volume should be regarded as further acknowledgments of indebtedness and appreciation.

Many social scientists and a few biologists have been kind enough to provide critical comments on, and suggestions for, one or more of the five editions of *Human Societies* thus far. The social scientists include Francis R. Allen, E. Jackson Baur, Rae Lesser Blumberg, William R. Catton, Jr., Ronald Cosper, David Featherman, George Furniss, Walter Goldschmidt, Robert Bates Graber, Gareth Gustafson, Thomas D. Hall, Amos Hawley, Paul Heckert, Joan Huber, Donald Irish, Charles K. Warriner, Norbert Wiley, Philip Marcus, Patrick D. Nolan, Ross Purdy, Leo Rigsby, Norman Storer, and Everett K. Wilson. The biologists include Alfred E. Emerson, Richard E. Lenski, and Edward O. Wilson. We extend sincere thanks to each of them for valuable suggestions, but remind readers that the final responsibility for the contents is ours alone.

Gerhard Lenski
Jean Lenski

HUMAN SOCIETIES

An Introduction to Macrosociology

PART I

Theoretical Foundations

CHAPTER 1

Starting Points

One of the most important developments in human societies in recent centuries has been the rise of modern science. Its aim is to understand the world in which we live. As scientific knowledge has increased, scientific activity has become more specialized. Each branch of science has its own special subject matter and its own special set of problems. *Sociology is the branch of science concerned with the study of human societies.*

In this volume, our analysis of human societies will be (1) *historical,* (2) *comparative,* and (3) *macroorganizational.* It will be historical because a temporal perspective is essential if we are to understand the processes of change and development that have been—and continue to be—so important. Moreover, we must never forget that most of the intellectual and organizational resources on which societies today depend are products of the efforts of previous generations, and even those that are our own creations have all been developed on foundations laid by earlier generations. As René Dubos, a distinguished biologist, wisely observed, "The past is not dead history; it is living material out of which man makes himself and builds [his] future."[1]

Our study of human societies will also be comparative, because *comparison is the basis of all scientific knowledge.* A scientific understanding of anything depends on comparisons of it with other things. To understand a pine tree, we have to compare it with other kinds of trees, and then compare trees with other kinds of plants, and plants with other forms of life, noting the similarities and differences

3

involved in each comparison and using them to draw inferences about their causes and consequences. Only in this way can we begin to understand what a pine tree is and why it is as it is. The same is true of human societies: we can understand them only by comparing them with one another and with other things, especially other kinds of societies, such as other mammalian societies or insect societies.

In making comparisons, the most important task for scientists is to discover *differences that make a difference.* In medicine, for example, the aim is to discover the actual causes of diseases, not just their symptoms. The same is true in other sciences: the goal is to discover the causes of things.

This search for the causes of things leads to the development of theory. *Scientific theories* are explanations of various aspects of the world of nature; they are explanations of why things are as they are. Theories also provide a coherent set of principles that form the basic frame of reference for a field of inquiry.

One of the most important characteristics of scientific theories is that they are *falsifiable.* This means that they are stated in such a way that they can be tested and shown to be wrong by observations of the hypothesized relationships if, indeed, they are wrong. To win acceptance in the scientific community, a theory must have withstood repeated tests and must be supported by a substantial body of observations that are consistent with its explanation of relationships.

Sometimes it seems as though science is merely the patient accumulation of facts. But facts, by themselves, are meaningless; they explain nothing. For scientists, the collection of facts is the means to a much more important end, namely, the development and testing of theories designed to explain some aspect of the world of nature.

Our study of human societies in this volume will be guided by such a theory— *ecological-evolutionary theory.* As its name suggests, this theory is concerned with two things. First, it is concerned with the relation of societies to their environments and with the relations of the parts of a society to one another. Second, the theory is concerned with the evolution of societies—how and why they change and how these changes create differences among societies.

Ecological-evolutionary theory provides a *macroorganizational* (or *macrosocial*) perspective on human societies. This means that it focuses on *societies as a whole* rather than on their component parts, such as individuals, families, and communities. But this does not mean that ecological-evolutionary theory ignores these components or regards them as unimportant. Far from it! Instead, these components are analyzed in the context of the larger society, or type of society, of which they are parts.

Human Societies: Their Place in Nature

Often in the past, and still today, many people have thought of human societies as though they stood apart from the world of nature that science studies. This is easy to do, because modern industrial societies are much like giant cocoons that stand between us and the surrounding environment. As a result, we seldom encounter anything that has not been processed and transformed by human actions. Nevertheless, the first premise of ecological-evolutionary theory is that *human societies* are a part of the global ecosystem and cannot be adequately understood unless this fact is taken fully into account.[2]

As many scholars have observed, the world of nature is structured like a system of wheels within wheels. Larger things are made up of smaller things, and these, in turn, are made up of still smaller things. Figure 1.1 provides a greatly oversimplified view of the structure of the world of nature as understood by modern science. Elementary particles, such as protons and electrons, form the lowest level. These are combined in various ways to form atoms, such as carbon and radium. Atoms, in turn, are organized into molecules, such as water, salt, amino acids, and proteins. Though Figure 1.1 does not show it, molecules constitute more than a single level in the hierarchy, because some of the simpler molecules, the amino acids, for example, are the building blocks for more complex and more inclusive molecules, such as the proteins.

Once we go beyond the level of molecules, we encounter the important division between living and nonliving things. Since our concern is with human societies, there is no need to consider all the levels of nonliving matter. Suffice it to note that the structure leads by degrees to the level of the giant galaxies that wheel through space and ends with the universe itself.

Societies, however, are part of the biotic world: they are one of the ways in

FIGURE 1.1 Levels of organization in the world of nature.

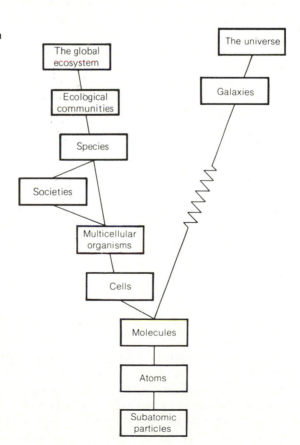

which living things are organized. More specifically, they are a form of organization found in some species of multicellular organisms. Because many kinds of multicellular organisms do not form societies, however, there is also a line in Figure 1.1 that bypasses that block and directly connects multicellular organisms to species.

This brings us to the question of why some species are organized into societies while others are not.

The Basic Function of Societies

The development of the societal mode of organization has been called "one of the great steps in evolution, as important as the emergence of the cell, the multicellular organism, and the vertebrate system."[3] Actually, societies evolved not once, but a number of times, independently and in widely scattered parts of the animal kingdom. They are concentrated in three areas: (1) many species of vertebrates, especially among mammals, birds, and fish; (2) the social insects (ants, termites, and many species of wasps and bees); and (3) the colonial invertebrates (such as corals, sponges, and Portuguese man-of-war).[4]

Why did so many and such diverse species develop this particular mode of organization? Quite simply, because being organized this way helped these species survive. In other words, the societal mode of life became common in the animal kingdom for the same reason that wings, lungs, and protective coloring became common: they are all important *adaptive mechanisms*.

But societal organization is different from adaptive mechanisms that enable species to perform some particular activity—the way wings, for example, enable creatures to fly, or lungs enable them to exchange oxygen and other gases with the air. What distinguishes social species from all the rest is a characteristic that has the potential for being used in a great variety of ways: an *enhanced capacity for cooperation*.

To those who study animal behavior, "cooperation" means simply that the individuals in a given species associate with and interact with one another for their mutual benefit. It does not mean they cooperate in every activity, nor does it imply the absence of competition and conflict.

The types of cooperative activities in which the various social species engage include reproduction, nurture of their young, securing food, and defense against predators and other dangers.* Some social species rely on cooperative behavior in virtually every facet of life; others are less involved in, or less dependent on, social activities. But every social species benefits substantially from the fact that its members are genetically programmed to solve at least some of their problems by acting together instead of individually.

Once we recognize that human societies are, first and foremost, adaptive mechanisms that are vital to the survival of our species, we see why we cannot

---

*Even *nonsocial* animals display cooperative activity in the area of reproduction (i.e., they reproduce sexually). But a species is not classified as "social" if its cooperative activity is limited to this single, though important, area.

FIGURE 1.2 Elephant society as an adaptive mechanism: adult members forming a protective ring around their young.

divorce our study of them from the study of the rest of the biotic world.* We see, too, why it is imperative that students of human societies have a clear understanding of the biological foundations of the societal mode of organization in general and of human societies in particular.

A Definition of Human Societies

A prominent zoologist recently defined a society as "a group of individuals belonging to the same species and organized in a cooperative manner."[5] This definition has the virtue of simplicity and, at the same time, encompasses the fundamental points of concern to biologists.

Sociologists, however, need to add something to this definition before it can be applied to human societies. Virtually every human society of which we have

---

*This is not to suggest that the study of human societies should be swallowed up by the biological sciences. It simply means it is necessary to take the biological foundations of human life fully into account when analyzing human societies.

knowledge has had subgroups within it—families, communities, and specialized associations of various kinds—and the definition above does not differentiate between these subgroups and the societies of which they are a part. To do this, we need to specify that human societies are *autonomous groups,* that is, free from outside political control. Thus, a human society may be defined as *a self-governing group of people engaged in a broad range of cooperative activities*. This clearly applies to American society, Soviet society, or Brazilian society, while excluding such subgroups as America's AFL-CIO, Soviet Jewry, and the population of Rio de Janeiro. None of the latter is autonomous: all are politically subordinate to the societies of which they are part.

Sometimes it is difficult for biologists to say for certain whether a particular group of animals does or does not comprise a society. This is because social species engage in cooperative behavior *in varying degrees*. For example, apart from the nurture of their young, many mammals expend little time or energy on social activities, while some of the social insects are immersed in them. Thus, between the extremes represented by solitary animals and highly social ones, there are countless gradations.

In the case of human societies, there are gradations not only in terms of the cooperative behavior displayed by their members, but also in terms of the *autonomy* of the groups. Consider, for example, a more or less typical American Indian society of the sixteenth or seventeenth century, an autonomous group whose members were caught up in a complex system of social activity. In time, the group established trade relations with Europeans or Americans and eventually came under their political control. This process often involved the gradual absorption of the Indian society by the larger, more powerful society, but it would be impossible, in such a case, to say precisely when the Indian society ceased to exist (i.e., lost its autonomy) and became merely a subgroup within American society. Autonomy is not an "all or nothing" matter. Rather, like cooperative behavior (and like many other phenomena, such as weight and temperature), its existence is a matter of degree.

The Biological Basis of Human Societies

The foundation of every society in the biotic world is the genetic heritage of the creatures who form it—which explains why the structure of a termite society and the activities that go on within it are so different from those of a society of wolves or birds. If we want to understand the structure of human societies and what goes on in them, we obviously have to begin with the genetic heritage of humans. Thus, we will spend the rest of this chapter examining that heritage. Our goal is not to understand how we, as individuals, differ from one another, but to understand those more fundamental and important characteristics that we all possess simply because we are members of Homo sapiens and not some other species.

During the last hundred years, there has been a lot of confusion and controversy on this subject of human nature. One view was popularized by some of Charles Darwin's more enthusiastic followers, who argued that science had proved Homo sapiens was not, after all, the exalted being humans so long imagined themselves to be, but merely an animal that could be understood in purely biological terms.

Most scholars have since rejected this view on the grounds that it involves what a leading evolutionary theorist, George Gaylord Simpson, once termed the "nothing but" fallacy. In his words:

> To say that man is nothing but an animal is to deny, by implication, that he has essential attributes other than those of all animals. This would be false as applied to any kind of an animal; it is not true that a dog, a robin, an oyster, or an amoeba is nothing but an animal. As applied to man the "nothing but" fallacy is more serious than in application to any other sort of animal, because man is an entirely new kind of animal in ways altogether fundamental for understanding of his nature. It is important to realize that man is an animal, but it is even more important to realize that the essence of his unique nature lies precisely in those characteristics that are not shared with any other animal.[6]

In reacting against the "nothing but" fallacy, many social scientists backed into the equally unsatisfactory position of ignoring or minimizing the biological foundation of human societies. Many seemed almost to deny our animal heritage. Fortunately, however, there is a third view which recognizes that our species has some characteristics in common with all living things, some that we share with certain other species but not with all, and some that are uniquely human. In the pages that follow, we will consider each of these in turn so that we may better understand the biological foundation on which human societies rest.

Characteristics Humans Share with All Other Species

When we first consider the world of living things in all its diversity and variety, it is hard to imagine that there is anything that *all* plants and animals share. Yet beneath the obvious and immense differences, the human, the slime mold, the rose, and the amoeba are alike in some very important ways.

To begin with, biologists have found that all living things have the same underlying structure.[7] Every organism is composed of one or more cells, and all cells are composed of the same basic materials: water, mineral solids, and various kinds of organic compounds (e.g., fats, proteins, carbohydrates, and their derivatives). In addition, the same basic activities go on in every organism, from the simplest to the most complex. For example, nutrition, respiration, and synthesis are metabolic processes found in every kind of organism.

Why are these and other characteristics shared by all forms of life? Simpson answers that it is because "all living things . . . have arisen from one source and have been developed within the divergent intricacies of one process."[8] In other words, *the most basic thing that all forms of life share is involvement in the process of biological evolution.*

Biological evolution is the process of gradual genetic change and development through which every species of plant or animal has developed out of a preexisting species.[9] This process has been going on for approximately 3.5 billion years, ever since life began on our planet. Every change in the characteristics of a species— whether it has involved appearance or behavior*—has been a manifestation of

---

*"Behavior" refers to *any response by an organism to internal or external stimuli.* Thus, behavior includes chemical processes like digestion and suntanning, and activities like hearing and thinking, as well as overt movements like crawling or biting.

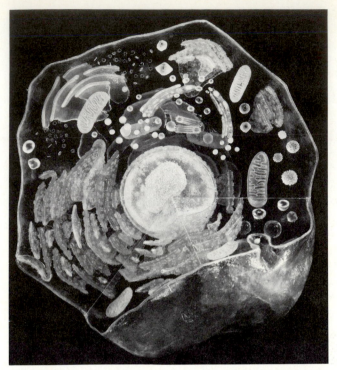

FIGURE 1.3 Every organism is composed of one or more cells: model of the structure of a cell magnified more than 10 million times.

change in its genetic makeup. The enormous complexity and diversity of plants and animals today testify to an incredible number of such changes.

Genes, the basic units of heredity, are complex chemicals that are present in every cell of every organism. An organism may have as many as 3 or 4 million genes in every cell. Rather like sets of built-in commands, genes trigger a variety of chemical processes in various parts of a plant or animal and, in so doing, determine its structure, how it functions, and how it differs from other organisms. When it reproduces, the organism passes on to its offspring precise copies of some or all of its own genes.* This is why the basic life processes are so orderly and predictable— why elephants do not give birth to butterflies, mushrooms do not grow as tall as oaks, and pigs do not produce chlorophyll.

To understand how evolutionary change occurs, we must focus on a *population.* This term refers to an aggregation of organisms of the same species that tend to interbreed because of geographic proximity. A herd of bison, the sparrows on an offshore island, and the earthworms in a local patch of forest are all examples of a population. Although most reproductive activity takes place *within* a population, there is almost always occasional interbreeding with nearby populations of the same species.

---

*The copies are precise, except in the event of mutation (see below).

The members of a population are fundamentally alike in both appearance and behavior, but they are not identical. This means that some genes in a population are found in every member, while others are found in varying proportions of the population. Since the genetic heritage of a population consists of all these varied individual heritages, biologists have coined the term *gene pool* to refer to the genes of all the members considered collectively.

The ultimate origin of genetic variation, and of every gene in biotic history, is *mutation*. A mutation is essentially an accident: a slight alteration occurs in the chemical structure of a gene as it is being replicated, with the result that the "copy"—the gene that is transmitted to the offspring—does not carry quite the same chemical message as the original—the gene of the parent.

Mutations occur continually in every population,* but they are never purposive. For example, a new gene in a white moth population does not arise for the purpose of making the insects a color that blends with the tree bark on which they alight, thus making them safer from predators. Rather, mutations are *random,* or chance, occurrences. Most of them, in fact, are actually harmful to the genetic makeup of the offspring into which they are introduced—much the way a random bit of metal substituted for a small part in a smoothly running machine is far more likely to harm than improve its operation. But every now and then, a mutation *does* produce an "improved" gene, a gene that gives its bearer an advantage (usually a very slight one) in the competition to survive and reproduce. In this way, some new genes eventually become established in a gene pool and may even become part of the genetic makeup of every individual in the population.

But mutations are only the beginning of genetic variation in species that reproduce sexually, as nearly all species do. Because this mode of reproduction involves the genes of two individuals, genes and sets of genes are, in effect, shuffled and reshuffled over the generations, creating ever new combinations, or *recombinations,* as they are called.

Just as important in the evolutionary process as a genetically varied population is the *environment*. This term refers to everything external to a population that influences it or is influenced by it. Its environment includes inorganic matter, physical phenomena (such as climate), other living things (among them, other populations of the same species), and everything the population requires to survive: food, moisture, air, light, and so on.

This relationship between population and environment is the most basic one in the biotic world. It is an intimate and dynamic relationship in which each contributes to, and is affected by, change in the other. And it is *this relationship that shapes evolution*.

We can understand how this happens if we focus on the gradual change that takes place in a population's genetic attributes—or, more precisely, on the change in the composition of its gene pool. Over a period of time, some genes become more frequent, others become less so, and some become rare or even disappear. This happens because some members of the population are reproducing their genes more frequently than others.

---

*The cause of most mutations is still unknown, although some have been found to result from exposure to x-rays and certain chemicals.

FIGURE 1.4 *"Broderick, what do you know about evolution?"*

In most populations, the great majority of organisms do not reproduce at all. They die before reproductive age because of the universal tendency of living things to have more offspring than the environment can support. (An oyster, for example, lays more than a million eggs per season, a tapeworm 120,000 per day.) The survivors, meanwhile, not only have different numbers of offspring, but offspring with different genetic potential for surviving and reproducing themselves.

Over the long run, the thing that determines this differential reproduction is the adaptive value of the various genes and sets of genes in the population. The genetic traits that "work best" for a particular species in a particular environment are "selected" for reproduction through a natural process (i.e., one not contrived by humans): hence the term *natural selection*. Each new generation of individuals in a population is essentially like the parental type, and it must cope with essentially the same environment. But each new generation also has a supply of genetic innovations that will be put to the test, and discarded or used in the never-ending process of maintaining an adequate relationship with the environment or achieving a better one.

All the populations of a species normally change in unison—that is, the species *as a whole* evolves. This is what we would expect of reproductive units that share with one another, at least occasionally, their different genetic "solutions" to the challenges of similar environments. A population that is well adapted to its environment is more likely to reject genetic alterations than to accept them, and the same is true of the species as a whole: it tends to resist change. As a result, a species does not usually experience major structural change during its span on earth. Its change is gradual and not dramatic.

The story may be different, however, during *speciation,* the process by which a new species splits off from its parental line. Speciation usually occurs in a small population that has become reproductively isolated from others of its kind. This is typically a consequence of a growth in numbers that causes a species to spread over such a wide area that some of its populations are struggling to survive in marginal areas to which the species is not well adapted. Eventually, one of these peripheral populations may be completely cut off from the rest and forced to adapt to an environment quite different from that in which the species had previously lived.

In a small, marginal population like this, one that barely manages to obtain its basic needs, any useful new genetic trait spreads rapidly. In effect, the rate of natural selection speeds up because of the peculiar circumstances. If such a population survives (and most do not), it will probably change more quickly than the other populations of its species, and not in unison with them. In a span of time that by evolutionary standards is very brief indeed (i.e., only hundreds or thousands of years), it may become so different genetically from the parental stock that effective interbreeding would no longer be possible if the separated populations were re-united. Two species would now exist where there was one before.

Over the mind-boggling expanse of time since life first appeared on our planet, these same natural forces have been constantly at work, producing genetic variation purely at random, and then selecting from it through a process that is *not* random, but is shaped by the relation of living things to their environments. The genetic heritage of every extant species, *including our own,* is thus quite literally the product of billions of years of biological experimentation. *It is a biochemical storehouse of information that guides and directs the responses of a population to the daily challenges of life in its environment.*

Characteristics Humans Share with Some Other Species

We humans obviously have more in common with some living things than with others. As evolutionary theory would lead us to expect, the closer our biological kinship with other species, the greater the range of characteristics we share with them. Thus, we have more in common with other members of the animal kingdom than with plants, and more in common with other vertebrates than with inverte-brates.

For the same reason, we are more like other mammals than like nonmammalian vertebrates, such as reptiles, birds, and fish. We share with other mammals a wide assortment of traits that include warm-bloodedness; body hair; lungs; four limbs (or vestiges of them) with nails; claws, hoofs, or digits; external genitalia; internal fertilization; teeth that come in only twice and that are differentiated according to use; a bony palate that permits breathing and chewing at the same time; a relatively elaborate brain; a marked capacity for learning; and, in the female, mammary glands that secrete milk. In addition, *all mammals are social animals:* there is, at a mini-mum, the cooperative behavior displayed by mothers in the nurture of their young, and in many mammalian species patterns of cooperation go far beyond this (e.g., hunting by a pack of wolves, or grouping for mutual defense by a herd of elephants).

When we compare ourselves to other primates, the range of common traits is even more striking. In addition to those we share by virtue of our common mam-malian ancestry, there are other characteristics such as upright posture and flexible arms, flexible hands with separated fingers and opposable thumbs, year-round sexual readiness, prolonged immaturity, greater reliance on the sense of sight than of smell, an enlarged neocortex, and a high order of intelligence. As the author of a leading biology text recently wrote, "Primates are the most intelligent and also the most curious, inventive, mischievous, and destructive of the mammals."[10]

One cannot compare humans with other species in this way without recognizing the extent to which basic patterns of human life are rooted in our genetic system. For it is not just a matter of similarities between our anatomy and physiology and that of the other primates: it is also a matter of behavioral tendencies and predispositions. If we humans are cooperative and live in societies, it is not simply because we choose to be social creatures, but because of our genetic heritage. Similarly, if we rely on learning as a basic mode of adaptation to the world we live in, it is not because we decided it was the best thing to do, nor did we invent learning. Rather, these are basic expressions of our mammalian and primate heritage.

Modern research has shed a good deal of light on the way we and the rest of the primate line came to be distinguished by the particular characteristics that set us apart from other species. The basic elements in our package of adaptive traits began to be forged about 65 million years ago when a mouse-sized ancestor of modern primates moved into a new environmental niche and began living in trees.[11] Manual dexterity and good vision were clearly of greater importance for tree-dwellers than for their cousins on the ground. Safe movement from tree to tree depended far more on sight than on smell, which is more important to the survival of ground-dwelling mammals. At the same time, as a consequence of the dangers inherent in arboreal life, there was a developing solicitude for the young which gradually led to stronger social ties between mothers and their offspring. The small individual whose agility, good vision, and vigilant mother kept him safely in the treetops would be more likely to reproduce the genes governing these critical traits than would the youngster, slightly less well endowed in these respects, who fell to the ground. The forces of natural selection thus began shaping the emerging primate line.

That basic combination of traits (i.e., manual dexterity, excellent vision, and stronger social ties) apparently provided the foundation for further genetic change, particularly growth of the forebrain and increasing reliance on learning and intelligence as basic adaptive mechanisms. Although these traits are found in some degree in all mammals, the evolution of nonprimates took them in other directions, and quite different traits became critical components of their genetic makeup. Great strength, stealth, and fecundity, for example, are important supplements to the ability to learn among, respectively, elephants, cats, and mice. But the primate line came to rely primarily on intelligence and learning. In fact, when the anatomy of primates is compared to that of other mammals, it is considered to be relatively unspecialized except for a single organ: the brain.[12]

Learning is the process by which an organism acquires, through experience, information with behavior-modifying potential.[13] This means that when it comes to solving problems, an animal that can learn is not completely dependent on instinct (i.e., the behavioral repertoire provided by its genetic heritage). Instead, its own experiences become a factor shaping its behavior. In the case of humans and some of the higher primates, the evolution of the forebrain has reached the point where they are able to store such a wide range of memories that they can learn by *insight;* in other words, they can analyze a situation in their minds and thereby avoid the time-consuming, costly, and often painful process of trial and error.[14]

The adaptive value of the ability to learn is greatly enhanced when animals live together in groups. This gives the individual more opportunity to observe, and to communicate with, others of its kind. In effect, social animals benefit from the experience of their fellows as well as from their own personal experience. Social life

FIGURE 1.5 All mammalian species have a marked capacity for learning: among primates, this is enhanced by the prolonged physical immaturity of the young. Chimpanzee family, with sister nuzzling brother in mother's arms.

thus multiplies the amount of information available to a population. In the words of two leading students of primate life, "The [primate] group is the locus of knowledge and information far exceeding that of the individual member. It is in the group that experience is pooled."[15]

The adaptive value of the ability to learn is also greatly enhanced among primates by the prolonged physical immaturity of their young. The young of most species are genetically equipped to fend for themselves from the moment of birth. For mammals and birds, however, there is a period in which the young depend on sustained contact with one or both parents. In the case of primates, this period of dependence is especially prolonged, a fact which is linked both with their enhanced capacity for learning and with their dependence on a societal mode of life.

Characteristics Unique to Humans

We do not require science to tell us that our species is unique. Only humans build skyscrapers, set off nuclear explosions, philosophize, compose symphonies, travel in space, and do a thousand other things no other species can do. This seems to suggest that our genetic makeup is profoundly different from that of every other species.

Such is not the case, however: recent immunological research has shown that chimpanzees are as close genetically to humans as horses are to zebras, and closer than dogs are to foxes. One estimate is that humans and chimpanzees share 99 percent of their genetic material, and other research suggests that gorillas may be even more closely related to us than chimpanzees.[16]

Since it is now clear that a species' behavior is intimately related to its genetic makeup, why is it that the life of the great apes is not more like our own? The explanation is that at some point in the evolution of one primate line, there occurred a series of genetic changes that, although relatively few in number, had revolutionary consequences for behavior.

These critical changes altered the structure of the brain. Although they are not fully understood, it is certain that one change involved the relocation of the center of vocalization. In every other species, including chimpanzees and gorillas, this voice-control center lies in an old part of the mammalian brain that is intimately involved with instinct and strong emotion. But in the hominid line,* the processes of biological evolution shifted this center to the neocortex, the newer part of the brain, where learning takes place and where learned information is stored.[17] In effect, a new and far more intimate relationship was forged between the past experiences of an individual and the sounds which that individual produced. The consequence of such changes in brain structure was that *hominids acquired the ability to create and use symbols.*

Because of this unique ability to create and use symbols, and eventually to develop complex symbol systems, or *languages,* our ancestors' capacity for learning, and for sharing what they learned with others of their kind, was increased tremendously. And this enormous capacity for learning was, in turn, the foundation for a totally new kind of adaptive mechanism, one without parallel in the biotic world: *culture.*[18]

Because culture is such a basic and crucial feature of human life, it is important that we understand precisely what it is. This term has been defined in a variety of ways over the years, but implicit in every definition has been a recognition that culture rests upon our species' tremendous capacity for learning. Scientists, both social and biological, have increasingly come to speak of culture in terms of a *learned heritage* that is passed on from generation to generation. Moreover, they recognize that a human society's cultural heritage is as important to its survival as its genetic heritage. The essential distinction between them is in the way they are transmitted: one is passed on through genes, the other through symbols. Thus, we can best define culture by saying that it consists of *symbol systems and the information they convey.*†

---

*Hominid refers to humanlike creatures. There were once other hominid species, but ours is the only one that exists today.

†A number of anthropologists and sociologists have included behavior and material artifacts in their definitions of culture, but it seems more appropriate to regard these as *products* of culture. This is in keeping with the recent trend described by Milton Singer in his article on culture in the *International Encyclopedia of the Social Sciences.* He reports that increasingly, in definitions and analyses of culture, "behavior, observed social relations, i.e., social structure, and material artifacts . . . are not themselves considered the constituents of culture."[19]

What are symbols that they have made such a difference to our species? After all, the members of other species also communicate among themselves, using *signals* to convey information. Both signals and symbols are *information conveyers*. But there is a vital difference: the meaning of a signal is wholly or largely determined by genetics; the meaning of a symbol is not.

The best way to understand this distinction is to look at examples of the two kinds of information conveyers, beginning with signals.[20] Animals signal with movements, sounds, odors, color changes, and so on, and the signals they produce vary greatly in the amount of information they convey. The simplest type of signal is one that is used by an organism in only a single context and that has only one possible meaning—the sexually attractive scent released by the female moth, for example. In contrast, some species are able to transmit more complex information by varying the frequency or intensity of a signal or by combining different signals simultaneously or in sequence. Thus, a foraging honeybee returns to her hive and performs the "waggle dance" to direct fellow workers to the food source she has located.[21] By varying the movements and vibrations that comprise the dance, she communicates enough information about direction and distance to enable her sisters to land remarkably near the target, and at the same time adds a comment on the quality of the food supply and the state of the weather.

In some species, especially birds and mammals, the use of, and response to, signals is partially learned. The young of certain species of birds, for example, must learn some elements of their territorial songs from adults.[22] Humans, too, learn to modify and use signals in different ways. Thus, we learn to pretend to yawn to indicate boredom. But whether it is simple or complex, and whether or not there is learning involved, a signal is *an information conveyer whose basic form and meaning are genetically determined.*

Symbols, by contrast, are not genetically determined. The ability to create and use symbols does depend on genetics, but the form of a symbol and the meaning attached to it do not. Thus, a symbol is *an information conveyer whose form is arbitrary and whose meaning is determined by those who use it.*

Humans share the ability to create symbols with no other species. Over the course of history, a variety of animals from plow horses to circus seals have been trained to recognize, respond to, and even use, after a fashion, a number of symbols. In recent years, chimpanzees and gorillas have proved to have a remarkable ability in this regard, learning to use up to 750 different symbols, even combining a few of them to convey more complex meanings.[23]

It is important to recognize, however, that none of these animals has ever created a symbol, that is, has ever deliberately assigned its own meaning to a gesture, sound, or object. Rather, the symbols they use were designed by humans and taught to them. What is more, these creatures show no prelanguage features in the wild.[24] Thus, while their accomplishments are impressive, they cannot compare with humans. For we not only quickly master the language of the group into which we are born but are capable, at a very early age, of devising new symbols and even entire symbol systems. Small children concoct names for their stuffed animals and sometimes go on to make up "secret codes." And at least one case has been well documented in which a set of twins, first thought to be retarded because no one understood their speech, proved to have invented an entirely original and complex language by which they communicated with one another.

We can appreciate the significance of symbols only when we understand their "genetic independence." Take the sound of the third letter of our alphabet, for example. We use that sound to refer to the act of perceiving, to a bishop's jurisdiction, and to a large body of water, as well as to the letter itself. Spanish-speaking people, meanwhile, use it to say "yes" and "if," and French-speaking people to say "yes," "if," "whether," and "so." Obviously there is no logical connection between these various meanings, nor is there any genetically determined connection between the meanings and the sound. They are simply arbitrary usages adopted by the members of certain societies.

Further evidence that symbols are determined by their users and not by genes is the ease with which we alter them. When Chaucer wrote "Hir nose tretis, hir yen greye as glas," he meant to say—in fact, he did say—"Her nose well-formed, her eyes gray as glass." English-speaking people have simply altered many of their symbols since his day. Slang is created by the reverse procedure: the symbol itself remains unchanged, but it is given a new meaning. The words "bread" and "dough," for example, have both come to be used to refer to money.

Although linguistic symbols are the most basic and important, they are not the

---

FIFTEEN WAYS TO SAY "I LOVE YOU"

Because there is no necessary connection between the sounds people make and their meaning, different languages use different combinations of sounds to express the same idea. Thus, every language has its own distinctive way of saying "I love you." In some languages, the phrase varies slightly when a woman addresses a man; these variants are shown in parentheses below.

Arabic: Ana b'hibbik (Ana b'hibbak)
Cambodian: Bon sro lanh oon
Chinese: Wo ai ni
Danish: Jeg elsker Dig
English: I love you
French: Je t'aime
German: Ich liebe dich
Hebrew: Ani ohev otakh (Ani ohevet otkhah)
Hindi: Maiñ tumheñ piyar karta huñ
Hungarian: Szeretlek
Italian: Ti voglio bene
Japanese: Watakushi-wa anata-wo aishimasu
Korean: Tangsinŭl sarang hä yo
Navaho: Ayór ánósh'ní
Russian: Ya tebya liubliu

Source: Charles Berlitz, *Native Tongues* (London: Panther, 1984), p. 54.

only kind we use, since anything to which humans assign a meaning becomes a symbol. Thus, the cross has become a symbol of Christianity, the hammer and sickle a symbol of Russian communism. Every nation in the world today has a flag to represent it, and standardized symbols communicate basic traffic directions on our highways.

Because they are not genetically determined, symbols can be combined and recombined in countless ways to form symbol systems of fantastic complexity, subtlety, and flexibility. The only limits are set by the physical characteristics of those who use them, that is, by the efficiency and capacity of the human brain and nervous system and the accuracy of our senses. And symbol systems help to overcome even these limitations. For example, our species' memory (i.e., its capacity for storing information) has been greatly increased by the use of written symbols and written records.

In the final analysis, the importance of symbol systems lies not in what they are, but in what they have made it possible for our species to become. Although we are all born into the human family, we become fully human only through the use of symbols. Without them, we are unable to develop the unique qualities we associate with humanness. For symbols are more than a means of communication: they are the basic tools with which we think and plan, dream and remember, create and build, calculate, speculate, and moralize.

The difference between a human mind without symbols and that same mind with them is eloquently described in Helen Keller's account of her early life.[25] Miss Keller became both deaf and blind before she learned to talk. By the age of seven, after years devoid of meaningful communication with other people, she had become very much like a wild animal. Then, a gifted teacher, Anne Sullivan, began trying to communicate with Helen by spelling words into her hands. Helen learned several words, but she did not yet comprehend the real significance of symbols. Finally, in a moment that both women later described in moving terms, Helen suddenly realized that *everything* had a name, that *everything* could be communicated with symbols! In her own words, she felt "a thrill of returning thought." At last, the world that exists only for symbol users began to open to her.

Miss Keller's experience helps us understand why the ancients, in their accounts of creation, so often linked the beginning of language with the beginning of the world. One of the oldest written texts from Egypt, for example, tells how Ptah, the creator of the world and the greatest of the gods, "pronounced the names of all things" as a central part of his act of creation.[26] Language also figures prominently in Chinese and Hindu creation myths. The book of Genesis tells us that the first thing Adam did after he was created was to name all the beasts and birds; and the Gospel According to St. John opens with the famous lines "In the beginning was the Word, and the Word was with God, and the Word was God." Significantly, the original Greek for "word" was *logos*, which meant not merely word, but meaning and reason. And *logos* is the root of our own word "logic," and of the suffix *-logy*, used to denote science, as in biology or sociology.

The German scientist Alexander von Humboldt once said, "No words, no world," and it is true that the human world, the world of human societies, would not exist without words. Without symbols, human societies would lack their most distinctive feature: *culture*. With symbols, however, each of them has developed a rich cultural heritage to supplement its genetic heritage.

The Common Genetic Heritage of Humans

Attributes we share with the amoeba, attributes we share with the ape, attributes we share with no other living thing—these are the elements that make up our species' common genetic heritage. We have examined some facets of this heritage in detail, and we have barely alluded to others. Now it is important to look at this heritage *as a whole* and consider its implications. For the complex cluster of traits that is part of every human is also *the biological foundation of every human society.*

Summarizing these traits is not easy, however, for two reasons. First, there is no way to observe and study normal humans, except possibly newborn infants, *apart from culture.* After that, cultural influences become so pervasive that it is extremely difficult to distinguish between their effects and those of genetics.

The other reason it is so hard to identify our common traits is because of the *complexities* of human genetics. For example, an observable trait (i.e., a behavioral or physical characteristic) does not typically result from one particular gene, as we might suppose, but reflects the interaction of a number of genes. Any given gene, meanwhile, usually affects not a single trait, but a number of different traits. What is more, most traits are not determined by heredity alone, but by the interaction of genetic endowment and environmental factors. Because of these complexities, many things are still poorly understood. Which genes or sets of genes are common to us all? Which are variable (i.e., either not present in everyone, or present in different forms)? And what is the relative contribution of inheritance and environment to the variance observed in a particular trait? Answers are beginning to emerge in all these areas, but they are still just a beginning.

Enough is now known, however, to put to rest some older views of human nature. One of these, the "tabula rasa" hypothesis, held that the newborn infant's mind is like a blank piece of paper and that its eventual content is supplied entirely by experience.[27] This view was extremely popular in the eighteenth, nineteenth, and early twentieth centuries because it provided the basis for a highly optimistic view of the future. For if babies are so malleable, it should be possible, with careful planning and proper education, to eliminate selfishness, greed, aggression, and all the other unpleasant elements in human nature. Recent studies of the brain and of language acquisition, however, as well as political developments in the twentieth century (e.g., wars, terrorist attacks on innocent civilians, the use of torture, concentration camps, etc.), have all cast doubt on the "tabula rasa" hypothesis.[28]

Meanwhile, the work of scientists and scholars in widely scattered disciplines has produced a clearer understanding not only of the human brain but of many other components of our common genetic heritage. At the risk of oversimplifying a very complex and still controversial subject, we will try to identify those elements that are most relevant to the study of human societies.

First, all humans have *the same fundamental needs.* These include the basic physical requirements for food, water, sleep, oxygen, elimination, et cetera that must be satisfied if we are merely to survive. We also have a variety of other common needs, needs whose satisfaction is not essential for individual survival or whose intensity varies greatly from one stage of life to another. These include sexual needs, the need for play, the need for new experience, and the need for social experience.[29] That these needs have as much of a genetic base as our "survival needs" has been well documented. The need for new experience, for example, is evident in the newborn infant, who exhibits a decided preference for visual variety and contrast and has "a bias to explore" that it begins to satisfy almost from the moment of birth.[30] The newborn also has such a fundamental need for social contact and stimulation that, if it is not satisfied, the child may even die.[31]

Second, humans everywhere develop a *variety of derivative needs*. Our common genetic heritage provides us with the potential for developing many needs and desires in addition to those above—needs and desires that are largely the result of our social and cultural experiences. Because this experience varies from one society to another and among individuals in the same society, and also because genetic variations play a role in their development, the intensity of these needs varies greatly. But all of us have the potential for at least minimal development of any number of needs beyond those required for mere survival. These include the need to control people and events, to possess things, to give and receive affection, to express oneself aesthetically and in other ways, to be respected and admired, to have emotional, aesthetic, or religious experiences, and to discern order and meaning in life.

Third, we all have the same basic resources to use in satisfying our needs. To begin with, there is such obvious physical equipment as legs, fingers, teeth, ears, bowels, heart, brain, and so on. The brain is a particularly impressive resource: it provides us with the means of recording "memory traces" equivalent to the content

FIGURE 1.6   The human brain is an impressive resource: it can record "memory traces" equivalent to 1,000 twenty-four-volume sets of the *Encyclopaedia Britannica*. Compare the size of the cerebral cortex of humans with that of other primates.

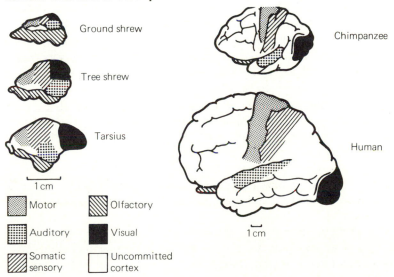

Ground shrew

Chimpanzee

Tree shrew

Tarsius

Human

1 cm

▦ Motor   ▨ Olfactory

▤ Auditory   ■ Visual   1 cm

▧ Somatic   ☐ Uncommitted
sensory   cortex

of a thousand 24-volume sets of the *Encyclopaedia Britannica* and is far more densely packed with information than a computer.[32] In addition, we are all genetically programmed for the automatic performance of a variety of activities (e.g., digestion, growth, ovulation, circulation, etc.) and have many valuable response sets and reflex actions (e.g., we draw back when we touch something hot). Paradoxically, some resources are hard to distinguish from needs. This is true, for example, of the "exploring tendency," which is both an expression of an innate need for new experience and a resource (i.e., an attribute that serves to satisfy other needs).

Because the members of all societies have essentially the same resources to use in satisfying the same basic needs, we all behave in strikingly similar ways and develop strikingly similar social patterns. For example, because of the universal need for sleep, and because our eyes, unlike those of many species, are poorly designed for seeing in the dark, every human society has been geared to the same basic cycle of heightened daytime activity and reduced activity at night.

Fourth, humans all depend on the *societal mode of life,* especially during the formative years. The human infant is born in a condition of extreme immaturity and helplessness. In fact, for its first year it experiences growth patterns (e.g., bone ossification, brain growth) that are part of *fetal* development in other primate species.*[33] Maturation proceeds at a slow pace: children require much longer to reach maturity than the young of other species (e.g., even the anthropoid apes reach sexual maturity by about the age of nine). And even as adults, most of us cannot satisfy all of our basic needs except through cooperative activities.

Fifth, as we have already seen, we humans have *an immense capacity for learning, and for modifying our behavior in response to what we learn.* The result is a remarkable flexibility of behavior and freedom from the constraints of genetically programmed behaviors, which so restrict the lives of other animals. Thus, we are able to devise alternative patterns of action for virtually every situation we encounter and create countless new ways of satisfying our needs.

Sixth, all humans have *the capacity to create and use symbol systems and cultures.* This uniquely human ability is dependent on a variety of genetic attributes, including such organs of speech as lips, tongue, palate, sinuses, and vocal cords. Equally important, however, are peculiarities of the human brain, specifically those unique areas of the cerebral cortex that control speech and abstract thought.[34] Most linguists now believe that despite the many differences among the 3,000 spoken languages humans employ, there is a single common "deep structure" that is shared by all.[35] This is thought to be the only explanation for the amazing speed and ease with which young children are able to learn any language to which they are exposed.[36] In other words, the human brain has evolved in such a way that it is genetically equipped to ensure comprehension of the basic underlying structure of any language, and all that must be learned are the specifics of vocabulary, grammar, and phonetics.

Seventh, our species' genetic heritage includes not only the ability to learn from experience, to reason, and to devise cultural solutions to problems, but also *power-*

---

*The reason humans enter the world in an essentially fetal state is apparently related to the size of the brain. If the infant were to develop in the womb an additional seven to twelve months, its increased head size would make birth impossible.

ful emotions and appetites which evolved in the distant past in our remote prehuman ancestors and which we have inherited from them. These are preserved in that portion of our brain which physiologists refer to as "the old brain" or "the animal brain." The precise nature of the relation of the old brain to the cerebral cortex, or reasoning part of the brain, has yet to be discovered, but it is obvious to even the most casual observer that under conditions of stress the emotions often take control of human actions and rationality is sacrificed—or forced to serve ends that are dictated by the emotions.

Eighth, humans have a *highly developed awareness of self and an acute consciousness of our situation with respect to the rest of the world.* This aspect of human nature has been called both a blessing and a curse. Because of it, we are able to picture ourselves in situations we have never experienced, and thus we have the capacity to plan for the future and develop goals. But with this awareness and foresight comes the realization that we are responsible for our actions, and thus we acquire the capacity for making moral judgments and creating a moral order. A famous geneticist once remarked that no other animal has to bear anything comparable to the tragic discord that self-awareness has created in the human soul.[37]

Ninth, and finally, we are *strongly motivated to put our own needs and desires ahead of those of others, especially when the stakes are high.*[38] The genetic basis of this becomes obvious when we compare human societies with the societies of the social insects. Social relationships in the latter are invariably harmonious because these creatures are genetically programmed to respond to other members of their society in a wholly cooperative and altruistic manner. The worker bee cannot alter its activities or vary its routine; nor can it choose between its own way of life and that of the drone. Individuality is genetically suppressed in these insects and cooperative behavior is unavoidable.

From an evolutionary standpoint, self-awareness and self-serving behavior both appear to be by-products of our species' tremendous dependence on learning. Learning, by its very nature, is a differentiating and individuating experience. No two individuals can possibly share exactly the same set of experiences over the course of their lives, and since experience shapes both our values and our perceptions of ourselves, a highly developed awareness of self and self-serving behavior become unavoidable. This does not mean, of course, that cooperation is lacking in human societies. As most individuals discover early in life, the benefits of cooperation usually exceed the benefits of conflict. Thus, enlightened self-interest ensures a substantial degree of cooperation in every society.

The late Abraham Maslow, a psychologist, once theorized that there is a genetically based hierarchy of human needs that each of us possesses. Our physiological needs are the most basic, followed by the need for safety, and then, in turn, by the need to belong and be loved, the need for esteem and respect, and the need for "self-actualization."[39] The more basic needs, according to Maslow, remain dominant in a person's life until they are satisfied, but the more fully they are satisfied the stronger the higher needs become. Thus, the most urgent need of one accustomed to having all of his or her physical and safety needs met will be the need to be loved and accepted by others. And the person whose needs are satisfied in every other respect may be driven by the need for "self-actualization"—the need for self-expression, perhaps, or for power, or for aesthetic experience. Although Maslow's theory is still unproven, it appears consistent with what can be observed of human behavior and helps us understand how our common genetic heritage can lead to such varied values and behavior.

By now it should be clear why we have had to examine our biological heritage before we could examine our societies. When a single species combines such diverse and often contradictory attributes as ours does, we must expect its societies to be complex and difficult to understand, and the principles we have established in this chapter will illuminate much that we encounter in the chapters that follow.

As many of the great novelists and poets have recognized, a fundamental tension is built into the very fabric of human life: Homo sapiens is, by nature, both a social animal and an individualistic, self-centered animal. It is this, more than anything else, which creates the drama in human life, and the uncertainties. And it is this which justifies one early sociologist's characterization of human societies as systems of "antagonistic cooperation."[40]

Excursus: A Brief History of Sociology

Before going further in our analysis of human societies, it may be well to pause and take a closer look at sociology itself—its origins and history, its recent trends and current status. This brief excursus will also provide an opportunity to consider the relationship between sociology and the other social sciences.

Though sociology is a relatively recent addition to the scholarly world, its roots can be traced back to the writings of Plato and Aristotle. Philosophers then were already speculating about societies—comparing one with another and trying to understand the forces that shaped them.

The more immediate origins of modern sociology, however, lie in the sixteenth, seventeenth, and eighteenth centuries. This was a period during which the peoples of Western Europe, especially the educated minority, were confronted with a tremendous amount of new information that could not be assimilated into their traditional belief systems. They learned that the earth was not, as they had long supposed, the center of the universe. And they also learned, through the discovery of whole new continents populated by peoples with cultures radically different from their own, that Western Europe was not the center of the earth. At the same time, European societies were themselves changing. The Protestant Reformation had divided Western Europe, and the bitter religious wars that followed undermined much of the moral and intellectual authority of the clergy. Meanwhile, urban populations were growing in size and influence. All this led to the questioning of older theories and to renewed speculation about the nature of human life.

Among the consequences were two more or less independent developments, which laid the foundation for modern sociology. The first of these was the revival of interest in the systematic study of man and society, fostered by writers such as Thomas Hobbes, John Locke, Jacques Rousseau, Adam Smith, and Thomas Malthus. Before the eighteenth century ended, these men had established the independence of social theory from theology and had laid the foundations of the modern social sciences. Some of them even went so far as to identify the phenomenon of sociocultural evolution—long before Darwin's day—and to formulate explanations for it.[41]

During this same period, others began making systematic, quantitative studies of various social phenomena. Birth and death rates were an early object of research; later there were studies of class, family income, jury verdicts, election results, and a variety of other phenomena. Sometimes those who were involved in developing theory were also involved in research, though this was usually not the case. By the end of the century, the quantitative tradition was firmly established; ties to theory were still imperfectly developed, but a basis had been established for the eventual integration of these two essentials of science: theory and research.[42]

The term "sociology" first appeared in the 1830s in the writings of a Frenchman, Auguste Comte. As a result, Comte is often referred to as the founder of modern sociology. This is an unmerited honor, however, since his writings were in an already established tradition and his own contribution was not that great.

The most famous nineteenth-century sociologist, and the most influential in his own day, was an Englishman, Herbert Spencer. Through his writings, which were translated into nearly all of the major languages, he brought sociology to the attention of the educated classes throughout the world. Like others before him, Spencer was profoundly interested in sociocultural evolution, though he saw it as merely one manifestation of a universal cosmic process linking the physical, biotic, and human worlds. Interest in evolution was further stimulated in that period by the writings of Charles Darwin, a contemporary of Spencer.

Another major contributor to the study of human societies in the nineteenth century was Karl Marx. Unlike Spencer, he stood apart from the emerging discipline of sociology, with the result that the relevance of his work to the discipline went unrecognized for many years. With the passage of time, however, this has changed. One reason has been the belated appreciation of the importance of the material base of human life—people's need for food, shelter, and the like, and the techniques for meeting these needs. Most of the other pioneer social scientists neglected or underestimated this factor.

Ironically, despite its European origins, sociology found more rapid acceptance in the United States. A number of leading American universities established professorships even before the turn of the century, and by the early decades of the present century, many institutions had established full-fledged departments of sociology. During the period between the two world wars, sociology continued to expand in the United States but failed to grow in Europe, partly because of attacks by totalitarian governments, especially in Germany and the Soviet Union, partly because of greater resistance to change and innovation by the faculties of European universities. As a result, sociology became primarily an American enterprise.

Following World War I, sociology underwent a number of important changes. Under American leadership the discipline became increasingly concerned with contemporary American society. Interest in other societies declined, as did interest in the historical dimension of human experience. To a large extent these changes reflected the desire of a new generation of sociologists to make the discipline more scientific. The result was a greatly heightened interest in field research, especially studies of local communities and their problems—crime, poverty, divorce, juvenile delinquency, illegitimacy, prostitution, the problems of immigrants, and so forth.

With this shift in interest, sociologists gradually abandoned the earlier evolutionary approach. In part, this was because of criticisms leveled against it, but primarily it was because the older approach seemed irrele-

vant to the concerns of the newer generation. Sociologists were forced to find a substitute for evolutionary theory—some new theoretical approach that could organize the growing but diffuse body of information on American society. By the late 1930s, *structural-functional* theory emerged as the apparent successor to evolutionary theory.

Structural-functional theory is, in effect, the sociological counterpart of anatomy and physiology in biology. Like anatomists, structural-functionalists are concerned with the identification and labeling of the many different parts of the things they study and with the structural relations among them (e.g., the structural patterns formed within business organizations, families, etc.). Like physiologists, they are interested in the functions each of the parts performs. Just as physiologists are concerned with the functions of organs, such as the liver, heart, and spleen, structural-functionalists are interested in the functions of institutions, such as the family, and of moral rules, such as the taboo against incest.

Since World War II, sociology has grown substantially not only in the United States but in Europe, Japan, and Canada, and it has begun to take root in other areas as well. One significant development has been the changing attitude of Communist authorities. During the Stalin era, sociology was outlawed throughout the communist world. Later, however, restrictions were removed and interest in the subject has grown considerably, especially in Poland, Yugoslavia, and Hungary.[43] This growth of sociology in other countries has reduced the unhealthy concentration of the discipline in the United States that characterized the decades of the 1930s and 1940s.

Another notable development has been the movement of sociology beyond the confines of the academic community. Prior to the 1940s, sociologists were employed almost entirely by universities and colleges. Beginning in World War II and continuing to the present, there has been a growing demand for their services by government, industry, and other kinds of organizations.

Intellectually, too, sociology has made substantial progress. Two of the more important developments have been the increasing use of quantitative techniques and the revival of interest in *macrosociology*. The first of these was a natural outgrowth of efforts to achieve greater precision in describing social phenomena and greater rigor in analysis. This trend was given an enormous boost by the invention of computers, which enable researchers to handle large volumes of data and carry out complex statistical analyses that would otherwise be impossible.

The revival of interest in macrosociology has come about for a number of reasons. Above all, there is a growing recognition that the most pressing problems of our time—the threat of war, the spread of revolution, the distress of Third World nations, the problem of poverty—are all macroorganizational problems that require macrosociological theory and research if solutions are to be found. Moreover, there is a growing recognition that many microorganizational problems and developments—the changing role of women, the changing nature of the family, the growing incidence of crime—cannot be understood adequately, or dealt with effectively, unless they are viewed within the context of broader societal trends. One response to this renewal of interest in macrosociology has been a revival of interest in societal development and change and the formulation of ecologically oriented developmental theories of the kind that provides the foundation and framework for the present volume.[44]

Sociology and the Other Social Sciences

The study of human societies has never been exclusively a sociological concern. All the social sciences have been involved in one way or another. Most of the others, however, have focused on some particular aspect of the subject. Economics and political science limit themselves to a single institutional area. Human geography studies the impact of the physical and biotic environments on societies. Social psychology is concerned with the impact of society on the behavior and personality of individuals.

Only sociology and anthropology have been concerned with human societies per se. That is to say, only these two disciplines have interested themselves in the full range of social phenomena, from the family to the nation and from technology to religion. And only these two disciplines have sought to understand societies as entities in their own right.

In matters of research, there has been a fairly well established division of labor between sociology and anthropology. Sociologists have, for the most part, studied industrial societies; anthropologists have concentrated on preliterate societies. This division of labor has made

good sense, since the skills needed to study a remote tribe in the mountains of New Guinea are very different from those needed to study a modern industrial society.

From the standpoint of teaching and the development of theory, however, the separation of sociology and anthropology has been far less satisfactory. Many problems, especially those involving long-term evolutionary processes, require the contributions of both disciplines. Ignoring either leads to incomplete analyses and biased interpretations. As a consequence, there has been a long tradition of intellectual "borrowing" between sociology and anthropology, and this volume follows in that tradition.

With the revival of evolutionary theory, scholars in these fields came to recognize that both disciplines were neglecting agrarian societies—those societies which occupy the middle range in the evolutionary scale between primitive preliterate societies and modern industrial societies. More recently, therefore, both sociologists and anthropologists have undertaken research on these groups in Southeast Asia, the Middle East, and Latin America.

The growing concern with agrarian societies has also led to increased cooperation between sociologists and historians. Since history is the study of written records of the past, historians have been the experts on agrarian societies of earlier centuries. Much of the older work by historians, with its heavy emphasis on the names and dates of famous people and events, is of limited value to students of human societies. But that discipline has been changing too, and historians today are increasingly concerned with the basic social processes and patterns that underlie the more dramatic but often less significant events on which their predecessors focused. As a result history and sociology have become more valuable to each other.

This trend toward interdisciplinary cooperation is evident today in all the social sciences, and even beyond. Scholars are coming to recognize that no discipline is sufficient unto itself. To the degree that any field cuts itself off from others, it impoverishes itself intellectually. Conversely, to the degree that it communicates with other disciplines, it enriches itself and them.

CHAPTER 2

Human Societies as Biosociocultural Systems

Much of the fascination of human societies is due to their extraordinary complexity and variability. Some societies have a hundred million or more members who are differentiated from one another on the basis of age, sex, occupation, education, income, wealth, religious beliefs, political beliefs, and numerous other personal characteristics. Within such societies, the members are organized into many kinds of groups—families, communities, religious groups, political parties, work organizations, schools, and more—and each involves complex patterns of conflict, competition, and cooperation. Each society is unique, and the differences among them often appear as enormous as the differences among unrelated species of plants or animals.

The extraordinary variability and complexity of human societies is due primarily to their symbol systems and the cultures based on them. The need for sociology as a discipline separate from biology arises precisely because these cultural differences enable humans to create such diverse and complex societies. If human societies, like those of other species, were shaped almost exclusively by their members' genetic heritage, they would be far less variable and complex—and far less interesting as well.

To appreciate the difference that variations in culture can make, one need only compare contemporary American society with any of the thousands of tiny Indian societies that occupied the same territory only a few hundred years ago. Were it not for culture, differences of this magnitude would be impossible; all human societies would be very much alike, just as all elephant societies are, and all chimpanzee societies.

Because human societies combine biological, social, and cultural elements, they are sometimes referred to as *biosociocultural* systems. This contraction is more than a semantic convenience: it is also a reminder that these three elements are inextricably intertwined and that we will badly misunderstand human societies if we ignore any of them.

In this chapter we will examine each of the major components of human societies individually and then see how they combine to form the complex and variable biosociocultural systems that will be our primary concern in this volume. First, however, we need to consider the minimum conditions that must be met if human societies are merely to survive.

The Needs of Societies

As we saw in the last chapter, human societies are, above all else, adaptive systems on which their members depend for the satisfaction of their many needs and desires, and, ultimately, for survival itself. *But societies also have needs of their own that must be met.* These needs are known as *functional requisites*.[1]

First and foremost among them is the need for *population and population replacement*. No society can survive without a sufficient number of mature adults of both sexes who are capable of reproducing and also of performing the work that is required to satisfy the essential needs of the members—including dependent children. This means that a society requires not only an adequate number of members (a dozen seems to be about the minimum), but also a population that has a reasonably balanced distribution in terms of age and sex.

Second, the population must be equipped with a substantial store of *information*. Information is a record of experience that is retained in the memory systems of organisms and machines and that guides their actions. Without such a guide, their actions would be random and unrewarding. Human societies make use of three very different kinds of information: (1) genetic, (2) neurological, and (3) cultural. The first of these is a record of the experience of thousands of generations of our ancestors—human and prehuman—and it has been acquired over hundreds of millions of years through the biological processes of variation and natural selection. This information is stored biochemically in our genes. The second is a record of experience that each individual acquires for himself or herself through personal experience over the course of a lifetime, and it is stored electrochemically in memories in the brain. The third is a record of experience that is acquired and *shared* by members of a society during their society's existence, and it can be stored in various ways, such as in the memories of members, in books, in organizational files, in computer data banks, on films, or on musical tapes, to mention some of the more familiar means. But what is essential in all of these information systems—genetic, neurological, and cultural—is the record of experience that they contain.

Energy is a third functional requisite for human societies, since without continuous inputs of energy all activity would come to a halt. Even thought requires energy. Food is the most basic source of energy in all societies, but in modern industrial societies it is supplemented by enormous inputs of energy from mineral sources, especially coal, petroleum, and natural gas. Dependence on information and on energy are characteristics that human societies share with all other living populations.

Fourth, every human society requires *materials.* In the simplest societies, these include wood, stone, and bone that can be fashioned into tools and weapons, as well as materials that can be used to construct shelters and to provide clothing. In more advanced societies, the quantity of materials required is far greater and more varied. Modern industrial societies, especially, consume vast quantities of materials of diverse kinds.

A fifth requirement of every society is a *system, or systems, of communication.* This is essential if cooperative activities among the members are to be sustained. It is also essential if cultural information is to be shared and if the society's store of such information is to be preserved or expanded. At a minimum, every human society has a spoken language, but as societies have grown more complex other systems of communication have had to be added. These include writing, musical notation systems, computer languages, braille, and others.

Sixth, every society must have a *system, or systems, of production.* Information, energy, and materials must be coordinated so as to provide the goods and services that the members of a society need and desire. One of the universal features of systems of production is a division of labor. At a minimum, this involves differentiation of work activities based on age and sex. In more complex societies there is also extensive occupational specialization, as well as a division of labor among organizations (e.g., schools, churches, labor unions), communities, and even regions. Systems of production also require capital goods and human capital. Capital goods are goods that are used for the production of other goods. They include not only tools, but also buildings that house tools and workers (e.g., factories), transportation systems that move materials from one stage of production to the next or from producers to consumers, and communication systems (e.g., telephone systems) that facilitate the productive process. *Human capital* is a term which refers to the knowledge, skills, and other attributes of the labor force which contribute to the production of goods and services.

Seventh, every society must have a *system, or systems, of distribution.* Because goods and services are produced by means of a division of labor, the person who produces a good or service is usually not the person who consumes it. In simple societies, distributional systems are simple: producers usually exchange goods and services directly with consumers. In large and complex societies, however, this is not possible and a medium of exchange—usually money—is created to facilitate the much more complex and far more numerous exchanges that are required. In addition, some individuals become specialists in the exchange process (e.g., merchants, brokers).

Eighth, every society must develop a *system of social organization.* In other social species, systems of social organization are genetically determined. In insect societies, for example, individuals are genetically programmed to perform various specialized tasks and to coordinate their activities with the activities of other members of the society. Humans lack this kind of genetic programming: individuals must learn the roles they are to perform and societies must create a system of social organization to coordinate these roles. Two of the most basic components of any human system of social organization are the family and the local community. The family brings together into a single cooperative system individuals of both sexes and varying ages. The community brings together into a larger cooperative system entire family groups. In larger and more complex societies, systems of social organization become still more complex as other kinds of social systems are created—religious groups, economic organizations, political organizations, and many more. The basic function of all of them is to preserve and extend the network of cooperative activities that is the essence of society.

A ninth requisite of societies is *a system of social control.* The socialization

FIGURE 2.1   Socialization occurs in play as well as in situations where adults attempt to train the young.

process is the most important part of this system. This is the process by which most newborn infants are gradually transformed, over a period of years, into responsible adult members of the group. This is accomplished through a complex system of formal and informal rewards and punishments that are triggered by the actions of individuals. From infancy on, we find that certain of our actions produce smiles, praise, and other rewards, while other actions generate hostile reactions ranging from verbal rebukes to poor grades at school, denial of promotions on the job, even prison sentences. As a result, certain patterns of behavior are reinforced while others are gradually extinguished. Because of our exposure to the socialization process, we not only learn the culture of our society, but adopt its standards and principles as our own. To the degree that the socialization process is successful and individuals "internalize" the norms of their society, external controls on their behavior become less necessary. In effect, the individual now polices his or her own behavior. When that is not sufficient, however, other members of society exert controls of the kinds just mentioned.

Tenth, and finally, every society must provide *protection for its members against threats to their health and welfare*. These include threats from physical hazards, such as droughts, floods, storms, excessive heat or cold; threats from other species, such as viruses, bacteria, crop-destroying insects, large carnivores; and threats from other human societies. To protect its members, societies have developed multiple defenses ranging from shelters that protect against the weather to military systems that protect against human enemies. No society is ever completely successful in defending its members, but every society must defend enough of them long enough so that they are able to raise the next generation to adulthood and thus ensure the survival of the group.

The Basic Components of Human Societies

By now it should be clear that even the simplest of human societies are complex systems made up of many different kinds of parts. Before proceeding further, therefore, we need to examine each of their basic components. These include (1) population, (2) culture, (3) material products of culture, (4) social organization, and (5) social institutions.

Population

Population is a term that refers to *the members of a society considered collectively*. For purposes of sociological analysis, there are three aspects of any population that must be considered: (1) the genetic constants, (2) the genetic variables, and (3) the demographic variables.

Genetic Constants The genetic constants are attributes of a population that are products of our species' common genetic heritage. They are the same for every human society and, for all practical purposes, the same from one generation to the next. There is no need to repeat here the material summarized in the latter part of

Chapter 1 (see "The Common Genetic Heritage of Humans," pages 20 to 24). There is, however, one additional point that needs to be made.

Humans, like the other forms of life on this planet, have a reproductive capacity that substantially exceeds what is necessary merely to maintain their numbers. Thus, human populations tend to grow, unless growth is checked by either environmental constraints, such as insufficient food and other resources; biological constraints, such as breast-feeding and low body fat ratios; or human actions, such as delay of marriage, contraception, abortion, infanticide, or war. This capacity for population growth has been a *profoundly destabilizing force* throughout human history and may well be the ultimate source of most social and cultural change. Population growth makes it difficult for societies to establish and maintain a stable relation with the biophysical environment. It increases pressure on resources, and this necessitates some kind of social or cultural adjustment—a lower standard of living, some technological innovation that makes new resources available, some organizational change that makes for a more efficient use of existing resources, war and the conquest of another society's resources, or migration to new territories. Whatever the response, however, the result of population growth is usually societal change.

Genetic Variables In addition to the core of traits which all humans share and which comprise the major portion of our species' genetic heritage, each of us also has thousands of genes that are absent, or occur in somewhat different forms, in other individuals. Because these genes are not distributed equally among societies and their populations, there are *variable* aspects to the genetic heritage of human societies. These include skin color, hair texture, eye shape, blood type, incidence of color blindness, and taste sensitivity, to name a few of those that have been identified thus far.[2] The *direct* impact of these variables on the life of human societies appears to have been of somewhat limited importance. However, because of social and cultural responses to them, such as ethnic stereotyping and prejudice, their *indirect* effects have sometimes been substantial.

Although prior to the modern era human populations in different regions of the world had no direct contact with one another and therefore could not interbreed for long periods, no fully human group (i.e., Homo sapiens) was ever isolated long enough, or became genetically differentiated enough, to become a separate species. During prolonged periods of isolation, however, human populations did become genetically differentiated in a number of highly visible ways, such as skin, hair, and eye color; hair type; body build; and shape of face and head. These differences, which tend to be interrelated, eventually became the basis of our modern concept of race. A race is simply a part of the human population in which some of these highly visible traits occur with a frequency that is appreciably different from that of other parts of the human population. Racial differences, it may be noted, are found in many species, not just in humans.[3]

Members of modern societies often have difficulty appreciating the adaptive value of racial characteristics, because we no longer depend on them for our survival or well-being. When we encounter unpleasantly strong sunlight, for example, we adapt *culturally:* we create artificial shade, or we apply artificial "pigment" to our eyes (sunglasses) and, if we are lightly pigmented, to our skin (suntan oil). Throughout most of human history, however, a population's *genetic* attributes were its primary means of adapting to the hazards of its environment, and even minor variations in relevant characteristics, such as the ability to store body fat as an insulation against extreme cold, could determine which individuals survived and which did not.

This explains why many genetic variables, from skin color to body and facial form, are not randomly distributed across the globe, but occur in discernible geographical patterns.[4] For example, the pigment in our skin determines how dark it is and protects underlying cells from exposure to ultraviolet light. Darker skin is universal in hot, sunny regions, with the heaviest pigmentation of all in the African Sudan, where solar radiation is the most intense and constant.[5] In contrast, light pigmentation in countries with limited sunshine facilitates the synthesis of vitamin D, which protects against rickets.[6]

The "sickling gene," found chiefly in populations of Africa, the Middle East, and India, in areas where a particularly deadly form of malaria occurs, provides a somewhat different illustration of the adaptive value of genetic variables. An individual who inherits this gene from *both* parents will develop sickle-cell anemia, a disease that is normally fatal before adulthood. But a far greater number of people in the population inherit the gene from only one parent, develop only mild symptoms of the anemia, and are likely to be highly resistant to certain virulent forms of malaria. Thus, in areas with a high incidence of malaria, the sickling gene has adaptive value: its benefits to a population clearly outweigh its costs.[7]

Most genetic variables are not as easy to identify as the ones we have discussed so far. This is because most of our characteristics result from the action of more than one gene and, in addition, are not determined by genes alone. Genes provide the *potential,* but the reality is determined by the interaction of genes and environment. And environment includes that of the prenatal period, even the preconception experience of sperm and egg. This interaction of genetics and environment has been dramatically illustrated many times, as in the case of Jewish children born in Israeli kibbutzim and Japanese children born in America who tower over parents born in the ghettos of Europe and in Japan. It is clear that most biological characteristics, from longevity to musical aptitude, are shaped by both genes and environment. But so far, at least, efforts to separate the two and measure their relative influence have generally proved frustrating and unprofitable.

One thing has been clarified, however: the relation between racial and non-racial genetic variables. Studies have been made, for example, of color blindness and blood characteristics, which are variables that can be precisely identified and are minimally affected by environmental factors, and whose gene frequency in a population can therefore be precisely calculated. When the distributions of these genes are plotted geographically, they cut across racial lines. For example, the frequency of the gene for type B blood is essentially the same in the gene pools of the South Chinese, the Russians, and the West Africans.[8] Findings like these make it clear that the traits used to define race are an extremely limited set of variables that are not correlated to any appreciable degree with other genetic variables that have been carefully analyzed.

Demographic Variables   The demographic properties of a population include such things as its size, its density, how it is dispersed or concentrated (e.g., to what extent its members are concentrated in a few areas or spread out more evenly over its entire territory), the patterns of migration into and out of the society, its composition in terms of age and sex, and its birth and death rates. These characteristics, like certain clusters of genes, vary from one society to another. But these variations, unlike most genetic variations, have direct, demonstrable, and far-reaching consequences for human societies.

Population size is by far the most variable of the demographic properties of human societies, which have ranged in numbers from 20 members or less (in some preliterate societies of the recent past) to more than 1 billion (China's current population). Variations in other demographic characteristics often appear insignificant beside such variations in size. For example, two societies with stable populations (i.e., neither growing in size nor declining) and with annual death rates of 14 per 1,000 and 40 per 1,000, respectively, may not seem very different. But this variation actually means that the average life expectancy at birth of the members of the first society is seventy-one years, and in the second only twenty-five years.

In later chapters, we will have frequent occasion to consider demographic variables, since they play an important part in the evolution of human societies. By contrast, we will have very little to say from here on about the genetic variables discussed in the previous section, since there is little to indicate that they have played a significant role in sociocultural evolution.

Culture

The second basic part of biosociocultural systems is *culture, a society's symbol systems and the information they convey.* As we saw in Chapter 1, symbols are information conveyers that enable us to handle information in ways that are impossible for other creatures. We can *extract* more information from an experience (i.e., *learn* more) because symbols permit us thought processes denied other species. We can also *share* more information, because symbols enable us to express so much of the subtlety, complexity, and diversity of our experiences. We can, in fact, do more with information *whatever* is involved: in recording it, accumulating it, storing it, combining it, or applying it, symbol users have a fantastic advantage over signal users.

The symbol systems and store of information that comprise a society's culture are like a foundation laid down by previous generations. Because each new generation has this base on which to build, it can avoid repeating many of the experiences of earlier generations. If a group has already learned how to make and use fire, or invented the plow, or devised a system of numbers, its members need not repeat the time-consuming and often unrewarding experiences by which that particular element of culture was first acquired. Instead, they can address new challenges, which may result in further enrichment or modification of their culture.

We will examine both of the basic parts of culture in some detail, beginning with symbol systems.

Symbol Systems   The most basic symbol system in any society is its *spoken language.* No matter how many other symbol systems a society creates, this remains the one employed by its members in their basic thought processes, and the one that bears the major burden of transmitting information among them.

At the heart of every spoken language is a mass of social conventions, or customary practices, that govern its vocabulary and its grammar. The vocabulary is a set of sounds with meanings attached to them, and the relationship between a sound and its meaning is embedded in the history of its use by those who share that language. To those who speak English, the word "bed" means a place to sleep, not because of any logical or necessary connection between the sound and the activity, but because this is the convention that has evolved in English-speaking populations. Similarly, grammatical conventions tell us how words must be combined if they are to be meaningful and intelligible to others. Thus, it means one thing to say, "The bear ate Jack," something quite different to say, "Jack ate the bear," and nothing at all to say, "The ate bear Jack."

Until we study a foreign language, most of us have the impression that there is something natural—even inevitable—about the way our own society and its language separate experience and thought into the bits of meaning we call words, and that learning another language is only a matter of learning the sounds another society applies to those same "units of experience." Yet as people conversant in two or more languages are well aware, words in one do not necessarily have an equivalent in the other. Americans and Russians were reminded of this some years ago during talks between President Kennedy and Chairman Khrushchev. Kennedy repeatedly said that the Russians should not miscalculate the will and intentions of the American people, and every time the word "miscalculate" was translated, Khrushchev flushed angrily. Kennedy later learned that the Russian language has no precise equivalent of this word, and the translator had seized on a Russian word, normally applied to a small child or uneducated person, meaning "unable to count." Khrushchev naturally assumed that Kennedy was implying he was not very bright![9]

One reason languages separate experience into different units is because the experiences of the people who *create* and *use* the languages are so different. For example, gauchos, the famous horsemen of the Argentine prairies, have 200 words to denote the different colors of horses, but only 4 for all the plants known to them: *pasto,* fodder; *paja,* bedding; *cardo,* wood; and *yuyos,* all others.[10] Meanwhile, the Eskimos have numerous terms to refer to the various phenomena that we call simply "snow." They have one word for dry-wind-driven snow, one for dry-packed-suitable-for-cutting-into-blocks-and-building-igloos snow, another for ice-crust-surface snow, and so on.[11] In yet another part of the world, the Dugum Dani, Stone Age horticulturists on the island of New Guinea, have seventy different words that refer to sweet potatoes, their staple crop,[12] and in the Middle East, Arabic is reputed to have a thousand words for sword, indicative of that culture's stress on poetry and emphasis on synonyms and figures of speech.[13] English is a language rich in numbers and units of measurement, perfect for describing and recording mathematical and scientific data. In short, a language reflects the needs and concerns of those who use it.

Another reason languages differ in the way they categorize and classify experience is the haphazard and spontaneous manner in which they evolve. Consider the evolution of the word "bureau," for example. A bureau was originally something made of baize, a thick green cloth. Because these bureaus were often put on writing tables and chests of drawers, the word was eventually extended to mean the furniture as well as the cloth. Later, because many government offices were equipped with bureaus, or writing tables, the offices themselves came to be known by that term (e.g., the Federal Bureau of Investigation).[14]

This process of change in language is so much a matter of chance that it is unlikely that the same pattern would occur in two societies. Even if two societies begin with the same language, as when a small group separates from the parent group to settle a new territory, linguistic differences are bound to develop unless a high level of communication is maintained between them. There is no better example of this in the modern era than in the differences between English as it is spoken in England, Australia, Canada, Jamaica, and the United States. For Australians, for example, "Don't come the raw prawn," means "Don't try to put one over on me," and "Fair and dinkum" means true and honest.

So far we have discussed spoken language as if it were merely a neutral and passive vehicle for transmitting information. But as political leaders, propagandists, and advertisers have long recognized, individual words often acquire, through the process of association, powerful emotional connotations that enable them to convey more than is embodied in their formal definitions. Words like "communist," "racist," and "sexist," for example, have such strong negative associations for many Americans that they respond unthinkingly to the emotional content of the symbol. Words can also acquire strong positive associations, and these, too, may be used to manipulate emotions. For example, linking kinship terms with organizations, as in "Mother Russia," "Mother Church," or "Uncle Sam," can stimulate warm feelings of affection.

A leading linguist of the last generation, Edward Sapir, went so far as to claim that the way people perceive reality "is to a large extent unconsciously built upon the language habits of the group," and that, as a result, different societies live in different worlds, "not merely the same world with different labels attached."[15] Though most scholars today would not go this far, they recognize that language is an important part of our experience, and therefore it helps to determine what we feel, what we perceive, and what we do.[16]

Supplementing the spoken language, every society uses conventional gestures and facial expressions whose meanings are evident to members of the group. This "body language" should not be confused with facial expressions and body movements that are genetically determined, such as our involuntary reaction when we touch something hot, or the way we pucker up when we taste something bitter. True body language is symbolic, just as words are, for the form and meaning of the gestures and expressions are determined by those who use them. Consider, for example, the shrug of the shoulders. Various groups use it to convey indifference, uncertainty, or a lack of information on the subject in question, with the specific meaning being indicated by the context in which it is used.

Body language may be the oldest type of symbol used by our species, and it probably once played a greater role in communication than it does today. Yet even now, it can be an invaluable source of information: people convey so much with a smile or frown, a tilt of the head, a movement of the hands. This is one reason many of us avoid the telephone when we have an emotionally charged message to deliver, such as news of the death of a loved one. We know we can communicate our own

FIGURE 2.2 Two sides of a limestone tablet found in Mesopotamia, bearing some of the oldest known picture writing
(about 3500 B.C.). Included are symbols for head, hand, foot,
threshing sledge, and several numerals.

feelings more effectively, and read those of others more clearly, when we combine
words, body language, and signals.

A third kind of symbol system in many societies is written language, a relatively
recent development in human history. Some of the oldest written records in existence today were prepared thousands of years ago by temple authorities in Mesopotamia to enable them to keep a record of their business transactions.[17] These
priests were stewards of their god's resources, and when they loaned out his animals
or grain, it was imperative to get them back again. Even though the priest who made
a loan might die, the god expected it to be recovered. To keep track of their god's
property and thereby avoid his wrath, the priestly community devised a primitive
system of writing that involved a mixture of numerals, pictographs, and ideograms.

The arbitrary and symbolic nature of this writing is clear. Even when a pic-
tograph (essentially a picture) was used to represent a bull, it was a stylized representation that excluded many of the animal's features that might have been included.
Moreover, the same features were used consistently, indicating that conventional
forms of notation had already been established. From a very early date, the pic-
tograph of a jar came to represent a certain quantity of grain, rather than the jar itself.
And finally, among these early examples of writing are a number of ideograms,
which are "pure" symbols, since they are completely arbitrary and based solely on
convention. They lack any visual resemblance to the objects they represent, just as
our dollar sign bears no resemblance to the currency it symbolizes.

As new uses for writing were discovered, new efforts were made to translate
spoken language into written form. At an early date, kings and princes recorded their
successes for posterity, priests their sacred rites and traditions. At first, as the
Mesopotamian priests' experience makes clear, a society's written symbols could
express only a small part of what was possible with its verbal symbols. Gradually,
however, written languages developed until they were able to convey the same
information as spoken ones, and writing came into its own as a means of storing
information, for communication across the barriers of space and time, and eventually as a medium of artistic expression, education, and entertainment.

As societies have acquired more information, it has often become necessary to go beyond such basic symbols as letters and numerals. Thus, new symbol systems have evolved that greatly facilitate the handling of specialized kinds of information. For example, musicians devised musical notation so they could express the information that they create and use, and mathematicians and scientists developed a wide variety of symbol systems to express abstract ideas, complex numbers, and so on. The specialized symbol systems now found in modern societies include languages for the deaf, the blind, engineers, stenographers, computer scientists, and others too numerous to mention.

Over the course of history, the relative importance of the three basic types of language—body, spoken, and written—has altered considerably. Body language, including symbolic gestures and facial expressions, may well have been dominant at an early date, declining only when true speech evolved. Then, until quite recently, verbal symbols remained the primary means of transmitting information from one person to another and from one generation to the next. With the invention of the printing press and the subsequent spread of literacy, written language steadily increased in relative importance, largely because it could overcome space and time, the historic barriers to communication. During the last century, thanks to such devices as the telephone, radio, motion pictures, and television, the spoken language, too, has overcome those barriers, altering the balance once again. And in the most recent, most dramatic development of all, a plethora of languages have been created for computers, enabling them to handle fantastic amounts of information of diverse kinds. More important than these shifts in the relative importance of different types of language, however, is the fundamental trend that has persisted from early prehistoric times: *the continuing expansion of old symbol systems and the creation of new ones has steadily increased the capacity of human societies to handle information.*

Information   Cultural information is *knowledge acquired through experience and conveyed through symbols.* A society's information, is, in effect, a product of its experience: its experiences in the remote past and in the recent past; its experiences with its environment and with itself. Needless to say, no society's culture preserves every experience of every member throughout its entire history. Rather, a society gleans what it considers valuable and attempts to preserve it.

Because every society has a unique past, every culture is unique. We can say this another way: out of diverse experience, diverse information emerges. This means that human societies not only have different amounts of information on a given subject; they frequently have different "facts" as well. Since we know that human senses and intellect are limited and fallible, this should be no surprise. Even hard scientific "facts" in modern societies must often be revised in the light of later research.

Cultural information is not limited to the kinds of ideas whose truth or accuracy is capable of being proved or disproved, however. It includes a group's total perception of reality: its ideas about what is real, what is true, what is good, what is beautiful, what is important, what is possible. When we discussed symbol systems, we saw that they, too, are so rooted in subjective experience that even individual symbols may become "units of experience"—which explains why a word like "mother" can be so emotionally charged. We also saw that the kind of information conveyed by symbol systems ranges from historical and statistical data to concepts of deity, attitudes toward horses (and plants), characteristics of snow, poetic inclinations, even music itself. Cultural information includes, quite literally, *everything humans are capable of experiencing and able to translate into symbolic form.*

Because all human societies have certain fundamental kinds of experiences in common, and because they all have the same basic needs to satisfy, all cultures include information on certain basic subjects:

- Every culture has a substantial store of information about the biophysical environment to which the society must adapt, including its plant and animal life, its soils and terrain, its mineral resources and water supply, its climate and weather conditions.

- Every culture includes information about the group's social environment, the other human societies with which the group has contact.

- Every culture contains information about the society itself: its origin, its people, its heroes, its history.

- Every culture contains information that seeks to explain the ultimate causes of events.

FIGURE 2.3 All cultures contain information created solely to satisfy culturally activated and intensified needs, such as the desire for artistic expression and ritual: Indonesian dancers performing the sacred dance drama of The Witch and The Dragon.

- Every culture has a lot of information that enables the members to cope with recurring problems, from feeding themselves to resolving intragroup conflict.

- Every culture contains information that guides individuals in making judgments about what is good and what is right and what is beautiful.

- Every culture has information created solely to satisfy culturally activated and intensified needs, such as the desire for artistic expression, for example, or for ritual.

Although this list is neither exhaustive nor detailed, it conveys something of the breadth of culture.

Much of the information contained in cultures is ideological in nature. We might say it is information that results from efforts to make sense out of human experiences.[18] For *ideology is information used to interpret experience and help order societal life.* Because humans are users of symbols and creatures of culture, life can be overwhelming. We think, feel, hope, enjoy, and suffer as no other creatures can. We imagine what we cannot know and yearn for what may not exist. We live simultaneously in three worlds: the past, the present, and the future. We alone, apparently, live out our lives aware that death is inevitable. To make things more difficult, we create for ourselves a profusion of cultural alternatives, in the face of which our genetic heritage is an inadequate guide. It is not surprising, therefore, that as individuals we need help in interpreting experience, finding meaning, and making choices. And, as we have seen, societies need help in regulating and ordering their collective life.

Medieval Christianity is a good example of a highly developed and comprehensive ideology, the kind that answers virtually all of these individual and societal needs. At its center was a vision of a universe inhabited by many kinds of spiritual beings (seraphim, cherubim, humans, demons, devils, etc.) mostly under the dominion of God. God was perceived as the King above all earthly kings, but because His authority was challenged by Satan, the prince of evil, people were confronted with a choice as to which to serve. Those who chose God (who would ultimately prevail) were obliged to accept the Church's doctrines and conform to its code of morality. The latter enjoined Christians to be charitable to one another, honest, sober, hardworking, monogamous (better yet, celibate), obedient to all in authority, and regular in devotions and worship. Since no one could adhere perfectly to these requirements, the Church provided opportunities for people to confess their sins, do penance, and obtain absolution.

When we look closely at medieval Christianity, we find the three basic elements that comprise *every* ideology. First, there is a system of *beliefs* about the kind of world we inhabit. Second, there is a system of general *moral values* that emanate from, or are justified by, those beliefs. Finally, there is a system of *norms* that apply those general values to specific situations and spell out how the members of the group are to act in various circumstances, what they should and should not do.

There are two basic kinds of norms in every society and they have evolved in very different ways. Some are part of official or legal codes of conduct that are enforced by an authority, such as a government, a church, or other organization. We refer to such norms as *laws, regulations,* or *rules,* and they are sometimes accompanied by explicit statements of the sanctions that will be used to punish those who violate them. A city ordinance, for example, may specify a fine of $25 for littering streets or sidewalks.

In contrast, many norms are informal and unofficial, and violations of them are not officially sanctioned. Thus, every society and every subgroup in a society, from corporations to families, has many informal rules, or *customs,* which define for the members acceptable and unacceptable behavior. They may apply to such diverse things as modes of dress, hairstyles, food preparation, the selection of marriage partners, the performance of various tasks, proper grammar, and attitudes toward children or older people—to name only a few. These informal norms are as important in shaping behavior as more formal ones. As we noted previously, norms and their related sanctions (i.e., rewards and punishments) are basic components of every system of social control.

Sometimes it is difficult to determine, or even to imagine, how certain elements of ideology originated, or what they can possibly tell us about the past experience of a society. This is true, for example, of one of the central beliefs of Hinduism, the belief in the sacredness of the cow. The boxed insert explains how this seemingly

---

INDIA'S SACRED COWS: THE ADAPTIVE VALUE OF AN IDEOLOGY

In a society where tens of millions of people go to sleep hungry every night, devout Hindus, who constitute the vast majority of India's population, would not dream of killing any of that country's 54 million cows for food. To a Hindu, even murder is not as great a sacrilege as killing a cow.

Marvin Harris, a leading proponent of ecological-evolutionary theory, examined this seeming paradox in an effort to find a rational explanation. He rejected the view that an ideology evolves arbitrarily, unrelated to the rest of societal life or to the experiences of its members in the past. Rather, he suspected that any belief that has been as widespread and as persistent as the Indian taboo against cow slaughter must have significant adaptive value for the society.

In a volume titled *Cows, Pigs, Wars and Witches: The Riddles of Culture,* Harris reported the results of an analysis of this subject. He found that the cow is of enormous economic value to the members of Indian society. A peasant's cow is, in effect, a factory that provides food (milk, butter); fertilizer; fuel for cooking (dried manure is excellent for this purpose, producing a clean, low heat); flooring material (a paste of manure and water hardens into a smooth surface that holds down dust and can be swept clean); and, most important of all, oxen to pull the peasant's plow. Harris also found that less than 20 percent of the food consumed by Indian cattle is edible by humans. In short, the cow converts substances of little worth to the peasant into extremely valuable products.

Although Indian peasants recognize that a living, productive cow is vastly more valuable to them and to their children than the same cow consumed as food, it would be only natural for them to ignore this fact when they are desperately hungry. The religious taboo against killing cows is a powerful cultural mechanism that helps to protect these animals even in times of famine and thereby preserve an invaluable resource. In short, Hinduism's conception of the cow as sacred is based on the experience of countless generations of the Indian people and continues to serve them well.

strange belief has, for centuries, helped the members of Indian society cope with some of their basic and recurring problems in a highly adaptive way.

Another crucial body of information in every culture is *technology*. This is *information about how to use the material resources of the environment to satisfy human needs.* Compared to ideology, technology seems rather prosaic and uninteresting. Historians and social scientists have tended to ignore it,[19] and until recently people seldom came to blows over the relative merits of different technologies. As we will see in the next chapter, however, the influence of technological information on the course of history and on the process of societal change and development has been out of all proportion to the recognition usually accorded it.

In every society, a large component of technological information concerns food: where and how to get it and how to process it for consumption or storage. There is also information about the other material resources available to the society and how they may be converted into useful forms—into fuel for heat, cooking, and other purposes; into clothing and shelter; into tools, weapons, ornaments, and other things the group needs or values.

Because a distinctive body of information tends to build up in response to each set of human needs, we sometimes speak of various technologies in the same society, such as a military technology or a communications technology. Often, however, we speak of a society's technology in the singular, because there is an underlying unity to this store of information. The principles of metallurgy, for example, are used in virtually every area of technological activity in a modern industrial society, and the same is true of other basic elements of technology.

Material Products of Culture

The third part of biosociocultural systems consists of the material products of culture, the result of the use of technological information to convert environmental resources into things the members need or want. These range from perishable items that are consumed within hours of production (such as certain foods) to things that may endure for centuries, such as pyramids, cathedrals, and plastic containers. They range, too, from utilitarian objects like horseshoes, hammers, and houses to frivolous items like hula hoops and Frisbees. And they include products, such as works of art, whose significance may persist beyond a single generation or extend beyond a single society.

Capital goods are some of the most important material products of a culture. These are things that are devoted to the production of other things. Thus, the more capital goods a society possesses, the more goods of various kinds it is able to produce, and the wealthier it tends to become.

The first capital goods were simple tools made of stone, wood, and bone, which enabled our ancestors to produce such essentials as fire, food, shelter, and more tools. Later, as the store of cultural information increased and as new environmental resources became available, the character of tools changed. Metals were especially important in this respect because they combined strength and durability with malleability. This culminated in the last two hundred years in the production of the kinds of capital goods that are vital in modern industrial societies: machines and instru-

FIGURE 2.4 **The more capital goods a society possesses, the more goods of various kinds it is able to produce and the wealthier it tends to become: aerial view of industrial complex at Westfalenhuette, West Germany.**

ments of many kinds, railroads, motorized vehicles, electrical power systems, factory complexes, and more.

Early in human history another environmental resource was gradually transformed by human societies into *living* capital: domesticated animals. Their contribution to production has been crucial in every society that depended upon oxen or horses to pull plows and wagons, cattle or goats to provide milk and cheese, or sheep to provide wool. Domesticated animals have often been a society's primary capital investment and its medium of exchange as well. This was true, for example, in ancient Greece and Rome. Our word "pecuniary," which means "relating to money," derives from *pecus,* the Latin word for cattle.

Social Organization

The fourth basic component of human societies is social organization. This refers to *the network of relationships among the members of a society*. These relationships make it possible for the members to satisfy their own individual needs as well as the collective needs of the society as a whole.

The kinds of relationships found in human societies are, to some extent, biologically determined. Social relationships in all mammalian societies, for example, are organized to take account of age and sex differences. Human societies, however, rarely stop there. In most instances, they go much further, developing elaborate kinship networks and other complex social arrangements that reflect cultural influences. Thus, as we think about social organization in human societies, we should view it as a product of the interaction of culture and genetics.

Individuals   The two basic building blocks in social organization are the individuals who make up the society and the roles they fill. Little need be added to what we have already said concerning the nature of individuals. Each person has a genetic heritage that is partly distinctive and partly shared, and each has a cultural heritage that is also partly distinctive and partly shared. From society's standpoint this is sometimes an asset and sometimes a liability. On the one hand, it ensures a high rate of individuality as a consequence of countless combinations and recombinations of genetic and cultural elements in different individuals. This can have great adaptive value for a society, especially when it is confronted with new circumstances to which it must adjust. On the other hand, intrasocietal conflict results from this individuality, as we have seen. Clearly, individuality is a mixed blessing.

Roles   *Roles* are positions in societies that can be filled by individuals. They develop in response to the recurring needs of societies. Young children, for example, require care and attention, and the roles of mother and father have evolved in response to this need. In large and complex societies, there is a continuing need for political leadership, and a variety of roles, ranging from city councilman to president or prime minister, have developed in response.

Roles in society, like roles in the theatre, have distinctive behavioral expectations and requirements attached to them.[20] Thus, just as a man may play the role of Macbeth on the stage, so he may "play" the roles of husband, father, and doctor in his home and community. In both instances, people expect him to act in certain ways and not in others, simply because of the roles he occupies. When he meets those expectations, he is applauded or rewarded. When he fails to meet them, he is criticized, or worse.

The behavioral requirements and expectations that are attached to "real life" roles are the norms we discussed on page 40. As we saw then, they may be quite formal, as in the laws forbidding theft and murder, or they may be informal, as in a neighborhood's expectations concerning property maintenance. They may involve fundamental moral issues, or they may involve the minutiae of etiquette. Norms also vary in their scope. Some apply to everyone, as in the law forbidding bigamy; others apply to only a few, as in the rules governing the conduct of members of the Canadian Parliament.

As we will see in later chapters, roles change as societies change. New roles are added and older ones disappear. Even when roles persist, their content often changes. Thus, prior to the development of modern technology, the feeding of infants was entirely the work of women. Today, this is a responsibility often shared with men.

Roles serve many functions in societies, but four of these functions are of crucial importance. First, roles are an important mechanism of social control. They harness people's energies to the tasks that must be accomplished if the system is to survive and the needs of the members are to be met. Roles also ensure the performance of less essential tasks that the society as a whole, or its more powerful members or subgroups, regard as necessary or desirable.

A second function of roles is to encourage specialization. This tends to increase the efficiency of the members' efforts, since no one can do everything well.

Third, roles and role specialization increase cooperation among the members of society. Specialization increases interdependence and thereby strengthens the group.

Finally, roles are a mechanism for cultural transmission, for passing traditions on from one generation to the next. Individuals are mortal; roles are not: they can persist indefinitely. The role of rabbi, for example, has existed for over 2,500 years, contributing immeasurably to the survival of the Jewish group and to the preservation of its cultural heritage.

Groups In most societies, individuals are organized into a variety of units we call *groups*. These range from small family units and cliques to giant corporate entities of various kinds. In popular usage, the term "group" is often applied indiscriminately to any aggregation of people, regardless of their other characteristics. Sociologists, however, limit the term to *an aggregation whose members (1) act together in a common effort to satisfy common, or complementary, needs, (2) have common norms, and (3) have a sense of common identity*.

As this definition suggests, human aggregations differ in their *degree* of "groupishness." While some aggregations clearly qualify as groups (e.g., Jehovah's Witnesses) and others just as clearly do not (e.g., all the redheads in the United States), many are on the borderline (e.g., Americans of Irish descent). This last example reminds us that the degree of "groupishness" of an aggregation is not permanently fixed. Aggregations may take on more of the qualities of a group, or they may lose some. Their members may come to work together more closely; develop new, stronger, and more generally shared norms; and acquire a stronger sense of common identity; or just the opposite may occur, as has happened with Irish-Americans during the last hundred years.

Despite the exclusion of aggregations such as redheads, the concept "group" still includes such a wide variety of organizations that it is necessary to differentiate among them. The most familiar way of doing this is by their basic function in society. Thus, we differentiate between families, churches, schools, political parties, and so forth.

Sociologists have also found it useful to differentiate among groups on the basis of their size and the intensity of the social ties among their members. Small groups in which there are face-to-face relations of a fairly intimate and personal nature are known as *primary groups*. Primary groups are of two basic types, *families* and *cliques*. In other words, they are organized around ties of either kinship or friendship. Larger, more impersonal groups are known as *secondary groups*.

Secondary groups are of three basic types: associations, communities, and social movements. An *association* is a formally organized secondary group that performs some relatively specialized function or set of functions. A political party, a church, a labor union, a corporation, and a governmental agency are all associations.

Communities, in contrast, are less formally organized and perform a wider range of functions. Basically, there are two types of communities, geographical and cultural. *Geographical communities* are those whose members are united primarily

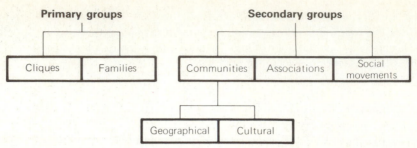

FIGURE 2.5 Types of human groups.

by ties of spatial proximity, such as neighborhoods, villages, towns, and cities. *Cultural communities* are those whose members are united by ties of a common cultural tradition, such as racial and ethnic groups. A religious group may be considered a cultural community if its members are closely integrated by ties of kinship and marriage and if the group has developed a distinctive subculture of its own.

As this last example indicates, associations may give rise to communities. The opposite can also happen: communities can give rise to associations (for example, in the United States during the 1960s, a number of new black political associations, such as CORE, emerged within the larger black community). When either of these developments occurs, the membership of the community and the membership of the association overlap to some extent. Usually, however, the community is larger because its membership requirements are less stringent, with membership often being automatically conferred by virtue of birth. For example, many who belong to the Jewish community by virtue of birth do not belong to any synagogue or other Jewish association.

Social movements are loose-knit groups that hope to change society in some way. The women's movement is a good example of such a group. Social movements, like cultural communities, often give rise to associations. Thus, the women's movement in the United States has given rise to various associations, such as the National Organization for Women (NOW).

Classes   The term *class* is used in two different, though related, ways.[21] Sometimes it refers to an aggregation or group of people who are similar with respect to their status, or rank, in society. When we use the term in this way, we usually speak of upper, middle, and lower classes; or, if we divide the hierarchy more narrowly, of upper-middle, lower-middle, and so on. Members of the same class have roughly the same degree of power, privilege, and prestige in their community or society.

Class can also be used to mean an aggregation or group of people who are alike with respect to some resource that affects access to power, privilege, and prestige. In other words, people can be classified according to their education, occupation, ethnic background, wealth, or political position, each of which either helps or hinders individuals in their efforts to attain greater power, privilege, or prestige. This use of the concept is generally more precise than that described in the previous paragraph. It enables us to identify such entities within a society as the working class, the governing class, and the propertied class, and it makes it possible to discuss the nobility and the peasantry in societies of the past, for example, or the rich and the poor in societies today.

One question that arises is whether classes are groups. The answer is, sometimes. In many instances, classes are simply aggregates whose members, though in a similar position with respect to some important resource, have no sense of common identity, have no common behavioral expectations, and do not act together to satisfy common, or complementary, needs. This is true of American office workers, a rapidly growing occupational class that does not constitute a group. On the other hand, American blacks, a racial-ethnic class, *are* a group: they have long been a cultural community with a strong sense of common identity.

Taken together, all the classes within a society form what sociologists call a *system of stratification*. The basic function of such a system is to allocate the things of value that society produces. These "valuables" include not only *material products* but also *services* (e.g., education and medical care) and *psychic gratifications* (e.g., prestige and popularity).

Because no society has yet been able to produce enough of all these things to satisfy fully the needs and desires of every individual, systems of stratification usually generate dissatisfaction and even conflict. This problem is impossible to resolve to everyone's satisfaction, because there is no obviously "right" or "fair" way to distribute things that are produced by the cooperative actions or efforts of many different people. It is equally reasonable to argue, for example, that a given product should be distributed on the basis of (1) how much a person needs it, (2) how much effort a person invests in producing it, or (3) how much skill a person contributes, to name only three of the possibilities.

Even if a society settles on one of these principles, disputes are still likely. If the members apply the principle of effort, for example, they must still decide how to measure effort. Should it be calculated by the hours spent on the job, by the foot-pounds of energy expended, or by how hard a person tries? Or, if the group adopts a different criterion, how do they measure and compare such dissimilar skills as those of a nurse, a statesman, and a computer programmer? In brief, there is no simple way, no one "right" way, to allocate rewards in human societies, and arbitrary standards are inevitable. But arbitrary or not, there must be standards.

Not surprisingly, efforts to explain social stratification and inequality have led to a major controversy in sociology.[22] The basic issue is whether distributive systems develop in response to the needs of society as a whole or in response to the wishes and desires of its most powerful members. One group of sociologists argues that inequality is necessary in order to motivate abler individuals to accept the responsibilities that are inherent in the more important positions in society. A second group argues that inequality is the result of the use of force and fraud by a minority that exploits other members of society for its own benefit. A third group sees elements of truth in both views and seeks to synthesize them.[23] Though we cannot resolve this controversy here, there will be materials in later chapters that shed light on this issue.

Social Institutions and Institutional Systems

The last of the five basic components of human societies is social institutions and institutional systems. These differ from the other components we have considered in

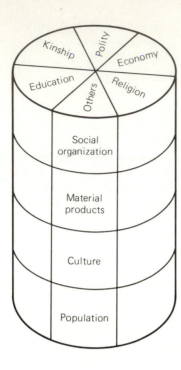

FIGURE 2.6 Relations among the basic components of human societies. Each major institutional system brings together people, culture, the material products of culture, and social organization.

one basic respect: they are combinations of the other four components, bringing together population, culture, the material products of culture, and social organization.

A British sociologist once described social institutions as "frozen answers to fundamental questions."[24] Although it is an exaggeration to call them "frozen" answers, institutions are durable and persisting elements of sociocultural systems. For purposes of definition, we may think of them as *persistent answers to important and persistent problems.*

One reason for their persistence is that their value to society is impressed on individuals at an early age. Thus, we grow up thinking of them as natural and inevitable. Another reason for their persistence is that the different elements of institutional systems are intricately intertwined and it is often impossible to change one element without being compelled to change countless others, making the cost of change too great.

Modern industrial societies have literally thousands of institutions. These include such things as marriage, the jury system, secret ballot elections, the rights of private property, the freedom to practice religion or not to practice it as one sees fit, the right to privacy, and many more.

For many purposes, sociologists are less interested in specific social institutions than in institutional systems. As the name implies, *institutional systems* are *systems of interrelated institutions.* There are five such systems that are of major importance in the study of human societies, and much of our analysis in later chapters, especially Chapters 5 to 13, will be organized around them. They are: (1) kinship, (2) the economy, (3) the polity, (4) religion, and (5) education. These are like major slices of the biosociocultural "pie." Each provides answers to a set of interrelated, important, and persistent problems. Kinship is the oldest of these systems, but all of them have existed for thousands of years and all seem likely to continue for as long as human societies endure.

Human Societies as Systems

Throughout this chapter we have made frequent use of the word "system." In the section above, for example, we discussed institutional systems. Prior to that, we discussed systems of stratification. And the chapter itself is titled "Human Societies as Biosociocultural Systems."

What, then, is a system?

"System" is a word that most of us use rather often, but seldom stop to consider. We recognize that it can be applied to many different kinds of things, but often fail to appreciate that it can be applied to *most* things. Thus, in the world of nature there are physical systems, such as the solar system, star systems or galaxies, weather systems, and systems of lakes and rivers. Every living organism is a system, and there are systems *within* organisms (e.g., digestive systems, reproductive systems), systems *of* organisms (e.g., populations, societies), and systems that include populations of organisms and their environments (i.e., ecosystems). In addition, there are systems created by humans, such as mechanical systems (e.g., automobiles and player pianos), electronic systems (e.g., computers and household security systems), and institutional systems.

In every instance, the term "system" refers to *an entity made up of interrelated parts*. The key word in the definition is "interrelated." In the words of one expert, a system is a "bundle of relations."[25] For this reason, what happens to one of the parts of a system has implications for other parts and for the system as a whole. Too much beer in the stomach, for example, affects the feet and brain, just as defective brakes on an automobile can have consequences for the fenders. Francis Thompson, the poet, captured the systemic quality of the universe as a whole when he wrote, "Thou canst not stir a flower without troubling of a star."[26]

The nature of systems is best understood, however, if we focus on a smaller, more familiar "bundle of relations," such as an automobile. When it is in normal working order, we think of it as an entity. But each of its components (wheels, frame, gears, drive shaft, battery, carburetor, transmission, engine, etc.) is also an entity— and each remains an entity even if the automobile is dismantled. But when the relations among these components have been destroyed—even if all the components are carefully preserved—the entity that was the automobile ceases to exist. A *system*, therefore, is more than the sum of its parts: it is *the sum of those parts plus the relations among them*.

Systems vary greatly in the degree to which the actions of the parts are coordinated with one another and with the actions of the system as a whole. Mechanical systems are among the most nearly "perfect" systems that exist. Consider the automobile again. When functioning properly, the actions of its parts all work together harmoniously.

Some animal societies are much like the automobile in this respect. The various parts of a termite colony, for example, work together as harmoniously as the parts of a well-tuned automobile; their actions all serve the interests of the society as a whole and there is almost total interdependence among the parts.

In human societies, the situation is quite different. For one thing, the coordination among their components is often poor. For another, their components do not always function in ways that are conducive to the well-being of the system. As we have seen, the members tend to be self-assertive. They resist efforts to coordinate and control their actions, and they do not readily subordinate their interests to the interests of the group. In short, a genetic blueprint that is very different from that of a termite society—but just as compelling—*prevents* human societies from achieving the strict ordering of relations among the parts that characterizes many other kinds of systems.

Modern scientists—including sociologists—are often content merely to dismantle and dissect a system in the belief that by examining its individual parts they will eventually learn everything they want to know about the system. In his book, *So Human an Animal,* René Dubos maintains that this process, known as *reductionism,* leads the scientist

> . . . to become so involved intellectually and emotionally in the elementary fragments of the system and in the analytical process itself, that he commonly loses interest in the phenomena or the organisms which had been his first concern. For example, the biologist who starts with a question formulated because of its relevance to human life is tempted, and indeed expected, to progress seriatim to the organ or function involved, then to the single cell, then to subcellular fragments, then to molecular groupings or reactions, then to the individual molecules and atoms.[27]

While acknowledging that the reductionist method has led to many valuable discoveries, Dubos argues that "The most pressing problems of humanity . . . involve . . . situations in which systems must be studied as a whole in all the complexity of their interactions. This is particularly true of human life."[28] Dubos goes on to say that to be fully relevant to life, the biological sciences must deal with the responses of total biotic systems to their total environments.

Dubos's advice, though aimed at biological scientists, is equally applicable to social scientists. It is easy for us, too, to become so absorbed in "the elementary fragments of the system"—individuals, roles, symbols, norms, and all the rest—that we neglect societal systems as a whole. To say this is not to minimize the importance of understanding these components. It only means that we must never allow our interest in any of the component parts of human societies to divert us from our primary concern, the study of human societies as biosociocultural systems.

The World System of Societies

Before we conclude this discussion of human societies as biosociocultural systems, there is one more system that needs to be considered. Every human society is, itself, part of a larger and more inclusive system that sociologists have come to call the *world system of societies.*

Throughout history, human societies have established and maintained relations with one another. They have exchanged ambassadors, carried on trade and commerce, sent out missionaries, translated books, exacted tribute, and in countless other ways developed and maintained a network of social and cultural ties. During much of the past, direct ties were limited to neighboring societies, since direct relations with distant societies were not possible. But even then, indirect relations existed. Society A maintained ties with Society B, which, in turn, maintained ties with Society C, and so on throughout the system. No society was ever totally cut off from the world system of societies for long, since even the most isolated societies had occasional contacts with others. With advances in transportation and communication during the last five thousand years, relations between societies have increased greatly and direct relations have been established between societies far removed from one another. As a result, the world system of societies has grown more integrated and more complex, and has come to exercise a greater influence on the life of individual societies.

As we will see in later chapters, one of the striking features of the world system of societies is its *dynamism*. Unlike many of the systems with which we are familiar (e.g., mechanical systems), relations among the parts of this system have changed tremendously over time. Were we to ignore this process of change and development, we would miss one of the most important characteristics of the world system.

CHAPTER 3

Societal Continuity and Change

Human life has changed tremendously in recent millennia. Ten thousand years ago, all human societies were tiny nomadic groups obliged to forage for the basic necessities of life. The practice of farming had not yet begun, and there were no cities or towns, and very few permanent settlements of any kind. Most societies were compelled to move about every few weeks or months in order to obtain sufficient food. The largest societies at that time had only a few hundred members at most, and the average society had only 25 or 30 members. Recent research indicates that the total human population at that time numbered no more than a few million, divided among 100,000 to 300,000 tiny societies.[1]

Today, conditions are remarkably different. The human population has increased a *thousandfold,* numbering nearly 5 billion, and the average size of societies has increased a *millionfold* to 25 or 30 million. The number of human societies, however, has dropped precipitously to fewer than 200. For the vast majority of humans, hunting wild animals and foraging for edible plants were replaced long ago by farming as the basic means of subsistence. Permanent settlements are almost universal, and there are a number of individual cities today with populations of 15 million or more.

These differences are only a few of the more obvious changes that have occurred. There have been thousands of others that are just as remarkable—changes in culture, changes in the material products of culture, changes in social organization, and changes in institutions and institutional systems. These changes, which we often forget or take for granted, are especially remarkable if we compare the experience of human societies with that of other primate, or other mammalian, societies during the same period. Chimpanzee societies today, for example, are hardly distinguishable from chimpanzee societies of 10,000 years ago, and the same is true of insect societies, fish societies, and the rest. Where significant changes have occurred, such as the growth of rat populations or the decline of wolf populations, they are largely the result of human activity, by-products of the changes that have occurred in human societies.

Ten thousand years is an enormous amount of time when judged by the standard of a single human life span, but it is a very short time by evolutionary standards. In the case of a species such as ours, which has few offspring and decades between generations, one does not expect to encounter major evolutionary changes in such a short period. Rapid change is also unlikely in a species with a population as large as the human population has been throughout this period.

Thus, the changes that have occurred in human societies in the last 10,000 years are not what biological theory would lead us to expect, and they raise important questions that we need to explore. Above all, we need to ask: What has caused these changes?

FIGURE 3.1 Ten thousand years ago, all human societies were tiny nomadic groups obliged to forage for the basic necessities of life. A few have survived into the twentieth century. The Tasaday, a recently discovered society in the Philippines, is one such group. This photograph shows two-thirds of all the members of this tiny, cave-dwelling, Stone Age society.

The Great Paradox

Before we attempt to answer this question, there is a puzzling paradox that must be considered. *Despite the tremendous changes that have occurred in human life during the last 10,000 years, the majority of societies successfully resisted change throughout their existence.* In other words, contrary to what we might infer from the changes that have occurred in the world system of societies—or from our own experience of life in the twentieth century—rapid social and cultural change has been the exception rather than the rule in individual societies until recently. In most societies, life changed very little from one generation to the next, or even from one century to the next.

When first considered, this paradox seems to pose a logical contradiction, but actually it does not. A system can change greatly even when the majority of its parts resist change—*provided that the parts that do not change do not survive.*

This is exactly what has happened in the world system of societies. The great majority of individual societies changed very little during the course of their existence, but almost none of those societies have survived into the present century. Furthermore, almost all of the societies that have survived have been societies that have changed greatly.

Table 3.1 provides a simplified illustration of what has happened in the last 10,000 years. Of the ten hypothetical societies in the illustration, only two changed from Time 1 to Time 4. During the course of their existence, the other eight did not change at all in terms of size. Nevertheless, as the bottom line of the table shows, the size of this hypothetical world system steadily increased, and by Time 4 it was almost eight times larger than it had been in Time 1.

As this illustration suggests, a process of natural selection has been at work in the world system of societies, favoring innovative societies at the expense of those

TABLE 3.1 The Great Paradox Illustrated: While the Majority of Societies Have Remained Unchanged throughout Their Existence, the World System of Societies Has Changed Tremendously

	Population Size			
Societies	Time 1	Time 2	Time 3	Time 4
A	100	1,000	2,000	5,000
B	100	500	1,000	2,500
C	100	100	100	100
D	100	100	100	100
E	100	100	100	*
F	100	100	100	*
G	100	100	*	*
H	100	100	*	*
I	100	*	*	*
J	100	*	*	*
World System Total	1,000	2,100	3,400	7,700

*This society no longer exists.

that resisted change. As we will see later in this chapter and in other chapters, this process has favored those societies that have been most successful in accumulating useful information, especially information relevant to subsistence. When societies have come into conflict with one another for territory and other vital resources, those that have been technologically more advanced have usually prevailed. Thus, even though the vast majority of individual societies have resisted social and cultural change, the world system of societies has been dramatically transformed.

Continuity and change are obviously *both important,* and both must be taken into account if we are to understand human societies. It is also obvious that we will need to differentiate carefully between the processes that have shaped the majority of individual societies and those that have shaped the world system of societies. This will become a major concern shortly, but first we need to consider several basic principles that will guide our analysis.

Environment, Heredity, and Human Societies: The Basic Model

The first premise of ecological-evolutionary theory, as stated in Chapter 1, is that human societies are a part of the world of nature and cannot be understood unless this fact and its implications are taken fully into account. This means that we must begin our inquiry into the causes of societal continuity and change by reviewing the general model of adaptation developed in the biological sciences to explain the characteristics of all living things.

Stripped to essentials, this model asserts that *all of the characteristics that we observe in any population of plants or animals arise in response to the interaction of the population with its environment and reflect the combined influence of environment and heredity. Environment* is a term that refers to everything which is external to a population and which exercises an influence on it. It includes other populations of plants and animals, climate, mineral and water resources, the topographic and locational characteristics of the territory occupied by the population, and much more. In the case of human societies, other human societies are an especially important part of the environment.

As a result of prior interaction with its environment, every plant and animal population possesses a record of experience that is stored in its members' genes. Because of the processes of mutation and recombination, different individuals have somewhat different sets of genes. Through the process of natural selection, those with genes that are more advantageous in a given environment are more likely to reproduce and transmit their genes to future generations. Those with harmful genes die before they are able to reproduce, thus causing their genes to disappear.

Prior to the 1950s, the nature of genes was still unknown. During that decade, however, geneticists discovered that genes are minute bits of the chemical molecule deoxyribonucleic acid, or DNA for short.[2] Within the two intertwined strands of this molecule, information is encoded in the form of varied sequences of four crystalline bases. These four (adenine, guanine, cytosine, and thymine, or A, G, C, and T, as they are known) are like the letters of an alphabet and can be combined in different

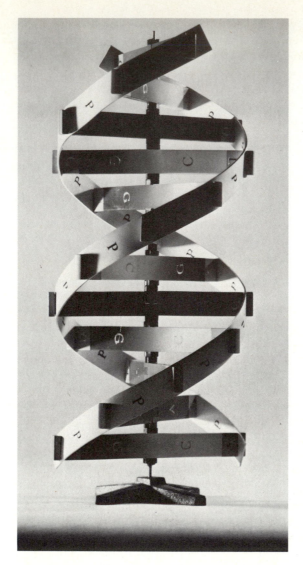

FIGURE 3.2 **Genes are minute bits of the chemical molecule deoxyribonucleic acid, or DNA for short. Within the two intertwined strands of this molecule, a wealth of information is encoded in the form of varied sequences of four crystalline bases, adenine, guanine, cytosine, and thymine, or A, G, C, and T.**

different ways to convey limitless amounts of information.* With these four chemicals, a fantastic amount of information is recorded in genetic code within the cells of every living thing, and it is this information which is translated into the chemical "messages" that guide and control an organism's development and behavior. For example, scientists have found that sickle-cell anemia is caused by the shift of a single "letter"—a T instead of an A—at one point in a 438-letter sequence of As, Cs, Gs, and Ts that is responsible for the beta-globin molecule.[3]

This genetic alphabet, working in combination with the process of natural

---

*Because our alphabet contains twenty-six symbols, it might be supposed that it can handle more information than the four-symbol genetic code. This is not true, as becomes obvious when we consider the Morse code, which, with just two symbols (dots and dashes), can handle as much information as our twenty-six-symbol alphabet.

selection, has made it possible for populations of plants and animals to create and transmit to future generations *a precious record of experience*—a record of the various physiological and behavioral traits that "work" in the environment in which they live. This record of experience, or store of information, directs both their physical development and their behavior.

This record of ancestral experience which organisms carry in their genes is extraordinarily complex in even the simplest of creatures. A single bacterium, for example, carries in its genes an amount of information equivalent to approximately 3,000 typed pages, and a single insect, depending on its species, possesses the informational equivalent of between 300,000 and 3 million typed pages.[4]

For plants, and for some species of animals, this is the only record of experience available. As a result, their physical life processes (e.g., metabolism, reproduction, behavior) are completely determined by their genetic heritage and by the influence of the environment. Thus, we say of these creatures that their behavior is "genetically programmed."

In many species of animals, however, this genetic record of experience is supplemented by individual learning, as we have seen. This allows individuals to profit from personal experience and to modify some of their actions in the light of circumstances.* Thus, learning leads to greater flexibility in the behavior of individuals and to greater variability within populations.

For humans, the potential for building a record of *their* species' experience took an enormous leap forward with the creation of symbol systems. These systems— which are the functional equivalent of the genetic alphabet—combine the flexibility of learning with the limitless storage capacity of genetic systems. Thus, the concept of heredity takes on an expanded meaning in the study of human societies: human societies have a *cultural* heritage as well as a genetic heritage. This means that when we apply the general biological model to human societies, it must be modified to take account of this unique, and critical, resource. In short, we are led to the conclusion, as Figure 3.3 indicates, that the social and cultural characteristics of

---

*Even in humans, however, many actions, such as digestion and other metabolic processes, are only marginally, if at all, subject to modification based on learning.

FIGURE 3.3   An ecological-evolutionary model of the determinants of the characteristics of individual societies.

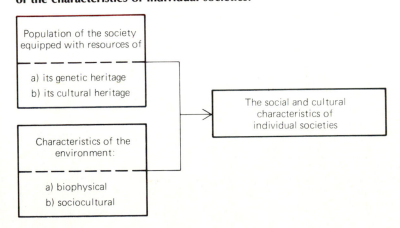

each individual society arise in response to the interaction of its population with its environment and reflect the combined influence of (1) its genetic heritage, (2) its cultural heritage, (3) the characteristics of its biophysical environment, and (4) the characteristics of its sociocultural environment.

Continuity and Change in Individual Societies

As we have seen, human societies are essentially adaptive mechanisms by means of which human populations endeavor to satisfy their varied needs and desires.* Sometimes this is accomplished by preserving traditional ways of doing things, and sometimes by adopting new and innovative practices. Thus, in the study of human societies we find ample evidence of both continuity and change.

Social and Cultural Continuity

In the world of nature as a whole, continuity is much more in evidence than change. As we noted earlier, apart from human societies, primate and mammalian societies have changed very little during the last 10,000 years except in response to changes initiated by humans. When we look further afield, the evidence of continuity is even more striking: many simple forms of life have survived almost unchanged for hundreds of millions of years.

In human societies, too, there is abundant evidence of continuity. Regardless of how rapidly a society seems to be changing, most social and cultural elements do not change. Many elements of contemporary cultures are hundreds of years old, and some, such as the alphabet, the calendar, the numeral system, many basic moral and religious beliefs, and various techniques of farming and metallurgy, are thousands of years old. The same is true of many elements of social organization, such as the roles of village headman, prime minister, king, queen, priest, and rabbi, and the even older roles of mother, father, husband, wife, child, cousin, and grandparent.

There are a number of reasons for the persistence of social and cultural elements in a society, but one of the most important is *the conscious recognition of their adaptive value*. People are naturally reluctant to do away with something they depend on when they have nothing better to take its place. Thus, every society preserves its spoken language, its basic medical, military, and subsistence technologies, and many of its norms and customs because they are recognized as workable solutions to some very important needs of the society as a whole. Cultural elements

---

*This does not mean, of course, that human societies endeavor to satisfy the needs and desires of all their members equally or impartially. On the contrary, as we will see in later chapters, all societies are more responsive to the needs of some than to the needs of others. In part, these differences are because of the varying importance of individuals to the society, and, in part, because of their varying power or influence.

α	β	γ	δ
ε	ζ	η	θ
ι	κ	λ	μ
ν	ξ	ο	π
ρ	σ	τ	υ
φ	χ	ψ	ω

FIGURE 3.4   Many elements of contemporary cultures are hundreds of years old, and some, such as the Greek alphabet, are thousands of years old.

are also preserved if they are perceived by enough people as useful in answering their individual needs. This accounts for the persistence of many elements of art, music, literature, and religion, and for the persistence of a great variety of customs and norms, including even such antisocial patterns of behavior as speeding or drug use.

Sometimes elements of culture are preserved not because they are superior solutions to problems but simply because they ensure *standardized behavioral responses* in situations where these are essential. For example, although driving a car on the right side of the road is inherently neither safer nor easier than driving on the left, this choice cannot be left to the individual. Every society must have a norm to ensure that all of its drivers follow the same procedure.

Another cause of continuity is *the cost involved in changing*. Change can be financially expensive; no one knows how many millions of dollars it will cost Americans to change to the metric system, for example. And change can also be costly in terms of time and energy, since it takes both to learn new rules and techniques and new ways of relating to others and performing one's job.

Change also exacts a *psychic* toll. This can affect people at any age when they encounter new environments, as when a child moves to a new neighborhood or a young woman enters military boot camp. But *new information* can be even more threatening. People in the past were reluctant to believe the world was round because it contradicted the evidence of their senses; people today are often just as loath to part with the comfortable thought that our earth is the center of the universe or that the world was created in six days. For new information can threaten one's view of life, making it necessary to restructure one's thinking on many other subjects in order to accommodate it.

Not surprisingly, the longer one lives with a set of ideas and beliefs, the more difficult and traumatic such "restructuring" becomes. This is why older people tend to be more conservative—that is, less open to new information and less eager for change—than young people. The *biological process of aging* is thus a very real force for continuity in every society, and its effects are magnified by the fact that older people often have the greatest power and influence. The result is a considerable resistance to change.

But aging is not the only process that makes the members of a society conservative. The *socialization process* is probably the greatest force of all for continuity within societies. For it is through this process that the members of a society acquire the belief that their culture is a precious resource and worth preserving. During their prolonged immaturity, children are obliged to master many of the most basic elements of their culture. This is essential for their survival, and their only road to any degree of independence. Before they learn to talk, for example, children are almost totally dependent on other people; after they master their society's language, they have an invaluable tool to help them get what they want. The same is true of other elements of culture: it pays the child to master them. Thus, the desire of members of the adult generation to preserve their culture by transmitting it to their offspring is more than matched by their offspring's eagerness to learn it, especially during the formative years. Since this cycle necessarily repeats itself as each generation matures, the result is a tremendous force for continuity.

These efforts to pass culture on to the next generation are reinforced by most *ideologies*. One of their chief functions is to preserve for the future basic insights of the past. Since these insights usually include the belief that the existing social order is a moral order that ought to be preserved, a society's values, norms, and leadership all acquire an aura of the sacred and thus become less vulnerable to efforts to alter them. Ironically, even revolutionary ideologies like Marxism eventually acquire a sacred and conservative character: once they win acceptance, they, too, become a force for continuity.

Finally, *the systemic nature of human societies* is a major force for continuity. This is because most of the elements in a sociocultural system are linked to other elements in such a way that change in one area often makes change in other areas necessary. As a result, the members of a society do not adopt change casually, especially when they are aware of how extensive—and expensive—that change may ultimately be. When Sweden shifted to driving on the right-hand side of the road, for example, this "simple" change meant not only that cars and other vehicles had to be redesigned, but that traffic signals and road signs throughout the country had to be relocated, traffic laws revised, and the deeply ingrained habits of millions of people altered. A society naturally hesitates to make changes that might have such far-reaching consequences, and this is a considerable force for preserving the status quo. As we saw in Chapter 2, the systemic nature of human societies is especially evident in its institutions and institutional systems, and it is there that we can see most clearly many of the basic forces for continuity and conservatism.

Social and Cultural Change

In spite of the strength of the forces promoting social and cultural continuity, some change occurs eventually in every society. Even in the simplest and most tradition-minded societies, changes occur in the pronunciation of words, and legends are altered inadvertently as they are transmitted by word of mouth from one generation to the next.

Social and cultural change is of two basic types. Sometimes it involves the addition of new elements to the existing system; sometimes it involves the elimination of older elements. In the first instance, we refer to social and cultural *innovation*; in the second, we speak of social and cultural *extinction*.

Forms of Innovation Social and cultural innovation takes various forms. Often it takes the form of borrowing from other societies, a process known as *diffusion*. This occurs more often than most of us realize. In fact, there is good reason to believe that most elements in most sociocultural systems have been borrowed from other societies.

Some innovations, of course, are independent creations produced within the society itself. These are of several types. *Alterations* are the least important type of innovation. These are innovations whose adaptive value is no greater than that of the things they replaced, as in new styles of dress or new musical fashions. Alterations are often unintentional changes, such as gradual changes in the pronunciation of words or inadvertent errors in the transmission of stories and legends.

Discoveries and inventions are much more important types of innovations. *Discoveries* provide the members of a society with new information that has adaptive value, while *inventions* are new combinations of already existing information.[5] Thus, Columbus was a discoverer, while Gottlieb Daimler, who built the first automobile, was an inventor. What Daimler did was to combine in a new way a number of things that were already part of the technological heritage of western societies (e.g., the gasoline engine, the carriage body, running gears, the drive shaft, brakes). The "only" thing that was new about the automobile was the automobile itself. As we will see shortly, we must understand the nature of inventions if we are to understand why societies differ in their rates of innovation and change, and why these rates have changed over the centuries.

Causes of Innovation Persius, a Roman poet, once wrote of hunger as "the teacher of the practical arts and the bestower of invention." Plato put the matter even more succinctly when he described necessity as the mother of invention.

One does not need to be a social scientist to recognize the stimulus that hunger and other human needs provide. Throughout the ages, men and women, prodded by unfulfilled needs and desires, have dreamed of ways of satisfying them. Most dreams have remained just dreams, but sometimes individuals have transformed them into realities and something new and useful has been added to the sum of human knowledge.

While most of us have little difficulty in recognizing the role that unsatisfied needs play in the innovative process, we often find it difficult to appreciate the role of *chance,* or accident. Based on our experience as members of a modern industrial society, we tend to think of inventions and discoveries as products of planning and forethought. Yet from earliest times to the present, chance has been an important

FIGURE 3.5 "If this doesn't result in one or two first-class inventions, nothing will."

factor in the innovative process. Thus, in a primitive society, someone with a high fever may dream of a visit by a long-dead grandmother and awaken to find the fever abated. Nothing would be more natural, under the circumstances, than for the individual to assume that the "visit" was the cause of the cure and, in future illnesses, to pray to the grandmother for help. Should such prayers be followed by cures, the practice might well spread and eventually become a permanent feature of the society's culture.

Chance has also played an important role in *technological* innovation. Random strikes by lightning, for example, were almost certainly an important part of the process by which humans first learned about fire and became aware of its uses and dangers. More recently, the great scientist Louis Pasteur discovered the principle and technique of immunization only after he accidentally injected some animals with a stale bacterial culture of chicken cholera. When the animals unexpectedly survived, it occurred to Pasteur that a weakened bacteria might immunize against the very disease that the bacteria, at full strength, were responsible for. Similarly, a key problem in the development of modern photography was solved when Louis Daguerre put a bromide-coated silver plate into a cupboard where, unknown to him, there was an uncovered container of mercury. When he returned the following day, he found that a latent image had begun to develop and correctly surmised that fumes from the mercury were responsible.[6]

While these and many other examples illustrate the role that chance has played in the process of discovery, it would be a mistake to suppose that chance *alone* was responsible in most of these cases. Not just anyone could have made the discoveries made by Pasteur and Daguerre. Both men were already working on the problem and both were highly knowledgeable on the subject. Moreover, both were members of a society that already possessed a substantial store of relevant information.

The importance of the existing store of relevant information is difficult to exaggerate where technological and scientific innovations are concerned. This can be demonstrated by the fact that two or more individuals, working independently, but with knowledge of the same body of information, have often made the same invention or discovery at about the same time. More than half a century ago, two sociologists had already compiled a list of 148 of these independent inventions and discoveries, and there have been more since then.[7] Examples from their list included:

Sunspots: Fabricius, Galileo, Harriott, Scheiner, 1611

Logarithms: Napier, 1614; Buergi, 1620

Calculus: Newton, 1671; Leibnitz, 1676

Nitrogen: Rutherford, 1772; Scheele, 1773

Oxygen: Priestley, Scheele, 1774

Water as H_2O: Cavendish, Watt, 1781; Lavoisier, 1783

Telegraph: Henry, Morse, Steinheil, Wheatstone and Cooke, 1837

Photography: Daguerre and Niepce, Talbot, 1839

Natural selection: Darwin, Wallace, 1858

Telephone: Bell, Gray, 1876

Because of culture, human needs and desires seem limitless. Each problem that is solved and each need that is satisfied seems to generate new needs and new desires as people come increasingly to take the satisfaction of their former needs and desires for granted. This is the basis of the so-called revolution of rising expectations that is such a striking feature of life in the twentieth century. Despite the fact that standards of living have risen more in the last century than in any previous century, discontent and dissatisfaction have probably never been greater. Recognition of this important aspect of human nature has led some observers to note that while Plato was certainly correct in his observation that necessity is the mother of invention, it is also true that *invention is the mother of necessity.* In other words, the process of innovation and change seems to feed on itself so that once it is set in motion it tends to continue, and even to accelerate.

One of the major reasons for this is *the systemic nature of sociocultural systems.* Because the various components of these systems are interdependent, a change in any one of them generates pressure for change in others. The invention of the automobile, for example, created the need for innumerable changes in the law and for the construction of a vast new highway system. More important still, it led to the transformation of cities by encouraging the growth and spread of suburbs and the construction of thousands of new suburban shopping centers, which often helped to kill older central business districts. In addition, the automobile spawned a tremendous number of other changes in the business world, including the fast-food industry, motels, and the trucking industry, to name but three.

Not all cultural innovations generate the same degree of pressure for change in the rest of the system. Some create very little pressure for further change, while others generate tremendous pressure. A new style of painting, for example, may have no impact on society outside a small circle of artists and critics. A new political movement, however, can have far-reaching consequences, depending on the number of people who join it and the seriousness with which they take it. But one kind of innovation that never fails to have far-reaching consequences is change in a society's *basic subsistence technology*. For reasons that will become clear shortly, changes in subsistence technology have ramifications that are felt in most other aspects of life in a society.

Many changes in human societies arise in response to *prior changes in either the biophysical or sociocultural environments*. Archaeologists have found, for example, that changes in climate in the past (e.g., at the end of the last Ice Age) led to changes in diet, in technology, and probably in other characteristics as well.[8] Similarly, changes in the sociocultural environment (e.g., increasing contacts among societies or the rise of expansionistic neighbors) can create new problems for societies and lead to social and cultural innovations of various kinds.

Finally, one of the most neglected causes of change has been *human fecundity*. Human populations, like other populations, are able to produce many more offspring than environmental resources can sustain. In other species, this merely leads to high death rates among the young, except in those rare instances when a genetic mutation, or set of mutations, enables a population to utilize some new environmental resource (e.g., a mutation that enables a population to digest and assimilate some new kind of food). Human societies, however, are able to respond to population pressures by developing technological and other innovations. These have enabled them to utilize new and different resources and thereby adjust to population pressures—at least for a time.

In summary, the causes of innovation are quite varied. When examined closely, however, we see that they all arise out of the interaction of populations with their environments. This is no surprise, of course, since as we noted earlier (see Figure 3.3) all of the social and cultural characteristics of human societies can be traced to this relationship.

The Rate of Innovation When we compare different societies, we find that they produce innovations at greatly different rates. Some, such as American society, have had extremely high rates of innovation. In others, however, the rate of innovation has been negligible.

There are a number of reasons for this difference, but one of the most important is *the difference in the amount of information societies already possess*.[9] One of the most important forms of innovation—invention—is the act of combining already existing elements of culture. This means that a society's potential for invention is a mathematical function of the number of elements, or amount of information, already present. Table 3.2 illustrates this principle. It shows how various numbers of units, or elements, of information can be combined. Although two units can be combined in

TABLE 3.2 Number of Combinations Possible for Various Numbers of Units

No. of Units	2 at a Time	3 at a Time	4 at a Time	5 at a Time	6 at a Time	7 at a Time	8 at a Time	9 at a Time	10 at a Time	Total
					Total Number of Combinations					
2	1	0	0	0	0	0	0	0	0	1
3	3	1	0	0	0	0	0	0	0	4
4	6	4	1	0	0	0	0	0	0	11
5	10	10	5	1	0	0	0	0	0	26
6	15	20	15	6	1	0	0	0	0	57
7	21	35	35	21	7	1	0	0	0	120
8	28	56	70	56	28	8	1	0	0	247
9	36	84	126	126	84	36	9	1	0	502
10	45	120	210	252	210	120	45	10	1	1,013

only one way, three units can be combined in four ways, and four units in eleven ways. In other words, *the addition of each new unit more than doubles the number of possible combinations*. Thus, a mere fivefold increase in the number of units from two to ten leads to a *thousandfold* increase in the number of possible combinations, and when the number of units reaches twenty, over a million combinations are possible!

Of course, not all elements can be combined in a useful way. It is difficult, for example, to imagine a useful combination of the hammer and the saw. The number of potential combinations, therefore, is much greater than the number of useful ones. This does not, however, affect the relationship between the number of units and the number of combinations. Thus, the amount of available technological information is a major factor in a society's rate of innovation.

A second cause of variations in the rate of innovation is *population size*.[10] Because every member of a society has somewhat different needs and abilities, the more people there are, the more new ideas and information are likely to be produced. Larger populations, especially when they are more complex, are also likely to generate more varied patterns of social interaction, leading to more new customs, norms, laws, and other kinds of information required to control and regulate relationships. In the case of technological innovations, the more people there are who are aware of a problem and looking for a solution, the more quickly it will be found, other things being equal. Since societal populations vary so greatly in size, this is another factor of considerable importance.

A third factor affecting the rate of innovation is *the stability of the environment to which a society must adapt*. The greater the rate of environmental change, the greater the pressure for change in culture and social organization. This is true with respect to both the biophysical and the sociocultural environment. And any change in the latter that upsets the balance of power among societies (e.g., large-scale migrations, empire building, a new weapons system) is an especially potent force for further innovation and change.

A fourth factor influencing the rate of innovation in a society is *the extent of its contact with other societies*. The greater the amount of its interaction, the greater its opportunities to appropriate their innovations. In effect, contact enables one society to take advantage of the brainpower and cultural information of other societies through the process of diffusion.

The importance of diffusion was beautifully illustrated some years ago by an anthropologist, Ralph Linton, who wrote:

> Our solid American citizen awakens in a bed built on a pattern which originated in the Near East but which was modified in Northern Europe before it was transmitted to America. He throws back covers made from cotton, domesticated in India, or linen, domesticated in the Near East, or wool from sheep, also domesticated in the Near East, or silk, the use of which was discovered in China. All of these materials have been spun and woven by processes invented in the Near East. He slips into his moccasins, invented by the Indians of the Eastern woodlands, and goes to the bathroom, whose fixtures are a mixture of European and American inventions, both of recent date. He takes off his pajamas, a garment invented in India, and washes with soap invented by the ancient Gauls. He then shaves, a masochistic rite which seems to have been derived from either Sumer or ancient Egypt. . . .

Linton followed this individual as he went through his daily round of activities using cultural elements most of which originated in other societies. As the day comes to a close and "our friend has finished eating," Linton wrote,

> he settles back to smoke, an American habit, consuming a plant domesticated in Brazil in either a pipe, derived from the Indians of Virginia, or a cigarette, derived from Mexico. If he is hardy enough he may even attempt a cigar, transmitted to us from the Antilles by way of Spain. While smoking he reads the news of the day, imprinted in characters invented by the ancient Semites upon a material invented in Germany. As he absorbs the accounts of foreign troubles, he will, if he is a good conservative citizen, thank a Hebrew deity in an Indo-European language that he is 100 per cent American.[11]

A fifth factor in a society's rate of innovation is *the character of its biophysical environment.* As we have seen, the potential for development and change in some societies has been severely limited by environmental factors over which they have no control. Thus, desert and arctic societies have been unable either to develop the techniques of plant cultivation themselves or to learn them from others. The absence of vital resources, such as an adequate water supply or accessible metallic ores, can also hinder innovation, as can endemic diseases and parasites that deplete people's energy.[12] Topography has played an important role in shaping patterns of inter-societal communication. Oceans, deserts, and mountain ranges have all prevented or seriously impeded the flow of information between societies, while navigable rivers and open plains have facilitated it. Considering the importance of diffusion, enormous differences in the rate of innovation can be explained by this factor alone.

Sixth, the rate of innovation is greatly influenced by *"fundamental" innovations.* Not all discoveries and inventions are of equal importance: a few pave the way for thousands more, while the majority have little effect.[13] The invention of the plow and the steam engine and the discovery of the principles of plant cultivation, animal domestication, and metallurgy were all fundamental innovations. So, too, were the inventions of writing and of money.

Sometimes a fundamental innovation will cause the rate of innovation to rise because it involves a principle that can be applied, with minimum effort and imagination, in hundreds, even thousands, of areas. This was true, for example, of the steam engine, metallurgy, printing, and the silicon chip. Sometimes, however, an invention or discovery is considered "fundamental" because it so drastically alters the conditions of human life that hundreds or thousands of other changes become either possible or necessary. This was the case with the principle of plant cultivation, which, as we shall see in a later chapter, led to revolutionary changes in every area of human life.

A seventh factor influencing the rate of innovation is *the society's attitude toward innovation.* In many societies, there has been such a powerful ideological commitment to tradition that innovation of any kind has been discouraged. In contrast, most modern societies have a much more positive attitude toward innovation.

Though the problem has not been studied as carefully as it deserves, a society's attitude toward innovation seems to be greatly influenced by its prior experience. A society that has already benefited from change is usually more receptive to innovation than a society that has not. Attitudes toward innovation also vary according to the nature of the dominant ideology in the society. Some ideologies generate a very conservative outlook and oppose change; Confucianism is an example of such a faith. Capitalism and Marxism, in contrast, have been much more supportive of innovation and change.

Before we leave the subject of the rate of innovation, it is important to note a tendency that is especially evident where technological innovation is concerned: it often occurs at an accelerating pace. Figure 3.6 illustrates this speedup for human societies as a whole during the period from 1000 to 1900 A.D. The majority of

FIGURE 3.6   The number of important technological innovations by century, 1000 to 1900 A.D.   Technological innovations tend to occur at an accelerating rate, because each new element increases the probability of acquiring more.

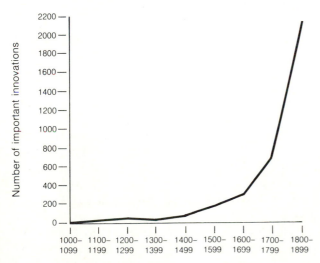

societies, however, have never experienced such an acceleration. But those that have experienced it have had an influence on human history out of all proportion to their numbers.

The explanation of the acceleration is that *each new bit of useful technological information acquired by a society increases the probability it will acquire still more.* This is partly a function of the potential of technological elements for being recombined in new ways. But in addition, technological advance tends to *mutually reinforce* several of the other basic factors that influence the rate of innovation. Throughout history, for example, advances in a society's subsistence technology have typically led to an increase in the size of its population, which, in turn, contributed to further innovation (since there were more people aware of problems and alert to possible solutions). Similarly, technological advance has led to increased intersocietal contact, resulting in greater diffusion and thus enhancing the rate of technological innovation.

In short, technological innovation and advance tend to make *further* technological innovation and advance increasingly likely. It is hardly surprising, therefore, that societies in which this happens come to be increasingly different from societies in which it does not.

Social and Cultural Extinction   Because of social and cultural innovations, societies are often faced with choices between competing alternatives, and this leads to a *process of selection.* Earlier in this century, for example, the members of many societies were confronted with a choice between the horse and carriage and the new horseless carriage. Gradually, the horseless carriage, or automobile, as it came to be known, replaced the older means of transportation.

This process of selection is like the process of innovation in that it, too, can be rational and deliberate, as in the adoption of the automobile and the rejection of the horse and buggy. But, again, as in the process of innovation, chance and irrational factors may play a part.

Although it is the members of a society that make the choices which shape and alter their society, everyone does not have an equal voice. "Who decides" depends on the kind of decision involved and the nature of the relevant power structure. For example, the teenaged members of an industrial society may choose, at one level, which songs make it into the top ten, but their range of choices has already been substantially narrowed by the people who control the recording industry and who pay disc jockeys to promote certain records and otherwise manipulate the selective process. Similarly, all of the members of a democratic society may have equal opportunities to cast their votes for public officials, yet the choice among candidates has already been narrowed by elites in the mass media and the political system.

This raises the question of whether or not a society's culture and social organization can be considered truly adaptive. While much of it is adaptive for the society as a whole (i.e., it satisfies the basic needs of the system and its members), many elements have been selected by and for the benefit of special segments of the society and are "adaptive" only, or largely, for them. Thus, the process of selection may result in the retention of many elements that are *nonadaptive* or even *maladaptive* for the society as a whole. Drug pushers and users select elements which they find rewarding, but which create serious problems for society (e.g., crime and illness).

FIGURE 3.7 Intrasocietal selection often occurs imperceptibly, as one element of technology gradually replaces another: in the first several decades of the present century, the horseless carriage gradually replaced the horse-drawn carriage.

Similarly, major corporations make decisions that lead to the adoption of maladaptive elements in a society, such as sugar-coated cereals, tobacco, and alcohol.

Societal Growth and Development

Most societies, as we have seen, changed little during the course of their existence. Moreover, most of the changes that occurred were of little importance—gradual changes in the pronunciation of words, minor alterations in the content of rituals and legends, changes in etiquette, and so on.

Occasionally, however, more substantial and more important changes have occurred. Some societies have experienced substantial growth in size. Some have shifted from a nomadic way of life to permanent settlements in villages and some have shifted from a predominantly rural mode of life to a predominantly urban one. Such changes have usually been accompanied by important changes in social organization—substantial increases in organizational complexity, marked increases in the division of labor, and significant increases in social inequality. In short, some societies have experienced a process of substantial growth and development while others have not.

One of the important tasks for sociologists is to explain this process of growth and development and why it has occurred in some societies but not in others.

Technology's Role in Societal Development   Viewed historically and comparatively, it is clear that significant societal growth and development cannot occur unless they are preceded or accompanied by advances in subsistence technology. In other words, *advances in subsistence technology appear to be a necessary precondition for any significant increase in the size, complexity, wealth, or power of a society.*

The reason for this is that subsistence technology is the body of information that a society depends on to provide its members with the *energy* required to sustain their varied activities.[14] No activity is possible without it: even thought requires energy. The more energy available to a society, the more things its members are able to do. Thus, one of the basic principles of ecological-evolutionary theory is that *subsistence technology defines the limits of the possible within a society and determines the relative cost of each of the options within those limits.*[15]

Societies that depend on hunting and gathering as their chief means of subsistence cannot sustain populations nearly as large as those that depend on farming; and those that depend on slash-and-burn horticulture, a more primitive method of farming, cannot sustain populations as large as those that depend on plow agriculture. These differences in the limits set on the size of societies by subsistence technology are matched by differences in the limits set on other aspects of societal development, such as the extent of the division of labor, the degree of social inequality, the size of communities and associations and the degree of their complexity, the wealth of societies and the standard of living within them, and the power of societies over the biophysical environment and over other societies.

Advances in subsistence technology are also important because *they stimulate advances in other kinds of technology.* For example, advances in subsistence technology tend to be accompanied or followed by advances in other productive technologies and in the technologies of transportation, communication, and warfare. These developments reinforce the effect of the initial advance in subsistence technology, as shown in Figure 3.8.

In effect, the tools and machines that societies construct on the basis of the technological information available to them are the functional equivalent of improvements in the organs with which their members are endowed—eyes, ears, voice

FIGURE 3.8   Model of the effects of advances in subsistence technology on other technologies and on societal development.

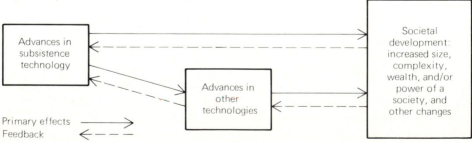

box, arms, legs, brain, nervous system, and the rest. Microscopes, telescopes, and television all extend the range of our vision, just as telephones and radios extend the range of our hearing, and bicycles, automobiles, and airplanes increase our mobility. Where technological advances have occurred, they have enabled the members of societies to act as if they had acquired a new and improved genetic heritage—improved sight, more acute hearing, new powers of locomotion, and so forth. Thus, technological advances—especially advances in subsistence technology—are functionally equivalent to the kinds of changes that occur in speciation (i.e., when genetic change creates a new species of plant or animal).

One important feature of the process of societal development that should not be overlooked is indicated by the feedback* loops shown in Figure 3.8. Advances in subsistence technology stimulate advances in other technologies and lead to growth in the size, complexity, wealth, and power of a society. But these developments, once they have occurred, increase the probability of further advances in subsistence technology. Population growth, for example, increases the number of potential innovators, and while few individuals ever make an invention or discovery of practical value, the greater the number of potential innovators in a society the greater tends to be the rate at which innovations occur. Thus, as this example suggests, *once the process of societal development is set in motion, it tends to become self-sustaining*. While this is not inevitable, the probabilities of continued development clearly increase.

Societal growth and development, while advantageous to societies in many ways, are not unmixed blessings. They create new problems and these often lead to changes that many members of society would prefer not to make—changes in beliefs and values, changes in patterns of social organization, changes in institutional arrangements. Among preliterate societies, for example, technological advance leads to population growth, and population growth necessitates changes in social organization. As Robert Carneiro has shown, population growth forces these societies to choose either to split up into smaller independent groups in order to preserve their traditional kin-based system of governance or to remain united but adopt a more authoritarian political system that is dominated by a small elite minority.[16] In short, in order to sustain the larger population, a new and less attractive system of social organization becomes necessary.

Ideology's Role in Societal Development   Although technology's influence on societal growth and development is substantial, it is far from complete. Other factors also play a role, and a society's beliefs and values are especially important. Whether or not the members of a society are receptive to innovation and change often depends to a considerable degree on ideology.

It is true, of course, that ideologies tend to reflect the past experience of a group and societies that have already enjoyed the benefits of societal growth and development are more likely to favor further growth and development. And it is also true that

---

*Feedback is a special kind of causal relationship. It is one in which a part of the effect produced by the initial cause or event reverts back to, and alters, its source. For example, illness may cause a loss of appetite, and the resulting failure to eat may then aggravate the illness.

subsistence technology sets limits on what is possible within a society and its culture—including its ideology.

But ideologies are not merely reflexive responses to prior developments in technology. Different ideologies may develop within a society whose members share a common technology, as happened in Germany at the time of the Reformation. Sometimes such differences can be explained by differences within the society and the resulting differences in the experiences of its members: farmers may adopt one set of beliefs, city dwellers another.[17]

But even if that were the whole story—and it seldom is—the formulation of the ideology as a clearly defined set of beliefs has significant consequences, as evidenced by the Hindu belief in the sacredness of the cow (see page 41). As we have seen, this belief has greatly helped to protect a precious resource in times of crisis. Other beliefs have had equally important effects in other societies. Thus, even though ideologies that come to be widely accepted reveal the influence of subsistence technologies, they still may have a significant impact on societal growth and development.

Change in the World System of Societies

As we have seen, change has been a basic characteristic of the world system of societies for the last ten thousand years. In that period, the human population has grown a thousandfold and the average size of individual societies has increased a millionfold. Meanwhile, the number of societies in existence has declined dramatically. These changes have been accompanied by countless other changes in the conditions of human life and in the characteristics of human societies—changes in family life, in the social roles of both men and women, in religion, in politics, in art, and more. Today, in the latter part of the twentieth century, we are witnessing signs of what appears to be the emergence of a single global culture, as societies around the world increasingly adopt similar patterns of dress, similar tastes in music, similar ambitions and aspirations, and, increasingly, a single language for intersocietal communication (i.e., English).

Societal Variation and Intersocietal Selection

The key to the major changes that have occurred in the world system of societies in the last ten thousand years is the process of intersocietal selection that has drastically reduced the number of societies.[18] Were it not for this process, in which the units that survive (or become extinct) are entire societies, human life would not have changed nearly as rapidly as it has.

This process of selection presupposed the existence of differences among societies. Such differences were inevitable, however, once the human population began to spread out geographically and to occupy new and different kinds of environments. Chance also contributed to the process of societal differentiation, so that even when two societies confronted similar environmental challenges, they did not always respond in the same way. Differences in vocabulary provide a good

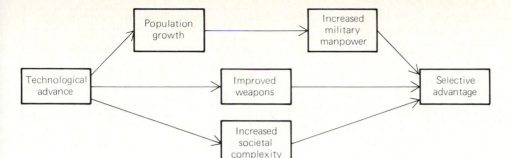

FIGURE 3.9 **Model of the effects of technological advance on the process of intersocietal selection.**

example of this: even when all societies were confronted with exactly the same experiences, such as birth and death, or the differences between males and females, they created different symbols to represent them. More important still, different beliefs developed to explain and interpret these experiences, and varied norms evolved to guide behavioral responses.

Not all the differences that have developed among societies have been of equal importance from the standpoint of intersocietal selection. Some have been much more important than others. This has been especially true of differences that had feedback effects on societal growth and development, because *societies that have grown in size, and developed in complexity, wealth, and power, have been much more likely to survive and transmit their cultures and institutional patterns than societies that have preserved traditional social and cultural patterns and minimized innovation.*

The reasons for this are not hard to find. To survive, societies must be able to defend their populations and their territorial bases against a variety of threats. These include the ravages of epidemics, natural disasters of other kinds, and, above all, threats from other societies. One only need consider the history of the United States, Canada, Australia, Brazil, or the Soviet Union to see what happens to smaller and less developed indigenous societies (i.e., the American Indians, the Australian aborigines, and various tribal groups in Siberia and Soviet Asia) when they compete for territory with larger and more developed societies. Larger societies have far greater manpower and can much more easily absorb military casualties. In addition, their more advanced technology has a variety of military applications so that their soldiers have more deadly weapons, better logistical support, and greater mobility. Finally, their more complex patterns of social organization can easily be adapted to military needs and this, too, provides an important competitive advantage. Thus, while it would be a mistake to suppose that more developed societies always prevail over their less developed rivals, the odds are strongly in their favor (see Figure 3.9).

Intersocietal selection is not always a violent process. Sometimes societies collapse simply because of insufficient support from their members. This is especially likely to happen when a less developed society comes into contact with one that is much more highly developed. Many members of the less developed society become impressed with the wealth and power of the more advanced society and

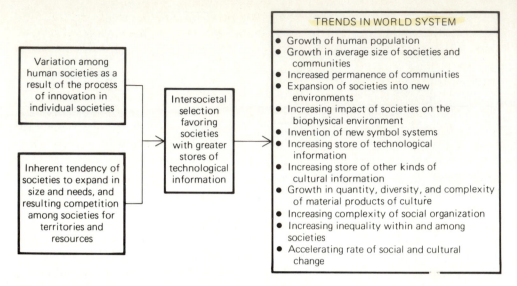

FIGURE 3.10 **Model of the causes of the evolution of the world system of societies.**

either migrate to it or begin to adopt its customs. If these tendencies become widespread, the institutional fabric of the less developed society begins to fray and a process of societal disintegration begins. There are a number of well-documented cases of this in India, where primitive tribes in the hill country have simply disintegrated and their former members have been absorbed into Indian society.[19]

A Model of the Evolution of the World System of Societies

Building on what we have learned about the process of intersocietal selection, we can now construct a model of the evolutionary process that explains the basic trends in the world system of societies in recent millennia. As Figure 3.10 indicates, the model is based on two premises. First, it assumes the existence of variation, or differences, among societies. Second, it assumes an inherent tendency of societies to develop an increased need for resources, either because of growth in population or because of the growth of its members' culturally generated needs and desires. The combination of these two conditions sets the stage for a deadly process of competition that has resulted in the survival of a small minority of societies and the extinction of the vast majority.

Because technologically advanced societies have had the advantage in this process of intersocietal selection, *their characteristics have increasingly come to be the characteristics of the world system as a whole.* Thus, because technologically advanced societies tend to be larger than other societies, the average size of societies has been increasing for the last 10,000 years. Similarly, because technologically advanced societies are structurally more complex than other societies, the trend in the world system has been in the direction of increasingly complex societies. The same logic applies to all of the trends shown in Figure 3.10.

There is, of course, nothing inevitable or unalterable about these trends. A number of factors could disrupt them. For example, a deadly new disease could sweep through human societies and, in a short period of time, reverse most of the trends of the last ten thousand years. The Black Plague of the fourteenth century had this effect in a number of societies, and it is not inconceivable that something comparable could happen on a global scale. An unpredictable catastrophe involving the biophysical environment could also reverse the trends of history. But a more likely possibility than either of these is that disaster will result from modern military technology. Both nuclear warfare and biochemical warfare have the potential for producing a global catastrophe, and there is no technological antidote for either of them. Thus, ecological-evolutionary theory provides no grounds for complacency regarding the future.

Although we cannot predict the future, we can say that, so far, the process of intersocietal selection has favored technologically advanced societies. Like the old game of musical chairs, it has eliminated first one, then another of the less developed societies. The result is a world system that, with the passage of time, increasingly consists of what were once the exceptions—innovative and developing societies.

Sociocultural Evolution Defined

By now it is clear that *sociocultural evolution is the process of change and development in human societies that results from cumulative growth in their stores of cultural information*. Although sociocultural evolution is an extraordinarily complex phenomenon, it becomes much easier to understand once we recognize that it combines the subprocesses of continuity and change, and that change is the result of innovation, which produces variations, and selection, which determines the fate of these variations.

It is also important to recognize that sociocultural evolution operates on two distinct levels simultaneously. First, it occurs within individual societies. Second, it occurs within the world system of societies. But while these two processes are separate and distinct, they are also related since the changes that occur in individual societies produce the variations on which the process of intersocietal selection operates. This is the process that determines which societies and which cultures survive and which become extinct, and the role that each of the survivors plays within the world system.

The consequences of sociocultural evolution have been very different for different human societies: when we look at them individually, we see many different patterns of development. But when we look at the world system, we see that at that level sociocultural evolution has produced *one dominant pattern* for at least the last ten thousand years. In the chapters that follow, we will explore both the diversity of patterns in individual societies and the dominant pattern of the world system.

Excursus: A Comparison of Biological and Sociocultural Evolution

During recent decades, our understanding of biological evolution and sociocultural evolution has advanced dramatically. It is now clear for the first time that both types of evolution are based on records of experience that are preserved and transmitted from generation to generation in coded systems of information. In the case of biological evolution, the record of experience is preserved and transmitted by means of the genetic code. In the case of sociocultural evolution, the record is preserved and transmitted by means of symbol systems. Both the genetic alphabet and symbol systems provide populations with the means of acquiring, storing, transmitting, and using enormous amounts of information on which their welfare and, ultimately, their survival depend. Thus, *symbol systems are functional equivalents of the genetic alphabet.*

It is hardly surprising, therefore, that there is a fundamental similarity in the way the two evolutionary processes operate. Continuity and change are present in both, and change takes the form of both innovation and extinction. Both processes also involve the subprocesses of variation and selection.

Despite these important similarities, there are a number of equally important differences in the way the two systems of evolution operate. Some of these are of special significance for students of human societies, such as the difference that results from the way information is transferred and spread in the two evolutions. The only way genetic information can be transmitted is through the process of reproduction. Because different species cannot interbreed, they cannot share genetic information with one another.* Thus, biological evolution is characterized by continued differentiation and diversification, a process much like the branching of a tree or shrub. Cultural information, by contrast, is easily exchanged between the members of different societies. Not only can human societies exchange information, but two or more can merge into a single system—the equivalent, were it possible, of the merging of separate species in biological evolution. Thus, sociocultural evolution is likely to eventuate in even fewer and less dissimilar societies than exist today.

This is related to a second important difference. In biological evolution, the emergence of more complex species of plants and animals has not had the effect of eliminating, or reducing the number of, simpler species. One-celled organisms thrive alongside, and indeed *inside,* complex multicellular organisms. In sociocultural evolution, on the other hand, the emergence of new and more complex kinds of societies has usually led to the extinction of older, simpler ones, as illustrated by the destruction of thousands of small American Indian societies since 1492. Thus, while biological evolution produces the pattern of a richly branched shrub, sociocultural evolution approximates the pattern of a pine tree that gradually loses its lower branches as new, higher branches appear and overshadow them.

A third basic difference involves a population's ability to incorporate into heritable form the useful information its members have acquired through the process of individual *learning.* In sociocultural systems, this is easily done; it is, as we have seen, the basis of their evolution. But it has no counterpart in biological evolution. Most biologists prior to Darwin believed that something analogous *did* occur in the biotic world. Jean Baptiste Lamarck, Darwin's most famous predecessor, argued that if an organism continually repeated a certain behavior, not only would this produce structural change in the organism, but the change would be inherited by its offspring.[20] It has long since been clear that biological evolution does not work that way: giraffes do not have long necks because their ancestors stretched day after day to reach high leaves, but because short necks were a liability in their ancestors' environment; animals with the genes for short necks were unable to survive and reproduce. In the cultural world, however, a kind of Lamarckian evolution *does* occur. Just about anything a population learns and considers worth preserving can be incorporated into its cultural heritage.

Springing from the easy flow of cultural information among societies and the ease with which it is incorporated into heritable form is yet another way in which sociocultural evolution differs from biological: it has a capacity for much higher rates of change in our species. An evolution whose mechanism is genetic change is necessarily a slow process in a species that has a long generation span and relatively few offspring. But cultural information, relative to genetic, can be rapidly acquired, exchanged, recombined, and accumulated, with the result that substantial alterations in a society's culture may occur within a single generation. Moreover, sociocultural evolution does not require that every society go through step-by-step sequential stages of development, which are the essence of biological evolution. Rather, a society may compress or even skip stages.[21] In the Third World today, for example, some nations have

---

*Closely related species do occasionally interbreed, as when lions and tigers produce "ligers" or "tiglons." These hybrids are usually sterile, however, at least in the animal kingdom, and therefore their importance in the total process of biological evolution has been minimal.

gone directly from human porters and pack animals to trucks and airplanes as the primary movers of goods, largely bypassing the stage of dependency on wagons and railroads that was part of the evolutionary experience of those societies in which the newer methods of transportation were first developed.

One other important difference involves the conditions under which major evolutionary change occurs. In the biotic world, most *major* change happens when a population becomes reproductively isolated and cannot receive new genetic information from other populations (i.e., during speciation; see page 12). In contrast, human societies that are isolated almost invariably experience a *low* rate of cultural change. In short, isolation tends to have opposite effects in the two modes of evolution.

Finally, sociocultural evolution has a greater potential than biological evolution has for being brought under rational human control. So far, however, this process is far from complete. One of humanity's most urgent tasks in the years ahead is to increase our understanding of the dynamics of sociocultural evolution so that we can find the means of controlling its direction and make it more responsive to human needs and ideals.

The Evolution of Evolution

The most important lesson to be learned from a comparison of biological and sociocultural evolution is that *the evolutionary process itself evolves*. In other words, evolution is not a fixed, unchanging process that merely produces a variety of new products (e.g., animals that swim, animals that fly, animals that walk; animals that eat plants, animals that eat other animals, etc.). It does this, of course, but it does much more. The process of change itself has been changed as a result of prior changes. More specifically, the evolutionary process has several times generated completely new "mechanisms" of change that did not exist previously.

One of the most important examples of this is the change that has occurred in the ways biological populations acquire the information on which they depend for survival and welfare. The oldest and most basic method, as we have seen, employs the biological processes of mutation and natural selection to alter the content of the gene pools of populations. In time, however, this evolutionary process gave rise to populations of mobile animals equipped with sensory organs and a central nervous system that enabled them to acquire information directly from individual experience through the process we call "learning"—a radically new and different method of acquiring and storing information. Still later, when human populations developed the ability to create symbol systems, a third method of acquiring and storing information evolved. Thus we see that evolution is not simply a stable and unchanging process that generates a sequence of new products. *The evolutionary process itself is evolving*.

CHAPTER 4

Types of Human Societies

The basic aim of science, as we have seen, is to explain how the world works. To this end, scientific research—whether it is focused on butterflies, galaxies, or human societies—seeks to discover patterns and regularities in the world we inhabit. This requires countless observations, all of which seek to discover how things resemble one another, how they differ, and why—*a process of systematic comparison*.

Classifying Human Societies

Over the years, this process of comparison has given rise to many systems of classification in the various sciences. The periodic table in chemistry, the Linnaean taxonomy and its successors in biology, and the paleontological and petrological systems in geology are several of the more familiar. All of these systems help us to make sense of the wealth of data that has been generated by research, and each serves as a guide to scientists, suggesting new comparisons for study and new lines of research. But most important of all, each of these systems of classification has stimulated the development of theories designed to explain the patterns and regularities that have been discovered.

The system of classification that we will use in studying human societies is based

FIGURE 4.1 Bushmen of southwest Africa: members of a twentieth-century society of hunters and gatherers.

on the *subsistence technologies* that they employ. The origins of this system, like the origins of ecological-evolutionary theory itself, lie in the work of seventeenth- and eighteenth-century scholars in Europe who responded to the discovery of less developed societies in the New World, Africa, and Asia by rethinking age-old questions about human origins and history. This led some of them to comparisons of societies and to efforts to classify them. Already in the eighteenth century, a number of scholars recognized the crucial importance of subsistence technology and based their systems of classification on it.[1]

The system of classification used in this volume grows out of that early work. It divides human societies into ten basic categories, with individual societies classified on the basis of their primary mode of subsistence.[2]

Hunting and gathering societies

Simple horticultural societies

Advanced horticultural societies

Simple agrarian societies

Advanced agrarian societies

Fishing societies

Maritime societies

Simple herding societies

Advanced herding societies

Industrial societies

For a system of classification to be useful in science, it should be as simple as possible so that the classification of cases can be as unambiguous as possible. For example, a society is classified as a hunting and gathering society if the hunting of wild animals and foraging for uncultivated plant foods are its primary means of subsistence. Horticultural societies are societies which engage in farming, but do not use the plow.[3] Advanced horticultural societies employ metal tools and weapons, while simple horticultural societies use wood and stone. Agrarian societies also engage in farming, but they make extensive use of plows. Advanced agrarian societies employ iron tools and weapons, while simple agrarian societies use copper and bronze, which are softer metals and less plentiful. (See Table 4.1.)

Fishing, herding, and maritime societies are different from the other types of societies in that they are *environmentally specialized* types. Each of them is distinguished from other societies at roughly the same level of development, not so much in terms of the technological information they *possess,* but rather in terms of what they *use* in their subsistence activities. Each relies disproportionately on those elements in its technology that are especially suited to the distinctive features of its particular environment. Thus, a fishing society relies primarily on the part of its technology that is most useful to a people located on a body of water. A herding society relies disproportionately on those elements of its technology that enable it to subsist on open grasslands with sparse rainfall. Maritime societies, like fishing societies, utilized their proximity to water, though in a different way: being technologically more advanced, they adapted their technology to the use of waterways for trade and commerce at a time when the movement of most goods was much cheaper by water than by land (see Figure 4.3, page 82).

Technologically, there is more variation among herding societies than among either of the other specialized types.[4] For this reason, the category is divided into simple and advanced types. The basic distinction is that the latter employ horses or camels for transportation in work and warfare, while the former lack this important resource.

TABLE 4.1 Criteria for Classifying Primary Types of Human Societies

Type of Society	Plant Cultivation*	Metallurgy*	Plow*	Iron*	Inanimate Energy Sources*
Hunting and gathering	−	−	−	−	−
Simple horticultural	+	−	−	−	−
Advanced horticultural	+	+	−	−	−
Simple agrarian	+	+	+	−	−
Advanced agrarian	+	+	+	+	−
Industrial	+	+	+	+	+

*The symbol + means that the trait is widespread in the type of society indicated; the symbol − means it is not.

FIGURE 4.2 Hybrid societies depend on elements of technology from two or more of the basic societal types: contemporary India, an industrializing agrarian society, combines elements of the older agrarian technology with elements of modern industrial technology.

Industrial societies are the newest type of society and technologically the most advanced. The distinguishing feature of these societies is their heavy dependence on machine technology and on the inanimate sources of energy—coal, petroleum, natural gas, and nuclear power—that drive the various machines. Because of their highly advanced technology, industrial societies are the most powerful and productive societies the world has ever seen.

Not all societies fit neatly into the ten types of societies listed above. Some are *hybrids* that combine, in roughly equal proportions, the characteristics of two or more of the basic types. Often—though not always—hybrid societies are in a state of transition from one mode of production to another and from one level of development to another. Thus, many Third World societies today are beginning to industrialize, but still depend heavily on preindustrial technology. These industrializing agrarian and industrializing horticultural societies will be examined in some detail in Chapter 13.

Societal Types and Environment

Human societies have had to adapt to many kinds of environments. Some have had to adapt to near-desert conditions where food resources have been hard to obtain,

81

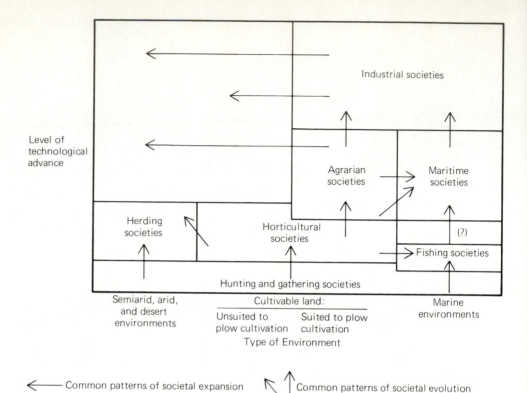

FIGURE 4.3   An ecological-evolutionary taxonomy of societies.

while others have had the good fortune to be located close to large bodies of water where they have had access to abundant supplies of fish in addition to all the resources of the land they occupied.

The great majority of societies, however, have occupied territories that were neither as rich in resources as the latter nor as impoverished as the former. Most have occupied territories the major part of which was suitable for farming of one kind or another. Many, however, have occupied territories that have been suitable only for the less productive form of farming known as horticulture.[5] In many tropical and semitropical regions, poor soils, inappropriate crops, and other factors have made plow agriculture impossible or unprofitable until recently.*

In summary, then, *the most basic differences among societies that have developed over the course of human history are a reflection of two things: (1) differences in their subsistence technologies, and (2) differences in their environments.*

Figure 4.3 illustrates how these two factors have combined to produce the various types of societies we have identified. *The vertical dimension* indicates how

---

*In recent years, heavy use of chemical fertilizers and other products of modern industrial technology has begun to make plow agriculture possible and profitable in some of these areas, but even now horticulture still remains the most profitable form of farming in most of these areas.

differences in the level of subsistence technology lead to differences among societies. For example, maritime societies occupy the same kind of environment as
fishing societies, but differ from fishing societies because they are technologically
more advanced. *The horizontal dimension* of Figure 4.3 indicates how differences in
environmental conditions lead to further differences among societies. Thus, although
maritime societies and agrarian societies are quite similar in their levels of technological development, they differ in important ways because of differences in the
environments to which they have adapted.

The vertical arrows in Figure 4.3 indicate the usual patterns of societal evolution. Thus, we see that fishing societies and horticultural societies have evolved out
of hunting and gathering societies. On the other hand, some herding societies,
which are roughly similar in level of technological advance to horticultural societies,
may have evolved from horticultural societies.[6] Usually, however, technologically
more advanced types of societies have evolved out of less advanced types.

One feature of Figure 4.3 that requires special comment is the absence of arrows
flowing upward from herding societies and from horticultural societies in areas that
are not suitable for plow cultivation. Further development by these societies seems to
have been blocked by environmental constraints. The presence of more advanced
kinds of societies in these kinds of environments, when it occurs, is the result of
societal *expansion* rather than societal evolution. Thus, the presence of an industrial
society in the arid regions of the southwestern part of the United States is the result of
the geographical expansion of an industrial society—American society—whose
origins were in the eastern part of North America, an area that was well suited to
plow cultivation.

Societal Types Through History

Throughout most of its history, the entire human population lived in hunting and
gathering societies. This period of relative social and cultural uniformity ended only
within the last 10,000 to 12,000 years.

The first new type of society to emerge was fishing society (see Figure 4.4).
Though the practice of fishing seems to have begun thousands of years earlier, the
invention of fishhooks, nets, traps, boats, and paddles was required before any
society could make the shift from hunting and gathering to fishing as its primary
means of subsistence.[7]

Simple horticultural societies probably came next, first appearing in the Middle
East around 7000 B.C.[8] Though people began to use copper within the next 1,500
years,[9] it was not until nearly 4000 B.C. that metal tools and weapons became
common enough to permit us to call any of these societies *advanced* horticultural.[10]

The plow was invented late in the fourth millennium, and this innovation also
occurred in the Middle East.[11] By 3000 B.C. it was used widely enough by societies
in Mesopotamia and Egypt to justify calling them simple agrarian.

Iron was discovered early in the second millennium B.C. but, like copper, did
not become the dominant material in tools and weapons for a long time.[12] Thus, the
first *advanced* agrarian societies did not appear until the early years of the first
millennium B.C.

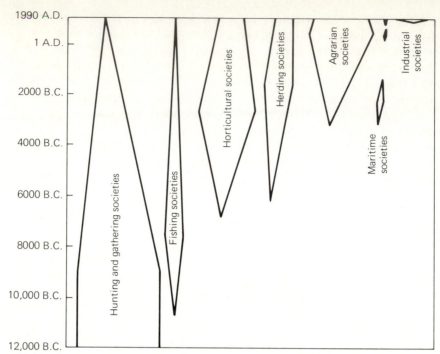

FIGURE 4.4 **Societal types from 12,000 B.C. to the present: changes in the size of each of the figures reflect the growth or decline in numbers of each of the types of societies.**

The origin of herding societies remains something of a mystery. Evidence of animal domestication dates from about 9000 B.C., but evidence from the earliest site suggests a hybrid technology.[13] While we cannot say for certain when any society first came to depend on herding as its chief means of subsistence, it was probably sometime after horticultural societies appeared.

Maritime societies date from the end of the third millennium B.C. Minoans on the island of Crete were apparently the first people to rely on overseas commerce as their primary economic activity.[14] Unlike other major societal types, maritime societies have not had a *continuous* history. After flourishing in the Mediterranean world for 2,000 years, they were destroyed by the growth of Roman power. During the Middle Ages, they enjoyed a brief revival for a few centuries, only to disappear again until the present century, when they reemerged in Singapore and elsewhere.

The last major societal type is industrial. Although the basic inventions that mark the beginning of the modern technological revolution occurred in the eighteenth century, it was not until early in the nineteenth that Britain, which pioneered in industrialization, reached the point where it could be classified as a truly industrial society. Since then, nearly thirty others have followed Britain's lead.

Historical Eras

As Figure 4.4 makes clear, the types of human societies in the world system have changed greatly in the last 10-12,000 years. There was a time when every society was at the hunting and gathering level of development; today, we have everything from hunting and gathering to industrial societies.

To understand a given society, past or present, it is not enough to know what type of society it is or was. It is equally important to know when it existed, since this tells us a great deal about its social environment. For example, the situation of hunting and gathering societies in the last hundred years has been far more precarious than the situation of hunting and gathering societies 10,000 years ago. Such groups have found themselves in the unenviable position of interacting with far more advanced, and hence far more powerful, societies. No matter where they have been located, agents of industrialism have penetrated, using their vast resources in ways that have transformed the conditions of life for less advanced groups. This has often been done with the best of intentions—as in the establishment of medical, educational, or religious missions—but that has made little difference. The ultimate effect has been to transform and eventually destroy the social and cultural systems of technologically primitive peoples.

In studying societies, therefore, it is usually necessary to specify the historical era involved. The various eras are named according to the type of society that was politically and militarily dominant at the time. Thus, the long period in which all human societies were hunting and gathering societies is designated as the hunting and gathering era, while the period in which we live today is the industrial era.

From the standpoint of ecological-evolutionary theory, the four major eras in human history have been:*

1. The hunting and gathering era (from the origins of our species to approximately 7000 B.C.);

2. The horticultural era (from approximately 7000 B.C. to approximately 3000 B.C.);

3. The agrarian era (from approximately 3000 B.C. to approximately 1800 A.D.);

4. The industrial era (from approximately 1800 A.D. to the present).

As Figure 4.5 suggests, the best way to learn what sociocultural evolution has meant is to examine in sequence the four types of societies whose dominance in successive eras has defined the upper limits of technological advance. In them, we can trace all the basic trends in population, culture, the material products of culture, social organization, and social institutions, not simply those in subsistence technology.

The reason for these trends, as Figure 4.5 reminds us, is that the rise of the technologically more advanced societies contributed directly to the decline of less advanced societies. For when horticultural societies appeared, the chances for survival of neighboring hunting and gathering societies were substantially reduced unless they also adopted the new technology. The same was true for both hunting and gathering and horticultural societies when agrarian societies appeared. The less

---

*These dates are for the world as a whole. In many parts of the world, the horticultural and agrarian eras began later. For example, the agrarian era did not begin in the New World until the sixteenth century, A.D., after European colonization and settlement.

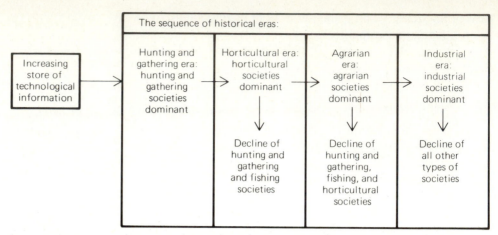

FIGURE 4.5 Model of the impact of the growing store of technological information on the sequence of historical eras.

advanced societies lacked both the numbers and weapons needed to defend themselves against the more advanced societies that coveted their territories and other resources. Those that managed to survive did so only in remote and isolated areas protected by oceans (e.g., islands) or other geographical barriers, or in territories judged undesirable by members of the more advanced societies (e.g., deserts, tropical rain forests, mountainous areas). In recent times, the pattern of military conquest and expansion has greatly declined, but the pattern of cultural penetration by technologically more advanced nations has certainly not declined. If anything, it has become more pronounced, as we will see in later chapters.

Differences among Types of Societies

One of the most important propositions in ecological-evolutionary theory is the one which asserts that advances in subsistence technology are a necessary condition for any significant increase in the size, complexity, wealth, or power of a society (see page 70). In Chapters 5 to 13 we will put this proposition to the test as we examine each of the major types of societies.

Before plunging into the detailed evidence that bears on this proposition, it may be helpful to consider a much more limited body of evidence that was assembled over a period of years by George Peter Murdock, with the aid of students and colleagues. Together, they assembled and codified a tremendous amount of information on approximately a thousand societies. These data permit us to classify most of these societies in terms of the taxonomy described earlier in this chapter, and they also make it possible to compare the various types of societies in a number of important ways.[15] Since the societies differ considerably in their levels of technological advance, this allows us to see whether they also differ in some of the ways that ecological-evolutionary theory asserts that they should.

Size of Societies

One of the most important consequences of technological advance, according to ecological-evolutionary theory, is an increase in the size of societies. Table 4.2 confirms this. Technologically more advanced types of societies have, on average, larger populations. Thus, the median size (see "Science and Measurement" on page 88) of agrarian societies is larger than the median size of advanced horticultural societies, which is larger than the median size of simple horticultural societies, which is larger than the median size of hunting and gathering societies. The median sizes of fishing and herding societies are also about what one would expect in view of their places in the taxonomy of societies (see Figure 4.3) and in view of the average sizes of hunting and gathering and horticultural societies. Fishing societies are larger, on average, than hunting and gathering societies, but smaller, on average, than horticultural societies. Herding societies are intermediate in size between simple and advanced horticultural societies.

Permanence of Settlements

Ecological-evolutionary theory also predicts that technological advance leads societies to establish more permanent settlements.[16] Because the hunting of wild animals and the gathering of wild vegetable products soon deplete the supply of foodstuffs in the immediate area surrounding human settlements, hunter-gatherers are forced to move about with considerable frequency. In contrast, societies that practice horticulture or agriculture should, according to our theory, be able to establish more permanent settlements.

Murdock's data confirm this. Of the 147 hunting and gathering societies for which data were available, *only 10 percent* were reported to have permanent settlements, and all of these enjoyed unusually favorable environmental conditions

TABLE 4.2 Median Size of Societies, by Type of Society

Type of Society	Median Size of Societies	No. of Societies
Hunting and gathering	40	62
Simple horticultural	95	45
Advanced horticultural	5,850	84
Agrarian	Over 100,000	48
Industrial	14,000,000	27
Fishing	60	22
Herding	2,000	22

Source: Derived from George Peter Murdock, "World Ethnographic Sample," *American Anthropologist*, 59 (1957), pp. 664–687, and *World Almanac, 1985*, pp. 518–594.

SCIENCE AND MEASUREMENT

Science requires the precise and accurate comparison of phenomena. In most cases, it is not enough simply to say, for example, that X is larger than Y, or that it is hotter, or faster, or growing more rapidly. For this reason, scientists in every field use mathematical tools to measure things, and the precise language of mathematics to describe them and to analyze relationships among them.

Sociology is no exception. In comparing different human societies, for example, it is not enough to say merely that one type of society is larger than another; this could mean that it is 1 percent larger or a thousand times larger. Imprecise statements do little to clarify the nature of relationships that exist among phenomena and thus hamper the search for patterns and their explanation.

Sociologists and other social scientists make great use of a set of mathematical tools known as *statistics,* the most basic of which are called *summary measures.* A summary measure reduces a number of different measurements to a single measure that "summarizes" them all. The most widely used are *measures of central tendency*—or what are popularly known as "averages."

The most familiar measure of central tendency is the *arithmetic mean.* The arithmetic mean is determined by adding the measurements of the individual units and dividing the sum by the number of units. For example, if 5 hunting and gathering societies have 25, 32, 39, 48, and 56 members respectively, the sum of the individual measurements is 200; and when this is divided by the number of societies—5—we obtain the mean of 40.

Another widely used measure of central tendency is the *median.* We determine the median by arranging the individual measurements in order and identifying the one that is in the middle. In the example above, the median is 39. The median is often a more meaningful measure of central tendency than the mean, because it minimizes the effect of a single, highly discrepant case. If the sizes of the 5 societies in the example above had been 25, 32, 39, 48, and 156 (instead of 56), we would have obtained a mean of 60, which would have been a poor "summary" of the situation. But the median would remain 39, a truer reflection of the size of most of the societies.

or partial reliance on horticulture, fishing, or other more advanced technologies. In contrast, *96 percent* of the 377 horticultural and agrarian societies had permanent settlements.

Societal Complexity

A third important prediction of ecological-evolutionary theory is that technological advance will be linked to greater complexity of the social system. Murdock's data permit us to test this hypothesis in two ways. First, we can compare societies on the basis of the degree of occupational specialization present in them, and second, we can compare them on the basis of the complexity of their status systems. Thus, we can test the complexity of both the vertical *and* the horizontal dimensions of social organization.

Table 4.3 shows the frequency with which several kinds of occupational specialists are found in seven different types of societies. In hunting and gathering

TABLE 4.3 Frequency of Craft Specialization, by Type of Society (in Percentages)

Type of Society	Metalworking	Weaving	Leather Working	Pottery	Boat Building	House Building	Average
Hunting and gathering	*	0	0	0	0	0	0
Simple horticultural	*	0	3	2	4	2	2
Advanced horticultural	100	6	24	24	9	4	28
Agrarian	100	32	42	29	5	18	38
Industrial	100	100	100	100	100	100	100
Fishing	*	0	0	0	9	4	2
Herding	95	11	22	*	*	0	21

*The activity in question is seldom found in this type of society.
Source: See note 15, page 440 and our estimates for industrial societies.

societies, technologically the least advanced, there are no specialists in the six areas indicated. Specialization in those areas occurs in a tiny minority of simple horticultural societies, but becomes considerably more common in advanced horticultural and agrarian societies. In industrial societies, there are specialists in all of these fields. In fishing societies, the level of occupational specialization is comparable to that in hunting and gathering and simple horticultural societies, while in herding societies it more closely resembles that in advanced horticultural societies.

Figure 4.6 shows the relationship between subsistence technology and the complexity of status systems. Once again, as ecological-evolutionary theory would lead us to expect, there is a steady progression from hunting and gathering to

FIGURE 4.6 Percentage of societies having complex status systems, by type of society.

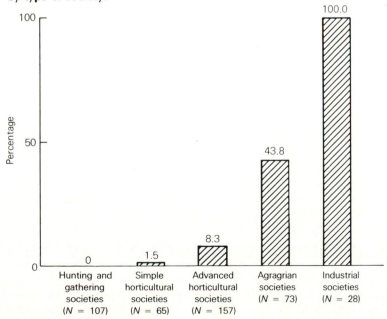

TABLE 4.4   Beliefs Concerning God, by Type of Society (in Percentages)

Type of Society	Beliefs*				Total	No. of Societies
	A	B	C	D		
Hunting and gathering	60	29	8	2	99	85
Simple horticultural	60	35	2	2	99	43
Advanced horticultural	21	51	12	16	100	131
Agrarian	23	6	5	67	101	66
Fishing	69	14	7	10	100	29
Herding	4	10	6	80	100	50

*A—no conception of Supreme Creator; B—belief in a Supreme Creator who is inactive or not concerned with human affairs; C—belief in a Supreme Creator who is active in human affairs but does not offer positive support to human morality; D—belief in a Supreme Creator who is active and supports human morality.
Source: See note 15, page 440.

industrial societies, with complex status systems totally absent in the former and universally present in the latter. The three intermediate types of societies occupy intermediate positions on the scale, with the technologically more advanced also the more likely to have complex status systems.

Ideology

Finally, ecological-evolutionary theory leads us to expect that technologically advanced societies will differ from less advanced societies in matters of ideology. Here again, Murdock's data provide the information we need to test this hypothesis with respect to one important aspect of ideology: the religious beliefs of preindustrial societies.

As Table 4.4 indicates, the basic religious beliefs of the technologically less advanced societies—hunting and gathering, simple horticultural, and fishing—tend to be quite different from those of the more advanced, especially agrarian and herding societies. Few societies in the first group have even developed the concept of a Supreme Creator, and those that have, usually assume him to be remote and indifferent to human concerns. In contrast, the majority of advanced horticultural societies believe in a Supreme Creator, but they, too, see him as inactive or indifferent to the affairs of humans. Finally, the majority of agrarian and herding societies believe not only in a Supreme Creator, but in one who is actively concerned with this world and provides support for those patterns of conduct he finds pleasing.[17]

Societal Types: What They Are and What They Are Not

By now, it should be clear that the societal types with which we will be concerned throughout this volume are sets of societies, the individual members of which resemble one another more than they resemble societies belonging to other types. The societies that make up one of these types are not identical, however. They differ from one another in many ways. Often, in fact, a number of societies of one type resemble some of the societies of another type *in certain respects* more than they resemble the majority of societies of their own type. For example, as Table 4.4 indicates, the religious beliefs of a small minority of herding societies (4 percent) resemble the beliefs of the majority of hunting and gathering societies more than they resemble the beliefs of the vast majority (80 percent) of other herding societies.

The differences between societal types are similar to the differences between age categories within a population. Every society finds it useful—even necessary—to differentiate between children and adults, and many societies go further and differentiate between infants, children, adolescents, young adults, the middle-aged, and the elderly. These distinctions reflect real and important differences within the population, but we recognize that the distinctions do not apply to all of the characteristics of all of the individuals in each of the categories. For example, a few elderly individuals are in better physical condition than many middle-aged individuals, and some adolescents may already be employed while some adults are still students in school. But these exceptions do not prevent us from using age categories as a useful tool in helping to understand and anticipate the different ways in which individuals respond to various situations.

The reason that we are able to use age categories in this way is because the physiological process of development and aging has such a profound impact on the daily lives of individuals. It sets limits on what is possible for individuals at various ages, and within those limits it makes some patterns of action more likely than others. Furthermore, it has a very similar impact on everyone who is at the same stage in the life cycle: this is why the members of a given age category resemble one another more than they resemble the members of other age categories. This is also why the members of adjacent categories resemble one another more than they resemble members of more distant categories (e.g., why adolescents resemble children or young adults more than they resemble the elderly).

Obviously, however, the physiological process of development and aging is not the only force that shapes our lives and personalities. This is why all the members of a given age category are not exactly alike and why there are always differences among them.

Societal types are much like age categories in all these ways. The reason they are so valuable is because subsistence technology has such a profound impact on the life of societies. It sets limits on what is possible for individual societies at every stage of development, and within those limits it makes certain social and cultural patterns more likely than others. Furthermore, it is a force which has a similar impact on all societies that share a common mode of subsistence: this is why societies of a given type tend to resemble one another more than they resemble societies of other types. This is also why societies of adjacent types (see Figure 4.3) resemble one another more than they resemble societies of more distant types (e.g., this is why simple horticultural societies resemble hunting and gathering societies more than they resemble industrial societies).

But subsistence technology is not the only force that influences the nature of societies any more than the physiological process of development and aging is the only force that influences individual personality and behavior. This is why there are differences among societies within a given societal type just as there are differences among individuals in the same age category.

In summary, then, societal types are analytical tools that help us to understand societies, both individually and collectively. They are sets of societies that share a single common characteristic, subsistence technology. But subsistence technology is not just any characteristic chosen at random from the almost endless list of societal characteristics. On the contrary, it appears to be *the single most powerful force responsible for the most important differences among human societies.* This is why societal types are such a valuable analytical tool.

Technological Determinism Rejected

Today, as in the past, efforts to understand the role of technology in human life are hindered by the tendency of some scholars to take extreme positions on the subject. Over the years, one group has argued the case for technological determinism, saying, in effect, that technology explains almost every sociocultural pattern.[18] To combat this exaggerated view and to uphold the importance of ideological and organizational factors, other scholars have minimized or even denied the importance of technology.[19] The unreasonableness of *both* positions has apparently escaped many social scientists, with the result that sociology and anthropology have both been slow in coming to a realistic assessment of technology's role in the evolutionary process

Much of the confusion results from the failure to think in *probabilistic* and *variable* terms. Few, if any, significant social patterns are determined by a single factor. Where human societies are concerned, one can rarely say that A, and A alone, causes B. Usually B is due to the combined effect of a number of factors, and, although A may be the most important, it alone is not likely to be strong enough to dictate the outcome. The most we can say, as a rule, is that if A is operative, B will occur with *some degree of probability.*

The problem is further complicated because so many of the B's we deal with are *variables.* For example, when we talk about a society's population, we are not interested in whether it exists, but in its relative size. The same is true of most of the other things we are concerned with—the *degree* of occupational specialization, the *frequency* of warfare, the *extent* of the authority vested in leaders, and so forth. To think in categorical, either-or terms about such matters is bound to be misleading.

While modern ecological-evolutionary theory emphasizes the tremendous importance of technology and technological innovation in the life of human societies, it does not take a deterministic view or claim that technology can explain everything in sociocultural evolution. It recognizes that other forces have also played a part—often an important part. Its view of technology's role in human affairs can best be summarized in the following propositions:

1. Because subsistence technology sets limits on what is possible within a society, an advance in subsistence technology is a necessary precondition for any substantial growth or development in terms of size, complexity, power, and wealth; this is true both for individual societies and for the world system.

2. Because subsistence technology sets limits on what is possible within a society and also determines the relative cost of each of the options within those limits, it is the single most important cause of the sum total of the differences among societies (although not necessarily of each individual difference).

3. Because societies that have grown substantially in size, complexity, wealth, and power enjoy a great advantage in intersocietal competition and are therefore better able to transmit their social and cultural characteristics to future generations, the nature of the world system has been increasingly shaped by the process of technological advance and reflects increasingly the characteristics of those societies that are technologically the most advanced and most innovative.

If these propositions are correct, then students of human societies can ill afford to ignore or neglect subsistence technology and the role it plays in human life. In fact, these propositions indicate that the first step in analyzing any society should be to identify its primary subsistence technology. This will insure that we take into account, from the outset, the most powerful single variable affecting it.

Our basic task for the rest of this volume will be to apply these principles in a broadly comparative study of human societies. We will examine each of the major societal types that have emerged in the course of history, seeing how technological advance has influenced its social institutions, and how these institutions have reacted on technology and influenced its development. We will, for obvious reasons, give special attention to the industrial and industrializing societies of our own day. Our ultimate goal is to achieve a better understanding of the forces that influence human societies, in the hope that this will help us to understand and eventually control the process of change that is such a striking, and, at times, threatening, feature of the contemporary world.

PART II

Preindustrial Societies

CHAPTER 5

Hunting and Gathering Societies

For the first 4 million years of hominid history, our ancestors all lived in hunting and gathering societies. This was the only type of society in existence during this period. Only in the last 10,000 to 12,000 years—the last one-fourth of 1 percent of hominid history—have other types of societies evolved.

Already, however, the end is in sight for hunting and gathering societies. They simply have not been able to compete with technologically more advanced kinds of societies for territories and other vital resources. As a result, hunting and gathering societies have survived in recent centuries only in remote and isolated regions. And now, in the twentieth century, with the aid of new technologies, members of advanced industrial societies have penetrated even these areas. Thus, it seems unlikely that any of the few remaining hunting and gathering societies will survive into the twenty-first century.

Fortunately, during the last hundred years or more, ethnographers, missionaries, colonial administrators, and others have had opportunities to observe more than 150 of these societies and provide us with detailed reports of their way of life. For a time, some questioned the relevance of these reports for our understanding of hunting and gathering societies of the prehistoric past. Today, however, most scholars who study the prehistoric past regard modern hunters and gatherers and prehistoric hunters and gatherers of the last 20,000 years or so as "analogous peoples" with much in common.[1] The chief differences between them are the result of (1) the contacts of modern hunters and gatherers with technologically more advanced societies (e.g., the acquisition of metal knives and other things in trade), and (2) the exclusion of modern hunters and gatherers from many of the more fertile regions of the world.*

In our analysis in this chapter, we will not assume that hunting and gathering societies of both eras are alike, but will instead present the findings of archaeology and ethnography separately. Only after we have done this will we explore the question of whether they provide consistent or contradictory images of hunting and gathering societies.

Hunting and Gathering Societies Prior to 40,000 B.C.

It is easy to speak of "the dawn of human history," but it is not so easy to assign a date to it, or even to say precisely what it means. The same evolutionary process that produced our species, Homo sapiens, first produced a number of others (e.g., Ramapithecus and Homo erectus) that were, in varying degree, "humanlike." Thus, it is impossible to say that human history began at some particular point. What *is* possible is to identify the patterns that gradually began to form during the long era of "morning twilight" that ultimately produced *fully* human creatures and *truly* human societies.

Our species, Homo sapiens, is part of the genus *Homo,* which is, in turn, part of the family *Hominidae,* better known as the hominids. This family split off from the ancestors of the modern chimpanzees and gorillas at least 4 million years ago, according to the best available evidence,[2] and has subsequently pursued a separate and increasingly unique evolutionary course. The process of natural selection, operating on a succession of hominid species, gradually shaped this line in certain fundamental and important ways and culminated in Homo sapiens, the sole surviving representative of the hominid family.

If we could look across the great abyss of space and time to a grass-covered plain in Africa several million years ago, we would see that the hominids were already on an evolutionary course that was distinct, in a number of important respects, from that of other primates. By then, according to fossil evidence, they had abandoned their ancestors' arboreal and largely herbivorous life for a bipedal, terrestrial, and omnivorous one. In other words, our ancestors had come out of the trees; they were walking on two feet and moving about much as we do today; and they were eating fruits, vegetables, and meat obtained by hunting smaller animals or by scavenging the remains of larger ones that had died or been killed by carnivores.[3]

This drastic set of behavioral changes had involved many genetic changes, especially in the skull, mouth, hips, and limbs. The most critical of these was the new upright stance, for this meant that hominid hands were no longer needed to propel their bodies through trees or over ground, but were freed for other kinds of

---

*The latter point may not be as important as it seems, since our present conception of "fertile" regions is based on their potential for farming. Yet many areas that are unsuited to farming have supported substantial populations of game animals (e.g., the Kalahari desert, various polar regions), and thus supported populations of hunters and gatherers about as well as many areas that we think of today as much more fertile.

FIGURE 5.1 **"This could mean the end of civilization as we know it."**

activity—to manipulate sticks, stones, and other objects as tools, and eventually to construct tools of their own invention.[4] This was a crucial development contributing to the evolution of our brain, for much of the development of that organ was a response to what hominids did with their hands during that long era.

Throughout hominid evolution, the attributes being selected as elements in their basic genetic heritage developed more or less in concert, not independently of one another. These included not only greater overall brain size, but an enlarging cerebral cortex (see Figure 1.6, page 21); large physical size (the earliest hominids appear to have weighed only about fifty pounds); improvement in hand-eye coordination; a variety of other advances in the nervous system; and increased cooperation and communication.

The hominids' shift to an omnivorous diet, interestingly, seems to have had implications for the emergence of important new elements of social structure in hominid societies. To begin with, hunting probably played a role in the early evolution of the division of labor. Because of pregnancy, lactation, and care of the young, females were probably somewhat handicapped in hunting activities. This may have led, at a fairly early date, to the beginnings of a pattern found in every hunting and gathering society of modern times: males have primary responsibility for providing meat, females for vegetables, fruits, shellfish, and other materials that may be more easily "gathered." This hypothesis is supported by recently discovered evidence that, as early as 2 million years ago, hunter-scavengers in east Africa transported their meat from the place where they obtained it to an "eating-place."[5] This practice, which is so unlike that of any living species of nonhuman primate, suggests a division of labor in acquiring food, as well as the sharing of food and the organization of activities around a "home base."

The division of labor along sexual lines may well lie behind yet another development in hominid societal life that distinguished hominids from other primates: the formation of durable bonds between males and females. Most other primate societies are organized around groups of mothers and their offspring; adult males do not maintain sustained contact with the group. The sustained association between the sexes that is such a fundamental part of human life may thus have had its origin in that ancient diversification of hominid diet.

The scavenging, and later hunting, of large animals also confronted hominids with the problem of how the meat should be distributed. Recent studies of chimpanzees have shown that the time they communicate most intensely is when they are dividing up meat,[6] and it is not unreasonable to assume that our ancestors reacted much the same way. Their increasing dependence on meat may thus have been an early factor in stimulating the development of symbol use as a supplement to signals.

As the ages passed, hominids came to be more like humans, in both appearance and behavior. But the rate of change was extremely slow. Archaeologists speak of the "almost unimaginable slowness of change" during this period.[7] Eventually, however, as a consequence of their increasing use of, and dependence on, tools, and as a result of the further evolution of their brains, hominids reached a point where, as the "brainiest" of the mammals, they began to make more effective use of the resources of their environment.

One of the manifestations of this was the beginning of big-game hunting, an activity with numerous repercussions on hominid societies. First of all, the pursuit of larger animals would have required a greater capability for planning, maneuvering, remembering, communicating, and cooperating, and the males that did this best were likeliest to survive and reproduce. Thus, there appears to be an important link between this activity and continuing evolution of the brain, especially in its development of more memory units and interconnecting nerve cells.[8]

There is also good reason to believe that the greater degree of cooperation demanded by big-game hunting strengthened the social bonds that united the adult members of hominid societies. Adult males could no longer be as independent as they are in other primate societies. And the new activity probably served to reinforce the division of labor between the sexes. Females would have been even more disadvantaged in this kind of hunting, because, as the hominid brain increased in size, their hips had to become wider to enable them to accommodate the infant's head at birth; running thus became slower and more awkward for them.

The use of fire was another significant technological innovation of this period. Fire was the first important natural force to be, in any sense, brought under control. Although humans may not have been able to generate fire during this era, they could preserve it after it was started by natural causes. And fire did far more than warm these societies. It set humans apart from all other animals, giving them some control over the cycle of day and night, and giving them a little more freedom of movement. It was also important for protection, and was a powerful weapon for driving predators away from camp or out of an attractive cave that humans wanted to use. Fire was also used to harden the points of wooden spears, and possibly to kill large animals by driving them over cliffs or into swamps.

The use of fire for cooking may have further affected the evolution of our teeth, and even the shape of our faces, since cooked food requires so much less chewing than raw. It was probably also involved in the beginnings of religious experience, as a basis of ritual, even as an object of worship. But most important, fire strengthened

FIGURE 5.2 Fire was the first great natural force to be brought under human control. Artist's conception of the earliest known use of fire by cave dwellers near Beijing, China, about 400,000 B.C.

the network of interrelationships within these societies, drawing the group together at the end of a day to communicate, to remember, and to plan.

No one can say with any certainty when Homo sapiens first appeared on the scene, but the best available evidence indicates that it was at least 100,000 years ago.[9] If we look for some dramatic change in human societies at this point, however, we are in for a disappointment. Though the archaeological record for this period is sparse, there is nothing to suggest that there were any significant new developments until much later. Living remained precarious, and life expectancy short. An authority who analyzed the remains of forty individuals who lived as recently as 50,000 to 100,000 years ago found that only one of them apparently reached the age of fifty, and only 10 percent the age of forty. Half of them died before their twentieth year.[10]

Within the last 100,000 years, hominids began to bury their dead, often placing in the grave with them artifacts that strongly suggest belief in life after death: food, flowers, implements, and red ocher, which some scholars suspect was believed to have the life-giving properties of blood.[11] At least one grave held animal bones and cinders, suggesting either burnt offerings or the remains of a funeral feast. This era also provides us with our first evidence of intraspecies violence. Several skeletons have been found with wounds that were almost certainly inflicted by other humans (e.g., a flint projectile embedded in a rib cage and a pelvis with a spear hole in it.)[12]

Although human societies of this era were clearly becoming more dependent upon culture, cultural change was still not as important in their adaptive response as

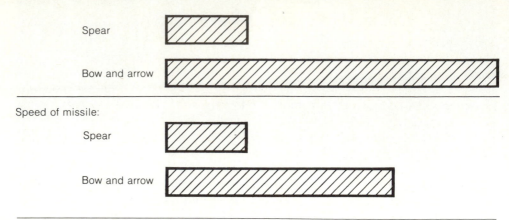

FIGURE 5.3 **Two comparisons of the spear and the bow and arrow.**

genetic change. But the situation altered later. Since our subspecies (Homo sapiens sapiens) emerged, about 40,000 years ago, there has been no major change in our species' genetic heritage, and cultural evolution has taken its place as the dominant mechanism of change.

Hunting and Gathering Societies from 40,000 B.C. to 7000 B.C.

The clearest indication of the quickening pace of sociocultural evolution is the rapid proliferation of new and improved tools and weapons. The spear, for example, had been in use for hundreds of thousands of years, with no significant improvements except for the use of fire to harden the point. Then, in the period from 40,000 B.C. to 7000 B.C., hunters made several major improvements. First, they developed the spear-thrower, which applies the principle of the lever and doubles the distance a spear can be hurled.[13] Second, at the other end of the spear they began using sharpened bone points to increase the penetrating power. Finally, they added barbs to the spearhead to create a much more serious wound.[14]

The most important innovation in weapons, however, was the bow and arrow. Employing the principle of the concentration of energy, hunters in this period created a weapon of great usefulness and versatility. Its effective wounding range is roughly four times that of the spear and twice that of the spear thrown with the aid of a spear-thrower.[15] Furthermore, an arrow travels two and a half to three times faster than a spear. This is important not only because of the time advantage it affords the hunter, but also because the force of the blow is a function of the missile's speed.* Finally, unlike the spear, the bow and arrow permit the hunter to sight the missile at eye level, which greatly increases the accuracy of the hunter's aim.

---

*These advantages are partly offset by the greater weight of the spear, which means that it remained best for some purposes.

Other technological improvements, though less dramatic, were no less important. As one writer puts it, people of this era "began to make the tool fit the task with an altogether new precision."[16] Innovations included such diverse tools as pins or awls, needles with eyes, spoons, graving tools, axes, stone saws, antler hammers, shovels or scoops, pestles and grinding slabs (for grinding minerals to obtain coloring materials), and mattocks.

In colder regions, people usually lived in caves. This was not always possible, however, as in the case of the mammoth hunters who ranged from Czechoslovakia to Siberia and whose way of life forced them to remain in caveless country even during the winter. Figure 5.4 shows a modern reconstruction of one of their settlements. Some societies also built earthen houses.[17]

The discovery of such settlements has provided us with information on the size of human societies in that era. In general, they were quite small, many with as few as six to thirty persons. The largest settlement of hunters and gatherers ever found was spread out along a two-mile stretch of river in France and may have housed as many as 400 to 600 persons,[18] but this was exceptional and may have been only a temporary gathering of a number of societies taking advantage of a salmon run or other special situation.

The best known innovation of that period is its art (see Figure 5.5). The drawings on the walls of caves in Western Europe are world famous, but they are only one of the new art forms developed at that time. There was sculpture of various kinds as well as bone and ivory carvings, often on the handles of weapons and tools.[19]

It would be hard to exaggerate the importance of these artistic remains, for they provide many insights into the evolution of human thought and the rapidly growing body of nontechnological information. Drawings of men dressed to resemble ani-

FIGURE 5.4 **Modern reconstruction of mammoth hunters' settlement in Czechoslovakia, about 25,000 B.C.**

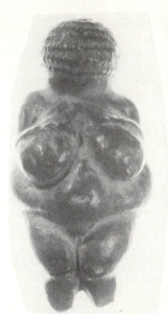

FIGURE 5.5a   The stag hunt: cave wall painting, Spain.

FIGURE 5.5b   The Venus of Willendorf, Germany.

FIGURE 5.5c   Handle of spear-thrower, France.

mals strongly suggest magical or religious practice and a belief in sympathetic magic. This belief—that anything done to an image, or a part, of a person or animal will affect that person or animal—is further suggested by the fact that a great number of the drawings have spears or darts drawn or scratched into animals' flanks.[20] Sympathetic magic was apparently also used in an attempt to produce fertility, in both humans and animals. At least this is the most likely explanation for the numerous female figures with exaggerated evidences of pregnancy (see Figure 5.5b). Most scholars think it is no coincidence that the artist ignored the facial features and focused on the symbols of fertility.

Many examples of the art of this period indicate the development not only of new beliefs, but of ceremony and ritual. This is suggested by the drawings of men dancing and by engravings of processions of men standing before animals, heads bowed and weapons resting on their shoulders in a nonthreatening position. It has been suggested that they are following the practice of some modern hunters and are asking the forgiveness of the animals they plan to kill.[21] In summary, the art of this era reveals the growth of human consciousness and the effort of people to understand and control their environment, and it attests to the growing gulf developing between them and the rest of the animal world.

By the close of the hunting and gathering era (about 7000 B.C.), human societies possessed a far greater store of cultural information than they possessed 30,000 years before. They had, in fact, acquired more information in those last 30,000 years than in all the previous millions of years of hominid history.

Table 5.1 shows how dramatic the change was in the rate of technological innovation alone. It lists all the known technological innovations of importance from the beginnings of the hominid family to the end of the hunting and gathering era. The four time intervals involved correspond to the periods which archaeologists label the Lower Paleolithic, Middle Paleolithic, Upper Paleolithic, and Mesolithic, and it should be noted that they differ tremendously in their duration (from 3,000 years to 3.9 *million* years).* By dividing the number of innovations by the approximate time required to produce them, we arrive at the figures in the right-hand column, which are a rough measure of the relative *rate* of innovation during the successive periods.

The rapid acceleration in the rate of change in the last 30,000 years of the hunting and gathering era cannot be explained by genetic change alone, since our species, Homo sapiens, had already evolved by 100,000 B.C. and was present for the whole of the second time period in Table 5.1, and our subspecies, Homo sapiens sapiens, was present for the whole of the third period. What, then, was the cause?

In recent years, a growing number of scholars have concluded that the explosive growth in the rate of technological innovation in this period resulted from critical advances in *language*.[22] While symbol use almost certainly began much earlier than this, earlier symbol systems were probably much more primitive and much less effective as instruments for the acquisition, storage, and transmission of information. According to proponents of this view, the relatively modest genetic changes that were involved in the transition from Homo sapiens neanderthalensis (Neanderthal

---

*We have set the point of hominid origins at the latest possible date, judging from current evidence, thus making our estimates of the rise in the rate of technological innovation low and conservative.

TABLE 5.1 The Rising Rate of Technological Innovation: 4,000,000 B.C. to 7,000 B.C.

Time Periods and Their Major Technological Innovations		No. of Major Innovations	Innovations Per Thousand Years
4,000,000 to 100,000 B.C.		6	.0015
Hand ax	Wooden spear		
Use of fire	Constructed shelters		
Fire-hardened spear point	Paints		
100,000 to 40,000 B.C.		3	.0500
Use of bone for tools	Skin clothing (probable)		
Built-in handles on tools			
40,000 to 10,000 B.C.		16.5*	.5500
Spear-thrower	Bow and arrow		
Lamps	Harpoon heads		
Fish gorgets	Pins or awls		
Needles with eyes	Antler hammers		
Shovels or scoops	Mattocks		
Stone saws	Graving tools		
Spoons	Stone ax with hafted handle		
Separate handles	Pestles and grinding slabs		
Boats (?)			
10,000 to 7,000 B.C.		15.5*	5.1660
Boats (?)	Fishhooks		
Fish traps	Fishnets		
Adzes	Sickles		
Plant cultivation	Domestication of sheep		
Basketry	Domestication of dog		
Grinding equipment	Leather-working tools		
Paving	Sledge		
Ice picks	Combs		

*Since the date for the invention of boats is uncertain, half credit has been assigned to each of the latest periods.

Sources: This table is based on data in Grahame Clark and Stuart Piggott, *Prehistoric Societies* (New York: Knopf, 1965); S. A. Semenov, *Prehistoric Technology* (New York: Barnes and Noble, 1964); John Pfeiffer, *The Emergence of Man*, 3d ed. (New York: Harper & Row, 1978); Jacquetta Hawkes, *Prehistory*, UNESCO History of Mankind, vol. 1, part 1 (New York: Mentor, 1965); and Alexander Marshak, *The Roots of Civilization* (New York: McGraw-Hill, 1972).

man) to Homo sapiens sapiens (fully modern man) paved the way for the explosive growth of culture that occurred at the end of the Old Stone Age, and for all the revolutionary social and cultural changes that followed. In other words, there was a critical "threshold effect"* involved: until a certain point was reached in biological evolution, the development of full-fledged symbol systems was impossible. But once that point was reached, the development of language could proceed rapidly.

The striking advances in technology at the end of the hunting and gathering era coincided with, and probably led to, an equally striking growth in the size of the human population. According to estimates based on recent archaeological research,

---

*The term *threshold effect* refers to a situation in which a small incremental change in one variable produces a much larger change in another. For example, on a stormy day a person may take a thousand steps to escape the rain without reducing his exposure to it at all, but if he takes just one or two more steps and enters a building, he is out of the rain altogether.

TABLE 5.2   The Growth of Human Population During the Hunting and Gathering Era

Approximate Date	Estimated Human Population	Average Percentage Increase in Human Population Worldwide Per Thousand Years*
1,800,000 B.C.	400,000	
150,000 B.C.	800,000	0.04
40,000 B.C.	1,200,000	0.40
7,000 B.C.	8,500,000	6.10

*These figures are our own calculations.
Source: Adapted from Fekri Hassan, *Demographic Archaeology* (New York: Academic Press, 1981), table 12/3.

the rate of growth of the human population increased substantially after 40,000 B.C. (see Table 5.2). This growth of population may also have had a feedback effect on technology and have been an added factor contributing to the rising rate of innovation.

Despite the rapid increase in the rate of growth during this period, the human population at the end of the hunting and gathering era still numbered less than 10 million and the rate of growth was still less than 0.1 percent per year (compared with 1.7 percent per year today). The reason for this was the inability of societies to provide adequately for their members and to protect them against disease and other dangers. A recent study of more than 300 skeletons of adults from Europe and Africa during the hunting and gathering era indicates that the average age at death was just 33 years for men and 28 for women.[23] Thus, the reproductive years for women were far fewer than they are today. With the high rates of infant mortality that also prevailed,[24] it is no wonder that the rate of growth of the human population was still extremely low at the end of the hunting and gathering era, despite the gains that had recently been made.

Hunting and Gathering Societies of the Recent Past

Even after the emergence of more advanced types of societies, hunting and gathering societies continued to flourish in many parts of the world. A hundred years ago, there were still large numbers of them in both the New World and Australia, and smaller numbers in southwest Africa, in parts of the rain forest in central Africa, in certain remote areas in southeast Asia and neighboring islands, and in Arctic Asia.[25] As recently as 1788 there were probably 5,000 hunting and gathering societies in Australia alone[26] and almost certainly as many in North America. Although the settlement of these areas by Europeans and the spreading influence of industrialization are now destroying the last of them, we have detailed descriptions of many of these groups.

In our review, we will concentrate on hunting and gathering groups whose way of life had been least affected by contact with agrarian and industrial societies at the time they were studied. Our primary concern will be with the more remote and isolated groups, and with groups that were studied before social contacts and cultural diffusion transformed or destroyed their traditional social patterns.

Even with these limitations, the societies in our sample are by no means all alike. Of the 151 hunting and gathering societies in Murdock's sample (see page 86), 13 percent relied on hunting and gathering for their entire subsistence, while 11 percent relied on these techniques for only about half. Most groups (80 percent) depended on fishing to some extent, and a few (15 percent) obtained nearly half their food from this source. A minority (23 percent) derived part from horticulture, and a few (less than 5 percent) almost half. In short, some were pure hunting and gathering societies, but most of them incorporated limited elements of fishing or horticulture or both.

Population

Size and Density Despite these variations in subsistence technology, modern hunting and gathering societies* have a lot in common. For example, none of them supports a large or dense population. Even in the most favorable environments, such as north central and northern California prior to white settlement, the population density for small localities rarely reached 10 people per square mile and, over larger areas, seldom exceeded 3 per square mile. In less favorable environments, such as Australia, much of which is desert, population density has been well below 1 person per square mile.[27] Communities, therefore, are necessarily small. And, since communities are almost always autonomous, societies are equally small. The average size of those that survived into the modern era is somewhere between 25 and 50.[28] As ecological-evolutionary theory would lead us to expect, the more completely societies depend for their subsistence on hunting and gathering, the smaller they tend to be, while those that incorporate fishing, horticulture, or herding as secondary means of subsistence are larger (see Table 5.3).

TABLE 5.3   Average Size of Hunting and Gathering Societies, by Percentage of Food Supply Obtained through Hunting and Gathering

Percentage of Food Supply Obtained through Hunting and Gathering	Median Size	Number of Societies
86–100*	29	32
50–85*	48	61

*These figures are estimates made by Murdock and his associates, based on nonquantitative statements in ethnographic sources.
Source: See note 15, page 440.

---

*When referring to "modern" hunting and gathering societies, we mean those that survived into the modern era (i.e., the last several hundred years). In writing about these societies, the present tense is usually used for convenience even though most of the studies were conducted some years ago.

FIGURE 5.6 Bushman mother carrying infant while digging roots.

The rate of population growth in hunting societies is so low as to be virtually nonexistent. The number of births each year seems to be matched by the number of deaths. In part, this is because of high death rates from natural causes, such as accidents and disease.[29] But it is also the result of biological processes which slow the birthrate: women who are nursing infants and women with little body fat are both less likely to ovulate than other women.[30]

The most important factor in producing an equilibrium in population size may be cultural, however, rather than biological. Infanticide and abortion are extremely widespread in these societies. One study revealed that infanticide was practiced in 80 of 86 hunting and gathering societies examined, while another study found that abortion was practiced in 13 of 15 societies studied.[31] Some scholars estimate that between 15 and 50 percent of all live births end in infanticide in societies at this level of development.[32]

The members of hunting and gathering societies are not, of course, less loving than the members of other societies. Their norms and values, like those of every society, simply reflect the past experience of the group. And this has taught them that any other course of action can be disastrous. When a mother already has one child at the breast, and may have to keep it there for several years because there is no safe alternative source of nourishment,[33] another baby can mean death for both children. This is especially likely to be true if the food supply is variable, that is, if hunting and gathering provide a glut of food at some times and a shortfall at others. If, in addition, the mother must participate regularly in the search for food and watch over her children at the same time, and if she must carry all her possessions as well as her children to a new campsite every few weeks or months (the usual practice), the logic of abortion and infanticide becomes obvious. They are simply measures that ensure the health and survival of mothers and children, and thus the survival of the society.

Nomadism Modern hunting and gathering societies are usually nomadic. Some groups are reported to remain in an area for periods as short as a week.[34] On the other hand, a few occupy permanent settlements, but all of these either rely on fishing or horticulture as important secondary sources of subsistence or are located in areas with high concentrations of game and other food resources.[35]

The nomadic character of most hunting and gathering communities is an inevitable result of their subsistence technology. One anthropologist described the basic problem when he said of a group of African Pygmies that "after a month, as a rule, the fruits of the forest have been gathered all around the vicinity of the camp, and the game has been scared away to a greater distance than is comfortable for daily hunting."[36] He went on to say that since "the economy relies on the day-to-day quest, the simplest thing is for the camp to move."

Hunters and gatherers may also change campsites for other reasons. A recent study of the Hadza in east Africa, for example, indicates that they often move to the place where a large animal has been killed simply to avoid carrying the meat.[37] Since their possessions are few, such a move requires little effort. The Hadza also move to a new site when someone dies, or even when a member becomes sick or has a bad dream, because these are all regarded as bad omens.

Many hunting and gathering groups disperse for a part of the year, with individual families striking out on their own. This pattern has been observed in such widely scattered groups as the Bushmen of southwest Africa, the Eskimo, and the Australian aborigines. Sometimes seasonal changes in flora and fauna make it more advantageous for the group to split up and do their hunting and foraging in smaller groups. Sometimes the splitting up of the group seems to be a response to controversies and conflicts that require a cooling-off period—after which the attractions of greater opportunities for socializing bring the group together again.[38]

Despite their nomadism, hunters and gatherers usually restrict their movements to a fairly well defined territory. When the society moves, it usually settles in or near some former campsite. There may even be a regular circuit of sites that the group uses year after year. A group is usually deterred from entering new territories because they are already occupied by others. Moreover, hunters and gatherers normally have a strong attachment to their traditional territory, which has acquired a sacred or semisacred character that is maintained through song and legend.

Kinship

Ties of kinship are vitally important in most hunting and gathering groups. It is hard for members of modern industrial societies to appreciate the tremendous significance of these ties, because so much of our own social interaction is organized independently of kinship, in terms of roles such as teacher and student, clerk and customer, or friend and friend.

In contrast, social interaction in hunting and gathering societies is usually organized around kinship roles. A student of the Australian aborigines reports that "in a typical Australian tribe it is found that a man can define his relations to every person with whom he has any social dealings whatever, whether of his own or of another tribe, by means of the terms of [kinship]."[39] Another writer says of these people that "every one with whom a person comes in contact is regarded as related to him, and the kind of relationship must be ascertained so that the two persons concerned will know what their mutual behavior should be."[40] He adds that kinship ties are the anatomy and physiology of aboriginal society and "must be understood if the behavior of the aborigines as social beings is to be understood." Though there are exceptions, *kinship is usually the basic organizing principle in hunting and gathering societies.*[41]

Viewed in evolutionary perspective, the family has often been described as the matrix, or womb, from which all other social institutions have evolved. This points to a basic truth: in hunting and gathering societies, kin groups perform many of the functions that are performed by schools, business firms, governmental agencies, and other specialized organizations in larger, more advanced, and more differentiated societies.

Kin groups in hunting and gathering societies are of two types, nuclear and extended families. A nuclear family includes a man, his wife or wives, and their unmarried children. Polygyny is widespread; only 12 percent of the hunting and gathering groups in Murdock's data set are classified as monogamous. It does not follow, of course, that 88 percent of the *families* in this kind of society are polygynous: this is impossible, given the roughly equal numbers of men and women. Usually only one or two of the most influential men have more than one wife, and they seldom have more than two or three. This limited polygyny is possible because girls usually marry younger than boys, and some men are obliged to remain bachelors. Multiple wives appear to be an economic asset in these societies and, to some extent, a status symbol as well.

Divorce is permitted in virtually all hunting and gathering societies and is fairly common in some.[42] In others, however, it is made relatively difficult. The most we can say is that there is great variability in this matter.

The nuclear family is usually part of a larger and more inclusive kin group known as the extended family.[43] In the majority of modern hunting and gathering societies the extended family includes *both* maternal and paternal relatives—a pattern that is not found in the majority of horticultural, herding, and agrarian societies. Compared with extended family systems that emphasize ties with either maternal or paternal kin, this bilateral, or two-sided, system effectively doubles the number of people to whom an individual can turn for help and assistance in time of difficulty, an arrangement that appears to have considerable adaptive value in societies that are quite small.[44]

The extended family is also important because the ties of kinship among its members encourage the practice of sharing. When the daily acquisition of food is uncertain, as it is in many hunting and gathering societies, a nuclear family could easily starve if it had to depend exclusively on its own efforts. A family might be surfeited with food for a time and then suddenly have nothing. Or all the adult members of the family could become ill or injured at the same time. In either case the family would be dependent on the generosity of others. Although sharing can, and does, take place between unrelated persons, kinship ties strengthen the tendency. In this connection, it is interesting to note that many hunting and gathering peoples create what we would call fictional ties of kinship when there is no "real" relationship by blood or marriage. These ties are just as meaningful to them, however, as "true" kinship ties and they serve to strengthen the bonds uniting the group—much like the role of godparent in some more developed societies.

Through marriages with people in nearby groups (a practice known as exogamy), a society gradually establishes a web of kinship ties with neighboring groups. According to one anthropologist, "One of the important functions of exogamy is that of opening up territories so that peaceful movements can take place among them, and particularly so that any large temporary variations in food resources can be taken advantage of by related groups."[45] This is also the explanation for the custom of wife lending, practiced by hunting and gathering peoples as diverse as the Eskimo and the Australian aborigines.[46] As in the case of exogamy, the purpose seems to be to strengthen, restore, or create bonds between the men involved. Thus, if two individuals or two groups have had a quarrel, they may settle it by lending one another their wives. The practice is predicated on the assumption that women are prized possessions that one does not share with everyone. It would be a mistake to suppose, however, that women are merely property in these societies; they often have considerable influence in the life of the group and are by no means mere chattels.

The Economy

Economic institutions are not highly developed in hunting and gathering societies. One reason is that the combination of a primitive technology and a nomadic way of life makes it impossible for most hunting and gathering peoples to accumulate many possessions (see Figure 5.7). In describing the Negritos of the Philippines, one observer reports that "the possessions of a whole settlement would not be a good load for a sturdy carrier."[47] The situation is the same among the Bushmen of southwest Africa. As one ethnographer explains, "It is not advantageous to multiply and accumulate in this society. Any man can make what he needs when he wants to. Most of the materials he uses are abundant and free for anyone to take. Furthermore, in their nomadic lives, without beasts of burden, the fact that the people themselves must carry everything puts a sharp limit on the quantity of objects they want to possess."[48] The minority of hunting and gathering groups that are able to establish permanent settlements may accumulate more possessions, but even they are severely limited by their primitive technology.[49]

The quest for food is an important activity in every hunting and gathering society. Since most of these societies have no way to store food for extended periods, the food quest must be fairly continuous. Moreover, unlike the situation in more advanced societies, every adult member of the group, except some of the elderly, participates and makes a contribution in this most basic part of the economy.

FIGURE 5.7   **Home and possessions of Paiute family in southern Utah in the 1870s.**

Until recently, most studies of hunting and gathering societies emphasized the uncertainty of the food supply and the difficulty of obtaining it.[50] A number of more recent studies, however, paint a brighter picture. Reports from the Pygmies of the Congo, the aborigines of Australia, the Tasaday of the Philippines, and even the Bushmen of the Kalahari Desert in southwestern Africa indicate that they all secure an ample supply of food without an undue expenditure of time or energy.[51] This has led some anthropologists to swing to the opposite extreme and refer to hunters and gatherers as "the most leisured people in the world" and to their way of life as "the original affluent society."[52]

Neither view does justice to the diversity and changeability of the situations reported by the numerous observers who have lived among these peoples. Conditions vary considerably from group to group, and within a group they may vary from season to season. For example, the Indians of northern California usually had an abundance of food, and yet even they occasionally encountered a shortage so severe that some of them starved.[53]

WHY WERE WOMEN NOT THE HUNTERS?

The revival of the women's movement in recent decades and its claim that biological differences between the sexes should be irrelevant in the division of labor invites the question of why men were the hunters and women the gatherers in hunting and gathering societies. Why not the reverse, or perhaps a sharing of responsibilities?

In recent years, a number of social scientists have reexamined these questions and have concluded that the biological differences between the sexes made a role reversal, or even a sharing of responsibilities, impossible in technologically limited societies such as these. Hunting with bows and spears requires speed, agility, and upper-body strength, and women, *on average,* are biologically disadvantaged in all three respects.

These disadvantages are linked to the special role of women in the reproductive process. The later stages of pregnancy, for example, reduce the speed and agility of women in obvious ways. But the requirements of reproduction have other, more subtle, consequences. Because of the physiological demands of pregnancy and lactation on a mother's body, women have a higher ratio of fat to muscle than men. This provides them with nutritional reserves on which they can draw during food shortages, both for their own sustenance and for that of a nursing infant. But this has the effect of reducing upper-body strength. Recent tests by the U.S. Army indicate that, on average, women have 42 percent less upper-body strength than men and that only 3 percent of women can perform "very heavy" tasks compared with 80 percent of men.

With training, women can obviously develop their muscles to a level that exceeds that of the average man. For example, when Candy Csencsits placed second in the 1983 Ms. Olympia Contest, she was down to 7 percent body fat (champion male body builders have even less, 3 to 5 percent). But when women drop below 15 percent body fat, they often cease to ovulate and become infertile. Thus, muscular development in women appears to conflict with their societally more essential role of child-bearing. In other words, if there ever were societies that used women extensively in hunting, they probably did not survive because of low birth rates.

In addition to all this, women in most hunting and gathering societies must nurse their babies for at least two to four years, because society is unable to provide a safe and adequate substitute for mother's milk. And, since nursing infants need to be fed often, mothers are not able to roam as widely or as fast as hunting requires. Finally, in most of these societies, women are usually either pregnant or lactating and thus have little opportunity to develop and maintain the many complex skills required in hunting. The end result, therefore, has been the classic division of labor in which men hunt and women gather.

Sources: Ernestine Friedel, *Women and Men* (New York: Holt, Rinehart, and Winston, 1975); Joan Huber and Glenna Spitze, *Sex Stratification* (New York: Academic Press, 1983); Janet Saltzman Chafetz, *Sex and Advantage* (Totowa, N.J.: Rowman and Allanheld, 1984); Michael Levin, "Women as Soldiers—The Record So Far," *The Public Interest,* 76 (Summer 1984), pp. 31–44; and Blythe Hamer, "Women Body Builders," *Science 86,* 7(March 1986), pp. 74–75.

A very few societies, such as the recently discovered Tasaday, do not practice hunting. For the rest, hunting usually provides less food, in terms of bulk, than gathering. According to one estimate, the gathering done by women accounts for 60 to 80 percent of the food supply of hunters and gatherers, except in arctic regions.[54] Yet hunting is valued more highly than gathering in virtually all these groups for several reasons. To begin with, meat is generally preferred to vegetables.[55] Whether this reflects a genetically based need or preference, we do not know; certainly not everyone feels this way. In some groups, preference for meat may simply reflect its scarcity. Hunting may also be valued because it requires greater skill and involves more uncertainty regarding the outcome. Added to all this is the fact that meat, unlike vegetables, is commonly shared beyond the immediate family, so success in hunting may be rewarded by widespread respect and deference. One leading anthropologist even suggests that sharing meat "is basic to the continued association of families in any human group that hunts."[56]

Because of the primitive nature of its technology, the division of labor in a hunting and gathering economy is largely limited to distinctions based on age and sex. Almost all hunting and military activities fall to the male, as do most political, religious, ceremonial, and artistic activities. The collection and preparation of vegetables and the care of children are women's responsibilities.[57] Some activities, such as constructing a shelter, may be defined as either men's or women's work, depending on the society.[58] Still other activities may be considered appropriate for both sexes. Further division of labor results because both the very young and the aged are limited in their capabilities.

There are no full-time occupational specialties in hunting and gathering societies, although there is usually some part-time specialization. For example, most groups have at least a headman and a shaman or medicine man. When their services are required, they function in these specialized capacities, but, as one writer says of the headmen of the Bergdama and the Bushmen, "when not engaged on public business they follow the same occupations as all other people."[59] He adds that this is most of the time.

Within hunting and gathering societies, the family or kin group is normally the only significant form of economic organization. Sometimes, when the practice of sharing is widespread and hunting and gathering are carried on as communal activities, even the kin group ceases to be economically important.

With respect to subsistence, each society is virtually self-sufficient. Trade between societies often occurs, but except where contacts have been established with more advanced societies, the bartered items tend to be nonessentials—primarily objects with status or aesthetic value. Such exchanges usually involve things that are scarce or nonexistent in one group's territory but present in the other's (e.g., certain kinds of shells, stones, or feathers).

Trade with advanced societies is more likely to involve economically important items. For example, many groups obtain metal tools and weapons this way.[60] In the past, these imports were seldom on a scale sufficient to alter the basic character of hunting and gathering societies.[61] In the last century, however, as contacts with industrialized and industrializing societies have increased, the volume and importance of such items have often greatly distorted traditional patterns of economic life and done much to undermine the sociocultural system as a whole.

The Polity

The political institutions of modern hunting and gathering societies are very rudimentary. As we have seen, most local communities are autonomous and independent entities (i.e., they are societies as well as communities) even though they have populations of fewer than fifty people. Because they are so small, hunting and gathering societies have not developed political mechanisms of the kind required to control and coordinate large or diverse populations.

The primitive nature of the political systems of these societies can be seen clearly in their limited development of specialized political roles and in the equally limited authority vested in them. In most cases, there is simply a headman, who provides minimal leadership for the group.[62] Allan Holmberg, who lived among the Siriono of eastern Bolivia, wrote a description of their headmen that, except for details, is a portrait of the "typical" headman in a hunting and gathering society.

> Presiding over every band of Siriono is a headman, who is at least nominally the highest official of the group. Although his authority theoretically extends throughout the band, in actual practice its exercise depends almost entirely upon his personal qualities as a leader. In any case, there is no obligation to obey the orders of a headman, no punishment for nonfulfillment. Indeed, little attention is paid to what is said by a headman unless he is a member of one's immediate family. To maintain his prestige a headman must fulfill, in a superior fashion, those obligations required of everyone else.
>
> The prerogatives of a headman are few. . . . The principal privilege . . . if it could be called such, is that it is his right to occupy, with his immediate family, the center of the [communal] house. Like any other man he must make his bows and arrows, his tools; he must hunt, fish, collect, and [so forth]. He makes suggestions as to migrations, hunting trips, etc., but these are not always followed by his [people]. As a mark of status, however, a headman always possesses more than one wife.
>
> While headmen complain a great deal that other members of the band do not satisfy their obligations to them, little heed is paid to their requests. . . .
>
> In general, however, headmen fare better than other members of the band. Their requests more frequently bear fruit than those of others because headmen are the best hunters and are thus in a better position than most to reciprocate for any favors done them.[63]

There are similar reports on headmen in most other hunting and gathering societies.[64] In a number of instances it is said that the headman "held his place only so long as he gave satisfaction."

Occasionally the headman enjoys a bit more power and privilege. For example, among the Arunta of Australia the headman "has, ex *officio*, a position which, if he be a man of personal ability, but only in that case, enables him to wield considerable power. . . ."[65] Among the Bergdama of southwest Africa, the headman "is treated with universal respect, being specified as a 'great man' by adults and 'grandfather' by children; he usually has the most wives (sometimes three or more); he has the pick of all wild animal skins for clothing himself and his family, and only his wives wear necklaces or girdles of ostrich eggshell beads; and he receives portions of all game killed in the chase, and tribute from men finding honey."[66]

At the opposite extreme are a number of hunting and gathering societies, including 12 percent of those in Murdock's data set, that do not even have a headman. In these societies, decisions that affect the entire group are arrived at through informal discussions among the more respected and influential members, typically the heads of families.[67]

The limited development of political institutions in hunting and gathering societies contrasts markedly with the situation in more advanced societies (see Table 5.4). The small size and relative isolation of these societies make it possible for them to handle their political problems very informally. Consensus is achieved much more readily in a small, homogeneous group of a few dozen people (of whom only the adults, and often only the adult males, have a voice) than in larger, more heterogeneous communities with thousands of members. A headman is valuable to such a small group only if he contributes special knowledge, insight, or skills.

Even if the leader of a hunting and gathering band were ambitious and eager to increase his power, he would not get very far. Unlike leaders in technologically more advanced societies, he would find it impossible to build and maintain an organization of dependent retainers to do his bidding, or to obtain a monopoly on weapons. The materials for making weapons lie ready at hand, and every man is trained to make and use them. If worse comes to worst, a man can usually leave the band he is in and join another.[68] Thus, there are no opportunities for building political empires, even on a small scale.

Given the rudimentary nature of political institutions in hunting and gathering societies, one might suppose that there are few restrictions on an individual. In one sense this is true; there are few rules imposed by political authorities—no courts, no police, no prisons. The individual is hardly free, however, to do as he wishes. No society is indifferent to the actions of its members, and even in the absence of formal political authority, the group controls their conduct through informal norms and sanctions.

Though there are minor variations from one hunting and gathering society to another, similar patterns of social control have developed in groups as far apart as the Kaska Indians of the Canadian Northwest, the Andaman Islanders of southeast Asia, and the Bushmen of southwest Africa.[69] First, there is the custom of blood revenge, whereby the injured party, aided, perhaps, by his kinsmen, punishes the offender himself. As one student of the Bushmen put it, "when disputes arise between the members of the band . . . there is no appeal to any supreme authority [since] . . . there is no such authority. . . . The only remedy is self-help."[70] This mode of social control is usually invoked only when the victim of the offense is a single individual or a family. In contrast, when an entire band suffers because of a member's actions, group pressure is used to sanction the individual. For example, if

TABLE 5.4 Degree of Power of Political Leaders, by Societal Type

Societal type	Degree of Power (in Percentages)				No. of Societies
	Substantial	Moderate	Slight	Total	
Hunting and gathering	9	18	73	100	11
Horticultural	50	33	17	100	24
Herding	88	13	0	100	8

Source: Derived from data in Leo Simmons, *The Role of the Aged in Primitive Society* (New Haven, Conn.: Yale, 1945).

FIGURE 5.8   Bushman hunter.

a man refuses to do his fair share in providing food, he is punished by losing the respect of others.[71] In the case of more serious offenses, the penalty may be ostracism or even banishment. The third method of control is a deterrent that applies primarily to violations of ritual prescriptions. In such cases, the group's fear of supernatural sanctions provides the needed restraint. Bushmen, for example, believe that girls who fail to observe the restrictions imposed on them at puberty turn into frogs.[72] All three methods of social control are very informal and would not be sufficient except in small, homogeneous groups in which ties among the members are intimate and continuous, and contradictory ideas are absent.

Stratification

The rudimentary nature of the political system and the primitive nature of the economic system contribute to yet another distinctive characteristic of modern hunting and gathering societies: *minimal inequality in power and privilege.* Differences between individuals are so slight, in fact, that a number of observers have spoken of a kind of "primitive communism." To some extent this is justified. As we have seen, political authority with the power to coerce is virtually nonexistent. Differences in *influence* exist, but only to the degree permitted by those who are influenced, and only as a result of their respect for another individual's skills or wisdom. When individuals lose this respect, they also lose their influence.

In most hunting and gathering societies, differences in wealth are very minor. Many factors are responsible for this. For one thing, as we have seen, the nomadic way of life prevents any substantial accumulation of possessions. Moreover, the ready availability of most essential resources (e.g., wood for bows, flint for stone tools, etc.) precludes the need to amass things, while technological limitations greatly restrict what can be produced. Finally, there is the widespread practice of reciprocity, or sharing, in most of these groups.

As a general rule, the concept of private property has only limited development among hunting and gathering peoples. Things that an individual uses constantly, such as his tools and weapons, are always recognized as his, but fields and forests are the common property of the entire society (see Table 5.5). These territorial rights of societies are often taken quite seriously, and outsiders are frequently obliged to ask permission to enter another group's territory to seek food.[73] Animals and plants are normally considered the common property of the entire society until they are killed or gathered, at which time they become the property of the individual. Even then, however, the use of them is hedged about by the rule of sharing.[74]

A successful hunter does not normally keep his kill for himself alone or even, in most cases, for his family.[75] The reason for this seems to be the same as that which underlies insurance systems in industrial societies: *it is an effective method of spreading risks.* As we have seen, poor hunting conditions, ill health, or just a streak of bad luck can render any individual or family incapable of providing for itself, and sharing food greatly enhances the entire group's chances of survival.

Despite near equality in power and wealth, there is inequality in *prestige* in most hunting and gathering societies. The interesting thing about this, from the viewpoint of a member of an industrial society, is the extent to which prestige depends on the *personal* qualities of an individual rather than on impersonal criteria, such as the offices or roles he occupies or the possessions he controls. This is, of course, a natural consequence of the limited development of specialized offices and roles and the limited opportunities for accumulating possessions and wealth. But it sharply differentiates these societies from our own.

Writing of the Andaman Islanders, A. R. Radcliffe-Brown reports that they accord honor and respect to three kinds of people: (1) older people, (2) people endowed with supernatural powers, and (3) people with certain personal qualities, notably "skill in hunting and warfare, generosity and kindness, and freedom from bad temper."[76] Although he does not say so explicitly, men are apparently more likely than women to become honored members of the group. Similar types of

TABLE 5.5 Frequency of Private Ownership of Land, by Societal Type

Societal type	Frequency of Private Ownership of Land (in Percentages)				Total	No. of Societies
	General	Frequent	Rare	Absent		
Hunting and gathering	0	0	11	89	100	9
Horticultural	36	23	23	18	100	22

Source: Derived from data in Leo Simmons, *The Role of the Aged in Primitive Society* (New Haven, Conn.: Yale, 1945).

people are accorded honor and prestige in most other hunting and gathering societies, and skill in oratory is often honored as well.[77]

Because personal characteristics are so important, systems of stratification in these groups have an openness about them not often found in more advanced societies. Almost no organizational or institutional barriers block the rise of talented individuals. For example, even where the office of headman is inherited, as it is in approximately half the societies,[78] others can surpass the headman in achieving honor, and he may fail to win even a modicum of it. The study of the Siriono Indians cited earlier tells of a headman who was a very poor hunter and whose status, as a result, was low. The importance attached to age also contributes to the openness of the system. Almost anyone who lives long enough usually ends up with a fair degree of honor and respect.

Religion

In almost every carefully studied hunting and gathering society of the modern era, there is evidence that its members have grappled with the task of explaining the world around them, especially those aspects of it that influence their own lives. Up to a point, their explanations and their interpretations of reality are the same as ours: animals run when they are frightened; people become hungry when they do not have enough to eat; and serious illness can cause death.

Because their store of information is so much more limited than ours, however, members of these societies quickly reach the limits of their ability to explain things in naturalistic terms. Insufficient food causes hunger; but why is there insufficient food? Illness is the cause of a death; but what caused the illness? To answer questions such as these, members of hunting and gathering societies, like people in every society confronted with what they do not fully understand, have developed their own sets of explanations. These explanations invoke concepts associated with a type of religion known as *animism*.[79]

The central element in animism is the belief that spirits inhabit virtually everything in the world of nature: rocks, stones, trees, lakes, and other inanimate things, as well as animals and humans. These spirits are constantly intervening in human affairs, sometimes helping, sometimes harming. They cause the arrow to strike the deer, or they warn the animal so it bolts; they enter the body to heal a wound, or they settle in the intestines to twist and burn them. Furthermore, these spirits can be influenced by humans who know the proper rituals, sacrifices, and magic charms. Some humans, however, are more skillful at this than others, and when people fail in their efforts to appease a spirit, as when a sick child fails to improve, they turn to the expert in such matters, the *medicine man* or *shaman*.

Shamans are not specialists in the strict sense of the term, any more than headmen are specialists. They are individuals who spend most of their time doing the same things as others of their sex (most shamans are men, but some are women), serving in their more specialized role only when the need arises.

While a shaman uses his powers in various ways, one of the most common is in healing.[80] He may also use them to ensure the success of hunting expeditions, to protect the group against evil spirits and other dangers, and generally to ensure the

FIGURE 5.9   Bushman shaman in trance.

group's well-being. Shamans do not always use their special powers for the benefit of others, however. Sometimes they employ them to punish people who have offended them.[81]

Because of their role, shamans usually command respect and often are more influential than the headman.[82] Sometimes, as with the Northern Maidu in California, the headman "was chosen largely through the aid of the shaman, who was supposed to reveal to the older men the choice of the spirits."[83] The role of shaman also tends to be profitable, since others are usually happy to offer gifts in exchange for help or to maintain goodwill. One early observer of the Indians of Lower California wrote that successful shamans in that area were even able "to obtain their food without the trouble of gathering it . . . for the silly people provided them with the best they could find, in order to keep them in good humor and to enjoy their favor."[84]

Education

Socialization of the young in hunting and gathering societies is largely an informal process in which children learn both through their play and through observing and imitating their elders. At a relatively early age, boys are allowed to join the men on

TABLE 5.6 Child-Rearing Emphases, by Societal Type, in Percentages

Societal Type	Self-Reliance Stressed More than Obedience	Self-Reliance and Obedience Stressed Equally	Obedience Stressed More than Self-Reliance	Total	No. of Societies
Hunting and gathering	72	14	14	100	22
Horticultural and herding	11	3	87	100	39

Source: Adapted from Herbert Barry III, Irving L. Child, and Margaret K. Bacon, "Relation of Child Training to Subsistence Economy," *American Anthropologist* 61 (February 1959), table 2.

the hunt, participating in any activities of which they are capable. Fathers commonly make miniature bows as soon as their sons can handle them, and encourage the boys to practice. Girls assist their mothers in their campsite duties and in gathering vegetables and fruits. Thus children prepare for their future roles.[85]

This informal socialization is often supplemented by a formal process of initiation that marks the transition from childhood to manhood or womanhood.[86] Initiation rites vary considerably from one society to another, though girls' ceremonies are usually linked with their first menstruation. The rites for boys commonly involve painful experiences (e.g., circumcision, scarification, or knocking out a tooth), which prove their courage and thus their right to the privileges of manhood. As a rule, these rites are also the occasion for introducing young men to their group's most sacred lore, and this combination of experiences helps to impress on them its value and importance.

Compared with horticultural and herding societies, hunting and gathering societies put more stress on training the child to be independent and self-reliant, less on obedience (see Table 5.6). This is apparently a cultural response to a subsistence economy in which it is imperative to have venturesome, independent adults who take initiative in finding and securing food.[87] In contrast, venturesomeness and independence are much less often encouraged in technologically more advanced horticultural and herding societies.

The Arts and Leisure

Modern hunting and gathering peoples have produced a variety of artistic works. Some are strikingly similar to the cave drawings and carvings of hunters and gatherers of prehistoric times. The motivation behind these efforts is not always clear, but in some cases it is plainly religious, in others, magical.[88] And sometimes it appears to be purely aesthetic.

Music, too, plays a part in the lives of at least some hunters and gatherers. Turnbull has written in detail of Pygmy hunter festivals, in which songs and the music of a primitive wooden trumpet are central.[89] These festivals have great religious significance and express the people's devotion to, and trust in, the forest in which they live and on which they depend. And, as with the visual arts, music may be used purely for aesthetic purposes, self-expression, and enjoyment.[90] Dancing is another valued feature of life in many of these societies, and, again, the motives for it are varied.

FIGURE 5.10 Contemporary cave art by Australian hunter: the water snake and turtle are important in the society's religious beliefs.

Another popular leisure activity is storytelling. Turnbull reports that the Pygmies "are blessed with a lively imagination."[91] Stories range from accounts of the day's hunt (often embellished to hold the listeners' attention) to sacred myths and legends passed down over many generations. Legends commonly deal with the origins of the world and the group, which are often considered contemporaneous. Stories about the exploits of great heroes of the past are popular and are often used to explain the group's customs. Sacred myths and legends, as we have seen, frequently enter into initiation rites, especially for boys, and they are sometimes accompanied by music and dance. This complex interweaving of art, religion, entertainment, and education provides a strong foundation for tradition and for sociocultural continuity.

Hunters and gatherers, like people everywhere, also enjoy gossip, small talk, and other nonessential activities. Games are played in virtually all these societies, but it is interesting to note that games of strategy are rare or unknown, while games of chance are more common than in any other type of society (see Table 5.7, page 124). Since a society's games, like the rest of its culture, reflect its experiences, the absence of games of strategy suggests that hunters and gatherers feel less sense of control over the events in their lives than the members of more advanced societies feel.

Tribal Ties: Links between Societies

As we have noted a number of times, each band, or local group, of hunters and gatherers is usually autonomous. Rarely are even two of them brought together under

TABLE 5.7   Types of Games, by Societal Type

Type of Society	Physical Skill	Chance	Strategy	No. of Societies
	Percentage of Societies Having Games of:			
Hunting and gathering	96	83	0	117
Simple horticultural	83	33	7	30
Advanced horticultural	90	37	68	41
Agrarian	92	60	60	25
Fishing	93	63	3	30
Herding	89	44	56	9

Source: See note 15, page 440.

a single leader, and when this does happen, it usually involves groups that are no longer completely dependent on hunting and gathering.

Despite the virtual absence of formal political organizations that extend beyond the local community, there are often informal social and cultural ties. The most inclusive of these, and one that is nearly universal, is the *tribe*—a group of people who speak a distinctive language or dialect, share a culture that distinguishes them from other peoples, and know themselves, and are known, by a definite name.[92] Unlike a society, a tribe is not necessarily organized politically. On the contrary, among hunting and gathering peoples almost none are.

Most tribes appear to have been formed by the process of societal fission or division. When the population of a hunting and gathering band grows too large for the resources of the immediate area, it divides. Division may also occur because of conflict within a band.[93] In either case, although a new group is formed, its members will naturally continue to share the culture of the parent group. Normally the new group locates somewhere near the old one, if for no other reason than because its technology and accumulated experience become less relevant the further it moves and the more the environment differs from the one its members have been used to. As this process of fission continues, it creates a cluster of autonomous bands with the same language and similar stores of information, and a tribe develops.

As this suggests, among hunters and gatherers the tribe is more important as a cultural unit than as a social unit. One writer, describing the Bushmen, reports that the tribe "has no social solidarity, and is of very little, if any, importance in regulating social life. There appears to be no tribal organization among the Bushmen, nothing in the nature of a central authority whose decisions are binding on all the members of the tribe, nor is collective action ever taken in the interests of the tribe as a whole. The tribe, in fact, is merely a loose aggregate of hunting bands which have a common language and name."[94] This description applies to most tribes of hunters and gatherers. Sometimes, as in Australia, an entire tribe gathers together occasionally for rituals and ceremonies, but this is not typical.

From the organizational standpoint, the chief significance of these tribal groupings lies in their evolutionary potential: with technological advance, they may become political units. Even among societies still on the hunting and gathering level, there is some evidence of movement in this direction. In a few of the more favorably situated sedentary groups, for example, several villages have been brought together under the leadership of a single individual.[95] This development is greatly facilitated by their common cultural heritage.

Hunting and Gathering Societies in Theoretical Perspective

Archaeological and Ethnographic Evidence Compared

Now that we have completed our review of both the archaeological and the ethnographic evidence, we can consider the relationship between prehistoric hunting and gathering groups and modern ones. Though indiscriminate comparisons of the two can be misleading, our evidence indicates that careful comparisons can be extremely valuable.[96] To begin with, we must recognize that we cannot equate modern hunters and gatherers with early hominid hunters and gatherers of a million or more years ago—before Homo sapiens had evolved and before the basic tools and weapons of modern hunters and gatherers had been invented. We can, however, reasonably compare modern hunters and gatherers with those that have lived during the last 15,000 years.

We can see why, now that we are familiar with both sets of evidence. The similarities between these two sets of hunters and gatherers are many and basic; the differences are fewer and much less important. The societies of the two periods are similar in such crucial matters as subsistence technology, size, relative equality,* and minimal occupational specialization. In addition, similarities in art suggest similarities in religious belief and practice.

The differences are largely of three types. First, in many modern hunting and gathering societies there are some elements that originated in more advanced societies (e.g., metal tools and some religious ideas). Second, modern hunters and gatherers have had no opportunity for territorial expansion, which means that population growth has been impossible for them and the number of deaths and births must balance. Prehistoric hunters and gatherers were not always subject to this harsh restriction. Finally, technologically advanced societies have often forced modern hunters and gatherers out of territories that were suitable for farming and herding.†

As we have seen, the archaeological record is much less complete than the ethnographic, being silent on many subjects about which the latter provides a wealth of information. Therefore, when the ethnographic record shows patterns that are

---

*This is indicated by the absence of differentiation in the burial remains of prehistoric hunters and gatherers. In contrast, in technologically more advanced societies of later eras one finds clear evidence of distinctions between rich and poor, the former having rare and costly objects buried with them.

†See footnote on page 98. Moreover, hunters and gatherers in both the New World and Australia still occupied good farming and herding lands until fairly recently, so we are not entirely without information on societies that existed under such conditions.

consistent for all or most modern groups and when these patterns do not depend on conditions peculiar to the industrial era, archaeologists now tend to regard them as applicable to most of the hunting and gathering societies of the last 15,000 years. This reflects the growing awareness of the *limiting* nature of a hunting and gathering technology,[97] and the realization that the range of variation in the basic characteristics of societies that depend on it will inevitably be small. In short, except where relevant conditions have changed significantly, we can probably assume substantial similarity between the advanced hunting and gathering societies of late prehistoric times and those of recent centuries.

A Model of Limited Development

In Chapter 2, we saw that human societies are systems of interrelated parts. In Chapters 3 and 4, we identified subsistence technology as the most powerful single variable influencing the other characteristics of the system. Now that we have completed our analysis of the first of the major societal types, we are in a better position to appreciate both the systemic nature of societies and the critical role of technology.

Figure 5.11 portrays the systemic qualities of a hunting and gathering society, and the relationships among its most important characteristics. The key element is the subsistence technology on which the members of these societies depend for their survival and well-being. Because of their dependence on a hunting and gathering technology, such groups are destined to be nomadic and to have a low level of productivity and a limited store of other kinds of technological information.

These characteristics lead, in turn, to other, second-order effects. Nomadism

FIGURE 5.11   Model of relations among the characteristics of hunting and gathering societies.

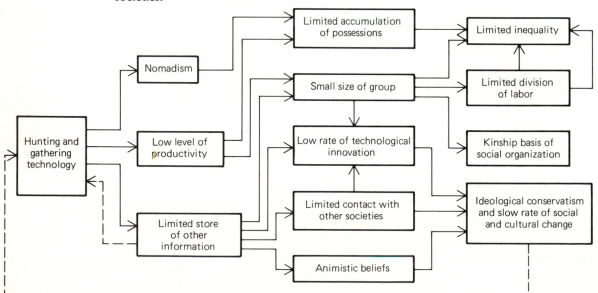

and the low level of productivity combine to limit possibilities for the accumulation of possessions. The low level of productivity and the limited store of other technological information, especially information relevant to transportation and communication, combine to keep hunting and gathering societies small. The limited development of the technologies of transportation and communication also limits contacts with other societies. These characteristics combine with the small size of these societies to keep the rate of technological innovation low. The limited store of other information also contributes to the spread of animistic beliefs about the causes of natural phenomena.

Finally, these second-order effects, individually and collectively, produce a series of third-order effects. These include the low level of inequality that is characteristic of hunting and gathering societies, their limited division of labor, the kinship basis of their social organization, and their ideological conservatism and slow rate of social and cultural change. The latter, through a process of feedback, acts to reinforce the dependence of these societies on hunting and gathering as their basic mode of subsistence. Thus, the system tends to be self-perpetuating.

The causal linkages indicated in Figure 5.11 may actually *understate* the degree to which the various characteristics of a hunting and gathering society are interrelated: some arrows that should have been included may have been omitted. The more important point, however, is not the completeness of the model, but the fact that it illustrates the systemic nature of these societies and shows the consequences of technology for every major component of the system, including basic beliefs and values.

Ecological-evolutionary theory asserts that technology sets limits on "the range of the possible" for a society, and in the case of hunting and gathering societies, it is clear that that range is remarkably narrow. We do, of course, find differences among these societies, but not in their most basic characteristics. Many of these differences, as in modes of dress and housing, simply reflect the kind of environment to which the society must adapt. Sometimes, as in the case of marriage practices—which vary considerably—we have to assume that hunting and gathering technology sets very broad limits on what is possible, and that it is largely the varied and unknown past experiences of individual societies that have led them to develop the differences we observe.

But where the basic characteristics and development of hunting and gathering societies are concerned, technology sets strict and seemingly inviolable limits. These limits are less restrictive when the technology is applied to a particularly favorable environment. A society's biophysical environment, for example, may be especially rich in the resources on which it depends, or its social environment may provide limited competition for those resources. But the only way the limits set by its technology can be *expanded* is for a hunting and gathering society to increase its store of technological information, as some of them have done by incorporating elements of fishing and horticulture.

The Last Hunting and Gathering Societies

In the summer of 1975, death came to the last full-blooded member of the Ona, a tribe of hunters and gatherers that had inhabited the southern tip of South America

FIGURE 5.12 One of the last photographs of the Ona of Tierra del Fuego, a tribe of hunters and gatherers that no longer exists.

since at least the days of Ferdinand Magellan, the famed sixteenth-century explorer, and probably for centuries or even millennia before that.[98] It is estimated that in Magellan's day there were 2,000 Ona, divided into about thirty societies. Despite the remoteness and harshness of their homeland, the Ona were destroyed not by that, but by their contacts with technologically more advanced societies. Disease, loss of territory, and loss of members to other societies all took their toll. The last Ona society died years ago; now the last Ona is also dead.

The experience of the Ona has been the experience of tens of thousands of hunting and gathering societies during the 9,000 years since hunters and gatherers first began competing for territories and other resources with technologically more advanced societies. Hunters and gatherers have had only one defense: retreat to lands that other groups regarded as worthless or inaccessible.

Today, even this defense is crumbling and the last outposts of this ancient way of life are doomed. The speed of the process is demonstrated by the experience of an anthropologist who pioneered in the study of the Bushmen of the Kalahari Desert in southwest Africa. She reports that to reach them in 1951 required an arduous trip across the desert by truck, lasting eight days from the final outposts of civilization until contact with the Bushmen was made.[99] There was no road of any kind, not even a track across the sand and bush country. When she returned in 1962, only eleven years later, she reached them in one day over a well-cleared track. As Bushmen come more and more in contact with, and under the influence of, more advanced societies, their traditional way of life is doomed. According to a recent report, less than 5 percent of the 30,000 Kung Bushmen are still hunters and gatherers.[100]

128

By the end of this century, perhaps sooner, the last hunting and gathering society will have vanished—and with it, an irreplaceable link to our past. For thousands of years, these societies maintained a highly successful relationship with their environments and a highly rewarding way of life. Relying entirely on cultural information that they could carry in their brains, hunters and gatherers adapted to a wide variety of biophysical environments; and, until the advent of societies with larger populations and more sophisticated technologies, they also adapted successfully to their social environments. The process of change in each part of these sociocultural systems occurred slowly enough that answering changes could occur in other parts without serious social unrest or upheaval. In short, this dying way of life served our species extremely well.

CHAPTER 6

Horticultural Societies

Before the hunting and gathering era ended, 9,000 years ago, human societies had accumulated substantial stores of information about plants and animals. People were as familiar with the behavior patterns of some animals as they were with their own, and probably understood them almost as well. They had also identified hundreds of varieties of edible plants and become familiar with their processes of reproduction and growth. Some hunters and gatherers in the Middle East even harvested wild grains with stone sickles. Thus, shifting from hunting animals to herding them and from gathering fruits and vegetables to cultivating them was not as great, or as difficult, a step as one might imagine.[1]

But what induced societies to take that step? Why, after hundreds of thousands of years of hunting and gathering, did the members of some societies abandon that ancient, time-hallowed way of life? Above all, why did they do it when the new mode of production meant more work and less freedom?

Causes of the Shift from Hunting and Gathering to Horticulture

Until fairly recently, scholars tended to assume that, because of human intelligence and unsatisfied human needs, technological innovation and societal development were normal and natural and required no special explanation. By shifting from hunting and gathering to horticulture, societies assured themselves of a greater and more stable supply of food, and the members of any society would naturally make the shift, once the principles of plant cultivation came to be understood. Furthermore, it was generally assumed that horticulture required less labor than hunting and gathering. Thus, by adopting horticulture—that is, farming without plows—societies traded a precarious and onerous way of life for a much more secure and satisfying one—or so it seemed. Some scholars hypothesized that the shift to horticulture may also have been stimulated by the changes in climate that occurred at the end of the last Ice Age.

More recently, however, doubts have been cast on these explanations. To begin with, a growing body of archaeological research indicates that the members of many hunting and gathering societies understood the basic principles of plant cultivation thousands of years before horticulture was adopted as the primary mode of subsistence. Furthermore, ethnographic studies of modern hunting and gathering societies have made it clear that their members place a high value on their way of life: they cherish the challenge and excitement of the hunt, and the freedom and other benefits their way of life affords. Finally, it has also come to be recognized that most societies have not shared the positive view of innovation and change that prevails in industrial societies today (see page 245). On the contrary, they place a high value on tradition and continuity.

As a result, most scholars now doubt that hunters and gatherers abandoned hunting and gathering and adopted horticulture unless they were compelled to do so by circumstances beyond their control. Instead, they have come to believe that the gradual growth of human population over millions of years (see Table 5.2, p. 107) eventually created a situation in which it became imperative to increase the supply of available food. This was probably done gradually, with plant cultivation serving initially as merely a minor means of supplementing the food resources obtained by hunting and gathering. But more food meant more babies surviving and still larger populations, thus necessitating still greater dependence on horticulture. Eventually, after hundreds or thousands of years the point would have been reached where horticulture had replaced hunting and gathering as the dominant mode of subsistence. But the whole process would have been so gradual that the people involved would have been largely unaware of the changes that were occurring.[2]

There is also evidence which suggests that in some areas of the world, this process was speeded up by advances in the weapons technologies used by hunters. Improved weapons appear to have led to increasing kills, and the eventual extinction, of many species of the slow-breeding, larger mammals on which many societies had come to depend for much of their food. In North America, for example, thirty-two genera (i.e., sets of species) of large mammals became extinct between 13,000 and 7000 B.C.[3] These included horses, giant bison, oxen, elephants, camels, antelopes, pigs, ground sloths, and giant rodents. The pattern was similar in northern Europe, where the woolly mammoth, woolly rhinoceros, steppe bison, giant elk, and others vanished.[4] A recent study in northern Spain provides striking evidence that, around 8500 B.C., there was significant substitution of fish and shellfish for the meat of big-game animals in people's diets, and that there was also an apparent decrease in the average size of the shellfish caught, indicating overkill and the apparent depletion of that resource.[5]

In summary, then, several newer lines of evidence now suggest that the shift from hunting and gathering to horticulture was essentially a response forced on human societies by population growth. Overall, the shift seems to have occurred gradually, but in some areas at least, the pressures to adopt horticulture appear to have been intensified by advances in weapons technology that led to the depletion, and eventual extinction, of many species of big-game animals that previously had been important sources of food.

The shift from hunting and gathering to horticulture, though "merely" a change in one aspect of life, was destined to have profound and far-reaching consequences for human life as a whole. We will examine the more immediate consequences in the present chapter, and the longer-term consequences in Chapters 7 through 13. Before doing this, however, we must first consider the new technology itself.

Horticulture

Horticulture is a method of farming that differs greatly from agriculture, the more familiar method of farming for Americans and Europeans.[6] Where agriculturalists depend on the plow, horticulturalists employ the digging stick or hoe, and where agriculturalists cultivate large fields continuously for decades, or even centuries, horticulturalists cultivate a succession of small gardens, each of which is abandoned after a few years.

Sometimes the practice of horticulture is referred to as *swidden cultivation*, and sometimes it is known as *slash-and-burn cultivation*. These terms call attention to the widespread practice of clearing new gardens by cutting and then burning existing vegetation, especially shrubs and small trees. Larger trees are often left standing, but are killed by girdling them, or cutting away a circular strip of bark all the way around the tree, thereby stopping the flow of nutrients from the roots to the branches.

After existing vegetation has been burned away, the resulting layer of ash provides fertilizer for the crops that are planted. Good yields can be expected for a year or two, but after that, as the nutrients in the ash are consumed, yields decline. Also, because of the absence of plows, weeds eventually take over. Thus, after only a few years, gardens must be abandoned and new plots cleared.

The length of time a garden can be cultivated by horticulturalists varies considerably, depending on environmental conditions and on the length of time since the land was last cultivated. The longer the period the land remains uncultivated, the greater is the amount of vegetation that grows on it and the thicker is the layer of ash and nutrients when it is burned. Allowing the land to revert to jungle or forest is especially important because this destroys the weeds which spring up when land is cleared and which choke out the cultivated plants of the gardeners.

Because of the necessity of allowing the land to revert to wilderness, horticulturalists are able to cultivate only a small fraction of the territory they occupy. Thus, horticultural societies seldom achieve the high levels of population density that are typical of agrarian societies. Nevertheless, their mode of subsistence is much more productive than hunting and gathering in terms of yield per acre, and their societies, as a result, almost always have larger and denser populations.

In the horticultural system of farming, men are usually responsible for clearing

FIGURE 6.1 Women planting taro in a simple horticultural society in New Guinea. Note the tree stumps in the cultivated area: most horticulturalists do not clear the land as thoroughly as agriculturalists, who use the plow.

the land when new gardens are needed, while women are responsible for planting, tending, and harvesting the crops. This division of labor is almost certainly linked to the earlier division of labor in hunting and gathering societies, where women were responsible for providing the vegetable materials that people consumed. Men continue to hunt in many horticultural societies, but hunting is a much less productive and rewarding activity, since the ratio of game animals to humans is much lower (partly because of the greater density of human population, partly because game animals tend to avoid areas of permanent human settlement). Overall, men's contribution to subsistence is much less than that of women in horticultural societies and requires much less time. Thus, men in these societies often have substantial amounts of time at their dispoal—a fact that has had important social and cultural consequences, as we will see.

In many respects, horticulture can be considered a more primitive form of farming than agriculture. The plow is both a more sophisticated and a more powerful tool than the digging stick and the hoe, and agricultural societies are usually more productive economically than horticultural societies. It should be noted, however, that plow agriculture has not been feasible in many tropical regions and efforts to introduce it there have usually failed. Thus, while it is legitimate to say that horticulture is a more primitive form of farming than agriculture, there are some areas in the world where horticulture is the only form of farming possible. This is why, in Figure 4.3 (page 82), one of the environmental categories was labeled "areas unsuited to plow cultivation."

In the analysis of horticultural societies that follows, we will employ the same format that we employed in the last chapter: we will begin with a survey of the archaeological record of the past, and then turn to the evidence from horticultural societies that have survived into the nineteenth and twentieth centuries. Finally, at the end of the chapter, we will return to ecological-evolutionary theory to help us formulate a coherent model of horticultural societies.

Simple Horticultural Societies in Prehistoric Asia and Europe

In Asia Minor, Palestine, and the hill country east of the Tigris River, archaeologists have found the remains of ancient settlements, dating from about 7000 B.C., in which horticulture appears to have been the primary means of subsistence.[7] During recent years our knowledge of these early horticultural societies has been advanced substantially by developments in the field of archaeology, including the excavation of new sites and the more extensive exploration of older ones. Biologists and geologists have made important contributions to our understanding of the biophysical environment during that era. Most important of all, greatly improved techniques for dating archaeological remains have been developed since World War II. With these techniques, prehistoric materials of up to 50,000 years of age can now be dated with a substantial degree of accuracy, and many once unanswerable questions can now be answered.[8]

In traditional archaeological usage, the period in which simple horticultural societies were dominant in a region was known as the Neolithic, or New Stone Age. This name was chosen because in early research in Europe and the Middle East, some strata in excavated sites yielded distinctive stone axes, adzes, and hammers that, unlike earlier stone tools, had been smoothed by grinding or polishing. Prior to the discovery of radiocarbon dating, these tools were one of the best indicators of the relative age of strata and their place in evolutionary history.

As research progressed, however, and more and more sites were excavated, it became increasingly clear that these tools were neither the most distinctive feature of Neolithic societies nor their greatest technological achievement. Rather, their most important innovations were in the area of subsistence technology: for the first time in history, people were mainly dependent on horticulture, and hunting and gathering was relegated to a secondary role. In this connection, it is important to recognize that these early horticultural societies had a mixed economy. Horticulture was their basic means of subsistence, but it was supplemented by herding, hunting, and gathering in various combinations.[9] The presence of livestock in many of these early societies was especially important, as we will soon see.

The First Great Social Revolution

Although many scholars today describe the emergence of horticultural societies as the first great social revolution in human history, it would be wrong to assume that the rate of change seemed revolutionary to those involved. As far as we can judge today, the process was so gradual that the changes occurring during a lifetime were neither very numerous nor overwhelming. For example, people in the Middle East had been using wild grains for a thousand years or more before the horticultural era began. Techniques of harvesting, storing, grinding, and cooking grains were well established long before the techniques of cultivation were adopted. Furthermore, as we have noted, hunting, and to some extent gathering, continued to play a part in the lives of early horticulturists. There was almost certainly considerable continuity in other areas of life as well, especially in kinship, religion, and politics. The survival of fertility cults, indicated by the widespread presence of female figurines in Neolithic remains, is one evidence of this.[10] Our use of the term "revolutionary" in connection with the rise of horticultural societies, therefore, is based primarily on the long-term consequences of the change.

Permanence of Settlements One immediate and very important consequence of the shift to horticulture was the greater permanence of settlements. No longer did groups of people have to move about constantly in search of food; on the contrary, the practice of horticulture forced them to stay in one place for extended periods. In the Middle East and in southeastern Europe, many permanent settlements seem to have been established. In most areas, however, simple horticulturalists usually have had to move their settlements every few years.[11] Why this was not necessary in the Middle East and southeastern Europe is still a mystery, since only continuing fertilization (by alluvial deposits or by man), the use of the plow, and crop rotation permit land to be kept under continuous cultivation,[12] and so far there is no evidence of these practices. We do know, however, that these early horticulturalists kept livestock, and it is possible that the value of manure was discovered at an early date.[13] This practice may not have spread to other areas simply because of the greater availability of arable land elsewhere.

FIGURE 6.2 Artist's reconstruction of farmhouse in Denmark during the horticultural era (about 2700 B.C.). Compare this with the dwellings of the Bushman and Paiute hunters (Figures 4.1 and 5.7, pages 79 and 113).

In any case, the shift from hunting and gathering to horticulture substantially increased the permanence of human settlements, thereby enabling people to accumulate many more possessions than ever before. This is evident in the archaeological remains left by horticulturalists of the Neolithic era. Tools and weapons are much more numerous and varied than in older sites, and for the first time there are large, bulky objects such as stone cups and bowls and pottery.[14] Dwellings also became more substantial. Some buildings contained several rooms and a small courtyard and were made of materials like sun-dried clay blocks, capable of lasting for as long as two generations.[15] Even more noteworthy is the appearance of such things as religious shrines or ceremonial centers, village walls, and occasional paved or timbered (corduroy style) roadways or alleys; though none of these is typical of simple horticultural communities, they are not rare.[16]

The change from hunting and gathering to horticulture also resulted in larger settlements and denser populations. Jarmo, one of the oldest horticultural villages yet discovered, contained twenty to twenty-five houses and an estimated population of 150,[17] nearly four times that of the average hunting and gathering band. Neolithic villages in Europe had from eight to fifty houses, suggesting populations ranging up to at least 200.[18] In several cases there were even more striking concentrations of population. One of the most famous was a town located on the site of Jericho 5,000 years before the days of Joshua. Excavations there have uncovered a community that apparently housed 2,000 to 3,000 inhabitants.[19] More recent excavations of Çatal Hüyük, in what is now Turkey, revealed a community occupying an even larger area with, presumably, a larger population.[20]

Growth of Trade and Commerce   These two communities, though obviously exceptional, illustrate another development associated with the rise of horticultural societies—the rapid expansion and growing importance of trade and commerce.[21] Modern scholars feel that the "great" size of Jericho and Çatal Hüyük was not simply the result of the practice of horticulture. As one writer has put it, "It is . . . most unlikely that [horticulture] should have flourished more at Jericho, 200 metres below sea-level, than elsewhere in Palestine. Some other resource must have existed, and this was probably trade."[22] As he points out, Jericho commanded the resources of the Dead Sea, including salt, bitumen,* and sulfur, all useful materials in simple horticultural societies and not available everywhere. This view of Jericho as an early center of trade is supported by the discovery there of products such as obsidian from Asia Minor and cowrie shells from the Red Sea. In the case of Çatal Hüyük, obsidian (i.e., volcanic glass, a material much sought after for use in weapons and other things) seems to have been the key local resource responsible for its growth. Even in small villages far removed from such centers as Jericho and Çatal Hüyük, there is evidence of trade. For example, shells from the Mediterranean have been found in the sites of horticultural villages and in graves in northern Europe.[23]

The growth in trade and commerce, combined with the increasing quantity of material products, may well have led to the beginnings of formal record keeping. Archaeologists have found a variety of clay tokens in horticultural sites from modern Turkey to Iran, but until recently no one could identify their use. Then it was discovered that the markings on many of the tokens were remarkably similar to symbols used in the oldest forms of writing (which date from the early years of the agrarian era) for such words as "sheep," "wool," "cloth," "bread," "bed," and a variety of numerals.[24] This strongly suggests that the tokens were used to represent those same objects and numbers. Since they were often stored in small clay containers, they were probably records of early business transactions (e.g., outstanding loans). But whatever their precise use in the societies of the time, those tokens tell us of a major breakthrough in the ability of human societies to store information.

Another probable consequence of the growth in trade and commerce was an increase in occupational specialization, at least in the chief commercial centers. Direct evidence of this has been found at several sites. For example, excavation of a community south of Jericho yielded a number of small workshops where specialized craftsmen, such as a butcher, a bead maker, and a maker of bone tools, worked.[25] This kind of specialization, however, was limited.[26] Most communities remained largely self-sufficient, and most families still produced nearly everything they used.[27] Innovations continued in the domestic arts, with the invention of pottery and weaving being especially important.[28]

---

*Bitumen was used to fix blades in handles, mend pottery, etc.

Increase of Warfare   There is little evidence of warfare in early horticultural societies. Graves rarely contain weapons, and most communities had no walls or other defenses.[29] Some, it is true, had ditches and fences, but these were more suitable for protection against marauding animals than against human enemies. Later in the horticultural era the picture changed drastically and warfare became increasingly common. In this period battle-axes, daggers, and other arms appear in the grave of every adult male. The reason for this change is not clear, but some scholars think it was linked with the growth of population and the resulting scarcity of new land suitable for horticulture. It may also have been related to declining opportunities for hunting, a traditional male activity. Warfare, with its demands for bravery and skill in the use of arms, would be a natural substitute, and if women were doing most of the work of tending the gardens, as is the case in most modern horticultural societies, men would have had substantial amounts of time to spend in this activity.[30] Moreover, the frictions created by growing pressure for land would provide a ready-made justification. Finally, some experts suspect that the increase in warfare was linked with the increase in wealth, especially in the form of cattle, which could be easily stolen.[31]

One consequence of horticulture was that, as more and more societies adopted the new technology, it became increasingly difficult for other societies in the same area to continue hunting and gathering. As the population grew in a horticultural society, new settlements would form on the outer fringes. When they moved into territory occupied by hunters and gatherers, the horticulturalists would, by remaining in one place for a number of years, deplete the supply of game to the point that it could no longer support the hunters. Were the latter tempted to fight for their "rights," they would usually find themselves outnumbered by a ratio of more than two to one, if the populations of contemporary groups are any indication.[32]

The Chinese Experience   The horticultural societies of China are of special interest because there the shift to that mode of subsistence began late enough, and writing developed early enough, that some memory of the horticultural era was preserved in legends that were eventually written down. For a long time scholars thought this material was entirely fictional, but modern archaeological research has substantiated enough of it so that it is now regarded as a mingling of fact and fiction.[33]

According to the legends, China's earliest inhabitants were hunters, but the increase of population eventually forced a shift to horticulture. As one source recounts, "The ancient people ate meat of animals and birds. At the time of Shen-nung [an early legendary ruler and culture hero] there were so many people that the animals and birds became inadequate for people's wants and therefore Shen-nung taught the people to cultivate."[34] Other legends relate that Shen-nung introduced pottery and describe the era as a period of peace and self-sufficiency. "During the Age of Shen-nung people rested at ease and acted with vigor. They cared for their mothers, but not for their fathers. They lived among deer. They ate what they cultivated and wore what they wove. They did not think of harming one another." This preference for mothers is especially intriguing, because it is so contrary to the later Chinese tradition, yet conforms to one of the distinctive features of contempo-

FIGURE 6.3 Ubaid settlement about 4000 B.C. Note the large temple in the center of the community.

rary horticultural societies (see page 149). Finally, there is a legend describing the Age of Shen-nung as the last era in which people were free from coercive political authority. "People were administered without a criminal law and prestige was built without the use of force. After Shen-nung, however, the strong began to rule over the weak and the many over the few."

The Ubaid Culture   During the horticultural era, technological progress was almost continuous, especially in the Middle East. In addition to the invention of pottery and weaving, metals were discovered and the basic principles of working them were developed. Thus, many of the simple horticultural societies of the latter part of the era were appreciably more advanced than their predecessors 3,000 years earlier.

The societies that flourished throughout Mesopotamia around 4000 B.C. illustrate how far these simple horticulturists had advanced. These groups apparently shared a common culture, known today as the Ubaid culture, named after one of the archaeological sites where its remains are found. This culture was notable in many ways. To begin with, large settlements were relatively common. This is indicated by the size of cemeteries (one of which contained more than 1,000 graves) as well as by the large temples that dominated these communities.[35] A variety of technical skills were highly developed. Some copper tools and weapons were used, as well as sickles and other tools made from clay fired at high temperatures, a process that produced a remarkably efficient substitute for the stone that was lacking in that area.[36] Trade became extensive throughout Mesopotamia, facilitated by simple sailboats plying the myriad waterways.[37] This undoubtedly contributed to the wide diffusion of Ubaid culture. As one writer says, "Never before had a single culture been able to influence such a vast area, if only superficially."[38]

Advanced Horticultural Societies in Prehistoric Asia and Europe

Each of the inventions and discoveries of the horticultural era increased, to some degree, the ability of human societies to utilize the resources in their environments. But none had such far-reaching effects as *the use of metal in weapons and tools*. This is why metallurgy is used as the criterion for differentiating between simple and advanced horticultural societies. Societies are classified as advanced horticultural only when the use of metal weapons and tools was widespread. Societies in which it was rare, or in which metals were used only for artistic and ceremonial artifacts (as in some pre-Columbian South and Central American Indian societies where gold was the only metal known), are better classified as simple horticultural, since the impact of metallurgy on societal life was limited.

The Shift from Stone to Metals

To the non–technically inclined, the shift from stone to metal may suggest a radical break with the past and the introduction of something completely new. Actually, however, the use of metals evolved from the use of stone by a series of surprisingly small steps.

For thousands of years, people had been well aware of differences among rocks and stones. They had learned that some were better for tools and weapons because they were harder and held a cutting edge longer. They were also aware of the colors in rocks and used the more unusual for beads and other ornaments, and also as a source of pigments for paints.

This interest in unusual rocks undoubtedly attracted people to copper. In its native form, copper appears as a purplish green or greenish black nugget which, when scratched or rubbed, shows a yellowish kernel of pure copper. At first, copper was simply hammered cold into small tools and ornaments such as awls, pins, and hooks. A few articles made by this method have been found in Middle Eastern sites dating from the seventh millennium B.C.[39] Later, between 5000 and 4000 B.C., the technique of annealing was discovered.[40] Copper, when alternately heated and hammered, was made less brittle and thus could be used for a wide variety of purposes. The heat from a simple wood fire was sufficient for annealing. Later still, people discovered techniques for extracting copper from ore by means of smelting, and they also found ways to melt "pure" copper and cast it in molds.[41]

These discoveries illustrate again the cumulative nature of technological progress. Both smelting and melting copper require higher temperatures than a simple wood fire can produce. This suggests that these important discoveries came after the invention of pottery and the pottery kiln.[42] And these inventions, in turn, presupposed settled communities where heavy and bulky objects could be accumulated. Figure 6.4 summarizes the complex chain of causation involved and reminds us again of the systemic nature of human societies.

As far as we can judge, the use of copper tools and weapons increased rather slowly, for a variety of reasons.[43] For one thing, until smelting was discovered, the supply of copper was extremely limited; even then, the ore often had to be carried

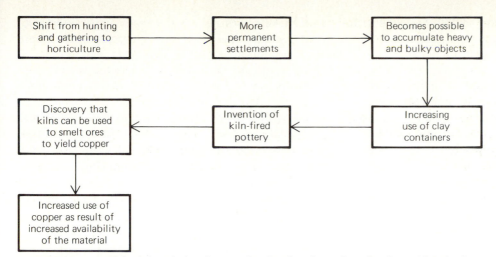

FIGURE 6.4 Model of the chain of causation leading from the adoption of horticulture to the widespread use of copper in the manufacture of tools, weapons, and other artifacts.

some distance by primitive and costly methods of transportation. In addition, metal-working (particularly smelting and casting) was probably mastered by only a few specialists, who may have treated their skills as a kind of magic (as smiths in modern horticultural societies often do) to protect a lucrative monopoly. Finally, since any man could make his own tools and weapons out of stone, people were undoubtedly reluctant to switch to the costlier product.[44] Thus, though copper was discovered as early as the seventh millennium B.C., no truly advanced horticultural society (i.e., one in which metal tools and weapons were widespread) seems to have developed until about 4000 B.C.[45]

The archaeological record provides an inadequate picture of European and Middle Eastern societies at the advanced horticultural stage of development. To see what the widespread adoption of metal tools and weapons meant for the life of a horticultural society, we must turn to China.

Social Consequences of Metal Tools and Weapons

Advanced horticultural societies flourished in China from the middle of the second millennium B.C. to the middle of the first.[46] The plow, for reasons that are unclear, was slow to appear in China, thus delaying the emergence of agrarian societies. This prolongation of the advanced horticultural era was undoubtedly a major reason why the overall level of technological development in China's horticultural societies surpassed that of most other horticultural societies.

One indication of this is the fact that the dominant metal in China during most of this era was not copper, as in the Middle East and Europe, but bronze. This is significant, because bronze, whose manufacture represents an important advance in metallurgy (involving, as it does, the principle of alloying), is a great deal harder than copper and thus can be used for many purposes for which copper is unsuitable. In the Middle East, the technique of making bronze was not really understood until some time *after* the first agrarian societies had made their appearance.[47] These variations in the sequence of such major innovations as bronze and the plow warn us of the inadequacy of *unilinear* theories of evolution, which assume that all societies follow exactly the same evolutionary path. Some variation is the rule, not the exception.

When the advanced horticultural era in China is compared with the simple horticultural period, the differences are striking. During the earlier era, northern China was covered with numerous small, mostly self-sufficient, autonomous villages. In the later period, the villages were no longer autonomous, and a few had become urban centers of some size and substance.

The emergence of these urban centers was largely the result of the military success of villages that had one important advantage: the possession of bronze weapons. As one scholar summarized this period, "In the course of a few centuries the villages of the plain fell under the domination of walled cities on whose rulers the possession of bronze weapons, chariots, and slaves conferred a measure of superiority to which no [simple horticultural] community could aspire."[48]

The importance of this development can hardly be exaggerated. For the first time in Chinese history, people found the conquest of other people a profitable alternative to the conquest of nature. Much the same thing happened in other parts of the world at this stage of societal development. Thus, beginning in advanced horticultural societies and continuing in agrarian, we find almost as much energy expended in war as in the more basic struggle for subsistence. One might say that bronze was to the conquest of people what plant cultivation was to the conquest of nature: both were decisive turning points.

From the military standpoint, China's advanced horticulturalists enjoyed a great advantage over simple horticulturalists. Recently excavated burial remains show that their warriors wore elaborate armor, including helmets. They also carried shields, and were equipped with spears, dagger-axes, knives, hatchets, and reflex bows capable of a pull of 160 pounds.[49] In addition, they used horse-drawn chariots carrying teams of three men (see Figure 6.5).

These societies also enjoyed substantial *numerical* superiority over simple horticultural societies and every victory brought more people under their control, enabling them to enlarge their armies still further.[50] This could not have been accomplished by a hunting and gathering society, whose primitive technology would make it impossible for conquerors to incorporate a defeated people into the group. At that level of development, the *economic surplus* (i.e., production in excess of what is needed to keep the producers healthy and productive) was small and unpredictable. But with the introduction of horticulture, the situation changed dramatically. *For the first time, the conquest, control, and exploitation of other societies had become possible—and profitable.* All that was needed to transform this possibility into a reality was an advance in military technology that would give one society a definite advantage over its neighbors. That advance was bronze. It tipped the balance of military power decisively in favor of advanced horticulturalists.

The earliest advanced horticultural society in China of which we have any knowledge was established around 1600 B.C., and its structure was basically feudalistic.[51] In most regions, especially those remote from the capital, power was in

FIGURE 6.5 Chariots, together with bronze weapons, gave the advanced horticulturalists of China a great advantage over their simple horticultural neighbors. Burial remains
of a warrior with his horses and chariot, eleventh century B.C.

the hands of a warrior nobility that ruled the people in their immediate area. They
paid tribute to the king and supported him militarily, but otherwise enjoyed great
independence.[52] They were so independent, in fact, that they often waged war
among themselves.

Marked social inequality was the rule in these societies. There were two basic
classes, the small warrior nobility and the great mass of common people.[53] The
warrior nobility was the governing class and lived in the walled cities which served
as their fortresses. It was they who enjoyed most of the benefits of the new technology and the new social system. The chief use of bronze was to manufacture
weapons and ceremonial objects for the benefit of this elite class. Almost none of this
scarce material was made available to the common people for farm tools.[54] The
situation was much the same in the Middle East and Europe for 2,000 years or more.
As one writer put it, this was a world in which metals played a major role in the
military, religious, and artistic spheres, but not in subsistence activities.[55]

Kinship was extremely important in the political systems of advanced horticultural China. Membership in the governing class was largely hereditary, and as
far as possible leading officials assigned the major offices under their control to
kinsmen.[56] The origins of these noble families are unknown, but it seems likely that
they were descendants of early conquerors and their chief lieutenants.

The walled towns where the aristocracy lived, though small by modern standards, were nonetheless an important innovation. One recently excavated town,

**FIGURE 6.6   The Great Wall of China: this 1,500-mile-long fortification, begun late in
China's horticultural era, illustrates the growing ability of political elites to mobilize labor
on a massive scale.**

probably the capital of an early state, covered slightly over one square mile.[57] The
size of the walled areas, however, does not tell the full story of these towns,
especially in the earlier period, for many of the common people had their homes and
workshops outside the protected area and cultivated nearby fields.

The walled area, while basically a fortress and place of residence for the
governing class, was also a political and religious center. Religious activities were
quite important and were closely tied to the political system—so closely, in fact, that
one writer describes the state as "a kind of theocracy."[58] Though this appears to be
an overstatement, ancient inscriptions prove that the ruler performed major religious
functions and was what we today would call the head of both church and state.

The physical structure of those early urban centers was impressive and reflected
the evolution of the state and its newly acquired ability to mobilize labor on a large
scale. One scholar estimates, for example, that it required the labor of 10,000 men
working eighteen years to build the wall around the capital of one early state. Such
massive undertakings apparently utilized large numbers of captives taken in war,
many of whom were used later as human sacrifices.[59]

Not much is known about the daily life of the common people, but their chief
functions were obviously to produce the economic surplus on which the governing
class depended and to provide workers and soldiers for various projects and military
campaigns. Not all labor was of the brute, physical type, however. Some people

were craft specialists who provided the new and unusual luxury goods that the governing class demanded for display and for ceremonial purposes; others produced military equipment.[60] Although many of these specialists were probably also part-time farmers, the growth of occupational specialization was undoubtedly accompanied by a significant growth in trade.

Despite their increasingly exploitative character, the advanced horticultural societies of China made important advances in a number of areas. The more important innovations included writing, money, the use of the horse, probably irrigation, and possibly the manufacture of iron at the very end of the horticultural era. In addition, there were lesser innovations too numerous to mention, some of them Chinese inventions or discoveries, others products of diffusion. In most cases, it is impossible to determine which were which.

Horticulture in the New World: Testing Ground for Ecological-Evolutionary Theory

No one knows for certain when humans first settled the New World. Using radiocarbon-dating techniques, archaeologists have calculated remains from one site in Alaska to be about 27,000 years old, and experts believe there may have been human settlements in the New World as early as 40,000 years ago.[61] In any case, the original settlers were almost certainly hunters and gatherers who migrated from Asia by means of the land bridge that once connected Siberia and Alaska.

When the last Ice Age ended and the waters locked in the glaciers melted, the level of the oceans rose and the land bridge was submerged. As a result, the inhabitants of the New World were cut off from the inhabitants of the Old World during those crucial millennia associated with the horticultural revolution. Thus, there was no way that information about the techniques of plant cultivation could have spread from Asia to the Americas.

Despite this, horticultural societies did develop in the New World, and some of them achieved a level of technological advance comparable to that of early agrarian Mesopotamia and Egypt. Space limitations prevent us from tracing these developments in detail, and much of the account would be repetitive if we did. But in the New World, as in the Old, the shift from hunting and gathering to horticulture was preceded by the growth of population, and it led to more permanent settlements, more substantial dwellings, increased wealth and possessions, increased inequality, the development of pottery and later of metallurgy, the beginnings of full-time craft specialization, the appearance of permanent markets and increased trade, the beginnings of urbanism, the establishment of permanent religious centers, the construction of massive temples and temple complexes (see Figure 6.7), and a marked increase in both militarism and imperialism.[62]

There were also some differences: New World horticulturalists were not as successful in domesticating animals, for example, nor was their metallurgy as advanced. On the other hand, they developed a numerical system that included the concept of zero centuries before this was invented in the Old World. Overall, however, the similarities far outweigh the differences.

FIGURE 6.7 **Mayan temple at Tikal, Guatemala. Some horticultural societies in the New World achieved a level of technological advance approaching that of ancient Egypt and Mesopotamia in the early agrarian era.**

The fact that horticulture developed at all in the isolated New World is the important point, for it provides an independent test of some basic ideas. For a long time, scholars debated whether the striking similarities in patterns of societal development in the Middle East, China, and Europe were due to the independent operation of the same basic laws of sociocultural evolution or merely the result of the diffusion of ideas from a single source. The issue was impossible to resolve as long as only Old World societies were involved, because the possibility of diffusion could never be ruled out. The New World, however, is a different matter. Its contacts with the Old World ended several thousand years before horticulture began there, and contact was not resumed until about 1000 A.D., when Leif Ericson briefly visited Vinland, somewhere on the northeast coast of North America.*

In short, the New World has been a kind of "Second Earth," where ideas about sociocultural evolution suggested by studies of the Old World can be put to the test.[64] The remarkable parallels between developments in the New World and the Old apparently indicate that there are limits to the amount of variation that is possible in the sequence of basic technological innovations. People must know certain things about both fire and rocks, for example, before metallurgy is possible, and a society must possess the hoe before it can invent the plow. In addition, major technological innovations have fairly predictable consequences for other aspects of sociocultural systems—especially for social organization, the demographic variables, and material production.

This is not to say that sociocultural evolution compels societies to march in lockstep. But much is predictable about the critical early stages of societal development. Marvin Harris, a major contributor to ecological-evolutionary theory, put the matter as well as anyone, *"Similar technologies applied to similar environments tend to produce similar arrangements of labor in production and distribution, and these in turn call forth similar kinds of social groupings, which justify and coordinate their activities by means of similar systems of values and beliefs."*[65]

Simple Horticultural Societies in the Modern Era

In recent centuries, simple horticultural societies have been confined almost exclusively to the islands of the Pacific and the New World. All of these societies have practiced some version of slash-and-burn horticulture. In most matters where comparisons are possible, the simple horticultural societies of modern times are strikingly similar to those of prehistoric times. In other words, they are usually small, mostly self-sufficient, politically autonomous villages with populations ranging from a few dozen to a few hundred.[66] Compared with modern hunting and gathering societies, their settlements are larger and much more permanent, as we saw in Chapter 4.[67] As in prehistoric times, their relative permanence permits a greater accumulation of goods and the construction of more substantial buildings.[68] There is also a more diversified production of goods and services and an increase in trade.[69] Finally, as in the simple horticultural societies of the later horticultural era, warfare is fairly common.[70]

---

*Though attempts have been made to prove other contacts, they have not been successful. Moreover, careful studies of the evolution of plant cultivation in the New World convince scholars that this was entirely an indigenous process. For example, the transformation of maize, or corn, from a wild plant to a cultivated plant took much longer than one would expect if the process had been guided by information on the techniques of plant cultivation brought from the Old World.[63]

The Continuing Importance of Kinship

As with hunting and gathering societies, the ethnographic record not only supports the view provided by archaeology but broadens and extends it. For example, ethnographic studies show that kinship ties are extremely important in simple horticultural societies. In most instances, these ties provide the basic framework of the social system.[71] This is hardly surprising in view of the small size of these groups: almost everyone is related in some way to almost everyone else. Kinship obligations must constantly be taken into account in relations between individuals. The virtual absence of competing social organizations (e.g., craft guilds, political parties, etc.) further enhances the importance of kinship.

Kinship systems in these societies are sometimes very complex, with intricate systems of rules governing relations between numerous categories of kin. Extended kin groups, or *clans,* are common and usually very important, since they perform a number of essential functions for their members.[72] Above all, they function as *mutual aid associations,* providing the individual with protection against enemies and with economic support. Although both functions are important, the former is critical, for the political system is too limited at this level to provide police services. Clans also perform important regulatory functions in the area of marriage, and they sometimes have important religious functions as well. Finally, the most powerful or respected clan often assumes leadership of the entire community, with its head serving as headman for the village.

In horticultural societies, both simple and advanced, the concept of the kin group includes the dead as well as the living. This manifests itself in many ways, but especially in the form of religious rituals designed to appease the spirits of dead ancestors. Nowhere is ancestor worship more common than in horticultural societies (see Figure 6.8).

FIGURE 6.8   Incidence of ancestor worship, by societal type.

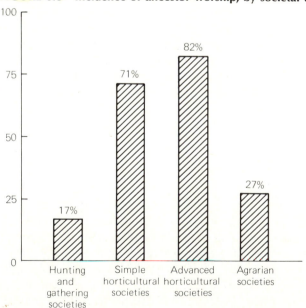

TABLE 6.1   The Division of Labor between the Sexes in Horticultural and Agrarian Societies

	Percentage Distribution				
Type of Society	Cultivation Primarily a Female Responsibility	Both Sexes Share Equally	Cultivation Primarily a Male Responsibility	Total	No. of Societies
Simple horticultural	37	49	14	100	51
Advanced horticultural	50	27	23	100	142
Agrarian	7	37	56	100	43

Source: See note 15, page 440.

The reason for such a high incidence of ancestor worship among horticulturalists, relative to hunters and gatherers, is probably tied to the greater permanence of their settlements. Because of this, the living remain in close physical proximity to their buried dead and carry on their daily activities in the very same settings in which their ancestors once lived. Under such circumstances, ancestors are less easily forgotten. In agrarian societies, more awesome and more powerful polytheistic and monotheistic deities usually displaced ancestors from the central position they occupied in most horticultural societies, though ancestor worship continued to be important in many of them (e.g., China, Rome).

Another distinctive feature of kinship systems in horticultural societies is the importance many of them attach to ties with the mother's relatives. This can be seen in Murdock's data, where the percentage of societies having *matrilineal* kin groups (i.e., descent traced through the maternal line) is as follows:[73]

Hunting and gathering societies	10%
Simple horticultural societies	26%
Advanced horticultural societies	27%
Agragarian societies	4%

This unusual pattern is apparently linked with women's contribution to subsistence in horticultural societies: in many of these groups, women do most of the work of cultivation (see Table 6.1). In horticultural societies where men also make a substantial contribution—by hunting or herding, for example—the matrilineal pattern is not as likely to develop (see Table 6.2).[74]

Developments in Polity, Stratification, and Warfare

Though village autonomy is still the rule, multicommunity societies are much more common than at the hunting and gathering level.[75] When a society does have more than one community, there are usually only a few, seldom more than ten.[76] Such societies were usually formed by a process of confederation of villages belonging to the same tribe,[77] and the motivation to unite was a military one.

The power of political leaders remains quite limited in nearly all simple horticultural societies. Even in the larger, multicommunity societies, local villages enjoy virtual autonomy except in matters of war and relations with other societies. Both the

TABLE 6.2 Matrilineality among Simple Horticultural Societies, by Percentage of Subsistence Obtained from Hunting and Herding

Percentage of Subsistence Obtained by Hunting and Herding*	Percentage of Societies Matrilineal	No. of Societies
26 or more	13	16
16 to 25	25	28
Less than 15	39	23

*These figures are estimates made by Murdock and his associates and are based on qualitative statements in ethnographic reports.
Source: See note 15, page 440.

village headman and the tribal chief (i.e., leader of a multicommunity society) depend more on persuasion than on coercion to achieve their goals. This is partly because of the limited development of the governmental system; a leader has few subordinates so dependent on him that they are obliged to carry out his instructions. Also, since men make their own weapons, no one can monopolize them and thereby dominate the others. The absence of weapons that only a few can afford limits the growth of political inequality.

In some simple horticultural societies, shamans also serve as headmen or chiefs because of the awe or respect in which they are held.[78] In others, secular leaders assume important religious functions and become quasi-religious leaders. As one writer notes, a "chief's influence is definitely enhanced when he combines religious with secular functions."[79] In short, in many simple horticultural societies of the modern era, just as in the prehistoric past, "church" and "state" are closely linked and sometimes almost become one.

The only other important basis of political power in these societies is membership in a large and prosperous kin group. As we noted earlier, the senior member and leader of the largest, most powerful, or most respected clan often becomes the village headman or tribal chief.[80] He can usually count on the support of his kinsmen, and that is a substantial political resource in this kind of society.

Social inequality is generally rather limited in most simple horticultural societies of the modern era. Although extremes of wealth and political power are absent, substantial differences in prestige are not uncommon. Political and religious leaders usually enjoy high status, but this depends far more on personal achievements than on mere occupancy of an office. There are few sinecures in these societies. Other bases of status include military prowess (which is highly honored in nearly all societies), skill in oratory, age, kinship ties, and in some cases wealth in the form of wives, pigs, and ornaments.[81] Each society has its own peculiar combination of these criteria.

The more advanced the technology and economy of one of these groups, the greater social inequality within it tends to be. Societies that practice irrigation, own domesticated animals, or practice metallurgy for ornamental and ceremonial purposes are usually less egalitarian than groups without these characteristics. We see this clearly when we compare the villagers of eastern Brazil and the Amazon River

TABLE 6.3 Incidence of Warfare, by Societal Type (in Percentages)

Type of Society	Perpetual	Common	Rare or Absent	Total	No. of Societies
Hunting and gathering	0	27	73	100	22
Simple horticultural	5	55	41	100	22
Advanced horticultural	34	48	17	100	29

Source: Adapted from data in Gregory Leavitt, "The Frequency of Warfare: An Evolutionary Perspective," *Sociological Inquiry*, 14 (January 1977), appendix B.

basin with their more advanced neighbors to the north and west who, in pre-Spanish days, practiced irrigation and metallurgy. Hereditary class differences were absent in the former, but common in the latter, where a hereditary governing class of chiefs and nobles was set apart from the larger class of commoners.[82]

Ethnographers have found warfare to be much more common among horticulturalists than among hunters and gatherers (see Table 6.3). This finding parallels the evidence from archaeology, where all the signs indicate that warfare increased substantially during the horticultural era. Now, as in the past, combat appears to serve as a psychic substitute for the excitement, challenge, and rewards which hunting previously provided and which were so important in the lives of men in hunting and gathering societies.

FIGURE 6.9 In horticultural societies, combat appears to provide a psychic substitute for the excitement, challenge, and rewards that hunting once provided. Yanamamö men intoxicated on ebene, a hallucinogenic drug, prepare for a "friendly" duel with men from a neighboring village. Such duels often turn violent and lead to war.

Warfare also functions as an important mechanism of population control in these groups. In addition to the direct loss of life in combat, warfare provides an impo.tant stimulus for female infanticide, which provides an even greater check on population growth.[83] In societies in which warfare is the normal state of affairs, it is imperative that the group be able to field the largest possible number of warriors, and female infanticide seems to be the best method of accomplishing this. By reducing the number of girls, the group can devote its resources to the care and nurture of a larger number of boys. A survey of studies of 609 "primitive" societies found that the sex ratio among the young was most imbalanced in those societies in which warfare was current at the time of the study and most nearly normal in those societies in which warfare had not occurred for more than twenty-five years.[84] In the former group, boys outnumbered girls by a ratio of seven to five on the average, indicating that nearly 30 percent of the females born in these societies had died as a result of female infanticide or neglect. If allowance is made for some degree of male infanticide (as in the case of male babies born with deformities or born before an older male sibling has been weaned), the actual rate of female infanticide may be 40 percent or more.

As warfare grows in importance in a society, several new patterns tend to develop. Above all, there is the cult of the warrior, which heaps honors on successful fighters. Record keeping and publicity are no less important to these warrior heroes than to modern athletes, and, in the absence of statisticians and sportswriters, they invent techniques of their own—especially trophy taking. Trophies include such things as skulls and shrunken heads, which are preserved and displayed like modern athletic trophies (see Figure 6.10).[85]

Ceremonial cannibalism, a surprisingly widespread practice in simple horticultural societies, may have developed as a by-product of trophy collecting. Utilitarian cannibalism, or eating other humans to avoid starvation, is an ancient practice, traceable to distant prehistoric times, but ceremonial cannibalism seems to be a more recent innovation. The basic idea underlying it is that one can appropriate the valued qualities of a conquered enemy by eating his body. Ceremonial cannibalism is usually surrounded by a complex, and often prolonged, set of rituals, as the following account from South America indicates.

> The prisoners taken by a Tupinamba war party were received with manifestations of anger, scorn, and derision, but after the first hostile outburst, they were not hampered in their movements nor were they unkindly treated. Their captors, whose quarters they shared, treated them as relatives. The prisoners generally married village girls, very often the sisters or daughters of their masters, or, in certain cases, the widow of a dead warrior whose hammock and ornaments they used. They received fields for their maintenance, they were free to hunt and fish, and they were reminded of their servile condition by few restrictions and humiliations.
>
> The period of captivity lasted from a few months to several years. When, finally, the date for the execution had been set by the village council, invitations were sent to nearby villages to join in the celebration. The ritual for the slaughter of a captive was worked out to the most minute detail. The club and cord which figured prominently in the ceremony were carefully painted and decorated in accordance with strict rules. For three days before the event, the village women danced, sang, and tormented the victim with descriptions of his impending fate. On the eve of his execution a mock repetition of his

FIGURE 6.10 **Record keeping and symbols of success are
no less important to warriors in horticultural societies than
they are to modern athletes. The Jivaro Indians of South
America collected heads as trophies and developed a
special technique for shrinking and preserving them.**

capture took place, during which the prisoner was allowed to escape but was immediately retaken; the man who overpowered him in a wrestling match adopted a new name,
as did the ceremonial executioner.

The prisoner spent his last night dancing, pelting his tormentors, and singing songs
which foretold their ruin and proclaimed his pride at dying as a warrior. In the morning
he was dragged to the plaza by old women amidst shouts, songs, and music. The
ceremonial rope was removed from his neck and tied around his waist, and it was held at
both ends by two or more men. The victim was once more permitted to give vent to his
feelings by throwing fruit or potsherds at his enemies. The executioner, who appeared
painted and dressed in a long feather cloak, derided the victim, who boasted of his past
deeds and predicted that his relatives would avenge him.

The actual execution was a cruel game. The prisoner was allowed sufficient
freedom of movement to dodge the blows aimed at him; sometimes a club was put in his
hands so that he could parry the blows without being able to strike back. When at last he
fell, his skull shattered, everyone shouted and whistled. Old women rushed in to drink
the warm blood, children were invited to dip their hands in it, and mothers smeared their

nipples so that even infants could have a taste. While the quartered body was being roasted on a babracot the old women, who were the most eager to taste human flesh, licked the grease running from the sticks. Certain delicate or sacred portions, such as the fingers and the grease around the liver, were given to distinguished guests.[86]

The high incidence of warfare in simple horticultural societies helps to keep the channels of vertical mobility open. Almost every boy becomes a warrior and thus has a chance to win honor and influence. Nevertheless, the channels of vertical mobility are somewhat more restricted in horticultural societies than in hunting and gathering societies, because status advantages can more easily be passed from parent to child. This is partly due to the greater amount of private property in horticultural societies, and its increased importance. In addition, there are the beginnings of inequality among kin groups: it is a distinct advantage to be born into a large, powerful, and wealthy clan. Finally, the institutional structures of these societies frequently evolve to the point where they can, to some extent, supplement the personal attributes of their leaders. No longer need a headman be the best man in his group; he need only be competent, because he now has assistants who support and help him. As a consequence, the headmanship is more likely to be inherited than in hunting and gathering societies. This growth in the heritability of status, though modest in scope and of limited importance in simple horticultural societies, marked the beginning of a trend that was destined to become of tremendous importance in more advanced societies.

Advanced Horticultural Societies in the Modern Era

For several centuries, advanced horticultural societies have been limited to two parts of the world, sub-Saharan Africa and southeast Asia. Until recently, they occupied most of sub-Saharan Africa. In southeast Asia, on the other hand, agrarian societies have occupied most of the land, and the practice of horticulture has been limited to the hill country.

These advanced horticulturalists of modern times differ in one important respect from those of prehistoric times: the dominant metal in their societies has been iron rather than copper or bronze. This is important, because iron ore is so much more plentiful than copper and tin* that it can be used for ordinary tools as well as weapons. However, because it is much more difficult to reduce the ore to metal, the manufacture of iron was a later development.

The history of Africa proves once again that the evolutionary process does not compel societies to follow exactly the same pattern of development. Bronze was never the dominant metal in most of Africa below the Sahara. During the period when bronze was dominant in the Middle East, where it originated, cultural contacts between Egypt and the territories to the south were minimal. By the time there was sufficient contact to permit diffusion of specialized skills like metallurgy, iron had become dominant.[87] Thus, most of Africa seems to have moved directly from the Stone Age to the Iron Age.

---

*Bronze is an alloy made of copper and tin.

FIGURE 6.11 Trade and commerce are much more important in horticultural societies than in hunting and gathering societies. The marketplace in Ougadougou, Burkina Faso.

Increased Size and Complexity

Compared with hunting and gathering or simple horticultural societies, advanced horticultural societies are usually larger and more complex. Table 4.2 (page 87) summarizes the evidence from Murdock's data set: on average, advanced horticultural societies are 60 times the size of simple horticultural and 140 times the size of hunting and gathering societies.

As one would expect, advanced horticultural societies are also structurally more complex. For example, more than two-thirds of them contain 2 or more villages, compared with just a fifth of the simple horticultural societies and almost none of the hunting and gathering. In fact, the average advanced horticultural society in Murdock's data set contains slightly more than 20 villages.

Further evidence of structural complexity is the extent of occupational specialization. Table 4.3 (page 89) shows that craft specialization is much more common in advanced horticultural societies than in either simple horticultural or hunting and gathering societies. For the six types of activities dealt with in that table, craft specialization occurred 28 percent of the time in advanced horticultural societies, compared with 2 percent and 0 percent in the other two types of societies.

Murdock's data also show that social inequality increases markedly at this level of societal development. Slavery, for example, is found in 83 percent of the advanced horticultural societies, but in only 14 percent of the simple. Hereditary systems of inequality are found in 47 percent of the former, but in only 15 percent of the latter. And finally, classes are reported in 54 percent of the advanced horticultural societies and only 17 percent of the simple.

TABLE 6.4   Economic Transaction Associated with Marriage, by Societal Type

Type of Society	Percentage of Societies Requiring Economic Transaction with Marriage	Number of Societies
Hunting and gathering	49	148
Simple horticultural	61	74
Advanced horticultural	97	265

Source: See note 15, page 440.

One consequence of the more fully developed economy and stratification system in advanced horticultural societies is their increased emphasis on the economic aspect of marriage. In almost every one of these societies, marriageable daughters are viewed as a valuable property, and men who want to marry them must either pay for the privilege or render extended service to their prospective in-laws. Fortunately for young men with limited resources, extended kin groups usually view marriage as a sensible investment and are willing to loan suitors part of the bride price. This economic approach to marriage is much more common in advanced horticultural societies than in either hunting and gathering or simple horticultural societies (see Table 6.4).

Political Development

The growth in social inequality is closely linked with the growth of government. A generation ago, Meyer Fortes, one of the pioneers in the study of African political systems, argued that most traditional African societies fell into one of two basic categories: those "which have centralized authority, administrative machinery, and judicial institutions—in short, a government—and in which cleavages of wealth, privilege, and status correspond to the distribution of authority," and those which have none of these attributes.[88] Though recent studies suggest that this twofold division was something of an oversimplification, they confirm that African societies differ in the ways Fortes described and that there is a strong relationship between the development of the state and the growth of social inequality.[89]

African societies afford a valuable opportunity to study the early stages of political development. A leading student of east African political systems suggests that a critical step in the process occurs when the head of a strong clan begins to take on, as retainers, men who are not related to him, thereby overcoming one of the traditional limitations on power and its expansion.[90] These retainers are usually individuals who have been expelled from their own kin group for misconduct or whose group has been destroyed in war or by some natural disaster, and they offer their allegiance and service in exchange for protection and a livelihood.

Since there is a natural tendency for men in this position to turn to the strongest families, power begins to accumulate. This is reinforced by the wealth of such a group, which permits it to buy more wives to produce more sons and warriors, and by the development of myths that attribute the group's success to the magical powers of its leader. The final link in this chain of *state building* is forged when less powerful families, and even whole communities, are brought under the control of the head of a strong kin group—either by conquest or by the decision of the weaker groups to put themselves under the strong group's protection. When this happens, each of the subordinate groups is usually allowed to retain its land, and its leader his authority within his own group, but the group is compelled to pay tribute. The leader of the dominant group then uses these revenues to support his kinsmen and retainers, thereby increasing their dependence on him and, he hopes, their loyalty to him as well.

Sometimes this state-building process is stimulated by intrafamily and inter-family feuds that get out of hand. Where strong political authority is lacking, feuds can be a serious matter. Individuals and families are forced to settle their own grievances, which often sets off a deadly cycle of action and reaction. More than one east African group has voluntarily put itself under the authority of a strong neighboring leader just to break such a cycle and reestablish peace among its members.

One might imagine that these processes, once set in motion, would continue until eventually all Africa came under a single authority. But powerful countervailing forces have prevented this. Technological limitations, especially in transportation and communication, were most important. Advanced horticulturalists in Africa, as in the New World, had no knowledge of the wheel and did not have draft animals until contact with Europeans. As a result, the farther a ruler's power was extended into outlying areas, the weaker it became. These areas were vulnerable to attack by other

FIGURE 6.12   In almost every politically advanced society of horticultural Africa there was a sharp cleavage between a hereditary nobility and the mass of common people: early bronze casting of Dahomean chief and his entourage of relatives and retainers. Note the fine workmanship and compare this with the scene in Figure 13.10, page 391.

societies, and, even more serious, they were likely to revolt. From the territorial standpoint, Songhay was probably the largest kingdom that ever developed in sub-Saharan Africa. In the early fourteenth century, it controlled approximately 500,000 square miles in the western Sudan (i.e., twice the size of present-day France).[91] Most African kingdoms were much smaller.

By the standards of modern industrial societies, the governments of Africa's advanced horticultural societies were extremely unstable. Revolts were a common occurrence, not only in outlying provinces but even in the capitals. These were seldom, if ever, popular risings. Rather, they were instigated by powerful members of the nobility, often the king's own brothers. This pattern was so common that the Zulus had a proverb that "the king should not eat with his brothers lest they poison him."[92]

In virtually every politically advanced society of horticultural Africa there was a sharply defined cleavage between a hereditary nobility and the mass of common people. Historically, this distinction grew out of the state-building process.[93] Nobles were usually descendants either of past rulers and their chief lieutenants, or of hereditary leaders of subordinated groups. They comprised a warrior aristocracy supported by the labor of the common people. Below the commoners there was often a class of slaves, many of them captives taken in war, and, as in other horticultural societies, they were frequently slaughtered as human sacrifices.

In the advanced horticultural societies of Africa, as in the New World and elsewhere, religion and politics were intimately related. In many instances the king was viewed as divine or as having access to divine powers.[94] This served to legitimate tyrannical and exploitative practices. It also helps explain why no efforts were made to establish other kinds of political systems: given their ideological heritage, such a thing was inconceivable. These beliefs did not protect a ruler against attacks from his kinsmen, however, because they shared his special religious status and thus were qualified to assume the duties and privileges of the royal office—if they could seize it.

A comparison of the politically complex societies of sub-Saharan Africa with those which remained autonomous villages shows that the former were more developed in other ways as well. They were far likelier to have full-time craft specialization, for example, and they were also more likely to have urban or semiurban settlements—a few with populations of 20,000 or more.[95]

Before concluding this discussion of advanced horticultural societies in the modern era, a brief comment on those in southeast Asia is necessary. The striking feature of these societies is their organizational backwardness, especially from the standpoint of political development. In most instances, villages have been autonomous, and when multicommunity societies have developed they have invariably been small.[96] Urban or semiurban settlements are absent.

The reason appears to be ecological. Centuries ago, after this region came under the domination of more powerful agrarian societies, horticultural societies survived only in hill country where transportation was difficult and the land unsuited for the plow and permanent cultivation. This combination of more powerful neighbors and the deficiencies of their own territories apparently prevented all but the most limited development and caused these groups to be looked down upon, and often exploited, by their agrarian neighbors. Ecological factors of a different type had a similar effect

FIGURE 6.13 **Recent view of the old city of Kano in northern Nigeria: Kano has been
an important commercial and political center for more than 500 years. The style of
architecture remains much as it was centuries ago.**

in certain parts of Africa: political development was quite limited in the tropical rain
forests. Apparently the lush vegetation and other hindrances to the movement of
armies and goods made it impossible to build and maintain extensive kingdoms.[97]

Horticultural Societies in Theoretical Perspective

Few events in human history have been as important as the shift from hunting and
gathering to horticulture. It is no exaggeration to say that the adoption of horticulture
in the realm of technology was comparable to the creation of symbols in the realm of
communication: each was a *decisive break with the animal world.* Hunting and
gathering, like the use of signals, are techniques our species inherited from its
prehuman ancestors. In contrast, horticulture and symbols are uniquely human.

Of all the changes in human life that resulted from the horticultural revolution,
the most fundamental—the one with the greatest repercussions for other change—

was the creation of a *stable economic surplus*. Hunting and gathering societies were rarely able to create such a surplus: food producers and their dependents usually consumed all the calories that they were able to provide. With nothing left over to support *non*producers of food, only the most limited occupational specialization was possible. There could be no governmental or religious institutions staffed by full-time officials and priests, nor could there be full-time artisans and merchants. And this, in turn, ruled out the development of towns and cities, since these are based on populations that have been freed from the necessity of producing their own food.

The shift from hunting and gathering to plant cultivation provided societies with the means of establishing an economic surplus, but only if the growth in productivity was not nullified by a corresponding growth in population size. To translate the potential for a stable surplus into a *reality,* a society needed an ideology that would motivate the producers of food to turn over part of their harvest to an individual in authority who could dispense it as he saw fit.

Religious beliefs often answered this need. In a number of societies, people were already accustomed to offering sacrifices, and nothing was more natural than that they should continue this practice as they shifted to plant cultivation, giving part of their yield to the priests. With greater productivity, rituals became more elaborate and more frequent, and priestly activities became full-time, for one man at first, and eventually for others. In this way, small proto-urban communities began to develop around important shrines—communities that could exist only if a stable economic surplus was maintained.

In other societies, the development of a stable surplus appears to have evolved out of an older tradition of turning over to the headman part of the fruits of the hunt to distribute to the families of unsuccessful hunters. Here, too, the increase in productivity resulting from the shift to plant cultivation made full-time employment possible, first for a headman, later for his aides. Thus, the foundation was laid for the emergence of the state as a specialized entity, distinct from the rest of society.

In either case, the outcome was the same: the potential of an economic surplus became a reality, opening up important new possibilities for the organization of societal life. The possibilities would not all be realized in horticultural societies, however. The most dramatic and the most revolutionary would be realized only in agrarian and industrial societies, where the size of the economic surplus would be many times greater.

It is important to note that in horticultural societies we see, for the first time, ideology playing a significant role in shaping evolution. In hunting and gathering societies, the limits set by technology are so narrow that ideology's role is negligible (i.e., it does not contribute to societal growth and development). But the picture changes with horticultural societies, where ideological differences sometimes give rise to significant differences in patterns of development.

Figure 6.14 summarizes the effects of the shift from hunting and gathering to horticulture for societies. Not all of these consequences occurred in every horticultural society, but the model indicates the possibilities inherent in the new subsistence technology.

At a minimum, the shift to horticulture meant more permanent settlements and an increased production of goods and services. These, in turn, were likely to lead to the adoption or spread of ancestor worship, increased accumulation of possessions, growth in population, and the possibility of a sustained economic surplus. If that possibility became a reality, there would probably be a series of further developments, including growth of the state, the emergence of urban communities, the greater accumulation of weapons, a greater division of labor, increased warfare, expansion in societal size as a result of conquest, development of the cult of the warrior, increased female infanticide, increased trade and commerce, and, in some societies, the invention of a system of protowriting. Even in societies that did not establish a stable economic surplus and whose increased production of goods and services was totally consumed by population growth, some of these developments— including an increase in warfare, the cult of the warrior, and increased inequality— were still likely to occur, though the changes were seldom as pronounced.

Figure 6.14 also traces the causal connections from more permanent settlements to the beginnings of metallurgy, and from there *to the speedup in the rate of intersocietal selection*. The latter was one of the most critical developments of the horticultural era, for two reasons. It meant the beginning of the end for hunting and

FIGURE 6.14   Model of the effects of the shift from hunting and gathering to horticulture.

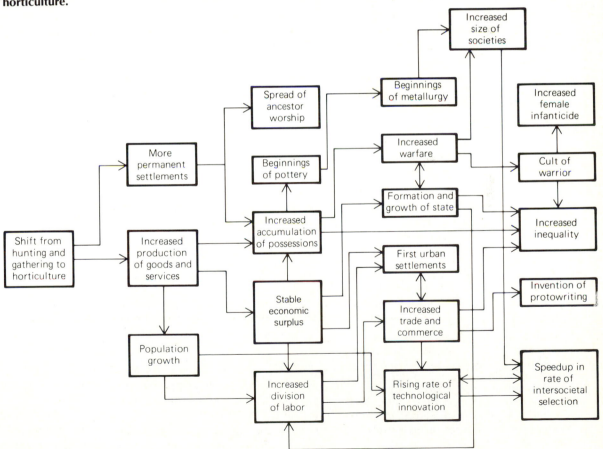

FIGURE 6.15   Human sacrifice, from carving on the Mayan Temple of the Jaguars, Chichén Itzá, Mexico.

gathering societies. And it meant that all of the basic trends in the world system of societies shown in Figure 3.10 (page 74) were now under way.

Before concluding this summary, a brief comment on the ethical consequences of the horticultural revolution is needed, lest anyone still suppose that the technological and structural advance of horticultural societies implies ethical progress. As numerous scholars have noted, it is one of the great ironies of evolution that progress in technology and social organization is often linked with ethical *regress*. Horticultural societies provide several striking examples. Some of the most shocking, by the standards of modern western culture, are the increases in head-hunting, cannibalism, human sacrifice, and slavery, all more common in technologically progressive horticultural societies than in the more primitive societies of hunters and gatherers.

Another development many would regard as ethical regression is the decline in the practice of sharing and the growing acceptance of economic and other kinds of inequality. This is not as simple a matter as it seems on the surface, however. Although inequality is an inevitable accompaniment of an economic surplus, the establishment of that surplus seems to have been a prerequisite for the development of civilization—with all that implies—and for subsequent improvements in the standard of living. In other words, without an economic surplus, all the benefits of technological advance would have been consumed by population growth, and there would simply have been more people living at the subsistence level. Our judgment concerning the growth in inequality, therefore, depends largely on whether we take a short-term or a long-term view.

Excursus: Race and Societal Development

Ever since the first explorers returned to Europe from Africa, the Americas, and Asia, Europeans have been intrigued by differences in the level of development of societies in various parts of the world. Interest in these differences led, quite naturally, to efforts to explain them.

Over the years, the most popular explanation has been the racialist. Racialist theories assert that societies differ in their level of development, and in other ways, because the members differ in their culture-building abilities.[98] Translated into modern scientific terminology, these theories assert that societies differ in their levels of development because of differences in the genetic heritages of their populations.

These theories have had great appeal because they seem to fit the evidence rather well. During the last several hundred years, societies dominated by Europeans have been technologically the most advanced and organizationally the most complex and powerful. Societies dominated by Asians have ranked next, while societies dominated by Africans have been the least developed technologically and organizationally. Since the level of societal development is obviously not responsible for the race of a population, racialist theorists have argued that the race must be responsible for the level of development.

Racialist theories can be quite compelling as long as one fails to employ an ecological and evolutionary perspective. However, if one adopts such a perspective a number of difficulties arise. To begin with, we find that the recent ranking of societies in terms of development has not always prevailed. For thousands of years, Middle Eastern societies—not European societies—were the most highly developed.[99] Also, for many centuries China equaled or surpassed northwestern Europe. And, finally, for several centuries before and after the start of the Christian era the center of civilization was in the Mediterranean basin, and North African societies, such as Carthage and Egypt, were much more advanced than the barbarian societies of northwest Europe. While there have been some changes in the racial composition of some populations during this period (e.g., in ancient times the proportion of fair-haired and fair-skinned individuals in Greek and Roman societies seems to have been appreciably higher than today), they do not appear to have been great enough to cause the substantial changes that have occurred in the relative level of societal development.

If we conclude, then, that the evolutionary record undermines the credibility of racialist theories, where do we look for an explanation? Here, the ecological perspective comes to our aid. It suggests that environmental differences offer a promising alternative. Recent research has made it clear, as we have seen, that many tropical and semitropical regions are poorly suited to plow agriculture.[100] Although the lushness of tropical rain forests suggests rich and fertile soils, modern research has found the opposite: the soils of tropical rain forests are among the poorest in the world. While it is possible to clear small and temporary gardens in these forests, as horticulturalists have done for centuries, it is not possible to clear permanent fields and cultivate them continuously as agriculturalists do. The fertility of these soils is quickly exhausted, and, worse yet, some of the soils harden and become compacted to the point where cultivation of any kind is impossible. In addition, large-scale clearing of the rain forest appears to break the hydrological cycle and rainfall declines. In short, *indigenous* development beyond the level of horticultural societies seems to have been impossible in much of sub-Saharan Africa and much of Latin America.

In addition, recent research has shown that human populations in tropical regions are exposed to many more tiny predators than are populations in temperate regions.[101] In fact, the number, variety, and seriousness of the parasites (bacteria, viruses, worms, etc.) that prey on human populations seem to increase steadily as one moves from polar regions to the tropics. In the tropics, the problems created by these micropredators have often been overwhelming. Large portions of the population have been affected by debilitating diseases of one kind or another—diseases such as malaria, onchocerciasis (which causes blindness), and schistosomiasis (which causes people to become listless and lacking in energy).

Prior to the invention of the microscope, the causes of all these diseases were not only unknown, but *unknowable*. Societies afflicted by them were badly handicapped, but they had no method of overcoming their handicap. Thus, the most serious challenges that confronted horticulturalists in the tropics were profoundly different from those that confronted horticulturalists in temperate areas, such as Europe. In the latter, the basic challenge was to increase the food supply, and this could be achieved through the gradual improvement of tools of various kinds—in other words, through the exercise of ordinary human intelligence. In contrast, in tropical regions this was impossible. Because of environmental constraints that were beyond human control, the usual course of evolution, from horticulture to agriculture, was impossible in most tropical societies, and human health and vitality were constantly undermined by forces that would remain unknowable until the development of modern industrial technology—a late stage in an evolutionary process that presupposes an earlier agricultural stage.

Thus, the adoption of an ecological and evolutionary perspective provides quite a different explanation of the relationship of race and societal development than that provided by earlier racialist theories. Moreover, because this explanation fits more of the facts than the latter, it has greater scientific credibility. Although it would be premature to suggest that we now fully understand the causes of the complex relationship between race and societal development, it appears that ecological-evolutionary theory can substantially advance our understanding of it.

163

CHAPTER 7

Agrarian Societies

"The thousand years or so immediately preceding 3000 B.C. were perhaps more fertile in fruitful inventions and discoveries than any period in human history prior to the sixteenth century, A.D."[1] So wrote V. Gordon Childe, the most influential archaeologist of the twentieth century. The innovations of that period included the invention of the wheel and its application both to wagons and the manufacture of pottery, the invention of the plow, the harnessing of animals to pull wagons and plows and their use as pack animals, the harnessing of wind power for use in sailboats, the invention of writing and numerical notation, and the invention of the calendar.[2]

Collectively, these innovations substantially transformed the conditions of life for societies in the Middle East, and eventually for societies throughout the world. With these new cultural resources, societies expanded their populations, increased their material wealth, and developed social organizations far more complex than anything known before.

Simple Agrarian Societies

Technology

Although all of the innovations that Childe referred to were important, the *plow* surpassed the rest in its potential for social and cultural change. To a modern city dweller, the plow may not sound very exciting, yet without it, we would still be back

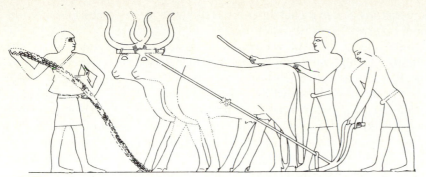

FIGURE 7.1 **Early Egyptian ox-drawn plow (about 2700 B.C.). Note the primitive method of harnessing the animals—a simple bar attached to the horns.**

in the horticultural era. To appreciate the importance of the plow, we need to keep in mind two basic problems that confront farmers everywhere: controlling weeds and maintaining the fertility of the soil.[3] With traditional horticultural tools and techniques, both problems become more severe the longer a plot of ground is cultivated. Weeds multiply faster than horticulturalists with their hoes can root them out, while the soil's nutrients seep deeper into the ground, below the reach of plants and too deep to be brought back to the surface with hoes or other simple tools. Within a few years, the yield from a garden usually becomes so small that the cultivator is forced to abandon it and clear a new one.*

The plow, if it did not eliminate these problems, at least reduced them to manageable proportions. Because it turns the soil over to a greater depth than the hoe, the plow buries weeds, not only killing them but adding humus to the soil. Deeper cultivation also brings back to the surface the nutrients that have seeped below root level. Thus, the plow made permanent cultivation of fields a common practice for the first time in history and led to the replacement of horticulture (from the Latin *horticultura,* or the cultivation of a garden) by agriculture (from *agricultura,* the cultivation of a field).

The invention of the plow also paved the way for the harnessing of animal energy.[4] As long as the digging stick and hoe were the basic tools of cultivation, men and women had to supply the energy. But the plow could be pulled, and it did not take long for people to discover that oxen could do the job. The importance of this discovery can hardly be exaggerated, since it established a principle with broad applicability. In Childe's words, "The ox was the first step to the steam engine and the [gasoline] motor."[5]

More immediately, however, the harnessing of animal energy led to greatly increased productivity. With a plow and a pair of oxen, a farmer could cultivate a far larger area than was possible with a hoe.[6] In addition, the use of oxen led, in many societies, to feeding them in stalls, and this in turn led to the use of manure as fertilizer.[7] In short, the shift from hoe to plow not only meant permanently cultivated

---

*In a few instances, horticulturalists have been able to maintain continual cultivation by means of irrigation (natural or artificial) or fertilization.

fields and larger crops; it also meant the potential for a larger economic surplus and new and more complex forms of social organization.[8]

The earliest evidence of the plow comes from Mesopotamian cylinder seals and Egyptian paintings dating from a little before 3000 B.C.[9] Modern research indicates that the plow, like so many other innovations in the last 10,000 years, presupposed certain earlier inventions and discoveries—underlining again the cumulative nature of technological change. The first plows of the Mesopotamians and the Egyptians were simply modified versions of the hoe, the basic farm implement of all advanced horticultural societies. In the earliest period, the plow was probably pulled by men, but before long, cattle and oxen began to be used. These plows, like all plows in simple agrarian societies, were made of wood, though sometimes the plowshare was made of bronze for greater strength.

The plow and related techniques of agriculture apparently spread by diffusion until agrarian societies were eventually established throughout most of Europe and much of North Africa and Asia. The plow did not spread to sub-Saharan Africa until the period of European colonialism, and in the New World, too, it was unknown until introduced by Europeans.

The full impact of the new technology was not felt immediately in either Mesopotamia or Egypt. Even so, the shift to agriculture was followed quickly by several important developments, notably the invention of writing, the rise of urban communities,[10] and the beginnings of empire building (which in Egypt led to the unification of the entire country under a single ruler for the first time in history). This was the period that historians have often referred to as "the dawn of civilization."

Similar developments occurred (though at later dates) in horticultural societies in China and Mexico, showing that an agrarian technology is not a necessary precondition for literacy, urbanism, and large-scale imperialism. But the rarity of these developments in horticultural societies and their frequency in agrarian societies indicate that the shift to agriculture, by increasing productivity, greatly increases the probability of their occurrence.

Religion and the Growth of the Economic Surplus

In the earliest simple agrarian societies, religion was an extremely powerful force. Mesopotamian theology held that "man was . . . created for one purpose only: to serve the gods by supplying them with food, drink, and shelter so that they might have full leisure for their divine activities."[11] Each temple was believed to be, quite literally, the house of a particular god, and each community had its own special deity. Priests and other attendants constituted the god's court or household, and their chief task was to minister to his needs. Another responsibility was to mediate between the god and the community, trying to discover his will and appease his anger. In order to perform these tasks, temples and their staffs had to be supported by a steady flow of goods. Over the years, the temples were continually enlarged and became increasingly costly. In fact, they became, in many respects, substantial business enterprises, a development that apparently provided the stimulus for the *invention of true writing*, which was originally a means of recording the business activities of temples.[12] Many scholars have described the early Mesopotamian city-

FIGURE 7.2   The temple of Luxor, Egypt, built about 1400 B.C.

states as theocracies, since the local deity was regarded as the real ruler and the king merely as his "tenant farmer."[13]

Egypt was also a theocracy, but of a different type. Pharaoh was himself a god.[14] To his subjects, he "was the incarnation, the living embodiment, of the god of any district he happened to be visiting; he was their actual God in living form, whom they could see, speak to, and adore."[15] Like the gods of the Mesopotamian city-states, he was the owner of the land and entitled to a portion of all that was produced, and, as in Mesopotamia, these revenues supported a small army of specialists (e.g., officials, craftsmen, soldiers).

In later years there was a secularizing trend, especially in Mesopotamia.[16] By then, however, societies had developed other institutional arrangements—notably political ones—to ensure the continued transfer of the economic surplus from the peasant producers to the governing class. Nevertheless, religion continued to play an important role as a legitimizing agency: it provided a rationale to justify the operation of the political system and its often harsh economic consequences.

The experience of Mesopotamia and Egypt thus supports the impression gained from horticultural societies concerning the importance of religion in the formation of an economic surplus. *Technological advance created the possibility of a surplus, but to transform that possibility into a reality required an ideology that motivated farmers to produce more than they needed to stay alive and productive, and persuaded them to turn that surplus over to someone else.* Although this has sometimes been accomplished by means of secular and political ideologies, a system of beliefs that defined people's obligations with reference to the supernatural worked best in most societies of the past.

Population: Growth in Size of Communities and Societies

In the first few centuries after the shift to agriculture, there was striking growth in the size of a number of communities, especially in Mesopotamia.[17] These became *the first full-fledged cities in history.* The largest of them were the capitals of the largest and most prosperous societies. Although it is impossible to determine exactly the size of the cities and towns of the third and second millennia B.C., scholars believe that one or more of these cities had a population of at least 100,000.[18]

Egypt was the largest of the simple agrarian societies of ancient times and politically the most stable. It enjoyed the unique distinction of being a united and independent nation throughout almost the entire simple agrarian era. This achievement was due to its unique environmental situation: no other society had such excellent natural defenses (i.e., the surrounding desert) and was so little threatened by powerful neighbors.

In the second half of the second millennium, Egypt embarked on a program of expansion that extended its boundaries from Syria to the Sudan. There were also other important empires in this era, especially those established by the Babylonians in the eighteenth century B.C. and the Hittites in the thirteenth century B.C. Babylonia succeeded briefly in uniting most of Mesopotamia, while the Hittites conquered much of what is now Turkey and Syria.

The Polity: Growth of the State

These conquests posed serious organizational problems for the rulers of early agrarian societies. Traditional modes of government based on ties among the members of an extended kin group were no longer adequate for administering the affairs of societies whose populations now sometimes numbered in the millions. Though rulers continued to rely on relatives to help them govern, they were forced to turn increasingly to others. One solution was to incorporate a conquered group as a

FIGURE 7.3 Egyptian painting of soldiers attacking a fortress (about 1940 B.C.).

subdivision of the state, leaving its former ruler in charge, but in a subordinate capacity. Eventually, however, all of the more successful rulers found it necessary to create new kinds of governmental structures, not based on kinship alone.

We can see these newer patterns evolving in both military and civil affairs. For example, the first armies in agrarian societies, like those in horticultural, were simply militia made up of all the able-bodied men in the society.[19] During this period, wars were of short duration and were fought only after the harvest was in. In fact, the period following the harvest came to be known as the "season when kings go forth to war." This limitation was necessary because, with the shift to agriculture, men's responsibilities in farming were much greater than they had been in horticultural societies.

As long as wars were brief and limited to skirmishes with neighboring peoples, this system was adequate. But once rulers became interested in empire building, it was no longer workable, and a new variety of specialist emerged. As early as the middle of the third millennium in Mesopotamia, would-be empire builders established small, but highly trained, *professional armies*. For example, Sargon, the famous Akkadian king, had a standing army of 5,400 men who "ate daily before him."[20] As far as possible, recruits were sons of old soldiers, and thus a military caste was gradually created. The Egyptians followed a similar policy except that they relied chiefly on foreign mercenaries. These new armies soon came to be *royal*, rather than national, armies. Their expenses were paid by the king out of his enormous revenues, and the profits resulting from their activities were his also. Not only were these armies useful in dealing with foreign enemies, they also served as a defense against internal threats.[21]

In civil affairs, too, the casual and informal practices of simpler societies proved inadequate. As states expanded and the problems of administration multiplied, new kinds of governmental positions were created, and a *governmental bureaucracy* began to take shape.[22] In addition to the many officials who comprised the royal court and were responsible for administering the king's complex household affairs, there were officials scattered throughout the countryside to administer the affairs of units ranging from small districts to provinces with hundreds of villages and towns. Each official had a staff of scribes and other lesser officials to assist him, and written records became increasingly important as administrative problems grew more complex.[23]

169

**FIGURE 7.4 Model of a royal granary, found in an Egyptian tomb (about 2000 B.C.).
Note the scribes sitting by the door recording the deliveries of grain.**

Throughout most of the history of the simple agrarian societies of antiquity, writing was a complex craft mastered by only a few individuals after long apprenticeships.[24] This is easily understood, considering the complex prealphabetic systems of writing then in use. Even after a 2,000-year process of simplification, Mesopotamian cuneiform script still had between 600 and 1,000 distinct characters. Before a person could learn to read or write, he had to memorize this formidable array of symbols and learn the complex rules for combining them. The Egyptian hieroglyphic and hieratic scripts were equally complicated. Thus, those who could write formed a specialized occupational group in society—the scribes—and their services were much in demand. For the most part, this occupation was filled by the sons of the rich and powerful, since only they could afford the necessary education.[25] Because of the political importance of their skill and the limited supply of qualified personnel, most scribes were at least members of the small middle class.

One consequence of the growth of empires and the development of bureaucracy was the establishment of the first formal legal systems. Over the centuries every society had developed certain concepts of justice, as well as informal techniques for implementing them. The most common solution, as we saw in the survey of hunting and gathering societies, was to rely on blood revenge by the injured party and his relatives. Because of the anarchic tendencies in such a system, people began to seek settlement by arbitration, and quite naturally turned to the most respected and powerful members of the community. In this way, headmen and other political leaders gradually acquired judicial powers (i.e., the power to administer justice). Then, as empires grew, peoples of diverse cultures were brought within the framework of a single political system. In many instances, the official appointed to rule over an area was not a native and was therefore unfamiliar with local conceptions of justice (which varied considerably from place to place). This generated pressure to clarify and standardize judicial practice, which eventually led to the promulgation of the *first formal codes of law*. The most famous of these was the Code of Hammurabi, the great Babylonian empire-builder of the early second millennium.

The Economy: The First Monetary Systems and the Growth of Trade

Money as we know it was absent in the first simple agrarian societies. There were, nevertheless, certain standardized media of exchange. Barley served this function in ancient Mesopotamia, wheat in Egypt. Wages, rents, taxes, and various other obligations could be paid off in specified quantities of these grains.[26]

As media of exchange, grains were less than ideal, since they were both perishable and bulky. So, from a fairly early date, various metals, particularly silver and copper, were adopted as alternatives.[27] Initially, they were circulated in the form of crude bars of irregular size and weight, and their use was restricted to major transactions, since metal was still relatively scarce. Later, as the production of metals increased, smaller units were introduced in local trade, and their sizes and weights were gradually standardized. As the final stage in the process, governments assumed the responsibility for manufacturing metallic currencies, and full-fledged monetary systems took shape. This did not occur, however, until the very end of the simple agrarian era.

The growth of monetary systems had tremendous implications for societal development. *Money has always facilitated the movement, the exchange, and ultimately the production of goods and services of every kind.* The establishment of a money economy greatly enlarges the market for the things each individual produces, because products can then be sold even to people who produce nothing the producer wants in exchange. Thus the demand for goods and services is increased.

One immediate consequence of the emergence of a money economy is the growth of opportunities for *merchants*, or middlemen, who purchase goods which they do not want for themselves, but which they know are in demand. Once a class of merchants has come into being, it serves not only to satisfy existing demands but to create new ones. By displaying new and unusual articles, merchants generate new needs and desires and thereby stimulate economic activity.

In the long run, a money economy subverts many of the values of simpler societies, especially the cooperative tendencies of extended kin systems. It fosters instead a more individualistic, rationalistic, and competitive approach to life, and lays a foundation for many of the attitudes and values that characterize modern industrial societies.

All of these developments were still very limited, however, in the simple agrarian societies of the ancient Middle East. The newly emerging monetary economies barely penetrated the rural villages, where most of the people lived. Even in the cities and towns, the role of money was quite limited compared with what we are accustomed to. The full impact of a money economy lay far in the future.

Stratification: Growing Social and Cultural Cleavages

In most simple agrarian societies of the ancient world, newly emerging social and cultural differences created cleavages within society, and sometimes conflict. Three cleavages were especially serious. First, there was a cleavage between the small governing class and the much larger class of people who had no voice in political decisions and who had to turn over all or most of their surplus to the governing class. Second, there was a division between the urban minority and the far more numerous rural population. Finally, there was a cleavage between the small literate minority and the illiterate masses.

Because these three lines of cleavage tended to converge, their impact was greatly magnified. The small and often literate urban governing class lived in a strikingly different world from that of the illiterate, rural, peasant majority—despite the fact that they were members of the same society. Each group had its own distinct subculture.[28]

The subculture of the common people was a mixture of primitive superstition and the practical information they needed in their daily lives. It was extremely parochial in outlook and knew little of the world beyond the village. The subculture of the governing class, in contrast, incorporated many of the refinements we identify with "civilization." It included elements of philosophy, art, literature, history, science, and administrative techniques. Above all, it included a contempt for physical labor of any kind (except warfare) and for those who engaged in it. Thus, the governing class was influenced by a body of cultural information that differed radically from that of the peasant class.

In many respects the differences within simple agrarian societies were greater than those between them. Apart from the problems of language, an Egyptian peasant in the latter half of the second millennium B.C. could have adapted far more easily to the life of a Babylonian peasant than to the life of a member of the governing class of his own society. As this gulf widened, members of the governing class found it increasingly difficult to recognize the ignorant, downtrodden peasants as fellow human beings. The scribes of ancient Egypt were fond of saying that the lower classes lacked intelligence and had to be driven like cattle, with a stick.[29]

Slowdown in the Rate of Technological Innovation

Another significant development in these societies was a marked slowdown in the rate of technological innovation and progress, beginning within a few centuries after the shift from horticulture to agriculture. V. Gordon Childe described the change this way:

Before the [agrarian] revolution comparatively poor and illiterate communities had made an impressive series of contributions to man's progress. The two millennia immediately preceding 3,000 B.C. had witnessed discoveries in applied science that directly or indirectly affected the prosperity of millions of [people] and demonstrably furthered the biological welfare of our species by facilitating its multiplication. We have mentioned the following applications of science: artificial irrigation using canals and ditches; the plow; the harnessing of animal motive-power; the sailboat; wheeled vehicles; orchard husbandry; fermentation; the production and use of copper; bricks; the arch; glazing; the seal; and—in the earliest stages of the revolution—a solar calendar, writing, numerical notation, and bronze.

The two thousand years after the revolution—say from 2,600 to 600 B.C.—produced few contributions of anything like comparable importance to human progress. Perhaps only four achievements deserve to be put in the same category as the fifteen just enumerated. They are: the "decimal notation" of Babylonia (about 2,000 B.C.); an economical method for smelting iron on an industrial scale (1,400 B.C.); a truly alphabetic script (1,300 B.C.); aqueducts for supplying water to cities (700 B.C.).[30]

Childe went on to note that two of these four innovations, the smelting of iron and the development of the alphabet, "cannot be credited to the societies that had initiated and reaped the fruits of the [agrarian] revolution" but rather were the products of somewhat less advanced neighboring societies.[31]

At first glance this slowing of the rate of cultural innovation seems an unlikely development. Larger populations, increased intersocietal contacts, and the greater store of information available to potential innovators should have produced higher rates of innovation, especially in technology. The fact that they did not poses an interesting problem.

To explain this unusual development, we need to return to the concept of feedback. This, as we have seen, is the effect produced when some part of an initial force reverts back to, and influences, the initial force itself. Until now, however, we have only seen examples of *positive feedback,* in which the secondary effect enhances or strengthens the original force. This is the type of feedback that has been involved in all of the major social and cultural changes we have examined so far. Now we are seeing one of the rare instances in sociocultural evolution in which major technological advances generated *negative feedback.* In other words, this is a case in which the secondary effect diminished or weakened the original force.

As Figure 7.5 indicates, changes in social organization and ideology that were themselves consequences of technological advance had the effect of *slowing* the rate of technological innovation and advance. As the older system of an armed militia that included all able-bodied men was replaced by a system of professional armies, there was a substantial increase in the power of the governing class, which controlled the new armies. New beliefs and values emerged that served to justify the new system, and at the same time served to perpetuate it and make it even worse. Thus, the governing class found it increasingly easy to extract most of the economic surplus from the peasants, so that peasants were left with little more than the barest necessities of life.[32]

As a result, the peasants lost all incentive for creativity, knowing that any benefits that resulted from their inventions and discoveries would simply be appro-

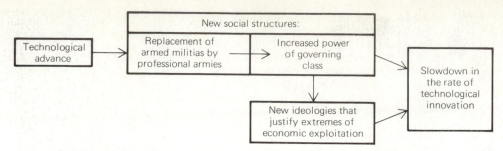

FIGURE 7.5   Model of the causes of the decline in the rate of technological innovation during the first two millennia of the agrarian era.

priated by the governing class.* At the same time, the governing class, though it had a vested interest in a more productive economy, no longer had the necessary knowledge of, and experience with, subsistence technology and thus was in no position to make creative innovations. In short, *expertise and incentive were inadvertently divorced,* with disastrous results for technological progress.

Under the circumstances, it is hardly surprising that members of the governing class turned increasingly to warfare and conquest as the best way to increase their wealth. Warfare was something they understood; moreover, in their system of values, waging war was one of the few occupations considered appropriate for their class. The energies of this powerful and influential class were thus turned *from the conquest of nature to the conquest of people.*[33] And this, thanks to the new, more productive technology, could be a highly profitable enterprise. With vast numbers of peasants producing more than they needed to survive and remain productive, there was a large economic surplus that could be obtained in the form of taxes, tribute, tithes, and rents and used to support the host of servants and artisans who catered to the whims of the governing class and the army of soldiers and officials who ensured the flow of revenues.

These developments help to explain the growing complexity of social organization during this period. Having cut themselves off from the sweaty world of work and having turned their efforts instead to conquest, members of the governing class found a new challenge for their creative talents in the area of social organization. The exercise of power and the manipulation of others were activities in keeping with their dignity. Moreover, they were rewarding: the better organized an army or government, the greater its chances of success in struggles with other groups.[34]

By the end of the period when simple agrarian societies were dominant, substantial changes had occurred in societies that had adopted the new technology. The largest of them were substantially larger than any horticultural society had ever been, and substantially more complex. There was a much greater division of labor within them, and social inequality had also increased. But as impressive as they

---

*It is possible that the process was even more complicated and that the mental capacities of many peasants may also have been impaired by protein-deficient diets and by environments not conducive to learning in early childhood. Thus, the basic intelligence of many peasants may have been permanently impaired.

FIGURE 7.6 One consequence of the growth of empires was an increase in the economic surplus extracted from conquered peoples in the form of tribute. Egyptian carving of tribute bearers (about 2000 B.C.).

were, these changes were only the prelude to what was yet to come in the remainder of the agrarian era.

Advanced Agrarian Societies

Technology

During the period in which simple agrarian societies dominated the Middle East, the most important technological advance was the discovery of the technique of smelting iron. Prior to this, bronze had been the most important metal. But since the supply was always limited* and the demands of the governing class always took precedence over the needs of peasants, bronze was used primarily for military, ornamental, and ceremonial purposes. It never really replaced stone and wood in ordinary tools, certainly not in agricultural tools, and so its impact on the economy was limited.

---

*This was because of the scarcity of tin, an essential component of bronze.

People knew of iron at least as early as the first half of the third millennium B.C., but apparently only in its meteoric form, which is very scarce.[35] Sometime during the second millennium, the Hittites of Asia Minor discovered iron ore and invented a technique for smelting it. For centuries they kept this a closely guarded secret, which gave them a monopoly on a highly valued commodity. Then, about 1200 B.C., their nation was destroyed. This led to the rapid dispersal of both the Hittite people and the technology of smelting iron.

As one would expect, in view of the class structure of simple agrarian societies, the initial use of iron was limited largely to the governing class. Some of the earliest iron objects recovered from Egypt were a dagger, a bracelet, and a headrest found in the tomb of the pharaoh Tutankhamen. Prior to the military collapse of the Hittite empire, iron was five times more expensive than gold, forty times more than silver. It was not until about the eighth century B.C. that iron came into general use for *ordinary tools*. Thus, it is not until this period that we can speak of true advanced agrarian societies, although many Middle Eastern societies of the previous three or four centuries were certainly transitional types.

During this transitional period two further discoveries greatly enhanced the value of iron. First it was found that if the outer layers of the iron absorbed some carbon from the fire during the forging process, the metal became somewhat harder. Later it was discovered that this carburized iron could be hardened still further by quenching the hot metal in water, thus producing steel. With these developments, iron became not only more common than bronze but also more useful for both military and economic purposes. As one writer has said, "After the discovery of quench-hardening, iron gradually passed into the position from which it has never subsequently been ousted; it became the supremely useful material for making all the tools and weapons that are intended for cutting, chopping, piercing, or slashing."[36]

From its point of origin in the Middle East, iron-making spread until eventually it was practiced in nearly all of the Old World, even in many horticultural societies. By the time of Christ, advanced agrarian societies were firmly established in the Middle East, throughout most of the Mediterranean world, and in much of India and China. Within the next thousand years, the advanced agrarian pattern spread over most of Europe and much of Southeast Asia, and expanded further in India and China. Still later it was transplanted to the European colonies in the New World.

Compared with simpler societies, advanced agrarian societies enjoyed a very productive technology. Unfortunately, the same conditions that slowed the rate of technological advance in simple agrarian societies continued to prevail. As a result, their progress was not nearly what one would expect on the basis of their size, the degree of contact among them, and, above all, their store of accumulated information.[37]

Nevertheless, over the centuries quite a number of important innovations were made. A partial list would include the catapult, the crossbow, gunpowder, horseshoes, a workable harness for horses, stirrups, the wood-turning lathe, the auger, the screw, the wheelbarrow, the rotary fan for ventilation, the clock, the spinning wheel, porcelain, printing, iron casting, the magnet, water-powered mills, windmills, and, in the period just preceding the emergence of the first industrial societies, the workable steam engine, the fly shuttle, the spinning jenny, the spinning machine,

FIGURE 7.7 Throughout the agrarian era, societies depended on humans and animals as their chief sources of energy: Indian peasants raising water from ditch to irrigate field. The man on the post moves back and forth on the crossbeam to raise the water and to allow the bucket to be lowered again to the ditch below where the other man refills it.

and various other power-driven tools. As a result of these and other innovations, the most advanced agrarian societies of the eighteenth century A.D. were much superior, from the technological standpoint, to their predecessors of 2,500 years earlier.

The level of technological development was not uniform throughout the agrarian world, despite diffusion. Information still spread slowly in most cases, and some areas were considerably ahead of others. During much of the advanced agrarian era, especially from 500 to 1500 A.D., the Middle East, China, and parts of India were technologically superior to Europe.[38] In part, this was simply a continuation of older patterns: the Middle East had been the center of innovation for more than 5,000 years following its shift to horticulture. An even more important factor in Europe's relative backwardness, however, was the collapse of the Roman Empire. For centuries afterward, Europe was divided into scores of petty kingdoms and principalities that had only enough resources to maintain the smallest urban settlements and the most limited occupational specialization. Therefore, Europeans were inactive on many of the most promising and challenging technological frontiers of the time. Though they made relative gains during the later Middle Ages—thanks largely to the diffusion of knowledge from the East—they did not really catch up until the sixteenth century and did not take the lead until even later.

Population: Continuing Trends

Size of Societies and Communities   The populations of advanced agrarian societies were substantially larger than those of any societies that preceded them. This was due partly to advances in agricultural technology that permitted greater population densities, and partly to advances in military technology that aided the process of empire building. The largest simple agrarian society, Egypt, probably had fewer than 15 million members.[39] In contrast, the largest advanced agrarian society, mid-nineteenth-century China, had approximately 400 million.*[40] While that was exceptional, India reached 175 million in the middle of the nineteenth century, and the Roman and the Russian empires each had at least 70 million people.[41]

Similar differences are found in communities. The populations of the largest cities in simple agrarian societies were probably not much over 100,000, if that. By comparison, the upper limit for cities in advanced agrarian societies was about a million (see Table 10.6, page 274).[42] Only the capitals of major empires ever attained such a size, however, and they maintained it but briefly. Cities of 100,000 were more numerous than in simple agrarian societies, though still quite rare by modern standards.

Fertility and Mortality   Birthrates in both simple and advanced agrarian societies have averaged 40 or more births per 1,000 population per year, nearly triple that of modern industrial societies.[43] In general, there seems to have been little interest in limiting the size of families, since large families, particularly ones with many sons, were valued for both economic and religious reasons. From the economic standpoint, children were viewed by peasants as an important asset, a valuable source of cheap labor.[44] Members of modern industrial societies are usually unaware of the amount of work required on a peasant farm. Children were also important as the only form of old-age survivor's insurance available to peasants. Religion added yet another incentive for large families, either by encouraging ancestor worship, in which perpetuation of the family line was essential, or simply by declaring large families to be a sign of God's favor.[45] The chief deterrent to large families was the

---

*Growth in China's population *after* the middle of the nineteenth century was due increasingly to the beginnings of industrialization. The same was true in India.

reaction of women to the strains and risks of repeated pregnancies; but because they were subordinate to their husbands, their feelings usually had little effect.[46]

Despite their high birthrates, advanced agrarian societies grew slowly. Sometimes they failed to grow at all or even declined in size. The reason, of course, was that death rates were almost as high as birthrates and sometimes higher. Wars, disease, accidents, and famine all took their toll. Infant mortality was especially high before the development of modern sanitation and medicine. Recent studies show that the average child born in Rome 2,000 years ago could not expect to live more than 20 years.[47] Even as recently as the seventeenth century, the children of British queens and duchesses had a life expectancy of only 30 years, and nearly a third were dead before their fifth birthday. Youngsters of the elite who survived the dangerous infant years still had a total life expectancy of only a little more than 40 years.[48] For the common people, conditions were even worse. With death rates averaging nearly 40 per 1,000 per year, life expectancy at birth was barely 25 years, and even those who reached adulthood usually died young (see Table 7.1).

The larger cities were notoriously unhealthy places, especially for the common people. The citizens of Rome, for example, had a shorter life expectancy than those in the provinces.[49] England in the early eighteenth century presented a similar situation. During the first half of that century, there were an estimated 500,000 more deaths than births in London.[50] Some of the reasons for this become clear when we read descriptions of sanitary conditions in medieval cities. As one historian depicts them:

> The streets of medieval towns were generally little more than narrow alleys, the overhanging upper stories of the houses nearly meeting, and thus effectually excluding all but a minimum of light and air . . . In most continental towns and some English ones, a high city wall further impeded the free circulation of air . . . Rich citizens might possess a courtyard in which garbage was collected and occasionally removed to the suburbs, but the usual practice was to throw everything into the streets including the garbage of slaughter houses and other offensive trades . . . Filth of every imaginable description accumulated indefinitely in the unpaved streets and in all available space and was

TABLE 7.1 Average Age at Death of Adults During Agrarian Era

	Males	Females
Early Bronze Age, 3000 B.C.	33.7	29.5
Middle Bronze Age, 2000 B.C.		
Commoners	36.3	30.8
Royalty	35.9	36.1
Late Bronze Age, 1500 B.C.	39.5	32.1
Early Iron Age, 1150 B.C.	38.6	31.3
Imperial Rome, 120 A.D.	40.2	34.6
Medieval Byzantium, 1400 A.D.	37.7	31.1

Sources: J. L. Angel, "Ecology and Population in the Eastern Mediterranean," *World Archaeology*, 4 (1972), pp. 88–105; and J. L. Angel, "Paleoecology, Paleodemography, and Health," in Steven Polgar, *Population, Ecology, and Social Evolution* (The Hague: Mouton, 1975), pp. 167–190.

FIGURE 7.8 **The streets of medieval towns were generally little more than narrow alleys, the overhanging upper stories of the houses nearly meeting, and thus effectually excluding all but a minimum of light and air: view of Dubrovnik, Yugoslavia, from the city wall.**

trodden into the ground. The water supply would be obtained either from wells or springs, polluted by the gradual percolation through the soil of the accumulated filth, or else from an equally polluted river. In some towns, notably London, small streams running down a central gutter served at once as sewers and as water supply . . . In seventeenth century London, which before the Fire largely remained a medieval city, the poorer class house had only a covering of weatherboards, a little black pitch forming the only waterproofing, and these houses were generally built back to back. Thousands of Londoners dwelt in cellars or horribly overcrowded tenements. A small house in Dowgate accommodated 11 married couples and 15 single persons . . . Another source of unhealthiness were the church vaults and graveyards, so filled with corpses that the level of the latter was generally raised above that of the surrounding ground. In years of pestilence, recourse had to be made to plague pits in order to dispose of the harvest of death.[51]

FIGURE 7.9 Sanitary standards were low in most agrarian societies: open-air butcher shop in the Middle East.

This account calls attention to one of the striking demographic characteristics of advanced agrarian societies: the disasters that periodically overtook them and produced sharp increases in the death rate.[52] The most devastating of all, the Black Plague that hit Europe in the middle of the fourteenth century, is said to have killed between a quarter and a half of the population in a four-year period.[53]

Crop failures and famines seldom affected such large areas, but they were much more frequent and could be just as deadly. One Finnish province lost a third of its population during the famine of 1696–1697, and many parts of France suffered comparable losses a few years earlier.[54] Even allowing for a considerable margin of error in the reports of such disasters, it is clear from other kinds of evidence—for example, the severe labor shortages and the abandonment of farms that followed plagues and famines—that the number of deaths was huge. For these reasons, the growth of advanced agrarian populations was anything but continuous.

The Economy: Increasing Differentiation

Division of Labor   The growth in both territorial and population size that came with the shift from the simple to the advanced agrarian level brought with it an increase in

FIGURE 7.10 Occupational specialization in an advanced agrarian society: silversmith at work in his shop.

the division of labor. For the first time, there was significant economic specialization by regions and by communities, and this was accompanied by increased occupational specialization.

The Roman Empire provides a good illustration of both regional and local specialization. North Africa and Spain were noted as suppliers of dried figs and olive oil; Gaul, Dalmatia, Asia Minor, and Syria for their wine; Spain and Egypt for salted meats; Egypt, North Africa, Sicily, and the Black Sea region for grain; and the latter for salted fish as well.[55] The tendency toward specialization at the community level is illustrated by a passage from a manual for wealthy farmers, written in the second century B.C., which advised:

> Tunics, togas, blankets, smocks and shoes should be bought at Rome; caps, iron tools, scythes, spades, mattocks, axes, harnesses, ornaments and small chains at Cales and Minturnae; spades at Venafrum, carts and sledges at Suessa and in Lucania, jars and pots at Alba and at Rome; tiles at Venafrum, oil mills at Pompeii and at Rufrius's yard at Nola; nails and bars at Rome; pails, oil urns, water pitchers, wine urns, other copper vessels at Capua and at Nola; Campanian baskets, pulley-ropes and all sorts of cordage at Capua, Roman baskets at Suessa and Casium.[56]

Similar patterns are reported in other agrarian societies.[57] Even at the village level a measure of specialization was not uncommon. In the agricultural off-season, peasants often turned to handicrafts to make ends meet, and certain villages often developed a reputation for a particular commodity.

In the larger urban centers, occupational specialization reached a level that surpassed anything achieved in simpler societies. For example, a tax roll for Paris from the year 1313 lists 157 different trades, and tax records from two sections of Barcelona in 1385 indicate a hundred occupations (see Table 7.2).[58] The clothing industry alone contained such specialized occupations as wool comber, wool spinner, silk spinner (two kinds), girdle maker, and headdress maker (seven kinds, including specialists in felt, fur, wool and cotton, flowers, peacock feathers, gold embroidery and pearls, and silk). Though such specialization was found only in the largest cities, smaller cities often had forty or fifty different kinds of craftsmen, and even small towns had ten or twenty.[59] In addition to craft specialists, urban centers also had specialists in government, commerce, religion, education, the armed forces, and domestic service. There were also specialists in illegal occupations (e.g., thieves), which were a normal part of urban life in advanced agrarian societies.

Command Economies Because politics and economics were always highly interdependent in advanced agrarian societies, the people who dominated the political system also dominated the economic system. The leading officeholders in government were usually the chief landholders as well, and in these societies land and control of those who worked it was the most important economic resource. As one economic historian has written, this was a time in which "true wealth consisted in being master."[60]

In these societies, the answers to basic economic questions—how resources should be used, what should be produced and in what quantities, and how the products should be distributed—were determined less by the forces of supply and demand than by the arbitrary decisions of the political elite. These were *command economies*, not market economies.[61]

The economy of an advanced agrarian society consisted of two distinct parts: its rural agricultural sector and its urban commercial and industrial sector. These were not of equal economic importance, however: one historian has estimated that the Roman state derived approximately twenty times more tax revenue from agriculture than from trade and industry. He went on to say that "this apportionment of the burden of taxation probably corresponded roughly to the economic structure of the

TABLE 7.2 Occupations of Householders in Two Sections of Barcelona in 1385 A.D.

Sailors	227	Longshoremen	50	Silversmiths	29
Merchants	151	Innkeepers	49	Curriers	29
Shoemakers	108	Brokers	45	Notaries	28
Tailors	96	Carpenters	43	Tavern-keepers	27
Fishermen	94	Bakers	40	Spicers	26
Seamen	73	Janitors	39	Bargemen	25
Wooldressers	70	Hucksters	36	76 other occupations	525
Weavers	63	Butchers	34		
Tanners	61	Scriveners	32	Total	2000

Source: Adapted from Josiah Cox Russell, *Medieval Regions and Their Cities* (Bloomington: Indiana University Press, 1972), p. 170.

empire. All the evidence goes to show that its wealth was derived almost entirely from agriculture, and to a very small extent from industry and trade."[62] The same could be said of every agrarian society. This does not mean, of course, that the urban economy was of little interest to members of the governing class. On the contrary, it was of great interest because it provided luxuries they valued highly. The urban economy, however, depended on the ability of the rural economy to produce a surplus that could support the urban population.

In many respects the economy of the typical agrarian society resembled a tree with roots spreading in every direction, constantly drawing in new resources. The pattern was similar to that shown in Figure 7.11. At the economic center of the society was the national capital, controlled by the king or emperor and the leading members of the governing class. Surrounding it were various provincial or regional capitals controlled by royal governors and other members of the governing class. Each of these, in turn, was surrounded by smaller county seats and market towns controlled by lesser members of the governing class. Finally, each of these towns was surrounded by scores of small villages.

In this system, there was a steady flow of goods from smaller units to larger, or from villages to county seats, and from there to regional and national capitals. Basically this flow was through taxation, but it was supplemented by rents, interest on debts, tithes and other religious offerings, and profits, all of which helped to transfer the economic surplus from the peasant producers to the urban-based governing class, its allies, and their dependents.

FIGURE 7.11 **In agrarian societies, there was a steady flow of goods from villages to county seats and from there to regional and national capitals: model of the flow of goods in these societies and of the accumulation of the economic surplus in the society's capital.**

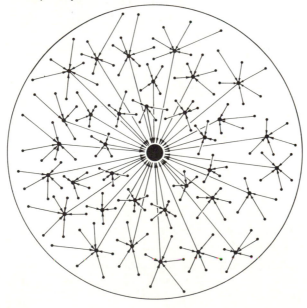

Some scholars have argued that this was a symbiotic relationship in which the villagers freely exchanged the goods they produced for goods and services produced in the urban centers. Although there is an element of truth in this, the historical record shows that the relationship was largely one-sided and that the peasants were forced to give far more than they received. The peasants obviously resented this, as indicated by the frequency of their protests and revolts.[63]

With what they retained of their surplus after paying taxes, rents, interest, and other obligations, peasants could go to the urban centers and trade for commodities that were not available in their villages (e.g., metal tools, salt, etc.). Many towns and cities were also religious centers, and the peasants often used these facilities. Finally, the peasants did benefit to some degree from the maintenance of law and order provided by urban-based governments, even though the law was used disproportionately to protect the rights of the governing class and keep the peasants in their place. The maintenance of order is extremely important in an agrarian society because so much depends on the success of each harvest, and each harvest depends on months of effort. Disruption at any point in the agricultural cycle can be disastrous for everyone.

The Rural Economy In most advanced agrarian societies, the governing elite (which included religious leaders) owned a grossly disproportionate share of the land. Although there are no precise figures for earlier times, the traditional pattern could still be seen recently in many parts of Latin America, the Middle East, and Southeast Asia. Typically, a minority of 1 to 3 percent of the population has owned from one-third to two-thirds of the arable land in these societies.[64]

Not only did the governing class usually own most of the land, but it often owned most of the peasants who worked it. Systems of slavery and serfdom have been common in agrarian societies, with large landholdings and large numbers of slaves or serfs normally going hand in hand. Thus, one nineteenth-century Russian nobleman who owned 2 million acres of land also owned nearly 300,000 serfs. Rulers, understandably, had the largest holdings. Prior to the emancipation of the serfs in Russia, the czar owned 27.4 million of them.[65]

But even when the peasant owned his own land and was legally free, he usually found it difficult to make ends meet. A bad crop one year, and he had to borrow money at usurious rates, sometimes as high as 120 percent a year.[66] In any event, there were always taxes, and these usually fell more heavily on the peasant landowner than on his wealthier neighbor, either because of special exemptions granted the latter or simply because of his greater ability to evade such obligations.[67] If a peasant did not own his land, he had to pay rent, which was always high. In addition, he was often subject to compulsory labor service, tithes, fines, and obligatory "gifts" to the governing class.[68]

Because the number and variety of obligations were so great, it is difficult to determine just how large the total was, but in most societies it appears to have been not less than half the total value of the goods the peasants produced.[69] The basic philosophy of the governing class seems to have been to tax peasants to the limit of their ability to pay.[70] This philosophy is illustrated by a story told of a leading Japanese official of the seventeenth century who, returning to one of his estates after an absence of ten years and finding the villagers in well-built houses instead of the

FIGURE 7.12   Peasant using traditional plow, Iran.

hovels he remembered, exclaimed, "These people are too comfortable. They must be more heavily taxed."[71]

Living conditions for most peasants were primitive, and it is doubtful that they were as well off as most hunters and gatherers had been thousands of years earlier. For example, the diet of the average peasant in medieval England consisted of little more than a hunk of bread and a mug of ale in the morning; a lump of cheese and bread with perhaps an onion or two to flavor it and more ale at noon; and a thick soup or pottage with bread and cheese in the evening. Meat was rare and the ale thin. Household furniture consisted of a few stools, a table, and a chest to hold the best clothes and any other treasured possessions.[72] Beds were uncommon; most peasants simply slept on earthen floors covered with straw.

Even later in France, toward the end of the agrarian era,

> Great masses of the people lived in a state of chronic malnutrition, subsisting mainly on porridge made of bread and water with some occasional, home-grown vegetables thrown in. They ate meat only a few times a year, on feast days or after autumn slaughtering if they did not have enough silage to feed the livestock over the winter . . . For most peasants village life was a struggle for survival, and survival meant keeping above the line that divided the poor from the indigent.[73]

But many did not survive and lost their farms. "Then they took to the road for good, drifting about with the flotsam and jetsam of France's *population flottante* ('floating population'), which included several million desperate souls by the 1780s." The same author concludes by saying that "The human condition has changed so much since then that we can hardly imagine the way it appeared to people whose lives really were nasty, brutish, and short."[74]

In China, conditions were so wretched that female infanticide was widely

MOTHER GOOSE REVISITED

Most of us today think of Mother Goose rhymes and stories as charming survivals from a simpler, happier world of the past. Yet if we look at them more closely, and at other older folk tales, a very different picture emerges. It is a picture of widespread poverty and despair, except for the fortunate few who lived in palaces.

Recall for a moment old Mother Hubbard who went to the cupboard to fetch her poor dog a bone, or the old woman who lived in a shoe and had so many children she didn't know what to do. But one of the saddest of all tells that

> There was an old woman
> And nothing she had,
> And so this old woman
> Was said to be mad.
> She'd nothing to eat,
> She'd nothing to wear,
> She'd nothing to lose,
> She'd nothing to fear,
> She'd nothing to ask,
> And she'd nothing to give,
> And when she did die
> She'd nothing to leave.

We can also learn something of life in agrarian societies from the story of Tom Thumb. In a late seventeenth-century French version, the story begins, "Once upon a time there was a woodsman and his wife, who had seven children, all boys . . . They were very poor, and their seven children were a great inconvenience, because none was old enough to support himself . . . A very difficult year came, and the famine was so great that these poor folk resolved to get rid of their children." Shades of Hansel and Gretel! In the French version of "The Sorcerer's Apprentice," a poor father sells his son to the devil in exchange for an ample supply of food for twelve years.

Though fairy tales often had happy endings, these endings depended on magic, trickery, or uncommon luck—not ordinary hard work. Cinderella had her fairy godmother; Jack (of beanstalk fame) combined a generous mix of magic, trickery, daring, and luck to win his fortune; and the miller's son in Puss 'n Boots, who inherited only a cat, had the luck to inherit a most remarkable cat indeed.

If Mother Goose has powers to charm, it is because we overlook the poverty and despair that are portrayed, or we imagine that they are just part of the world of make-believe, like the fairy godmothers who provided the happy endings. But if we look closely at the conditions of life of ordinary people in agrarian societies, we find that there is at least as much truth as fiction in these old rhymes and tales.

practiced. One nineteenth-century scholar indicated that in some districts as many as a quarter of the female infants were killed at birth.[75] Sometimes signs were posted near ponds, reading, "Girls may not be drowned here."

To compound the misery created by their economic situation, peasants were often subjected to further cruelties. Families were sometimes split up if it served their master's economic interests.[76] Peasants often found it difficult to defend their wives and daughters from the amorous attentions of the governing class, and in some areas the lord of the manor maintained the notorious *jus primae noctis* (i.e., literally, the right of the first night, meaning the right to have sexual relations with all brides on their wedding nights).[77] Finally, peasants were subject at all times to the whims and tempers of their superiors, who could invoke severe punishments even for minor offenses. Petty thievery could be punished by death, often by cruel and frightful means.[78]

To the governing class, all this seemed only fitting and proper, since most of them, like their predecessors in simple agrarian societies, viewed peasants as sub-human. In legal documents in medieval England, a peasant's children were listed not as his *familia*, but as his *sequela*, meaning "brood" or "litter."[79] Estate records in Europe, Asia, and the Americas often listed peasants with the livestock.[80] Even so civilized a Roman as Cato the Elder argued that slaves, like livestock, should be disposed of when no longer productive.[81]

As shocking as these views seem today, they were not illogical, but simply one facet of the belief systems that emerged in this kind of society. These new beliefs and values reflected the cleavages within societies and the increasingly diverse experiences of their members. So divergent were the ways of life of the governing class and the peasantry, and so limited their contacts (normally a class of supervisory officials and retainers stood between them[82]), that it may be more surprising that some members of the privileged class recognized their common humanity than that the majority did not.

Despite the heavy burdens laid on them, not all peasants were reduced to the subsistence level. By various devices, many contrived to hide part of their harvest and otherwise evade their obligations.[83] A small minority even managed, by rendering special services to the governing class or by other means, to rise a bit above their fellows, operating larger farms and generally living a bit more comfortably.[84]

For the majority, however, the one real hope for a substantial improvement in their lot lay, ironically, in the devastation wrought by plagues, famines, and wars. Only when death reduced their numbers to the point where good workers were scarce was the governing class forced to bid competitively for their services, thus raising the average income above the subsistence level.[85] Usually, however, high birthrates kept this from occurring, or, when it did, soon brought about a return to the former situation.

The Urban Economy   When we think of the famous societies of the past, most of us conjure up images of Rome, Constantinople, Alexandria, Jerusalem, Baghdad, Babylon, and the other great cities that loom so large in the historical record. Thus it is with a sense of shock that we discover that rarely if ever did all the urban communities of an advanced agrarian society contain as much as 10 percent of its population, and in most cases they held less.[86]

How can this be? Why are our impressions so wrong? The reason is that history was recorded by literate men—men who nearly always lived in cities and towns and

FIGURE 7.13 Servants were far more numerous in advanced agrarian societies than in modern industrial societies, both because of the absence of laborsaving devices in homes and because the governing class considered it degrading to do manual work of any kind: slaves transporting a wealthy Roman matron.

regarded the life of the rural villages as unworthy of attention. Thus, the historical record is primarily a record of city life, particularly the life of the governing class.

The most striking feature of the cities and towns of these societies was the great diversity of people who lived in them. City residents ranged from the most illustrious members of the governing class to beggars and other destitute people who barely managed to stay alive. Unlike so many cities and towns in modern industrial societies, these were not primarily centers of industry. Though considerable industrial activity was carried on in them, their political and commercial functions, and frequently their religious ones, were more important.

Since cities and towns were the centers of government, and social and cultural centers as well, most members of the governing class preferred to live in them.[87] As a result, urban populations included not only civil and military officials, but the extensive households of the governing class as well. Servants were far more numerous in these societies than in ours, both because of the absence of laborsaving devices and because the governing class viewed manual work of any kind as degrading. Furthermore, one of their chief forms of status competition was to see who could maintain the most luxurious household. The household staff of the head of one small kingdom, Edward IV of England, numbered 400.[88] A more important ruler, such as the Roman emperor at the height of empire, had thousands. As one historian put it, one "is dumbfounded by the extraordinary degree of specialization [and] the insensate luxury."[89] One group of servants was responsible only for the emperor's palace clothes, another for his city clothes, another for those he wore to the theater, yet another for his military uniforms. Other servants attended to eating

FIGURE 7.14   **The souk, or market, Fez, Morocco; compare with the market in Ouagadougou, Figure 6.11, page 155.**

vessels, a different group to those used for drinking, another to silver vessels, and still others to gold vessels and those set with jewels. For entertainment, the emperor had his own choristers, an orchestra, dancing women, clowns, and dwarfs. Lesser members of the Roman governing class obviously could not maintain household staffs as elaborate as this, but many had staffs of hundreds, and some had a thousand or more. All this was made possible by the labors of the peasantry.

   Part of the peasants' surplus also went to support two important groups that were allied with the governing class yet separate from it. The first of these was the clergy, of whom more will be said shortly. The second was the merchant class. Merchants were a peculiar group in the structure of agrarian societies. Although some of them were extremely wealthy, they were rarely accepted as equals by members of the governing class—even by those less wealthy than they. For merchants worked to obtain their wealth, and this, by the values of the governing class, was unpardonable.[90] Nevertheless, the latter avidly sought the goods that merchants sold and coveted their wealth, acquiring it whenever they could by taxes, marriage, or outright confiscation.[91] The attitude of the merchants toward the governing class was equally ambivalent: they both feared and envied them, but, given the chance, they emulated their way of life and sought to be accepted by them.

   Like modern merchants, the merchants of agrarian societies often created the demand for their goods, thereby spurring productivity. And like modern advertisers, they were primarily interested in creating a demand for luxuries. One reason for this was the high cost of moving goods from town to town. With the primitive transportation available,[92] only lightweight, luxury items, such as silks, spices, and fine swords, could be moved far without the costs becoming prohibitive.

A report on China shortly after World War II indicates what an enormous difference modern methods of transportation have made in the cost of moving goods. To ship a ton of goods one mile at that time, the costs were as follows (measured in United States cents):[93]

Steamboat	2.4	Pack mule	17.0
Railroad	2.7	Wheelbarrow	20.0
Junk	12.0	Pack donkey	24.0
Animal-drawn cart	13.0	Carrying by pole	48.0

Figures from Europe are strikingly similar: in 1900, for example, it cost ten times more to move goods by horse-drawn wagon than by rail.[94] In short, modern methods of transportation have slashed this cost by 80 to 95 percent.

The prosperity of the merchant class was due in no small measure to the labors of another, humbler class with which they were closely affiliated—the artisans, who numbered approximately 3 to 5 percent of the total population.[95] Except for the peasantry, this class was the most productive element in the economy. Most artisans lived in the urban centers and, like the rest of the urban population, were ultimately dependent on the surplus produced by the peasants. Craft specialization was rather highly developed in the larger urban centers, as we have seen.

The shops where artisans worked were small by modern standards and bore little resemblance to modern factories. In Rome in the first century B.C., a shop employing fifty men was considered very large.[96] A pewter business employing eighteen men was the largest mentioned in any of London's medieval craft records, and even this modest size was not attained until the middle of the fifteenth century.[97] Typically, the shop was also the residence of both the merchant and his workmen, and work was carried on either in the living quarters or in an adjoining room.[98]

The economic situation of the artisans, like that of the merchants, was variable. In Peking at the time of World War I, wages ranged from $2.50 a month for members of the Incense and Cosmetic Workers Guild to $36 a month for members of the Gold Foil Beaters Guild.[99] Those in highly skilled trades and some of the self-employed fared moderately well by agrarian standards. Apprentices and journeymen in less skilled trades, however, worked long hours for bare subsistence wages. In Peking, for example, a seven-day workweek and ten-hour workday were typical, and many artisans remained too poor ever to marry.

Merchants and artisans in the same trade were commonly organized into *guilds*. These organizations were an attempt to create, in an urban setting, a functional approximation of the extended kin groups of horticultural societies. Many guilds spoke of their members as brothers, for example, and functioned as mutual aid associations, restricting entry into the field, forbidding price cutting, and otherwise trying to protect the interests of their members.[100] But a guild included merchant employers as well as artisan employees, and the employers were naturally dominant, controlling key offices and formulating policies that benefited them more than the artisans.[101]

Beneath the artisans in the class structure of the cities were a variety of other kinds of people, including unskilled laborers who supplied much of the animal energy required by the system. The working conditions of these men were usually terrible, and injuries were common. As a result, their work life was short. For example, early in the present century, the average Peking rickshaw man was able to work only five years, after which he was good for little except begging.[102] The class of unskilled laborers shaded off into still more deprived groups—the unemployed, the beggars, and the criminals. The high birthrates of agrarian societies resulted in a perennial oversupply of unskilled labor, and such people usually migrated to the cities, hoping to find some kind of employment. As long as men were young and healthy, they could usually get work as day laborers. But after they were injured or lost their youth and strength, they were quickly replaced by fresh labor and left to fend for themselves, usually as beggars or thieves. No agrarian society ever found a solution to this problem. But then, the leading classes were not especially interested in finding one. The system served their needs quite well just as it was.

Many of the sisters of the men who made up the urban lower classes earned their livelihood as prostitutes. Moralists have often condemned these women as though they elected this career in preference to a more honorable one. The record indicates, however, that most of them had little choice: their only alternative was a life of unrelieved drudgery and poverty as servants or unskilled laborers, and many could not even hope for that.[103] The men they might have married were too poor to afford wives, and the system of prostitution was often, in effect, a substitute for marriage that was forced on people by society. To be sure, the poor were not the only ones to avail themselves of the services of prostitutes, nor were all girls in that "profession" because of poverty. But economic factors were clearly the chief cause of its high incidence in agrarian societies.

The number of profitable working years for prostitutes was hardly longer than that for the rickshaw boys, porters, and others who sold their physical assets for a meager livelihood. As a result, the cities and towns in agrarian societies often swarmed with beggars of both sexes. Estimates by observers suggest that beggars comprised from a tenth to as high as a third of the total population of urban communities.[104] The proportion was not nearly so high for society as a whole, of course, since many of the rural poor migrated to the cities and towns in the hope of finding greater opportunities.

The Polity: Continuing Development of the State

In nearly all advanced agrarian societies, government was the basic integrating force. It was inevitable in any society created by conquest and run for the benefit of a tiny elite that coercive power was required to hold the society together. Not only did the natural antagonisms of the peasant masses have to be kept in check, but diverse groups of conquered people often had to be welded together politically. The scope of this problem is suggested by the geographical size of some of these societies. Whereas the largest simple agrarian society was probably Egypt, which controlled roughly 800,000 square miles (much of it desert and uninhabited), several advanced agrarian societies covered between 2 and 8 million square miles.

Nearly every advanced agrarian society was a monarchy: it had at its head a king or an emperor, a position that was usually hereditary. Republican government, in which power was divided among a small ruling elite, was an infrequent exception limited almost entirely to the least powerful and least developed agrarian societies.[105] The prevalence of monarchical government seems to have been the result of the militaristic and exploitative character of societies at this level. Governments were constantly threatening, or being threatened by, their neighbors. At the same time, they were in danger from internal enemies—dissatisfied and ambitious members of the governing class, eager to seize control for themselves, and restless, hostile members of the numerically dominant lower classes. Under such conditions, republican government was nearly impossible.[106]

Because of the tendency to romanticize the past, many people today are unaware of the frequency of both internal and external conflict in the great agrarian empires. In Rome, for example, 31 of the 79 emperors were murdered, 6 were driven to suicide, 4 were forcibly deposed, and several more met unknown fates at the hands of internal enemies.[107] Though Rome's record was worse than most, internal struggles occurred in all advanced agrarian societies.[108]

Peasant uprisings were also indicators of internal stress. One expert states that "there were peasant rebellions almost every year in China," and an authority on Russia reports that in the short period from 1801 to 1861, there were no less than 1,467 peasant uprisings in various parts of that country.[109] Most of these disturbances remained local only because authorities acted swiftly and ruthlessly. Had they not, many would have spread as widely as the famous English revolt of 1381 or the German Peasants' War of 1524–1525.[110]

External threats were no less frequent or serious, and warfare was a chronic condition. A survey of the incidence of war in eleven European countries in the preindustrial period found that, on the average, these countries were involved in some kind of conflict with neighboring societies nearly every second year.[111] Such conditions obviously required strong centralized authority. Societies without it were eliminated in the selective process, unless they happened to occupy a particularly remote and inaccessible territory.

Most members of the governing class considered political power a prize to be sought for the rewards it offered rather than an opportunity for public service, and the office of king or emperor was *the supreme prize*. This is the only interpretation one can put on the perennial struggle for power within agrarian states or the use made of it after it was won. Efforts to raise the living standards of the common people were rare, efforts at self-aggrandizement commonplace.[112] In many of these societies, government offices were bought and sold like pieces of property, which purchasers used to obtain the greatest possible profit. Officeholders demanded payment before they would act on any request, and justice was typically sold to the highest bidder. No wonder the common people of China developed the saying "To enter a court of justice is to enter a tiger's mouth."[113]

These practices reflected what is known as *the proprietary theory of the state*, which defines the state as a piece of property that its owners may use, within broad and ill-defined limits, for their personal advantage.[114] Guided by this theory, agrarian rulers and governing classes saw nothing immoral in the use of what we (not they) would call "public office" for private gain. To them, it was simply the legitimate use of what they commonly regarded as their "patrimony." It is said of the Ptolemies of Egypt, for example, that they showed the first emperors of Rome "how a country might be run on the lines of a profitable estate."[115] In the case of medieval Europe, we read:

FIGURE 7.15 One use of the economic surplus in an agrarian society: the Taj Mahal, a tomb erected by the Mogul emperor Shah Jahan in memory of his favorite wife.

The proprietary conception of rulership created an inextricable confusion of public and private affairs. Rights of government were a form of private ownership. "Crown lands" and "the king's estate" were synonymous. There was no differentiation between the king in his private and public capacities. A kingdom, like any estate endowed with elements of governmental authority, was the private concern of its owner. Since *"state" and "estate" were identical,* "the State" was indistinguishable from the prince and his personal "patrimony."[116]

The proprietary theory of the state can be traced back to horticultural societies and, in a sense, even to hunting and gathering bands. In those simpler societies, no distinction was made between the private and public aspects of political leadership. When a surplus first began to be produced, at least part of it was turned over to the leader, who held it as trustee for the group. As long as the surplus was small and in the form of perishable commodities, there was little the leader could do with it except redistribute it, thereby winning status for his generosity. Eventually, however, as we saw in Chapter 6, it grew large enough to permit him to create a staff of dependent retainers who could be used to enforce his wishes. At this point, the proprietary theory of the state was born. Later rulers merely applied it on an ever-expanding scale, as productivity and the economic surplus steadily increased.

Recent research provides a good picture of the extremes to which rulers and governing classes have carried the proprietary principle. In late nineteenth-century

China, for example, the average income for families not in the governing class was approximately 20 to 25 taels per year. By contrast, the governing class averaged 450 taels per year, with some receiving as much as 200,000.[117] The emperor's income, of course, was considerably larger even than this. To cite another example, the English nobility at the end of the twelfth century and early in the thirteenth had an average income roughly 200 times that of ordinary field hands, and the king's equaled that of 24,000 field hands.[118] Putting together the evidence from many sources, it appears that the combined income of the ruler and the governing class in most advanced agrarian societies equaled *not less than half of the total national income*, even though they numbered 2 percent or less of the population.[119]

Despite their many similarities, the polities of advanced agrarian societies varied in a number of ways, the most important being the *degree of political centralization*. In some societies the central government was very strong; in others its powers were severely limited. In the main, these differences reflected the current state of the perennial struggle between the ruler and the other members of the governing class. The king or emperor naturally wanted the greatest possible control over his subordinates, and the subordinates just as naturally wanted to minimize his control. Since land (including the peasants who worked it) and political office were the most valuable resources in agrarian systems of stratification, most of the struggles between rulers and the governing class were over them. In a few instances, very powerful rulers gained such great control over these resources that both land and political offices were held solely at their pleasure and were subject to instant confiscation if an individual's services were judged unsatisfactory.[120] A Dutch traveler of the early seventeenth century left a vivid picture of the situation in the Mogul empire in India:

> Immediately on the death of a lord who has enjoyed the King's [favor], be he great or small, without any exception—sometimes even before the breath is out of the body—the King's officers are ready on the spot and make an inventory of the entire estate, recording everything down to the value of a single piece, even to the dresses and jewels of the ladies, provided they have not concealed them. The King takes back the whole estate absolutely for himself, except in a case where the deceased has done good service in his lifetime, when the women and children are given enough to live on, but no more.[121]

In Turkey, under Suleiman, the chief officers of state were specially trained slaves over whom the sultan held life-and-death power.[122]

At the other extreme, during much of the medieval period in Europe, the governing classes were very independent. Though their lands were typically royal grants given in exchange for pledges of service, their monarchs usually lacked the power to enforce these pledges.[123] Although examples of both extremes can be found, the usual pattern was something in between, and in most cases the powers of the ruler and the governing class were fairly evenly balanced.

Religion: The Emergence of Universal Faiths

During the era in which advanced agrarian societies were dominant, there were a number of important developments in the religious sphere. The most important by far was the emergence and spread of three new religions, Buddhism, Christianity, and

FIGURE 7.16 Working equipment for member of the governing class in sixteenth-century Europe.

Islam. Each proclaimed a *supranational or universal faith,* and each succeeded in creating a community of believers that transcended societal boundaries. In the older religions, people's beliefs and loyalties were determined by the accident of birth. Where one lived determined the god or gods one worshiped, for the prevailing view was that there were many gods and that, like kings, each had his own people and territory.

The ancient Israelites were some of the first to reject this view and move toward a more universalistic outlook. Centuries before the birth of Christ, the prophets proclaimed that there was only one God and that He ruled over the entire world. For

FIGURE 7.17 Islam is one of the universal faiths that emerged in the agrarian era: interior of mosque in Baghdad, Iraq.

a time, Judaism was a missionary religion and won converts in many parts of the Roman world.[124] This phase ended, however, when the early Christian missionaries won most of these Gentile converts to their faith. From then on, implementation of the universalistic vision became the mission of Christians and Muslims, who eventually converted, at least nominally, most of the population of Europe, North Africa, and the Middle East, and some of the people of India, Central Asia, China, and Southeast Asia.

Buddhism, the other great universal faith, began in India as a heretical offshoot of Hinduism and spread through most of Southeast Asia, China, Korea, and Japan, though it later died out in the land of its origin. The older ethnic faiths, such as Hinduism, Confucianism, and Shintoism, still survived in much of Asia, but even they now incorporated some elements of universalism in their thought.

The emergence and spread of universal faiths reflected the broader social and intellectual horizons that came with improved transportation and the spreading web of trade relations. Empire building, by bringing diverse populations under a single government, also helped to weaken parochial or "tribal" views. As people's knowledge of other societies increased, and with it their awareness of the essential unity of all humanity, the basic postulate of the older ethnic faiths (i.e., the belief in tribal deities) was gradually undermined.

Another important development was the growing separation of religious and

FIGURE 7.18 This eighteenth-century French
cartoon attacked the clergy and nobility for "riding
on the back" of the peasantry.

political institutions.[125] Compared with the situation in advanced horticultural and
simple agrarian societies, the governments of advanced agrarian societies were
much more secular. Kings and emperors were, it is true, still said to rule "by the
grace of God"; the divine right of kings was still generally accepted; and occasionally a ruler even claimed to be a god. But few rulers functioned as high priests, and
theocracies (i.e., states in which a priesthood rules in the name of a god) were almost
unknown. This separation of church and state was part of the more general trend
toward institutional specialization that has been so basic in the evolutionary process
from the horticultural era on.

Despite the growing organizational separation of politics and religion, leaders of
the two systems continued to work closely together. This was especially evident in
struggles between the governing class and the common people. When rebellious
voices challenged the right of the governing class to control the economic surplus
produced by the peasants, the clergy usually defended the elite, asserting that their
power had been given them by God and any challenge to it was a challenge to His
authority.[126] By legitimizing the actions of the governing class in this way, the clergy
reduced the need for costly coercive measures.

In appreciation for this, and also because of their own religious beliefs, agrarian rulers were often extremely generous with religious groups, giving them large grants of land and special tax exemptions. In effect, a symbiotic relationship was established, with a religious organization legitimizing the actions of the governing class in return for generous financial support. Modern research indicates that religious groups frequently owned as much as a quarter or a third of a nation's land.[127]

Despite such profitable alliances, most religions of the agrarian era fostered some concern for distributive justice. This is especially evident in Judaism and Christianity.[128] One historian captured the contradictory nature of medieval Christianity in this discerning characterization: "Democratic, yet aristocratic; charitable, yet exploitative; generous, yet mercenary; humanitarian, yet cruel; indulgent, yet severely repressive of some things; progressive, yet reactionary; radical, yet conservative—all these are qualities of the Church in the Middle Ages."[129]

Magic and Fatalism   Two other aspects of the beliefs of agrarian societies deserve comment: (1) the widespread belief in magic and (2) the equally widespread attitude of fatalism.[130] Logically, these are contradictory. If magic really works, people do not need to be fatalistic, and if they are true fatalists, they should have no confidence in magic. But people are not always logical: in their more optimistic moments they are inclined to hope for things they know are impossible. Considering the tremendous pressures operating on the common people in agrarian societies, and their limited sources of information, it is hardly surprising that many of them held these mutually contradictory views.

Fatalism and belief in magic both contributed to the slowdown in the rate of technological advance in agrarian societies. One encouraged people to look to supernatural forces for the answers to problems; the other convinced them that control was out of their hands. Neither attitude motivated people to strive to build better tools or devise better techniques for satisfying their needs.

Kinship: Declining Importance in Society

For individuals, kinship ties remained of great importance throughout the agrarian era. For societies, however, they ceased to be the chief integrating force. In most horticultural societies, the largest and most powerful clan in a society, aided perhaps by dependent retainers, could still provide enough people to staff the important political offices. But by the level of advanced agrarian societies, this was no longer possible. Civil and military offices were so numerous that not even the largest of extended families could fill them all.

The fact that kinship ties were no longer the chief integrating force in societies did not mean, however, that they were no longer politically significant. The royal office itself was inherited in most societies, as were numerous other political offices. Many of these, civil and military offices alike, were a family's patrimony, handed down, like any other family possession, from father to son (or, sometimes, daughter). Offices that were not actually owned might still be closed to anyone who was not a member of the nobility or who did not qualify as coming from one of the "right families."

Even in the allocation of offices to which such restrictions did not apply, families continued to play an important role. Family funds might be used to purchase an office, for example. And those who had it in their power to assign an office were naturally influenced by their own family's interests. Although nepotism still occurs in modern industrial societies, it is usually a violation of the law and lacks public approval. But in advanced agrarian societies, it was an accepted part of life, and there was little criticism, and still less punishment, of those who practiced it.

During the agrarian era, the family remained very important in the economic sphere as well. It was usually *the basic unit of economic organization.* Businesses were almost always family enterprises; the corporate form of enterprise, owned jointly by unrelated persons, was virtually unheard of, even in the largest cities. And in rural areas the peasant family was the basic work unit.

The family's economic significance can be demonstrated in many ways. For instance, because of its economic implications, marriage was considered much too important to be decided by young people; even among the peasantry, marriages were usually arranged by parents, often with the aid of marriage brokers.[131] Sometimes the young couple did not even meet until the ceremony itself. In selecting spouses for their children, parents were primarily concerned with the economic and status implications of the match and only secondarily with other matters. Marriage arrangements often involved an outright economic transaction. The husband would pay the parents for the bride, or her parents would provide her with a dowry.[132]

As one would suppose, marriages contracted in this way did not necessarily produce sexual or psychological compatibility between the spouses, but this was not seen as the primary purpose of marriage. Ties between man and wife usually endured because of the value that was placed on the relationship by society, and because the economic arrangement was usually of critical importance to the individuals involved. Within families thus established, male dominance was the rule, for obedience was generally held to be one of the prime virtues in women and children.[133] In this, the family simply reflected the general authoritarian pattern of life in agrarian societies.

Leisure and the Arts

Although the life of the peasant was hard, even harsh, there were occasional opportunities for leisure and recreation.[134] Weddings and religious festivals, for example, were important occasions for people to get together for a good time. Singing and dancing were the basic entertainment at such festivities, and, in most societies, alcoholic beverages added to the merriment. People also amused themselves with games and contests, courtship and lovemaking, gossiping and storytelling, and a host of other activities.

Class distinctions were evident in leisure activity as in any other, with falconry, jousting, and chess among the activities favored by the governing class. But some forms of entertainment, such as archery and dice, had a universal appeal. Gambling in particular was popular with every class.

The rise of professional entertainers was part of the general trend toward occupational specialization. Actors, minstrels, jesters, clowns, acrobats, jugglers, and geishas are some of the more familiar. In general, the status of such people was

FIGURE 7.19 Recreation was frequently brutal and violent in agrarian societies, and the Romans were probably unsurpassed. In their so-called games, tens of thousands came to watch wild animals devour helpless victims, and armed gladiators maim and kill one another.

extremely low, probably because of their economic insecurity and their excessive dependence on the favor of others. Yet entertainers who had a powerful patron might find their work quite lucrative.

Recreation was frequently raucous and crude. It could also be brutal and violent, and in this the Romans were probably unsurpassed. In their so-called games, first in the Circus Maximus, later in the Colosseum, tens of thousands came to watch wild animals devour helpless victims, and armed gladiators maim and kill one another. When the Colosseum was first opened in 80 A.D., the Emperor Titus promised the people of Rome 100 consecutive days of such games, with fights to the death between more than 10,000 prisoners and 5,000 wild animals (including lions, tigers, and elephants), and a naval battle between 3,000 men in an arena especially flooded for the occasion.[135]

In agrarian Europe, cockfights and dogfights were very popular, and public hangings often drew large and exuberant crowds. Wedding parties and other festivities frequently ended in drunken brawls. In fact, violence typically followed drinking. From what we know of life in agrarian societies, it would appear that alcohol simply removed a fragile overlay of inhibitions, revealing people's frustrations and bitterness.

But if the agrarian world at play was often unattractive, its artistic accomplishments were quite the opposite. In their sculpture, their painting, and their architecture, these societies left monuments of lasting beauty. Thousands of cathedrals, churches, mosques, pagodas, temples, and palaces, and the treasures within them, testify to an impressive development of the arts during that era. Achievements in literature were probably no less impressive, though language barriers make it diffi-cult for us to appreciate them as fully.* Developments in music during most of the agrarian era seem to have been less spectacular than in the other arts. Toward the end of the era, however, the invention of new instruments and the genius of composers like Bach, Handel, Mozart, and Beethoven combined to produce an outburst of magnificent music that has transcended societal boundaries in unprece-dented fashion.

Most artists were subsidized by the governing class or by the religious elite, drawing on the economic surplus extracted from the peasant masses. Thus, the artistic achievements of agrarian societies were a product of the harshly exploitative social system. Yet, if the peasants had been allowed to keep the surplus, the result would simply have been more poor people. Again, as with horticultural societies, this link between an exploitative class system and impressive cultural achievements reminds us of the difficulty we face in passing ethical judgments on complex sociocultural systems.

Stratification: Increasing Complexity

The basic cleavages in advanced agrarian societies were much the same as they had been in simple agrarian societies, and, as a consequence, so were the basic patterns of inequality. The principal division in society was still the one between the govern-ing class and the great mass of peasants and other people of low status over which it exercised control both politically and economically. But the system of stratification had altered in one respect from that of simpler societal types: it had become more complex.

This growing complexity can be seen in two areas. First, in advanced agrarian societies there were more people in occupations whose status fell somewhere between the extremes. These people were either directly employed by the governing class (e.g., household servants, stewards, men-at-arms) or served them indirectly (e.g., merchants, artisans).

Second, advanced agrarian societies experienced a growing overlap in the status of different categories of people, especially in terms of wealth and property. Some merchants, for example, now had more wealth than some members of the governing class, and a tiny minority of peasants, by luck and hard work, actually amassed greater wealth than some impoverished members of the nobility. Although members of the governing class still had greater wealth, *on average*, than merchants or any other group, this was no longer true of every member of the class. Similarly, although merchants were, *on average*, wealthier than peasants, there were excep-tions.

Figure 7.20 depicts the status system of advanced agrarian societies. The ruler was invariably the most powerful, prestigious, and wealthy individual in society: he was, in fact, literally in a class by himself. For example, the English kings Richard I and John, who ruled in the last decade of the twelfth century and the first decade of

---

*Robert Frost once said that "poetry is what gets lost in translation," and anyone who has ever seriously tried to translate a poem understands the complexity of the language problem.

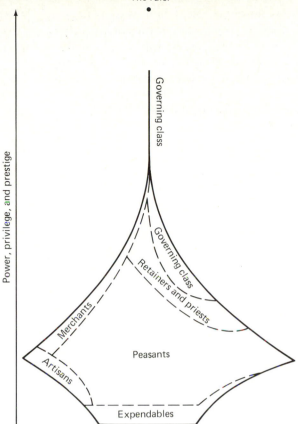

The ruler

Power, privilege, and prestige

Governing class

Governing class

Retainers and priests

Merchants

Artisans

Peasants

Expendables

FIGURE 7.20   **Model of the class structure of advanced agrarian societies.**

the thirteenth, had incomes thirty times that of the wealthiest nobleman of the day.[136] By the reign of Richard II, at the end of the fourteenth century, the king's income had risen to forty times that of the wealthiest member of the governing class. In late fifteenth- and early sixteenth-century Spain, the king was reputed to enjoy one-third of all the revenues of the land (meaning, apparently, one-third of the economic surplus). Similar patterns are reported in virtually every advanced agrarian society.

At the opposite extreme in the system of stratification was a wretched class of individuals for whose labor the society had no need. These were mostly peasant sons and daughters who were unable to inherit land or to marry anyone who did, and thus were forced out on their own in a society that suffered a chronic labor surplus. As we have seen, these individuals could usually eke out a living while they were young and healthy, but most of them soon joined the ranks of the expendables and died at an early age.[137]

On the whole, the class divisions within advanced agrarian societies were more serious than those within simple agrarian societies. In particular, they were more likely to lead to violence. Earlier, we noted the frequency of peasant risings. Though most of these were local incidents involving small numbers of people, some spread to become large-scale insurrections. In either case, they were something new in history and foreshadowed revolutions to come. Nor was it only the peasants who revolted against the governing class. The artisans followed suit on a number of occasions, as did the merchants,[138] and these groups, unlike the peasants, sometimes emerged victorious. In Europe, the merchants were so successful in their challenges to the governing class that eventually *they* became the governing class in many cities and towns. From an evolutionary perspective, this proved to be a very important development indeed, as we will see.

Variations on Agrarian Themes

In surveying societies at the same level of development, it is natural to emphasize those characteristics which are found in all or most of them, and to slight the differences. This may give an impression of greater uniformity than really exists. Obviously there were variations in every area of life in advanced agrarian societies, and we have noted many of them, or at least hinted at them in qualifying phrases, saying that a particular pattern was found in "most" or "many" of these societies.

To begin with, advanced agrarian societies varied technologically. The first to emerge resembled their simple agrarian predecessors more than they resembled the advanced agrarian societies of Europe on the eve of the Industrial Revolution. Furthermore, the size of advanced agrarian societies ranged all the way from tiny principalities to giant empires. Most were monarchies, but a few were republics. Some were governed by enormously powerful autocratic rulers; in others, power was diffused more widely among members of the governing class. Similar variations occurred in almost every area of life.

Clearly, then, there has been variation among societies at the advanced agrarian level—indeed, at *every* level of societal development. There is, however, one important difference. In the less advanced societal types (i.e., hunting and gathering, fishing, and simple horticultural), intratype variation results primarily from differences in the *biophysical environment*. We see this clearly when we compare the Eskimo with the Australian aborigines, or the Bushmen of the Kalahari Desert with the Pygmies of the rain forest. In advanced agrarian societies, on the other hand, differences in the biophysical environment have not been as important a cause of intratype variation. This is exactly what ecological-evolutionary theory would lead us to expect, since the further a society advances on the evolutionary scale, the greater is its ability to overcome the limitations imposed by the biotic and physical world and the more likely it is, because of geographical expansion, to include within its borders a variety of environments, thus making its own environment less distinctive.

In studying advanced agrarian societies, historians have often focused attention on religion as the chief source of the differences among them. Thus, they have contrasted Christian societies with Islamic societies, for example, or Buddhist societies with Hindu societies.

There is, of course, no doubt that each of these religions was responsible for social and cultural variations among advanced agrarian societies. Christianity and Islam, like Judaism, had a special day of worship and rest each week, while the

Oriential religions did not. Most of the religions encouraged monasticism, but Protestantism and Islam did not. Islam sanctioned the practice of polygyny, which Christianity forbade; Confucianism encouraged ancestor worship; Buddhism encouraged all families to send their sons to live in monasteries for a year or two before assuming adult responsibilities; and Hinduism had a hereditary priestly caste. Theologically, there were tremendous differences among the various religions, and members of advanced agrarian societies often fought and died in order to extend or defend their faith.

Without denying the importance of these and other religious influences, we cannot fail to note that no faith was able to break the "agrarian mold" that shaped the basic patterns of life in these societies. For regardless of its dominant religion, every advanced agrarian society was much like the rest with respect to its fundamental characteristics. Class structure, social inequality, the division of labor, the distinctive role of urban populations in the larger society, the cleavage between urban and rural subcultures, the disdain of the governing class for both work and workers, the widespread belief in magic and fatalism, the use of the economic surplus for the benefit of the governing class and for the construction of monumental edifices, high birth and death rates—all these patterns and more were much the same in all advanced agrarian societies.

The greatest variations among advanced agrarian societies stemmed not from ideological differences, but from differences in their *social environments*. The latter involved both proximity to trade routes and the influence of frontier territories.

From the standpoint of trade, the most advantageous location for a society was at the point where several trade routes intersected.[139] Having such a location ensured continuing contact with a large number of other societies and increased opportunities for acquiring useful information through diffusion. It also provided a valuable source of income and fostered economic growth and development. Societies that were not so well situated were handicapped and tended to be less developed, unless some compensating factor offset this handicap. Because of the importance of trade routes, societies in the Middle East, where routes from Europe, Asia, and Africa converged, remained at the forefront of social and cultural development for most of the agrarian era. Toward the end, however, when trade with the New World became important, the advantage shifted to western European societies.

A different kind of variation, *the frontier society*, developed when an agrarian society expanded into territories that were either uninhabited or inhabited by pre-agrarian societies. The first known instance of this occurred when the nation of Israel was established in the previously uninhabited hill country of Palestine in the thirteenth century B.C.[140] More recently, this process was repeated in the settlement of North and South America by migrants from various European societies, in the British settlement of Australia and New Zealand, in the Norwegian-Irish settlement of Iceland, in the Dutch (or Boer) settlement of South Africa, and in the Cossack settlement of the Russian steppes.[141] In each instance, the social environment of the frontier consisted of small, technologically less advanced societies that could not adequately defend their territories. As a consequence, substantial amounts of land became available to low-status members of agrarian societies who were willing to risk their lives and endure the hardships of frontier life.

Frontier societies are of special interest to ecological-evolutionary theorists because they show the extent to which the agrarian way of life was shaped by an oversupply of labor and an undersupply of land. When these conditions were eliminated even temporarily, as they were in frontier regions, many deviations from the usual patterns of agrarian life developed.

To begin with, the settlers themselves tended to be the poor, the dispossessed, the noninheriting sons and daughters, troublemakers, misfits, and even criminals deported by the parent society. Frontier regions held little attraction for the rich and powerful, who preferred to remain close to the traditional centers of power and influence. Thus, in frontier regions established authority was usually weak or absent, and because societal life was not under the control of the governing class, traditional agrarian patterns tended to break down and new patterns of life emerged.[142]

One of the most significant changes that occurred was the breakdown of the traditional class system. Except where the native population was enslaved or enserfed (as in much of Latin America) or where slaves were imported (as occurred in the Caribbean and the southern United States) a highly egalitarian system of family farms and ranches was likely to develop. This is what happened in Canada, the United States outside the southern region, Australia, New Zealand, and South Africa. In such areas there was a serious shortage of labor; workers were much more valuable than they were in the older, settled areas, where there was usually a surplus of labor. On the frontier, there were neither enough farmers to cultivate the newly opened land nor enough fighters to defend it. It is not surprising, then, that frontier life generated a striking independence of spirit and a stubborn resistance to authority. Having risked their lives to establish themselves in a new land, frontiersmen were not prepared to hand over their surplus to anyone. Thus, frontier conditions usually broke down the sharp inequalities and exploitative patterns that characterized all traditional agrarian societies.

This condition was usually temporary, however. As the resistance of the native population came to an end and the population of settlers grew in number and density, as roads were built and governmental authority was established, there was a waning of the spirit of independence and individualism and the traditional system began to assert itself. To be sure, this did not happen overnight. On the contrary, it usually took a century or more. But in the end, the typical agrarian pattern prevailed.

Only one thing ever prevented this from happening—the onset of industrialization. In a number of instances during the last century and a half, the Industrial Revolution generated a new demand for labor before the frontier was fully absorbed into the old system. This happened in the United States in the nineteenth century, and then in Canada, Australia, and New Zealand. These societies were thus spared the agony of slowly sliding into the classic agrarian pattern in which a massive, impoverished peasantry is dominated and exploited by a small, hereditary aristocracy.

In the United States, this process had actually gotten well under way in much of the South with its system of slavery. But the Confederacy's defeat in the Civil War and the South's eventual industrialization halted the restoration of the old agrarian system. In other parts of the country, the process had barely begun before the forces of industrialization intervened.

Looking back, it seems clear that the frontier experience was excellent preparation for the Industrial Revolution. Above all, it established a tradition of innovation and a receptivity to change that were lacking in other agrarian societies. Also, by creating a more egalitarian class system, the frontier prepared the way for the more open and fluid class systems of modern industrial societies. These developments help explain the relative ease with which the overseas English-speaking democracies (i.e., the United States, Australia, Canada, and New Zealand) made the transition to the industrial era, and why they have so long been in the forefront with respect to productivity, standard of living, and political stability. It is interesting to speculate on what the situation in these societies might be today if they had been settled a thousand years sooner and a more typical agrarian social system had had time to take root.

Agrarian Societies in Theoretical Perspective

The most basic effect of the shift from horticulture to agriculture, as we saw at the beginning of this chapter, was the increase in food production. Societies that adopted the plow were able to produce substantially more food in a given territory than those that relied on the hoe and the digging stick.

This increase in productivity could be used, as Figure 7.21 indicates, either to expand the economic surplus of the society or to expand its population. Actually, the historical record shows that in most agrarian societies *both* of these things happened. The expansion of the economic surplus was more significant than population growth, however, since it was prerequisite for so many social and cultural changes. Figure 7.21 makes no attempt to portray all of these changes, or all of their

FIGURE 7.21 **Model of the effects of the shift from horticulture to agriculture.**

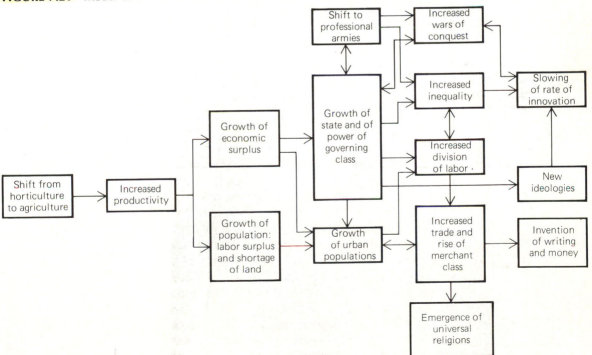

interrelationships, since that would require an impossibly complex diagram. Instead, the figure focuses only on the most critical developments.

The single most important consequence of the greater economic surplus was further *growth in the state and the power of the governing class* that controlled it. This contributed, directly or indirectly, to most of the other important social and cultural changes of the agrarian era. It lay behind the shift from militias to professional armies, the increase in wars of conquest, the growth of inequality and of the division of labor, the expansion of urban populations, the growth of trade and the rise of the merchant class, the invention of writing and of money, and the emergence of the new universal religions. And finally, it was responsible for the lagging rate of technological innovation.

Many of the changes in agrarian societies were essentially a continuation of trends that began in horticultural societies. But the shift to agriculture magnified those trends dramatically. To cite a single example, the largest societies ever constructed on a horticultural foundation appear to have been the Incan empire in the years immediately preceding the Spanish conquest of Peru, and Songhay, a west African empire of the sixteenth century. Both of these, at the peak of their power, had populations of several million.[143] In contrast, mid-nineteenth-century China, before it began to industrialize, had a population of approximately 400 million, and the Roman and Russian empires each had at least 70 million.[144]

As great as they are, these differences in population size are probably no greater in degree than differences in many other basic features of these two types of societies. Their numbers, in other words, are but a reflection of the vastly different potentials inherent in the subsistence technologies on which horticultural societies and agrarian societies were built.

CHAPTER 8

Some Evolutionary Bypaths and a Brief Review

Specialized Societal Types

Up to this point in our survey of human societies, we have concentrated on those types which have been in the mainstream of evolutionary history, those which developed their technologies around the resources of fields and forests. The types of societies to which we now turn have adapted to *less typical environments*—two to aquatic environments, the third to semidesert grasslands and other arid environments. Though these specialized societies have contributed to sociocultural evolution in many important ways, their contributions have been more limited than those of the mainstream societies. This is because of the specialized nature of the problems with which they have dealt in their subsistence activities. For these reasons, we will not examine them in the same detail as the others.

Fishing Societies

It is something of a misnomer to call any group a "fishing" society, for none ever depended exclusively on fishing for its food supply.[1] Except in the Arctic, nearly all fishing peoples obtain fruits and vegetables by foraging or cultivation. Many of them

FIGURE 8.1   African fishing village, Benin.

also supplement their diet by hunting, and occasionally by raising livestock. To call a society a fishing society, then, merely indicates that fishing is its most important subsistence activity.

In recent centuries, fishing societies have been found in many parts of the world, but the majority have been in the northwestern part of North America—Oregon, Washington, British Columbia, Alaska, and the arctic regions of Canada. There have also been some in northeastern Asia, among the islands of the Pacific (though most of the Pacific peoples have been simple horticulturalists), in scattered parts of Africa and South America, and elsewhere.

Historically, fishing societies are probably the second oldest type, emerging about a thousand years before the first horticultural societies. The actual practice of fishing is, of course, even older and more widespread and has provided a supplementary source of subsistence in many societies for at least 12,000 years.

In some ways fishing societies might be regarded as hunting and gathering societies that have adapted to aquatic environments rather than terrestrial. One might argue that the chief difference is simply that fish, rather than land animals, are the object of the chase and that the technology of the group is modified accordingly. But there is a reason why fishing societies must be considered a separate societal type: a fishing economy has the potential for supporting a larger, more sedentary population than a hunting and gathering economy.

This is a consequence of the fact that primitive fishing peoples are much less

210

likely to deplete the food resources of their environment than are hunters and gatherers. For one thing, fish have much higher reproductive rates than most land animals. In addition, most fishing peoples work only a small part of their food-gathering territory. Even if they catch all the fish in their immediate area, the supply is quickly replenished by the great surplus spawned in adjacent areas. This could not happen with land animals, at least not after hunting and gathering bands became numerous and occupied most of the habitable territory.

Thus, although fishing societies are only a bit more advanced technologically than hunting and gathering societies, we would expect them to be somewhat larger, more sedentary, and more complex.[2] This is, in fact, precisely what we find. With respect to size, they are half again as large: Murdock's data set shows that the average size of fishing communities is approximately 60, the average size of hunting and gathering groups only 40.[3] With respect to settlement patterns, only 10 percent of the hunting and gathering societies live in permanent settlements, compared to 49 percent of the fishing societies.

Their political systems also indicate the greater potential inherent in a fishing economy. Less than 10 percent of hunting and gathering societies have two or more communities, in contrast to nearly a quarter of fishing societies. Social inequality, too, is both more common and more pronounced. A system of hereditary nobility is found in 32 percent of fishing societies and in only 2 percent of hunting and gathering societies. And slavery occurs in slightly over 50 percent of fishing societies, but in only 10 percent of hunting and gathering. Finally, as another indication of their greater economic development and wealth, fishing peoples are much more likely to link marriage with some economic transaction. This happens in 77 percent of these groups but in only 48 percent of hunting and gathering societies.

In terms of structural development, fishing societies have about as much in common with simple horticultural societies as with hunting and gathering societies.[4] Depending on the criterion, they sometimes resemble one, sometimes the other. For example, in community size they more closely approximate hunting and gathering societies,[5] while in frequency of multicommunity societies they are almost indistinguishable from simple horticultural.[6] In permanence of settlements, they are midway between hunting and gathering and simple horticultural.[7]

Unlike hunting and gathering societies, fishing societies seldom evolved into a more advanced type.* The reasons for this are quite simple. To begin with, territories suited to a predominantly fishing economy are not only limited, they are strung out along thin coastal strips, so that it has been virtually impossible to consolidate several groups into one large, defensible, political entity.[8] Instead, when neighboring horticultural societies became powerful enough, fishing societies were usually conquered and absorbed. Then, even though fishing continued in the area, it became only a minor part of the economy of the larger society, and the leaders of the fishing groups were reduced to the status of minor officials, too weak to hold on to the local surplus. As a result, fishing communities in *agrarian* societies have often been socially and culturally less advanced (except in subsistence technology) than

---

*It is possible that some evolved directly into maritime societies, but there is no real evidence of this. Maritime societies seem, instead, usually to have evolved out of advanced horticultural or agrarian societies.

FIGURE 8.2 The Shui-jen, or water people, of southern China are descended from fishing peoples of an earlier time. They still depend on fishing for their livelihood and remain largely separate from the mainland population.

fishing communities in more primitive *fishing* societies. Typically, their situation was no better than that of peasant villages, and for the same reason—their surplus was confiscated by more powerful elements in the society.[9]

Herding Societies

Herding societies, like fishing societies, represent an adaptation to specialized environmental conditions. Other than that, the two have little in common. Their environments are radically different, and the technology of herding societies is usually more advanced.

Herding societies cover the same range of technological development as horticultural and simple agrarian societies. Animals were first domesticated about the same time plants were first cultivated, and the two practices typically went hand in hand in the horticultural and agrarian societies of the Old World.* In some areas, however, crops could not be cultivated because of insufficient rainfall, too short a

---

*This was not true in most of the New World, where there were almost no large animals suitable for domestication.

growing season (in northern latitudes), or mountainous terrain. This was true of much of central Asia, the Arabian peninsula, and North Africa, and also parts of Europe and sub-Saharan Africa. Because it was possible to raise livestock in many of these areas, however, a new and different type of society emerged.*

A pastoral economy usually necessitates a nomadic or seminomadic way of life.[10] In fact, "nomad" comes from an early Greek word meaning a "herder of cattle."[11] In the sample of herding societies in Murdock's data set, more than 90 percent are wholly or partially nomadic. In this respect they closely resemble hunters and gatherers.

Herders are also like hunters and gatherers in the size of their communities. On average, their communities are a bit smaller than fishing communities and much smaller than simple horticultural, as the following figures show:

Hunting and gathering communities	40
Herding communities	55
Fishing communities	60
Simple horticultural communities	95

The explanation for this is primarily environmental. Given the sparse resources of their territories, large and dense settlements are impossible.[12]

Despite the small size of their communities, herding *societies* are usually fairly large. Whereas the typical hunting and gathering, fishing, or simple horticultural society contains only a single community, the average herding society contains several dozen.[13] Thus, the median population of herding societies far surpasses those of the other three types:

Hunting and gathering societies	40
Fishing societies	60
Simple horticultural societies	95
Herding societies	2,000

The size of herding societies results from the combined influence of environment and technology. Open grasslands, where the majority of herders live, present few natural barriers to movement and, therefore, to political expansion. Furthermore, since early in the second millennium B.C., many of the herding peoples have ridden horses or camels, which greatly facilitated military conquest and political expansion.

The basic resource in these societies is livestock, and the size of the herd is the measure of a man. Large herds signify not only wealth but power, for only a strong man or the head of a strong family can defend such vulnerable property against rivals and enemies. Thus, in most of these societies, and especially in the more advanced (i.e., those with horses or camels and herds of larger animals such as cattle), marked social inequality is the rule. Hereditary slavery, for example, is far more common in herding societies than in any other type.[14] Other kinds of inequality are also very common, especially inequality in terms of wealth.[15]

---

*Most of these societies have also had some secondary means of subsistence, frequently horticulture or agriculture on a small scale.

FIGURE 8.3 Herding societies have adapted to environments where crop cultivation is not possible. Bedouin shepherd with his flock, near Jericho.

With respect to kinship, herding societies are noteworthy on at least two counts. First, they are more likely than any other type of society to require the payment of a bride price or bride service.[16] Second, they are the most likely to require newly married couples to live with the husband's kinsmen.[17]

These strong patriarchal tendencies have several sources. To begin with, they reflect the mobile and often militant nature of pastoral life. Raiding and warfare are frequent activities, and as we have noted before, these activities stimulate the growth of political authority. Moreover, the basic economic activity in these societies is men's work. In this respect they stand in sharp contrast to horticultural societies, where women often play the dominant role in subsistence activities. It is hardly coincidence that horticultural societies are noted for their frequent female-oriented kinship patterns, herding societies for the opposite.

Herding societies are extremely interesting from the religious standpoint. Their concept of God corresponds to the Jewish and Christian concept more often than that of any other societal type. In forty of the fifty herding groups for which Murdock provides data, there is belief in a supreme Deity who created the world and remains actively concerned with its affairs, especially with the moral conduct of humans. This combination of beliefs is rare in other kinds of societies, except agrarian, where it occurs in two-thirds of the cases.[18] But even there, as Table 8.1 indicates, its occurrence varies directly with the importance of herding activities within the society.

For those familiar with religious history, this relationship is not surprising. Herding was an important secondary activity in the life of the early Hebrews, who played such a critical role in the rise and spread of monotheism. And Islam, the most uncompromisingly monotheistic of faiths, enjoyed its earliest successes among the herding peoples of the Arabian peninsula.

TABLE 8.1 Religious Beliefs of Agrarian Societies, by Percentage of Subsistence Derived from Herding

Percentage of Subsistence from Herding	Percentage Believing in Active, Moral Creator God	Number of Societies
36–45	92	13
26–35	82	28
16–25	40	20
6–15	20	5

Source: See note 15, page 440.

Why this relationship developed is far from clear, but the relation itself is undeniable. One can find repeated evidence of the affinity between the pastoral way of life and these religious concepts in biblical texts that describe God as a shepherd and his people as sheep (e.g., Psalm 23). The shepherd's simultaneous awareness of his flock's dependence on him and of humanity's dependence on forces beyond its control may have suggested answers to the perennial questions about the nature and destiny of humans, and the power that ultimately controls them. Such answers have not been obvious to all herding peoples, however; a number of pastoral groups in Asia and Africa have come up with very different ones. The most we can safely say is that pastoral life seems to increase the probability that a society will develop or adopt this kind of explanation.

One of the most important technological advances made by herding peoples was the utilization of horses, and later camels, for transportation. This practice originated in the eighteenth century B.C., when certain herding groups in the Middle East began harnessing horses to chariots.[19] This gave them an important military advantage over their less mobile agrarian neighbors and enabled them to win control of much of the Middle East—at least until the new technology was adopted by the more numerous agrarian peoples. Herders later learned to *ride* their horses, which led to a new wave of conquests, beginning in the ninth century B.C.[20]

During the next 2,500 years, a succession of herding groups attacked agrarian societies from China to Europe, and frequently conquered them. The empires and dynasties they established include some of the largest and most famous in history— the great Mongol empire, for example, founded by Genghis Khan early in the thirteenth century A.D. and expanded by his successors. At the peak of its power, the Mongol empire stretched from eastern Europe to the shores of the Pacific and launched attacks in places as distant as Austria and Japan. Other famous empires and dynasties founded by herding peoples include the Mogul empire, established in India by a branch of the Mongols, the Manchu dynasty in China, the Ottoman empire in the Middle East, and the early Islamic states established by followers of the prophet Muhammad.

Despite their frequent military victories, herding peoples were never able to destroy the agrarian social order. In the end, it was always they, not the agrarian peoples, who changed their mode of life. There were a number of reasons for this, but it was primarily because the economic surplus that could be produced by

agricultural activities was so much greater than what could be produced by convert-
ing the land to herding activities. After a few early conquerors tried to turn fields into
pastures, they realized they were, in effect, killing the goose that laid the golden
eggs, and abandoned their preferred way of life for economic reasons. Thus, despite
many impressive military victories, the limits of the herding world were not permanently enlarged.

Although herding continued to be an important secondary source of subsistence
in the agrarian world, it was the primary source only in areas not suited to plant
cultivation. In recent centuries, even these areas have, in most cases, been brought
under the control of agrarian or industrial societies, and herding societies, like other
preindustrial types, are vanishing.

Maritime Societies

Maritime societies have been the rarest of all the major societal types. Never have
there been more than a small number at a time. Yet once they played an important
role in the civilized world.

Technologically, maritime societies were very much like agrarian societies.
What set them apart was the way they used their technology to take advantage of the
opportunities afforded by their environmental situation. Located on large bodies of
water in an era when it was cheaper to move goods by water than by land (see page
191), these peoples found trade and commerce far more profitable than either fishing
or the cultivation of their limited land resources and gradually created societies in
which overseas trade was the chief economic activity.

The first maritime society in history was probably developed by the Minoans on
the island of Crete, late in the third millennium B.C. We are told that the wealth and
power of the Minoan rulers "depended more upon foreign trade and religious
prerogative than upon the land rents and forced services."[21] The island location of
Minoan society was important not only because it afforded access to the sea, but also
because it provided protection against more powerful agrarian societies. Maritime
societies usually developed on islands or peninsulas that were difficult to attack by
land (see Figure 8.4). Their only military advantage was in naval warfare.

During the next 1,500 years a number of other maritime societies were established in the Mediterranean world. These included the Mycenaeans, or pre-Hellenic
Greeks of the second millennium B.C., the Phoenicians, the Carthaginians, and
possibly some of the later Greek city-states. The spread of the maritime pattern in this
period was largely, perhaps wholly, the result of diffusion and the migration of
maritime peoples. Eventually, all of these societies were conquered by agrarian
societies and either destroyed or absorbed as subunits. This was not the end of
overseas trade and commerce, of course, since these remained important activities
in advanced agrarian societies. It was, however, a temporary end to societies in
which they were the *dominant* economic activities.

Then, more than a thousand years later, there was a revival of maritime societies
during the Middle Ages. Venice and Genoa are the best known, but there were
others (e.g., Danzig and Luebeck in northern Europe). Later, Holland became an
important maritime society, and during the seventeenth and eighteenth centuries

FIGURE 8.4 Maritime societies usually developed on islands or peninsulas that were difficult to attack by land: aerial view of the Lebanese city of Tyre, once an important maritime society. When Tyre was a Phoenician city-state, no land bridge connected it to the mainland.

apparently derived the major part of its income from overseas trade.[22] Britain moved far in this direction in the seventeenth, eighteenth, nineteenth, and early twentieth centuries but probably never quite reached the point where it depended more on overseas commerce than on, first, agriculture and, later, industry. Nevertheless, because of the great growth of overseas commerce, Britain acquired a number of the characteristics of maritime societies.

In many ways, maritime societies resembled advanced agrarian societies, particularly their urban centers. But there were also important differences. To begin with, most maritime societies were much smaller, often containing only a single city and the area immediately around it. Only two maritime societies, Carthage and Holland, ever developed empires worthy of the name and, significantly, both of these were *overseas* empires.[23] In each case the empire was created more as an adjunct of commercial activity than as a political venture.

This curious feature is linked with another, more basic peculiarity of maritime societies. In a largely agrarian world in which monarchy was the normal—almost universal—form of government, maritime societies were usually republics. There were some monarchies, but this pattern was most likely to occur early in a maritime society's history, suggesting a carryover from a premaritime past.

The explanation for the republican tendency in maritime societies seems to be that commerce, rather than warfare and the exploitation of peasant masses, was the chief interest of the governing class. Being less concerned than the typical agrarian

217

FIGURE 8.5   A Venetian merchant's bedroom reveals the wealth that commercial activities brought to leading citizens of most maritime societies.

state with conquest and the control of large peasant populations, these nations had less need for a strong, centralized, hierarchical government. An oligarchy of wealthy merchants could do the job, since their primary responsibilities would be to regulate commercial competition and to provide naval forces to defend their access to foreign ports.

Another peculiarity of maritime societies was their unusual system of values and incentives. As we saw in the last chapter, the governing class in agrarian societies typically viewed work of any kind as degrading. Since this was the class that all others looked up to and emulated, its view of economic activity rubbed off on the rest. This was especially evident in the case of merchants, who, when they became wealthy, usually gave up their commercial activities. As we noted, this antiwork ethic undoubtedly contributed to the slowdown in the rate of technological innovation and progress. In maritime societies, in contrast, the merchants were the dominant class, and a very different view of economic activity prevailed. Though much more research is needed on the subject, there is reason to believe that the rate of technological advance was greater in maritime societies than in agrarian, and that maritime societies made disproportionate technological and economic contributions to the emergence of modern industrial societies. Moreover, the rate of technological advance in *agrarian* societies seems to have been correlated with the social and political strength of their merchant class. In other words, *the greater the social status and political influence of its merchants, the higher the rate of technological and economic innovation in a society tended to be.*[24]

A Brief Review: Sociocultural Evolution to the Eve of the Industrial Revolution

Now that we have completed our survey of the various types of preindustrial societies, we need to pause and briefly review the ground we have covered. In particular, we should consider how well the evidence we have examined conforms to ecological-evolutionary theory.

As we saw in Chapter 3, the central thesis of this theory is that subsistence technology is the key to societal growth and development, both for individual societies and for the world system of societies. Technological advance expands the limits of what is possible for a society and thereby increases its advantage in the process of intersocietal selection. As a consequence, technological advance has also been the basic determinant of the patterns of sociocultural evolution in the world system.

Figure 3.10 on page 74 suggests that this evolutionary process has generated a number of trends in the world system. These trends provide us with an excellent means of checking the validity of ecological-evolutionary theory as it applies to the experience of human societies through most of human history. What exactly *had* happened with respect to those trends by the time the agrarian era was coming to a close?

Growth of human population   In the opinion of the experts, there were between 3 and 10 million people at the end of the hunting and gathering era (7000 B.C.). By the end of the agrarian era (1800 A.D.), there were more than 700 million.

Growth in average size of societies and communities   At the end of the hunting and gathering era, the average size of both societies and communities appears to have been somewhere between 25 and 50. Although it is impossible to obtain reliable estimates of average societal and community sizes for the entire world system at the end of the agrarian era, there is no doubt that both were substantially larger because by then there were so many horticultural, herding, maritime, and agrarian societies. We also know that, whereas the largest society prior to the horticultural era had no more than a few hundred members at most, by the end of the agrarian era there was one with 400 million, and a number with over 10 million.

Increased permanence of communities   Before the first fishing and horticultural societies appeared, nearly all human communities were nomadic. By the end of the agrarian era, only a small minority of them were nomadic.

Expansion of societies into new environments   Most of this trend occurred either before the end of the hunting and gathering era or during the industrial era. The horticultural and agrarian eras, however, did see greatly heightened activity in marine environments. By the end of the agrarian era, oceans, lakes, and rivers had become important both as sources of subsistence and as trade routes.

Increasing impact of societies on the biophysical environment Prior to the horticultural era, the most notable impact of human societies on the biophysical environment seems to have been their apparent extermination of a number of species of large mammals. Societies of the horticultural and agrarian eras had a far more profound effect on the physical landscape, clearing vast forests, damming rivers, irrigating arid areas, and mining an increasing variety of minerals.

Invention of new symbol systems During the horticultural era, the first primitive record-keeping systems were invented. These were followed, during the agrarian era, by prealphabetic and eventually alphabetic systems of writing, numeral systems, measurement systems, systems of musical notation, and monetary systems.

Increasing store of technological information During the horticultural and agrarian eras, the store of technological information increased enormously, a fact amply documented by the great growth of human population. Striking technological advances occurred in plant cultivation, animal domestication, metallurgy, construction, transportation, and communication. By the end of the agrarian era, societies could produce enormous quantities of foods, fibers, and other goods; move people and products over great distances; build monumental edifices of great durability; and inflict great damage on one another, to cite but four of the more significant consequences of the expanded store of technological information.

Increasing store of other kinds of information During the horticultural and agrarian eras, the store of nontechnological information increased dramatically. By the close of the agrarian era, many societies had amassed great amounts of political, economic, philosophical, ideological, historical, aesthetic, scientific, and other kinds of information. Much of this new information emerged as a by-product of the growing size and complexity of societies, a process that created new problems requiring new solutions and new information and that led to the emergence of new norms, beliefs, and values.

Growth in the quantity, diversity, and complexity of material products No brief statement can do justice to this trend, though there are many areas that provide dramatic illustrations. Compare, for example, the greatest structures created by advanced agrarian societies—cathedrals, temples, palaces—with the greatest created by the members of hunting and gathering societies—shelters made from rocks and branches as temporary protection for one or more families. More important, by the end of the agrarian era, human societies were providing the food and other material necessities required to sustain a population of 700 million people, or 100 times the population at the end of the hunting and gathering era.

Increasing complexity of social organization In hunting and gathering societies, full-time occupational specialization was extremely rare, possibly nonexistent. The usual pattern was a division of labor by age and sex, with part-time specialization by a headman and/or a shaman. In agrarian and maritime societies, in contrast, occupational specialties numbered in the hundreds, and there was a complex division of labor that often involved specialization by communities and even regions. In hunting and gathering societies, the only organized groups were families, whereas in agrarian societies, there were numerous communities, often organized into provinces, plus a great variety of specialized associations, especially religious, political, economic, and educational. Political and religious associations, in particular, were often extremely complex.

Increasing inequality within and among societies In hunting and gathering societies, there were only minor status distinctions among individuals. The members of agrarian and maritime societies, however, were usually born into one of a number of classes, which profoundly influenced their opportunities in life. Similarly, prior to the horticultural era, differences among societies were minimal; but by the end of the agrarian era, advanced agrarian and maritime societies were far wealthier and far more powerful than other societies in the world system (i.e., surviving hunting and gathering, horticultural, herding, and fishing societies).

Accelerating rate of social and cultural change During the last 9,000 years of the hunting and gathering era, the rate of social and cultural change was greater than it had previously been, yet the changes in those years could not compare with the changes that occurred in the next 9,000 years. Although there was a temporary slowing of the rate of *technological* innovation during the first part of the agrarian era, it accelerated again well before the end of the agrarian era, as shown in Figure 3.6 (page 67).

By 1800 A.D., near the close of the agrarian era, the patterns of human life had been dramatically altered for all but the relative handful of people who still lived in hunting and gathering societies in remote areas. The vast majority of humans were now living in either agrarian or advanced horticultural societies, with smaller numbers in simple horticultural, herding, and fishing societies. This was not, of course, a stable world system: the deadly process of intersocietal selection that had begun thousands of years earlier was still working to the disadvantage of the technologically less advanced. And every time advanced agrarian societies took another step forward, they tilted the balance a bit more in their favor and against the rest.

This was the situation on the eve of the Industrial Revolution.

PART III

Industrial Societies and Industrializing Societies

CHAPTER 9

The Industrial Revolution

Throughout much of the agrarian era, the rate of technological innovation was less than one would expect in view of the size of agrarian societies, the amount of information available to them, and the extent of contact among them. As we have seen, the cause of this lay in their highly exploitative social systems and in the ideologies that shaped their members' economic attitudes and activities. Not surprisingly, these produced *negative feedback effects* on both technology and the economy.

Late in the agrarian era, however, the rate of innovation in western Europe increased substantially within a relatively short period of time, and by the latter part of the eighteenth century the Industrial Revolution was well under way. Not long thereafter, England became the first truly industrial society—that is, the first society to derive most of its income from productive activities involving machines powered by inanimate energy sources. With this, a new era of far more rapid and pervasive social and cultural change was launched.

What was responsible for this important development? What happened to break the agrarian mold and produce this burst of technological innovation in societies that had been so resistant to change? What happened, in other words, to turn the system of negative feedback into a *positive* one?

225

Causes of the Industrial Revolution: Prior Technological Advance and Its Consequences

The Accumulation of Information in the Agrarian Era

Probably the least heralded of the major causes of the Industrial Revolution was the gradual accumulation of technological information during the agrarian era. For despite the slowdown in the rate of innovation, discoveries and inventions did not cease. Evidence of significant advances can be found in agriculture, mining, metallurgy, transportation, construction, and various other fields.[1] Advances in construction and engineering, for example, can still be traced if one compares the churches and cathedrals built in western Europe in successive centuries. As a result of many such advances, the store of technological information available in the eighteenth century was far greater than in the thirteenth, just as it had been far greater in the thirteenth century than in the eighth. This enormous store of information held obvious potential for an increase in the rate of technological innovation when other conditions within societies became favorable.

Advances in Water Transport and the Discovery of the New World

Some innovations of the late agrarian era were more important for sociocultural evolution than others, and those with a potential for altering agrarian social structure and ideology were most important of all. In this respect, improvements in ships and navigation proved to be some of the most critical.

Prior to the introduction of the compass in Europe, late in the twelfth century, navigation beyond the sight of land was so hazardous that it was undertaken only for short distances or in familiar areas, as in crossing the English Channel or the Mediterranean. Acquisition of the compass was followed, over the next several centuries, by a series of important advances in the technology of shipbuilding. These included the invention of the stern rudder (which replaced steering oars attached to the sides of ships), the construction of larger ships with multiple masts, the substitution of several smaller sails for a single large sail on each mast, and a reduction in the width of ships relative to their length.[2] All of these innovations made ships more responsive and more manageable, and therefore safer on stormy seas.

With such ships at their command, and with the compass to guide them, western European sailors increasingly ventured out into the open seas for extended periods of time. During the fifteenth century, they began a series of voyages designed to open new trade routes to India and China that would enable Europeans to bypass the merchants of the Middle East. Instead, of course, they discovered, and quickly subdued, the New World. Less than fifty years after Columbus first set foot in America, Spain had conquered the two most powerful societies in the New World, the Incan empire in Peru and the Aztec empire in Mexico.

Almost immediately the new conquerors began to ship vast quantities of gold and silver back to Europe. This had a number of consequences, one of which was a tremendous growth in the money economy and a decline in the older barter system.[3]

FIGURE 9.1 Recent reconstruction of the Santa Maria, flagship of Christopher Columbus's first voyage to the New World, illustrates advances in shipbuilding in the late medieval period. Note the multiple masts and sails, the stern rudder, and the relatively narrow beam.

Although money had been used for more than 2,000 years, the supply of precious metals was so limited that many payments were still made in goods rather than in cash—especially in rural areas, but by no means only there. This situation seriously hindered economic and technological advance, because an economy that operates on the basis of barter is not flexible and the flow of resources from areas of oversupply to areas of short supply is sluggish. Furthermore, it is difficult to determine what is economically most advantageous in a barter system. The more widely money is used, however, the easier it is for people to calculate their costs and incomes and determine which of the alternatives open to them is likely to yield the greatest profit.

This is extremely important in breaking down barriers to technological innovation. In societies where technological progress has been halting and uncertain for centuries and where there is no efficient accounting system, people with money are reluctant to invest in new and unproven enterprises. Also, where money is scarce, people tend to state obligations (e.g., wages, rents, debts) in relatively inflexible and traditional terms, which makes the economy unresponsive to changing conditions and new opportunities. But all of this began to change in western Europe during the sixteenth and seventeenth centuries because of the flow of precious metals from the New World.

This influx of gold and silver had a second important effect: it produced inflation.[4] This was a natural consequence of the greatly increased supply of money together with the much more limited increase in the supply of goods. Prices doubled, tripled, even quadrupled within a century. As is always the case when this happens, some people prospered and others were hurt. In general, those with fixed incomes, especially the landed aristocracy, were hurt. But merchants and entrepreneurs tended to benefit. This meant a marked improvement in the position of the merchants relative to the governing class. More of the economic resources of European societies wound up in the hands of people who were interested in, and knew something about, both economics and technology. More than that, *these were people oriented to rational profit making (not a typical orientation in agrarian societies) and therefore motivated to provide financial support for technological innovations that would increase the efficiency of people and machines.* The rise in prices in the sixteenth century was simultaneously a stimulant to feverish enterprise and an acid dissolving traditional relationships.[5]

The benefits to Europe from the discovery of the New World were even greater in the eighteenth and nineteenth centuries than they had been earlier. As the population of European colonists increased, so did opportunities for trade. The colonists provided a growing market for manufactured goods, paying for them with a swelling flood of cheap and abundant raw materials.[6] Between 1698 and 1775, Britain's trade with its colonies increased more than fivefold,[7] and that was only the beginning. As a result, *the center of world trade shifted for the first time in more than 5,000 years, as western Europe replaced the Middle East in the favored position.*

Looking backward, it is difficult to exaggerate the importance of the discovery and conquest of the New World with respect both to the rise of European power in the world system of societies and to the subsequent occurrence of the Industrial Revolution. Suddenly, a handful of societies had access to an enormous treasure house of resources. In addition to the gold and silver, western European societies quickly gained control over vast territories whose forests were a source of great quantities of cheap lumber and, when cleared, provided seemingly endless acres of rich farmland. Contact with the native peoples of the Americas also provided Europeans with information about new plants—especially corn and potatoes—that became valuable new food resources. Never before in history had technologically advanced societies enjoyed such a favorable ratio of resources to population. It was almost as though a new Garden of Eden had been created, but for the benefit of a favored few.

The Printing Press and the Spread of Information

The printing press was another technological innovation that played an important role in helping western European societies break out of the traditional agrarian mold. Printing sped the dissemination of both new technological and new ideological information, and thus was a major factor in overcoming the historic resistance to innovation and change.[8]

Printing apparently originated in China about the fifth century A.D.[9] This early method of printing was extremely expensive, however, because it required a highly skilled craftsman to engrave the contents of every page on a separate block of wood.

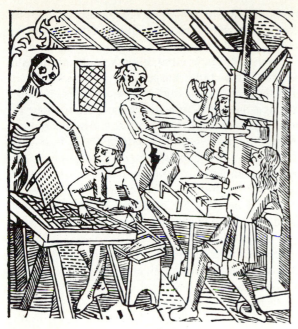

FIGURE 9.2 **The earliest known picture of a printing press, dating from 1499. The typesetter is
reading copy on the left, the press and the press-
man are on the right. The large figures in the rear
symbolize the constant presence of death, a recurring theme in medieval art.**

As a result, printed materials remained a luxury until Johann Gutenberg, a goldsmith
and engraver, invented a system of movable type in the middle of the fifteenth
century.[10] Thus, the expense of skilled engraving was eliminated from printing,
except in the manufacture of the type (i.e., letters and other symbols), which could
be combined in various ways and used over and over again.

Gutenberg's invention resulted in a tremendous increase in the quantity of
printed materials in western Europe. In medieval monasteries, it took 10 to 15 years
to produce a single copy of the Bible using traditional methods. One historian has
concluded that more books were printed in the first 50 years after the invention of the
printing press than all the scribes of Europe had produced in the previous thousand
years.[11] Among the materials that achieved wider circulation were treatises on the
new scientific theories of men like Copernicus and Galileo in the sixteenth and
seventeenth centuries and books on farming that revolutionized English agriculture
in the eighteenth. One of the most significant applications of the printing press,
however, occurred less than a century after its invention, when it was used to spread
the teachings of the Protestant reformers. Historians today regard the printing press as
a major factor in the success of the Protestant movement.[12]

As many scholars have observed, a number of the new Protestant doctrines
substantially altered the thinking of many members of agrarian societies in ways that
were conducive to economic and other kinds of change.[13] In the first place, the

reformers taught that work is an important form of service to God. Martin Luther, for example, insisted that all honest forms of work are as truly Christian callings as the ministry or priesthood. This challenged both the medieval Christian view of work as a punishment for sin and the traditional aristocratic view of work as degrading and beneath the dignity of a gentleman. At the same time, it supported the merchants and craftsmen in their efforts to upgrade their status. Second, the new Protestant faiths undermined fatalism and trust in magic and encouraged the growth of more rationalistic thought processes. Though the reformers dealt with these things only in the area of religion—and even there imperfectly—they strengthened a trend that ultimately had far-reaching consequences. Some branches of Protestantism, for example, encouraged their adherents to plan their lives rather than simply live from day to day, as the name "Methodism" reminds us. Third, many of the newer Protestant faiths emphasized the value of denying the pleasures of this world and living frugally, a practice that enabled those who became economically successful to accumulate capital.

To the extent that people followed these teachings, they developed a new outlook on life: they worked harder, acted more rationally, and lived more thriftily. In short, the Reformation remolded the attitudes, beliefs, and values of many people in ways that helped to undermine the traditional agrarian economy and stimulated economic and technological innovation. Related to this, certain branches of Protestantism, notably Calvinism, elevated the activities of merchants and other businessmen to a status they had not previously enjoyed in any agrarian society. As one scholar has noted, this was not surprising in a faith which had its headquarters in Geneva and its most influential adherents in leading business centers, such as London, Antwerp, and Amsterdam.[14]

Protestantism was also important to economic development because of the insistence of the reformers that people should be able to read the Bible for themselves and thus have direct access to God's Word. This meant that literacy assumed a new significance in societies that became Protestant: it became a religious obligation for the masses rather than an option for elites. But while the initial motivation for the spread of literacy among the masses was religious, its major long-term effects were secular. More literate populations proved to be more innovative and creative than their less literate competitors, and societies that encouraged literacy at an early date appear to have gained an important advantage over other societies in the developmental process.[15]

In summary, it seems more than coincidence that the Industrial Revolution had its beginnings in predominantly Protestant nations. The new Protestant ideology, like the conquest of the New World, undermined belief systems and social structures that had been formidable barriers to innovation and change. Above all, it encouraged a new respect for work and rational planning and discouraged both fatalism and reliance on magic. But it is important to recognize that the success of the Reformation movement and its influence on the subsequent course of European history were due in no small measure to prior changes in technology and economics and to the discovery and conquest of the New World with its vast treasure of natural resources. The latter development was especially important because it enabled many of those who adopted the new work ethic to prosper to a degree that otherwise would not have been possible. Thus, while the Protestant Reformation was one of the links in the chain of causation that led to the Industrial Revolution, it was not the critical link that some have suggested.

Advances in Agriculture

Throughout the agrarian era, the chief restraint on societal growth and development was the backward state of agricultural technology. The rural elite, so long as it managed to extract a surplus sufficient to maintain its customary lifestyle, was content to preserve the status quo. And the peasants, so long as they managed simply to survive, were content to follow the practices inherited from their forebears—or, if not content, at least not motivated to change them. Thus agriculture, which was the basis of the economic surplus, remained largely the same from one century to the next.

In the sixteenth century, however, the situation began to change in much of western Europe.[16] The growth of trade, the increased use of money, and, above all, inflation began to undermine the traditional system. On the one hand, a growing number of large landowners found that, as transportation costs declined in the wake of advances in shipping, markets for certain farm commodities (e.g., wool, grain) were expanding. On the other hand, the effects of inflation were threatening the profitability of their farms, which depended on rents and other obligations established long before the rise in prices. Many landowners realized that if they hoped to maintain their traditional standard of living under the new economic conditions, they must try something new. Some of them subsequently brought new land under cultivation by draining swamps, or by enclosing land that had previously been "common pasture" and at the disposal of peasants and elite alike. Others turned to raising sheep in an effort to benefit from the growing trade in wool. Still others eliminated traditional modes of payment by which tenants fulfilled their obligations to their landlord through customary services or by supplying him with goods or produce, and began to require instead payments of money, which had become more important in economic relationships and which could more easily be adjusted to take account of inflation. Thus, during the sixteenth and seventeenth centuries, agriculture in Europe, and particularly in England, gradually became a more rational and less traditional enterprise.

Then, in the eighteenth century, a new wave of inflation hit western Europe, and landowners were again faced with a choice between innovation and a declining standard of living.[17] In England, where the traditional system of agriculture had already been seriously weakened, a number of other important innovations were adopted. Early in the century, for example, one landowner devised a system of crop rotation that enabled farmers to keep all of their land continuously under cultivation; previously, farmers had to leave land fallow, or uncultivated, a quarter of the time in order to restore its fertility. A little later, another landowner discovered the principle of selective breeding, simultaneously making a fortune for himself from his stud farm and greatly improving the quality of British livestock. Other members of the rural elite invented a variety of simple machines that increased the efficiency of farm labor, while still others published books expounding the new techniques. The practice of enclosing "common lands," meanwhile, continued.

By the end of the eighteenth century, the traditional system of agriculture had been replaced in most of England by a new system of larger, more efficient farms operated on rational and capitalistic principles. But the adoption of this new system meant the massive displacement of poor rural families whose labor was no longer needed and whose right to "common lands" was no longer protected by tradition. Some of these people migrated to the new frontiers overseas. Many others, however, migrated to the cities and towns, where they became a source of cheap labor in the new mills and factories that were beginning to appear.

A Model of the Causes of the Industrial Revolution

Figure 9.3 provides a model of the principal causes of the Industrial Revolution. As the model indicates, *the basic cause was the growing store of technological information in the latter part of the agrarian era.* Advances in navigation and shipbuilding were especially important because, without them, the societies of western Europe could not have gained control of the resources of two vast continents. This revolutionary development, abetted by the success of the Protestant Reformation, led to the changes in economics, social organization, and ideology which made it possible for these societies to break out of the historic agrarian mold. Because of this, the long-time agrarian pattern of negative feedback from social organization and ideology to technology was transformed into a positive one, thereby freeing creative forces that had been curbed for centuries.

It is interesting to note that England, the first society to become industrialized, experienced significant change in several of the factors that are primarily responsible for shaping a society's development. Its environment was drastically altered through the discovery and conquest of the New World, and its store of both technological

FIGURE 9.3 **Model of the causes of the Industrial Revolution in western Europe.**

Summary
of
Chpt. 9.

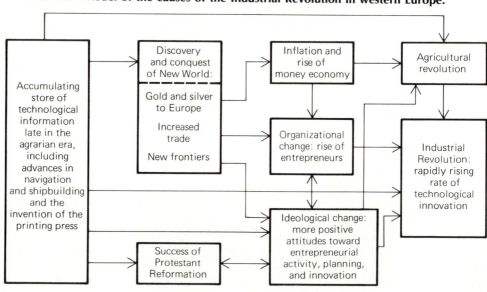

and ideological information underwent substantial change in the sixteenth, seventeenth, and eighteenth centuries. These developments combined to produce major changes in the processes of innovation and selection. These developments will also provide us with useful clues when, in a later chapter, we ponder the question of why societies trying to industrialize today find it so much more difficult than did the societies that industrialized a hundred years or more ago.

A Brief History of the Industrial Revolution

Before the end of the nineteenth century, economic historians were already beginning to use the term "Industrial Revolution" to refer to the series of dramatic technological and economic innovations that had occurred in England during the period from about 1760 to 1830. In their judgment, the mechanization of the textile industry, the technical advances in, and expansion of, the iron industry, the harnessing of steam power, the establishment of the factory system, and other, related developments of that period had transformed English society. What was still essentially an agrarian society (or agrarian-maritime hybrid) in the middle of the eighteenth century had become an industrial society by the middle of the nineteenth.

The time limits that early writers assigned to the Industrial Revolution have subsequently been questioned. Many scholars today believe it is a mistake to put a terminal date (i.e., 1830) on a revolution that is still continuing.[18] Others argue that 1760 is too late a starting date, since the acceleration in industrial activity began not in the middle of the eighteenth century but in the middle of the sixteenth or earlier.[19]

There is some merit in both criticisms. The rate of technological advance did, in fact, begin to accelerate long before 1760, as we have seen. But it does not follow that we should treat those earlier developments as part of the Industrial Revolution. To be meaningful, this term should be limited to *the period during which the productive activities of societies were rapidly transformed by the invention of a succession of machines powered by newer, inanimate sources of energy, such as coal, electricity, petroleum, and natural gas.* Using this criterion, we cannot put the start of the Industrial Revolution much, if any, before the middle of the eighteenth century.

The other criticism of the dates is sounder: the Industrial Revolution definitely was *not* over by 1830. Only its first phase ended at that time. Subsequently, there have been three other phases, and each has contributed substantially to the importance of industrial activity in the societies involved, and to their general transformation.

We cannot assign precise dates to these phases, since they are all rather arbitrary divisions in what has been essentially a continuous process of development. However, by organizing our review in terms of phases, we can see more clearly the progression of events. In the first phase, which began in mid-eighteenth-century England, the revolution was centered in the textile, iron, and coal industries, and the invention of the first true steam engine was probably the most important innovation. The second phase got its start in the middle of the nineteenth century and involved rapid growth in the railroad industry, the mass production of steel, the replacement of sailing ships by steamships, and use of the new technology in agriculture. Around the turn of the century, the Industrial Revolution entered a third phase, with rapid growth in the automobile, electrical, telephone, and petroleum industries. World War II marked the beginning of the fourth phase, distinguished by remarkable developments in aviation, aluminum, electronics, plastics, nuclear power, computers, and automation.

These four phases should not be thought of as stages that each society must pass through to become industrialized. On the contrary, many societies in recent decades have skipped over certain phases, or at least part of them, and combined elements from different phases. For example, a Third World nation today will often develop its railways, highways, and air transportation system simultaneously. But a review of the way things happened *initially* enables us to see how one innovation often makes further innovations possible, even imperative.

First Phase

The first phase of the Industrial Revolution, as we noted, began in the middle of the eighteenth century and lasted about a hundred years. Geographically, it was centered in England. Many of the best known innovations occurred in the textile industry and were of two kinds: machines that increased the efficiency of human labor, and machines that harnessed new sources of energy. The flying shuttle is a good example of the first—and a good example, too, of the way one invention stimulated others. Because it enabled one weaver to do the work formerly done by two, spinners could no longer keep up with the demand for yarn. This disruption of the traditional balance between spinning and weaving triggered a succession of further inventions. First, the traditional spinning wheel was replaced by the spinning jenny, which enabled a worker to spin 4 threads simultaneously and, after a number of modifications, 120 threads. But although the spinning jenny was a tremendous improvement

FIGURE 9.4   James Hargreaves's spinning jenny.

from the standpoint of speed, its yarn was so coarse and loose that flax had to be mixed in with the cotton to produce a satisfactory fiber. This was remedied with the water frame, a machine that could satisfactorily spin pure cotton, and later with the spinning mule, whose cotton threads were stronger and finer. All these advances in spinning reversed the earlier situation: now weaving was the bottleneck in the industry—until a new series of innovations in weaving machines helped restore the balance.

By the end of the eighteenth century, the new looms had become so large and heavy that they were almost impossible to operate. To work the treadle even at a slow speed required two powerful men—and they had to be relieved after a short time.[20] This led to a search for alternative sources of power. One possibility was waterpower, which had already been used for a variety of purposes for many centuries.[21] But England was poorly supplied with suitable streams and rivers, and the wheels and troughs used in water systems were extremely inefficient.[22] Eventually, James Watt developed the first true steam engine,[23] a source of power that could be employed anywhere, and by the end of the century it had been adapted for use in the textile industry.

The net effect of these innovations was such a rapid expansion of the British textile industry that between 1770 and 1845 its contribution to the national income increased more than fivefold.[24] This was a striking rate of growth by the standards of traditional agrarian societies. The actual increase in production was even larger, since per unit costs of production dropped considerably during this period.

One of the immediate consequences of advances in textile production was *the creation of the factory system*. Prior to the Industrial Revolution, and even during its early years, spinning and weaving were cottage industries. Entrepreneurs provided the raw materials, and poor families, working in their own homes and using their own spinning wheels and looms, provided the labor. But after heavier and more expensive machines came to be used, this arrangement was impossible: families could neither afford the new equipment nor power it. Businessmen were forced to buy their own machines, construct buildings to house them, and provide engines to run them, thereby creating the factory system that has become such a prominent feature of modern industrial societies.

Another industry that expanded greatly during the first phase of the Industrial Revolution was iron manufacture. Despite increasing demand for iron by both the textile industry and the military, technical difficulties greatly restricted its manufacture until late in the eighteenth century. One problem was England's growing shortage of wood, which was needed to make charcoal for smelting and refining. This problem was partially solved earlier in the century, when it was found that coke (derived from coal) could be substituted for charcoal, at least in the smelting process. But a serious bottleneck remained. Because it is hard and brittle, pig iron must be converted into wrought, or malleable, iron before it can be used for most purposes. This process required charcoal and was very time-consuming until the traditional forge was replaced by the newly invented coal-fired blast furnace. These innovations opened the way for rapid expansion: in 1788, England produced only 68,000 tons of iron; by 1845, it produced twenty-four times that.[25] The new blast furnaces also made it possible to perform all the processes of iron making in a single establishment. Thus, the factory system spread from the textile industry to the iron industry.

FIGURE 9.5   Prior to the Industrial Revolution, and even during its early years, entrepreneurs provided poor families with raw materials for spinning, weaving, and garment making in their own homes: early 19th-century print of English family sewing uniforms for the army under the domestic, or putting-out, system that preceded the factory system.

Between them, the iron industry and the steam engine substantially increased the demand for coal. At the same time, the steam engine helped alleviate the ancient problem of flooding in coal mines, providing power to pump out the water that constantly seeped into shafts and tunnels. The growth of the coal industry, though not quite so dramatic as that of the iron industry, was still impressive: in 1760, Britain produced barely 5 million tons; by 1845, the figure had risen over ninefold.[26]

No discussion of developments in this period would be complete without mention of the machine-tool industry. Although never as large or financially important as the textile, iron, and coal industries, it was crucial for technological progress because it produced the increasingly complex industrial machinery. This industry, which began undramatically with the invention of the first practical lathe, was soon producing machines capable of precision work to the thousandth of an inch.[27] For many years a single tool was used for drilling, boring, grinding, and milling; but special tools were gradually designed for each operation.

Another basic advance in the eighteenth century was the production of machines with interchangeable parts. This greatly facilitated industrial growth, since damage to one part of a complex machine no longer meant that the entire machine had to be discarded or a new part specially made. Spare parts could now be kept on hand and replacements made on the spot by mechanics with limited skills and equipment.

During this initial phase of the Industrial Revolution, shortly after 1800, Britain became the first nation in which machine-based industry replaced agriculture as the most important economic activity, and thus the first industrial society.[28] The United States would not reach this point until 1870.[29]

Second Phase

The second phase of the Industrial Revolution began in the middle decades of the nineteenth century. Expansion continued at a rapid pace in the textile, iron, and coal industries, but now there were breakthroughs in a number of others as well. By the end of the century industrialization had occurred in most segments of the British economy. Meanwhile, the Industrial Revolution began to make significant headway in some of the other countries of northwestern Europe and in the United States.

One of the most important developments during this phase was the application of the steam engine to transportation, something inventors had been trying to accomplish for decades. Finally, about 1850, most of England was linked together by a network of railroads.[30] The results were tremendous: the greatly reduced cost of moving goods by rail contributed to a significant reduction in the price of most heavy, bulk commodities, and this in turn led to greater demand. In addition, railroads helped break down local monopolies and oligopolies (i.e., markets with only a few sellers), which added to competition and further lowered prices. Thus, England gradually became a single giant market for an increasing number of commodities, a development destined to have far-reaching consequences.

Even before the steam engine was adapted to land transportation, it had been used on water. For many years, however, it was limited to coastal and river shipping, because inefficient engines made it impossible to bunker enough wood or coal for long voyages and because paddle wheels worked poorly in high seas. Then, in only a few decades, more efficient compound engines reduced substantially the amount of fuel required; iron and steel began to replace wood in ship construction, permitting longer and larger vessels with greater carrying capacity (the upper limit in length for wooden ships was only about 300 feet); and the screw propeller replaced the cumbersome and easily damaged paddle wheel.[31] After this, steamships increased so rapidly that by 1893 world steam tonnage exceeded sailing tonnage.

In the iron industry, meanwhile, a way was finally found to produce steel

FIGURE 9.6   Model of the DeWitt Clinton, built in New York in 1831. On its first run between Albany and Schenectady, it traveled twelve miles in less than an hour. Note the similarity of the coaches to stagecoaches and the similarity of the engine to an ordinary steam engine of the kind already in use in factories and mines.

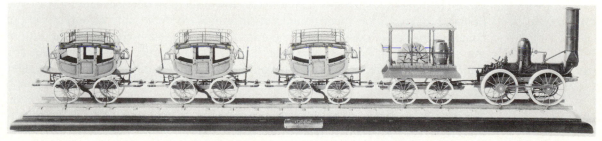

cheaply and in large quantities, making it available for many new purposes.[32] Between 1845 and the early 1880s, Britain's production of iron and steel increased more than fivefold.[33] This meant that in less than a century, from 1788 to the early 1880s, the increase was 100-fold, and the quality of the product was vastly improved.

The tremendous growth in railroads and steamships and the expansion of the iron industry all combined to increase the demand for coal. Though there were no spectacular breakthroughs in mining techniques, improvements in engines and in the quality of steel tools pushed production up fivefold.[34]

A number of new industries emerged in addition to the railroads, none as important at the time, but some destined to surpass them later on. The rubber industry developed after Charles Goodyear discovered the technique of vulcanization, which prevented rubber goods from becoming sticky in hot weather, stiff and brittle in cold. About the same time, Samuel Morse and several others invented the telegraph, and this quickly became the basis of another new industry. Then, in the 1860s, the electric dynamo was invented, and the door was opened to the use of electricity in industry. A second critical development in this field, the invention of the transformer, helped alleviate one of the greatest impediments to the use of electricity: the loss of energy during long-distance transmission. The petroleum industry also got its start in these years, chiefly by providing a substitute for whale oil in lighting homes.

The Industrial Revolution began to have an impact even on agriculture, through improved equipment (e.g., sturdier steel plows), new kinds of machines (e.g., threshing machines, mowers, reapers, steam plows), and synthetic fertilizers from the growing chemical industry. The result was a substantial increase in productivity. In Germany, for example, production per acre rose 50 percent in only twenty-five years. In the United States, the number of man-hours required to produce corn and wheat was cut in half between 1840 and 1900.[35]

An important organizational development in this second phase of the Industrial Revolution was the formation of the *multidivisional enterprise with its hierarchy of salaried managers*.[36] This happened first in the new railroad, steamship, and telegraph industries, which required workers in widely scattered locations. No longer was it possible for a single family to fill all or even most of the managerial positions needed to supervise its employees and coordinate their activities: hired personnel had to assume this responsibility. This was an important step in the development of the modern *corporation*.

Another spur in this direction was the great quantity of new material products that had become available to the members of society. As further advances in production and transportation continued to lower the cost of goods and increase the demand for them, the sheer volume of sales made it impossible for the owners of some businesses to oversee all of the transactions. For example, around the turn of the century, Sears, Roebuck was processing 100,000 orders a day, more than any merchant of an earlier generation would have handled in a lifetime.[37] As sales increased, so did the number of retail outlets in a wide variety of businesses, each requiring a local manager at first, and eventually intermediate layers of management.

All during this period, industrialization was spreading rapidly in northwest Europe and North America. Before the century closed, Britain had lost its position of economic and technological leadership. The iron and steel industry illustrates the trend: although Britain nearly doubled its production of pig iron between 1865 and 1900, its share of the world market dropped from 54 to 23 percent.[38] Its chief rivals were the United States and Germany, whose respective shares rose from 9 to 35 percent and from 10 to 19 percent.

As these figures indicate, though industrialization was spreading, it was still largely limited to a few countries. The United States, Britain, Germany, and France, for example, produced 84 percent of the world's iron in 1900. A similar picture emerges when we look at national shares of all manufacturing activity. In 1888, the percentages are estimated to have been as follows:[39]

United States	32%
Britain	18%
Germany	13%
France	11%
All other countries	26%

The fact that "all other countries" contributed more to *all* types of manufacturing than they did to iron production reflects the fact that the new technology was spreading faster in light industries, such as textiles, than in heavy industries. This was because light industries required less capital and because the rate of innovation in them had already slowed considerably, reducing the need for highly skilled and innovative personnel.

The last factor points to a final characteristic of this phase of the Industrial Revolution: a growing dependence on science and engineering. Before 1850 most of the major advances were made by simple craftsmen or gentlemen amateurs. After that date, key inventions came primarily from people with formal technical or scientific training. This was especially true in the chemical industry, but it was evident in others as well.

Finally, near the end of the nineteenth century, the innovative process began to be institutionalized, and laboratories were built to enable teams of trained people to work together to solve technical problems.[40] The laboratories established by Thomas Edison are an example of the new trend, and the successes he and others achieved led many to emulate them, especially in Germany and the United States. These developments also contributed to the growth of scientific study in universities, to the training of engineers, and to increasing cooperation between innovative industries and institutions of higher education. Most of these developments did not come to full flower, however, until the third and fourth phases of the Industrial Revolution.

Third Phase

Around the turn of the century, the Industrial Revolution entered a phase that lasted until the beginning of World War II and was characterized by major advances in *energy technology*. The foundation for some of the twentieth century's most dis-

FIGURE 9.7 **Early automobile assembly line: dropping the engine into the Model T chassis, Highland Park, Michigan.**

tinctive innovations had been laid in the late nineteenth century with the invention of the internal combustion engine and of machines capable of generating and transmitting electricity in quantities great enough, and at prices cheap enough, to be industrially useful and commercially profitable.

One of the most dramatic developments was the tremendous expansion of the automobile industry. In 1900 no more than 20,000 cars were produced in the entire world, most of them in France.[41] By 1929, the total was over 6 million, 85 percent of them made in the United States.[42]

Just as remarkable as the automobile industry's rate of growth was its impact on other industries. In 1937, for example, the manufacture of cars in the United States consumed 20 percent of the nation's steel, 54 percent of its malleable iron, 73 percent of its plate glass, and 80 percent of its rubber.[43] More striking yet, 90 percent of its gasoline went to run those vehicles.

The electrical industry was another that mushroomed during the third phase as electricity came to be used widely for industrial purposes. This was also the period in which small electric motors began to be used widely to power household appliances. Between 1900 and 1940 the capacity of all the generating plants in the world increased 200-fold.[44] Again the United States led the way, producing 40 to 45 percent of the world's electric power.

The proportional growth of the petroleum industry was less dramatic, because it had already grown substantially before 1900. Even so, production in 1940 was thirteen times larger than it was in 1900.[45]

The telephone industry also grew rapidly in this period. The number of telephones in the United States increased from 1.4 million in 1900 to 20.8 million in 1940, by which time the industry had investments valued at $5 billion.[46]

During this phase, as during the second, the Industrial Revolution was felt not only in new sectors of the economy but in new parts of the world as well, which meant some change in the relative ranking of nations. While the United States continued to lead, Britain, Germany, and France all lost ground relatively (see Table 9.1) despite substantial growth in absolute terms. The chief gains were registered by nations that were just beginning to industrialize, especially Russia and Japan.

Fourth Phase

No previous war was as dependent on industrial activity as World War II, as every major nation made tremendous efforts to increase its output of military supplies. One of the long-term consequences was the great stimulus given to the aviation industry. In the United States, the production of aircraft rose from 3,600 in 1938 to more than 96,000 in 1944.[47] Though the manufacture of new aircraft declined substantially at the end of the war, the air transportation industry expanded rapidly. Between 1940 and 1982, the number of passenger-miles flown by scheduled airlines rose from 1.2 billion to 259 billion, and the number of ton-miles flown in hauling freight and mail rose from 14 million to over 6.8 billion.[48] The year 1958 marked a significant shift in transportation patterns: for the first time, planes covered more passenger-miles in the United States than trains, and they also replaced steamships as the chief carriers of transatlantic passengers.

Just as automobiles spurred the petroleum industry, so aviation spurred aluminum. Though it was first manufactured in the nineteenth century, its production was

TABLE 9.1 Percentage Distribution of World Industrial Output (Excluding Handicrafts), in 1888 and 1937, by Society

Society	1888	1937
United States	32	34
United Kingdom	18	10
Germany	13	11
France	11	5
Russia	8	10
Japan	No data	4
All others	17	26

Source: Calculated from W. S. Woytinsky and E. S. Woytinsky, *World Population and Production: Trends and Outlook* (New York: Twentieth Century Fund, 1953), pp. 1003–1004.

quite limited until Germany and Italy began building their air forces in the 1930s. In just four decades (from 1938 to 1980), world production increased twenty-five times, and it is still increasing as new uses continue to be found.[49] As in most of the rapidly expanding industries of the third and fourth phases, American production has been a major share, varying from a third to a half of the world's aluminum output since World War II.

The plastics industry is another that came into its own during this fourth phase. Its origins go back to 1861, when nitrocellulose was plasticized with camphor to produce artificial ivory and used as a substitute for horn in frames for eyeglasses. Thanks to many subsequent developments, plastics have become the most versatile of modern materials: they can now be manufactured to almost any set of specifications. Not surprisingly, the industry has mushroomed: as recently as the late 1930s, world output was under 200,000 tons; by 1980, it was nearly 50 million and growing, with American production a quarter of the total.[50]

The nuclear power industry has also grown tremendously since World War II. Although the atomic age began with Hiroshima, the world's first nuclear power facility did not begin operating until 1955, when the Soviet Union opened a small installation with a 5,000-kilowatt capacity.[51] By 1983, there were 250 reactors operative in at least twenty nations (data on the Soviet Union and some other nations were not available) with a capacity of 800 billion kilowatts.[52] In recent years, however, the rate of growth of the industry has slowed substantially in many countries (France and the U.S.S.R. are notable exceptions) for a variety of reasons.

Electronics is another industry with a spectacular rate of expansion, and its impact on daily life has been as dramatic as its growth. Its products include radio and television equipment, video and stereo tape recorders, high-fidelity systems, computers, calculators, testing and measuring equipment, industrial control equipment, and microwave communications systems, to name but a few. With the development of servomotors—small power units that respond instantly to signals of various kinds (e.g., a temperature change)—machines that not only act but *react* became possible, and the foundation was laid for automation.

The most revolutionary innovation of the fourth phase, however, has been the computer, which is the functional equivalent of a radical advance in certain capabilities of our species' most valuable tool, the human brain. The first electronic digital computer was built in 1946, barely forty years ago. A massive piece of equipment weighing thirty tons and occupying an entire room, it required 140,000 watts of electricity and had a memory of only 20 ten-digit numbers. Today, a far greater information-handling capacity resides in the circuits of a tiny quarter-inch silicon chip, while one of the newer computers can perform 30 to 40 million information-processing operations per second.[53]

Such leaps in capability dwarf the other technological advances of the fourth phase,* and carry with them a staggering potential for change in human societies. One indication of this is the use of computerized robots in the automobile industry, first in Japan and more recently in the United States. Although early reports greatly

---

*It is reported that if the automobile industry had made comparable advances, a Rolls-Royce would now cost only $70.

FIGURE 9.8 **The most revolutionary innovation of the
fourth phase of the Industrial Revolution has been the
computer, which is the functional equivalent of a radical
advance in certain of the capabilities of our species'
valuable genetic resource, the brain.**

exaggerated the impact of this innovation on the size of the labor force in the plants
where it has been adopted thus far,[54] some experts believe that by the end of the
century "small robots" will be capable of replacing from 50 to 75 percent of all
factory workers, and at significantly lower costs.[55] Similar changes can be expected
in other areas where labor consists of relatively routine and repetitive operations.
Meanwhile, computers are already integral components in everything from children's toys to military weapons systems.

Several of the rapid-growth industries of the third phase maintained their high
rate of growth in the fourth. Between 1940 and 1980, world output of electricity
increased fifteenfold, world production of motor vehicles and petroleum tenfold.[56]
The United States was still a major producer, but its contribution to total world
production in these industries had declined considerably. For example, its share of
world automobile production dropped from 85 percent in 1929 to only 21 percent in
1981.

A comparison of Tables 9.1 and 9.2 shows some of the important changes that
have occurred in the last hundred years with respect to industrial development in the
world system. The most striking fact revealed by this comparison is the precipitous

TABLE 9.2 Percentage Distribution of Gross World Product, by Society, in 1980

Society	Percentage Share of Gross World Product
United States	23
Union of Soviet Socialist Republics	12
Japan	10
West Germany	7
France	6
China	5
United Kingdom	4
All others	33

Source: Adapted from *Statistical Abstract of the United States, 1984,* table 1509.

decline of Britain, which in 1888 still ranked as the second leading industrial power. Japan, on the other hand, has made impressive advances. The dynamic nature of modern industrial technology means that no society is assured of continuing leadership simply because it enjoys that status during a particular phase of the continuing Industrial Revolution. It means, too, that it has become increasingly difficult for any nation or set of nations to dominate the industrial scene. In 1888, the five most highly industrialized societies were responsible for 83 percent of the world's industrial output. But by 1980, the output of the top five was only 58 percent, reflecting the diffusion of industrial technology throughout the world as a whole.

Until recently, the fourth phase of the Industrial Revolution has been a period of tremendous economic growth throughout the world. Between 1950 and 1980, for example, gains in productivity ranged from 313 percent in East and Southeast Asia (with Japan excluded) to 422 percent in Latin America (see Table 13.3, page 365). These rapid gains were due largely to two factors: (1) the increasing availability of cheap energy sources prior to 1973, and (2) the movement of millions of people out of agriculture into modern industries.

The growing uncertainty concerning the future of energy costs, together with the appearance of several fundamental innovations, especially the computer, suggests that the world system may be on the threshold of a new phase in the continuing Industrial Revolution—a phase characterized by a shift to new energy sources and more energy-efficient machines. Because of its great relevance for the future, we will return to this subject in the final chapter.

New Energy, New Machines, New Materials: The Key Advances

In studying the Industrial Revolution, it is easy to become so immersed in the details of individual inventions and discoveries that we fail to see the larger picture. At the risk of oversimplifying an admittedly complex developmental process, it seems fair to say that three sets of innovations have been of critical importance. Together, they have provided a necessary foundation for most of the other innovations, and without these three, there would have been no Industrial Revolution.

First, the Industrial Revolution has greatly increased the amount of *energy* available to societies. New technologies have made accessible for the first time vast quantities of energy stored in coal, petroleum, natural gas, and certain radioactive materials. The importance of this development is difficult to exaggerate.

Second, the Industrial Revolution has involved the invention of thousands of *new machines* which use this energy to perform an enormous variety of tasks to satisfy human needs and desires. These machines now provide hundreds of millions of people with countless goods and services—many of which were previously unavailable to even the most powerful kings and emperors.

Third, the Industrial Revolution has made available many *new materials* from which new kinds of machines can be constructed and new products produced. Perhaps the most important and most useful of these will prove to be plastic, which is, by far, the most versatile material that humans have ever had.

Collectively, these three sets of innovations—the vast new stores of energy, the new machines, and the new materials—have transformed the world. As we will see in the next several chapters, these advances in technology have given rise to a social and cultural revolution which is unequaled in human history, not only in its scope and rapidity, but also in the enormity of its impact on human life.

Causes of the Continuing Industrial Revolution

As the twentieth century draws to a close, the technological revolution that began in the eighteenth century shows no signs of abating. On the contrary, the rate of innovation continues to accelerate. Thus, to understand the Industrial Revolution it is not enough merely to understand the forces that gave it its start several centuries ago. We also need to understand the forces that are responsible for its continuation still today.

Greater Informational Resources and a Larger Population

Many of these forces are ones that we first identified back in Chapter 3. For example, the existing store of useful information about the material world is far greater today than ever before. This means that the informational resources available to would-be inventors today are vastly greater than in the past (see again Table 3.2 and the related discussion, page 65). In addition, the human population is substantially larger today than it was two centuries ago, and this means more minds at work on the problems confronting human societies.

Changing Attitudes toward Innovation

In preindustrial societies, traditions have always been held in high esteem and change has generally been viewed as undesirable, even dangerous. Innovators, far from being praised or admired for their efforts, have commonly been accused of abandoning the hallowed ways of the past and of their forebears. Because of this strong attachment to the past, social scientists often refer to preindustrial societies as "traditional" societies.

In contemporary industrial societies, in contrast, the attitude toward innovation and change is almost always a positive one. Members of these societies are not just tolerant of innovation: *they actively promote and encourage it.* Many are *neophiliacs,* who love novelty for its own sake. In the arts, for example, innovation is often praised merely because of its novelty and without regard to aesthetic criteria (see "Neophilic Art"), with the result that on a number of occasions entries submitted to art exhibits as hoaxes have actually won prizes.

In the educational world, a strongly positive attitude toward innovation is also much in evidence. In preindustrial societies, the basic function of education was to transmit the cultural heritage of the past to successive generations, and great emphasis was placed on memorization of the classics and on rote learning of materials. Today, most educators scorn memorization and argue that the chief aim of schools should be to train young people to think creatively. And as increasing emphasis has been placed on science and engineering in institutions of higher learning, these have become more and more centers of research and innovation.

The institutionalization of innovation is equally evident in industry and government. Industrial enterprises and governmental agencies have created countless research centers within their own organizations, and often they also subsidize research in universities. As a result, expenditures for research and development have risen enormously. In the United States, for example, expenditures, even after adjustments for inflation, increased fiftyfold between 1953 and 1984.[57] Industrial societies are the first in history to search systematically and continuously for new technological answers to human problems.

The reasons for the modern attitude toward innovation and change are not hard to find. For the most part, the changes that have already occurred have meant improvements in the quality of life for the vast majority of people in industrial societies—greatly improved standards of living, improved health, and greater longevity. Under the circumstances, it would be much more surprising if attitudes toward change had *not* themselves also changed.

The Rise of Modern Science

The emergence of science as a major new institutional system is another development that has contributed greatly to the continuing revolution in technology. Although science is sometimes confused with technology, the two are not the same. Science is the search for general and abstract principles that explain the workings of the world we live in. Technology, in contrast, is information about specific ways in which the material world can be manipulated to satisfy human needs and desires. It is a much more practical and "down-to-earth" body of information.

Science and technology today are obviously interdependent. Almost all of modern science presupposes an advanced technology. Modern science is possible only because of technological advances which have enhanced the powers of our senses and of our brains, thus enabling us to learn things which would otherwise

FIGURE 9.9   While modern science is largely a product of the Industrial Revolution, it is also an important cause of its continuation: nuclear power, a controversial new technology, is the result of theoretical advances in physics earlier in the twentieth century.

remain forever unknowable. For example, modern molecular biology and modern medical science are possible only because of the invention of the microscope, which revealed for the first time the previously invisible and unknowable world of cells and molecules, bacteria and viruses. Similarly, modern astronomy is possible only because of the invention of the telescope and radio telescope, which extend the range of our vision far beyond what was previously possible.

But if modern science is a product of the Industrial Revolution, it is also an important cause of its continuation. Today, technological advance depends increasingly upon the kind of abstract, theoretical knowledge that is the special concern of the sciences. More and more, fundamental discoveries and major inventions are the work of men and women with advanced scientific training, and less and less the work of untrained mechanics. Without the contributions of modern science, it is hard to imagine that the rate of technological innovation would still be accelerating.

The Threat of War

Prior to the Industrial Revolution, military technology changed slowly. As a result, military success among societies at the same level of development depended largely on the size of armies and the organizational and tactical skills of their commanders.

Today, in contrast, military technology becomes obsolete in a very short time and the size of armies and their commanders' skills are less important than the productive capacity of a nation's economy and the skills of its engineers and scientists. To maintain their relative military preeminence, the leading military powers are obliged to invest substantial sums in technological research of many kinds.[58] Although the aim of this research is to create new and improved weapons systems, the new technologies that result often have significant nonmilitary applications. A classic example of this is the development of the silicon chip, which was developed in response to the need to reduce the size and weight of materials used in the space program (a program whose funding has depended greatly on its military relevance).

Environmental Feedback

For the first time in history, the most significant changes in the biophysical environments of most societies are not the result of spontaneous natural forces but, rather, the result of human actions. The global ecosystem now has to support a much larger human population than ever before, and the standards of living for much of this population are steadily rising. As a result, natural resources of every kind are being consumed much more rapidly than in the past, and supplies of many resources are threatened with depletion. In addition, many of the new technologies have had unanticipated side effects, such as acid rain, and these create new problems and the need for new technologies to solve them. Faced with this situation, societies have had no choice but to invest in further research in an effort to find solutions to the problems created by prior advances in technology. Thus, technological advance has itself become one of the most important causes of the need for continued technological advance.

The Desire for Ever Higher Standards of Living

Finally, it is clear that one of the major factors responsible for the continuing Industrial Revolution is the desire of most humans for ever higher standards of living. One might suppose that the tremendous improvements in living standards that have been achieved in industrial societies in the last two hundred years would satisfy their members. But, clearly, this has not been the case. The desire for goods and services seems to be insatiable: the more people have, the more they want.

This seems to be a part of our genetic heritage—an element of human nature that results from our enormous capacity for learning, and especially from our powers of imagination. No matter what we have, or what we are able to do, we can always dream of something more. And having dreamed of more, some are driven to make the dream a reality. Where this process will end—or if it will end—no one can say. For the present, however, it is one of the more powerful forces behind the continuing revolution in technology.

Levels of Industrialization in Contemporary Societies

Societies today differ enormously in the degree to which they have industrialized. Some now rely almost entirely on the newer energy sources, such as coal, oil, natural gas, and electricity, while others still depend primarily on older sources, especially human and animal power, wind, water, and wood. Some have become almost totally dependent on machine technology, while others still depend primarily on hand tools. And some are now heavily dependent on the new kinds of materials, while others still depend largely on traditional ones.

There is no single measure of industrialization that enables us to gauge perfectly the degree to which individual societies have adopted the new technology, but one of the best is *per capita annual energy consumption*. Societies that employ the newer energy sources extensively and depend on the new machines and the new materials invariably have high rates of energy consumption, while those that still depend on the older energy sources and on traditional tools and materials have low rates.

The chief defect in this measure is that it exaggerates somewhat the degree of industrialization of societies in colder climates (where heating needs consume large amounts of energy) and understates somewhat the degree of industrialization of societies in warmer climates. This measure also exaggerates somewhat the degree of industrialization of societies, such as the United States and Canada, that are large in size and rely heavily on automobiles (which consume large quantities of energy) for intrasocietal travel. Despite these limitations, per capita energy consumption is the best single indicator we have of the degree of industrialization achieved by individual societies.[59]

Table 9.3 documents the tremendous variation that exists among societies

TABLE 9.3   Energy Consumption Per Capita, by Society

Society	Energy Cons./ Capita	Society	Energy Cons./ Capita	Society	Energy Cons./ Capita
Canada	9,699	Venezuela	3,142	Egypt	618
United States	9,431	S. Africa	2,642	China	581
East Germany	7,385	Yugoslavia	2,331	Zambia	387
Australia	7,164	Spain	2,277	Thailand	364
Netherlands	5,830	Mexico	1,760	Philippines	329
Soviet Union	5,768	Argentina	1,653	Indonesia	229
West Germany	5,510	South Korea	1,442	Pakistan	211
Sweden	4,956	Portugal	1,327	India	200
United Kingdom	4,538	Iran	1,025	Nigeria	195
Poland	4,465	Algeria	737	Zaire	70
France	3,995	Brazil	704	Bangladesh	50
Japan	3,503	Iraq	680	Ethiopia	30

Source: *Statistical Abstract of the U.S., 1985,* table 1499.

today. At one extreme, there are some societies that consume 5,000 to 10,000 kilograms of coal, or its equivalent in other forms of energy, per person per year. At the other extreme, there are societies that consume less than 500 kilograms per person per year. Most societies fall somewhere between these extremes.

These differences are not randomly distributed in the different parts of the world. Rather, all of the highly industrialized societies, with a single exception, are either European or overseas English-speaking democracies (i.e., Australia, Canada, New Zealand, and the United States). Thus far, Japan is the only society with a non-European heritage that has successfully industrialized.

Not all European societies, however, are industrial societies. Several in southern and eastern Europe—specifically, Greece, Yugoslavia, Albania, Spain, and Portugal—are best described as hybrid *industrializing agrarian* societies. This category also includes most of the societies of Asia, North Africa, and Latin America. The societies of sub-Saharan Africa, Haiti, and Papua New Guinea are also hybrids, but of another kind—*industrializing horticultural.* These two sets of societies are often lumped together and referred to as the *less developed countries* (the *LDCs*) or the Third World; but as we will see in a later chapter, there are good reasons for differentiating between them.

For the remainder of the present chapter, and in the three chapters that follow, we will be concerned with the minority of societies that has already industrialized. Our goal in these chapters will be to see how the new technology which they have adopted has transformed the conditions of life for the hundreds of millions of people who live in them.

Consequences of the Industrial Revolution

From an early date it became clear that the Industrial Revolution would involve more than just a change in the techniques of production: it would also produce far-reaching changes in virtually every aspect of human life. Though our chief concern in this volume is with the long-run consequences of the revolution, we cannot ignore its impact on the lives of those who were first exposed to it and to the new social order to which it gave rise.

Initial Consequences

The first indication of serious change came with the invention of the new spinning and weaving machines in the late eighteenth century. Because of their great size and weight, they required specially constructed buildings and steam engines or waterfalls to power them. In short, as we have seen, the new technology necessitated the creation of the factory system.

Factories, however, required a concentrated supply of dependable labor. A few of the early factories were built in open countryside, but their owners quickly found they could not hire enough workers unless they built adjoining tenements and thus, in effect, created new urban settlements. Most factories were built in or near existing towns, and the cry that went out from them for workers coincided with the declining need for labor on the farms.

FIGURE 9.10   Early English industrial town, Staffordshire.

Although the ensuing migration to urban areas was not a new phenomenon, its *magnitude* was, and most communities were unable to cope with the sudden influx. The migrants themselves were badly prepared for their new way of life. Sanitary practices that had been tolerable in sparsely settled rural areas, for example, became a threat to health, even to life, in crowded urban communities.

Equally critical problems resulted from the abrupt disruption of social relationships. Old ties of kinship and friendship were severed and could not easily be replaced, while local customs and institutions that had provided rural villagers with at least a measure of protection and support were lost for good. Thus, it was an uprooted, extremely vulnerable mass of people who streamed into the towns and were thrown into situations utterly foreign to them, and into a way of life that often culminated in injury, illness, or unemployment. A multitude of social ills—poverty, alcoholism, crime, vice, mental and physical illness, personal demoralization— were endemic.

Town magistrates and other local officials had neither the means nor the will to cope with rampant problems in housing, health, education, and crime. Cities and towns became more crowded, open space disappeared, and people accustomed to fields and woodlands found themselves trapped in a deteriorating environment of

FIGURE 9.11   During the early stages of the Industrial Revolution, large numbers of children were employed in factories in both the United States and Britain: textile mill employees in North Carolina, 1908.

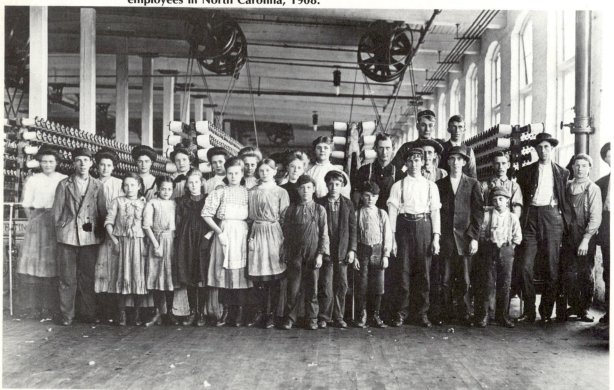

CHILDREN AND THE FACTORY SYSTEM

The following testimony was given by Peter Smart to a Parliamentary committee investigating working conditions in 1832. Similar testimony was provided by numerous others.

Q. Where do you reside?
A. At Dundee.
Q. Have you worked in a mill from your youth?
A. Yes, since I was 5 years of age.
Q. Had you a father and mother in the country at the time?
A. My mother stopped in Perth, about eleven miles from the mill, and my father was in the army.
Q. Were you hired for any length of time when you went?
A. Yes, my mother got 15 shillings for six years, I having my meat and clothes.
Q. What were your hours of labor, as you recollect, in the mill?
A. We began at 4 o'clock in the morning and worked till 10 or 11 at night; as long as we could stand on our feet.
Q. Were you kept on the premises constantly?
A. Constantly.
Q. Locked up?
A. Yes, locked up.
Q. Night and day?
A. Night and day; I never went home while I was at the mill.
Q. Do the children ever attempt to run away?
A. Very often.
Q. Were they pursued and brought back again?
A. Yes, the overseer pursued them and brought them back.
Q. Did you ever attempt to run away?
A. Yes, I ran away twice.
Q. And you were brought back?
A. Yes; and I was sent up to the master's loft, and thrashed with a whip for running away.
Q. Do you know whether the children were, in point of fact, compelled to stop during the whole time for which they were engaged?
A. Yes, they were.
Q. By law?
A. I cannot say by law; but they were compelled by the master; I never saw any law used there but the law of their own hands.

Source: *Parliamentary Papers, 1831–32, vol. XV.*

filthy, crowded streets and tenements, polluted air, and long workdays rarely relieved by experiences of either beauty or hope.[60]

The misery of the new urban dwellers was compounded by the harshness of the factory system, which often operated along quasi-penal lines.[61] Regardless of how hard life had been before, country folk had at least had some control over their own hour-to-hour movements; but now work was, if anything, longer, more arduous, and more confining. Women and children, though they had always worked extremely hard in homes and fields, now worked in factories with dangerous, noisy machinery or in dark and dangerous mines. Minor infractions of complex rules, such as whistling on the job or leaving a lamp lit a few minutes too long after sunrise, led to fines, more serious infractions to floggings. One observer of the period wrote poignantly of hearing children, whose families could not afford clocks, running through the streets in the dark, long before the mills opened, so fearful were they of being late.[62]

The immediate effects of industrialization have been traumatic for vast numbers of people in virtually every society that has made the transition from agrarianism. The details varied, but the suffering was no less acute in the Soviet Union than in

England. Whether life for the new urban working class was better or worse than it had been for the peasants and the urban lower classes of the old agrarian societies is still a matter of debate.[63] But one point is not debatable: the transition to an industrial economy has exacted a cruel price in terms of human suffering and demoralization for countless millions of people.

Long-Run Consequences: An Overview

In subsequent chapters, we will examine in detail the new societies and the distinctive life patterns that have resulted from two centuries of industrialization. For the moment, however, we will note just a few of the most important and most striking consequences outside the realm of technology. Collectively, these changes in population, social organization, ideology, and language add up to a revolution without parallel in human history, from the standpoint of scope as well as speed.*

1. World population has multiplied nearly sevenfold (from 725 million to 5 billion) just since 1750, a rate of growth more than fifteen times higher than the rate between the time of Christ and 1750.
2. The rural-urban balance in advanced industrial societies has been nearly reversed: agrarian societies were approximately 90 percent rural; several advanced industrial societies are more than 80 percent urban.
3. The largest urban communities of the industrial era are more than fifteen times the size of the largest of the agrarian era.
4. Women in industrial societies give birth to only about a third as many children as women in preindustrial societies.
5. Life expectancy at birth is almost three times greater in advanced industrial societies than it was in agrarian.
6. The family, for the first time in history, is no longer a significant productive unit in the economy.
7. The role of women in the economy and in society at large has changed substantially.
8. The role of youth has also changed, and youth cultures have become a significant factor in the life of industrial societies.
9. The *per capita* production and consumption of goods and services in advanced industrial societies is at least ten times greater than in traditional agrarian societies.
10. The division of labor is vastly more complex.
11. Hereditary monarchical government has disappeared in industrial societies, except as a ceremonial and symbolic survival.
12. The functions of government have been vastly enlarged.
13. Free public educational systems have been established and illiteracy has been largely eliminated in all industrial societies.
14. New ideologies have spread widely (notably socialism, capitalism, and na-

---

*Documentation for this assertion will be found in Chapters 10 to 13.

tionalism), while older ones inherited from the agrarian era either have been substantially altered or have declined.

15. Worldwide communication and transportation networks have been created that have, for practical purposes, rendered our entire planet smaller than England in the agrarian era.

16. A global culture has begun to emerge, as evidenced in styles of dress, music, language, technology, and organizational patterns (e.g., factories, public schools, small families).

17. Global political institutions (e.g., the United Nations, the World Court) have been established for the first time.

18. A number of societies have acquired the capacity to obliterate the entire human population.

All this in only 200 years!

In the next four chapters we will examine in detail the consequences to date of the Industrial Revolution, first in advanced industrial societies, and then in hybrid industrializing agrarian and industrializing horticultural societies of the Third World. Finally, in the last chapter, we will turn to the question of what the future may hold—if our species' remarkable new technological capabilities do not bring the unfolding drama of sociocultural evolution to an abrupt and tragic conclusion.

CHAPTER 10

Industrial Societies: I

There are nearly thirty industrial societies in the world today. The majority of them are in Europe, where all societies are now industrialized with the exception of Albania, Greece, Portugal, Spain, and Yugoslavia. The other industrial societies are the English-speaking democracies overseas (Australia, Canada, New Zealand, and the United States), Japan, and Iceland. Some of these societies, however, have only recently crossed the threshold of industrialization and still have many of the characteristics of preindustrial societies. For this reason, our primary concern in the next three chapters will be with those societies that have moved well beyond this threshold and therefore provide the clearest picture of what industrialization means for a society.

The Informational Base: Technology and Ideology

The same kinds of cultural information that are most important in shaping the patterns of life in other human societies are most important in industrial societies as well. First, there is technological information, which defines the "limits of the possible" for a society and the costs of the various alternatives within those limits. Because the technological bases of all advanced industrial societies are fairly similar, these limits and cost calculations are much the same in all of them, leading to important similarities in various aspects of societal life. Second, there is ideological

TABLE 10.1 Productivity of American Agriculture, 1800–1982.

Activity	Number of Man-Hours Required			Percentage Reduction in Man-Hour Requirements
	1800	1910–1917	1978–1982	
Production of 100 bushels of wheat	373	106	8	97.9
Production of 100 bushels of corn	344	135	3	99.1
Production of a bale of cotton	601	276	6	99.0
Production of 1,000 pounds of milk	n.a.*	38	3	92.1
Production of 1,000 pounds of beef	n.a.*	46	11	76.1
Production of 1,000 pounds of chicken	n.a.*	95	2	97.9

*Not ascertained.
Sources: U.S. Department of Commerce, *Historical Statistics of the United States: Colonial Times to 1970,* pp. 500–501, and U.S. Department of Commerce, *Statistical Abstract of the United States, 1985,* table 1156.

information, the basic system of beliefs and values that guides a society or its leaders in selecting from among the viable alternatives. Here, the differences are greater than the similarities, and these differences in ideology lead to a number of important institutional and organizational differences, as we shall see.

Technology

The best way to appreciate the dramatic difference between an agrarian society and an industrial one is to look at the measurable changes that have occurred as a result of the shift from the older technology to the new. There is no better place to begin than with *agricultural productivity,* on which everything else ultimately depends.

As Table 10.1 shows, the industrialization of agriculture has had a revolutionary impact on the production of foods and fibers, making it possible to produce a given quantity of grain, fiber, milk, or meat with only a tiny fraction of the labor required with the older agrarian technology.* The labor used to produce a given quantity of wheat, corn, cotton, and chicken has been cut approximately 98 percent. In the case of milk and beef, the reductions have been somewhat less, but still dramatic. Because of these advances in agricultural technology, tens of millions of people who would otherwise be required on farms are free to engage in other kinds of economic

---

*In this discussion, we will draw heavily on data from the United States because of the excellent statistical materials that make it possible to trace trends well back into the nineteenth century.

activities. As a result, the percentage of farmers and farm workers in the American labor force dropped from 72 percent in 1820 to 2 percent today.[1]

The basic factor responsible for this remarkable trend has been the harnessing of new energy sources. In agrarian societies, people and animals were the chief sources of the energy used in most work activity, such as pushing, pulling, digging, lifting, and cutting. Their efforts were supplemented to some extent by wind power and waterpower. As recently as 1850, these four sources still supplied over 87 percent of the energy used in work activities in the United States. Today, they account for less than 1 percent.[2] In their stead, industrial societies use coal, petroleum, natural gas, hydroelectric power, and nuclear power. Except for coal, these sources were still untapped in 1850, and even coal had not been used as a substitute for human and animal energy until the invention of the steam engine in the eighteenth century.

Not only have energy sources changed, but the quantities used have multiplied enormously. In 1850, all the prime movers in the United States (i.e., human bodies, work animals, steam engines in factories, sailing ships, etc.) had a capacity of less than 10 million horsepower; by 1983 this had risen to more than 30 *billion*—a 3000-fold increase in only a little more than a century, and a 300-fold increase in *per capita* terms.[3]

FIGURE 10.1   A basic factor responsible for the high standard of living and other revolutionary developments in modern industrial societies is their ability to harness enormous amounts of relatively cheap energy: offshore oil rig.

FIGURE 10.2   The Krupp steel works at Rheinhausen, West Germany, operates twenty-four hours a day, producing 2 million tons of steel a year.

This remarkable jump in the production and consumption of energy was closely linked with increases in the production and consumption of a wide variety of other raw materials. Consider iron and steel, for example: British production rose nearly 7,000-fold between 1750 and 1970,[4] while American production increased 12,000-fold between 1820 and 1974.[5]

Equally dramatic growth is evident in the production and consumption of many other raw materials. In one recent year, the United States produced 3.8 tons of stone for every man, woman, and child in the population, 4.6 tons of sand and gravel, 3.6 tons of coal, 1.9 tons of crude petroleum, 700 pounds of iron ore, 620 pounds of cement, 515 pounds of phosphate rock, 390 pounds of clay, 340 pounds of salt, 170 pounds of uranium ore, 165 pounds of lime, 100 pounds of gypsum, and 55 pounds of sulfur, to cite but a few items.[6] Altogether, mineral production equals about 14 tons per person per year.

Change in the gross national product (GNP) of a society, corrected for effects of inflation, is one of the best measures we have of the magnitude of the technological advance brought about by industrialization.* It tells us the extent to which the changes in technology have enhanced the society's ability to produce goods and services.

When we compare American society's GNP in 1878 (the first year for which reliable data are available) with current figures, we find that there has been a *45-fold*

---

*Change in *per capita* GNP is the more appropriate measure when comparing societies that vary greatly in size, such as China and Uganda. When comparing the same society at two different times, however, simple GNP may be preferable, especially when our concern is to identify the magnitude of change in the society's capacity to produce goods and services.

increase.[7] As striking as this figure is, it is considerably smaller than the British figure, which shows a *nearly hundredfold* increase since 1801.[8] As these figures demonstrate, the technologies of advanced societies are much more powerful than the technologies of even the most advanced agrarian societies of the past. Small wonder that the advances in technology have been accompanied by revolutionary changes throughout society!

Ideology

During the last five centuries, the bounds of human knowledge have expanded enormously. The voyages of exploration that began in the fifteenth century gave humans their first accurate picture of the earth as a whole. Astronomers of the sixteenth and seventeenth centuries did the same for the solar system. More recently, the natural sciences have given us a vision of a universe of incredible complexity, whose age must be measured in billions of years and whose size must be expressed in billions of light-years. And, finally, in the last hundred years, the social sciences have begun the task of demythologizing the social order, challenging ancient theories about the nature of man and subjecting virtually every aspect of human life to systematic scrutiny.

Theistic Religions   Not surprisingly, this flood of new information about ourselves and the world we live in has shaken and unsettled many traditional beliefs, and the institutional systems based on them. This is especially evident in the case of theistic religions. The thought forms of all the great historic faiths—Judaism, Christianity, Islam, Hinduism, Buddhism, and Confucianism—bear the imprint of the agrarian era during which they evolved. But beliefs about the natural world and the social order that were "self-evident" during the agrarian era often appear alien and antiquated to members of industrial societies. This has created an acute theological crisis for all theistic faiths in industrial societies. Religious leaders have tried, in many cases, to translate the most important elements of their traditions into modern terms, while steering a course between irrelevant orthodoxy and heretical innovation. The turmoil and controversy within the Roman Catholic Church since Vatican Council II is but the latest in a series of intellectual crises that began at the time of Copernicus and Galileo.

**TABLE 10.2   Trends in the Subject Matter of Books
Published in the United States, 1880–1975 (in Percentages)**

Subject Matter	1880	1975
Technology, natural science, and social science	10.5	28.5
Religion	11.5	4.5
All other areas, including fiction and poetry	78.0	67.0

Source: Adapted from Christopher Sterling and Timothy Haight, *The Mass Media: Aspen Institute Guide to Communicaton Industry Trends* (New York: Praeger, 1978), tables 510 A and B.

TABLE 10.3   Religious Beliefs in Fourteen Industrial Societies, in Percentages

Society	Belief in "God or Universal Spirit"	Belief in Life after Death	Religious Beliefs "Very Important"
United States	94	69	56
Canada	89	54	36
Italy	88	46	36
Australia	80	48	25
Belgium, Netherlands	78	48	26
United Kingdom	76	43	23
France	72	39	22
West Germany	72	33	17
Sweden, Norway, Denmark, Finland	65	35	17
Japan	38	18	12

Source: Gallup Poll report, Sept. 9, 1976.

While the majority of people in most industrial societies still profess a belief in God, many no longer accept the fundamental teachings of the historic faiths (e.g., belief in a life after death) or consider religious beliefs to be an important part of their lives (see Table 10.3). As the traditional sources of religious authority have come more and more into question, religion has become more privatized and individualized. There has also been a great proliferation of new sects and cults of many kinds, reflecting the growing spirit of neophilia. One of the important consequences of these trends has been the gradual elimination of ties between government and governmentally supported state churches. While some industrial societies (e.g., Britain, Sweden) still have an officially recognized state church, their governments now provide minimal support, and it appears to be only a matter of time until the relationship is finally dissolved.

The New Secular Ideologies   Beginning in seventeenth- and eighteenth-century Europe, a number of new ideologies appeared in which supernatural beliefs were substantially reduced or totally eliminated. While some of these new ideologies quickly died out—for example, eighteenth-century Deism—a number of them not only survived but have prospered in the industrial era. The most important of these new faiths are democratic republicanism, capitalism, democratic socialism, revolutionary socialism, nationalism, and pragmatism.

Democratic republicanism, as its name suggests, is a special form of the more general ideology known as republicanism. The basic doctrine of republicanism is its repudiation of hereditary monarchy—the type of government that prevailed in most agrarian societies of the past—and of the proprietary theory of the state (see page 194).

Although republicanism has existed as an ideology for thousands of years, republican governments have been rare, except in maritime societies. Prior to the nineteenth century, most influential republicans rejected democratic republicanism, preferring instead oligarchical republicanism. In other words, they advocated a form of government in which power was concentrated in the hands of a few individuals, as in maritime societies of the past. Oligarchical republicans have generally been distrustful of the masses of common people, fearful that they would misuse the powers of government if they ever gained political control.

The government of the United States in the first fifty years after the American Revolution provides a good example of oligarchical republicanism. Most members of the new political elite thought it wise to limit the exercise of political power to a small minority of the population—men of property, who therefore had, presumably, the greatest stake in the welfare of society and also the greatest capacity to govern. In the new constitution adopted by the state of North Carolina in 1776, for example, the right to vote was limited to men who owned at least 100 acres of land, and the right to sit in the General Assembly (i.e., the new state legislature) was limited to the even smaller group that owned 300 acres. To be eligible to be governor of the state, a man had to have a net worth of £1,000. Similar provisions were contained in the constitutions of virtually all of the other states in postrevolutionary America. While it is impossible to translate those figures into modern terms in any precise way, it may be noted that £1,000 was more than eight times the net worth of the average white adult male in the South at the time.

Not everyone in early America was satisfied with oligarchical republicanism, and even in the eighteenth century there were some who advocated democratic republicanism, or what Abraham Lincoln would later describe as "government of the people, by the people, and for the people." Not surprisingly, many of the most ardent advocates of democratic republicanism were people who lived on what was then the western frontier. As we saw in Chapter 7 (pages 205–207), frontier regions have long been noted for their egalitarianism and their resistance to established systems of authority. With strong support from this increasingly important part of the population, democratic republicanism won growing support in the early decades of the nineteenth century. With the election of Andrew Jackson in 1828, the fate of oligarchical republicanism in the United States was sealed. Property requirements for voting were gradually reduced, and soon eliminated altogether. This process was virtually completed by the late 1850s so that nearly all free white males were then eligible to vote.

Since that time, democratic republicanism has been the dominant political ideology in American society and has won the support of hundreds of millions of other people throughout the world. Nevertheless, even today only a small minority of societies are governed by democratic principles, and these are largely confined to the industrial societies of Western Europe, North America, Oceania, and Japan. One reason for this has been the rise of a new, competing ideology, Marxism-Leninism (see below, pages 264–267).

Capitalism is another important new ideology of the industrial era. Its intellectual father was Adam Smith, a Scottish professor of moral philosophy who combined a keen analytical mind with a crusading nature.[9] In his most influential work, a book published in 1776 and entitled *An Inquiry into the Nature and Causes of the Wealth of Nations,* Smith made a powerful case for the thesis that the intervention of government into the economic life of a society will only retard its growth and development. The only useful function government can perform in the economic sphere, according to Smith, is to enforce contracts that individuals enter into freely. Anything more than this is harmful. Smith backed up his argument with an im-

FIGURE 10.3   Adam Smith.

pressive analysis designed to show that the law of supply and demand, operating in a truly free market situation, would ensure that "the private interests and passions of men" are led in the direction "most agreeable to the interest of the whole society."[10] It would be a self-regulating system, but it would function, said Smith, as though an "invisible hand" were at work, ensuring the best possible outcome.

Smith's work laid the foundation for the emerging academic discipline of modern economics. More important, however, his basic beliefs about the harm done by governmental intervention in the economy became the basis of a powerful new ideology that for 200 years has exercised a profound influence on societies around the globe. Above all, it has provided moral justification for governmental policies that minimize public control of businessmen and business enterprises. In societies where capitalism is the dominant ideology, the term "free enterprise" has become a sacred symbol that is often invoked with considerable success to manipulate public opinion. As we will see shortly, the realities of contemporary capitalism are strikingly different from its ideals, as has been true, of course, of every ideology from Christianity to socialism.

Another important new ideology of the industrial era is *socialism*. While its underlying principle has been applied in many simpler societies for thousands of years, the modern concept dates from the nineteenth century and was an explicit response to, and reaction against, the realities of early capitalism. Socialists argued that the basic economic resources of a society should be the common property of all its members, and used for the benefit of all. Where proponents of capitalism praised free enterprise for the growth in productivity it generated, socialists attacked it for its harsh working conditions, its low wages and economic inequality, its unemployment, its child labor, its boom and bust cycles, and its alienating and exploitative character. Where capitalists advocated the private ownership of the means of production, socialists favored public ownership. Where capitalists argued for economic inequality to provide incentives for people to work productively, socialists insisted that a more egalitarian distribution would achieve the same result.

Since early in its history, the socialist movement has been split into a variety of warring sects that have often fought more with one another than with the advocates of capitalism and other ideologies.[11] In the long run, however, the most important split has been between *democratic socialism* and *revolutionary socialism*.

Democratic socialism, as its name implies, assumes that socialist principles have an inherent appeal to the vast majority of people. Its proponents therefore maintain that, in democratic societies, socialist governments should seek to achieve power through democratic means, and that, after coming to power, they should allow opposing political parties to compete freely for the support of the electorate and to return to power any time they can secure it. Democratic socialists believe that any other policy would defeat one of socialism's basic aims: to maximize the freedom of individuals. They argue that the practice of political democracy is as essential to socialism as public ownership of the means of production, and that failure to practice political democracy subverts the very nature of socialism.

During the twentieth century, parties adhering to these principles (e.g., the Labour Party in Britain, the Social Democratic Party in Germany, the Socialist Party in France) have developed large followings, and in many cases they have succeeded in electing governments. Because of the continuing appeal of capitalist principles, however, none of them has attempted to abolish entirely private ownership of the means of production. While these parties have taken some steps in that direction (i.e., they have nationalized some industries), the major thrust of their policies has become the creation of a *welfare state*. In other words, they have used the powers of government to tax the profits of privately owned enterprises in order to fund health, educational, and social service programs that benefit the masses of ordinary citizens who do not own any significant amount of the means of production. This allows everyone to share in the benefits of the productive system without totally abolishing private ownership and control.

In contrast, the other major faction within the socialist movement has denied the possibility of achieving socialism through peaceful, democratic means, even in democratic societies. In their view, socialism can be established only by the forcible overthrow of the bourgeoisie (i.e., the capitalist class) and by the expropriation of its properties.

The spiritual father of modern revolutionary socialism is Karl Marx, whose writings and political activities in the nineteenth century laid the foundation for the Communist parties of the twentieth. In contemporary societies controlled by his followers, he occupies an honored status not unlike that accorded great religious figures of the past. His doctrines are taught to children from an early age in all the schools, his writings are cited by the party elite to justify their policies, and pictures and statues of him are found in public places.

Marx believed that humans are inherently good and decent and that the evils found in societies can all be traced ultimately to the influence of the institution of private property. This institution stimulates greed and selfishness, exploitation, in-

FIGURE 10.4   Karl Marx.

justice, and oppression. By destroying it, humans could free themselves forever from all of these evils and set human societies on a new course that would lead, in time, to the development of a world in which freedom, justice, and equality would prevail and in which everyone's material and spiritual needs would all be met.

Marx based these beliefs on a complex and interesting theory of history in which he argued that capitalism contains the seeds of its own destruction and that socialist revolutions, led by members of the then-new and growing army of industrial workers, not only are inevitable but ultimately will prevail. In short, after a brief but bloody period of revolution, human societies will advance to a new stage of development in which all of the legitimate needs and desires of people will be fulfilled. In an initial phase of this new stage of development, people will be rewarded according to the socialist principle, "to each according to his *work*." In a later, higher phase of development, people will be rewarded according to the communist principle, "to each according to his *need*."

Marxist socialism is a far more comprehensive ideology than either capitalism or democratic socialism. Where these other ideologies allow people to make their own choices in most areas of their lives, Marxism imposes standards on everything from politics and economics to art and religion. In this respect, Marxism is closer to medieval Catholicism than to capitalism or democratic socialism. Maurice Duverger, a French social scientist, summarized this aspect of Marxist socialism when he wrote:

> The party not only provides [the militant Communist] with organization for all his material activities, more important still it gives him a general organization of ideas, a systematic explanation of the universe. Marxism is not only a political doctrine, but a complete philosophy, a way of thinking, a spiritual cosmogony. All isolated facts in all spheres find their place in it and the reason for all their existence. It explains equally well the structure and evolution of the state, the changes in living creatures, the appearance of man on the earth, religious feelings, sexual behavior, and the development of the arts and sciences. And the explanation can be brought within the reach of the masses as well as being understood by the learned and by educated people. This philosophy can easily be made into a catechism without too serious a deformation. In this way the human spirit's need for fundamental unity can be satisfied.[12]

Revolutionary socialism makes broad claims on the lives not only of its adherents but of all who come under its power. Despite its professed aim of maximizing human freedom, it has become the most authoritarian and repressive of all the major current ideologies. This seeming paradox reflects, to a considerable degree, the influence of Vladimir Ilich Lenin, Marx's foremost disciple. Lenin extended and modified certain key ideas of Marx's in ways that profoundly influenced the subsequent course of revolutionary socialism. It is no mere coincidence that in Marxist-Leninist societies today, Lenin is usually honored and revered more highly than Marx himself.[13]

Lenin's chief contribution to revolutionary socialism was to define the role of the Communist Party in postrevolutionary societies. Not surprisingly, since Marx died in 1883, thirty-four years before the first successful socialist revolution, his writings dealt primarily with prerevolutionary conditions. He had relatively little to say about postrevolutionary societies and was generally vague and unspecific in what he did say about them. Lenin, in contrast, wrote extensively on the subject. In his writings, he gave an important new meaning to a concept that Marx had mentioned only briefly and in an ambiguous manner: *the dictatorship of the proletariat.*

Marx had written that a dictatorship of the working class would probably be necessary for a brief period after a socialist revolution in order to effect the transition from capitalism to socialism.[14] Lenin took this concept and gave it a striking new meaning: for him, the "dictatorship of the proletariat" became the justification for a seemingly permanent dictatorship by the leaders of the Communist Party.[15] Lenin justified this on the elitist principle that the proletariat, or working class, is unqualified to govern and must depend on the Party's leaders, since only they understand the principles of "scientific" socialism.

Because of Lenin, modern revolutionary socialism is a curious combination of radical goals and reactionary means. Marxism-Leninism, as the dominant version of modern revolutionary socialism has come to be known, still claims its goal is the establishment of freedom, justice, and equality throughout the world, but it proposes to achieve this by the dictatorial rule of a tiny elite. Unfortunately, when Leninist means (i.e., the rule of this elite) and Marxist ends (i.e., freedom, justice, equality) come into conflict, as they often do, Party leaders invariably give priority to the means.* For them, the preservation of Party power, which also means their own power, has become the highest priority.[16] As a result, Marxism-Leninism provides a remarkably successful ideological justification for the establishment of elite rule and for the preservation of the political status quo in Marxist-Leninist societies everywhere. Thus, ironically, an ideology that began as a radical, idealistic, even utopian faith has been transformed into a remarkably reactionary and elitist political doctrine wherever its adherents have come to power.†

The fifth of the major new secular ideologies is *nationalism*.[17] As with other major ideologies, some of its elements have existed for thousands of years: group loyalty and tribalism, for example, are hardly new. During the agrarian era, however, the peasant masses, who made up 80 percent or more of the population, had little interest in politics beyond the village level.[18] The rise and fall of empires were of no consequence to them—unless, of course, they were drawn into these struggles against their will. This lack of interest in politics at the national level was only natural in societies in which the dominant ideology defined the state as the private property of the ruler.

With industrialization, the situation began to change. Expanded educational systems, increasing urbanization, shortened workweeks, an improved standard of living, and the new mass media all combined to bring politics within the sphere of concern of the average citizen. With this came a heightened sense of personal identification with the nation-state, especially in times of international tensions and conflict. Nationalism has been an especially potent ideology in colonial territories ever since the American Revolution, and it is important today in many societies of the Third World that have recently escaped colonial control. It has also become a potent force among ethnic and religious minorities in many industrial societies, such as the French in Canada, the Catholics in Ulster, the Lapps in Sweden, and the Basques in Spain.

In many societies in recent decades, nationalism has been combined with other ideologies. The Nazi (literally, National Socialist) regime in Germany prior to World War II was a good example. In American society, nationalism of a far more temperate variety is often linked to Christianity and capitalism to form what some have called this nation's "civil religion."[19]

The last of the major new ideologies, *pragmatism,* differs from the others in one essential respect: it offers no preconceived ideas as to how societies should be organized. It asserts that social institutions should be judged by their consequences:

---

*The elitist character of modern Communist parties cannot be attributed entirely to Lenin, since Marx himself provided a strong initial impetus in this direction.[15a] In his own participation in the revolutionary socialist movement of his day, Marx was extremely autocratic and unwilling to share power with those who disagreed with him. Nevertheless, Lenin seems to have been primarily responsible for institutionalizing elitist rule under postrevolutionary conditions. His doctrine of "democratic centralism," which places all power within the Party in the hands of a tiny elite of self-chosen leaders, has made efforts to democratize the Party all but impossible.

†In societies in which Marxist-Leninists are *not* in power, they are more easily able to project an image of idealism, since their primary role in these societies is that of critic of the existing elite, and every elite is vulnerable to criticism.

FIGURE 10.5   William James.

those that prove beneficial should be strengthened and preserved; those that are not should be eliminated.

The spiritual father of modern pragmatism was the American philosopher William James. Like Adam Smith and Karl Marx, he developed, expanded, and systematized certain basic ideas that had existed for centuries. But unlike those of Smith and Marx, his teachings have not given rise to any large or influential group of disciples. At the same time, however, the basic principles of pragmatism have been adopted widely in the modern world. In fact, it would be no exaggeration to say that most of the world's leaders today who profess to believe in other ideologies are also, to greater or lesser degree, pragmatists. They have discovered that no ideology provides a fully satisfactory blueprint for the organization and governance of society. If they hope to be successful, or just retain power, they have to improvise, and this means they have to adopt the pragmatic principle of judging policies and programs by their consequences.

The extent to which they do this varies considerably: Chinese Marxists, for example, have been much more pragmatic than Soviet Marxists, just as some Smithians are much more pragmatic and flexible than others. The more important point, however, is that the pragmatic principle of judging social arrangements by their results has become characteristic of an ever-increasing number of the leaders of modern societies.

Despite their many differences, the new ideologies of the industrial era all have one thing in common: *they are all predicated on the belief that human destiny is largely subject to human control.* This is in sharp contrast to ideologies that originated in the preindustrial past. Those ideologies asserted that events depended on forces beyond human control—fate, God, the gods—and taught that the best way to appease those forces was through magic, ritual, and adherence to tradition. Some ideologies held that every development in life was ordained by a higher power, and that mere mortals had no right to try to change conditions.

Members of modern societies are not nearly so passive. New information in areas ranging from science to history has improved their understanding of human nature and of the world they inhabit, while new technological information has increased their capacity to adapt to that world. The result has been a growing awareness of humanity's potential for shaping its own future. This basic belief underlies all of the new ideologies of the industrial era, and the members of modern societies have come to rely increasingly on these ideologies, and less and less on traditional ones, in their efforts to control their lives and to shape the life of society as a whole.

Despite this basic similarity, there are fundamental differences between these new ideologies, and these are of greater significance today than at any time in human history. For as technology has expanded the limits of the possible and increased the range of viable alternatives available to industrial societies, *the ideologies that guide them in choosing among these alternatives have become an important source of societal variation—and thus a significant factor in the process of intersocietal selection.*

Population

Growth in Size of Societies

Industrialization has led to a substantial increase in the size of most human societies since the beginning of the industrial era. Population growth in the most industrialized societies, however, has not been nearly as great as their technological advances and gains in productivity would lead one to expect. For example, England and Wales had a population of approximately 9 million at the start of the nineteenth century, and their current population is about 50 million.[20] While this fivefold to sixfold increase is impressive when compared to rates of population growth in preindustrial eras, it falls far short of the nearly hundredfold increase in Britain's gross national product during that same period. The same thing is true of other societies that have industrialized, with the exception of the United States, Canada, Australia, and other former frontier societies which entered the industrial era with abnormally small populations for their geographical size.

Improved Health, Increased Longevity, and Lowered Death Rates

Throughout the agrarian era, sickness and disease were a pervasive feature of human life. Prior to the invention of the microscope, it was impossible for anyone even to know of the existence of bacteria or viruses, much less to devise effective means of combating them. Sanitary and medical knowledge were not advanced much beyond what had existed at the end of the hunting and gathering era and, for most illnesses, people were forced to rely on faith healing, magic, or medical practices of dubious value (e.g., the use of leeches and bloodletting) when they became ill. Not surprisingly, as we have seen (page 179), average life expectancy at birth in even the most advanced societies ranged from 20 to 25 years, and even the children of royalty and other members of the upper classes did not have a much greater life expectancy at birth.

During the industrial era, however, there has been an explosive growth in the store of information concerning the prevention and cure of disease—especially communicable diseases, such as influenza, tuberculosis, diphtheria, and smallpox, that once killed large numbers of people and afflicted many more. As a result, the death rate from communicable diseases has dropped tremendously (see Table 10.4) and life expectancy at birth has tripled in advanced industrial societies. Today, newborns can expect to live 70 years or more, on average, in virtually all advanced industrial societies. Equally important, they will live far healthier lives than was possible in most preindustrial societies.

Lower Birthrates, Slower Growth, and the New Demographic Equilibrium

As health conditions improved and death rates declined, industrial societies began to experience rapid population growth. This was because birthrates remained for a time at traditional levels, which created a widening gap between birthrates and death rates.

TABLE 10.4 Death Rates for Communicable Diseases, 1860–1980

	Deaths per 100,000 Population per Year		
Cause of Death	Mass., 1860*	U.S., 1900	U.S., 1980
Influenza and pneumonia	†	202	24
Tuberculosis	365	194	1
Gastritis, enteritis, etc.	†	143	0
Typhoid fever	76	31	0
Diphtheria	68	40	0
Smallpox	27	†	0
Measles	18	13	0
Scarlet fever	†	10	0

*Massachusetts was the first state to keep reliable statewide records on the causes of death; reliable national data are not available until 1900.
†Not reported.
Source: *Historical Statistics of the United States: Colonial Times to 1970*, pp. 58 and 63; *Statistical Abstract of the United States, 1984*, p. 78.

Within a few decades, however, birthrates also began to move downward. During the last 150 years, technological advances on various fronts (e.g., the vulcanization of rubber, the development of the contraceptive pill, safe methods of abortion and sterilization) have made it possible for members of industrial societies to control the number of their offspring by safe and effective means. At the same time, technological advances in other areas, together with various social changes (e.g., the creation of social security programs, prohibitions against child labor), have virtually eliminated the historic *economic* incentive for having children. As a result, birthrates have dropped greatly in all industrial societies.

In recent years, there has been growing evidence that a new demographic equilibrium may be developing in industrial societies, with birthrates and death rates both stabilizing in the neighborhood of 13 or 14 per thousand population per year. Death rates have long been at this level in advanced industrial societies, and birthrates are now at or close to it in most of them (see Table 10.5).

TABLE 10.5 Crude Birthrates, Death Rates, and Rates of Natural Increase for Major Industrial Societies

Society	Crude Birthrate*	Crude Death Rate†	Rate of Natural Increase‡
Hungary	12	14	−0.2
West Germany	10	11	−0.1
Denmark	10	11	−0.1
Sweden	11	11	0.0
Austria	12	12	0.0
Italy	11	10	0.1
Belgium	12	11	0.1
United Kingdom	13	12	0.1
East Germany	14	13	0.1
Switzerland	11	9	0.2
Norway	12	10	0.2
Czechoslovakia	15	12	0.2
Bulgaria	14	11	0.3
Netherlands	12	8	0.4
France	14	10	0.4
Romania	15	10	0.5
Japan	13	6	0.7
United States	16	9	0.7
Canada	15	7	0.8
New Zealand	16	8	0.8
Australia	16	7	0.9
Poland	20	10	1.0

*Live births per 1,000 population per year.
†Deaths per 1,000 population per year.
‡Percentage growth of population due to excess of births over deaths (or percentage decline due to excess of deaths over births) per year.
Source: Population Reference Bureau, "1985 World Population Data Sheet."

The period of rapid population growth now seems to have ended for advanced industrial societies. Figure 10.6 illustrates the pattern of change that has occurred since the onset of industrialization—a pattern which demographers refer to as "the demographic transition."

The Rising Tide of Immigration to Advanced Industrial Societies

There is, of course, no guarantee that a new equilibrium will be established. It is possible that members of advanced industrial societies will so limit the number of their offspring that the population of these societies will actually begin to decline. The technology that would be needed is already available. Alternatively, population growth may occur as a result of increasing immigration. Evidence of this can be found not only in the United States and Canada, but also in most of the advanced industrial societies of Western Europe. The economic opportunities and high standards of living these societies offer, together with the growth of the welfare state with its many free services, are proving to be a powerful magnet that attracts great numbers of people from Third World societies.

In the years ahead, this immigration is likely to create serious political problems in many of these societies. No society today can possibly create enough jobs to satisfy the demand for them by all of the would-be immigrants from the Third World. Already, many advanced industrial societies are finding it difficult to create and maintain enough jobs to satisfy the demand of their own citizens. Under conditions in which there are not enough jobs for everyone, competition between natives and immigrants is an almost certain formula for racial and ethnic strife. Even when there is no competition for jobs, cultural differences between ethnic groups usually generate hostility.

In a few instances, the magnitude of the migration from Third World societies to advanced industrial societies has become so great that a single group of immigrants actually outnumbers the native population in large sections of a number of major

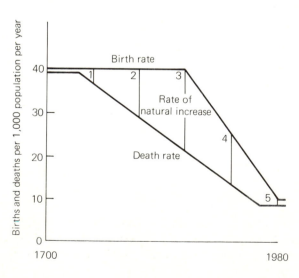

FIGURE 10.6 The demographic cycle experienced by advanced industrial societies: trends in fertility, mortality, and natural increase. The vertical lines indicate the rate of natural increase in different years.

FIGURE 10.7   Migration from Third World societies to advanced industrial societies has become so great that immigrants often outnumber natives in large sections of a number of major cities: Turkish shops in the Kreuzberg district of West Berlin.

cities. Thus, for example, Turks outnumber Germans in parts of West Berlin, Algerians outnumber French in parts of Paris, and Cubans outnumber Americans in much of Miami. These developments, and others like them, have already given rise to new nationalist movements in Western Europe and to renewed efforts to limit and control immigration in the United States. What further reactions develop remains to be seen.

Population Distribution: The Growth of Urban Populations

Another revolutionary demographic change has been the massive shift of population from rural areas to cities and towns. Even in the most advanced agrarian societies, the limitations of agricultural technology required that 90 to 95 percent of the population live in rural areas, where the basic raw materials were produced. Since urban communities were almost totally dependent on the surplus that could be extracted from the peasantry, they could never grow beyond 5 to 10 percent of the population.

Advances in agriculture in the last two hundred years removed this constraint on urban growth. Thanks to the new technology, farms required far fewer workers. Simultaneously, the new system of factory production, with its need for large concentrations of workers, stimulated the growth of cities and towns. As a result, three-quarters of the populations of most industrial societies now live in urban areas.

Not surprisingly, cities in industrial societies are much larger than cities in pre-industrial societies. In the agrarian era, capitals of a few great empires appear to have had populations numbering a million or slightly more at the height of the empire's power (see Table 10.6). Today, barely two centuries after the end of the agrarian era, there are at least twenty cities with populations of 5 million or more, and the largest of them, New York, with its urban and suburban satellites, has more than 16 million.[21]

The Economy

The economy of a society is, in effect, an institutionalized set of answers to the basic questions of production and distribution: What kinds of goods and services will be produced? In what quantities? At what prices? And by what means will they be allocated to the various members of the society?

The way in which these questions are answered reflects, to a large degree, constraints imposed by the environment, by the technology on which a society depends, and by the necessity of keeping the productive system functioning properly. But it also reflects the beliefs and values—the ideology—of those who control the society. Thus, among modern industrial societies there are important differences between the economies of the Marxist-Leninist societies of Eastern Europe and the economies of the others. There are also less important differences between the economies of most Western European nations and those of the United States,

TABLE 10.6   The World's Largest Cities, from 3000 B.C. to 1980 A.D.

Date	City	Population*	Date	City	Population*
3000 B.C.	Memphis	40,000	620 A.D.	Constantinople	500,000
2000 B.C.	Memphis	100,000	900 A.D.	Baghdad	900,000
1360 B.C.	Thebes	100,000	1300 A.D.	Hangchow	430,000
650 B.C.	Nineveh	120,000	1500 A.D.	Peking	670,000
430 B.C.	Babylon	250,000	1700 A.D.	Constantinople	700,000
200 B.C.	Patna	350,000	1800 A.D.	Peking	1,100,000
100 A.D.	Rome	650,000	1900 A.D.	London	6,500,000
360 A.D.	Constantinople	350,000	1980 A.D.	New York	16,500,000

*Population includes suburbs.
Sources: Tertius Chandler and Gerald Fox, *3000 Years of Urban Growth* (New York: Academic Press, 1974), pp. 300–341 and 362–363, and *World Almanac, 1983*, p. 590.

FIGURE 10.8   Cities in industrial societies are much larger than cities in agrarian societies. The population of greater New York is now approximately 16 million.

Canada, and Japan, reflecting the greater relative strength of democratic socialism in the former and of capitalism in the latter.

Before considering these differences, however, we need to consider the characteristics that are shared by the economies of *all* industrial societies. As we will see, there are a number of such features and they are quite important. These shared characteristics are due chiefly to constraints imposed by the new technology on which they all depend so heavily.

The Urbanization of Production

Prior to the Industrial Revolution, agriculture was the chief form of economic activity and production was centered in rural areas. Farmers were a substantial majority of the labor force. In addition to farming, the rural population often engaged in a variety of crafts during winter months, welcoming the opportunity that this provided for additional income. Urban populations were small, and many urban residents were members of the governing class and not gainfully employed (this was true of many of the men as well as almost all of the women and children). In addition, many of those who were gainfully employed in cities and towns produced nonessential goods and services for the enjoyment of the upper class.

The Industrial Revolution changed all this. As we saw in the last chapter, the new machines that were invented required the development of factories and large concentrations of industrial workers. At the same time that new urban industries were generating a growing demand for workers in cities and towns, technological advances in agriculture were reducing the need for workers on farms. As a result, industrialization led to a massive migration of people from rural areas to urban—a migration that only now seems to be nearing its end in the most advanced industrial societies.

The effect of these changes has been to shift the locus of production in societies from rural areas to urban. In advanced industrial societies today, less than 15 percent of Gross Domestic Product (GDP) is the result of agricultural activity, and in many cases it is less than 5 percent.[22] Equally important, the rural economy of industrial societies has been completely transformed. Many of the people who now live in rural areas commute to work in urban communities. In much of Eastern Europe, for example, there is a segment of the population that has come to be known as worker-peasants: the men commute to cities and towns where they work in factories during the week, while helping the women on the farms on weekends. (Women work on the farms during the week.) Similar patterns have also developed in western societies: already by 1970 the majority of American "farmers" earned more from nonfarm activities (e.g., work in factories) than from the sale of farm products.[23]

The traditional family farm is a dead or dying institution in most industrial societies. In the Soviet Union and in most of Eastern Europe it has been replaced by large, state-owned farms or by equally large collective farms (Poland is a notable exception, with the majority of its farms still small and privately owned). In the United States, the family farm is increasingly replaced by giant agribusinesses that employ managers and workers in the same way as factories. While family-owned farms have proven somewhat more durable in Western Europe and Japan, their future hardly seems assured even there. In fact, in most cases these farms have survived chiefly because of political actions that have protected them against competition from more efficient foreign producers. Without such protection, these family farms would have failed long ago.

Rise in Productivity and in the Standard of Living

The most striking characteristic of the economies of industrial societies is their remarkable productivity. As we noted earlier, Britain's gross national product has grown approximately a hundredfold since 1801, and that of the United States more than fortyfold just since 1878. Other highly industrialized societies have experienced comparable growth. Because most of this increase in productivity has not been consumed by population growth, there has been an enormous increase in the size of the economic surplus in every industrial society.

In agrarian societies, any new surplus would have been absorbed almost entirely by a small minority of the population. In industrial societies, the surplus is spread far more widely among the members.[24] In other words, the growth of the

FIGURE 10.9 Harvesting grain on a collective farm, USSR.

economic surplus has greatly improved the standard of living for the vast majority of people who live in these societies. Per capita income in Great Britain today is approximately sixteen times what it was in 1801, and in the United States it is nine times greater than in 1878.

That these figures reflect real gains in the living standards of the masses becomes apparent when we consider some of the basic characteristics of the lifestyle of the average member of an industrial society today—keeping in mind the situations of the typical agrarian peasant (pages 186–188) and of the workers during the early stages of industrialization (pages 252–254). To begin with, the vast majority of the members of every industrial society have a food supply that is larger, far more dependable (i.e., less subject to acute shortages), and of higher quality and greater variety than in any agrarian society of the past. They live in superior housing, with an indoor water supply, plumbing, electricity, usually central heating, and often air conditioning in warmer climates. The majority of their homes and apartments are equipped with furnishings and appliances that are far more than adequate for health and comfort, and some would have aroused envy in the elites of agrarian societies. Widespread educational opportunities are available, and so is vastly improved health care. Modern transportation and communication systems broaden and enrich their lives and provide them with entertainment and relief from boredom. And countless other goods and services too numerous to catalog, and unheard of in agrarian societies, are also available to the majority of people in every industrial society.

This is not to suggest that life in industrial societies does not have its deficiencies and worse: we will discuss the negative aspects of industrial societies in Chapters 12 and 14. But it is impossible to deny that industrialization has meant a remarkable improvement in the standard of living for the average individual compared with the average individual in preindustrial or early industrial societies. Relative to the peasants of the agrarian era, modern industrial workers live lives of unbelievable affluence and abundance. And there are very few people in these societies whose standard of living comes anywhere near that of the expendables of agrarian societies. Even those dependent on public welfare are much better off than that.

The Shift from Labor-Intensive to Capital-Intensive Industries

The basis of the enormous productivity and affluence of modern industrial societies is their fantastic store of technological information. But most of this information would be useless unless it were *converted into capital goods*. Without the complex machines, factories, transportation facilities, power plants, and other capital goods that are essential to production in an industrial society, the output of its workers would be little different from that of workers in agrarian societies.

We can see the importance of capital goods when we compare two contemporary industries, one capital-intensive and the other labor-intensive. The petroleum industry is a good example of the former, with expensive, highly automated machinery and a small labor force; the fast-food industry, utilizing simpler and less expensive machines, is far more labor-intensive. UNOCAL (formerly Standard Oil of California), for example, recently reported average annual sales of more than $750,000 *per employee,* while the sales of McDonald's hamburger chain amounted to only $17,400 per employee per year.[25]

One of the chief reasons for the tremendous growth in per capita GNP in industrial societies has been the massive movement of workers out of traditional subsistence agriculture and into capital-intensive industries during the last 150 years. In traditional subsistence agriculture, farmers raised cash crops only to the extent required to pay taxes, rent, and interest on loans, and to enable them to buy the simple tools and other necessities they could not produce themselves. Thus, only a small fraction of what they produced entered the larger economy. As these farmers abandoned their farms and joined the urban labor force, their economic contribution increased substantially. Since about 80 percent of the population of the typical agrarian society were food producers, in contrast to a tiny minority—in some cases less than 5 percent—in industrial societies, the impact of that shift is obvious.

Today, however, that flow has ended (and with it a major boost to economic growth). The small, traditional family farm has been largely replaced by huge agribusinesses, state farms, and collective farms that are as capital-intensive as urban industry.

To appreciate the changes that have occurred in farming, one need only consider First Colony Farms, a 375,000-acre, $600 million enterprise in northeastern North Carolina.[26] This highly mechanized, capital-intensive business employs less than 1,000 workers and operates on the same basis as any other large corporation. Its products are sold in national and international markets.

FIGURE 10.10   The petroleum industry is a classic example of a capital-intensive industry requiring heavy investment in machines and minimal investment in human labor: Soviet oil refinery in Kazakhstan.

Agricultural operations on this scale are still unusual in western societies. But when a single tractor may cost $150,000 or more, and when the *minimum* investment in land, buildings, and machines required for profitable farming in many areas has risen to the neighborhood of $1 million, there is not much choice.[27]

Changes in the Labor Force

The Shift from Primary Industries   From the onset of industrialization, there has been, as we have seen, an inevitable movement of workers out of primary industries. These industries, which produce raw materials, include farming, fishing, mining, and lumbering. In traditional agrarian societies these industries usually provided a livelihood for over 80 percent of the labor force. With industrialization, most of these people move into *secondary industries*, such as mills and factories, which process the raw materials and turn them into finished products, and into *tertiary industries*,

COWS AND COMPUTERS

Ron Van Zee and his brother, Bill, still like to think of their dairy farm as a "family farm," but a visit to the barn suggests otherwise. All of their 200 cows are now linked to computers that provide the Van Zees with a detailed set of records on each cow, and the computer is hooked to a radio transmitter that controls each animal's allotment of feed.

As the cows are milked mechanically, Ron Van Zee punches their ID numbers into the computer. If one light goes on, it means that the cow's milk is fit to drink, but if another light goes on it means that the cow is medicated and her milk must be discarded. Stored in the computer is a file on every cow in the herd, with eighty statistics on each, such as her milk production, milk-fat content, and the number of calves she has produced. There is even a measure of her disposition, on a scale from 1 to 9.

The Van Zees lease their computer system for $900 a month and believe their investment has been well worth the expense. Since introducing the computer, they have been able to reduce the feed their cows consume by 1,650 pounds per day by adjusting the amount each receives to take account of where she is in the calving cycle. Research has shown that there are times in the cycle when extra feed only produces useless fat, not more milk. When a cow sticks her head into a computerized feed trough, her four-digit ID number is transmitted to the computer, which scans the relevant data and determines whether more food is indicated. If she has not yet eaten her allotted amount, the feeder is instructed to crank out another serving. As a minor incidental benefit of the new system, the Van Zees have the computer programmed to alert them if the door to the feeding parlor has been left open by accident.

Source: *Wall Street Journal,* September 21, 1983.

which provide the varied and growing kinds of services found in industrial societies: education, health care, police and fire protection, social services, government, retail trade, and so on. As industrialization proceeds, the initial rapid growth in secondary industries slows down considerably, and tertiary industries become the chief area of growth in the economy.

Table 10.7 shows how striking this process has been in the United States, completely transforming the labor force in the last 140 years. From a 70 percent concentration of workers in primary industries, there are now 70 percent in tertiary industries, and growth in those industries continues at the expense of the other two. Similar trends are found in every industrial society, although growth in the tertiary industries has been much less pronounced in the Marxist-Leninist societies of Eastern Europe.

Growth of White-Collar Jobs Another striking change in the labor force has been the rapid expansion of white-collar, or nonmanual, jobs. This trend is especially evident in the United States. At the beginning of the present century, only 17 percent of American workers were employed in white-collar jobs; today, 54 percent are in such jobs.[28]

**TABLE 10.7 Changing Patterns of Employment in the
American Labor Force, 1840 to 1980: Percentages
Employed in Primary, Secondary, and Tertiary Industries**

Year	Primary Industries	Secondary Industries	Tertiary Industries	Total
1840	69	15	16	100
1870	55	21	24	100
1900	40	28	32	100
1930	23	29	48	100
1960	8	30	62	100
1980	3	24	73	100

Sources: Calculations based on *Historical Statistics of the United
States: Colonial Times to 1970,* series D152–166; and *Statistical
Abstract of the United States, 1985,* table 679.

The rapid growth of white-collar jobs has been associated with the growth of the
tertiary, or service, industries and the decline of the primary industries. As opportunities for farm employment have declined, opportunities for employment in clerical and sales work, the professions, and management have increased. More
recently, opportunities for employment in the secondary industries (i.e., manufacturing) have also begun to decline, both in absolute and in relative terms, and this has
meant a decline in opportunities for employment in blue-collar jobs. In 1960, for
example, 37 percent of American workers were employed in blue-collar jobs,
chiefly in the secondary industries. Today, less than 30 percent are in such jobs and
the percentage is still declining.[29]

Increased Employment of Women Outside of Households Until recently, most
women worked only within households—as wives, mothers, sisters, or daughters in
their own family's household, or as servants in someone else's. The Industrial
Revolution and the new technology, however, have changed all this. Today, the
majority of women in industrial societies are also employed outside households,
working for corporations, state enterprises, and other kinds of work organizations.

In many work organizations, especially in the service sector, a majority of the
workers are women. This is particularly true of white-collar jobs, some of which
have come to be identified as women's jobs (e.g., nursing, social work, elementary
school teaching, secretarial work, clerical work, retail sales work of most kinds).
Despite efforts by feminists to discourage this kind of sexual division of labor, it
seems remarkably persistent, in part, at least, because of the preferences of many
women and also because of the demands of marriage and family life.

Growth in the Size of Work Organizations Workers today find themselves increasingly in the employ of organizations of enormous size. Governments have
become the largest employers of all, even in nonsocialist societies. The federal
government of the United States, for example, currently employs 5 million people,[30]
while the governments of thirteen states and municipalities employ more than
100,000 each (the largest, New York City, employs 335,000).[31] Many private
corporations also employ large numbers of workers: General Motors employs

FIGURE 10.11 Extreme occupational specialization has been characteristic of industrial societies: women processing poultry.

690,000; IBM, 395,000; Ford, 380,000; American Telephone and Telegraph, 365,000; and General Electric, 330,000, to name a few of the largest.

Increase in Occupational Specialization   Growth in the size of work organizations along with advances in technology have been responsible for yet another important trend: the substantial increase in the level of occupational specialization. Contemporary industrial societies have an astonishing number of highly specialized occupations. The United States Department of Labor lists more than 20,000 different kinds of jobs that are found in American society today.[32] The meat-packing industry illustrates the extremes to which occupational specialization is often carried. Forty-hour-a-week jobs in that industry include:

belly opener	gut sorter	rump sawyer
bladder trimmer	head splitter	side splitter
brain picker	jowl trimmer	skull grinder
gland man	leg skinner	snout puller
gut puller	lung splitter	toe puller

("What does your daddy do, little girl?" "Oh, he's a snout puller at the packing house.")

Further increases in specialization seem unlikely in most blue-collar occupations, since extreme specialization appears to be counterproductive: workers quickly become bored and this often leads to carelessness, hostility, and even sabotage. In many industries, management has responded by diversifying work activities, thus reversing the historic trend toward greater specialization. Indiana Bell Telephone, for example, used to assemble its telephone books in twenty-one steps, each performed by a different clerk. Now, each clerk has responsibility for assembling an entire book, with the result that labor turnover (a sensitive measure of worker morale) has been reduced as much as 50 percent.[33] Volvo, the Swedish automobile manufacturer, developed two experiments to reduce boredom and improve morale: one is a system of job rotation involving work at a variety of highly specialized tasks; the other is a system of teamwork involving groups of three to nine workers who share a common set of responsibilities, choose their own leader, and are paid on the basis of group output.[34] These changes reduced Volvo's annual worker turnover from 40 percent to about 10 percent. Other industries are responding to the problem of boredom by replacing increasing numbers of their workers with robots and other automated machines. Because this solution not only avoids labor unrest but cuts costs, it may become industry's preferred solution.

While the trend toward greater occupational specialization is apparently waning in blue-collar occupations, it is still growing in many kinds of white-collar jobs. This is especially evident in professional and managerial occupations, where many people seem to derive greater satisfaction from their work when their areas of responsibility and expertise are more narrowly defined. This is because professional and managerial occupations usually involve such complex bodies of information that no one can master them entirely; as a result, frustration is more likely to come from too little specialization than from too much. Thus, general practitioners in medicine have been largely replaced by a variety of medical specialists, just as general historians in the academic world have been replaced by specialists in such fields as medieval English history and modern German history. In addition, some of the traditional components of most professional and managerial jobs are now being partially performed by machines, and more efficiently. This is true, for example, of some kinds of teaching (e.g., foreign-language instruction, elementary math) and medical diagnosis (e.g., CAT-scans, computerized laboratory tests).

Declining Self-Employment   One notable by-product of all the other technological and economic changes in industrial societies is a decline in the proportion of workers who are self-employed. Throughout most of the advanced agrarian era, merchants and many artisans and farmers were self-employed. In the Marxist-Leninist societies of Eastern Europe, self-employment has been all but eliminated as a matter of deliberate governmental policy. Even in Poland, which has been more tolerant of private enterprise than most of these societies, self-employed workers outside of agriculture number only 1.7 percent of the work force.[35] In the Soviet Union, the percentage is even lower.

In western industrial societies, despite ideological support of private enterprise and individual initiative, technological advances and economic forces have produced a similar result. In the United States, for example, less than 8 percent of the labor force outside of agriculture is currently self-employed.[36]

284

Industrial
Societies and
Industrializing
Societies

Market Economies, Command Economies, and Mixed Economies

In the prehistoric past, before societies were able to produce a sustained economic surplus, all economies were essentially subsistence economies in which each community provided for its own members' needs, and trade and exchange were limited to nonessentials (e.g., birds' feathers, amber, and other objects valued for ceremonial and aesthetic reasons). With the shift from hunting and gathering to farming, conditions changed in a number of important ways. No longer was it necessary for all adults to be primarily food producers. New and more specialized kinds of occupations developed, trade and commerce increased, and political systems developed that were able to impose the will of small political elites on the other members of society.

Because of these developments, the subsistence economies of societies came to be supplemented by market economies and by command economies. In a market economy, producers exchange most of what they produce for goods or services produced by others. Such exchanges are made freely, and the only constraints are those imposed by the market itself. Prices are set by the forces of supply and demand, that is, by the relative quantities of various goods and services that are available and by the relative eagerness of would-be buyers and sellers. As this suggests, a market economy resembles a democratic system of government in which individuals are free to express their preferences among competing alternatives. The comparison is imperfect, however, because a market system allows wealthy individuals to "vote" more often than poorer individuals, and therefore their preferences have more influence on the economy.

Command economies are even more elitist. In a command economy, basic choices among economic alternatives are made by a tiny political elite. Sometimes these decision makers claim to act on behalf of the population as a whole, but it is important to note that they are unwilling to transfer their enormous power to the larger population on whose behalf they claim to act. Thus, as imperfect as market systems are, their basic mechanism of decision making is more democratic than that of command systems.

The Rise of Market Economies

The origins of modern market systems can be traced back to the simple barter systems of prehistoric societies. But the development of a true market economy (i.e., one in which market forces shape the majority of major economic decisions) could not occur until the use of money became widespread and most of the goods and services people value were assigned a monetary value. In addition, the basic economic resources of land, labor, and capital had to be freed from traditional restraints on their use or transfer. People had to be free to sell ancestral lands when that was profitable; workers had to be free to leave their jobs and take new ones when they could get higher wages or better working conditions; and owners of businesses had to be free to use their capital however they wished. Restraints on economic activity based on family sentiments, religious taboos, social customs, or organizational restrictions (guild restrictions on output, for example, or legal restrictions on the migration of serfs and slaves) had to be substantially reduced or eliminated. In short, individual economic advantage, as measured in monetary terms, had to become the decisive determinant of economic action.

As we saw in Chapter 9, the discovery of the New World gave a powerful impetus to the first requirement: the great flow of gold and silver led to the emergence of a money economy in western Europe. At the same time, a series of ideological changes weakened traditional social bonds that had previously immobilized both people and property. These same factors also sparked the Industrial Revolution, and once that was under way and the economy had changed further, the effect became cumulative. Each change stimulated further change; the more resources that came under the control of western Europe's entrepreneurial class, the better they were able to promote further change.

By the end of the nineteenth century, it looked as if every industrial society would soon have a largely market economy. Industrial societies were coming increasingly under the control of political parties dominated by businessmen committed to the philosophy of laissez-faire capitalism, or free enterprise. Following the teachings of Adam Smith, this new governing class argued that the most productive economy, and the most beneficial, was one in which governmental restrictions were held to a minimum.

Shift toward a Mixed Economy

It was not long, however, before it became evident that the new market economy was not the unmitigated blessing its enthusiasts made it out to be. In the pursuit of profits, businessmen often adopted practices that were harmful to others. In an attempt to cut labor costs, many employers fired adult workers and replaced them with children, simultaneously creating adult unemployment and endangering the health and welfare of children. Efforts to reduce costs also led to dangerous working conditions and the production of shoddy, even unsafe, merchandise.

Protests soon began to be raised, sometimes by social reformers like Robert Owen, sometimes by poets and novelists like Thomas Hood and Upton Sinclair. Even before the middle of the last century, the British Parliament began enacting legislation to protect society against the extremes of free enterprise. The Factory Acts of 1833 and 1844, the Mines Act of 1842, and the Ten Hour Law of 1847 prohibited the employment of children under the age of 9 in textile factories, restricted children under 13 to six-and-a-half hours of work per day in factories, forbade the employment of women or of boys under 10 in the mines, limited women and young people aged 13 to 18 to ten working hours per day, and provided for inspectors to enforce these laws.[37] By 1901, the minimum age for child labor in England was raised to 12, and in 1908 limitations were finally imposed on the working hours of men. Other legislation forced employers to provide for the safety of their employees in dangerous industries and established the first minimum wage.

None of these reforms would have come about, however, without the efforts of workers themselves. Already by the latter part of the eighteenth century, small groups of workers had begun banding together to negotiate with their employers on wages, hours, and working conditions. During the nineteenth century, the labor movement had many ups and downs, but by 1900, there were 2 million members of

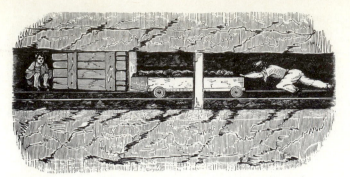

FIGURE 10.12   Children working in a British mine in the 19th century: the Mines Act of 1842 prohibited the employment of boys under the age of 10 in mines.

labor unions in Britain and nearly a million each in the United States and Germany.[38]

Before that date, however, another major defect in the market system had become evident. There was a tendency for it to lose its competitive character and evolve in the direction of monopoly. This danger was greatest in industries in which *fixed costs* were a significant part of total costs. Fixed costs are costs of production that do not increase in proportion to the quantity of goods produced. The costs of designing, tooling, and advertising a new model car, for example, are all fixed costs: they are essentially the same whether 5 million cars are produced or only 1 million. As a result, the company that sells 5 million cars can undersell its competitors, or offer a better product for the same money. Either way, the larger company tends to win its rivals' customers, further increasing its own advantage.

Table 10.8 illustrates how, in an industry in which fixed costs are relatively great compared to variable costs, the company that has the highest volume of sales to begin with will have *a growing competitive advantage*. Note that the amount that the three companies in the example spend on variable costs varies directly with the number of units each produces—one dollar per unit. But fixed costs are the same for each company—$5,000—regardless of how many units it produces. Thus, the differences in "cost per unit" are due entirely to the influence of fixed costs. Note also that the initial pricing advantage enjoyed by Company A because of its initial high volume of sales enables that company to acquire a growing share of the market, and, with it, a growing ability to undersell its competitors. As this example illustrates, if pure market forces were allowed to operate with no restrictions, smaller competitors would eventually be forced out of business in any industry in which fixed costs are a significant part of total costs.

In an effort to prevent the growth of monopolies, the United States passed the Sherman Antitrust Act in 1890. Although it has not been vigorously enforced, this act has served as a deterrent. A number of industries might now be dominated by a single company had not the managers of the leading firms been fearful of the legal consequences. For example, economists have testified before Congress that economies of scale have long made it possible for General Motors to undersell its American competitors by a substantial margin. But rather than face antitrust action, GM's managers have chosen to price their cars competitively, thereby increasing profits while, perhaps, offering their customers a bit more car for the money.

TABLE 10.8   Illustration of How Fixed Costs Contribute to the Growth of Monopoly in a Free Enterprise System

Time Period and Firm	Number of Units Sold	Variable Costs*	Fixed Costs*	Total Costs	Cost per Unit†
Time I:					
Company A	10,000	$10,000	$5,000	$15,000	$1.50
Company B	9,000	9,000	5,000	14,000	1.56
Company C	8,000	8,000	5,000	13,000	1.63
Time II:					
Company A	11,500	11,500	5,000	16,500	1.43
Company B	8,500	8,500	5,000	13,500	1.59
Company C	7,000	7,000	5,000	12,000	1.71
Time III:					
Company A	13,000	13,000	5,000	18,000	1.38
Company B	8,000	8,000	5,000	13,000	1.63
Company C	6,000	6,000	5,000	11,000	1.83

*Variable costs need not be exactly proportional to sales volume, and fixed costs need not be exactly identical for all firms, but they have been shown this way to make the essential principles clearer.
†Cost per unit equals total cost divided by number of units sold.

The situation in which an industry is dominated not by a single firm but by a very few of them is known as *oligopoly*. This has become common in capitalist societies. Table 10.9 provides some indication of the current situation in the United States. As a rough rule of thumb, economists consider an industry oligopolistic when as few as four companies control 50 percent or more of production.[39] This standard can be deceptive, however, because the degree of national concentration means different things in different industries, depending chiefly on whether the market is local, regional, or national. The newspaper industry in the United States, for example, might appear highly competitive, because according to government statistics the four largest companies produce only 19 percent of the papers. But a moment's reflection reminds us that most newspapers produce for a local market, and in most

TABLE 10.9   Percentage of Production by the Four Largest Companies in Selected Industries in the U.S.

Industry	Percentage	Industry	Percentage
Motor vehicles	93	Steel mills	45
Breakfast cereals	89	Petroleum refining	30
Washing machines	89	Pharmaceuticals	24
Turbines	86	Paints	24
Home refrigerators	82	Meat packing	19
Tires	70	Newspapers	19
Roasted coffee	61	Fluid milk	18
Aircraft	59	Poultry dressing	16
Distilled liquor	52	Fur goods	11
Radios and TVs	51	Women's dresses	8

Source: Adapted from U.S. Department of Commerce, Bureau of the Census, *Census of Manufacturing, 1977* (Washington, 1981), vol. 1, chap. 9, table 7.

communities, the paper or papers are owned by a single person or firm.[40] Since the same is true of a number of industries, Table 10.9 *understates* the extent of oligopoly.

Where oligopoly prevails, the law of supply and demand often stops functioning, primarily because collusion between firms is so easy. Collusion can take various forms. A fairly common practice in the construction industry is *bid-rigging,* whereby firms get together and decide among themselves who will take which job and then bid accordingly, with the "low" bid set as high as they dare. *Price leading,* a perfectly legal practice, appears to be standard procedure in several major industries: one firm, usually the largest, sets its prices at a level that ensures profits for all and maximizes profits for itself. In this situation, competition is largely restricted to secondary matters, such as design and advertising.

Another development which has weakened the role of market forces has been the increase in what is known as *vertical integration,* the process by which a company gains control of companies in other industries that either supply it with materials or buy its products.[41] A furniture manufacturer, for example, buys up a number of lumber companies and sawmills to provide its raw materials and then buys into retail establishments that sell the furniture it produces. In this way, it eliminates many of the uncertainties of the market situation. Another device with a similar purpose is to establish *interlocking directorates,* which bring the top officials or directors of a company on which one depends for some essential commodity onto the controlling board of one's own company. This device is widely used to bring officers of banks onto the boards of firms that require ready access to large amounts of capital.[42]

Finally, the market system has been weakened by the nature of military technology. Modern warfare requires the mobilization of all of a nation's economic resources. Obviously this effort cannot begin with the outbreak of hostilities; it must be planned and implemented far in advance. In societies that wish to maintain a strong military position, this inevitably leads to the development of a military-industrial complex from which most of the elements of the market system are eliminated. For one thing, there is only one buyer for the product, the government. In addition, there is frequently only one producer, and seldom more than a handful, for a particular weapons system. The situation is prejudicial to an open market in yet another way: the military is not inclined to shop around for bargains, because this increases security risks, while truly competitive bidding might cause companies to cut corners and turn out defective products. So long as the military has the taxing power of the government behind it, it has little motivation to economize. Thus, there is a natural tendency for market forces to be replaced by the principles of command in the vast and important area of military procurement, even in societies whose leaders are committed to the principles of free enterprise.

We can summarize most of the foregoing by saying that the last two hundred years have revealed *three basic flaws in market systems.* First, not only do they fail to protect the weaker and more vulnerable members of society, such as industrial workers and consumers; they compel the strong to act ruthlessly if they wish to remain strong. Second, the market system has what might be called a built-in tendency to self-destruct, which causes most free competitive markets to evolve into oligopolistic or monopolistic markets unless checked by governmental intervention.

Finally, the market system cannot respond adequately to many or most of the needs of society as a whole, as contrasted with the needs and desires of individuals.

This final flaw is particularly evident during societal crises, such as wars, depressions, or environmental crises. As long as individuals and organizations are free to act according to what they perceive as their own best interests, the more selfish ones tend to win out. A corporation that responded voluntarily to environmental problems by installing expensive anti-pollution devices, for example, would find itself at a competitive disadvantage with firms that did not.

For a variety of reasons, then, even those societies that have remained ideologically most committed to the market system and to the principle of free enterprise now have what can only be described as *mixed market-command economies.*[43] The role of government in the economic life of these societies is enormous. Privately owned businesses are obliged to operate within well-defined limits set by an increasingly complex system of governmental regulations. Minimum wage laws must be observed, governmentally prescribed safety standards maintained, and compulsory social insurance payments for workers made, to name but three of the many controls that governments now exercise.

A good measure of the greatly increased power of government in the economic life of western industrial societies is the growth in the percentage of national income that governments control through taxes and use to support their various activities.[44] As Table 10.10 indicates, this figure has, on average, nearly doubled since 1950 in the eleven societies for which data are available. And if the experience of the United States is at all typical, the percentage of the GNP spent by these governments as a whole has been increasing ever since the beginning of the century.[45]

Finally, it should be noted that in most of the so-called capitalist industrial

TABLE 10.10   Governmental Expenditures as a Percentage of National Income in Western Industrial Democracies

Society	1950	1980
Netherlands	30.3	59.8
Sweden	19.9	46.6
Denmark	16.6	45.5
United Kingdom	34.9	44.4
France	34.6	44.3
Finland	31.2	34.0
West Germany	17.1	32.3
United States	18.0	26.0
Canada	16.8	25.7
Switzerland	9.6	21.7
Japan	5.0	21.7
Average	21.3	36.5

Source: Adapted from United Nations, *Statistical Yearbook, 1955,* tables 156 and 167; and UN, *Statistical Yearbook, 1981,* tables 26 and 44.

societies of Europe, the basic means of production are usually operated as state enterprises. In a survey conducted by *The Economist* not long ago, it was found that the majority of the most basic industries in all but one of those societies were state owned (see Table 10.11).

Thus, while the socialist revolution that Marx predicted has never occurred in any of the historic centers of modern capitalism, capitalism of the kind advocated by Adam Smith has all but disappeared. What passes for capitalism today is really a mixed market-command economy that combines in a complex way elements of both capitalism and socialism. In fact, it even incorporates elements of communism (i.e., rewards allocated on the basis of need) in such areas as education, health, and welfare. The nature of the economic mix varies considerably from society to society, with governmental intervention in, and control of, the economy being greatest in Western Europe and least in Japan, the United States, and Canada.

Viewed from a sociological perspective, the mixed economies that have evolved in the majority of industrial societies in the last hundred years reflect an effort by the members of these societies to achieve simultaneously what appear to be, to some degree at least, mutually contradictory goals. On the one hand, they want economic growth and the higher standard of living that market systems and capitalism seem better able to provide. On the other hand, they also want the

TABLE 10.11 Percentage of Basic Industries* Owned by the State in Thirteen Industrial Societies

Society	Percentage
Austria	100
Britain	83
Italy	81
France	78
Sweden	69
Netherlands	63
Switzerland	61
West Germany	55
Australia	53
Belgium	44
Canada	28
Japan	22
United States	5

*The ten industries are telecommunications, electricity, gas, oil production, coal, railways, airlines, automobiles, steel, and shipbuilding. In societies where an industry is absent or makes a negligible contribution to GNP, the industry was not included in calculations.
Source: Adapted from *The Economist*, December 30, 1978.

economic security and attention to the corporate needs of society that command economies and socialism seem better at providing.

Small groups of ideologues continue to argue for a purer type of economic system, but the majority of citizens in the industrial democracies of Western Europe, North America, and Japan seem to prefer the more pragmatic approach represented by a mixed market-command economy. While people argue endlessly over details of the mix, there seems to be little popular support for proposals that would abandon or substantially reduce either of the two basic components of the mixed economy.

Evolution of the Modern Corporation

Before turning to the command economies of the industrial societies of Eastern Europe, we need to consider briefly the nature of the modern corporation, a strikingly new and important kind of organization that has evolved in recent centuries in the western world. During the last hundred years, this new kind of organization has replaced the proprietorship, the family-owned enterprise, and the partnership as the dominant form of private enterprise in the mixed economies of Western Europe, North America, and Japan. Its only serious rival in modern industrial societies is the state- or publicly owned enterprise.

The origins of the modern corporation lie in the sixteenth century, when English and Dutch merchants, trading in remote areas, banded together in what came to be known as joint stock companies.[46] This form of organization had several advantages over family enterprises and partnerships. Above all, it permitted people to pool their capital and thereby spread their risks. This was extremely important in ventures where risks were great and large investments essential. In addition, a joint stock company, unlike a family enterprise or a partnership, was not disrupted by the death of one of the owners.*

During the next several centuries, the joint stock company, or corporation, gradually spread to new fields of enterprise, and a series of changes made this form of organization safer and more attractive to investors. The most important change was the adoption of the principle of *limited liability*. Prior to the nineteenth century, stockholders in most corporations had unlimited liability: in case of bankruptcy they could lose not only their investment in the company but all their personal property as well. This naturally made investors extremely cautious; unless they had intimate knowledge of a business and those running it, they were taking a great risk. The passage of laws limiting the liability of stockholders to the investment itself greatly stimulated the flow of capital into this new form of enterprise.

In non-Marxist societies today, nearly all of the largest and most powerful private enterprises are corporations. In the United States in recent years, for example, nearly 90 percent of all business was done by corporations, and among larger concerns (i.e., those with annual receipts of $1 million or more), they accounted for 96 percent of the total.[47] The very largest concerns, those with annual profits in the hundreds of millions or billions of dollars, are all corporations.[48]

---

*The law requires, for example, that a partnership be dissolved on the death of any of the partners. This was not required of joint stock companies.

As corporations have grown, there has been a tremendous change in their character, especially with respect to their control. The largest are rarely controlled by the people who own them (i.e., the stockholders); they are controlled by employees who have been hired to manage them.[49] This shift is a consequence of the fragmentation of stock ownership which has accompanied the enormous growth in size of these organizations. In some corporations, no one owns as much as 1 percent of the stock, and most stockholders own only a minute fraction of 1 percent. Furthermore, the stockholders are scattered around the world. Mobilizing a majority of the voting stock to wrest control from the managers is extraordinarily difficult and expensive.

The character of the corporation has also been altered during the twentieth century by increasing government control. As we have seen, this intervention of government into capitalist economies has been a response to the inherent weaknesses of an unregulated market system. Over the years, the scope of government involvement in corporations has steadily increased, creating some problems while alleviating others. Many economic questions that were once resolved by the forces of supply and demand are now decided by government officials, much as they are in socialist societies. As a result of such changes, the owners of the largest corporations have become, in most cases, merely investors: *real power in these organizations now lies in the hands of management and government.*

The Economies of Marxist-Leninist Societies

All of the industrial societies that are governed by Marxist-Leninist elites are found today in Eastern Europe. These include the Soviet Union, East Germany, Poland, Czechoslovakia, Hungary, Romania, and Bulgaria.* In each of them, private ownership of the means of production has been largely eliminated and market forces play a very limited role in the economy. State enterprises and centrally planned command economies have taken their place.

In these Marxist-Leninist societies, most goods and services are produced in state enterprises. In Soviet society, for example, state enterprises produce all of the manufactured products and are responsible for their subsequent transportation and eventual sale through retail outlets. Schools, hospitals, the mass media, theatres, restaurants, and almost every other kind of service enterprise are also owned and operated by the state. The only private forms of enterprise appear to be farmers' markets, where certain kinds of agricultural products are sold; moonlighting (i.e., work done apart from an individual's regular job) by mechanics, doctors, teachers, and others with marketable skills; and some kinds of semilegal and illegal activities associated with the so-called "second economy."[50]

In recent years, private enterprise in the agricultural sector (which seems to be the most important form of private enterprise) has accounted for about one-fourth of total agricultural production, but that amounts to only about 3.7 percent of the Soviet Union's total GNP.[51] Thus, even if one were to add in all the various forms of private

*As noted elsewhere, Yugoslavia and Albania are classified as industrializing agrarian societies, not yet fully industrialized.

enterprise in which the urban populations engage, it seems unlikely that the total would reach as much as 5 percent of total Soviet production.

In Poland and Hungary, opportunities for private enterprise have been somewhat greater than in the Soviet Union. For example, in Hungary privately owned businesses may employ up to 18 workers, while in Poland most farms are still privately owned. But even in Poland some years ago, state enterprises accounted for more than three-fourths of the nation's GNP.[52]

In some respects, the state enterprises of Marxist-Leninist societies are remarkably like the large corporate enterprises of capitalist societies. Both are administered by a complex hierarchy of officials whose powers, responsibilities, and rewards vary according to level. Both have a highly complex division of labor, in which the duties of every specialist are carefully defined. And both require individuals in subordinate positions to follow the directives of their superiors.[53]

There are also, of course, important differences between corporations and these state enterprises. For one thing, Marxist-Leninist societies place great emphasis on central planning. The famous Five Year Plans of the U.S.S.R. are a classic example. Officials in the capital of each of the East European societies set production goals for everything that is produced, but these goals often prove unrealistic. Moreover, in an effort to meet their quotas and thereby win bonuses, the managers of these organizations frequently comply with the letter of the plan, while ignoring the spirit (e.g., they produce the required quantity, but cut corners on quality).[54] Several years ago, *Pravda* published a poll of more than 1,000 industrial managers, and 80 percent complained of interference in day-to-day operations by higher authorities, while 90 percent said they needed more flexibility in decision making to do a better job.[55]

Another way in which state enterprises in Marxist-Leninist societies differ from private enterprises is that their workers have no fear of being fired. As a result, work discipline is often slack, absenteeism high, and workmanship careless.[56] Job turnover is also a problem in many state enterprises.[57] If workers become bored with their jobs, they feel free to quit, knowing other jobs are always available as long as they avoid political difficulties.

State enterprises in Marxist-Leninist societies also differ from private enterprises in other industrial societies because of the nature of their trade unions. These unions are part of the central power structure of Marxist-Leninist societies, but subordinate to the authority of the Party and political elite. From a functional standpoint, they are similar to the company unions that managers in capitalist enterprises established in an earlier period in response to the growing threat of worker-organized unions. The basic task of trade unions in Marxist-Leninist societies is to maintain productivity. To achieve this, union leaders report labor problems both to management and to the Party, while providing various social services to their members (e.g., insurance, access to health and vacation facilities, counseling services). Strikes and collective bargaining are forbidden, but union leaders are supposed to bring workers' grievances to the attention of management. The response to these grievances apparently varies a great deal and depends, to some extent at least, on the motives and the negotiating skills of union leaders. It is clear, however, that labor unions in Marxist-Leninist societies have far less power and influence than labor unions in non-Marxist-Leninist societies. The Party's justification for this is that worker interests in these societies are protected by the Party itself.

FIGURE 10.13 The Kama Heavy Truck Works, a Soviet state-owned enterprise, has a capacity of 75,000 trucks per year. Note the similarity to western automobile plants: as one East European sociologist has written, "the socialist revolution does not change the relation of the worker to the machine, nor does it change his position in the factory."

Prior to the Russian Revolution, many critics of socialism argued that it would be impossible to operate an economy successfully without private ownership and the operation of market forces. Today, this argument is no longer heard, since the Soviet Union and other Marxist-Leninist societies have proven that a socialized economy is not incompatible with economic growth.

In addition, Marxist-Leninist economies have overcome unemployment, one of the great scourges of capitalist economies. In part, this is achieved by the creation of "busywork" (e.g., women ride the escalators of the Moscow subway system, hour after hour, wiping the handrails with a rag), and often, as we have seen, at the expense of economic efficiency. Nevertheless, it is a significant accomplishment. Closely related to this, the command economies of Marxist-Leninist societies have generally been successful in eradicating abject poverty, especially in urban areas. Finally, Marxist-Leninist societies have been relatively successful in reducing economic inequality—partly by reducing wage inequalities, partly by eliminating the private ownership of the means of production.

Despite these successes, the economies of Marxist-Leninist societies leave much to be desired, even from the standpoint of the working class in whose name the Communist Party claims to govern. As one leading East European sociologist describes conditions,

> . . . the workers are still hired labor. The socialist revolution does not change the relation of the worker to the machine, nor does it change his position within the factory. . . . His relation to the machine and to the organizational systems of work requires his subordination to the foreman and to the management of the factory. He receives wages according to the quantity and quality of work performed, and he must obey the principles and regulations of work discipline.[58]

Despite efforts to hide evidence of worker discontent, reports of strikes leak to western reporters even in the Soviet Union.[59] In Poland, of course, worker discontent has led not only to strikes but also to efforts to organize labor unions free of Communist Party control. In 1981, such efforts led to the enrollment of nearly 10 million Poles in the now outlawed independent labor union known as Solidarity.

Move Toward Market Socialism During the last twenty years, Communist Party leaders have become increasingly aware of the difficulties inherent in a completely planned command economy. The burden that falls on economic planners is an impossible one. In the Soviet Union, for example, planners must set prices for 8 to 9 million items as well as decide the quantity of each item to be produced.[60] To be effective, however, a plan must also take into account all of the interrelations among all of these items, and according to one Soviet estimate this would require that provision be made for more than 15 *billion* interrelations.[61] Because that is obviously impossible, it is inevitable that shortages repeatedly develop in some goods and surpluses in others.

The great virtue of the market system is its automatic mechanism for balancing supply and demand. When the demand for a product goes up, so does the price, giving producers an incentive to increase production. Conversely, a slump in demand lowers prices and reduces incentives. All of this is accomplished without costly centralized planning and the growth of bureaucracy.

Despite these attractive features, the market system had always been so closely identified with capitalism that Soviet leaders were long unwilling to consider its reintroduction. During recent decades, however, a number of Marxist economists have argued that the market mechanism is not necessarily linked to private enterprise, and that its introduction into socialist economies need not stimulate a revival of capitalism. Despite continuing skepticism by many Party leaders, the way has been cleared for experimentation. Elements of the market system have been reintroduced into areas of the economy from which they had been excluded for years.[62]

The use of market mechanisms in Marxist economies suggests that in the future there may be somewhat less variation in the economies of industrial societies than there has been in the past. Marxist and non-Marxist societies alike appear to be moving toward a mixed type of economy, in which the forces of both market and command will play important roles. Market forces will be used to achieve greater efficiency, while command will be used to protect the corporate interests of society and to limit the degree of social inequality. This is not to suggest, of course, that differences between economic systems will be eliminated (East European Communist leaders seem determined to prevent the reestablishment of large privately owned enterprises, for one thing), but differences will probably be reduced.

The Increasing Economic Integration of the World System

To be complete, our survey of the economies of modern industrial societies must take note of one further development: the growing web of economic ties among societies, industrial and nonindustrial, throughout the world.

TABLE 10.12   Imports as a Percentage of GNP in Selected Industrial Societies

Society	Imports as Percentage of Gross National Product
Belgium	59
Netherlands	44
Switzerland	32
Austria	31
Sweden	28
United Kingdom	27
Italy	27
Canada	24
West Germany	22
France	21
Japan	12
United States	9

Source: Adapted from *Statistical Abstract of the United States, 1984,* tables 1509 and 1513.

Human societies have exchanged goods with one another since prehistoric times, but the volume of trade was always small because of the limitations of technology. Since the cost of transporting goods was often greater than the cost of producing them, intersocietal trade was largely restricted, for thousands of years, to small items of substantial value, especially luxury goods produced for elites.

With advances in ship construction and navigational technology in the thirteenth, fourteenth, and fifteenth centuries, the volume of international trade began to increase. By 1850, the volume of goods exchanged was 6 times what it had been in 1750, and in 1950, it was 20 times what it was in 1850.[63] And for the last forty years, the volume of international trade (corrected for inflation) has been growing at a rate that would equal a 400-fold increase if it lasted a century.[64]

The result of this trend has been a substantial increase in the division of labor among societies, and the growing economic integration of the world system. The other side of the same coin, of course, is that societies are steadily declining in economic self-sufficiency. As Table 10.12 shows, the value of foreign trade now equals 20 to 50 percent of GNP in most industrial societies.

The societies of Western Europe have moved further in this direction than other industrial societies and have formed the European Economic Community, whose goal is the complete integration of the economies of the nine member societies. This development could be the prelude to political unification and the formation of a new multinational society embracing much of Western Europe.

In the world system as a whole, movement toward economic and political unification is far less advanced, but a number of international organizations—economic and political—have emerged. These include the International Monetary Fund, the Food and Agriculture Organization, the World Bank, the International Labor Organization, the World Health Organization, the International Court of Justice, and the United Nations. While the powers of these bodies are far more limited than those of the European Economic Community, they reflect the growing web of relations that binds all human societies together as a consequence of the technological advances of the industrial era.

297

Industrial
Societies: I

Excursus: Some Terms with Multiple Meanings

Is the Soviet Union a socialist society or a communist society? Is Sweden a capitalist society or a socialist society? And what about the United States: is it a capitalist society, or not?

The answer to each of these questions depends upon the criteria used to describe each of these societies. The Soviet Union is a communist society in the sense that it is governed by members of the Communist Party. But it is not a communist society in the sense that rewards are distributed to its members on the basis of need, or are shared equally. Rather, it is a socialist society in which rewards are distributed unequally in proportion to the value of individuals' contributions to society as judged by the ruling Communist elite. Also, it is a socialist society in the sense that the means of production are publicly owned—not privately.

In the case of Sweden, the label applied also depends on the criteria used. Sweden can be called a socialist society on the grounds that it is governed at present by members of the Socialist Party. But it can also be called a capitalist society on the grounds that the means of production are still largely in private hands. (Even though a majority of the firms in the most basic industries are now publicly owned, the revenues of all such enterprises provide only 21 percent of Sweden's GNP.[65])

The United States is often referred to as a bastion of capitalism, and indeed it is, when compared to most other industrial societies today. The proportion of the economy that is publicly owned is still quite small (see Table 10.11). However, as we have seen in this chapter, the role of government in the economic life of the society goes far beyond what Adam Smith and other classic proponents of free enterprise deemed appropriate. In fact, when account is taken of the extent of governmental regulation of business activities and of the percentage of the national income that government claims in taxes, the United States is better described as having a mixed market-command economy.

In summary, then, there is no single correct answer to the questions posed at the beginning of this Excursus. The Soviet Union is both a socialist society and a communist society; Sweden is both a capitalist society and a socialist society; and the United States both is and is not a capitalist society. It all depends on the way in which these terms are defined.

CHAPTER 11

Industrial Societies: II

The Polity

Prior to the start of the Industrial Revolution, nearly all of the largest and most powerful nations of the world were monarchies governed by hereditary kings and emperors. The power to govern was believed to be a God-given right and the state was viewed as the private property of the ruling family. The state and the ruler's estate were one and the same—and the heads of states were "rulers," not merely "leaders." In 1750, the republican idea that the powers of government are derived from the consent of the governed was still only an abstract principle for philosophers to debate, not an operative political principle.

Today, the older view of government has all but disappeared, especially in the new industrial societies. While a few of them still retain some of the trappings of monarchy, as in Britain, Sweden, and Japan, for all practical purposes industrial societies are now democratic republics. Even in the Marxist-Leninist societies of Eastern Europe, republicanism prevails—though in the more elitist form of oligarchical republicanism.

The Democratic Trend

People who are sensitive to the undemocratic elements that still exist in western industrial societies sometimes have difficulty appreciating the enormity of the change that has occurred. It includes not just the introduction of elections and the formation of political parties which mobilize the masses of people in support of particular leaders and policies, but—most important of all—it includes, for the first time, *the exercise of the powers of government to benefit the masses of ordinary people in countless ways.* Such use of these powers was almost unheard of in agrarian societies: in those societies, the powers of government were used almost entirely for the benefit of the governing class.

The nature of the change that has occurred in industrial societies may best be symbolized by the way in which the ordinary members of these societies are referred to in their legal codes. In agrarian societies of the recent past, they were referred to as "subjects"; in industrial societies today, they are referred to as "citizens."

Democracy as a Variable In discussing political systems, we should resist the temptation to think of them in categorical, either-or terms. To divide governments into those that are democratic and those that are not is to oversimplify. In the real world, governments differ by degree in the practice of democracy, and the degree of democracy often changes over time. Thus, we need to think of democracy as a variable like other societal characteristics, such as population size or economic productivity.

Thinking of democracy in this way helps us to recognize that no large and complex society can ever be completely and perfectly democratic. This would require that all its citizens participate fully and equally in every political decision: they would have to devote themselves almost entirely to politics and abandon most other activities. Even if the practical problems of communication among tens of millions of people could somehow be overcome, everyone would have to devote at least as much time to politics as professional politicians now spend, whether they wished to or not.

The system of representative democracy that has evolved in western industrial societies is, in effect, an effort to avoid the difficulties inherent in a fully democratic system (what some have called "participatory democracy"). It employs the ancient concept of a division of labor in an effort to minimize the costs of democracy while maximizing its benefits. Responsibility for day-to-day decision making is delegated to a relatively small group of individuals, while the population as a whole retains the right to select these individuals and to replace them.

The Democratic Trend in Western Industrial Societies Once we recognize the variable nature of democracy, we begin to appreciate the magnitude of the change that has occurred in the polities of western industrial societies in the last two hundred years. In Britain, for example, as recently as 1865, 76 percent of the members of Parliament were members of the aristocracy and gentry (i.e., the old governing class of preindustrial Britain) and nearly half of the seats were filled in uncontested elections.[1] One quarter of the members of Parliament belonged to just 31 families, a fact that led one writer of the period to refer to Parliament as "one vast cousinhood."[2]

In the United States, as we saw in Chapter 10, the government was originally an oligarchical republic, not a democratic republic. The right to vote was limited to men of property, as in Britain, and the great majority of people were denied this

FIGURE 11.1 The Founding Fathers of the United States created an oligarchical republic, not a democratic republic: the Constitutional Convention, Philadelphia, 1787.

right. This was still true even half a century after the republic was established. In the presidential election of 1824, only 350,000 votes were cast, indicating that less than 10 percent of the adult population was eligible to vote.[3] Since then, the elimination of property requirements for the right to vote and for the right to hold office, the abolition of slavery and the extension of the franchise (i.e., the right to vote) to blacks, the extension of the franchise to women and eighteen-year-olds, the passage of the civil rights acts, the direct election of senators, and the "one person, one vote" decision of the Supreme Court have not only increased greatly the percentage of Americans who are eligible to vote, but, equally important, have increased the effectiveness and importance of their votes. Today, as a result, more than half of all governmental expenditures in the United States are for social programs that benefit the masses of ordinary people.[4] This is a tremendous change from the practices of governments during the agrarian era.

Similar trends can be observed in the recent history of other western democratic societies, although nearly all of them lagged behind the United States in removing property requirements for the right to vote. In Sweden and Britain, for example, these requirements were not finally removed until after World War I (see Table 11.1).[5] On the other hand, the democracies of Western Europe now spend a higher percentage of their total income on social programs.

Democratic Tendencies in Marxist-Leninist Societies As noted earlier, Marxist-Leninist societies are, by far, the least democratic of modern industrial societies. In fact, they are really oligarchical republics in which tiny, self-chosen political elites dominate the decision-making process. Not all Marxists have been happy with

TABLE 11.1   Percentage of the British Population Age Twenty-One and Over Eligible to Vote

Before First Reform Act, 1831	5.0
After First Reform Act, 1832	7.1
After Second Reform Act, 1867	16.4
After Third Reform Act, 1884	28.5
After World War I, 1919	74.0
After Equal Franchise Act, 1928	96.9

Source: Judith Ryder and Harold Silver. *Modern English Society: History and Structure, 1850–1970* (London: Methuen, 1970) p. 74.

Leninist elitism, however. For example, the famous Polish Marxist Rosa Luxembourg, a contemporary of Lenin's, was highly critical of Lenin's elitist practices and policies. As she wrote at one point, while democratic institutions have their shortcomings,

> . . . the remedy Lenin [has] found, the elimination of democracy, is worse than the disease it is supposed to cure; for it stops up the very living source from which alone can come the correction of all the innate shortcomings of social institutions.[6]

She also wrote that unless all of the people were to take part in the building of socialist societies, these societies would be controlled by a handful of elitist intellectuals and bureaucrats.[7]

Despite such warnings, Lenin and his successors have vigorously resisted efforts to democratize the societies under their control. Nevertheless, the desire for democracy persists. In fact, sometimes it even surfaces within the Communist Party itself, as evidenced by the efforts of a group of Czech Party leaders in 1968 to reestablish multiparty democracy in that country (an effort which was halted only by a Soviet invasion) and by the efforts of a majority of the members of the Polish party in 1980 to introduce secret ballot elections for leadership positions within the Party (an effort which succeeded briefly, but was later reversed under threat of Soviet invasion). Meanwhile, outside the Communist Party, the desire for a more democratic political system appears to be very widespread in Eastern Europe, especially in Poland and Hungary.

Causes of the Democratic Trend

One of the more remarkable characteristics of the industrial era has been the tremendous strength and appeal of democratic ideology. In all the history of modern industrial societies, there has been only a single instance in which the members freely chose to abandon democracy in favor of another form of government. And in that one case, Germany in the 1930s, the society was confronted by an exceptional set of circumstances, both economic and political. Thus, the record suggests that the democratic trend in modern industrial societies is the work of a powerful set of forces which are not easily overcome.

**FIGURE 11.2   Luther nailing his famous 95 Theses to
the door of the castle church, Wittenberg, Germany,
1517. Luther's doctrine of the priesthood of all believers
had revolutionary implications; though Luther did not
recognize this, others soon did.**

For the most part, these seem to be the same forces—the Protestant Reformation, the conquest of the New World, and, most important of all, the Industrial
Revolution—that gave rise to all the major new ideologies of the industrial era.
Protestantism appears to have been especially significant in the early rise and spread
of democratic beliefs and values.[8] If it did nothing else, the Protestant Reformation
proved that established authority *could* be challenged and overthrown. But even
more important, the Protestant doctrine of the priesthood of all believers—the
doctrine that all believers are equal in God's sight and can relate directly to him
without the mediation of the clergy—had *political implications of a revolutionary*

nature. Though Luther and Calvin did not recognize the fact, others soon did, and the bitter German Peasants' Revolt of 1524–1525 and the Leveler movement a century later in England were both stimulated by it.

This new doctrine also led to the adoption of democratic or semidemocratic polities by many of the more radical Protestant groups, such as the Anabaptists, Mennonites, Baptists, Quakers, Puritans, and Presbyterians. It is no coincidence that democratization began in ecclesiastical (i.e., church) governments some generations before it began in civil governments. Nor is it just a coincidence that when it did begin in civil government, its early successes were chiefly in countries where ecclesiastical democratization had already made considerable headway. The first major and enduring victory of the democratic movement was in the United States, a country which since colonial days had been a refuge for the more radical and more democratic Protestant groups.

The conquest of the New World was another important factor in the spread of democratic government. Conditions in the frontier regions of the United States, Canada, Australia, and New Zealand were far more favorable to democracy than conditions in the older, heavily settled societies of Europe. It is no coincidence that the Jacksonian movement, which did so much to broaden the base of political participation in American society, had its greatest strength in what was then the western frontier. The conquest of the New World was also important because, as we noted in Chapter 9, it weakened the power of the traditional governing classes in European societies and strengthened the influence of the merchant class, which had long been noted for its republican tendencies.

As important as these influences were, however, the democratic movement could not have succeeded as it did without the Industrial Revolution. Industrialization eliminated the need for large numbers of unskilled and uneducated workers living at or near the subsistence level, and as new sources of energy were tapped and new machines invented, societies had to produce more skilled and educated workers. Such people, however, are much less likely to be politically apathetic and servile. On the contrary, they tend to be self-assertive, jealous of their rights, and politically demanding.[9] Such characteristics are essential in a democracy, for they counterbalance and hold in check the powerful oligarchical tendencies that are present in any large and complex social system.

Industrialization also made possible the remarkable development of the *mass media.* To a great extent, this has been a response to the spread of literacy and to the increased demand for information generated by the rising level of education. Through newspapers, magazines, radio, and television, the average citizen of a modern industrial society is vastly more aware of political events than his or her counterpart in agrarian societies. Although much of the information received is extremely superficial and distorted, nevertheless it generates interest and concern. Thus the media not only satisfy a need, they also help to create it.[10]

Finally, industrialization, by stimulating the growth of urban communities, further strengthened democratic tendencies. Isolated rural communities have long been noted for their lack of political sophistication and for their patriarchal, paternalistic political patterns. Urban populations, in contrast, have always been better informed and more willing to challenge established authority. Thus, merely by increasing the size of urban populations, industrialization contributed to the democratic trend.

Special Interest Groups

Modern industrial societies are made up of many groups, each with its own special interests. Labor and management are two of the more familiar, but there are many others. In American society, for example, there are blacks, Hispanics, Catholics, Protestants, Jews, welfare mothers, veterans, professional groups, retired people, women, men, pro-choice groups, pro-life groups, environmentalists, pro-handgun advocates, anti-handgun advocates, groups representing individual industries, and dozens more. All of them have interests that conflict, to greater or lesser degree, with the interests of other groups, and often with the interests of society as a whole.

One of the more difficult problems facing democratic societies today is that of protecting the interests of society as a whole against the claims and demands of these special interests. Paradoxically, it is far easier for politicians to rally support for programs that offer special favors to limited interest groups than for programs designed to promote the common good.* Since political survival in a democratic society depends on voter support, politicians tend to respond more readily to the appeals of special interest groups than to the needs of society as a whole. Some rationalize their actions by arguing that the interests of society are simply the sum of the interests of its parts, but that argument ignores the systemic nature of human societies.

Interest groups vary greatly in their ability to influence public policy. Success is largely a function of the political and economic resources that they control. In democratic industrial societies, the most important of these resources is the active support of large numbers of voters. Money is also essential in many societies, however, especially in ones where the allegiance of voters to political parties is weak and where large campaign contributions can be used to influence voters. Influence over the mass media—especially television—has become one of the most powerful of all resources in democratic societies (see pages 351–354).

In Marxist-Leninist societies, in contrast, the most important political resource is control of the state, and this is a monopoly of the Communist Party. For other groups, their most valuable resource is their usefulness to the Party. For this reason, the secret police, the military, the governmental bureaucracy, managers of industry, certain groups of scientists, and pro-Party intellectuals and artists tend to have more influence politically than other interest groups.

---

*The construction of the interstate highway system in the United States, for example, was primarily a response to a massive lobbying effort by the trucking industry, the highway construction industry, the cement industry, and the automobile industry, and only secondarily a response to the public desire for safer and faster highways.

Political Parties

The growth of democracy and the rise of industrial societies have produced a totally new kind of political organization, the mass political party, which serves to mobilize public opinion in support of political programs and candidates. Wherever there are more candidates than offices, there is a process of selection, and the candidates that are supported by parties are usually the ones that survive.

Party organizations differ in several respects. Some, such as the Republican and Democratic parties in the United States, are largely pragmatic, *brokerage-type parties*. They have no strong ideological commitments and no well-defined political programs. Their chief goal is to gain control of public offices in order to trade favors with special interest groups, giving preferential legislative treatment in exchange for electoral and financial support. In this type of party, discipline is weak or nonexistent, since each elected official is free to work out his or her own "deals." Some degree of party unity is maintained, however, because once an interest group establishes close ties with the officials of a certain party, it usually prefers to continue working with them. This is reinforced by the tendency of the more ideologically inclined to separate into opposing camps, liberals gravitating toward one party, conservatives toward the other. Sometimes the more ideologically inclined win control of the party machinery, as did Goldwater's followers in 1964 and McGovern's followers in 1972, but this is usually short-lived.

FIGURE 11.3   The rise of industrial societies has produced a totally new kind of political organization, the mass political party: the Republican Party Convention, Dallas, Texas, 1984.

In contrast to brokerage-type parties, many of which were formed in the nineteenth century, political parties formed in the twentieth century have often had strong ideological commitments. Such parties, including both fascist parties of the right and democratic socialist and revolutionary socialist parties of the left, have usually had well-developed programs designed to transform society; in most instances, the leaders of these parties were willing to be defeated again and again rather than compromise the principles they held sacred. Since World War II, however, many of these parties have become less ideological and more pragmatic.[11]

Nationalist ideologies have also given rise to political parties in several industrial societies. The most famous was the German National Socialist (Nazi) Party organized by Adolf Hitler following Germany's defeat in World War I. Nationalist ideologies are more likely, however, to be simply one of the elements in the overall program of the major conservative parties in democratic societies. Thus, the Republicans in the United States, the Conservatives in Britain and Canada, and the conservatives in France usually place more emphasis on national defense and other policies relevant to nationalist ideals than do their opponents.

In ethnically divided societies, minorities sometimes form nationalist parties to protect or promote their own group's special interests. This has happened among the French in Canada, the Scottish and Welsh in Britain, and the Basques in Spain.

Finally, religious groups in Western Europe and Japan have formed a number of political parties. The most successful of these have been the Christian-Democratic parties formed by Catholics in Italy, Germany, Austria, and several other countries. While the original aim of these parties was to defend the church's position on such issues as birth control, abortion, and tax support for church schools, they have often become the chief conservative opposition to social democratic and Communist parties.

Experience has taught professional politicians that parties which remain ideologically pure are likely to remain numerically small and politically weak, except in times of national crisis. Thus, some of the more successful Communist parties of Western Europe have softened their stance on some issues in recent years. The Italian Party, in fact, has gone so far as to support the continued participation of Italy in the NATO alliance and to pledge its support to the principle of western-style democracy.

Political Conflict and Stability

Every social system generates internal conflict, and industrial societies are no exception. Nevertheless, their success in channeling it into nonviolent forms is remarkable. Compared with agrarian societies in particular, they are much less prone to revolutions, coups, and other serious political upheavals. This is especially true of those societies which are past the transitional or early phase of industrialization. One study of 62 societies found an extremely strong statistical correlation between their levels of political stability and their levels of economic development.[12]

There are a number of reasons for this. First, the greater productivity of industrial societies and the resultant higher standard of living give the majority of the population a vested interest in political stability. Revolution and anarchy would be very costly for most members of advanced industrial societies. Second, a democratic ideology strengthens the allegiance of most segments of the population to their government and weakens support for revolutionary movements. Especially noteworthy in this connection is the loyalty shown by the military and the absence of military coups in the more advanced industrial societies. Finally, the very complexity of the structure of industrial societies seems to generate a readiness to compromise on controversial issues. This is partly because *there are so many people in intermediate positions between the contending groups.* Most of the population, for example, has modest property holdings. Such people are likely to benefit from peaceful compromise and therefore reject extreme or violent proposals. Contrary to Marx's expectations, this is true of the great majority of blue-collar workers. Moreover, since the complexity of industrial societies means that each individual simultaneously fills a number of different roles and often belongs to a variety of groups, people who are opponents in one controversy are often allies in another. For example, middle- and working-class blacks who are divided over labor-management controversies find themselves allied on racial issues. This, too, has a moderating effect.

Although political conflicts are restrained in industrial societies, they are still present in various forms and involve a wide range of issues. The most common type of conflict is between economic classes, and, in most democratic nations, this type of conflict has established the basic framework for partisan politics. Typically, some parties appeal to the working class and other disadvantaged elements in the population, promising improved conditions if they are elected. Opposing parties rely for support on the more privileged elements in the population and campaign for office on a platform promising economic growth.

Sweden provides a good example of a strong relationship between economic class and party preference. As Table 11.2 shows, support for Socialist and Communist parties is more than twice as strong in the working class as in the middle and upper classes. The strength of the relationship between party preference and economic class varies greatly in industrial societies, however. It is strongest in Scandinavian societies and weakest in North American, as Table 11.3 shows. The limited relation between class and party preference in the United States and Canada is due in

TABLE 11.2 Party Preferences of the Swedish Population in Elections Between 1956 and 1979, by Occupational Class, in Percentages

	Socialist and Communist	Other Parties
Upper and middle classes	30	70
Working class	74	26

Source: Adapted from Walter Korpi, *The Democratic Class Struggle* (London: Routledge & Kegan Paul, 1983), figure 5.3.

TABLE 11.3   Strength of Relationship between Occupational Class and Party Preference in Eleven Industrial Societies

Society	Percentage Point Difference*
Finland (average of 3 surveys)	50
Norway (average of 3 surveys)	46
Denmark (1 survey)	44
Sweden (average of 8 surveys)	44
Italy (1 survey)	37
Britain (average of 14 surveys)	37
Australia (average of 7 surveys)	35
West Germany (average of 7 surveys)	26
France (average of 2 surveys)	22
United States (average of 9 surveys)	17
Canada (average of 10 surveys)	7

* Specifically, the figures are the difference between the percentage of urban upper- and middle-class people who support Labor, Socialist, and Communist parties and the percentage of urban working-class people who do so. Canada's Liberal Party and the Democratic Party in the United States are also included, since there are no mass socialist parties in those societies.[13]

part to the absence of major working-class parties with strong ideological commitments. Their major parties are pragmatic, brokerage types, which tend to downplay class-related issues.*

Another factor that influences the relation between economic class and party preference is the presence of serious ethnic and religious divisions within a population. It is probably no coincidence that the countries in Tables 11.3 with the strongest relation between class and party preference are generally the most homogeneous from an ethnic and religious standpoint. In contrast, Canada has for years been divided by struggles between an English-speaking Protestant majority and a very large French Catholic minority. In both Canada and the United States, religion and ethnicity are important determinants of party preference.

Modern industrial democracies differ dramatically from traditional agrarian societies by virtue of their willingness to permit ethnic and religious minorities and the economically disadvantaged to participate in the political process. In agrarian societies, such groups had little or no political power. In industrial societies, in contrast, these groups have sometimes won control of the machinery of government, or at least a share in it, as the socialists have done in Scandinavia, the French in Canada, and the Catholics in the Netherlands.

---

*The New Democratic Party in Canada is a democratic socialist party, but it has not yet achieved the stature of a major national party.

Apart from the rise of democracy, the most important political change associated with industrialization has been the great growth of government. The range of activities and the diversity of functions performed by government are far greater in modern industrial societies than in any other type of society. In a traditional agrarian society, the government's chief functions were the preservation of law and order, defense, taxation, and the support of religion. In modern industrial societies, the last has usually been dropped, but dozens of new functions have been added.

The broader scope of government in industrial societies is closely linked to their increasing democratization. As the common people gain a voice in government, they demand services seldom, if ever, provided in agrarian societies. They want educational opportunities, job training, assistance when they are old or sick or unemployed, protection against dishonest business practices, recreational facilities, and many other things. The provision of these services further strengthens democratic tendencies, since an educated, economically secure population participates more intelligently and effectively in the democratic process and is less likely to be attracted by anti-democratic parties than is an illiterate and economically insecure population.[14]

Another factor contributing to the growth of government in an industrial society is the greater interdependence of its population. Occupational specialization has progressed to the point where virtually everyone is engaged in specialized work. Everyone, therefore, is dependent on the labors of others, and on the maintenance of the complex system of exchange by which goods and services reach their ultimate consumers. A disruption at any point has serious consequences for almost everyone, and people generally support governmental efforts to prevent it.

Similarly, in a society geared to a high degree of interaction among its members, dependable systems of transportation and communication are essential. And in its urban centers, where people live close together, well organized fire, police, and health services are imperative. Private individuals and organizations are unable to assume these responsibilities: only government can command the resources and exercise the authority needed to deal with such problems.

The Growth and Transformation of Government Bureaucracies   One of the best measures of the growth of governmental activity is the size of the governmental bureaucracy. In the United States, for example, the number of civilian employees of the federal government has risen steadily for the last century and a half:[15]

1821	7,000
1861	37,000
1901	239,000
1941	1,438,000
1981	2,865,000

FIGURE 11.4 "Now that the elections are over we can get back to the real business of government . . . Growing bigger!"

This increase far outdistanced the growth of the population as a whole. While the latter increased twentyfold, the number of federal employees shot up 400–fold. Contrary to what many people think, it is not only the federal bureaucracy that has been growing: between 1929 (the earliest year for which national totals are available) and 1983, the number of employees in state and local governments increased more than fourfold, while the general population grew only about 85 percent.[16]

The great growth in the powers of governments and in the size of their bureaucracies has made top administrative officials (i.e., civil servants) extremely powerful figures in industrial societies. Although this might be interpreted as simply a perpetuation of the old agrarian pattern with its dominance by a hereditary governing class, it is not. Government offices are no longer private property to be bought and sold and inherited by one's children. Rather, they tend to be assigned competitively on the basis of education and experience. Furthermore, in the exercise of the office, officials are expected to act on the basis of the public interest rather than of private advantage. Although reality falls far short of these ideals, there is nonetheless a marked contrast between the practices of officials in most modern industrial societies and the practices of those in traditional agrarian societies. The United States has discovered this repeatedly in its dealings with the officials of many of the governments of Southeast Asia, the Middle East, Africa, and Latin America, where bureaucratic corruption is widespread.

In large measure, the explanation for the change lies in the new democratic ideology, which asserts that the powers of government are derived from the people and should therefore be used for their benefit. This is in sharp contrast to the traditional ideology of agrarian societies, which defined the state as the property of the ruler. When modern officials use public office for private advantage, they are subject to a variety of official sanctions, including criminal prosecution. Such restraints were largely absent in agrarian societies.

Despite the less venal behavior of public officials in industrial societies, the growing size and power of government bureaucracies has become a matter of serious concern to many. A series of Gallup polls taken since 1967 shows that far more Americans fear big government than fear big business or big labor. In the most recent poll, 51 percent saw big government as a threat to the nation compared with 19 percent who saw big business as a threat and 18 percent who saw big labor as a threat.[17] In the Marxist-Leninist societies of Eastern Europe, both friends and foes consider the unsatisfactory performance of their entrenched bureaucracies to be one of their most serious defects.[18]

One of the chief problems of bureaucracies everywhere is maintaining a sense of public responsibility in their personnel. Officials in welfare agencies, for example, often become more concerned with enlarging their staffs, and hence raising their own rank and salary, than with delivering services to those whom the agency was created to serve. In most governmental bureaucracies it is also difficult to get individuals to accept responsibility for decisions. Buck-passing, paper-shuffling, and endless delays become standard operating procedures. Because of the tremendous division of labor, and hence of responsibility, within these organizations, it is frequently impossible to establish accountability, and as a result these patterns persist year after year, and generation after generation.

So far, critics of bureaucratic power have not come up with any feasible alternative. The sheer size and complexity of government in a modern industrial society make mass participation in decision making impossible. A substantial delegation of power, therefore, is inevitable, and those to whom the power is delegated generally do what they deem appropriate. As we have seen, there are serious limitations to the applicability of democratic principles in any large-scale organization.

Warfare

Compared to some of the wars of the agrarian era (e.g., the Thirty Years' War), wars among industrial societies have been of shorter duration. This is not an indication of the spread of pacifism, but rather of the awesome power of industrial technology. World Wars I and II caused over 23 million military deaths, maimed and killed many millions of civilians, and destroyed so much property that a reliable estimate is virtually impossible.[19]

Since the Second World War, weapons technology has advanced at a startling pace. The atomic bomb that fell on Hiroshima was the equivalent of 13,000 tons of TNT, while a single hydrogen bomb today may be the equivalent of 59 *million* tons.[20] Any future conflagration involving the major military powers would cause vastly more suffering and devastation than wars of the past. In fact, some experts believe that full-scale war between the United States and the Soviet Union would, *at a minimum,* cause industrial societies to regress permanently to a preindustrial state.[21]

The tremendous destructive power of the modern military machine is simply a corollary of the tremendous power of modern industrial technology. The invention of the automobile gave rise to the tank, the invention of the airplane to fighter planes and bombers. While the relationship is often reversed, with advances in weapons technology leading to important civilian innovations (as was the case with radar, for example), the point is the same: industrial societies, like societies before them, do

FIGURE 11.5 The tremendous destructive power of modern weapons is a corollary of the tremendous productive power of modern technology: the center of Hiroshima a year after the atomic bomb.

not segregate or separate the military and nonmilitary components of technology. As a consequence, technological advance carries with it the potential for greater destruction.

Unfortunately, industrial societies, like their predecessors, have failed to develop nonmilitary means of settling serious disputes. Some kind of world government appears to be a possible solution, but this raises difficult problems of its own, as we will see in Chapter 14. For the present, none of the major industrial societies seems inclined to move in that direction. Thus, the arms race, with all its hazards, continues.

Social Stratification

As we saw in Chapter 2, the basic function of any society's system of stratification is to distribute the things of value that people produce in their life together as members of society. These include not only material goods, but power and prestige as well.

Prior to the Industrial Revolution, every major technological advance led to an increase in the degree of social inequality within societies. This was true of the horticultural revolution, and it was true of the agrarian. During the early stages of the Industrial Revolution, it seemed that the historic pattern would be repeated once again and that industrial societies would prove to be the least egalitarian of all.

More recently, however, as a number of societies have reached a more advanced stage of industrialization, this 9,000-year trend toward greater inequality has begun to falter, even to show signs of a reversal. This has not meant a return to the highly egalitarian pattern of hunting and gathering societies. Far from it. But it has meant a less unequal distribution of power, privilege, and prestige within advanced industrial societies than has been characteristic of many technologically less advanced societies.

Evidence of this can be seen in Figure 11.6, which plots the relationship between the level of income inequality in contemporary societies and their level of economic development. While this figure does not show the historical trend, it does show clearly that the level of income inequality is lower in societies with the highest levels of energy consumption (one of the best measures of societal development) than in societies with intermediate levels of energy consumption. This is what one would expect to find if industrialization does, indeed, cause a decline in the level of income inequality within societies.

As we have seen previously, all societies must ensure that their productive members obtain the essentials needed to keep them healthy and productive—food, clothes, shelter, tools. When there is an economic surplus, however, its distribution

FIGURE 11.6   The relation of income inequality to the level of economic development in the modern world-system of societies. (Source: Adapted from Patrick D. Nolan, "Status in the World System, Income Inequality, and Economic Growth," *American Journal of Sociology, 89 (1983), pp. 410–419.*)

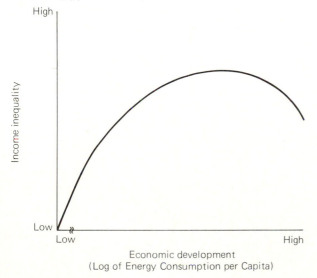

is largely controlled by the more powerful members of society. This does not mean, of course, that they consume all of the surplus themselves, but it does mean that they have the chief say in deciding for what purposes it is to be used and for whose benefit.

Therefore, to understand systems of stratification and patterns of inequality in industrial societies, we must ask, Who controls the economic surplus, and who decides the uses to which it will be put?

Control of the Economic Surplus

The Marxist-Leninist Societies of Eastern Europe   Control of the economic surplus is clear and unambiguous in the Marxist-Leninist societies of Eastern Europe. The Communist Party controls the surplus, and the Party itself is controlled by its top leaders, a handful of individuals (sometimes a single individual) within the Politbureau, which is the highest authority in the Party. These individuals not only decide Party policy, they also control the process of promotion within the Party and appointment to all important offices in society at large. When there are vacancies to be filled in the Politbureau itself, the leading member or members of that body choose the replacement. Although this decision is later ratified by a somewhat larger group of Party leaders known as the Central Committee, ratification is assured because appointment to the Central Committee itself is controlled by the same members of the Politbureau. As noted earlier, Marxist-Leninist societies are the most elitist of all modern industrial societies.

One of the most striking features of Marxist-Leninist societies is their use of a system of social control known as the *nomenklatura,* or nomenclature. This is a list of important positions that can be filled only by individuals who have been approved by Party leaders. These are the most powerful and important positions in the government, the economy, the military, the secret police, the mass media, education, and science, and control of appointments to these positions ensures control of society as a whole. In effect, the individuals who occupy *nomenklatura* positions, together with their families, constitute the governing class in Marxist-Leninist societies.[22]

Decisions concerning appointments to *nomenklatura* positions are made at varying levels within the Party. The most important positions are controlled by members of the Politbureau and Central Committee; less important positions are filled by Party leaders at regional and local levels. Political criteria are decisive in appointments to *nomenklatura* positions. Most of the people who are appointed are already trusted Party members, though exceptions are made occasionally for appointments to administrative posts in research institutes, universities, or health centers. In these kinds of organizations, non-Party people with outstanding technical qualifications are occasionally chosen if they are believed to be politically dependable.

Although the *nomenklatura* system has been in existence for decades, details concerning its size and operation are difficult to obtain. According to one recent estimate, approximately 750,000 positions in Soviet society are subject to *nomenklatura* control.[23] Reports from Poland indicate that there are approximately 100,000 *nomenklatura* positions in that country.[24] These figures indicate that the

**FIGURE 11.7   Members of the Politbureau and other high officials of the
Soviet Union laying wreath at the Tomb of the Unknown Soldier.**

governing class in Marxist-Leninist societies numbers a little less than 1 percent of
the population. Despite their limited numbers, the members of this "new class," as
some have called it, effectively control the organizational structures and institutional
resources of these societies.

Those who are a part of this new governing class enjoy many special privileges
that are denied to the rest of the population. Although their official salaries are not
unusually high compared to others in their societies, members of this class are able
to obtain at public expense, or at bargain prices, superior living quarters, second
homes, special schools for their children, vacations at the best resorts, automobiles,
servants, and many consumer goods that can be obtained only at special stores
closed to the general public.[25]

Beneath this small governing class there is a much larger class of lesser officials
who also enjoy special privileges, but on a more modest scale, including better
living quarters and the right to purchase goods that are not available to the general
public. This class includes, among others, members of the secret police and regular
police, lesser party and government officials, journalists and writers, and prominent
scientists, artists, and athletes. The basic function of this class, which numbers about
20 percent of the population in Poland, is to preserve Party control of the society.

Another group that shares in the economic surplus in Poland, and perhaps in other Marxist-Leninist societies, is workers in large industrial plants (steel mills, mines, etc.). One might suppose that these individuals benefit because the Communist Party claims to be the party of the working class. Poles are more cynical, however, and regard the benefits that these workers enjoy as merely a response by the Party elite to the threat which large concentrations of such workers pose. As some of them put it, "Lenin got it wrong when he said, 'Those who don't work don't eat'; in Poland, those who don't strike don't eat meat."[26]

Contrary to official claims, the distribution of the economic surplus in Marxist-Leninist societies does not appear to be guided by the socialist principle of "To each according to his work," but rather by the ancient conservative principle of "To each according to his contribution to the preservation of the political status quo."[27] Graphically, the stratification system in Marxist-Leninist societies resembles that in agrarian societies (see Figure 7.23, page 203) except that the nature of the classes has changed and the degree of inequality has been reduced—chiefly because industrialization makes the maintenance of an authoritarian system of control more difficult* and thus requires a somewhat wider sharing of the economic surplus.

The Western Industrial Democracies   In the western industrial democracies, control of the economic surplus is much more complex and, therefore, much more difficult to describe. Some believe that control lies in the hands of a tiny wealthy elite that owns and controls the great corporations. Others believe that control of these corporations, and of the economic surplus, has passed from the owners of these enterprises to their managers.[28] Still others insist that control lies in the hands of political leaders. And, finally, there are some who believe that no single elite controls the distribution of the economic surplus in western democratic societies but that control is divided among various elites who compete with one another as often as they cooperate.[29]

The last of these views appears to correspond most closely with the evidence. In the United States, for example, control of the economic surplus is divided among at least seven sets of elites: (1) major elected officials, (2) federal judges, (3) senior civil servants, (4) the heads of large corporations, (5) a small number of very wealthy individuals, (6) those who control the content of the mass media, and (7) the leaders of a few large associations who are able to influence large blocks of voters (e.g., heads of large labor unions, leaders of some religious and ethnic groups). The mix of elements in the dominant coalition varies somewhat from society to society, depending on the relative strength of the various interest groups and ideologies within a society. Also, the nature of the mix can change over time in response to technological and other changes. But most of these same elites are influential in most of the western industrial democracies and compete with one another for control of the economic surplus.

In a number of western democratic societies, there is a strong symbiotic relationship between politicians and economic elites. This is especially true in societies with brokerage-type political parties. In these societies, politicians constantly need

---

*A better-educated populace tends to be more demanding, and large-scale enterprises, such as factories and mines, create opportunities for organized opposition that were lacking in agrarian societies.

money to finance expensive election campaigns, while economic elites seek legislative favors, such as lower taxes, larger governmental subsidies, and less restrictive regulation, which only the politicians can provide. Although this kind of symbiotic relationship is strongest where brokerage-type parties are dominant, leaders of some of the more ideologically oriented parties (e.g., the French Socialists) have discovered that electoral success can depend on economic conditions and this often forces them to work more closely with economic elites than they might otherwise choose to do.

Control of the economic surplus in western societies is not simply a matter of elites versus the masses, as it is sometimes made to appear. Different sets of elites often come into conflict with one another (e.g., President Reagan's tax proposals in 1985 led to conflicts between the older "rust-belt" industries of the midwest and the newer high-tech industries in other parts of the country). Many political battles in western industrial societies are between interest groups representing different sectors of the economy, rather than between elites and the mass of ordinary citizens.

Another significant feature of the relation between elites and the masses in western industrial democracies is the amount of power which has been acquired by organizations which represent large blocks of ordinary citizens. The growth in power of labor organizations earlier in the century is a good example of this. By organizing politically and economically, union members were able to share significantly in the benefits of the rapidly expanding economic surplus. Traditional elites resisted less vigorously than they might have otherwise, because the rapid expansion of the surplus made it possible for them to avoid costly conflicts while still obtaining greater benefits for themselves. In other words, the great expansion of the economic surplus changed the nature of the conflict from the almost zero-sum game (see Glossary) it had been throughout most of the agrarian era to a positive-sum game from which everyone could benefit.

More recently, other kinds of organizations have been formed to promote the interests of other nonelite segments of the population—racial minorities, women, retired people, even welfare recipients. While these groups have never gotten all they wanted, they have won numerous concessions and a larger share of the economic surplus.

Today, because of the enormous productivity of western industrial societies and because of their democratic polities, *almost all parts of the population share to some degree both in the control of the economic surplus and in its benefits*. To be sure, they do not share equally in either the control of the surplus or in its benefits, but they do share in them. As a result, the vast majority of the members of these societies enjoy a standard of living far above the subsistence level. Even people who are classified as living in poverty in these societies usually live considerably above the subsistence level—which is why so many people in Third World societies are eager to migrate to the western democracies.

Because so many groups have a voice in decisions concerning the use of the economic surplus, no year passes without efforts to redistribute wealth and income. Although the political elite makes the final decisions, its members know that they can always be replaced at the next election if a majority of the electorate becomes dissatisfied with their actions—or inaction. This compels them to be attentive to the more basic interests of the masses of ordinary citizens.

This system does not please everyone by any means, but it has at least given the majority of people some influence in decisions concerning the economic surplus. That is no small accomplishment in a world in which other large and complex societies have uniformly denied the vast majority of their members even a limited voice in such decisions.

Technologically Based Similarities   Despite the important differences between the Marxist-Leninist societies of Eastern Europe and the western democracies, there are many important similarities between the two systems of stratification. The differences, as we have seen, stem primarily—though not entirely—from differences in *ideology* between elites in the two sets of societies; the similarities, in contrast, stem largely from the new industrial *technology* that they share and from organizational constraints imposed by their size (itself a result of technological advance).

Because of the technology they share, all industrial societies have a similar division of labor. There appears to be no alternative, if they are to take maximal advantage of the benefits the new technology can provide. Moreover, they seem to be similarly constrained in the ways in which they reward people in different occupations. If elites want to attract capable people to the more demanding and responsible professional and managerial roles, they have to provide material incentives. When such incentives were withdrawn for ideological reasons and income differences between occupational strata were minimized, as in the Soviet Union in the early 1920s and again in the late 1920s, or in Czechoslovakia in the early 1960s, the flow of qualified individuals into these positions declined and serious problems developed. Thus, despite ideological differences, patterns of stratification in all industrial societies are alike in some basic ways.

The Distribution of Income

One of the best measures of the level of social inequality in a society is the distribution of income among its members. This is especially true in western industrial societies, where money is a medium of exchange that can be used to purchase almost anything. The more money individuals have, the more easily they are able to satisfy their needs.

In Marxist-Leninist societies, the distribution of income is not nearly as good an indicator of inequality, since political power is much more valuable than money as a means of obtaining the good things of life, and the uses to which money can be put are much more limited than in other industrial societies. In the Soviet Union, for example, many goods and services are simply not available in stores which are open to the public and can be purchased only at special stores which are closed to everyone except members of the governing class. For those outside the governing class, they are not available except at black market prices, if at all. Many other things, such as housing, are generally not for sale, but are allocated by the authorities, and allocations are based largely on an individual's political clout.[30] Thus, the value of money is much more limited in Marxist-Leninist societies than in other industrial societies. Yet even in Marxist-Leninist societies, income distribution data provide some insights into the level of social inequality, as we will see.

In the western industrial democracies, incomes vary enormously. In the United States, for example, there are many families whose annual income totals less than $10,000 per year, even when the value of welfare payments, food stamps, housing subsidies, medical aid, unemployment compensation, social security, and other benefits is included. At the other end of the income scale, there are some athletes, entertainers, and business executives with incomes of $1 million or more per year. Beyond them, there is a tiny group of entrepreneurs who have made $10 million or more in a single year, and there are several families with enormous fortunes who should, at normal interest rates, have incomes in excess of $100 million per year. Thus, the range of family income in the United States appears to be as much as 10,000 to 1.

As large as this difference is, income inequality in industrial societies is not as great as in agrarian societies of the not-so-distant past. As we saw in Chapter 7, the top 1 or 2 percent of the families in those societies received not less than half of the total income. In contrast, the top 1.2 percent of the American population currently receives less than 10 percent of the total income and even the top 10 percent receives only a little more than a quarter of the total.[31]

Although the distribution of income in the United States is somewhat more unequal than in most other western industrial democracies, the difference is not great, as Table 11.4 indicates. Not surprisingly, there is a rough similarity between the ordering of societies in this table and in Table 11.3 (page 308), which suggests that class-based party systems tend to reduce income inequality somewhat.

It is also interesting to note that the distribution of income in the Marxist-Leninist societies of Eastern Europe appears to be surprisingly similar to the distribution of income in the nonsocialist societies of the West, despite the egalitarian ideals of the former. According to a recent estimate by a French scholar, there is a ratio of 10 to 1

TABLE 11.4   Income Distribution in Western Industrial Societies

Society	Percentage Share of Household Income by Percentile Groups of Households		
	Top 10 Percent	Bottom 20 Percent	Ratio of Top to Bottom
Sweden	21.2	7.2	2.9
Denmark	22.4	7.4	3.0
Finland	21.2	6.8	3.1
United Kingdom	23.8	7.3	3.3
Japan	27.2	7.9	3.4
Norway	22.2	6.3	3.5
Australia	23.7	6.6	3.6
West Germany	28.8	6.9	4.2
Italy	28.1	6.2	4.5
France	30.5	5.3	5.8
United States	26.6	4.5	5.9
Canada	26.9	3.8	7.1

Source: Adapted from World Bank, *World Development Report, 1982,* table 25.

between the highest-paid 10 percent of the Soviet population and the lowest-paid 10 percent; by comparison, the ratio for Britain is just 8 to 1, and for West Germany, 15 to 1.[32] If one could make an adjustment for the value of the nonmonetary benefits that members of the Soviet governing class enjoy, the Soviet ratio would almost certainly be as high as the ratio for West Germany, and perhaps even higher.[33]

One of the important new discoveries concerning income distribution in American society is that relatively few individuals remain persistently below the poverty level year after year. In fact, a major study found that only a little over half of the individuals living in poverty in one year were still living at the poverty level a year later, and less than 1 percent of the American population remained at the poverty level for an entire decade.[34] This is quite a change from the situation that existed not so long ago in agrarian and early industrial societies.

The Distribution of Wealth

One of the important differences between Marxist-Leninist societies and the western industrial democracies is that the former have numerous controls on the private ownership of wealth. Private ownership of land and capital goods is forbidden by law.[35] Citizens are allowed, however, to own their homes and furnishings—even second homes or vacation cottages. If they have good political connections or substantial financial resources, they may also own automobiles. Finally, they are allowed to have savings accounts in state banks, and there is no legal limit on the size of these accounts.

Unfortunately, Marxist-Leninist societies do not publish data on the distribution of wealth. The Soviet Union once published data on funds held in savings accounts, but discontinued the practice many years ago—perhaps because the data proved embarrassing. In the last year for which data were published, 3 percent of the depositors owned 43 percent of the money on deposit.[36]

In western industrial societies, data on the distribution of wealth are more readily available, though even in these societies they leave much to be desired. In the United States, for example, the chief source of information on the subject is data that the federal government gathers from estate (i.e., inheritance) tax returns, and these provide information only on individuals. Families, not individuals, are the more meaningful unit of analysis, however, because wealth tends to be shared within a family, or at least made available for the benefit of all the members. Furthermore, the data are gathered only at the time of death, when wealth is usually greater than earlier in life; and this, too, exaggerates the degree to which wealth is concentrated. Finally, estate tax returns are filed only for wealthy individuals; persons of more modest means do not have to pay this tax or file the return.

After corrections have been made for some of these deficiencies, it appears that in the middle 1970s the wealthiest 1 percent of the American population owned about 19 percent of the wealth.[37] If we make a further adjustment for the fact that spouses, children, and grandchildren usually share in the benefits of this individually owned wealth, and will eventually inherit most of it, the percentage would be somewhat less, but still substantial.

Research by a Royal Commission on the Distribution of Income and Wealth

TABLE 11.5   Distribution of Wealth in Britain

| | Percentage of Wealth Owned | |
Percentage of Population	Excluding Pension Rights	Including Pension Rights
Top 1 percent	28	17
Top 5 percent	54	35
Top 10 percent	67	46
Top 20 percent	82	59
Bottom 80 percent	18	41

Source: Royal Commission on the Distribution of Income and Wealth. Report No. 1. *Initial Report on the Standing Reference* (London: H. M. Stationery Office, 1975), tables 36 and 39.

yields a similar picture for Britain, though their more thorough study of the subject uncovered further problems with measures of the distribution of wealth. For example, as Table 11.5 indicates, when one takes into account the accumulated equity that workers have built up in governmental and private pension systems, the concentration of wealth is not nearly as great as it appears when this is ignored (as in most American data).[38] Nevertheless, it is still considerable.

Occupational Stratification

For the vast majority of the members of any industrial society, the chief determinant of their access to income and wealth is their position in the occupational system of stratification. Approximately 70 percent of the income in the United States today is distributed in the form of wages and salaries. All other forms of income—rent, profits, interest, dividends, capital gains, welfare payments, social security, unemployment compensation, food stamps, etc.—provide only 30 percent.[39]

The range of benefits received by people in different kinds of occupations varies greatly, as we have seen, with the top 10 percent enjoying incomes that are 10, 15, or more times larger than the incomes of those in the bottom 10 percent—the unemployed, part-time workers, and the unskilled. For individuals at the *very top* of the occupational ladder in the western democracies—business leaders, entertainers, and athletes—earnings are more than 100 times larger than the earnings of individuals at the bottom. In Soviet society, this ratio is reported to be "only" about 50 to 1 in recent years, but individuals holding *nomenklatura* positions enjoy many special benefits apart from their incomes, as we have seen.[40]

The basic structure of the occupational system of stratification is remarkably similar in Marxist-Leninist societies and in the western industrial democracies. In both sets of societies, managerial and professional occupations are the most highly rewarded, followed by manual workers in skilled occupations or heavy industries (e.g., tool and die makers, electricians, steelworkers, miners). These are followed by lower white-collar employees engaged in clerical and sales work, while unskilled manual workers are at the bottom of the occupational hierarchy.

As Table 11.6 indicates, the rank order of these major occupational groups is

TABLE 11.6   Relative Earnings of Four Major Occupational Groups in Six Industrial Societies

Society	Unskilled Manual Workers*	Lower White-Collar*	Skilled Manual Workers*	Professionals and Managers*
United States	100	108	146	169
Bulgaria	100	104	122	128
Czechoslovakia	100	133	136	164
East Germany	100	95	120	140
Hungary	100	114	123	156
Poland	100	113	110	144

*To facilitate comparisons among the six societies, the earnings of unskilled manual workers for all societies have been standardized at 100.

Sources: *Statistical Abstract of the United States, 1985,* table 699, and Gyorgy Akszentievics, "International Comparative Survey on the Situation of Industrial Workers," in Antal Boehm and Tomás Kolosi (eds.), *Structure and Stratification in Hungary* (Budapest: Institute for Social Sciences, 1982), p. 420.

basically the same in both the United States and the five Eastern European societies for which comparable data are available. The resemblance between the two sets of societies even includes an interesting reversal in the relative ranking of the two middle occupational classes. Prior to World War II, lower white-collar workers enjoyed, on average, higher incomes than skilled blue-collar workers in both the Soviet Union and the United States.[41] Since then, however, the relative rankings of these two classes have gradually been reversed, creating the present pattern, which favors skilled manual workers in all of the countries except Poland.

Another even more important change that has occurred in the occupational system of stratification in industrial societies has been the substantial growth in the relative number of high- and middle-status occupations. As Table 11.7 indicates, the percentage of upper white-collar jobs in the American labor force has more than

TABLE 11.7   Frequency Distribution of Adult Population among Occupational Classes in the United States, 1900 and 1980 (in Percentages)

Occupational Class	1900	1980
Upper white-collar	10	22
Upper blue-collar	11	13
Lower white-collar	7	30
Lower blue-collar	34	32
Farmer and farm laborer	38	3
	100	100

Sources: Figures based on data in U.S. Bureau of the Census, *Historical Statistics of the United States: Colonial Times to 1970,* series D182–232, and U.S. Bureau of the Census, *Statistical Abstract of the United States, 1985,* table 673.

doubled since the beginning of the century. There has also been relative growth in the two intermediate occupational classes—skilled manual workers and lower white-collar workers, especially the latter. These developments have brought about an important change in the class structure of American society, and, to a lesser extent, other industrial societies. No longer are the majority of people concentrated in the lower class, as in agrarian societies of the past (see Figure 7.21, page 203). Today, the majority of people in most industrial societies are members of the middle class. This is, of course, yet another consequence of the technological innovations that have so transformed the conditions of life for members of these societies since the beginnings of industrialization.

Educational Stratification

One of the great achievements of industrial societies has been the tremendous expansion of educational opportunities. Formal education is no longer a privilege limited to children of a small affluent minority. Today, all children not only are allowed to attend school for ten years or more at public expense, but are compelled by law to do so.

Despite the great increase in educational opportunities, inequalities in their utilization persist. Some young people drop out of school as soon as possible, while others go on to receive advanced degrees. The amount of education an individual receives is a function of many things—especially intelligence, motivation, health, peer influence, family tradition, and family resources.[42]

Differences in educational achievement, whatever the cause, have substantial consequences for subsequent achievement in the occupational system of stratification. Many jobs in modern industrial societies—probably the majority—have educational prerequisites, and insufficient years of education or lack of an appropriate diploma can bar otherwise qualified individuals from careers in many fields. In effect, modern personnel practices have created a civilian counterpart to the traditional military caste system, with its sharp distinction between officers and enlisted men. Just as the ceiling on promotion for enlisted men is normally the rank of sergeant, so the ceiling on promotion for less educated workers in industry tends to be the rank of foreman, or possibly plant superintendent. Higher-ranking positions in industry, and also in government, are usually reserved for people with a college or university degree who are recruited directly from outside the organization. Figure 11.8 illustrates the pattern.

The importance of educational stratification today is clearly evident in data on the relationship between education and income. Over the course of their lifetime, the most highly educated young Americans will receive two to three times the income of their least educated counterparts. Lifetime earnings (expressed in 1981 dollars) for young men are currently expected to vary as follows, depending on the amount of education they have received:[43]

Less than 12 years of education	$460,000
High school, 4 years	660,000
College, 1–3 years	724,000
College, 4 years	890,000
College, 5 years or more	968,000

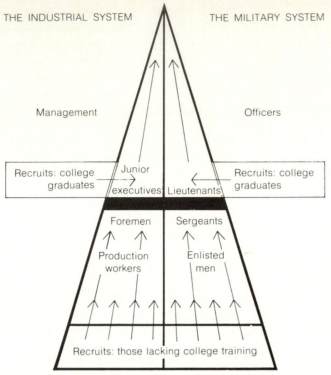

THE INDUSTRIAL SYSTEM   THE MILITARY SYSTEM

Management   Officers

Recruits: college / Junior \   Recruits: college
graduates \ executives | Lieutenants /   graduates

Foremen   Sergeants

Production   Enlisted
workers   men

Recruits: those lacking college training

FIGURE 11.8   Model of recruitment and promotional patterns in modern industry compared with those in the military.

For women, the level of expected income is lower for each level of education, but the ratio between the best educated and the least educated is even greater than for men.

Although comparable data are not available for any Marxist-Leninist society, available evidence indicates that the impact of educational differences on income and occupation in those societies is every bit as great as in the western industrial societies. Because of the great economic value of education in modern industrial societies, many economists and sociologists have begun to refer to it as "cultural capital." Like the more traditional forms of capital, it has the power to produce income.

Racial and Ethnic Stratification

Many industrial societies have racial or ethnic divisions within them. Canada, for example, has a serious cleavage between its French- and English-speaking populations, Belgium between Flemings and Walloons, and the United States between blacks and whites—to cite but three of the more serious instances. When membership in an ethnic or racial group has an appreciable influence on an individual's access to the benefits a society offers, the group has become, in effect, a class.

Classes of this kind are different, however, from most others in several respects. For one thing, the resource that is involved in ethnic and racial systems of stratification is *an ascribed characteristic*. Racial or ethnic background, unlike occupation and education, cannot be altered by individuals. For another thing, racial and ethnic classes usually have a greater degree of class consciousness than most others, more, say, than the educational class of people with high school diplomas, more even than the class of manual workers. Finally, because physical traits (i.e., appearance) and primary relationships (i.e., ties with family and close friends) are often involved, it is more difficult for an individual to move into or out of an ethnic or racial class.

The most striking example of this type of stratification in the United States involves the two major racial groups. Since colonial times, blacks have been a subordinate group. Before the Civil War this was evident in the legal position of the majority of blacks, who were slaves and, therefore, usually the property of members of the white group. Even before the Emancipation Proclamation, a few blacks established businesses and became wealthy (some even became slave owners themselves); but despite their achievements, they continued to suffer from handicaps imposed because of race. Their access to clubs, churches, housing, and services of almost every kind was much more limited than that of whites with comparable income and wealth.

Today, most of these limitations have been removed. Civil rights legislation ensures blacks equal treatment in stores, hotels, restaurants, and other business establishments, and affirmative action legislation even provides preferential treatment in college admissions, hiring, and promotions. But discrimination often continues in housing, club membership, and some other areas. Even more important, the general cultural and economic deprivation of recent centuries has left many blacks unable to take full advantage of the new opportunities. So much basic learning occurs while a child is small that large numbers of black children with poorly educated, low-income parents are already badly handicapped when they begin school. Many of these youngsters leave school poorly equipped to compete in the occupational system.

These problems are frequently aggravated by family situations in which the father is absent because of divorce, desertion, illegitimacy, or other reasons. In 1982, this was true of 42 percent of black families compared with 12 percent of white.[44] Children in these families are deprived not only of a father's contribution to socialization but of an important source of income as well. The average income of these families in 1982 was $10,424, compared with $22,719 for black families in which both parents were present. Whatever the underlying causes of the high proportion of broken families among blacks (the subject of a lively controversy), its impact on black children is undeniable.

Although the white population is sometimes thought of as a unit, it is, of course, divided along ethnic lines. People of British extraction enjoy the highest status, then those of other northwestern European ancestry, followed by those of southern and eastern European ancestry.[45] This reflects the historic dominance of those who first settled this country. Until about 1830, most of the white population was of British extraction, and these people naturally occupied the dominant positions in all the major institutions. Since most of the later immigrants were poor, had little education, and were unable to speak English, they tended to fill the more menial positions at first. The more they had in common with the older stock, the more readily they were accepted in marriage and in the better jobs, clubs, and neighborhoods. North-

FIGURE 11.9   Much basic learning occurs while a child is small: learning opportunities in Spanish Harlem.

western European Protestants were thus accepted more readily than southern and eastern European Catholics and Jews.

In Canada, the most serious cleavage is along ethnic lines and divides French-speaking Canadians from English-speaking ones. Although the French settled the country first, they were conquered by the British, who dominated the political system from the eighteenth century on. The problem was further aggravated because the English industrialized while the French clung to an agrarian way of life. As a consequence, the English also dominated the economy, even in Quebec, the home province of the French.[46] In recent years the French have succeeded in eliminating most discriminatory practices through political action, but a minority desires political independence.

Age and Sex Stratification

Inequalities based on age and sex have been present in every human society, past as well as present. In part, these inequalities reflect genetic differences among the members. On average, men have been stronger and more mobile than women, and they have not been burdened biologically by the responsibility for bearing and nursing children. Adults have been larger, stronger, and more knowledgeable than children, though aged adults have become disadvantaged whenever their health, vitality, and mental abilities have declined.

These biologically based differences have been reenforced and extended in most societies by cultural norms. Thus, the fact that the average woman is not as strong or mobile as the average man has usually led to norms that exclude *all* women from many kinds of activities for which a minority of women would be physically qualified.

With respect to age and sex stratification, modern industrial societies resemble preindustrial societies in many ways. Continuity can be seen most clearly in the frequency with which older men still control the more powerful organizations. Most members of the United States Senate, for example, are men and their average age in recent years has been 56 (the more powerful members of the Senate have been even older because of the seniority system that is used to select committee chairmen).[47] Most business leaders are also men, and a recent listing of the chief executive officers of 818 of the largest American companies indicated that they averaged 57 years of age.[48] Finally, a study of American military leaders, all of whom were male, found that their average age was 54.[49]

In Soviet society, and in most other Marxist-Leninist societies, the dominance of older males is even more pronounced, especially at the pinnacles of power. This is because of the enormous power leaders enjoy in those societies and because of the many barriers they have erected to protect themselves against potential challengers. As a result, the average age of the all-male Soviet Politbureau in 1984 was nearly 70 (in China in 1985, Politbureau members averaged an astonishing 75 years of age).[50]

In all the years of Soviet rule only one woman has ever become a member of that select group. Even in the less exclusive Central Committee of the Party, less than 3 percent of the members are women.[51] As one specialist on the subject has stated, "The position of Soviet women does not differ in principle from that of their counterparts in capitalist society."[52]

In nearly all of the industrial societies for which data are available, the income of women is substantially lower than that of men. As Table 11.8 shows, women usually earn about two-thirds as much as men.

There are a variety of reasons for this, but the most important appears to be the persistence of the division of labor between the sexes. In all industrial societies, there are certain occupations which are filled primarily by men and others which are filled primarily by women (in addition, there are some in which there is a more balanced representation of the sexes). The occupations filled primarily by women usually have lower wages or salaries than those filled primarily by men. They also tend to be occupations that offer fewer opportunities for promotion to more responsible positions.

The concentration of women in these lower-paying jobs is partly a heritage of the past when women seldom worked for long outside the home (see Figure 12.3, page 342) and when those who did were assumed (sometimes incorrectly) to be supplementing their husband's or father's income and, therefore, less in need of high wages than men, who were expected to be the primary providers for families. Once

TABLE 11.8 Women's Earnings as a Percentage of Men's Earnings in Industrial Societies

Society	Percentage
Sweden	86
Britain	68
France	68
West Germany	68
Czechoslovakia	67
Poland	67
Soviet Union	65
United States	63
Japan	58

Sources: Hilary Land, "The Changing Place of Women in Europe," *Daedalus*, 108 (Sept. 1979), pp. 80 and 84; *Statistical Abstract of the United States, 1985*, table 755; Michael Swafford, "Sex Differences in Soviet Earnings," *American Sociological Review*, 43 (1978), p. 661; Mary Brinton, lecture, University of North Carolina, Jan. 24, 1985.

established, this pattern has persisted because it tends to shape the expectations and aspirations of many women. Thus, the pattern of women's employment has become, in part, a matter of choice, with many women viewing marriage as a more attractive alternative than the job market and a commitment to family as more rewarding and more important than a commitment to career.[53]

Change is occurring, but it has been slow. In the United States, for example, women's earnings have risen from a little less than 60 percent of men's earnings in 1939, the first year for which data are available, to a little over 63 percent in recent years.[54] In Soviet society, the situation of women even appears to have regressed somewhat, since the percentage employed in lower-paying, predominantly women's occupations has risen from one-fifth to one-third in recent years.[55]

Overall, however, the situation of women has definitely improved as a result of industrialization. Laws that once restricted their right to own property have been eliminated, and women now own much of the wealth in all western societies.[56] Barriers to higher education have also been largely eliminated. Even in the political arena, women have made substantial gains. As recently as 1900, women were permitted to vote only in New Zealand and in four American states.[57] Today, they enjoy this right in every advanced industrial society, and women have served as prime ministers in both Britain and Norway.

ORGANIZATIONAL DISCRIMINATION OR INDIVIDUAL PREFERENCE?

Not long ago, a large American corporation was sued by several of its female employees for discriminating against women in promotions. In support of their claim they showed that while 82 percent of the entry-level clerical jobs in the company were filled by women, only 74 percent of the promotions had gone to women. This, they charged, was clear evidence of discrimination.

Management in this company had long prided itself on its policy of promoting on the basis of merit and was greatly distressed by the suit and by the allegation that it had failed in this regard. To find out whether it had, in fact, failed and, if so, how, the company hired a sociologist to study the matter.

Interviews with 850 employees of the firm demonstrated that women in entry-level clerical positions were much less likely than their male counterparts to seek, or even to desire, promotions (e.g., 39 percent of the women reported that they had no desire for a higher-level position compared to 21 percent of the men). Also, male employees in these positions were twice as likely as female employees to have requested promotion during the previous year (28 percent versus 14 percent). Females, however, were more likely to report that they had received encouragement from management when they sought promotion (70 percent versus 55 percent). These and other findings indicated that the lower rate of promotion for women in this company was the result of choices made by the women themselves rather than sex discrimination by the company.

These findings raised the obvious question of why women were less inclined to seek promotion than men. Further research indicated that both men and women saw promotions as requiring longer working hours and a greater burden of responsibility. This was a price that fewer women were willing or able to pay, especially married women. Whether by choice or necessity, they and their spouses had apparently developed a division of labor within the family that assigned primary responsibility for providing income to the husband and primary responsibility for child care and care of the home to the wife. Thus, the job was a secondary responsibility for the majority of married women in these entry-level positions and this led, not surprisingly, to lower rates of promotion.

This study also found, however, that among individuals already in supervisory positions, the rates of promotion were the same for both sexes. The authors of this study concluded that this was because the selective process operating in the entry-level positions weeded out those individuals of both sexes who were unwilling or unable to make the sacrifices required by supervisory responsibilities. This further supported the conclusion that it was a mistake to infer from the simple statistics on rates of promotion that the company was guilty of sex discrimination.

One cannot infer from this one study that all differences in rank and income between the sexes in industrial societies are the result of women's preferences, but it serves as a caution against the frequently made assumption that sex discrimination is the sole explanation, or even the chief explanation, for the underrepresentation of women in managerial positions.

Adapted from Carl Hoffman and John Shelton Reed, "Sex Discrimination?—The XYZ Affair," *The Public Interest,* no. 62, Winter, 1981, pp. 21–39.

FIGURE 11.10 "I didn't realize Akerman, Burbee & Smith had women in key jobs."

Vertical Mobility

Compared with agrarian societies, industrial societies offer many more opportunities for individuals to improve their status. In agrarian societies, high birthrates ensured an oversupply of labor in almost every generation. At every level in society, a certain percentage of the children were obliged to work in occupations of lower status than their parents' or to join the ranks of beggars, outlaws, prostitutes, and vagabonds. Although a few improved their situation, far more were downwardly mobile.

In industrial societies, conditions are strikingly different. Falling birthrates have helped to reduce the oversupply of labor, and if it were not for immigration from abroad, upward mobility would be substantially more frequent than downward mobility. As we have seen, technological advances have greatly increased the proportion of high-status, high-income jobs. Furthermore, because the upper classes now have smaller families than the lower classes, opportunities are created for many children of the latter to become upwardly mobile. Finally, flawed though they are, the systems of free public education in industrial societies provide talented and disciplined children from the lower classes with an opportunity to acquire skills that can help them move up the social ladder.

As a result of these developments, there is no industrial society in which the rate of downward mobility greatly exceeds the rate of upward mobility, the typical pattern in agrarian societies of the past. At worst, there are a few industrial societies in which the rate of downward mobility seems to be slightly greater than the rate of upward mobility (e.g., Britain, Denmark, and Poland).[58] In most industrial societies, however, there appears to be more upward mobility than downward, which is a remarkable change from the recent preindustrial past.

This development has undoubtedly been a factor in reducing the threat of working-class revolution predicted by Marx. If, in every generation, a quarter or more of the children of workers are able to rise into the ranks of the middle class, resentment against the system is almost certain to be less than if only a few percent move up the ladder, as Marx expected. Furthermore, since those who rise are generally the more talented and ambitious members, much of the potential leadership for protest movements is lost to the working class.

Social Inequality: Two Basic Trends

When we began our examination of stratification in industrial societies, we noted the trend toward greater social inequality that started with the horticultural revolution 10,000 years ago and continued into the early stages of the Industrial Revolution. We also noted that with further industrialization this trend was halted, and then reversed. Before concluding our review of stratification, we need to take a closer look at this important development, and at another important trend as well.

In agrarian societies of the past, systems of inequality were often built into the legal codes. There was no pretense that people were equal. Some were legally classified as members of a privileged nobility, some as commoners, others as slaves or serfs, and legal rights and privileges varied accordingly. Democracy as we understand it was unknown in these societies. Political decisions were the God-given prerogative of a tiny elite; the rest of the population had no voice in decision making. The only thing that limited the power of the governing elite was the knowledge that if conditions became too oppressive the masses might revolt. Because of their enormous power, the ruler and the rest of the governing class usually enjoyed not less than half of the national income and sometimes as much as two-thirds.[59]

In advanced industrial societies, legally based hereditary status has been virtually eliminated. In Britain and a few other societies, titles of nobility remain, but nearly all of the special rights and privileges that were once attached to them no longer exist. Equally important, the disadvantaged legal statuses of serfs and slaves have been completely abolished. Although social inequalities remain, they are no longer based solely on the accident of birth.

FIGURE 11.11   Public housing project for low-income families, Denmark.

In addition, except for the Marxist-Leninist societies of Eastern Europe, opportunities for participation in political decision making have been substantially increased in industrial societies. The franchise has been extended ever more widely until now virtually the entire population is able to vote in all of the western democracies. Although the system falls far short of equal influence for all, it is, by democratic standards, a tremendous advance over the situation that prevailed in agrarian societies not long ago.

Finally, economic inequality has been greatly reduced in *all* industrial societies. Though substantial inequalities still exist, the change has been tremendous. As we have seen, the top 10 percent of the population in the western democracies appears to receive only 20 to 30 percent of the national income compared to the 50 percent or more that was received by the top 1 or 2 percent of the population in agrarian societies. While comparable data on income distribution in Marxist-Leninist societies are not available, the evidence we do have indicates that the situation in those societies is roughly the same as in the western democracies.

Thus, *the overall level of inequality in industrial societies is considerably less than that in agrarian societies of the past or in most nonindustrial societies in the world today*. The best explanation for this egalitarian trend seems to be the enormous growth in productivity unleashed by the Industrial Revolution.[60] With national incomes increasing rapidly, the dominant classes found it was no longer in their interest to fight all of the claims of nonelite groups to a larger share of the economic surplus. Periodic concessions to the lower and middle classes could help them preserve much of their power and privilege. By giving ground in *relative* terms (i.e., by conceding a larger share of total income to nonelites), they could even improve their economic position in *absolute* terms (i.e., their total income and wealth actually increased). This was possible because technological advances had transformed the old zero-sum game that was characteristic of most preindustrial societies into a positive-sum game. Elites apparently concluded that it was better to settle for a smaller share of a much larger pie than to fight to preserve their historic share and, in the process, risk an end to economic growth and the loss of their privileged position in society.

But while the new technology has helped to reduce the level of inequality within industrial societies, it has had the opposite effect on the world system. *The gap between rich and poor nations has been widening ever since the start of the industrial era*. In the 120 years between 1860 and 1980, the wealthiest quarter of the nations increased their share of the world's income from 58 to 74 percent, while the share of the bottom quarter fell from 12.5 to 2.3 percent.[61] With the new technology gradually eroding the barriers between societies, the importance of this trend is bound to increase. We will return to this subject in Chapter 13, when we examine the complex problems of Third World societies which are struggling to industrialize in the shadow of far wealthier and more powerful societies.

CHAPTER 12

Industrial Societies: III

Kinship

The impact of industrialization on kinship has been no less dramatic than its impact on population, the economy, the polity, and stratification. The consequences for kinship, the oldest institutional system in human societies, can be seen in its declining functions, in the smaller size of nuclear families, in the high incidence of divorce, and in the changing roles of women and young people.

Declining Functions of the Family

In the simplest human societies, the basic integrative force in societal life was the kin group, an all-purpose organization that provided for the political, economic, educational, religious, and psychic needs of all its members. As societies grew in size and complexity, this had to change. No longer could an individual's relationships with other people always be defined in terms of kinship. New roles and organizations began to take shape, and, in the process, some of the functions of the kin group were eroded.

Although this process began thousands of years ago, kin groups remained of great importance throughout the entire agrarian era. Above all, the nuclear family (i.e., mother, father, and children) was still the basic productive unit in the economy. The peasant family was almost invariably a work unit, and this was also true of many other families. Place of work and place of residence were normally the same, and all of the members of a family, including the children, shared in the work.

Government, too, was still a family matter. Members of the political elite usually inherited their status, while the royal family considered the state to be its personal property. Education remained primarily a family responsibility: boys usually learned the male role and their productive skills from their fathers; girls learned theirs from mothers and aunts. Due to the growth of urban communities, the kinship system was not always as strong or pervasive as it had been in simpler societies. But family ties remained central in the lives of most individuals and provided the basic framework for societal life.

In industrial societies, many of the family's traditional functions have been eliminated or greatly altered. The family is an economic unit only in terms of consumption, not of production. Families no longer control the political system; nepotism may still occur, but it is not accepted as normal or legitimate. Schools, religious groups, and other organizations have assumed much of the responsibility for the education, socialization, and supervision of children, and a wide variety of organizations, from 4-H clubs to summer camps and from beauty colleges to universities, have taken over the task of providing young people with the skills they will need in their adult lives.

But the family has not been stripped of all its historic functions. Some of the most critical ones, including reproduction and the early socialization of children, still fall to the nuclear family. And as the larger kin system, or extended family, has diminished in importance, and as societal life has become increasingly complex and depersonalized, the nuclear family's responsibilities have in some ways become more important. For example, it usually bears the primary responsibility for fulfilling the psychic and emotional needs of its members. With respect to children, the nuclear family is still expected to be the major factor in personality development, instilling basic values, providing affection, providing guidance and encouragement in school and career decisions, training in the use of money, and much more. And all of this must be accomplished in a social environment that is far less homogeneous, and therefore far more difficult, than the one in which agrarian families raised their children.

Marriage today is undertaken for more personal reasons than in the past. Because most horticultural and agrarian societies viewed marriage largely in economic terms, marriages were often arranged by parents with economic considerations primarily in mind. The individuals most intimately involved were often denied even veto power. Sexual attraction and affection were not considered of primary importance: everyone knew that these might grow or wane, but the family's need for a firm economic base would persist.

In industrial societies, in contrast, marriage has become an arrangement that is undertaken primarily to enhance personal happiness and to permit individuals to fulfill personal goals, such as establishing a home or having children. Most people today view marriage as the union of a man and a woman who are attracted to one another both physically and emotionally and who hope to find pleasure, comfort, convenience, and companionship by sharing their lives. In short, marriage and the family are becoming more a matter of choice than of necessity. One indication of this is the growing number of individuals who live alone, apart from any family group. Currently, nearly 13 percent of American adults live this way.[1]

Causes of Change in the Family

Change in the family, like change in other institutions today, is essentially the result of technological advance and the trends that accompany it. One of the most fundamental and pervasive of these trends has been an enormous increase in specialization. As a result, specialized organizations of various kinds have steadily removed from home and family much of the responsibility for a wide range of service functions. These include not only educating and caring for the young, but caring for the ill and the aged, processing food and preparing meals, making and caring for wearing apparel, and much more. As a result, the nuclear family itself has become a more specialized institution.

Specific elements of the new technology have also had a great impact on the nuclear family, especially those that have given people control over fertility. Because of advances in methods of limiting family size, couples today have a much wider range of options available to them in almost every area of their lives than couples had in societies of the past. Nothing better illustrates how technological advance expands the "limits of the possible," for individuals and families as well as for societies, than these advances.

Industrialization has also served to undermine the traditional structure of the family with respect to authority. The father is no longer the head of the family in the way he was in agrarian societies, and parents do not have as much control over their children's conduct as they had either in agrarian societies or earlier in the industrial era. Peer group influence and the mass media have become much more powerful than family influences for many teenagers, and serious family conflict often results.

In large measure, the drastic decline in parental authority is the inevitable consequence of the technological and other societal changes that have destroyed the family's role as a productive unit, which once had to work together for the mutual benefit, even the survival, of its members. Related to this, industrialization has had the effect of drawing families apart both physically and psychologically. Most fathers and many mothers are away from home all day because of work, while schools and other organizations draw children out of the family for other purposes. Today, children in the lower grades may spend far more time with their teacher than with their mother, and teenagers often spend more time with their friends than with parents or siblings. Similarly, husbands and wives see less of one another or of their children than of their co-workers. One study of the fathers of 1-year-olds in the United States found that they spent an average of only 20 minutes a day with their infants.[2]

Another important cause of the decline of authority within the home has been the new democratic ideology which has permeated industrial societies, and which carries with it an individualistic bias that puts more emphasis on the rights of individuals than on their responsibilities to the groups to which they belong. Just as the democratic trend has altered roles within other institutions (e.g., political, economic, and educational), it has altered roles within the family. A final factor contributing to this trend is the greater number of options available to individuals who want to break family ties. Divorce is easier (see below), and so is economic independence for women. As a result of all of these factors—increased specialization, new ideologies, and new technologies—the nuclear family today is less cohesive than its agrarian predecessor.

Finally, the extended family has been substantially weakened by technological advances that make the populations of industrial societies highly mobile. Although the lower cost and greater ease of transportation and communication make it possible for individuals to maintain contact with relatives across greater distances, the relationships are not as intimate as when relatives lived within the same community.

The Nuclear Family in Industrial Societies

Size and Composition The most drastic change in the nuclear family is in the number of children, as Table 12.1 indicates. British marriages contracted around 1860 produced a median of six children. Only two generations later, the median had dropped to two. Families with eight or more children declined from 33 percent of the total to only 2 percent. Although the decline was more rapid in Britain than in most industrial societies, the general pattern has been quite similar.[3]

Comparisons like the one in Table 12.1 are somewhat misleading if we assume that they also reflect the degree of change in the number of children actually living within a family at the same time. In the earlier period the death rate among children was so much higher than it is today that there were considerably fewer children

TABLE 12.1   Number of Children Born to British Couples Married around 1860 and around 1925

Number of Children Born	Percentage of Marriages	
	Marriages around 1860	Marriages around 1925
None	9	17
One	5	24
Two	6	25
Three	8	14
Four	9	8
Five	10	5
Six	10	3
Seven	10	2
Eight	9	1
Nine	8	0.6
Ten	6	0.4
Over ten	10	0.3
Total	100	100.3

Source: Royal Commission on Population, *Report* (London: H. M. Stationery Office, 1949), p. 26.

FIGURE 12.1   During the nineteenth and early twentieth centuries, large families were the rule: the Dudleys of Richmond, Virginia.

living in an agrarian family than were born into it. Another factor that reduced the number of children living with their parents at any given time was the long duration of the childbearing period. Women who had eight, ten, or more children often bore them over a twenty-year period or longer. By the time the youngest children were five or ten, many of their older brothers and sisters had left home or died. Thus, although the nuclear family was certainly larger in agrarian societies, the number of its members who actually lived together at one time was not as different as the change in birthrates suggests.

A second noteworthy change in the composition of the family is the elimination of the last vestiges of polygyny. Industrial societies are the only major type in which polygyny has never been socially approved. Among preagrarian societies, only a minority, around 13 percent, insist on monogamy.[4] In agrarian societies, monogamy is more common, though still far from universal. For example, polygyny has been practiced throughout the whole of the Islamic world extending from Morocco to the East Indies. The pattern in industrial societies reflects the changing character of the family, especially the growing importance of affective ties between husband and wife and the declining importance of economic functions. Monogamy in industrial societies is also an expression of democratic, egalitarian values and a reaction against inequalities inherent in polygynous marital systems.

The modern nuclear family also has fewer extended kin living with it. Its household less frequently accommodates aged grandparents, unmarried aunts and uncles, and grown children. This is no longer as necessary because modern urban communities provide so many alternative facilities for single individuals—

apartments, nursing homes, restaurants, laundries, and so on. Moreover, as these facilities have developed, changes have occurred in societal values: most members of industrial societies are quite jealous of their privacy and value it more highly than the benefits they might enjoy as members of more inclusive households.

Disrupted Nuclear Families During the last hundred years, the divorce rate in virtually every industrial society has risen substantially. In the United States in 1890 it was only 0.5 per 1,000 population; by 1983 it had risen tenfold to 5.0.[5] In large measure, this trend is an inevitable result of the altered functions of the family, the changed perception of marriage which has accompanied it, the new options available to women, and the newer attitudes of society toward divorce. Half or more of all divorced people eventually remarry, however, which indicates that marriage is still considered a meaningful and valuable institution.

Despite the great increase in divorce, its impact on the nuclear family has not been as dramatic as one might suppose. This is because marriages during the agrarian era, and early in the industrial era, were disrupted about as often as they are today, but for a different reason: *the death of one or both parents*. In eighteenth-century Sweden, approximately 50 percent of nuclear families were broken in this way before all of the children had reached adulthood; in late eighteenth-century

FIGURE 12.2   Prior to industrialization, many marriages were broken during the child-rearing years by the death of one or both parents.

France, the figure was 60 percent, and in early twentieth-century India it was 70 percent.[6] Thus, despite the rising divorce rate, the percentage of ever-married women between the ages of 45 and 64 who were still living with their first husband remained virtually unchanged in the United States from 1910 to 1970.[7]

More recently, however, as the divorce rate has continued to rise and the death rate has leveled off, the picture has begun to change for the nuclear family. Most important, the proportion of children living with *both* of their natural or adoptive parents has begun to fall. In 1968, 12 percent of American children under 18 years of age were living with only one of their parents; fifteen years later, the figure had doubled.[8] This pattern is especially common among blacks: nearly 60 percent of black children under 18 live in one-parent households.[9]

Changing Role of Women

Nowhere are the effects of industrialization on society's norms, values, and sanctions seen more clearly than in the changing role of women.[10] Throughout recorded history most women were destined to spend their prime years bearing children, nursing them, caring for them when they were sick and dying, and rearing them if they survived; doing domestic chores; tending a garden; and often helping in the fields. It is hardly surprising, therefore, that women seldom played significant roles outside the home or made outstanding contributions to the arts.

The first signs of change came in the nineteenth century, when the economic benefits of large families came to be outweighed by their costs. Efforts to reduce fertility were soon aided by innovations in the area of birth control. During the nineteenth and early twentieth centuries, however, the average woman still produced a large family, still had babies for whom there was no alternative but prolonged breast feeding, still carried the full burden of child care and housework, and sometimes was obliged to work outside the home.

Because women were usually supplementary wage earners for their families, they were not trained for skilled jobs and were relegated to those that paid the least. Their availability for work at low wages posed a threat to the emerging labor movement and, as a consequence, women were virtually excluded from it. It was, in effect, a working*man's* movement, and its goal was to wrest a greater share of the growing economic surplus from the upper classes.

In contrast, the early women's movements in western societies were dominated by the better educated, more leisured, and economically more secure women of the upper classes, and their goals were primarily to obtain for women some of the legal and civil rights that already belonged to upper- and middle-class men: the right to vote, to hold public office, to own property, and to enter universities. Late in the nineteenth century, they also became concerned with the situation of working mothers and sought to have their hours of employment shortened and night work eliminated entirely.

By the 1920s, the original goals of the women's movements in western industrial societies had been largely achieved and these movements virtually disappeared. Changes continued to occur in the role of women, but chiefly as a result of technological innovations—not because of organized political efforts. These innovations included the invention of many laborsaving devices for the home, such as

THE YOUNG HOUSEKEEPER'S FRIEND

Women's liberation owes more to technological advance than many people appreciate. Cookbooks and other guides for nineteenth-century housewives are interesting reminders of the revolutionary transformation that has occurred in the care of a home and family.

Baking, for example, was a very time-consuming job in a day when homes had either a reflecting oven beside an open fire or a brick oven built into a chimney. Books written for young housewives often advised them to set aside a day or two each week for baking, and *The Young Housekeeper's Friend,* published in 1859, stressed the importance of careful planning. As Mrs. Cornelius, the author, advised, "The bread first—then the puddings—afterward pastry—then cake and gingerbread—lastly, custards." With respect to bread, Mrs. Cornelius wrote that "A half hour is the least time to be given to kneading the bread . . . and an hour's kneading is not too much."

Laundry was another time-consuming task, and an exhausting one as well. Water had to be carried from the well or cistern to the stove to be heated, and then carried to the washtubs. White items required boiling. Most items required scrubbing by hand while bending over a washboard. After washing, rinsing, boiling, blueing, and starching, everything had to be carried outside and spread on bushes or hung on a line to dry, and collected later. Ironing for a large family could easily consume most of a day. And from time to time the housewife had to prepare her own soap from wood ashes, fat, and grease.

Today, with a single twist of the dial on a modern gas or electric oven, an individual accomplishes the equivalent of cutting and splitting the firewood, hauling it in from the yard, and building and maintaining the fires, and "brown and serve" rolls are more likely to go into the oven than bread kneaded for half an hour. Similarly, automatic washers and driers and no-iron fabrics have reduced the expenditure of time and energy required by a family's laundry by 95 percent, even as standards of personal care and cleanliness have risen.

refrigerators, freezers, automatic washing machines and dryers, vacuum cleaners, electric irons, and frozen foods, all of which, taken together, greatly reduced the time and energy consumed by housekeeping. The development of a safe alternative to breast-feeding and more effective methods of birth control were especially important in freeing married women from historic constraints on their lives and in enabling substantial numbers of them to seek employment and to engage in other activities outside the home for the first time.

During the twentieth century, there has been a rapid increase in women's participation in the labor force in most industrial societies. Figure 12.3 shows the trend for the United States. Today, more than half of all American women are employed outside the home, including approximately two-thirds of the women between the ages of 20 and 45.[11] In Eastern Europe, the rates of female employment are even higher. In the Soviet Union, 82 percent of women between the ages of 15 and 55 are employed outside the home, and in Czechoslovakia, 87 percent.[12]

The tremendous increase in women's participation in the labor force, especially in recent decades, is the foundation for the new women's movement that began in the 1960s. This newer movement has had a diversity of goals, but one underlying objective: to break the restrictive molds in which societies have cast women. This

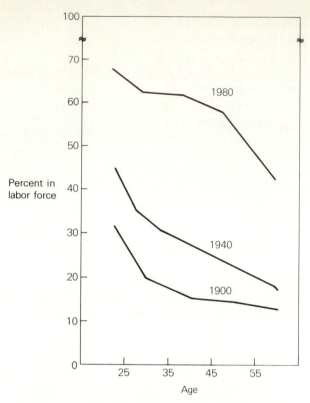

FIGURE 12.3 Female labor force participation in the United States by age: 1900–1980. (Sources: V. K. Oppenheimer, "Demographic Influence on the Employment and Status of Women," *American Journal of Sociology*, 78 (Jan. 1973), p. 948, and *Statistical Abstract of the U.S., 1985*, table 669.)

goal is based on the premise that with a single exception—women's capacity for childbearing—the differences between the sexes no longer provide a valid basis for the division of labor. Modern technology is able to compensate to a large degree for those differences which are physical (e.g., strength, lactation), while those differences which are psychological (e.g., emotional responses, competitiveness) are to an indeterminate degree the result of socialization rather than genetics.

The women's movement also emphasizes the fact that power and prestige in modern societies derive from activities outside the family and that if women are to have equal access to these rewards and share equally in shaping society's institutions, they must participate fully in both the economy and the polity. But women cannot have equal access to the more interesting and demanding jobs and to promotions, higher pay, political offices, and other opportunities outside the home unless the burden of responsibilities *within* the home is divided more evenly. Thus, the women's movement is seeking both to increase men's participation in household responsibilities and child care and to spread the burden of child care by tax rebates for working parents and by the creation of tax-supported child care centers.

TABLE 12.2 Average Hours Urban Americans Devoted Each Week to Work for Pay and to Care of Home and Family, by Employment Status, Marital Status, and Sex

Employment Status, Marital Status, and Sex	Work for Pay	Home and Family Care	Total
Employed married men	47.4	9.7	57.1
Employed married women	30.1	24.9	55.0
Full-time housewives	1.1	44.3	45.4

Source: U.S. Department of Commerce, Bureau of the Census, *Social Indicators, 1976*, table 10/1.

As Table 12.2 indicates, married men and women in the United States who are employed spend approximately equal amounts of time working (57 hours per week for men, 55 hours per week for women), but men spend a much higher percentage of time working for pay, while women spend proportionately more on family responsibilities. Similar patterns are reported in the Soviet Union and elsewhere.[13] This is, of course, one reason for both the differences in earnings between the sexes and the lower proportion of women who rise to supervisory and managerial positions. An interesting response to this problem has been the decision by an increasing number of employers to provide paternity leave for the fathers of the newborn. In the United States today, more than a third of employers are reported to provide such leave (usually unpaid leave for a period of up to three months).[14] In Sweden, the parents of a newborn child are given nine months paid leave, and the parents decide how to divide the leave between them.[15]

Despite efforts such as these to deal with the changing role of women, numerous problems remain. Many individuals find it difficult to combine the role of employee with the role of parent and spouse and to meet both sets of responsibilities. More often than not, the demands of the job take precedence and marital and parental obligations are sacrificed.

Efforts to expand nursery schools and other child care facilities have only partly met the need, even in Eastern Europe, where women's involvement in the labor force is greatest. East Germany, for example, is reputed to have the most extensive and the best child care system of any industrial society, but even it provides for only 60 percent of the children under three years of age.[16] Furthermore, despite strong Party support for this system, East Germans who are involved in it are cautious in evaluating the long-term effects of early separation of children from their mothers. As the head of one district hospital stated, "So far the children have not shown any damage, but how it turns out historically with a large number of people, we cannot say."[17]

For women themselves, the consequences of changes in their role are becoming increasingly evident. Not surprisingly, they indicate the erosion of many traditional differences between the sexes in areas beyond employment and family life. This is evident in everything from clothing to mental and physical health, and from tobacco and alcohol consumption to frequency of crime, automobile accidents, and suicide.[18] Betty Friedan has argued that middle-aged women suffer less from depression and insomnia today than fifteen or twenty years ago, and others report a decline in

FIGURE 12.4   Female locomotive engineer, USSR.

the use of tranquilizers by women. The once-large differences between the sexes in smoking habits has been all but eliminated, and among teenagers, more girls than boys now smoke. Similarly, differences in the incidence of heart disease between men and women are declining, and one recent study found that heart disease among middle-aged mothers employed in clerical and sales jobs was twice as frequent as among housewives.[19] And, finally, between 1932 and 1982, the percentage of women arrested for crimes doubled.[20]

Changing Role of Youth

In preindustrial societies, the transition from childhood to adulthood occurred swiftly and at an early age. Children were typically given chores to do while they were still quite young, and their responsibilities gradually increased. By the time they were in their middle teens, sometimes earlier, they were doing much the same work as their parents and other adults. Traces of this older pattern still survive in the rites of passage of certain religious groups (e.g., confirmation rites and bar mitzvahs), which occur around the age of thirteen. In an earlier era, these commonly signaled the end of childhood and the beginning of adulthood, a period in which the individual would be obliged to earn his or her own way and contribute to the support of others.

With the rise of industrialization, the need for human labor was reduced to such an extent that children came to be viewed as a threat to adults in the job market, and labor unions fought to make child labor illegal. Their efforts were reinforced by the passage of legislation to make school attendance compulsory, and young people were gradually edged out of the labor force or into marginal, part-time jobs. In the home, there were fewer siblings for older children to care for, and fewer chores to perform. In short, opportunities for participation in the adult world were drastically curtailed. As a consequence, a new age role was created. Whereas most people in their teens, and certainly those in their early twenties, had previously been viewed as young adults, they came increasingly to be seen as occupying an intermediate role, a role that is neither that of adult nor that of child.

Most of the individuals in this new age role are students. Table 12.3 shows how rapidly the school population in the United States increased during the last hundred years. By 1983, 95 percent of Americans aged 14 to 17 were enrolled in school, and 30 percent of those aged 18 to 24.[21] As this suggests, some industrial societies may have expanded their educational institutions beyond what is required to equip individuals for their roles in the economy, or even for their roles as citizens in a democratic society.[22] In addition, these societies have failed to take account of the fact that all individuals are not equally disposed to be students for such a long period. Many young people have little interest in the intellectual aspect of education, or even in its vocational relevance, but would rather move on into adult roles. They frequently discover, however, that there are no viable alternatives. Many who drop out of the educational system have trouble finding employment and getting established in the world of work.

As always happens when one segment of a population is cut off for an extended period from full participation in the life of the larger society, young people have developed their own subculture. Many of its more distinctive features (e.g., music, sports, experimentation with sex and drugs, etc.) are a natural consequence of the distinctive attributes of youth, such as vitality, curiosity, the desire for fun and excitement, and resistance to adult authority. The highly innovative nature of the youth culture, in areas such as music, language, and dance, is at least partly the

TABLE 12.3 Growth of the Student Population in the United States, 1880–1980

Date	Enrollment in Public Schools, Grades 9–12	Enrollment in Colleges and Universities	Total	Percentage of American Population Enrolled
1880	100,000	100,000	200,000	0.4
1930	4,400,000	1,100,000	5,500,000	4.4
1980	14,700,000	12,100,000	26,800,000	11.8

Sources: U.S. Department of Commerce, Bureau of the Census, *Historical Statistics of the United States: Colonial Times to 1970* (1975), series H 424 and H 706, and *Statistical Abstract of the United States, 1984*, table 214.

result of deliberate efforts to create a barrier between youth and adults. The faster the youth culture changes, the harder it is for adults to keep up with it, thereby forcing them to keep their distance and preventing them from moving in and dominating the youth scene.

At a more fundamental level, though, youth culture simply reflects some of the most distinctive characteristics of industrial societies themselves: their high rate of innovation, their affluence, their opportunities for leisure, their emphasis on individuality, and their tendency to specialize. The preoccupation of young people with changing fads and fashions, for example, can be viewed as simply another expression of their society's enormous economic surplus and its love of novelty.

The differences between the norms and values of the youth culture and those of the larger society can cause serious problems, however, especially when they involve decisions with long-term implications for young people and for others. Teenaged pregnancy is a compelling example of this. Every year in the United States alone, several hundred thousand unmarried girls in their teens become pregnant,[23] usually because they begin sexual activity without adequate information on reproduction and contraception. These individuals are thus forced to make decisions that neither experience nor the norms and values of the youth culture have equipped them to make. Should the girl have an abortion or have the child? Marry the father or remain single? Put the child up for adoption or struggle to raise it alone? One

FIGURE 12.5   The heavy investment in athletics that many boys make in high school rarely pays off in their adult years: only one high school football player in a thousand ever makes it to the National Football League.

consequence of young women's answers to these questions has been a dramatic increase in the United States in the number of small children raised by only one parent—21.7 percent of all children under 6 in 1983.[24]

Even when the decision to marry is made without the complications of an unexpected pregnancy, teenaged marriages are high-risk marriages, largely because the qualities that the youth culture values most highly in the opposite sex have little to do with the qualities an adult finds most desirable in a marriage partner. Similarly, because their peer group values success in sports more highly than success in academics, many boys make a heavy investment in athletics at the expense of their studies, only to find their skills no longer in demand once they are through high school or college. As Table 12.4 shows, no more than one high school varsity athlete in a thousand makes it into the ranks of the professionals.

In most industrial societies, great numbers of specialized youth groups have developed, each with its own distinct subculture. In the United States, these have included a wide variety of religious cults, counterculture groups, ghetto gangs, motorcycle gangs, homosexual groups, communes, and political groups of various persuasions.

Youth culture is now almost as much a part of the Marxist-Leninist societies of Eastern Europe as it is of other industrial societies. After trying for years to prevent the intrusion of what were viewed as degenerate products of decaying capitalist societies, Communist Party officials appear to have adopted the philosophy that "if you can't beat them, join them." Thus, the Komsomol (the party youth organization) now operates, in Moscow alone, more than 260 clubs where disco dancing and punk rock are featured.[25] State factories, meanwhile, produce great quantities of blue jeans. Despite this, a growing number of Soviet youth still seem determined to flout authority, turning to such unacceptable alternatives as church attendance or crime.

Crimes of violence have come to be associated with youth in all industrial societies. In Soviet society, for example, 80 percent of those convicted for assault with intent to rob are under 25 years of age.[26] In the United States, 75 percent of those arrested for robbery, the legal definition of which involves the threat or use of violence, are under 25 years of age, as are 56 percent of those arrested for all crimes.[27] Political violence is also largely the work of younger people, though older adults often guide such activity.

Many attempts have been made to explain the tendency toward violence among

TABLE 12.4 Number of Men and Boys Playing Basketball and Football in High School, College, and Professional Sports

Level of Competition	Basketball	Football
High School	700,000	1,100,000
College	18,000	43,000
Professional	264	1,260

Source: Adapted from Leonard Shapiro and Donald Huff, "The Games Always End," *Washington Post,* Mar. 20, 1977, p. D4. Professional football figure updated to 1986.

younger people, especially younger males, in industrial societies. In American society, scholarly explanations usually place the blame primarily on society (e.g., widespread unemployment among youth, racism).[28] In Soviet society, in contrast, blame is usually placed on individuals (e.g., the parents of the criminal, the criminal himself).[29] Soviet scholars also explain the problem as an inevitable by-product of the difficult transition from the submissiveness and obedience of childhood to the self-assertiveness and relative autonomy of adulthood.[30]

In trying to understand this phenomenon, it is important to keep in mind what many experts seem not to realize: young men were often involved in crimes of violence in agrarian societies, and most hunting and gathering and horticultural

FIGURE 12.6   No society of the past ever offered such rich and varied opportunities for recreation as industrial societies now provide, thanks to modern technology: scuba diving is but one of many opportunities available.

societies provided socially approved opportunities for violence in hunting or war-fare. While there can be no definitive explanation of violence in younger men, it is certain that the causes are many and complex. They probably include the biological influences of age and sex, distinctive characteristics of the individual, and a number of characteristics not only of his nuclear family and other associates but of the larger society as well.

Leisure, the Arts, and the Mass Media

Leisure and the Arts

No preindustrial society ever offered such rich and varied opportunities for recreation as modern industrial societies provide. With the aid of electronic devices, one can now "command" performances by the world's greatest symphony orchestras or the world's greatest artists (even some now dead), all in the comfort of one's own home. With other elements of modern technology, individuals can travel quickly and comfortably to distant lands or, alternatively, bring the sights and sounds of those places into their own living rooms via television or video recorders. For those who prefer physical activity, there are scores of opportunities ranging from miniature golf to hang gliding and snorkeling.

Industrial societies are also unique because of the extent to which they have commercialized recreation. Entertainment and the manufacture of equipment for leisure activities have become important industries. Ironically, even when members of industrial societies go camping to get "back to nature," they usually take with them many products of modern technology.

One of the attractive features of leisure in industrial societies is its relative democracy. Most members of these societies enjoy substantial amounts of leisure (see Table 12.5) and most can afford a wide variety of recreational activities.

TABLE 12.5 Average Hours Urban Americans Spend per Week on Leisure Activities and Personal Care, by Marital Status, Employment Status, and Sex

Marital Status, Employment Status, and Sex	Hours per Week of Leisure and Personal Care
Single individuals:	
Employed men	64.0
Employed women	58.3
Married individuals:	
Employed men	57.5
Employed women	57.9
Housewives	65.8

Source: Adapted from U.S. Department of Commerce, Bureau of the Census, *Social Indicators, 1976,* table 10/1.

FIGURE 12.7   The modern symphony orchestra is a triumph of technology as well as of art: the New York Philharmonic at Avery Fisher Hall.

Members of agrarian societies of the recent past would find the opportunities available to the average member of modern industrial societies unbelievable.

Although the influence of technology on the growth of leisure and on the creation of new recreational activities is obvious, its impact on the fine arts is not always so obvious. Yet the modern symphony orchestra, for example, is a triumph of modern technology, and recent trends in sculpture and painting reflect, in part at least, the influence of new materials and new processes that were not available to artists of an earlier era. But the most important consequence of the new technology in this area is an indirect one: traditional standards have given way to the belief that "newer is better" (see Neophilic Art, page 246). This could not occur except in societies that have benefited greatly from change in other areas.

The Mass Media

Some of the most striking technological advances of the industrial era have been in the field of communications. First the telegraph, and later the telephone, made it possible for individuals in widely separated places to communicate with one another almost as easily as though they were face to face.

Meanwhile, another set of inventions made *mass* communications a potent force in daily life for the first time. The printing press, which was invented late in the agrarian era, was a step in this direction. It enabled writers to reach many more people than had been possible previously. But books and pamphlets were an uncertain mode of communication, since there were no established channels of distribution. Moreover, the majority of people were still illiterate and books were expensive.

The first of the true mass media was the penny newspaper, and it got its start in New York in the 1830s. Published on a daily basis and selling so cheaply, the newspaper enabled a small group of journalists and advertisers to transmit ideas and information on a regular basis to a relatively large audience. The invention of the telegraph at about the same time made newspapers much more attractive than they would otherwise have been, since it enabled them to report events in distant places in a much more timely manner than had been possible before.

Later in the nineteenth century other inventions paved the way for new and psychologically more powerful means of communication that utilized visual images and sound. The first of these was motion pictures, which became technologically and commercially feasible shortly before 1900. Movies were followed by radio a quarter of a century later, and another quarter century after that by television—the most powerful of all the modern instruments of mass communication.

It is hard to exaggerate the impact of the mass media on industrial societies (and increasingly on other societies as well). Most adult members of industrial societies read one or more newspapers. Many also read a weekly newsmagazine, and specialized magazines of other kinds have wide circulation. Radio and movies are popular modes of entertainment, and sometimes a source of news and other information as well.

But it is television, most of all, that has transformed modern life. "By the time the average American youngster graduates from high school," according to one authority, "he has spent more hours watching the television screen than he has spent in school, or in any other activity except sleeping."[31] For most adults, too, television viewing is one of their chief activities. In Japan, the average family spends more than 57 hours a week in front of the tube, while in the United States the average is almost 50 hours.[32]

There are a number of reasons for the great appeal of television. Above all, it combines many of the most attractive features of the other media: like printed matter and the radio, it can be enjoyed in the comfort of one's home, and, like the movies, it presents material vividly. In addition, it informs and entertains while requiring little or no mental or physical effort on the viewer's part. This makes it especially attractive for people who are tired at the end of a day's work or who are simply unwilling or unable to engage in more demanding activities.

A leading historian of the broadcasting industry has written that television

> . . . is like a nervous system. It sorts and ignites memories. The impulses it transmits can stir the juices of emotion, and can trigger action. As in the case of a central nervous system, aberrations can deeply disturb the body politic.[33]

A study of the role of the mass media in the 1976 presidential election in the United States confirms this view.[34] This study found that the media, by the biases in their coverage, create a bandwagon effect that tends to throw elections to those who win the earliest primaries.* For example, Jimmy Carter won a very modest plurality in New Hampshire, where the first Democratic primary was held; he received only 28 percent of the vote, compared to 23 percent for the candidate who ran second. But he won an overwhelming victory in the media. *Time* and *Newsweek* both featured him on their covers and devoted 90 percent of their reports on the primary to him, dividing the remaining 10 percent among all of the other Democratic candidates. During the week that followed, television and the daily press gave Carter four times as much coverage as the average of his rivals. This proved to be a tremendous advantage, since a study of those who voted in the Democratic Party primaries showed that 95 percent voted for the candidate they felt they knew best— and, thanks to media coverage, this was Carter.

This bias in the allocation of media coverage was reinforced by bias in its content. A national sample of Democratic Party members interviewed prior to the primaries indicated that the two things they most wanted to learn about the candidates were their stands on policy questions and their leadership capabilities. Instead, the majority of the material offered by the media, and by television in particular, concerned the candidates' campaign tactics and styles, and reports on who was leading in the latest polls. It is hardly surprising that when the primaries were over and these same voters were interviewed again, 65 percent of the new information they had assimilated was about tactics and styles and only 35 percent involved policy issues and leadership ability. The deficiencies of campaign coverage by American television were especially evident to anyone who had an opportunity to compare it to Britain's: BBC's television reporters asked American presidential candidates exactly the kinds of questions which American voters wanted answered, but which their own networks were not asking.[34a]

As David Halberstam and others have noted, television news tends to focus on things that are visually exciting, regardless of their newsworthiness.[35] Among other things, this bias makes television reporting vulnerable to manipulation by small and unrepresentative groups that are willing to create visually dramatic effects (e.g., bombings, riots, demonstrations) in order to reach national and international audiences and thus bring pressure on political authorities.[36]

A growing number of observers, including some journalists, have also commented on the increasingly aggressive and adversarial role of the press in its relations with elected officials in democratic societies. According to the editor of one major newspaper,

> Every policy initiative [by elected officials], every action, has to run a gantlet of criticism that is often generated—and always amplified—by the press. In the searing glare of daily coverage, an official's every personal flaw, every act, every mistake, every slip of the tongue, every display of temper, is recorded, magnified, and ground into the public consciousness. . . . Controversy and conflict are sought out wherever they can be found, sapping energies and diverting attention from more urgent public business. In this whirling centrifuge of criticism and controversy, authority is dissipated . . . [and] the capacity to govern . . . is weakened further.[37]

---

*Thus, the "momentum" in election campaigns that TV newscasters are so fond of talking about is essentially the product of their own activities.

The adversarial relation between the media and public officials can be further aggravated if journalists and officials have conflicting political values. In recent years, this has often been the case in American society, where journalists and editors have been much more liberal than the voting public and many elected officials. A recent national survey by the Los Angeles Times found that reporters and editors on a sample of nearly 600 newspapers were more than twice as likely as a national sample of Americans to describe themselves as liberals (55 percent versus 24 percent), while an earlier study revealed that the most influential media news elites (those who controlled national TV network news broadcasts and the editors of major national newspapers and newsmagazines) had favored Democratic presidential candidates by more than a 4 to 1 margin in every election from 1964 on.[38]

Another aspect of the visual media that has been disturbing has been the prominence given to violence. A growing number of people have come to believe that this has contributed significantly to the increase in crimes of violence, the rate of which has grown nearly fivefold in the United States since the beginning of the television era.[39] Today, there is a substantial body of evidence that indicates that the portrayal of violence in movies and on television leads to imitative acts and other kinds of aggressive behavior by a minority of viewers.[40] Despite this evidence, media elites continue to resist efforts to modify the content of their programming. They believe, and probably correctly, that the portrayal of violence, both in news reporting and in entertainment, is one of the best ways to maximize the size of their audiences and, thus, maximize the profits derived from advertising.

Finally, another serious criticism of the visual media is that too often they present a distorted image of reality. For example, the machinists union did an interesting study of prime-time broadcasting in which they discovered that unions were almost invisible on television.[41] Moreover, when they were depicted, it was usually in an unfavorable light (e.g., on "Trapper John, M.D." nurses were forced to choose between going out on strike and caring for their patients). This study also found a grossly distorted view of the American labor force presented on prime-time television: over the course of a month, the networks showed twelve prostitutes for every machinist, two butlers for every government worker, and twelve times more detectives than production workers.

In summary, it is clear that the mass media have become a powerful force in modern life. While informing and entertaining, they also mold our ideas about the world and what it is really like; they influence our beliefs about good and evil, right and wrong. For a growing number of people, the media have replaced schools and churches, even families, as the primary agents of socialization. This process of socialization occurs not only in political news reporting and in docudramas about important historical events, but also in programs that seem intended merely to entertain. In fact, people may be most susceptible when viewing the latter, precisely because they consider it "merely entertainment" and therefore their mental defenses are down. By presenting in a positive light lifestyles and beliefs that the majority has traditionally rejected, or by holding up to ridicule lifestyles and beliefs that have been traditionally accepted, those who control the media can change a society's standards without public awareness until after the fact. For unless people have been trained to recognize the subtle biases and distortions—both intentional* and unintentional—that the media contain, they are very vulnerable to manipulation. No wonder the editors of *Webster's Third New International Dictionary* define the mass media as communications media *"that tend to set the standards, ideals, and aims of the masses."*

Intratype Variation: Trends and Prospects

In recent decades there has been a great deal of variation among industrial societies. As we have seen, the differences have been especially pronounced between the one-party Marxist-Leninist societies of Eastern Europe with their command economies on the one hand, and the multiparty, democratic societies of the West and Japan with their mixed market-command economies on the other. Thirty years ago, it seemed that these were fundamentally different kinds of industrial societies, both stable and durable, both with excellent chances of surviving for the indefinite future.

For a number of years, however, there have been increasing signs of some convergence. Since Stalin's death in 1953, and even more since the Twentieth Party Congress in 1956, there has been a slow and halting movement away from the extremes of totalitarianism and political repression in the U.S.S.R. Compared with the Stalin years, the present system seems almost liberal, even though political dissent still leads to prison sentences, exile, or commitment to a mental institution. In the economic area, there has been a shift away from more extreme forms of the command economy. For a number of years, market forces have been permitted to operate in certain areas of the economy, and the role of centralized planning has been somewhat curtailed. The latter trend, as we have noted, is especially evident in Hungary and Yugoslavia, but it is also evident to some extent in the Soviet Union.

---

*Richard Salant, a former president of CBS News, acknowledged the presence of intentional biases in television journalism when he stated that "our job is to give people not what they want but what we decide they ought to have." Roone Arledge, president of ABC News, is a bit more cautious and says that the media elite "can't decide *everything* that people should be allowed to see," (emphasis in original) but he asserts that they have the right and responsibility to impose their own judgments in presenting the news.[42]

Meanwhile, non-Marxist industrial societies have taken many steps to increase governmental intervention in their economies and to restrict the free play of market forces. Nor are signs of convergence restricted to the political and economic arenas. A declining birthrate, the movement of married women into the labor force, the growth of urban populations, the growing importance of education, the growth of tertiary industries, the generation gap, the emergence of a distinctive youth culture—these trends and many more are found in *all* industrial societies.

Industrial societies are not, of course, moving toward a single, uniform pattern. Differences will certainly remain; but they will probably be much less marked than those that separated Hitler's Germany or Stalin's Russia from the still largely laissez-faire, capitalistic western democracies of the 1930s. The reason for this seems to be that *the social, psychological, economic, and political costs inherent in these extreme systems are more than most citizens are willing to pay.* Public pressure thus led to the gradual erosion of both laissez-faire capitalism in the West and totalitarian rule in Marxist-Leninist societies. Although future crises may cause some industrial societies to return to the extremes of totalitarianism, this does not seem likely at present, and a return to the older forms of capitalism seems even less likely.

Problems and Progress

The members of contemporary industrial societies are in a paradoxical situation. They are, on average, far healthier, wealthier, and freer to choose among alternative lifestyles than were the vast majority of their ancestors of the last 5,000 years, and they are probably happier as well (see pages 404–405). Yet they are far more vocal concerning the shortcomings and problems of their societies.

Like so many other changes, this is basically a consequence of industrialization. The mass media and, in most industrial societies, multiparty political systems serve to keep social problems before the attention of the general public. Better education and new ideologies, meanwhile, provide people with an enhanced capacity for envisioning improvements in living conditions and also for expecting them, and if these are not constantly forthcoming, they often become critical of both their leaders and the social system. Finally, affluence gives people the means and leisure to voice their opinions, and democratic polities give them the opportunity. As a result, social problems receive far more attention and are far more salient in democratic industrial societies than in any other kind of society.

There are, of course, good substantive grounds for the concerns expressed by members of industrial societies. Their new high-information, high-energy technologies have a potential for creating more serious problems than those which confronted societies of the past. The threat of nuclear war is the most obvious, but it is not the only one. Others include the pollution of the environment, the rapid consumption of vital resources, the weakening of family ties, the growing use of drugs, the use of terrorist tactics as a means of achieving political goals, and more. In addition, many older problems persist, even though progress has been achieved in dealing with some of them.

Although there is considerable controversy concerning the amount of progress industrial societies have actually achieved in solving humanity's problems, there is general agreement on several points. First, despite the presence of many continuing problems from the past, the most serious problems facing industrial societies today are either new problems or old problems with major new dimensions. Second, these problems are largely by-products, or consequences, of technological advance. Third, although many of these problems are distressingly complex, most of them could be alleviated by rational human effort—though in many cases not without great cost to many people. Finally, a completely problem-free society is not likely ever to be achieved, partly because of our species' genetic heritage, partly because of the constraints of the environment, partly because of the extraordinary complexity of modern social systems, and partly because the very process of problem solving itself so often creates new needs and new problems.

Because the problems that remain unsolved by one generation define the agenda for the next generation, we will postpone our analysis of them until the final chapter. In that chapter we will be concerned primarily with the future and what we can, and cannot, say about it.

Industrial Societies in Theoretical Perspective

When we compare modern industrial societies with societies of the past, it is clear that they are a radically new type of sociocultural system. This is evident in everything from the family to the polity, and from ideology to technology. The foundation for these societies is, of course, their rich store of information, especially the technological information that enables them to harness vast amounts of energy to enormously productive machines.

If human societies had never created that technology, we would still be in the agrarian era. The vast majority of people would still be illiterate peasant farmers eking out a marginal existence, women's lives would still be dominated by the cycle of reproduction and child care, and authoritarian elites that knew little and cared less about the lives of the masses would still regard the economic surplus as their rightful property. If we imagine a different sequence of events—one in which industrial societies evolved, but subsequently, in the 1980s, were forced to return to agrarian life—we must add a further note: 75 percent or more of the world's current population would die. For an agrarian technology could probably sustain no more than one-third to two-thirds more people than were alive when the agrarian era ended.

We will not try to trace here all of the consequences of the shift from an agrarian to an industrial technology, or to detail all of the causal linkages, as we did at the ends of earlier chapters. These consequences are so numerous, and the linkages so complex, that a single diagram could not do justice to them. Instead, we will simply restate some of the basic points that have emerged from our analysis.

First, in industrial societies, as in their predecessors, *technological innovation continues to be the basic underlying force responsible for societal change and development.* Although other kinds of innovations also influence the course of social and cultural change, they are largely dependent on prior technological change. We have seen numerous examples of this, especially in the new beliefs and values which shape these societies' institutions—beliefs and values which had little or no impact prior to industrialization.

Second, *many of the trends of the industrial era are continuations of trends that began in earlier eras.* Although industrialization intensified them, each of the following was initiated by technological advance in the more distant past:

The growing store of information

The increasing power of energy sources

The growing productivity of societies

The expanding economic surplus

The growth of world population

The growth in size of societies and communities

The increasing diversity of material products

The growth of capital goods

The increasing division of labor within societies

The increasing division of labor among societies

The increasing economic interdependence of societies

The growing complexity of associations and communities

The relative decline in importance of kinship systems

The increasing number of symbol systems

The increasing impact of human activities on the biophysical environment

The increasingly destructive potential of military technology

Third, a *number of trends in industrial societies are new and represent a break with trends of the past.* The most significant of these involves inequality. During the long period between the close of the hunting and gathering era and the early stages of the industrial, technological advance was accompanied by a steady decline in both political and economic equality. As a result, either advanced agrarian or early industrial societies achieved the dubious distinction of having the greatest degree of inequality of any type of society in history. Advanced industrial societies have appreciably reversed this trend. Other new developments that are evident in industrial societies include greater democratization, greatly improved opportunities for education, more upward mobility, movement toward an equilibrium of birth and death rates at a level far below that of any other type of society, the institutionalization of innovation, and changes in the family and related roles.

Fourth, *industrial societies are the first in human history in which the greatest threats posed by the biophysical environment are products of prior human activity.* Before the Industrial Revolution, famine and disease were two of the greatest threats to a society. Technology and science have succeeded in eliminating the first of these scourges in industrial societies, and they have brought the second largely under control: the members of industrial societies now die primarily from degenerative diseases (e.g., cancer) that reflect the natural limits of our species' life span. Now, however, societies are threatened by the *feedback effects of their own technology* on the biophysical environment.

Fifth, and finally, thanks to the many advances in technology and the enormous growth in the economic surplus that these advances have made possible, the leaders of industrial societies today have far more policy options available to them than the leaders of preindustrial societies would have imagined possible. As a result, *the differentiating influence of ideology on industrial societies is far greater than on any other type of society.* One indication of this is the frequency with which we have found it necessary to differentiate between two basic variants, or subtypes, of industrial society, (1) the western democracies with their mixed economies, and (2) the Marxist-Leninist societies of Eastern Europe with their elitist polities and command economies. With preindustrial societies, ideologically based, intratype distinctions were not necessary because the differentiating impact of ideology on the political and economic systems of societies was not nearly so great.

Social Experimentation: Testing the Limits of the Possible

From the standpoint of the development of theory, Marxism-Leninism is extraordinarily important. Its goal, as we have seen, is the creation of a radically new type of society—a type of society which would be as different from the western industrial democracies as they are different from the agrarian societies which preceded them. Marxism-Leninism challenges many widely held assumptions about human nature and society and it purposes to test the limits of what is possible in human life. Equally important, its adherents have had almost total control over a number of societies and, thus, have been in the best possible position to implement their ideas. In effect, Marxist elites have conducted a series of tremendously important social experiments, and one of the most important tasks confronting sociology today is the analysis of their results.

That task has barely begun, and it is much too large and complex for our present summary. A few of the more important conclusions, however, can and should be noted here.[43] To begin with, we have learned that private ownership of the means of production is *not* essential in a modern industrial society and that, contrary to the expectations of many economists earlier in this century, a socialist society can achieve substantial economic growth. At the same time, we have also learned that elimination of private ownership does not mean the elimination of unequal control over property, nor does it ensure an equitable distribution of benefits among the members of a society. On the contrary, as the authors of one recent study concluded, public ownership of the means of production in the Marxist-Leninist societies of Eastern Europe has led to a system in which people are rewarded far more for their contribution to the preservation of the political status quo than for the value of their contribution to society and its welfare.[44]

We have learned, too, that the elimination of the private ownership of the means of production does not lead to the emergence of "the new socialist man" or bring selfishness and greed to an end. If anything, the tremendous concentration of power in the hands of political elites, which results when the private ownership of property is abolished, promotes an extremely selfish and ruthless struggle for power within societies.[45] And, finally, we have learned that it is exceedingly difficult to make a command economy function efficiently.

Thus, while Marx's goals of freedom, justice, and equality still have great appeal, the means that he and his followers have proposed for achieving those goals have been largely discredited among scholars who have studied Marxist-Leninist societies. Even the goals themselves, when viewed in light of the experience of Marxist-Leninist societies, appear unrealistic and utopian: they ignore the limits of what is possible even in highly productive modern industrial societies. For they ignore the constraints that are imposed on societies by our species' genetic heritage, by the biophysical and sociocultural environments to which societies must adapt, and by the limitations of existing technology.

This does not mean, of course, that human societies cannot be improved or that people must accept the world as they find it. The experience of modern industrial societies as a whole proves that this is not true. But the massive social experiments conducted by the Marxist-Leninist elites of Eastern Europe demonstrate that we are still a very long way from being able to create the ideal society of which we sometimes dream.

Ironically, then, despite the tremendous efforts of Marxist-Leninist elites to create a radically new and better type of society, we are forced to conclude that the societies of Eastern Europe are essentially a variant form of industrial society. Despite the differences between these societies and the western democracies, the two sets of societies have much in common with one another. These similarities will become much more apparent in the next chapter as we turn our attention to the less developed and still industrializing societies of the Third World.

CHAPTER 13

Industrializing Societies of the Third World

Despite the rapid spread of industrialization during the last two centuries, less than a third of the world's population lives in societies that can be called "industrial" as we have defined the term. The great majority, however, do live in societies that have been substantially altered as a consequence of the diffusion of modern industrial technology. These hybrid societies are best described as *industrializing agrarian and industrializing horticultural* societies—the ones we commonly refer to as the less developed nations of the Third World.

These nations are in a transitional phase, moving from an older agrarian or horticultural way of life to the modern industrial. Social scientists often refer to this as the *modernization* process, a process that involves all aspects of the life of society, not just the technological. Unfortunately, the transition period is proving to be longer and more difficult than most scholars had expected. For both theoretical and practical reasons, then, these societies merit careful study.

In most analyses, industrializing agrarian and industrializing advanced horticultural societies are lumped together indiscriminately. This is a serious mistake, since the two types of societies differ in a number of important respects. In this chapter, therefore, we will deal with them separately.

Although quite a number of hunting and gathering, fishing, and *simple* horticultural societies also survived into the modern era in remote and isolated areas, recent advances in transportation have opened up most of their territories and removed this source of protection. As a result, most of these groups have either been destroyed or herded onto reservations where they live as wards of their conquerors, usually under conditions that make the preservation of their traditional ways of life impossible. Even the few groups that still enjoy some degree of autonomy have usually adopted tools and other things from more advanced societies and thus are no longer pure types. But this does not make them *industrializing* societies; that implies something utterly beyond their adaptive capacities. Groups with such a limited technological base cannot possibly evolve into anything so advanced in the little time available to them. They are simply unusual hybrids with a very limited future.

Apart from agrarian and advanced horticultural societies, the only types of preindustrial societies that have a chance of surviving into the twenty-first century and successfully industrializing are maritime and herding societies. Because of limitations of space, we will not examine these two sets of societies but will concentrate instead on the more numerous, and more important, industrializing agrarian and industrializing horticultural societies.

Industrializing Agrarian Societies

Today, industrializing agrarian societies comprise most of Latin America, southern and eastern Asia, the Middle East, and North Africa, and are also found in parts of southern Europe. When we discuss industrializing agrarian societies, we are talking about China, India, Egypt, Yugoslavia, Portugal, Brazil, Cuba, Mexico, and several dozen others.

Naturally, these societies differ from one another in many ways, reflecting differences in their histories, in the social and biophysical environments to which they must adapt today, and in their level of technological advance. Yet despite their differences, they share a number of important characteristics because they all combine elements of the agrarian past and the industrial present. Recognition of this fact can be enormously helpful to us as we try to understand them and their problems.

By one criterion, at least, industrializing agrarian societies are the most important type in the world today: more people live in them than in any other type of society. But this is not the only reason for their importance. These societies have, for decades, been struggling with problems that often threaten to overwhelm them. Despite partial industrialization, many of their citizens are as poor as the common people ever were in traditional agrarian societies (see Table 13.1). At the same time, improved education and the mass media have raised their hopes and expectations and given them an awareness of the possibility of a better life. This contradiction has created a revolutionary situation that threatens to involve the entire world.

Sometimes it is suggested that the problem of the less developed countries is simply their technological and economic backwardness. The problem is much more complex than that, however, for it involves all of their social institutions—polity, economy, family, religion, education—as well as the attitudes and values of their people. In addition, their position in the world system creates further problems, as will become clear shortly.

TABLE 13.1   An Industrial and an Industrializing Agrarian Society Compared: The United States and India

	U.S.	India
Population (in millions)	237	746
Area (in millions of square miles)	3.6	1.2
Population density (population per square mile)	65	589
Birthrate per 1,000 population	15	34.5
Death rate per 1,000 population	9	13
Rate of natural increase (percent per year)	0.6	2.15
Infant mortality per 1,000 live births	11	125
Life expectancy at birth (in years)	74	50
Hospital beds per 10,000 population	56	7
Doctors per 10,000 population	18	4
GNP per capita, in dollars	12,482	235
Average annual percentage growth in GNP, 1960–1980	3.7	3.5
Average annual percentage growth in GNP per capita, 1960–1980	2.3	1.4
Hundreds of kilograms of energy consumed per capita per year	94	2
Petroleum production per capita, in pounds annually	4,414	58
Coal production per capita, in pounds annually	6,563	378
Steel consumption per capita, in pounds annually	783	36
Wheat, rice, and corn production in pounds per capita per year	2,755	331
Meat production in pounds per capita per year	158	2
Passenger cars per 1,000 population	673	2
Telephones per 1,000 population	789	5
Newspaper circulation per 1,000 population	282	20
Radios per 1,000 population	2,110	59
Televisions per 1,000 population	631	2

Source: Calculations based on data in *Statistical Abstract of the United States, 1985*, sec. 33, and World Bank, *World Development Report, 1982*, tables 1 and 2.

Technology and Productivity

Technologically, an industrializing agrarian society is a bewildering mixture of the ancient and the modern. Peasant farmers using techniques and tools very much like those their forefathers used 2,000 years ago work in sight of such marvels of modern technology as the Aswan Dam in Egypt or the Tata Iron and Steel Works in India.

The old technology is much more prevalent, however, especially in the agricultural sector of these societies. Not long ago, an average of 55 percent of the labor force of forty-six industrializing agrarian nations were still engaged in agriculture, and yet they produced only 26 percent of the gross domestic product.[1] The difference would have been even greater were it not for the income from relatively modern plantations (tea, rubber, etc.) operated by foreigners from industrial societies.

There is great variation in the level of technological and economic development in industrializing agrarian societies. Per capita GNPs range from only $133 per year in Bangladesh to $3,887 in Argentina. Unfortunately, the average for all industrializ-

FIGURE 13.1   The old and the new: Indian farmer plowing with oxen under high-power electrical transmission lines.

ing agrarian societies is closer to Bangladesh's: in 1982 the median for thirty-one of them was only $1,373.[2]

Many discussions of the less developed countries give the impression that they are technologically and economically stagnant or, at least, developing less rapidly than industrial societies. But the fact is that the productivity of industrializing agrarian societies has actually increased at essentially the same rate as that of industrial societies. Unfortunately, however, because they have far surpassed industrial societies in population growth, their gains in *per capita income* have often been small, as we will see.

Population Growth and Its Consequences

With the introduction of modern medicine and sanitation, death rates have been cut drastically in almost every industrializing agrarian society. Birthrates, however, have declined much more slowly. As a result, the rate of natural increase in these societies is high—in most cases it is more than 2 percent per year and in some cases it is more

TABLE 13.2   Crude Birthrates, Death Rates, and Rates of Natural Increase for Selected Industrializing Agrarian Societies

Society	Crude Birthrate*	Crude Death Rate†	Rate of Natural Increase‡
Nicaragua	44	10	3.4
Iran	41	10	3.1
Bangladesh	45	17	2.8
Egypt	37	10	2.7
Mexico	32	6	2.6
Peru	35	10	2.5
Turkey	35	10	2.5
Philippines	32	7	2.5
Brazil	31	8	2.3
Indonesia	34	12	2.2
India	34	13	2.1
Colombia	28	7	2.1
Sri Lanka	27	6	2.1
Thailand	25	6	1.9
Argentina	24	8	1.6
China	19	8	1.1
Yugoslavia	17	10	0.7
Spain	13	7	0.6
Portugal	14	9	0.5

*Live births per 1,000 population per year.
†Deaths per 1,000 population per year.
‡Percentage growth of population due to excess of births over deaths per year.
Source: Population Reference Bureau, "1985 World Population Data Sheet."

than 3 percent (see Table 13.2). Growth rates of 2 or 3 percent per year may not sound very high, but they are. In fact, they are *20 to 30 times higher than the average rate of growth of world population during the agrarian era.* A society that is growing at a rate of 2 percent a year will double in size in just 35 years, and a society growing at a rate of 3 percent will double in less than 24 years.

When societies grow as rapidly as this, it is extraordinarily difficult for them to find the resources needed to care for everyone and to create enough new jobs to provide employment for the growing numbers who are looking for work.* Table 13.3 shows the cost of rapid population growth for the industrializing agrarian societies of Asia and Latin America. Had these societies been able to avoid popula-

---

*Some Americans have used the history of their own country during the eighteenth and nineteenth centuries to argue that rapid population growth actually speeds economic growth and raises the standard of living in societies. They forget, however, that prior to the twentieth century the United States had a very small population in relation to its size and the wealth of its resources, and because of this the country suffered from labor *shortages.* This is not the situation in which Third World nations today find themselves. On the contrary, most of them are suffering from a *surplus* of labor.

TABLE 13.3   The Effect of Population Growth on the Growth of Per Capita GDP for Three Sets of Societies, 1950–1980

Sets of Societies	Percentage Increase in GDP 1950–1980	Percentage Increase in Per Capita GDP 1950–1980	Percentage of GDP Gain Consumed by Population Growth*
Western industrial societies and Japan	234	143	39
Industrializing agrarian societies:			
East and Southeast Asia	313	118	62
Latin America and Caribbean	422	138	67

*The figures in this column were arrived at by dividing the rate of population growth by the rate of growth of GDP.

Sources: Adapted from United Nations, *Statistical Yearbook, 1970*, table 4, and United Nations, *Statistical Yearbook, 1981*, table 3.

tion growth between 1950 and 1980, their standards of living would have risen even more rapidly than those of the western industrial societies (compare the growth of Gross Domestic Product or GDP—see Glossary—for the three sets of societies in Table 13.3). Instead, they fell further behind. In fact, as the right-hand column in Table 13.3 shows, more than 60 percent of the economic gains they achieved during those decades were wiped out by the effects of population growth and the necessity of providing for more people.

Population growth is a serious problem for industrializing societies, not only because it means so many more mouths to feed, but because of its implications for the entire process of development. For example, high birthrates make universal public education prohibitively expensive in these nations, and yet without it, the population is not equipped for most jobs in modern industry. This forces large numbers of people to find employment in traditional industries, especially farming. But this leads to the subdividing of already small farms to the point where they become hopelessly inefficient and the introduction of modern machinery is impossible. In Egypt, for example, 70 percent of the farm owners already had less than half an acre in 1950.[3] As one observer remarked, "Most of those who are working the land work not because the land requires their labor but because they require the work."[4] He went on to say that as early as 1939 it was estimated that 10 percent of Egypt's farmers could have supplied all the necessary labor if Egypt's farms had been even half as mechanized as America's. The story is much the same in other industrializing agrarian societies.

Another factor retarding economic development is the poverty of the excess population. Because they are unable to buy anything but the most basic commodities, they do not generate a demand for the kinds of products that are an essential component of the economy of every industrial society. Finally, this surplus population compounds all the other problems by its own productive achievements: an abundance of children. The society is thus trapped in a vicious circle.

In view of all this, it is hardly surprising to learn that there is a correlation of −0.49 between the birthrate and the annual growth of per capita productivity.[5] This indicates a fairly strong relationship between high birthrates and low rates of economic progress.

In recent years the leaders of a few industrializing agrarian societies have finally begun to grasp the seriousness of the population problem and its relation to economic growth, and have encouraged the use of modern methods of birth control. In most cases, however, their efforts have not been very successful, largely because children are still perceived as an economic asset by the average peasant farmer. While they are growing up, they are cheap labor, and when their parents become too old to work, the children can support them. If too many children survive to adulthood, they can be sent to the cities to look for work. Unfortunately, an increasing proportion of them are looking for jobs that do not exist, or jobs they can fill only while they are young and vigorous. After that they drift into the growing ranks of the underemployed and the unemployed and become a further drain on the economy. People like these occupy the squatter settlements and shantytowns that contain from one-fourth to two-thirds of the populations of most Third World metropolises.[6] These settlements are growing at an annual rate of 12 percent a year, which means they double in size in less than seven years.

By the middle 1970s, there began to be an increasing concern for the problems caused by unchecked population growth in a number of industrializing agrarian societies. In 1976, the Indian state of Maharashtra, which has a population as large as the population of France, adopted a law that provided jail sentences and fines for couples of childbearing age who had three or more children and refused sterilization.[7] Introducing the legislation, the state's minister of health said, "If the alarming rate of growth is not checked it will be impossible to remove poverty and realize the

FIGURE 13.2   According to a recent United Nations' study, one-fourth to two-thirds of the populations of most Third World cities live in squatter settlements and shantytowns, such as this one in Lima, Peru.

fruits of economic development." India's Minister of Health and Family Planning announced that this law was soon to be adopted nationwide, but plans for this were shelved because of the widespread reaction against the government's quota system for male sterilization. This public outcry soon led to the downfall of Indira Gandhi's government. Under the government that succeeded her, the number of sterilizations performed annually dropped by 90 percent, and the birthrate edged up from 33 per 1,000 population per year to 35.[8] After Mrs. Gandhi's return to power she did not dare to reinstitute her earlier program of population control and the Indian government is still reluctant to act in this sensitive area.

In contrast, the People's Republic of China, under Chairman Deng's leadership, has moved vigorously to check population growth. The government recently reported that if every woman of childbearing age had only three children, by the year 2080 China's population would rise to 4.3 billion, nearly the equivalent of the present *world* population![9] To avert this, the government has created a system of sanctions that encourage small families and discourage large. Contraceptives, abortions, and sterilizations are available at no cost. In most areas, women cannot register to marry until age twenty-three, and men until age twenty-five in rural areas and twenty-six in urban.[10] When women check into hospitals to have their first child, they are offered bonuses if they permit postnatal sterilization, and there is a national campaign to pressure young couples into signing a "one family, one child" pledge. Couples who marry late and those who have only one child are given top priority in housing assignments, while physicians, nurseries, and schools are instructed to give preference to children who have no siblings. There are punishments as well as rewards (see Shuai Xiu Rong Fined $200). Couples who have three

---

SHUAI XIU RONG FINED $200

Chengdu, China—Shuai Xiu Rong was fined $200 yesterday because she became pregnant without permission and then refused to have an abortion. The No. 1 Brigade of the Golden Horse Commune, where Mrs. Shuai, her husband, and their 4-year-old daughter live, has a population of 1,200 and is allowed only 9 births per year. Mrs. Shuai was one of five women who became pregnant last year without permission, but the other four chose to have abortions.

In addition to the fine, Mrs. Shuai was subjected to public scolding for selfish thinking and wrote a public self-criticism. Authorities have decided that her baby will not be registered for some years. This denial of a registration card means his family will have to stretch its present grain ration to provide for his needs or buy grain in the open market at higher prices. Also, until authorities issue such registration, he will not be eligible to attend school. It is expected that the boy will be registered in a few years, but that authorities have determined to make an example of Mrs. Shuai to discourage other women from following her lead.

Sichuan Province, where the Shuai family lives, is home to nearly 100 million Chinese, or nearly the population of Britain and France combined. Family planning authorities report that, by a system of incentives and penalties, the province's annual growth rate has been reduced from 3.1 percent per year in 1970 to 0.7 percent in 1980.

Adapted from Associated Press wire service report, August 4, 1980.

FIGURE 13.3 **During the last decade, the People's Republic of China has moved vigorously to check population growth: billboard promoting the one-child family principle, Chengdu.**

children, for example, are fined 10 percent of their pay for fourteen years, the time it takes for most children to join the labor force.

Taiwan is another industrializing society whose leaders have recognized the need for vigorous action. They have created a system whereby couples with two children receive a credit of $25 a year for a period of ten years, with the accumulated funds plus interest later made available for the children's education. If a third child is born, the annual payments are cut in half, and a fourth child disqualifies the family.[11] The most recent figures on the birthrate in Taiwan indicate striking success: births are down to 20 or 21 per 1,000 population per year, a figure that is not much above some advanced industrial societies. If other Third World nations are willing to initiate measures comparable to China's and Taiwan's, there is reason to hope that the era of runaway population growth will draw to a close and that standards of living in these nations will improve more rapidly.

The Economy

The economies of industrializing societies consist of two basic components. The traditional component is very similar to the economy of the typical agrarian society of the last 2,000 years. The tools and techniques are much the same, and so is the level of productivity. The modern—or at least modernizing—component has tools, techniques, and patterns of economic organization that have, for the most part, been borrowed from advanced industrial societies.

TABLE 13.4   Some Indicators of Regional Differences in Greece

Indicators	Attica or Greater Athens	Thrace
Per capita consumption of electric energy in kilowatt-hours	833	34
Private cars per 10,000 inhabitants	168	8
Percentage of households with inside baths or showers	30	2
Percentage of households with running water	72	21
Number of doctors per 10,000 inhabitants	33	3
Number of hospital beds per 10,000 inhabitants	142	17

Source: Nikos Mouzelis and Michael Attalides, "Greece," in Margaret Archer and Salvador Giner (eds.), *Contemporary Europe* (New York: St. Martin's, 1972), p. 187.

Obviously, such a division results in tremendous internal differences within a society. The people in some areas are living much the way their forebears did centuries ago, while in other parts of the same society, many people are living very much like the residents of Washington, London, or Moscow. Table 13.4 illustrates the kinds and degrees of differences that can separate the members of industrializing agrarian societies. A similar cleavage exists in most industrializing societies.

The modernizing sector of the economy of these societies is not simply a scaled-down version of the economy of the typical advanced industrial society, however. In other words, it is not likely to contain a representative sample of industries—some small steel mills, a small automobile plant or two, some textile mills, a variety of wholesale and retail distributors, and so on. Instead, this sector of the economy is often rather one-sided in its development, with heavy emphasis on one or two key industries.

To understand why this is, we have to bear in mind the tremendous difference in the circumstances under which these nations are industrializing and those under which western Europe and the United States industrialized. Today's developing societies are industrializing in a world that is dominated politically and economically by *already industrialized societies* with whom they are interdependent. Producers in the already industrialized societies have long had easy access to large and affluent home markets and thus are now able to spread their fixed costs (see page 286) over a large volume of goods. This gives them a great competitive advantage in many industries. Add to this the low cost of moving goods today, thanks to advances in transportation technology (see page 191), and it is easy to see that producers in industrializing societies are often left in a poor competitive position *even in their home markets*. Thus, European, American, and Japanese firms have come to dominate world markets for most manufactured products.

As a result, many of the industrializing societies have been forced into a distinctive ecological niche: they have become the producers of raw materials for the world economy. Furthermore, because of pressures generated by world markets and by their own desire to maximize income, they often become dangerously specialized (see Table 13.5).

A society that depends so heavily on just one commodity is highly vulnerable to

FIGURE 13.4 The economies of industrializing societies consist of two distinctive sectors, a traditional sector which has changed little from the preindustrial past and a modern sector that resembles industrial societies of the present. Two views of Yugoslavia: peasants plowing with oxen near Karlovac and city scene in Belgrade.

TABLE 13.5 Leading Exports of Selected Industrializing Agrarian Societies and Their Percentage Dependence on These Commodities for Foreign Exchange

Society	Commodity	Percentage Dependence
Iraq	Petroleum	99
Cuba	Sugar	84
Indonesia	Petroleum	69
Colombia	Coffee	52
Chile	Copper	49
Pakistan	Textiles	39
Honduras	Bananas	28
Burma	Wood	26
Bolivia	Tin	21
Thailand	Rice	14

Source: Adapted from United Nations, *Yearbook of International Trade Statistics, 1982*, vol. 1, table 5.

any shift in the world economy that affects its specialty. Technological innovations (e.g., synthetic fibers, synfuels, coffee or sugar substitutes) may permanently reduce, or even eliminate, demand for the product. This sensitivity to change often creates an unstable "boom or bust" atmosphere that is not conducive to rational economic planning and development by either business or government. Instead, it encourages a speculative attitude whose goal is to make quick profits and then transfer capital to safer investments abroad.

Despite such drawbacks, these specialized industries can help developing societies industrialize more rapidly. For one thing, they make it possible for more people to shift from traditional subsistence agriculture into jobs in the modern sector. Such people are thus introduced to the new world of machine technology, to new skills, and to new attitudes and values.[12]

Equally important, these industries can serve as a source of capital to finance further industrial development. Some of the Middle Eastern oil states have used some of their income for this purpose, creating their own steel mills, petrochemical plants, aluminum smelters, fertilizer plants, and other industrial establishments.[13] One result is that, whereas industrializing societies were obliged to import 30 percent of the steel they consumed as recently as 1970, they are now *net exporters* by a small margin.

It is still too early to say whether the benefits of specialized export industries will, in the long run, outweigh their costs. This will probably depend on the product involved. In the case of societies that export petroleum and natural gas, for which there is great demand, a finite supply, and low costs of production, the long-term prospects seem reasonably good. Despite recent difficulties, these societies should, in time, be able to industrialize if they have adequate political leadership.

In contrast, societies that produce commodities which are not essential or for which substitutes can easily be found, or commodities whose prices are highly

FIGURE 13.5   State-operated department store, Beijing, China. Such stores are now facing increasing competition from private enterprise.

unstable, will find industrialization much more difficult. The experience of Cuba under Castro is a classic case (see Table 13.5): despite the shift from capitalism to socialism, Cuba is still largely dependent on its sugar crop (and on a large, and seemingly permanent, Soviet subsidy in exchange for military services provided to Soviet allies in various parts of the Third World).[14]

As the case of Cuba reminds us, a number of industrializing agrarian societies are now controlled by Marxist-Leninist elites. In addition to Cuba, they are Yugoslavia, Albania, China, North Korea, Vietnam, Kampuchea, Laos, Afghanistan, Ethiopia, and Nicaragua. At present, these societies have various kinds of economies. Nicaragua still has a limited capitalist sector, though the authorities are trying to eliminate it by denying it access to the hard currency that is needed to buy machines and materials. Yugoslavia has developed a type of economy that it calls "market socialism," while China has moved substantially in the direction of a mixed economy. Albania, North Korea, and Vietnam, meanwhile, have classical command economies, while in Kampuchea, Afghanistan, and Ethiopia, conditions are in such turmoil that neither a market nor a command economy can function properly.

In addition to Marxist-Leninist societies, there are a number of other industrializing agrarian societies that have adopted command economies to a greater or lesser degree in recent decades. India is the most important example of such a society, but it is not the only one by any means.

Based on the experience of societies such as China, Cuba, and India—all of which maintained command economies for more than a quarter of a century—it is clear that such an economy is no panacea for industrializing societies. Often, it seems to have done more harm than good. By comparison with other industrializing agrarian societies, such as Taiwan and South Korea, that have relied much more on market mechanisms, the records of China, Cuba, and India are very disappointing. In fact, the performance has been so disappointing that China's leaders are now boldly reintroducing market mechanisms of various kinds. Between 1980 and 1985, the number of private businesses in that country increased from 660,000 to 10.6 million, and 14 percent of all retail sales now occur in the private sector.[14a] Furthermore, at least one large Chinese-owned private corporation has been re-established and several stock exchanges have opened.[14b]

Underlining the importance of these developments, the Chinese Communist Party newspaper, *People's Daily*, declared in a major editorial late in 1984 that the Chinese people cannot rely any longer on the writings of Marx and Lenin for answers to their problems, since these men never encountered or wrote about the kinds of problems that China faces today.[15] According to the new Party line, the Chinese people must become pragmatic and learn from experience. If these new policies prove successful in China, which long has been noted for its recalcitrant economic problems, other industrializing societies may well follow its example and rely more on market mechanisms and pragmatism and less on centralized economic planning and doctrinaire ideologies.

The Polity

In industrializing agrarian societies, one of the greatest hindrances to development has been the kind of governing class they inherited from the past. This class had a good thing going for centuries, and its members have seldom seen a need to change in the twentieth century. Their ideal is the kind of society that flourished before intellectuals, students, and the common people ever heard of liberty, equality, democracy, socialism, and communism. From their perspective, change is something to be resisted, or, when possible, exploited for their private benefit.

In the last hundred years, a growing number of voices have been raised against this backward-looking, exploitative class. In some instances proponents of development have seized control of the government, with the idea of using the power of the state as a force for political, economic, and social change. These modernizers have been a heterogeneous lot. Some have been military men with a strong spirit of nationalism, such as Egypt's Nasser; some have been civilians and democratic socialists, such as India's Nehru. A number have been Marxists, such as Tito, Mao, and Castro, while in at least one case—Iran—the monarch himself played this role.

Would-be modernizers have usually found, however, that it is not enough simply to win control of the government. To implement their plans, they need the support of thousands of lower- and middle-level officials who are both efficient and honest. Unfortunately, such people are hard to find in societies which for centuries provided education for only a few, and which viewed government office as a means for self-aggrandizement. The problem is further compounded by the political necessity of providing public-sector employment for large numbers of otherwise unemployable graduates of high schools and universities who might otherwise be attracted to destabilizing political movements, and by the inability of governments to pay them an adequate wage. Thus, older patterns of corruption and inefficiency are perpetuated and the plans of would-be modernizers frustrated.[16]

One of the most important issues facing the leaders of industrializing societies today concerns the role of the state in the developmental process. In recent decades there have been two contrasting models to choose between, one provided by the western industrial democracies, especially Britain, France, and the United States, the other by Marxist-Leninist societies, especially the Soviet Union.

Prior to World War II, and for some time thereafter, most would-be modernizers in the Third World chose the western democracies as their model. A democratic government with limited powers working in combination with a market economy seemed to offer the best hope for societal development. But the adoption of these institutions seldom produced the results expected. Industrializing societies that adopted this model often became bogged down in divisive party rivalries, corruption of officials frequently undermined public support, economic growth was generally slower than had been anticipated, and persisting economic inequalities led to social unrest. As a result, democratic governments in the Third World were toppled with increasing frequency by authoritarian elites of one kind or another.

Many times the new elites were army officers who had grown disgusted by the corruption and incompetence of democratic politicians. Sometimes they viewed their task merely as one of removing corrupt and incompetent leaders and of quickly restoring democratic government. Other times, however, they lost faith entirely in the democratic process and came to see their role as one of giving the nation new leadership on a permanent basis.

Following World War II, an increasing number of modernizers, both military and civilian, adopted Soviet society as the model to emulate. They were attracted both by the ideals of Marx and by the authoritarianism of Lenin. Marxism-Leninism promises to eliminate political conflicts of the kind that invariably arise in democratic societies. Instead, it concentrates political power in the hands of a tiny group of individuals who share a common vision of the future and who are prepared to use all of the powers of the state to implement that vision. Under the leadership of dedicated Marxist-Leninists, revolutionary socialist regimes came to power in Yugoslavia, Albania, China, North Vietnam, North Korea, and Cuba.*

For a number of years it seemed as if the Soviet model was able to provide effective solutions to the problems of industrializing societies. By carefully controlling the flow of information out of their societies, the new elites were able to project an image of substantial success.[17] More recently, however, as the facts have become better known, a very different picture has emerged. In China, the new leadership has openly acknowledged the failure of the Soviet model and has, as noted in the previous section, begun making drastic changes.[18] In Vietnam, where the leadership has continued to adhere to the Soviet model, the economic situation has deteriorated badly, and recent visitors to Hanoi report being stunned by the "grinding poverty." As one observer has written, "The frail bodies, the tattered clothing, the dilapidated buildings, and the scarcity of everything from meat to medicine is not what one expects in the capital of a legendary military power and the third largest Communist country."[19] Especially disturbing is the fact that conditions are not improving; on the

---

*Castro did not become a Marxist until the Cuban revolution was over, but some of his closest associates were already Marxists during the revolution.

contrary, the standard of living seems lower today than at the end of the war. Meanwhile, in Cuba, vast numbers of people seem eager to leave and evidence of economic progress is hard to find.[20]

In some industrializing agrarian societies, the failure of both the western and Soviet models of development has led to a revival of movements advocating a return to the past. This tendency has been especially evident in Islamic societies, with the Ayatollah Khomeini's program in Iran being the most striking example. While the negative aspects of this program (e.g., hatred directed at non-Muslims) have an obvious appeal for the masses of peasants and others who have been frustrated by the slowness of progress and angered by their continued poverty, it is hard to see how such movements will improve their standard of living or solve most of their other problems. Already, in fact, one hears reports that disillusionment has begun to set in in Iran, and one suspects that the same will happen in other societies after traditionalist regimes have been in power for a time and their own shortcomings have become more obvious.

Based on the experience of most industrializing agrarian societies thus far, it seems that there is no simple political solution to their many problems. No form of government can solve all of their problems, and every form of government is vulnerable to criticism and perhaps even to revolution. Thus, political instability may prove to be the unhappy fate of many of these societies—at least until they are able to provide a higher standard of living for more of their people.

Social Stratification

Systems of stratification in industrializing agrarian societies are as varied as the polities and economies to which they are linked. In a number of them, the class structure is still much as it was in agrarian societies of the past, though modified to some degree by industrialization. In others, the traditional class structure has been modified not only by industrialization but by socialism as well.

In societies of the first variety, the upper class is still largely an aristocracy of long-established, wealthy, landowning families that dominate the government, the army, the religious establishment, and other social institutions. The middle class is small and made up of merchants, lesser officials, lesser members of the clergy, and a few prosperous peasants. In addition, it includes increasing numbers of business and professional people with modern education and skills, members of the civil service with modern educational qualifications, and teachers trained in the newer disciplines, such as science and engineering. As industrialization and modernization progress, some members of the new middle class may penetrate into the upper class by virtue of their wealth or political success. In effect, however, there tend to be two separate systems of stratification in these societies. One is dominant in rural areas and reflects the old order; the other is dominant in urban areas and reflects the new. With the passage of time, the newer system of stratification, which is based on the industrial economy, tends to become dominant throughout the country as a whole.

In societies with Marxist-Leninist regimes, the transformation of the system of stratification is quicker and more ruthless. Many members of the old upper class are killed and the remainder have their properties taken from them. They are replaced by a new elite made up largely of leading Party cadres. Merchants and private entrepreneurs are also eliminated from the system of stratification and replaced by the managers of state enterprises, who make up a significant portion of the new middle and upper strata. Overall, the system of stratification in these societies closely resembles that in Marxist industrial societies, except that the proportion of peasants is much greater.

The value of modern education, especially training in engineering and science, is great in almost all industrializing societies. This places the younger generation in a relatively advantageous position, since they tend to be better educated. This advantage is often reinforced by the effects of political revolutions. Because they are usually the work of young people who distrust the older generation and prefer to

FIGURE 13.6   Large numbers of Bombay's poor have no place of residence and are compelled to cook, eat, bathe, and sleep on the sidewalks.

surround themselves with their age peers, revolutions are usually followed by a period in which youth is an asset and young people are promoted much faster than they would be otherwise. As the Chinese, Russian, and Cuban revolutions demonstrate, however, this is a temporary phenomenon, and revolutionary elites tend to become gerontocracies.

The major variations in the composition of the lower classes in industrializing agrarian societies are the result of differences in level of economic development. The less developed the society, the larger the peasant class and the smaller the urban class, especially persons working in factories and other modern industries. At one extreme, 80 to 95 percent of the labor force in Nepal, Afghanistan, and Ethiopia are still engaged in agriculture, and only a small percentage in industry. At the opposite extreme, countries like Mexico, Argentina, and Portugal have less than half of their workers in agriculture and 25 to 35 percent in manufacturing.[21]

Life is grim for large numbers of the lower classes in many industrializing agrarian societies. High birthrates, low death rates, and inadequate educational systems combine to ensure an oversupply of unskilled labor, a situation that is aggravated by the economy's shift from human labor to machines. The excess population typically migrates from rural areas to the cities, where there are at least some employment opportunities for the young and able-bodied. But, as in agrarian societies of the past, aging, accidents, and illness soon deprive them of their economic value, especially when there is a steady stream of fresh labor continually moving into the cities. The only industrializing agrarian societies that seem to have made much progress toward solving this problem are some of the Marxist-Leninist societies, where, according to reports, beggary, prostitution, and widespread unemployment have been greatly reduced by drastic authoritarian measures.

SATAHU SAHNI: RICKSHAW MAN

Satahu Sahni, one of Calcutta's poorer citizens, pulls a rickshaw for a living. He works from 6 A.M. to midnight, earning $3 a day. He lives in a one-room hut with his wife and two children. They spend about $2.50 a day for food alone, which provides tea and cookies for breakfast, a wheat cake for lunch, and rice and dried peas for supper. Satahu says of his work, "This job shouldn't be done by any human being, but I couldn't find any other thing to do."

Up and down hills, through broiling molten tar, across rough cobblestones, hauling heavy carts often loaded with more than one passenger as well as freight, Satahu and his fellow rickshaw men run day after day. Summer temperatures that are often above 100, and high humidity, cause a few each day simply to slip from between the shafts of their carts and drop dead. "It's really quite awful lately," said a British-educated Calcuttan, who has his own air-conditioned Mercedes and never rides in a rickshaw. "Not only do the poor runners die, but many passengers are injured when the rickshaws tip over backwards. Quite awful." But Satahu is fortunate compared to the hundreds of thousands of jobless persons and beggars in Calcutta who have no home at all and are forced to sleep on the open sidewalks at night and beg their food.

Adapted from a copyrighted story by Myron Belkind of the Associated Press, by permission.

Cleavages and Conflicts

Few societies in history have had such serious internal divisions as the majority of those now undergoing industrialization. Most of them are torn not only by ancient cleavages inherited from the preindustrial past, but also by some that are peculiar to societies industrializing at this particular time.

Most basic of the older cleavages in industrializing agrarian societies is that between the few who control the nation's resources and the vast majority who supply the labor and get little more than the barest necessities in return. The traditional cleavages between urban and rural populations and between the literate minority and the illiterate majority are also present, though they may be less pronounced now that advances in transportation and communication have reduced the isolation, and hence the ignorance, of the rural and the illiterate.

As we have already seen, the struggle to industrialize and modernize creates its own cleavages and conflicts. There is a split within the more favored classes, for example, between those educated along traditional lines and those with modern scientific and technical training. These groups have difficulty understanding one another and are mutually prejudiced against one another. Another new cleavage separates the old landowning aristrocracy and the new industrial entrepreneurs, who now often have greater wealth.

As the monarchical political system found in agrarian societies has broken down, many new groups have become politically active and many new issues have become politically relevant. For example, the political unrest and other changes associated with industrialization often exacerbate historic tensions between religious and ethnic groups. This has occurred in such widely scattered countries as Vietnam, Indonesia, Sri Lanka, India, Lebanon, Iraq, Iran, Egypt, Guyana, and others. The breakdown of the older political system and efforts to establish a modern regime can also produce serious tensions between civilian leaders and the military. Struggles between these groups have often caused crises in Latin American, Middle Eastern, and Asian nations. In democratic countries, mass political parties have introduced yet another cleavage. Although support for the various parties tends to follow other lines of cleavage, it is seldom a perfect reflection of them. Thus, it creates further divisions within already badly divided populations.[22]

Finally, the rapid rate of change characteristic of industrializing societies invariably creates a cleavage between the generations. This cleavage appears to be more serious than the generation gap in societies that have already industrialized. This is indicated both by the frequency and bitterness of the conflicts between students and political authorities in these nations and by the frequency of revolutionary activity by "young Turks" (e.g., the Kemalists in Turkey after World War I, Nasser's associates in Egypt, and Castro's associates in Cuba). We would expect this, of course, in societies that are changing so rapidly. The experiences of the different generations are so dissimilar that conflict is almost inevitable. Universities are often the centers of discontent, because they bring together large numbers of people who have maximum exposure to new ideas but little power to implement them. The result, not surprisingly, is often explosive.

Authoritarian governments of both the right and the left generally manage to suppress these conflicts so that often they are not visible to the outside world. Yet as the Chinese experience indicates, suppressing them is not the same as eliminating them. When Mao mistakenly assumed in the 1950s that the masses were solidly behind his revolution and announced a new policy of greater political freedom ("Let a hundred flowers bloom, let a hundred schools contend"), the situation quickly threatened to get out of hand. Cleavages within the People's Republic were revealed again during and after the Great Cultural Revolution of the middle 1960s, with violent conflicts between students and Party cadres, workers and managers, soldiers and civilians, young and old. Then, following Mao's death in 1976, dissension surfaced once more. The fact of the matter is that industrialization and modernization are extremely stressful processes and when the cleavages they generate are added to the historic cleavages inherent in an agrarian social order, the choice is often between harsh repression and chronic and endemic conflict.

Education

The importance of education for economic growth is abundantly clear: the most prosperous nations are those that have invested heavily in education. In the United States, Japan, and the Soviet Union—three of the most striking examples of economic growth—high levels of national expenditure on education preceded industrialization.[23] In czarist Russia as early as the end of the last century, 44 percent of the men between 30 and 39 were literate, and in urban areas the figure was as high as 69 percent. In Japan, half the male population was literate a generation before that; and in the United States, 90 percent of white adults were literate as early as 1840.

Recent studies of the relation between education and economic growth reinforce this conclusion. They indicate that expansion of primary and secondary school enrollments, especially the latter, has been linked to increases in per capita GNP since World War II.[24] However, these same studies found this relation did not exist in the case of the expansion of enrollments in *higher* education. The reasons for this are not clear, but it may reflect the fact that many industrializing societies have overemphasized training in the humanities and neglected training in fields required by industrialization. In both eastern and western Europe, for example, from one-third to one-half of university students study science or engineering, compared to only 23 percent of those in Asia and 16 percent in Latin America.[25]

These figures are important not only because industrializing societies so urgently need technical and engineering skills, but because they have so much trouble absorbing the nontechnical professionals their universities turn out. In India, for example, 58 percent of the students were recently enrolled in the humanities, fine arts, and law.[26] Most graduates simply cannot find jobs that utilize these skills. Unwilling to accept lesser employment (a reflection of the traditional value system of agrarian elites and would-be elites), they become a kind of intellectual proletariat with deep-seated hostilities toward the existing social order. Because such people are easily attracted to revolutionary movements, this leads to more political instability, and this in turn hampers economic progress. In short, far from aiding economic growth, an oversupply of nontechnically trained students in a society actually hinders it.*

Ideologies: Old and New

Most leaders of modernizing movements are convinced that social and economic progress requires more than increased capital and improved techniques of production. New creeds and new gods are needed to arouse and mobilize the common people who, after centuries of frustration, are often apathetic and fatalistic. Ironically, even so dedicated a Marxist as Mao Zedong came to place the spiritual struggle for people's minds and hearts ahead of the struggle to transform the economy.

Today, in all but the most backward parts of the industrializing agrarian world, there is an intellectual ferment and a clash of ideas between the advocates of traditional belief systems and the proponents of newer ones. The situation is often extremely complicated, because both traditionalists and modernizers are themselves divided on many points, while others favor various blends of the old and the new.

A lot of the intellectual and ideological resistance to modernization has come from leaders of the traditional faiths. In southern and eastern Asia, this means Buddhism, Hinduism, and Islam; in the Middle East, Islam. In all these areas, religious leaders have often been the leaders of conservative and traditionalist movements. This is hardly surprising, considering the historical role of these groups in agrarian societies and the nature of their beliefs. In general, they believe that the quest for truth is essentially complete: what people need to know has already been revealed—in the Vedas, or in the Koran, or to the Sangha. True wisdom, in their opinion, lies in turning to religious authorities for guidance and following their directions. In describing the traditionalist approach to education in the Middle East, one writer has said, "Education, as far as it is under the control of the ulema [the spiritual leaders of the Muslim community], is still bound up with authoritarianism, rote learning, and a rigid devotion to ancient authorities—providing only already known solutions to already formulated problems."[27] This approach sees little need for change, unless it is to root out whatever modernizing influences have crept in.

In the late nineteenth and early twentieth centuries, many western intellectuals thought these older faiths would simply die out as their adherents came to recognize the "obvious" superiority of western creeds such as Protestantism, humanism, and socialism. All three of these newer faiths were then winning converts, especially among the better educated, and it looked as if it were only a matter of time until the older faiths would vanish altogether.

Since World War I, however, and even more since World War II, the situation

---

*One may ask why the leaders of these societies allow this kind of educational imbalance to develop. There are two main reasons. First, in allowing the humanities to dominate their educational systems, they are following the example of the oldest and most prestigious educational institutions in the world—Oxford, Cambridge, and the famous continental universities—as well as their own native traditions. Second, it costs much more to provide technical education, and these nations have very limited resources.

FIGURE 13.7 Much of the intellectual and ideological resistance to modernization has come from leaders of the traditional faiths: the Ayatollah Khomeini, a leading opponent of modernization throughout the Islamic world, addressing a group of his followers.

has changed drastically in many areas. With the development of nationalist movements and a growing resistance to western ideas and influences, some of the traditional faiths have experienced a remarkable reinvigoration. After Sri Lanka won its independence, for example, a significant number of Christian converts there reconverted to Buddhism. In India, Hindu traditionalist forces became strong enough to pass laws forbidding the entry of foreign missionaries. In Egypt, Nasser imprisoned or executed most of the leaders of the Communist Party. In Iran, Khomeini led an Islamic revolution that overthrew the Shah and ended his program of modernization.

Although religious leaders have often been among the most conspicuous proponents of traditionalism, they have usually had strong support from the old governing class, especially the large landowners.[28] In fact, the rural population as a whole, emotionally involved in its traditional religion and unfamiliar with alternatives, has generally supported them. Members of such old "professions" as herbalists and practitioners of traditional medicine have also been strong supporters of traditionalist ideologies and belief systems, because they know their skills are rendered obsolete by newer technologies.

Ranged against traditionalists like these are individuals and groups who by virtue of educational, occupational, or other experience have been converted to the newer faiths. Early in a modernization movement, a disproportionate number of the leaders are people who were won over to the new outlook during visits to industrial societies, either as students or as workers. This was true, for example, of India's Nehru and of Vietnam's Ho Chi Minh.[29] Later, however, most of the leaders are people who were converted by experiences in their own countries. Frequently they are children of members of the old governing class, who rise to positions of leadership because of their superior training and other resources.

As we have noted earlier, there are usually competing movements within the camp of modernizers, some advocating western-style democracy, others the authoritarian Marxist-Leninist model, still others some kind of hybrid political system. The liberal democratic model was the first to be tried in most industrializing agrarian nations, as we also noted. It has had its greatest support from the more prosperous segments of the new middle class—professional people, managers in new industries, and others with modern education. Socialist movements were usually introduced next. Their support has been greatest among intellectuals, students, and the economically insecure—landless peasants and unemployed urban workers.

The most recent approach to modernization is nationalism, which reflects the dissatisfaction of many of the current generation of leaders with both of the other models. Their idea is to synthesize not only capitalism and socialism but modernism and traditionalism as well. Most of the nationalist ideologies that have flourished in industrializing agrarian societies since World War II have had a strong element of traditionalism (e.g., Khomeini's Iran). Usually, nationalism has been a reaction against colonialism, and this has been important in the process of nation building, especially in countries that were under foreign control until very recently. It is also a reaction against the continued technological and economic dependence of industrializing societies on the more advanced industrial societies.

There is more to modern nationalism than this, however: it is also an effort to reaffirm the importance of the cultural traditions of non-European peoples (in the case of Latin America, of peoples not in the Anglo-American tradition). Sometimes this helps to heal the breach between traditionalists and modernists by providing a position that is acceptable to both. Moreover, it gives dignity to a nation's leaders in their relations with European (or Anglo-American) peoples.

Unfortunately, the cultivation of nationalist sentiments can easily lead to the hatred of other nations. Even when this is not a spontaneous development, leaders of industrializing nations may encourage it to divert criticism from themselves and their policies. It can be very useful to blame foreigners for all the defects and shortcomings, inevitable and otherwise, of one's own policies.

Industrializing Horticultural Societies

During recent centuries, advanced horticultural societies flourished both in South-east Asia (from India to Vietnam) and in Africa south of the Sahara. In Southeast Asia, however, all of these societies have been either conquered or assimilated by neighboring agrarian societies.[30]

In Africa south of the Sahara things have been different. There, much of the traditional horticultural way of life has survived into the second half of the twentieth century, apparently because the period of European colonial rule was so brief and its impact on most of these societies relatively limited. The period of European rule in most of sub-Saharan Africa did not begin until the last decades of the nineteenth century and it ended early in the second half of the twentieth.

The problems of these societies are similar in a number of respects to those of industrializing agrarian societies. Both are confronted by a variety of radically new social and cultural elements introduced by technologically more advanced societies. Both find that these new elements throw traditional relationships out of kilter and create serious tensions. Furthermore, both experience an almost continuous state of crisis because conditions are changing so fast and because they lack the institutional and other resources to cope.

At the same time, there are a number of important differences between these two kinds of hybrid societies that reflect their horticultural and agrarian backgrounds and often cause them to react differently to the impact of industrialization. To avoid unnecessary repetition, our discussion of industrializing horticultural societies will focus mainly on these differences, referring only briefly to the points of similarity. Unless the similarities are kept in mind, however, the differences between industrializing agrarian and industrializing horticultural societies may appear to be greater than they actually are.

Technology and Productivity

Technologically, industrializing horticultural societies are much less advanced than industrializing agrarian, especially in their indigenous, or native, technology. This is revealed in a number of ways. For one thing, they are much less urbanized: in one recent year, industrializing agrarian societies had an average of 17 percent of their population in cities of 100,000 or more, while industrializing horticultural societies had only 5 percent in cities that large.[31] This is important, because the size of the urban population is a good indicator both of the size of the economic surplus and of the growth of specialized crafts and trade and commerce.

Per capita GNP is a useful summary measure of the level of both technological advance and productivity in the two types of industrializing societies. In the late 1970s, the median per capita GNP for 27 industrializing horticultural societies was slightly over $400; for 38 industrializing agrarian societies, it was slightly under $800.[32]

One of the most disturbing features of industrializing horticultural societies has been their inability to improve living standards. In a number of cases, real per capita income (i.e., per capita income after correction for the effects of inflation) has actually *declined* in recent years. In Ghana, Madagascar, Mozambique, and Zaire, for example, real per capita income dropped more than 20 percent between 1975 and 1982.[33] This is a shocking decline, especially in view of the low level of income to start with in all of these societies. Overall, the growth in per capita income in industrializing horticultural societies during the 1970s was only a little more than one-seventh as great as in industrializing agrarian societies.[34]

The reasons for the economic difficulties of the industrializing horticultural societies of sub-Saharan Africa are not hard to find. First and foremost, there is the runaway rate of population growth (see below). Second, governments, in many instances, are controlled by leaders who are either corrupt or repressive, or both.[35] Third, there are the environmental problems described earlier in the Excursus following Chapter 6—especially the problems caused by micropredators and poor soils. Fourth, and finally, the sociocultural heritages of these societies put them at a severe disadvantage in the modern world system: unlike societies with an agrarian heritage, few of these societies brought to the industrial era traditions of literacy and

TABLE 13.6 Crude Birthrates, Death Rates, and Rates of Natural Increase for Selected Industrializing Horticutural Societies

Society	Crude Birthrate*	Crude Death Rate†	Rate of Natural Increase‡
Kenya	54	13	4.1
Botswana	50	13	3.7
Rwanda	53	17	3.6
Tanzania	50	15	3.5
Uganda	50	15	3.5
Zimbabwe	47	12	3.5
Zambia	48	15	3.3
Ghana	47	15	3.2
Nigeria	48	17	3.1
Liberia	46	15	3.1
Zaire	45	16	2.9
Ivory Coast	46	18	2.8
Mozambique	45	17	2.8
Angola	47	22	2.5
Guinea	47	23	2.4
Chad	44	23	2.1
Gambia	49	29	2.0
Sierra Leone	47	30	1.7
Gabon	35	18	1.7

*Live births per 1,000 population per year.
†Deaths per 1,000 population per year.
‡Percentage growth of population due to excess of births over deaths per year.
Source: Population Reference Bureau, "1985 World Population Data Sheet."

formal education, experience with standardized monetary systems, bureaucratically organized governments, urban communities and urban institutions, and other social and cultural elements that are essential to success in the industrial era. This handicaps them badly as they struggle to compete in a world dominated by societies whose social and cultural heritages include all of these elements and more.[36]

Population and Economy

Industrializing horticultural societies are believed to have the highest rates of population growth of any major set of societies in human history. Collectively, they are growing at a rate of nearly 3 percent a year. At that rate, their populations would multiply 16-fold in less than a century. Small wonder that their economies are not able to keep pace and their standards of living are declining.

What is most disturbing about the current situation in sub-Saharan Africa is the unwillingness of governments and people to acknowledge the problem and to adopt programs that would slow this runaway growth in numbers.[37] Western governments are not altogether blameless in this matter either, since they have encouraged the idea that economic development alone could solve Africa's problems. Furthermore, western medical missionaries and others have worked to bring down the death rates in these societies without concerning themselves with the necessity of balancing these changes with corresponding changes in birthrates. The result, as Table 13.6 shows, is that death rates have been drastically reduced while birthrates have remained at preindustrial levels (in fact, there are some indications that birthrates in Africa are now even higher than in the preindustrial past).

Because of the extraordinarily rapid growth of population in African societies (compare Table 13.6 with Table 10.5, page 271), it has been almost impossible for the growth in productivity to keep pace. In fact, as Table 13.7 indicates, the growth of population has run well ahead of the growth of food production since at least 1970, with the result that the amount of food available to the average individual has steadily declined. The economic problems that African societies have faced in recent years cannot be explained away by droughts and natural disasters (though these have played an important part in some societies, at least since the middle 1970s). As Table 13.7 makes clear, the overall production of food has actually increased in these societies as a whole in recent decades. The problem of hunger arises because population has increased *even more rapidly*.

In certain ways, the economies of industrializing horticultural societies resemble those of industrializing agrarian societies. For one thing, they, too, are a mixture

TABLE 13.7   Average Annual Growth Rates for Food Production and for Food Production Per Capita in Sub-Saharan Africa, 1970–1983, in Percentages

	1970–75	1976–79	1980–83
Food production	1.6	1.1	1.9
Food production per capita	−1.2	−1.5	−1.1

Source: United Nations, *World Economic Survey, 1984: Current Trends and Policies,* table I–6.

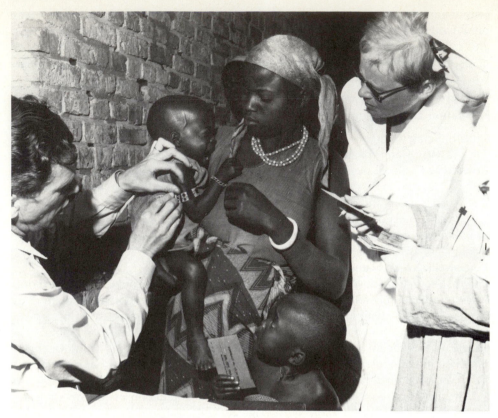

FIGURE 13.8 Western medical missionaries and others have worked to reduce death rates in industrializing societies without concerning themselves with the necessity of balancing these changes with corresponding changes in birthrates: Belgium nutritionist examining child in Zaire.

of traditional and modern elements, with the result that there may be little resemblance between the economic patterns in a nation's outlying villages and those in its largest cities. In addition, like many industrializing agrarian societies, the societies of sub-Saharan Africa are unable to compete in world markets with industrial societies in the production of most manufactured goods. Thus they, too, tend to become highly specialized and to be suppliers of raw materials in these markets (see Table 13.8). In fact, their economies are even more specialized than the economies of industrializing agrarian societies.[38]

Since their independence, many industrializing horticultural societies have proclaimed themselves socialist, or even Marxist-Leninist, societies. But African socialism is very different from European or Asian socialism. It is, in fact, as variable as the societies that have adopted it. Former President Senghor of Senegal, in a book entitled *African Socialism,* wrote, "We have rejected prefabricated models," and the economy of Senegal combines a communal system of agriculture with mixed public-private utilities, and private ownership of banks, commerce, and industry.[39] Although the details vary from society to society, this blending of public and private ownership of the means of production is widespread. There are a few societies, such

TABLE 13.8   Leading Exports of Selected Industrializing Horticultural Societies and Their Percentage Dependence on These Commodities for Foreign Exchange

Society	Commodity	Percentage Dependence
Nigeria	Petroleum	95
Uganda	Coffee	83
Zambia	Copper	82
Ghana	Cocoa	80
Madagascar	Coffee	65
Togo	Phosphate	50
Gambia	Groundnuts	48
Malawi	Tobacco	45
Zaire	Copper	36
Kenya	Coffee	33

Source: Adapted from United Nations, *Yearbook of International Trade Statistics, 1982,* vol. 1, tables 5.

as Kenya and Ivory Coast, that lean heavily toward private ownership, and a somewhat larger number, such as Tanzania, Angola, and Mozambique, that lean heavily toward state ownership. But the majority mix capitalist and socialist principles, together with a generous component of subsistence farming and other traditional African economic practices.

The economic development programs of the more idealistic African leaders, such as President Nyerere of Tanzania, have emphasized the need to improve the conditions of life for the common people and to minimize economic inequalities. According to western experts on whom he relied, this would lead to a burst of economic growth and prosperity. However, this has not happened. Despite the creation of an extensive educational system and greatly improved health and sanitary facilities in 8,000 villages, the production of cash crops for export (which is essential to the economy) has declined since 1965. Were it not for the infusion of huge amounts of foreign aid, the economy would be in desperate shape, since this aid provides 60 to 70 percent of the cost of the government's program of economic development.[40]

Because the urban sector of the economy in horticultural societies has historically been so much less developed than in agrarian societies, urban populations in industrializing horticultural societies have had less experience with such fundamentals of modern life as money, trade and commerce, markets, occupational specialization, literacy, and bureaucracy. This makes it very difficult for modernizing governments and businesses to find skilled personnel to staff their organizations. The problem is especially serious in societies in which national pride often demands that businesses and government be staffed with local personnel, regardless of the cost in terms of organizational efficiency.[41]

Data on literacy give some idea of the relative magnitude of this problem for the two types of industrializing societies. The most recent data available show that 71 percent of the adult population in the average (median) industrializing agrarian

FIGURE 13.9   Many industrializing societies have been forced into a specialized
ecological niche as producers of raw materials for industrial societies. In recent years, as
much as 80 percent of Ghana's foreign exchange has come from the sale of cocoa, which
is shown above being collected at a cooperative marketing society.

society was literate, while in industrializing horticultural societies the comparable
figure was only 47 percent.[42] If literacy is a minimum requirement for effective
participation in modern economic life, it is clear that it will be many years before
industrializing horticultural societies develop a fully qualified labor force.

Horticultural societies face still other problems in economic development. We
can see why when we consider the traditional nature and meaning of work in these
societies. Some years ago, the Inter-African Labour Institute characterized work
traditions in horticultural Africa this way:

1. Work is viewed in its relation to the basic institution of family or clan; within the
   family, it is divided on the basis of age and sex.

2. Work is linked with religious rites.

3. Work activities are considered and evaluated in the light of a subsistence
   economy rather than a profit economy (i.e., they are oriented more to the
   production of the necessities of life than to the production of an economic
   surplus).

4. Work requires neither foresight nor planning.

5. Time is largely irrelevant in work activities; no time limits are set for most tasks.

6. There is little specialization.

7. For men, work is episodic; when a task has to be done, men often do it without a break, but intervals of inactivity are long and frequent.

8. Men hardly ever work alone; work activities (e.g., hunting parties and work parties) often resemble a collective leisure activity in modern industrial society.[43]

These traditions do little to prepare the members of these societies, especially the men, for work in a modern industrial economy. A parallel list of the characteristics of work in industrial societies would, in fact, be an almost perfect contradiction.

One of the biggest problems is suggested by item 7. In analyzing horticultural societies in Chapter 6, we saw how often farming is primarily women's work. Men's responsibility tends to be limited to the occasional clearing of new gardens. While women do the sustained, tedious chores—planting, cultivating, and harvesting crops—men are free to do more interesting and exciting things—hunting, fighting, politicking, socializing, and participating in ceremonial activities. The disciplined, routinized patterns of work that are typical of an industrial economy are seldom encountered by men in these societies. In this respect, the peasant farmers of agrarian societies are far better prepared for industrialization. Yet even they have found the transition difficult.[44]

There is tremendous economic and social variation within every industrializing horticultural society in sub-Saharan Africa. A few tribes and villages are still largely untouched by the influences of industrialization, while in some of its cities the older patterns have been largely destroyed.[45] In addition, there is every conceivable combination of the old and the new—such as the woman in Nairobi who practiced witchcraft in order to earn the down payment on a truck so she could go into the trucking business.[46] A more common practice is for men to work for extended periods in factories in the cities, while their wives continue to practice traditional horticulture in the villages.

One observer reports that there have been four basic economic patterns in Africa in recent decades.[47] The first, which has become extremely rare, is a pure subsistence economy in which the local village consumes only what it produces or obtains through barter with its neighbors. The second pattern he calls "taxed subsistence," in which a village also raises a cash crop or sends its young men out to work for cash so it can pay the taxes levied by the government. The third is a mixed economy: villagers still rely on a subsistence economy for their basic necessities, but they also work for cash—not only because of taxes but so they can buy modern consumer goods. The fourth pattern is a predominantly cash economy in which even food is bought and laborers are hired to work on farms.

These patterns, which usually follow one another in sequence in a particular area, show how internal and external forces combine to transform a society's economy. On one side, there are the values, preferences, and desires of the villagers themselves; on the other are the demands made, and the attractions offered, by alien groups and institutions. It is easy to underestimate the power of the internal forces and interpret economic development as a process that is forced on reluctant villagers who would rather be left alone to live as their forebears did. But the problem is more complex than this. Given a choice, most of the members of horticultural societies choose the industrial way of life—not knowing, it is true, all the implications and ramifications of their choice. Sometimes they adopt it *in toto*, like the family that migrates to the city. In other cases, they adopt only part of it, like the family that stays in the village but earns all the cash it can to buy modern tools, cloth, soap, a sewing machine, a radio, a bicycle, and other products of an industrial economy; or the family in which the husband and father migrates to the city to earn money to buy such goods, which he brings back with him on his periodic visits.

The Polity

One of the striking features of sub-Saharan Africa is how new most of its societies are: almost without exception, they were established in the late nineteenth or the twentieth century. Most of them are products of European colonialism, and their boundaries are largely the result of the rivalries of colonial governments or missions, the outcomes of battles, the location of rivers, and other things that had little to do with the boundaries of the older societies they replaced. Actually, the process was not too different from the one that produced most other nations.

Because of their newness, however, and because of their recent horticultural past, most African societies suffer from serious internal divisions rooted in traditional tribal loyalties. Colonial powers seldom destroyed the older tribal groups. On the contrary, they usually preserved these groups in order to use them as instruments of administrative control, allowing tribal rulers to serve as lower-echelon officials. Colonial governments often pretended that these tribal groups were autonomous, because this enabled them to put the burden, and the onus, of political control on their leaders. They also encouraged tribal rivalries, applying the ancient principle "Divide and rule." As a result, even after independence was won, there was a fundamental tension between tribal loyalties and national loyalties in most parts of Africa. This is a problem that few industrializing agrarian societies have had to contend with.

The consequences of tribalism have been serious for sub-Saharan societies. Tribal divisions nearly destroyed the new nations of Zaire and Angola after they gained their independence. In Nigeria, Uganda, Zimbabwe, and others, the fuse burned more slowly, but the results were even worse. In most countries, tribalism remains a major divisive force, sometimes with the potential for civil war. When they were fighting for independence, many African leaders (as well as their friends in industrial societies) ignored or minimized the importance of these tribal loyalties, thinking that their compatriots valued them as little as they did and that the old ties were rapidly losing their vitality. Although this may have been true in a few countries, it proved a serious misjudgment in most.[48] Even in cities and towns, tribal loyalties are still meaningful.[49] In view of the ethnic and linguistic diversity in these societies (Cameroon's 10 million citizens belong to 200 tribes and speak 24 languages; Zaire has 700 languages and dialects[50]), and considering the virtual absence of any national institutions in these African societies until recently, this is hardly surprising. With increasing urbanization, with the establishment of schools that cultivate national loyalties, and with the growth of the mass media to reinforce these

FIGURE 13.10   Tribal chief on visit to Monrovia, capital of Liberia.

early lessons, tribal loyalties may eventually disappear. But this will take decades or even generations, and in the meantime these allegiances will produce bitter and often costly conflicts.

Except for the influence of tribal loyalties, the polities of industrializing horticultural societies have a lot in common with those of industrializing agrarian societies. The majority of them profess socialist ideals, but their planning efforts, and even their basic administrative activities, are often hamstrung by the lack of trained personnel and by commitments to rapid Africanization of the civil service. This is especially serious because most of these governments, like those of most industrializing agrarian societies, are committed to programs of economic planning and development, a notoriously difficult and complex business even for industrial societies.

Another important similarity is the trend that one writer has referred to as "the erosion of democracy."[51] Prior to independence, most of the political leaders in these countries professed to be democrats and to believe in parliamentary government, a multiparty system, and free elections. Subsequently, however, when the hostility that had previously been focused on the colonial regime came to be directed at them and their new governments and opposition forces threatened to turn them out of office, most African leaders became advocates of a one-party state with

391

control in the hands of a strong executive (i.e., themselves). Subsequently, in about half of these societies, the government was taken over by the military. Only two industrializing horticultural societies—Botswana and Gambia—have maintained stable democratic governments. Tanzanian President Julius Nyerere commented not long ago, "We spoke and acted as if, given the opportunity for self-government, we would quickly create utopias. Instead, injustice, even tyranny, is rampant."[52]

Related to this, the governments of many of the industrializing horticultural societies of Africa have had a major problem with corruption. In Zaire, for example, an international grant of $1.8 million to repair Kinshasa's broken-down city buses was reportedly "swindled down" to $200,000 by the time it reached the Transportation Ministry, while in Gabon the president built himself a $650 million marble palace with revolving rooms and walls that disappear at the touch of a button. For a number of years, oil-producing Arab nations were generous providers of foreign aid to sub-Saharan African societies, but they soon cut back on such aid after a series of bad experiences. A leading Arab publication reported, "In some cases now coming to light, for every $1 million of aid, less than $100,000 finds effective applications in African countries like Zambia and Zaire."[53]

Social Stratification

Although most industrializing horticultural societies profess to be socialist, the level of inequality in them tends to be higher than in the nonsocialist industrial democracies of Europe and America. In Tanzania, for example, government figures indicate that the top 10 percent of households receive 35.6 percent of the national income compared with 26.6 percent for the top 10 percent of American households.[54] In Zaire and in other societies where, unlike Tanzania, corruption has been widespread, the level of inequality is almost certainly greater, though no statistics are available.

Since independence from colonial rule was achieved, the composition of the upper class has been substantially altered in most sub-Saharan societies. In most of these societies, the upper class is now composed mainly of the new political elites whose control of the government is the basis of their wealth and power. Sometimes these elites are primarily military leaders, sometimes they are mainly civilians. Because of the continuing importance of kinship, the upper class includes many members of the extended families of these leaders. In addition, the upper class may include some intellectuals and some wealthy businessmen.

Beneath this politically and economically dominant class, there are two fairly distinct systems of stratification. In the rural areas, where traditional patterns still prevail, an individual's status is largely a function of his own and his family's relation to traditional authorities (especially the village headman and the tribal chief). In urban areas, where industrialization has had a far greater impact, the crucial criteria are education, occupation, income, and connections with the new political elite.

Religion and Ideology

The traditional religions of horticultural Africa were relatively undeveloped, both organizationally and intellectually, compared to those of agrarian Europe and Asia.

There were no complex organizations of priests or monks, no body of sacred writings to serve as the core of a common faith, no tradition of philosophical speculation, and, most important of all, no universal faith to provide a bond between members of different societies. As a result, these faiths could not easily defend themselves against the inroads of Islam and Christianity, especially when the latter were introduced by peoples who were politically and economically stronger and whose way of life, therefore, seemed so obviously worthy of emulation.

Africans who still cling to the older tribal faiths are usually residents of the more isolated rural areas or the less educated residents of the towns. Since this describes the majority of people in these societies, adherents of the older faiths are obviously still numerous. In Benin and Togo, for example, only 30 percent of the people are even nominally Christian or Muslim; in Gabon and Zaire, less than 40 percent.[55] In the cities, however, the picture is very different. In Dar es Salaam in Tanzania, 99.8 percent of the population claimed to be either Muslim or Christian twenty years ago, at a time when 40 percent of the society as a whole were non-Muslim and non-Christian.[56] Similarly, in Monrovia, the capital of Liberia, 72 percent were either Christian or Muslim at a time when only 25 percent of the nation as a whole were Christian or Muslim.[57]

Conversion to Islam and Christianity is often for nonreligious reasons. For many people, it is a status symbol, an effort to identify with modern ways and avoid being regarded as ignorant, backward country folk. In Dar es Salaam, for example, many pagan tribesmen "on arrival in town call themselves Muslims—some few call themselves Christians—in order to conform, not to be conspicuous in a [community] where Islam is supreme and where to 'have no religion,' as people put it, is the mark of the uncivilized. Some go so far as to be circumcised and to be formally admitted to Islam: most merely use a Muslim name instead of a tribal one; some have two names, a Christian and a Muslim, to cover all eventualities."[58] Under the circumstances, it is hardly surprising to find that "the outward observances of religion are strikingly absent in Dar es Salaam: it is rare to see an African Muslim praying his daily prayers [and] in Ramadhan [the Muslim month of fasting] people may be seen anywhere eating and drinking publicly during the daily hours [a forbidden practice]," and the consumption of alcohol, also forbidden, is almost universal.[59] In Monrovia, where Christianity is dominant, the pattern is not quite so pronounced, but even here "the professing of Christianity remains a basic requirement of 'civilized' status," and "for a great many of the civilized, church membership has become largely a question of social status."[60] In many areas, both urban and rural, those who have adopted Christianity or Islam often continue to practice traditional tribal religions as well.[61]

In the early years of colonial rule, Christian missions were an important force for modernization. This was primarily due to the mission schools, which introduced literacy and elements of western culture and, most important of all, opened up channels of communication with the larger world. As a result, the areas that came under Christian influence advanced more rapidly than those where paganism or Islam prevailed. In discussing Tanzania, one writer asserts:

> Mission schools and mission hospitals have been very important factors in changing tribal society, although their influence has been felt much more strongly in some areas than others. Very nearly a one-to-one correlation exists between mission influence, the cash-crop economy, fertile land, education, and the general desire for progress.[62]

Similarly, many people have commented on the singular economic success of the Christian Ibo of southeastern Nigeria compared with the Muslim and pagan tribes to the north.

With the rise of the independence movement after World War II, identification with Christianity became a somewhat ambiguous social attribute. Christianity was linked with colonialism, and colonialism was assumed to be a force detrimental to Africa. Missionaries came under heavy attack for dominating the churches and refusing to let native Christians assume positions of leadership. Furthermore, in an era of great social change and uncertainty, mission-brand Christianity often seemed too tame and too western. In many areas, new sects were founded, some basically Christian, others largely pagan, many a mixture of both.[63] These sects have their greatest appeal for individuals who are in mid-passage in the difficult transition from traditional culture to modern. Such people are subject to great insecurity, both economically and intellectually, and the sects often provide a link to the past. They also are popular because they permit polygyny and other traditional practices condemned by the missionaries.

There are also new nontheistic ideologies in sub-Saharan Africa, the most important of which is nationalism. In many cases, nationalism functions simply as a secular ideology. But sometimes, when it demands supreme loyalty, it assumes a truly religious character. In Ghana, for example, President Nkrumah assumed messianic titles, and his political party took on quasi-religious functions.[64] Whether nationalism will survive in this extreme form no one can say. Its chances are probably linked to the experience these new societies have with the modernization process. The quicker and easier it is, the poorer the chances for an extreme nationalism.

Kinship

In the horticultural societies of precolonial Africa, kin groups were extremely important. As one writer put it, in Africa "the [kin group] was the basic building block of society."[65] More than that, it was psychologically the center of the individual's world, establishing his identity and defining most of his basic rights and responsibilities.

Now the historic bases of power of the kin group are being undermined in these societies. In the modern sector of the economy, the kin group no longer controls its members' access to the means of livelihood, which it traditionally did through its control of the land. Similarly, the family plays a smaller role in the political system. And the once-important cult of the ancestors, centered in the kin group, has declined in importance as Christianity and Islam have grown.

In the past, most of the advantages of the kin group were enjoyed by the older generation, while the disadvantages fell disproportionately on the younger. Before the growth of cities and towns, young people had no choice but to accept the burdens and patiently await the day when they would become the privileged elders. The growth of cities and towns has changed all this: by migrating to these urban centers, young people can largely escape the control of their elders.[66] Although ties to the extended family are not entirely eliminated, they are greatly weakened, and this has become a fairly serious source of social instability in most industrializing horticultural societies.[67]

These changes in the kinship system also appear to have contributed to the runaway growth of population in these societies.[68] For example, the traditional stigma attached to unmarried mothers is no longer as powerful as it used to be when family controls over young people were stronger. In addition, the decline of polygynous households (a result of the influence of Christian missions) has apparently contributed to higher birthrates. As some Africans point out, although a few older, wealthy men could afford many wives and have large numbers of children, the practice of polygyny meant postponement of marriage for most men. Furthermore, the wives in polygynous households usually had fewer children than women in monogamous households. Thus, a pattern of marriage that might seem to increase the birthrate actually had the opposite effect.

Industrializing Societies in Theoretical Perspective

Not too many years ago, the prospects for industrializing societies looked bright. All they had to do, it appeared, was to follow the path blazed by the industrial societies of western Europe and North America. In fact, some people believed that because these societies had the experience of the others to go on, they would be able to avoid many of the problems of modernization and speed up the process.

A quarter of a century later, that prediction seems naive. In most Third World societies development has been disappointingly slow. Improvements in the standard of living of the masses of citizens in many of these societies have been especially disappointing. Hundreds of millions of people continue to live in poverty, with little prospect of any significant improvement in their situation.

Why were earlier predictions so inaccurate? Why have the majority of societies of the Third World not been able to take greater advantage of the vastly expanded store of technological information that is now available?

One answer, originally developed by a group of Latin American scholars in the 1960s and known as *dependency theory*, is that the problems of less developed societies are due to external influences, to forces in their social environment.[69] Specifically, their problems are the result of influences exercised by industrial societies. The backwardness and problems of the less developed societies, they argued, are an inevitable consequence of the economic growth and prosperity of industrial societies. Dependency theory is, in effect, an extension to the *global* level of Marx's theory that the growth of an increasingly impoverished proletariat is a necessary consequence of the growing wealth and power of the bourgeoisie or capitalist class.

There are currently a number of versions of dependency theory, each providing a somewhat different explanation of the Third World's problems, but all locate the source outside the industrializing societies themselves.[70] Some blame multinational corporations, some the governments of industrial societies, and others the capitalist world economy that has led so many of these nations to concentrate their production of exports in raw materials or in low-technology industries. Whatever the cause, dependency theorists blame the difficulties of the Third World on western industrial societies that drain away their economic surplus.

Another group of scholars, mostly American, has developed an alternative explanation of the Third World's problems. *Modernization theory* finds the source of these problems within the industrializing societies themselves.[71] As with dependency theory, there are a number of versions of modernization theory, but most of them focus on the attitudes and values of the members of Third World societies as the chief deterrent to industrialization. Thus, the difficulties of these societies, in their opinion, are due to the persistence of ideologies and institutional systems which were inherited from the preindustrial past and which are incompatible with the needs and requirements of industrialization. They point out, for example, the persistence of fatalism, trust in magic, resistance to innovation and change, and the conflict between traditional patterns of work (see page 388) and the requirements of modern industrial enterprises. They emphasize the consequences of illiteracy and the lack of information and skills of many kinds that are essential in the modern world. In short, modernization theory locates the causes of lagging development within the less developed societies themselves, rather than in their social environments.

In any attempt to evaluate the relative merits of dependency theory and modernization theory, it is important to keep two things in mind. First, there is little evidence to support the claim of some dependency theorists that life was better in most Third World societies before the industrial era. Such a view cannot be supported by the historical record of the last 5,000 years. It is a mistake, therefore, to ask, What has caused these societies to regress? Rather, the question must be, Why have the conditions in most of them been so slow to improve?

The second point to remember is that there is no reason to assume that the source of the problems in the Third World is *either* primarily internal *or* primarily external. On the contrary, ecological-evolutionary theory asserts that the characteristics of human societies—including the degree of their development—are the product of both internal *and* external forces (see Figure 3.3, page 58). To ignore or neglect either is to misunderstand and misinterpret the complex process of societal development.

One indication of the hazards of neglecting either set of forces is provided by the results of the foreign aid programs created by western industrial societies in recent decades. Because of the tremendous success of the Marshall Plan in rebuilding the German economy and German society following the massive destruction of World War II, some leaders assumed that large transfers of capital to the less developed societies of Asia, Africa, and Latin America would produce similar results. Unfortunately, however, the results of aid programs to most of these societies have been extremely disappointing. As noted earlier, much of the money was wasted on ill-conceived projects, and much simply vanished into the pockets of corrupt officials in the recipient societies. It has gradually become clear that the success of foreign aid programs depends as much on the characteristics of the recipient society as on the generosity of the donors. The effective use of large amounts of capital presupposes the presence in the recipient society of supportive institutions and ideologies, plus large numbers of people with modern administrative and technical skills and honest elites capable of organizing vast and complex programs.

The greatest deficiency of both modernization theory and dependency theory, however, is their failure to focus more closely on the role that demographic factors are playing in most Third World societies today. With runaway population growth, most of the economic gains they have achieved have been canceled out by the necessity of providing more food, more schools, more jobs, and more of everything for their burgeoning populations.

This problem, like most of their problems, is a product of both internal and external forces. Advanced industrial societies have introduced modern health and sanitation technologies that have cut death rates in industrializing societies by 50 percent or more, but they have been much slower to recognize the need to provide resources to curb birthrates and thus restore the demographic equilibrium. Moreover, the leaders and peoples of many of these societies—especially in sub-Saharan Africa—have been extraordinarily slow to recognize the nature of the problem confronting them. Thus, once again, internal forces have combined with external forces to create an extremely serious problem.

In the past, demographic imbalances were corrected through the play of natural forces. In an earlier chapter we saw how plagues and famines periodically reduced the size of the populations of agrarian societies whenever population growth got too far ahead of economic growth. In the Third World today, however, the western industrial democracies have repeatedly intervened and minimized the *immediate* effects of overly rapid population growth by supplying large amounts of food and other necessities. In doing so, they have laid the foundation for far more serious crises and far greater problems in the future.

From both the selfish and the altruistic points of view, it would appear that industrial societies should begin shifting the focus of their efforts to help the Third World. Instead of trying primarily to alleviate symptoms, such as hunger, malnutrition, and disease, they should be directing more of their attention toward eliminating the source of those symptoms. Sooner or later, they will have to recognize that it is irresponsible to provide aid programs that increase food production or improve infant health, without simultaneously providing powerful incentives and resources for lowering birthrates; industrial societies would be well advised to make rigorous population policies a precondition for aid.

One thing that the industrial democracies may have to accept in the years ahead is authoritarian Third World regimes. Democratic governments have difficulty handling the critical problems facing these societies. In fact, there is reason to believe that one-party governments, like China's, may be best adapted organizationally and ideologically to the needs of these societies, at least once the leaders of these governments acknowledge the critical importance of the population problem.

Of one thing we can be sure: the problems of the Third World are not going to be solved quickly. The basic reason is that the population of most Third World societies would increase 50 percent even if no couple ever again had more than two children. These societies have a heavily mortgaged future: *a 50 percent gain in GNP under these circumstances would translate into no gain at all in per capita income.* Thus, a quick fix is out of the question.

Industrializing societies provide a fascinating means of testing ecological-evolutionary theory, and other sociological theories as well. Their problems are so complex that they compel us to consider all of the components of these sociocultural systems, as well as the relationships among them. They also compel us to consider the relationship of each sociocultural system with the larger world system—which is good preparation for an analysis of the future, our primary concern in the final chapter.

CHAPTER 14

Retrospect and Prospect

When we study something as complex as sociocultural evolution, it is easy to become so immersed in details that we lose sight of the larger picture. For this reason, we begin this final chapter with a brief look back over the long sweep of human history. Then we go on to consider an important question that we could not address until this point: What has sociocultural evolution really meant for humanity? More specifically, how has technological advance affected the quality of human life? Has it brought greater freedom, justice, and happiness? Or have these qualities been unaffected by this progress, or even declined?

After considering these questions, we turn our attention to *the future*. What lies ahead for human societies? Can ecological-evolutionary theory help us anticipate the problems and prospects they will face ten, twenty, even thirty years from now? This is an important question, and a practical one as well. For most of us will live in that world, and it could be very different from the world we live in today.

Looking Back

When we look back over the long course of hominid history, we see that we and our societies are an integral part of the global ecosystem and that our species' development has always been part of the same grand process of biological evolution that shapes all life on this planet. Yet it is equally clear that our species' development has been different from that of the rest of the biological world in some fundamental ways.

If we can understand where, and how, our path diverged, we can better understand our problems and those of our societies, and perhaps, as a result, create a better, happier future.

The Divergent Path

For millions of years, there was little to suggest that our early ancestors were destined to be anything more than just another variety of primate. But genetic changes gradually provided our line with the ability to create symbol systems, a trait that is as much a product of natural selection as wings, gills, social instincts, and other adaptive mechanisms of the biotic world.

With the aid of symbol systems, hominids were able to use their primate capacity for individual learning to far greater advantage. They could now create and share vast amounts of cultural information gleaned from individual experience. Eventually, hominid societies came to depend far more on new cultural information than on new genetic information in their adaptive efforts. Thus, for the past 35,000 years, *humanity's evolution has been shaped primarily by the processes of cultural innovation and selection,* rather than by the processes of biological evolution.

The explanation of the tremendous adaptive capacity of cultural information is its potential for creating diversity. In this respect, it is like genetic information, which is responsible for the striking diversity in the biotic world. In the case of cultural information, however, *all of the diversity is concentrated within a single species.* As a result, despite a common genetic heritage, human individuals become, with culture, far more varied than the members of any other species. Human societies, too, are extremely varied, again unlike the situation in other social species. Though such diversity enhances our species' survival potential, it is a major source of problems, both within and among societies.

Another manifestation of culture's capacity for creating diversity is the great variety of needs and desires that humans have developed, *needs and desires not even related to the survival of either individuals or our species.* To satisfy these culturally triggered or intensified needs, societies have depended primarily on the kind of information—technological—that helps people utilize environmental resources in new ways and for new purposes. As technology advanced, however, it altered the conditions of life, and as that happened, further needs emerged. Efforts to satisfy these needs created further change, which led in turn to new needs, a process of positive feedback that has continued at an accelerating pace for at least 10,000 years.

Through this process, *humanity established a new and unique relationship with the biophysical environment.* Since every other species of plant or animal uses the resources of its environment to satisfy only a limited set of genetically programmed needs, this characteristic is perhaps the most fundamental divergence of all.

The Question of Progress

Despite the problems that have attended our species' reliance on culture, one thing is clear: *culture has been a highly successful adaptive mechanism.* Humanity has not only survived, it has flourished by biological standards: there are far more of us alive today than at any time in the past, and our numbers are growing rapidly. Moreover, humans have spread into an enormous variety of environments.

But mere numbers and dispersion are not enough on which to base an assessment of *human* evolution. We must also ask whether the process of sociocultural evolution has meant progress in terms of more uniquely human criteria and goals, such as freedom, justice, and happiness.

It is not easy, however, to assess progress in terms such as these. For one thing, these concepts are so broad that they apply to many aspects of human life. For another, the way we define such terms is the product of past experience, and this, as we have seen, varies greatly among individuals, groups, and societies. Nevertheless, because the subject is too important to ignore, we must at least make the effort to evaluate humanity's progress in terms of these goals and determine whether our species' growing store of cultural information has had the effect of advancing or hindering them.

Freedom   The high value that the members of modern industrial societies attach to freedom is revealed in the growing challenge to all forms of authority, not only in the liberal democracies of the West but in the authoritarian nations of Eastern Europe as well. Even those who are not in the forefront of the libertarian movement are likely to consider the degree of freedom accorded individuals one of the basic measures of the attractiveness, and hence the progress, of a society, and they would deny that a technologically advanced, politically repressive society is truly progressive.

But human freedom is more than the absence of repressive social controls; it is also freedom from restraints imposed by nature. People who must spend most of their waking hours in an exhausting struggle to produce the necessities of life are not truly "free"—even if there are few social restraints on their actions. A woman whose life is a long succession of unwanted pregnancies is not "free"—regardless of the kind of society she lives in. Disease, physical and mental handicaps, geographical barriers, and all the laws of nature restrict people and deny them freedom. For freedom does not exist where there are no alternatives; and freedom can be measured only by the range of choices that are available. The fewer the viable choices, the less freedom there is—and it matters little, from the standpoint of the individual, whether the restrictions are imposed by nature or by other people.

Once we recognize this, it becomes clear that humanity's long struggle to advance technologically is not irrelevant to the desire for freedom. Every technological innovation reflects the desire to overcome natural limitations on human actions. Thanks to this struggle, some of us are now free to talk across oceans, free to travel faster than sound, free to live longer lives in better health while enjoying a range of experiences that far surpass in richness and variety what was available to the greatest kings and emperors of the past.

There has been a price to pay, of course: technological progress has necessitated larger and more complex social systems. If we want the option of flying to another part of the country instead of walking there, or of watching the day's events on a screen in our home instead of hearing about them weeks later, we have to accept certain social controls. The goods and services essential for those options can be produced only where there are organizations with rules and with sanctions to enforce the rules, and individuals with authority to exercise the sanctions. And these organizations can function efficiently only within the context of a society with rules to govern the relationships between them, and an authority system to enforce the rules. The only alternative is anarchy—and the loss of all the freedoms that modern technology affords.

Critics of modern society often say that the price has been too high, that the increased social restrictions outweigh the gains in freedom we derive from modern technology.[1] They may be right—this is a matter each of us must decide for himself or herself. In doing so, however, we need to beware of romanticizing the past. Before deciding that people are less free than they used to be, we must read accounts of peasant life in agrarian societies and of the life of horticultural and hunting and gathering peoples. In doing this, we must resist the temptation to abstract the attractive features and ignore the appalling ones. We must remember that slavery and serfdom were not accidental characteristics of agrarian societies, but reflections of basic, inescapable conditions of that way of life, as were the high mortality rate and short life span of many hunting and gathering peoples. Finally, we must keep in mind that the restraints in those societies were not all physical ones; there were often powerful social controls operating too.

Once we recognize the danger of comparing some rosy version of life in less advanced societies with the negative side of life in industrial societies, we are in a better position to consider whether freedom is a correlate of technological advance. We can say, first of all, that technological progress has clearly raised the *upper* level of freedom in human societies. Individuals with the greatest measure of freedom in contemporary societies—that is, members of the upper classes—have a far wider range of choice than individuals with the greatest measure of freedom in agrarian societies, and the elites of agrarian societies had far more freedom than the elites of less advanced societies. This has been true with respect to everything from the individual's use of a leisure hour to the use of a lifetime. In this sense, then, there is a high positive correlation between technological advance and gains in human freedom.

The relation between technological advance and freedom for the *average* member of society is more complicated. If we compare the typical peasant in an agrarian society with a typical hunter and gatherer, it is not at all clear that there were any gains. In fact, the peasant had to live with a lot of new social controls, while gaining very little freedom from natural controls. Thus, during much of the course of history—especially after the formation of the state—the average individual probably experienced a decline in freedom. With industrialization, however, the pattern changes: once the difficult period of transition is past, technological progress and freedom for the average person are positively related, as Figure 14.1 illustrates. Whether people in industrial societies have more freedom than hunters and gatherers is less certain. Clearly they have more social restraints, but far fewer physical and biological ones.

Before leaving the subject of freedom, we should take note of the popular misconception that governmental activity necessarily results in a loss of freedom for the members of society. This is at best a half-truth. Laws do, of course, place restrictions on people, but in democratic societies, this is often done in order to increase freedom, not reduce it. The Pure Food and Drug Act, for example, was

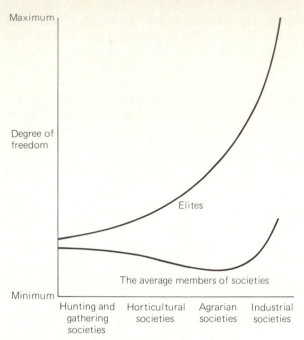

FIGURE 14.1 **Trends in freedom for elites and for the average members of societies.**

designed to restrict the freedom of businessmen who were willing to sell spoiled food and dangerous drugs for profit, but it increased the freedom of the rest of the population who used their products. Sometimes, of course, laws restrict everyone's freedom in one area—the freedom to proceed at will through a busy intersection, for example—in order to preserve it in others. In short, most legal norms *redistribute* freedom.

Justice   Justice has to do with the *fairness* of a society in its treatment of its members. Although no one would quarrel with the idea that a society should be "fair," we run into trouble when we try to define what this means. Is a society fair when it rewards people on the basis of their contributions to the common good, or is it more equitable to allocate rewards on the basis of individual needs? Should handicapped individuals, for example, be paid the same as those who are able to outproduce them with less effort? And how does one arrive at a fair evaluation of the relative contributions of people in dissimilar activities—a symphony conductor, a bricklayer, a housewife, a garbage collector, a student?

   And what about punishments? Does a "fair" society punish its members strictly in accordance with the letter of the law, or is it more just to take circumstances and intent into account? What of a parent's theft to feed a hungry child, for example, or a mercy killing? And should a society deal more severely with those in positions of power than with lesser members of society when they commit crimes, or should everyone be treated equally? Most important, perhaps, should a society seek to exact "an eye for an eye," or should it set a higher standard? Questions like these point up the difficulty of measuring progress with respect to justice. Since an adequate treatment of the subject would require volumes, all we will do here is call attention to basic trends and offer tentative conclusions.

To begin with, as we observed in earlier chapters, social inequality became more pronounced as societies advanced technologically and status became increasingly dependent on the family into which one was born. The result was a weakening of the link between a person's *efforts* and a person's rewards. Whereas every boy in a hunting and gathering group had a chance of becoming the best hunter (and hence the most important man) in his society, a peasant's son had little hope of advancing even a notch above his father's social level, no matter how hard he tried.

The relation between a person's *natural ability* and his or her rewards also declined with societal advance. For one thing, societies beyond the simple horticultural level frequently denied many of their members access to rewards because of their religion or ethnicity, thereby denying them the chance to use many of their abilities. In addition, increasingly rigid stratification systems locked people into roles and situations where they could neither develop nor use their gifts, while those with few or none to use might occupy positions for which they were grossly unsuited.

The trend in punishment, meanwhile, was toward increasingly harsh and discriminatory treatment. In most agrarian societies, the privileged were free to abuse members of the lower class without fear of reproof; if the reverse occurred, however, an individual would be punished swiftly and severely. A master involved in a conflict with his slaves or serfs was often both judge and prosecutor; he could beat them with impunity and, in many societies, kill them if he wished. Nor were there legal sanctions against the beating of children by parents, employers, or schoolmasters.

Courts of law were equally harsh. In eighteenth-century England, 222 different offenses could draw the death penalty, including such minor infractions as the theft of a handkerchief, the shooting of a rabbit, or the forgery of a birth certificate.[2] Nor was execution always a humane process: we are told that the hangman in Elizabethan England was "an artist, and the knife was his chief instrument; the art consisting in tossing his man off the ladder, hanging him, but cutting him down before he breaks his neck, so that he may be dismembered and disemboweled while still alive."[3]

In general, societies seem to have become less fair and less just as they advanced technologically. Since the Industrial Revolution, however, there are clear signs of a reversal. With respect to economic rewards, industrialization has resulted in some decline in the level of social inequality among the members of a society. Public education now provides at least some chance for almost all children to develop their abilities, and women and minorities have gained numerous legal and economic opportunities long denied them. Industrial societies are also more solicitous of their poor and their handicapped, and provide a far broader range of legal rights and protections for their members, whatever their social status. Criminal justice is far less harsh. Industrial societies today rarely execute their members, and never for minor infractions, nor do they maim them, as was common in the agrarian era. In short, after a long period of declining justice with respect to both rewards and punishments, there is finally movement in the other direction.

Happiness   Of all the possible measures of progress, happiness is the most elusive, for it depends so much—perhaps primarily—on the quality of interpersonal relations, whether there is love, mutual respect, cooperation, and so forth. And these things do not always depend on the level of technological development. Studies of modern hunting and gathering groups indicate that the most primitive peoples develop these qualities as surely as members of modern industrial societies do.[4]

There are several respects, however, in which technological progress is relevant to this kind of happiness. To begin with, some of life's greatest tragedies involve the premature death of a loved one—a cherished child, a parent, or a partner in a happy conjugal relation. We saw how common this was in most societies prior to the Industrial Revolution and can therefore appreciate how the recently expanded life span has contributed to human happiness.

Health, too, contributes to happiness. When we are seriously ill, life may not seem worth living. Disease was very poorly understood through most of human history, and it would be hard to argue that technological advance prior to the Industrial Revolution had any real impact in this area. More recently, however, advances in sanitation and medicine have dramatically improved the physical well-being of the members of many societies. Unfortunately, modern medical technology has also had a negative effect: it has been used to keep alive individuals who, in simpler societies, would mercifully be allowed to die. In balance, however, the result has undeniably been positive.

Hunger, another cause of enormous human misery over the centuries, has been drastically reduced in many societies as a result of industrialization. As recently as the eighteenth century, local crop failures in most parts of Europe could still result in starvation, because of an inadequate transportation network. Today, thanks to advances in technology, food supplies can be safely stored for long periods, or moved to areas of scarcity, in every industrial society and in an increasing number of industrializing ones.

The industrialization of agriculture has also meant a substantially improved food supply, with respect to quality, quantity, and diversity, for most members of industrial societies. During the winter, for example, people can now enjoy fresh fruits and vegetables shipped in from areas with different growing seasons. Nor do the members of industrial societies have to subsist on short rations in the months prior to harvest, as members of traditional agrarian societies had to do. As with improvements in health, it is easy to take such benefits for granted and to lose sight of the numerous links between technological advance and human happiness.

The increased production of other kinds of goods and services, especially nonessential ones, has probably had much less effect on happiness. The absolute quantity of luxuries we enjoy is certainly not as important in this regard as how they compare with what people around us have. Thus the headman in a simple horticultural society may be quite content with his few special possessions, because they are more than his neighbors own and as good as anything he knows about, while middle-class Americans, surrounded with goods and services the headman never dreamed of, may feel terribly deprived when they compare themselves with more prosperous neighbors. In other words, insofar as happiness depends on material possessions, *the degree of inequality* is probably more important than anything else.

TABLE 14.1 Degree of Happiness and Satisfaction with Life Expressed by Members of Societies around the World

	Percentage Very Happy or Fairly Happy	Percentage Highly Satisfied with Their Lives*
North America	91	50
Western Europe	80	41
Latin America	70	40
Africa	68	15
Far East†	48	11

*The values shown in this column are the arithmetic means of responses to questions about satisfaction with ten specific areas of life (see Table 6 of Gallup's article).
†The Far East includes both Japan and India, and Gallup notes that "the differences between Japan [an advanced industrial society] and India [an industrializing agrarian society] with respect to personal happiness are very large."
Source: Adapted from George H. Gallup, "Human Needs and Satisfactions: A Global Survey," *Public Opinion Quarterly*, 40 (Winter, 1976–1977), Tables 2 and 6, pp. 465 and 467.

When we take into account the advances in health, the greater abundance and improved quality of food, and the drastic reduction in premature deaths, it is clear that the Industrial Revolution has eliminated the sources of much of the misery of earlier eras. Putting it all together, we are again led to the tentative conclusion that the long-term trend for the average individual has been curvilinear, as shown in Figure 14.1 (page 402). Conditions seem to have been more conducive to human happiness for the average individual in hunting and gathering societies than in horticultural, and better in horticultural than in agrarian, or even in early industrial. But with further advances in industrialization, the situation of the average individual seems to have improved considerably, reversing the long-term trend.

Recent evidence, the first of its kind, tends to support this conclusion. In a study of almost seventy nations, containing two-thirds of the world's population, the Gallup Poll and its associates abroad found a striking relation between the level of happiness expressed by the people they interviewed and the level of technological advance of the societies in which they lived (see Table 14.1). The same relation was found between societal development and people's satisfaction with specific aspects of their lives (e.g., family life, health, housing, work). The results of this survey led George Gallup to comment: "For centuries, romantics and philosophers have beguiled us with tales of societies that were 'poor but happy.' If any such exist, the survey failed to discover them."

Concluding Thoughts   It should be clear by now that there is no simple one-to-one correspondence between technological advance and progress in terms of freedom, justice, and happiness. In fact, one may well ask whether technological advance has not proven to be a bitch goddess, luring societies into evolutionary paths where the costs often outweigh the benefits.

Had human history come to an end several hundred years ago, one would have been forced to answer affirmatively. During the last hundred years, however, technological advance has begun to make a positive contribution to the attainment of humanity's higher goals. Whether or not this will continue in the future is another question. We can say this, however: technology has at last brought into the realm of *the possible* a social order with greater freedom, justice, and happiness than any society has yet known.

Whatever our judgment about the wisdom of our species' pursuit of technological advance, one thing is clear: *for the evolution of human societies as a whole, technological advance can be equated with progress only in the restricted sense of growth in the store of cultural information, and the consequences of its use.*

Looking Ahead

For thousands of years, hoping for a glimpse into the future, people turned to shamans and oracles, prophets and astrologers. Despite the sorry record of predictions made by such people, interest in the subject has not abated. Never, in fact, has it been greater than in modern industrial societies, as evidenced by the many books and articles on the subject.

The reason for this concern is clear: culture makes us aware of the relation between the present and the future, and the increased pace of change in recent decades has heightened our concern with that relationship. But despite our desire to see into the future, and our need to do so, prediction remains a hazardous business. Only a hundred years ago, for example, Friedrich Engels wrote that warfare had reached the point where no significant advances in weapons could be expected. As he put it, "The era of evolution is therefore, in essentials, closed in this direction."[5]

There have been so many unsuccessful attempts to forecast the future that prediction might appear to be entirely a matter of luck. Successful prediction does, in fact, always involve an element of luck, for the future depends on the interaction of so many factors that no one can possibly assess them all correctly. Besides, a single critical factor in a situation may be so poorly understood that it upsets the most carefully reasoned analysis of the others. This is the case, for example, with certain aspects of the biophysical environment, on which all life depends. We simply do not have the ability to predict such things as natural shifts in climate (i.e., not caused by human activity) or the emergence of new and deadly viruses.

As we attempt to see what lies ahead for human societies, there are three basic guidelines we need to keep in mind. First, the shorter the time interval involved in a prediction, the greater the chance of success. Predicting events far in the future greatly increases the probability that some important but unforeseeable factor will intervene and completely upset one's calculations. It also increases the chance that minor errors will be compounded, through repetition, into major ones. The safest predictions, therefore, concern the immediate future. But these are also the least interesting and the least valuable. Because of this inverse relationship between accuracy and value, it makes sense to concentrate on predictions geared to *an intermediate time span.*

Second, the subject on which we can usually speak with the greatest confidence when discussing the future, especially the next twenty-five to fifty years, concerns *the problems societies will face.* The serious, unsolved problems of societies today will almost surely continue to be problems in the years ahead.

Third, and finally, the more thoroughly a prediction is *grounded in an analysis of the past and present,* the better its chance of success. This means we should not simply extrapolate current trends into the future. Rather, we must seek to discover the conditions that gave rise to each trend and the forces that sustained it—or caused it to waver or accelerate—so that we can anticipate reversals in trends and other shifts. For example, the birthrate in the United States dropped 40 percent during a twenty-year period, beginning in the late 1950s, but it would be as irresponsible simply to project that trend over the next 30 years as it would be to ignore it.

Applying the first of these guidelines, we will focus our analysis of the future on the next quarter century. This takes us beyond the point where we can simply say, "Things will still be pretty much the way they are today," yet it does not get us into the realm of science fiction or pure speculation. Applying the second guideline, we will devote much of our attention to the most serious problems facing the world system of societies today: the threat of nuclear war, uncontrolled population growth, energy needs, and environmental abuse. Finally, applying our third guideline, we will base our predictions of societal change on our analysis of sociocultural evolution up to the present, giving special attention to changes in technology, ideology, the biophysical environment, population, political and economic institutions, and the social environment.

This approach does not allow us to make flat, unqualified predictions of the kind that everyone would like. Rather, it leads to statements that say that, under conditions X, Y, and Z, outcome A is more likely than B, which in turn is more likely than C. The virtue of discussing the future in this way is that it puts the assumptions on which predictions are based out in the open where other people can examine them, and challenge or modify them as new information or insights become available. This should, in time, lead to progressively better predictions about human societies.

Prospects: Technology

Technological advance has been the most important factor in shaping the evolution of the world system in the past, and there is little reason to doubt that it will continue to be of major, perhaps paramount, importance in coming decades. Many of the most pressing problems of societies today have stimulated searches for technological solutions, and the new technologies that result will almost certainly give rise to social and cultural changes of many kinds.

Rate of Change   Benjamin Franklin once said that nothing is certain in this world but death and taxes. Were he alive today, he might add technological advance. A prediction of continuing advance at an accelerating rate does not depend simply on an extrapolation of the current trend. The basic factors responsible for the trend—the magnitude of the existing store of information, the great size of societal populations, and the amount of communication between societies—are still operative, and give every indication of providing even stronger impetus to innovation in the future than they do today. Furthermore, advanced industrial societies are engaging, for the first time in history, in a systematic, large-scale pursuit of new information. Investments in scientific and technological research and development have grown immensely, while computers and other devices that increase our ability to acquire, analyze, and process data add their own impetus to the rate of change.

The only thing that seems likely to slow the rate of technological innovation during the next several decades is a nuclear holocaust. War between the United States and the Soviet Union could easily mean the end of industrial societies, and even of human life itself. The rate of innovation could also be slowed by an acute energy shortage, since most of the activities on which modern technological innovation depends require large quantities of relatively cheap energy. But while energy shortages are possible in the next quarter century, they are not likely to be so acute that resources cannot be found for essential activities, including technological research and development.

Content of Change   The development of new sources of energy is one area in which advanced industrial societies have an enormous stake. Their way of life requires access to vast and ever-increasing quantities of energy. Unfortunately, however, many of these societies are poorly endowed with energy resources except for coal, and heavy use of coal is already creating serious environmental problems.

There are, of course, substantial supplies of petroleum and natural gas in the Middle East and some other parts of the Third World. But dependence on these sources is risky: wars and revolutions in those areas can quickly reduce the available supply with little warning, and even those supplies will begin to decline before long. According to a major U.S. government study, *The Global 2000 Report to the President,* world production of petroleum will be forced to decline before the year 2000 as the reserves in more and more fields are depleted.[6]

If this happens, the cost of this vital resource will rise sharply once again, just as it did in the 1970s. The only reason this is not already happening is because the sharp price increases of the 1970s led to a massive shift from the use of oil to the use of coal and because of the discovery of several important new oil fields (especially the North Sea and north shore Alaskan fields). These developments have temporarily altered the balance of supply and demand enough to bring prices down and to create a false sense of security. But the basic problem remains: there is only a limited quantity of petroleum available but a limitless demand for energy. Thus, before long petroleum will again be in short supply and prices will rise. When petroleum prices rise, other energy prices will probably follow as they did in the 1970s. And when this happens, the cost of living will rise and living standards will decline for many people, since energy costs are such an important part of the total cost of almost everything we use.

As noted above, the sharp price increases in petroleum in the 1970s led to massive conversions from the use of oil to the use of coal, especially in the production of electricity. Supplies of coal are far more abundant than supplies of petroleum and there is no danger of their exhaustion for a number of centuries at least.[7] Unfortunately, most of the coal that is available gives off large quantities of sulfur dioxide, nitrogen oxide, and carbon dioxide when it is burned. These chemicals have already caused serious damage to forests and to buildings, bridges, and other structures. But another, even more serious effect of the increased use of coal seems likely: the buildup of carbon dioxide (CO_2) in the atmosphere may alter the earth's climate in a dangerous way (see Prospects: the Biophysical Environment below). The burning of fossil fuels of all kinds has already increased the level of CO_2 in the atmosphere by 10 percent since the start of the industrial era, and the rate of increase should rise even more rapidly in the years ahead as the result of a shift from oil to coal, because coal emits 25 percent more CO_2 per unit of energy consumed than oil.[8] This suggests that, while coal will become increasingly important in the years ahead, it will not provide a long-term solution to the world's energy needs unless means can be found for controlling its harmful side effects.

In recent years, scientists and engineers have conducted a wide-ranging search for new energy sources that would reduce societies' dependence on fossil fuels. Among the possibilities that have been, or are being, explored are nuclear fission and fusion, solar energy, geothermal energy (i.e., energy derived from heat deep beneath the earth's surface), wind power, ocean wave power, shale oil, coal gasification, liquid hydrogen derived from water, manure and garbage (a source of methane gas), and just plain trash. Except for nuclear fission, none of these technologies is yet available at competitive costs for mass use, though some, such as solar energy, geothermal energy, wind and wave power, and trash and garbage, are already in use on a limited basis. Although some of these possibilities will eventually prove impractical or uneconomical, it will be surprising if one or more of them does not contribute significantly to the energy needs of societies in the twenty-first century.

Another major effort that will continue in the years ahead is the development of machines that use energy more efficiently. At present, the average *energy end-use efficiency* of the various technologies in use in industrial societies is estimated to be only 10 percent.[9] In other words, 90 percent of the energy is wasted (e.g., in the generation of heat by equipment intended to provide light) or consumed in the production and transmission of energy to the ultimate consumer. While anything approaching 100 percent efficiency will never be possible, even small improvements would be significant. If the efficiency of energy-using machines in the United States could be raised from the current 10 percent to just 11 percent, for example, this would free almost the amount of energy required today to power all American automobiles.[10] And if such improvements were adopted by other societies throughout the world, it would be the equivalent of the discovery of a major new energy source.

A recent study of energy use concluded that one-fourth of the energy currently consumed in manufacturing processes in the United States, or one-tenth of the nation's total energy consumption, could be saved merely by applying technologies that are already available, and at costs no greater than would be offset by the energy savings. For example, many of the heating processes required for the manufacture of metals, ceramics, glass, and cement are carried out in furnaces at very high temperatures. Exhaust gases from these furnaces, which currently go unused, could be employed to generate electricity. The history of modern technology provides us with ample grounds for optimism about the prospect for increasing the energy efficiency of many existing technologies. Figure 14.2 shows the steady improvement that has been achieved in the efficiency of both steam engines and forms of lighting, and the same could be demonstrated for other technologies as well.

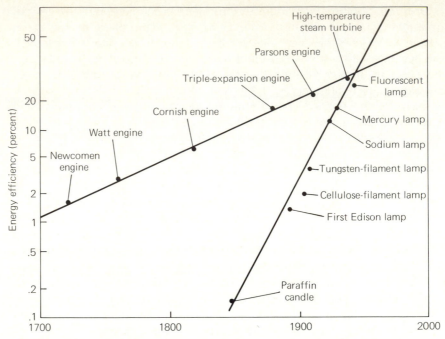

FIGURE 14.2 Increasing energy efficiency in two areas of modern technology: steam engines and illumination. Note that a logarithmic scale is used to plot energy efficiency in this diagram; if an ordinary linear scale were used, the trends would be much more pronounced.

Pollution of the environment, like the depletion of resources, will also provide a spur for technological innovation during the next twenty-five years. Some of these efforts will be directed toward the development of devices which more effectively control undesirable emissions from industry and other sources into the air, water, and soil. Other efforts will be aimed at developing more economical ways to recycle the refuse of societies that produce so many goods that quickly become obsolete. It should be possible during the next few decades to build profitable plants that not only burn waste to generate energy but also recover recyclable resources: iron, aluminum, glass, rubber, paper. Heat, too, is a pollutant, and methods of recycling it will not only save energy but benefit the environment.

Safer disposal of toxic substances will be another focus of research. Untold millions of containers of radioactive water, nerve gas, and other lethal materials are already buried or stored in unsafe containers. Scientists have recently made a breakthrough with respect to one of these problems: the disposal of plutonium, an extremely hazardous waste product of nuclear reactors that remains radioactive for thousands of years.[11] By slighting altering a molecule that occurs naturally in living organisms, they have devised a chemical means for removing plutonium from the wastewater in which it is stored, rendering it far more compact and thus much easier to dispose of. Similar techniques can probably be devised to aid in the safer handling of other hazardous wastes.

Another area in which there may be important technological innovations in the next quarter century is *population control*. Although the technology for limiting population growth is already available, the members of many societies have been slow to accept it, as we have seen. It is clear that ideological and economic changes will have to occur before the seriousness of this problem lessens appreciably, but the development of cheaper, safer, simpler, and more reliable methods of contraception, sterilization, and abortion would speed the process. For example, one new technique currently being tested is the administration of ovulation-controlling hormones by injection. Some women in Third World nations appear to be much more receptive to shots administered by medical personnel than to pills or devices they use at home.

The current effort to find technological solutions for *hunger*, which is so widespread in the Third World, will continue unabated in the years ahead. Although this problem is primarily the result of uncontrolled population growth in these societies, as we have seen (see Table 13.6, page 384), it is aggravated by dietary patterns in industrial societies. The heavy consumption of meat by the members of advanced societies has necessitated increased production of grain for livestock feed. Since 1 calorie of food energy derived from meat requires approximately 7 calories of grain to produce,[12] the average American today effectively consumes about 2,000 pounds of grain per year, compared to the 400 pounds consumed by the average person in a society with a predominantly cereal diet.[13]

At the present time, there are a number of new technologies at various stages of development that promise to increase the world's food supply. One of these, fish farming, is already in operation in several societies and promises to provide an increased supply of high-quality protein at relatively low cost.[14] Another promising innovation is soilless cultivation, which involves a recycled mixture of water and nutrients that is sprayed on the roots of plants suspended in frames. Developed in Israel, this technique should greatly increase food production in arid and semiarid areas. A bit further down the road, the new technology of recombinant DNA (see page 412) will probably provide new and improved strains of plants and animals.

As important as such advances may be, most agricultural experts believe that increases in the world's food supply during the next quarter century will come primarily from the diffusion of technologies already available. During one recent decade, 40 percent of the increase in food production in 90 industrializing societies came solely from the increased use of fertilizers, and much of the rest came from the diffusion of other older technologies.[15] This pattern seems likely to continue during the next quarter century.

The most depressing aspect of technological innovation is the amount of money and effort that will be invested in *weapons* research and development in the years ahead. The leaders of advanced societies argue that this is necessary for their defense; and it is true, of course, that military technology has been the major determinant of societal survival in the past. The situation today, however, is one in which the two nations already most advanced in this technology are in a race to keep ahead of one another, with the result that there is a relentless growth in the potential for mutual extermination—or even extinction of the entire human population.

Unless there is a major breakthrough in arms control negotiations in the years immediately ahead, we can continue to expect that any significant innovation by either the United States or the Soviet Union will serve to enhance the sense of urgency on the other's part to restore the balance. The areas in which innovative efforts by the major powers will probably be concentrated include the development of planes and missiles capable of eluding detection; the development of satellites and other monitors better able to detect and destroy attacking planes or missiles; improvements in nuclear weapons that make their limited use more feasible (e.g., the neutron bomb, which harms only people but leaves things intact); the development of new biochemical weapons, such as nerve gases, as well as better equipment for protecting military personnel from them; and the development of anti-missile weapons, such as laser beams and killer satellites. Nor will military technology be advanced only by the two major powers. Other societies are also active in devising improved weapons.

Another area in which we can expect technological innovations of major significance is in *the application of the computer and microcircuitry (i.e., the silicon chip) to new industrial tasks*. As we mentioned in Chapter 9, computers have already been devised to guide "smart robots" in spot-welding and other tasks in automobile assembly plants. Like other fundamental innovations, this one will undoubtedly be adapted for use in thousands of similar operations in a variety of industries, although the time frame for the widespread adoption of a technology which replaces so much human labor will probably be affected by such factors as the amount of unemployment in a society and the attitudes of labor leaders and other elites.

Microcircuitry's potential for a wide variety of nonindustrial applications is equally clear. By substituting microcircuitry for mechanical parts, a manufacturer of cash registers reduced the number of parts in its product from about 5,000 to several hundred. This, in turn, led to a reduction in the number of workers on its assembly line from about 400 to 15 or 20—an even more drastic reduction in labor than that achieved by the automobile industry's use of "smart robots."[16]

Yet another fundamental innovation with revolutionary potential for human societies in the next quarter century is the new technology of *recombinant DNA*. In the last few years, geneticists have learned how to remove a bit of genetic material from the cell of one kind of organism and implant it in the cell of another species. This new technology is particularly fascinating from the perspective of ecological-evolutionary theory, for it marks *a new stage in our species' capacity for handling information*. Until recently, the only information we could manipulate and recombine was cultural information. Now we can use the genetic alphabet in the same way (although only to a very limited extent so far) to create combinations of genetic information which do not exist in nature and which can serve as tools for accomplishing human purposes.

So far, most applications of recombinant DNA technology involve the transplantation of genes that govern the production of rare proteins from the cells of slower-breeding animals, including humans, into the cells of bacteria. These organisms grow and divide so rapidly that a single bacterium can produce 100 trillion identical cells in 24 hours, each one containing at least 100 molecules of the desired protein.[17] In this way, large quantities of rare and valuable chemicals can be produced at minimal cost.

The potential applications of recombinant DNA technology appear to be vast, but so far it has become important primarily in medicine. Diabetics, for example, do not produce enough insulin in their own pancreases and must rely on insulin derived from the glands of slaughtered cows and pigs. But it requires approximately 8,000 pounds of these pancreases to produce a single pound of insulin, and there has been grave concern that future supplies will prove inadequate to meet the needs of the growing number of diabetics in the world population. Now, bacteria-produced insulin is being tested on human subjects and will probably be produced commercially in the near future.[18]

Interferon is another chemical produced in the human body, but in minute amounts. Its function is to protect cells from the invasion of viruses, and it appears to have the potential for treating a broad spectrum of viral diseases, as well as some forms of cancer. It also enables the body to withstand larger and more effective doses of other anti-cancer drugs. Currently, interferon is produced by extracting it from human cells grown in the laboratory, with the result that it is enormously expensive (the amount required to treat a single cancer patient costs well over $10,000) and research is severely limited.[19] With recombinant DNA, the supply may become plentiful and the cost could plummet, thus allowing large-scale testing of this potential new wonder drug.

No one can say with any certainty just how the revolutionary new technology of recombinant DNA will develop, or where it will ultimately lead. Already in 1980, patents were pending for new forms of bacteria that can metabolize ethylene into ethylene glycol (antifreeze) and ethylene oxide (the basic component of plastics); for two new forms of wheat, one requiring only 10 percent of the water that wheat normally requires, the other providing twice the protein of ordinary wheat; for "bugs" that convert oil spills into harmless biodegradable materials; and for bacteria which produce an enzyme that eats away the salts in low-grade copper ore, leaving behind almost pure copper.[20] As the final example suggests, this new technology has a potential for saving energy by replacing traditional industrial operations that consume fuels with processes that are largely biochemical.

Many other kinds of technological innovations can also be expected during the next quarter century. Substantial resources are being invested in medical research of various kinds, including efforts to cure genetic diseases, such as sickle-cell anemia. Striking advances have recently been made in communications, data processing, and office automation, and further advances in these areas should be only a matter of time. In addition, it is very possible that some unanticipated breakthrough, comparable to the silicon chip or recombinant DNA, will lay the foundation, as all fundamental innovations do, for a host of new applications.

Prospects: Ideology

Ideology may well play an even greater role in human societies in the next quarter century than it has in the recent past. This larger role is possible because, as we noted in our retrospective summary of industrial societies (see page 358), technological advance and the resulting growth of the economic surplus have provided societies today with a far wider range of options than they had in the past. Thanks to advances made during recent decades, the "range of the possible" has come to include, along with greater freedom and happiness, basic and irreversible damage to the global ecosystem, the devastation of dozens of human societies in a matter of days or hours, and even the destruction of humanity itself. It is obvious that when technology makes so many things possible, the beliefs and values that guide people in using it become a critical factor in the process of sociocultural evolution.

To say that ideology is becoming a more important factor in sociocultural evolution does not mean there will be drastic or dramatic changes in ideology itself in the next several decades. In ideology, as in technology, change is usually gradual. Thus, except in societies that experience serious social upheaval or revolution, we can expect more ideological continuity than change. Most of the more influential belief systems today, together with most of their related norms and values, will continue to be influential. Certainly Christianity, Islam, Buddhism, capitalism, democracy, democratic socialism, revolutionary socialism, and nationalism will retain the loyalties of tens of millions of people and influence the actions of those in positions of power.

When ideological changes do occur in the decades ahead, pragmatism is likely to gain at the expense of the more inflexible and doctrinaire ideologies. As we have seen, this trend is already in evidence as ideologies have lost much of the aura of the "sacred" that once helped them to resist change. Ideological innovation and selection have become much more a matter of purposive creation and conscious choice than in the past, especially in the western industrial democracies.

The movement toward greater pragmatism is also evident, however, in industrializing societies and in societies that profess to be socialist. In China, for example, as we have seen, many of the institutional arrangements traditionally associated with socialism have been abandoned and replaced with others that seem more likely to contribute to economic growth. As noted in the last chapter, the Communist Party's official newspaper recently declared that the Chinese people should not look any longer to the writings of Marx and Lenin for answers to problems, since those men never encountered or wrote about the kinds of problems China is now facing.[21] Today, China's new "Marxist" elite seeks to achieve economic growth by such strikingly un-Marxist policies as the revival of private enterprise, the encouragement of greater economic inequality, and a rigorous program of population control. Similar pragmatic tendencies, though seldom so pronounced, are found increasingly in other societies, both capitalist and socialist.[22] The chief exceptions have been postrevolutionary societies, such as Khomeini's Iran or Pol Pot's Kampuchea, which is not surprising since revolutions, by their very nature, encourage fanaticism and tend to bring extremists to power. Shiite Muslim societies in general are another important exception.

One doctrinaire ideology that may spread in the decades ahead is dependency theory, which, as we saw in the last chapter, blames the ills of the Third World on the western industrial democracies. This ideology has proven extremely useful to the leaders of many industrializing societies. At home, it deflects criticism from the leaders and from flawed policies; abroad, it stimulates feelings of guilt among some influential members of more affluent societies and thus encourages the flow of economic aid. In addition, dependency theory helps to create a sense of solidarity among industrializing societies whose interests are otherwise often in conflict, and solidarity can be advantageous in international forums, such as the United Nations.

Further evidence of the trend toward more conscious, purposive development of systems of belief is the enormous ideological diversity that has emerged within many societies in recent years, largely in response to culturally activated and intensified needs. In the United States, for example, these newer ideologies include everything from neo-Nazism to various versions of revolutionary socialism, from transcendental meditation to Protestant fundamentalism, from pro- to anti-abortionism, and a host of others. These systems of beliefs, values, and norms reflect the great abundance of resources and the broad range of options that are available to the members of advanced societies today, especially to members of the industrial democracies.

There is little reason to expect that ideological diversity will decline in these societies in the next several decades, particularly in those that place the greatest value on individualism and freedom of expression. But it will undoubtedly continue to be a source of social problems, as it is today. Problems are inevitable when so many diverse, and often contradictory, beliefs find expression within a single society. Perhaps the most serious problem of all, however, is that it is becoming increasingly difficult for the leaders of democratic societies to establish broadly acceptable goals and policies when their members have such different motivations, and when so many of the newer ideologies place great emphasis on the rights and needs of individuals while ignoring their responsibility to the society of which they are part.

In the years ahead, ideological diversity will pose an even greater threat to societies that are trying to industrialize, because they must cope with so many other problems. It will be especially serious in societies that must contend not only with divisive new ideologies (e.g., those of political and economic movements and women's movements) but with major ethnic or religious differences inherited from the past. Unless an authoritarian regime is able to impose a dominant "unifying" ideology on the entire population, as the Communist Party has done in China, for example, the prospects for industrialization by societies so divided internally (e.g., Turkey, India) seem poor indeed.

Prospects: Biophysical Environment

During the next twenty-five years there will almost certainly be changes in the biophysical environment that will be of importance to human societies. Some will be the result of natural catastrophes, such as earthquakes, volcanic eruptions, and major storms. But others will be caused by the use of modern industrial technology, and it is these that are likely to have the greatest impact on human societies.

Such a prediction would not have been possible throughout most of human history. For the first several million years, human societies simply adapted to environmental conditions; they could do nothing to alter them. Then, late in the hunting and gathering era, advances in weapons technology enabled societies to make their first irreversible alteration in the biophysical environment, when hunters apparently destroyed a considerable number of species of large animals.

Following the horticultural revolution, societies gradually began making changes on the earth's surface, clearing forests and planting gardens in their place. Although the balance of nature was affected wherever this happened, the impact was not great, because horticulturalists usually had to move every few years and their abandoned gardens reverted to wilderness. The agrarian revolution, however, changed this. Fields became permanent and cultivated land no longer reverted to forests, while larger populations took increasing amounts of minerals and other natural resources from the earth. Even so, the impact of human societies on the environment was still limited.

Industrial technology, in contrast, has enabled human societies to change the biophysical environment in completely unprecedented ways. The landscape has been so drastically rearranged that large areas that once teemed with life have been virtually destroyed. Complex ecosystems that required tens of millions of years to evolve have been damaged beyond repair in a matter of decades. The earth has been plundered of many of its resources, some of them seriously depleted. Vast quantities of toxic matter have been poured into the earth's atmosphere and into its great bodies of water. Some experts now predict that as much as a fifth of all the species of plants and animals alive in 1980—some 500,000 to 2 million of them—may be extinct by the year 2000 as a consequence of pollution and loss of habitat.[23]

Environmentalists have been warning for years that our biophysical environment is vulnerable, that it does not have an unlimited capacity for renewing itself. Yet even as we have heard the warnings, our demands on the environment have risen at a fantastic rate. Between 1950 and 1985, an infinitesimal period of time by geological standards, the gross world product rose from approximately $1.5 trillion to $9 trillion. If we consider what this means in terms of our impact on the environment, no future crises will surprise us. For the simple fact is that the biophysical environment can sustain neither an infinite growth of the human population nor the endless demands of an advancing technology.

This is why it is difficult to be optimistic about the state of the environment during the decades immediately ahead. Barring a nuclear holocaust, the human population will probably increase by at least 2 billion during the next quarter century,[24] while simultaneously the technology of the world system becomes increasingly industrialized. Merely providing for the survival needs of that many more people will put a formidable strain on an already overworked environment. But at the same time, the factories of industrializing societies will be demanding ever greater quantities of raw materials, and their members ever more material products as they struggle to raise their standards of living. Nor is it reasonable to expect that the governments of those hard-pressed societies will rank environmental protection as a high priority.

What we *can* expect during the next quarter century, therefore, is new abuses of the environment by societies whose impact in the past has been relatively minor, and that these abuses will aggravate already serious problems on the global level. We can see how this will happen by considering a problem that is already of concern to scientists: the buildup of carbon dioxide in the earth's atmosphere. Too great a concentration of this gas would trap so much of the sun's heat that a "greenhouse effect" would result, causing a warming trend on the earth's surface. Some experts now predict an increase in average global temperature of 2 to 6 degrees Fahrenheit by the early to middle decades of the next century.[25] This would have devastating consequences for agriculture in some regions and would probably melt the polar icecaps, causing the flooding of many major cities and coastal regions.

The reason for the growing amount of carbon dioxide in the atmosphere is that more of it is being released than can be handled by natural mechanisms—the leaves of green plants and the oceans and lakes that absorb it. Societies are currently producing 20 billion tons of carbon dioxide every year, and, as they turn to greater use of coal, the problem can only grow worse.[26] What is more, lakes, oceans, and forests are themselves vulnerable and will apparently be able to handle even less carbon dioxide in the future than they do now. Although forests have been leveled in the past, it is now happening at an unprecedented rate. In their search for affordable energy and new acreage for farming, many Third World societies are destroying vast forest regions, leaving many of them unfit either for cultivation or for reforestation. It is now expected that 40 percent of the forests that still remain in the poorer nations will no longer exist in the year 2000.[27]

The loss of these forests will have consequences that go well beyond the greater pollution of the atmosphere and the loss of species that we noted earlier. It will also contribute to the accelerating deterioration and loss of the resources that developing societies so desperately need, both for agriculture and for industrialization. The depletion of forests will aggravate problems of flooding, cause siltation in streams and rivers, deplete groundwater, and create water shortages. To make matters worse, it is estimated that the world's need for fresh (i.e., not sea) water will triple in the final third of this century, with the majority of the increase needed for irrigation.[28] Meanwhile, an area the size of Maine becomes desert, and unsuitable for agriculture, every year. If this trend continues until 2000, there will be almost 20 percent more desert on our planet than there was in 1975.

Growing world population, increasing industrialization, and energy needs are not the only reasons for predicting growing problems with the environment. Another cause for concern is that so many elements of industrial technology are adopted before their full potential for harm can be determined. Just as societies of the past could not predict that the burning of fossil fuels would lead to a potentially dangerous buildup of carbon dioxide in the atmosphere, so contemporary societies are adopting practices that could produce serious, but still largely unsuspected, problems. No one can predict, for example, what the ecological consequences will be if higher levels of radiation are produced through continued nuclear weapons testing, or by a major accident in one or more of the world's 250 nuclear power plants—to say nothing of the fallout from nuclear warfare. Toxic chemicals are another largely unknown quantity. Because they are of such diverse kinds, have been so widely used, and are often so poorly stored or disposed of, chemical pollution could do far greater environmental and ecological damage in the near future than it has in the past. Among those substances, for example, are vast quantities of lethal nerve gases that are stored in containers vulnerable to decay, earth tremors, and accidents. In short, a big question mark must be inserted into any predictions about the biophysical environment, since it could already contain the seeds of a major disaster.

Another thing that makes it difficult to be optimistic about the state of the environment during the next twenty-five years is the response of advanced societies during the last twenty-five. Industrial societies are the ones that can best afford to develop and adopt new technologies to protect the soil, water, and air and help safeguard the finite store of resources on which they depend. Yet their responses have been fairly limited, and often dictated solely by short-term economic considerations.

Industrial societies will almost certainly become more active in this area in the years ahead, however. As the full impact of modern technology on the environment and the dynamics of the process become increasingly clear, so will the costs of continued neglect of the problem. Thus, we can expect that these societies will begin to weigh more carefully the hidden costs (e.g., illness, genetic damage, loss of farmland) and that they will also come to recognize that it is far more costly to rectify environmental damage than to prevent it in the first place.

Another reason industrial societies will probably become more environmentally concerned in the next quarter century is that growing scarcity in a number of natural resources will serve to make them more valuable economically. This should lead to greater conservation efforts—not only of energy and minerals but of wood and water as well. Conservation will involve far greater emphasis on *recycling*—of heat, of water, of wood, and of minerals. Recycling often produces multiple benefits. Not only does it reduce the quantity of materials that must be taken from the environment, it often saves energy as well (e.g., it takes only 4 percent as much energy to produce recycled aluminum as to produce "new" aluminum from bauxite ore) and reduces air and water pollution (e.g., the recycling of steel is estimated to cut air pollution 86 percent, and water pollution 76 percent).[29]

Recycling and other techniques for reducing the harmful impact of human societies on the environment will require substantial capital expenditures, and therefore it is unlikely that they will be widely adopted in industrializing societies. Although there have been some encouraging signs (China, for example, closed several plants causing pollution, and heavily fined another[30]), pollution and a host of other environmental problems are certain to become far worse in the Third World during the years ahead. With respect to industrial societies, there is no reason to believe that they, even with their new technologies, will *remove* more pollutants, contaminants, and hazardous materials from the biophysical environment during the next quarter century than they put into it. Thus, we can predict that, even without a nuclear disaster, the environment will deteriorate seriously before societies can effect a reversal of that trend.

Prospects: Population

As our analysis of the prospects for the biophysical environment makes plain, population growth during the decades ahead poses an ominous threat to the entire world system of societies. If our numbers continue to swell at the current rate, there will be 7.5 billion people by the year 2010. Even if we base our prediction on the optimistic assumption that there will be major shifts in public policy in the Third World that significantly increase access to family planning and lead to a substantial decline in fertility, there will still be at least 7 billion of us in another quarter century. If we look a little further into the future (again being optimistic in our assumptions), we can expect a global population of nearly 10 billion by 2030, and 28.5 billion by the end of the twenty-first century![31] The year 2030 is well within the expected life span of the majority of today's college students, so it is interesting to note that a National Academy of Science group believes that a population of 10 billion is "close to (if not above) the maximum that an *intensively managed* world might hope to support with some degree of comfort and individual choice."[32]

What will it mean to see the population climb from 4.8 to 7 billion or more in just 25 years? For one thing, it will mean that world population will increase by about 100 million *every year*. It will mean that the world system will have to find enough new resources to support the equivalent of two more Chinas in a very short amount of time. Since these additional people must all be fed with little or no increase in the amount of arable land available, it will mean far greater use of fertilizers, insecticides, and water.[33] In addition to the added strain this will place on the environment, it will almost certainly increase the cost of food worldwide. It may also mean an enormous increase in the number of hungry and malnourished individuals, because, despite predictions that the increased use of fertilizers and other technological advances will provide slightly more food per capita, it does not follow that food will be more equally distributed than it is today. The World Bank predicts the number of malnourished people in the Third World (where more than 90 percent of the population growth will occur) could rise from the estimated 500 million of the mid-1970s to 1.3 billion in 2000.[34]

Because of advances in agricultural technology, and because of rural overcrowding in Third World societies, most of the additional 2.2 to 2.7 billion people will be forced to live in cities. Overcrowding in urban areas, which is already a serious problem, will thus become far worse during the years ahead, and so will the attendant problems of poverty, disease, crime, and social unrest. Calcutta's population, for example, is expected to increase from its current 10 million to 20 million by 2000, and Mexico City's from 16 million to 32 million.[35] And most of this growth will occur in their already enormous and overcrowded slums.

It is obvious that our species' population growth must be halted at some point, and it is equally obvious that the consequences will grow more serious with every year that passes before this happens. Even if every couple in the world had no more than two children from now on, world population would continue to clinb for many years, simply because the combination of high birthrates and low death rates in the last two decades has given us today a world population with a disproportionate number of young people. In the case of Mexico, for example, more than half of its population is under 20 years of age. If we assume that 15 percent of the individuals in that age group will have no children and that the rest will produce only two per couple, Mexico's population will still rise from its present 82 million to 123 million before it levels off—assuming there is no increase in life expectancy. If life expectancy also increases, as it almost certainly will, then the predicted ceiling will be higher than 123 million.[36] And for every year that elapses before Mexico adopts a

YOU HAVE TO ADMIT, THEY GOT THE PART RIGHT ABOUT BEING FRUITFUL AND MULTIPLYING.

© 1984 by NEA, Inc. TM Reg. U.S. Pat. & TM Off.   THAVES 1-11 stringent population policy—which is very unlikely in the near future—the higher that figure will go.

The most critical question for human societies today may well be, When will the nations of the Third World take steps to bring their population growth under control? Although this is impossible to predict, there are reasons to believe that a growing number of societies will take serious steps to that end during the next quarter century. For one thing, there has been a significant shift in the attitudes of the leaders of industrializing societies on the subject of family planning and population control, from nearly universal indifference or condemnation only twenty-five years ago to almost universal approval today.[37] By now, many of the leaders of industrializing societies have come to recognize the futility of trying to improve living standards when population is increasing so rapidly.

Recognition of the problem has done little to halt population growth thus far, however, because few Third World leaders have yet taken substantial action. Some are apparently reluctant, for ideological reasons, to intrude in this traditionally private area of life and place sanctions on their people's reproductive activities. They hope that increased education and gradually changing beliefs and values will be enough to halt population growth before the consequences become disastrous. Others are more realistic—and pessimistic—in their assessment of the situation, but avoid imposing sanctions because they fear the consequences of doing so. They have not forgotten that after Indira Gandhi's government mandated forcible sterilization on a limited scale, she was swept from office. So far, China has been the only major Third World nation to develop a rigorous program of population control that shows promise of halting growth within the next several decades.

It is difficult to believe that other Third World governments will not also begin to instigate more rigorous—even coercive—programs in the next decade, but how many do so, and how effective their efforts will be, will depend on a variety of factors whose relative strength is often difficult to assess. They include ideological factors, such as the extent to which the elite is influenced by either Marxism or Catholicism (both traditionally opposed to population control), and the extent of the elite's commitment to planning. They also include such factors as the extent of hunger and poverty within the society, the degree of political unrest and the strength of the elite, and the amount of pressure applied by outside forces. The latter, as we noted earlier, might be in the form of offers of economic aid made conditional on the development of a rigorous program of population control. Until now, most aid has been given with the sole purpose of keeping people alive—and able to reproduce. It is difficult to believe that well-intentioned donors will not soon perceive that such aid does no lasting good unless it is linked to a program designed to check runaway population growth.

Another demographic trend we can anticipate is increasing migration from the Third World to industrial societies. This trend is already well under way, as evidenced by the growing numbers of Mexicans, Haitians, other Latin Americans, and Asians who enter the United States, often illegally, every year. There has been a similar migration of Turks and Yugoslavs into West Germany (Berlin now has the second largest Turkish population of any city in the world, including those in Turkey); of Algerians into France; and of Indians, Pakistanis, and West Indians into Britain. It is even possible to envision the day when the indigenous populations of some industrial societies will become minorities in their own homelands, a circumstance that would almost certainly have explosive political consequences.

Prospects: Economy

Barring a nuclear holocaust, there will probably be continuing economic growth for the world system as a whole during the next quarter century. The wider application of techniques that are already known should so improve energy efficiency that increased productivity will be ensured, even when energy costs begin to rise again. In addition, there will almost certainly be further advances in this area, which should boost world production higher still.

It is important to note that this prediction is for a rising GWP (i.e., gross world product), *not for a rising standard of living for the world's people*. Whether living standards also rise will depend on the number of people who must share the fruits of the increased productivity. The projected rates of population growth combined with rising energy costs could well offset the effects of the rise in GWP, and thus prevent improvement in living standards for the world as a whole. And even if per capita GWP rises, it does not necessarily follow that per capita GNPs (gross national products) will rise in every society. Improvements are unlikely in most African societies, where runaway population growth threatens economic disaster and widespread starvation. Although the situation may be alleviated temporarily by international aid programs, the basic problems in these societies will persist until their leaders face up to the problems confronting them. Unfortunately, there is little sign of this in Africa in the mid-1980s.

Increasing productivity in *industrial* societies during the next few decades could prove disappointing to them as well, though for a different reason. The new technologies that will be responsible for much of their economic growth (e.g., automation, computerization) will reduce the need for labor at a time when the number of people of working age in these societies will be increasing. The United States, for example, will have 30 million more individuals between the ages of 22 and 65 in the year 2000 than it had in 1980.

Unless the western democracies take steps to spread work among more people, unemployment rates will rise substantially. This could lead to political unrest and a variety of other problems, regardless of whether the unemployed in these societies are left to fend for themselves or become part of an hereditary welfare class dependent on a working population that feels ill-used because it is taxed to support them. The rational solution would be to shorten the workweek, which has been done in the past: in 1890, the average workweek in manufacturing in the United States was 60 hours, today it is only 40. To reduce it further could mean regular employment for millions of people who would otherwise be chronically unemployed.

One economic trend that seems almost certain to continue is the increasing division of labor in the world economy. Since 1750, the volume of international trade has increased 1,000-fold, which reflects the extent to which economic specialization at the societal level has grown during that time. This trend, a consequence of technological advances that have drastically reduced the costs of moving goods, has been highly beneficial for the most part. Societies now export what they can produce more cheaply than other societies and import what they find more costly to produce.

The world economy, which is essentially a *capitalist* economy, has not been without its disadvantages, especially for societies that specialize in products whose value on the world market tends to fluctuate sharply. Yet even these societies have found this system more rewarding than trying to produce for themselves everything they need. For a few of these societies, the oil producers in particular, the system has worked enormously to their advantage, greatly enhancing their position in the world economy. In the long run, however, they will not be able to rely exclusively on this one highly profitable product, and their future in the world economy will come to depend on the extent to which they have used their oil profits to build a modern industrial economy.

During the next quarter century, economic ties among societies will probably grow even stronger than they are today. As this happens, societies will gradually lose more and more of their economic independence. At some point, many societies, perhaps most, will find that these economic ties have become so vital that they cannot be left vulnerable to disruption by international disputes or war. When this point is reached, it will provide an enormous boost to proposals for the creation of a single world government. Although there is little likelihood that a true world government will be established in the next several decades, it could occur later in the twenty-first century (see Prospects: The World System below).

Prospects: Polity

During the next quarter century, political elites will be confronted with a number of critical problems. Some of the most difficult decisions will be made by leaders of the Third World, as they struggle to industrialize while coping with growing populations, rising costs, and shortages of key resources. At the same time, the leaders of industrial societies will be facing problems created by declining rates of economic growth, rising energy costs, chronic inflation, and environmental pollution. Meanwhile, looming over the entire world system will be the gravest problem of all: the threat of a nuclear holocaust.

In societies that suffer from widespread poverty and chronic economic crises, democratic polities are unlikely to survive the stresses of the years ahead. Judging from the experience of the last few decades, we can expect to see some further increase in the number of revolutionary socialist governments. Promises of freedom, justice, and equality have great appeal to downtrodden people, and once Marxist-Leninist elites seize power, they are seldom dislodged.

Despite the likely increase in the number of Marxist-Leninist regimes, they will probably not form a cohesive bloc. Marxism is like sixteenth-century Protestantism in this respect: just as Protestantism divided along national lines in the sixteenth century, so Marxism has divided in the twentieth, with each national party organization jealous of its autonomy. Although the Soviet Union, by virtue of its military power, maintains control over most of the parties of Eastern Europe, and exercises a more limited control over Party organizations in some other societies through financial subsidies, the basic trend has been one of increasing fragmentation. This has happened not only to the Party structure but to ideology as well, and we can expect these trends to continue. During the next quarter century, the political and economic alliances formed between societies are likely to cut across the old cold-war division between Communists and anti-Communists with increasing frequency.

It is harder to predict political changes for industrial societies than for those of the Third World, because in politics, as in other areas of societal life, so many things are possible for societies with advanced technologies and enormous economic surpluses. New computer and electronic technologies, for example, can be used for wholly different political ends. Used one way, they could improve a population's access to information, increase its leisure, and provide it with the means to have greater input into the political process, all of which would enhance democratic trends. Alternatively, they could be used as electronic surveillance equipment and police data banks to encroach on individual freedom and move a society in a more authoritarian direction.

Which direction the western democracies and Japan move in coming decades will depend to a great extent on the severity of their problems and the effectiveness of their leaders in coping with them. If a democratic regime is unable to resolve the problems that are of the greatest concern to the majority of its citizens, or if the problems confronting the society become unexpectedly severe (e.g., as the result of an environmental disaster or serious civil strife), its members may become willing to exchange some of their freedoms for stronger leadership.

For the Marxist-Leninist societies of Eastern Europe, probabilities seem to favor a very gradual increase in democracy. This will depend, however, on the ability of these societies to avoid major economic or political crises, and on some relaxation in political tensions between the United States and the Soviet Union. Under these circumstances, a new generation of Soviet leaders may feel greater confidence in themselves and in their system and become less resistant to the democratic tendencies within their society. If this occurs in the Soviet Union, it will almost certainly occur in other Eastern European Marxist-Leninist societies as well.

Prospects: The World System

Discussion of this, the final factor responsible for producing change in sociocultural systems, had to be left until last. For when we ask, What changes are most likely to occur in the world system during the next few decades? we have to draw on all of our analysis up to this point, and once again our predictions apply only if a major war can be avoided.

First, there will probably be somewhat fewer societies in the world system in the year 2000 or 2010 than there are today. This is less likely to be the result of military conquest than of the consolidation of some smaller societies for economic reasons and the elimination of the few small, primitive societies that still survive. Second, we can expect the world system as a whole to become more advanced technologically during the time in question.

Third, the average size of societies will be larger than it is today. This will be primarily the consequence of demographic trends now in progress in industrializing societies, but it will also reflect the demise of some smaller societies. Fourth, the societies of the world system will be even more economically interdependent than they are today. Fifth, the world system will be, for all practical purposes, a smaller system than it is now, since continuing advances in transportation and communication will further shrink the effective size of our planet.

Sixth, the level of intersocietal tensions will almost certainly rise during the decades ahead. Even if relationships among the major powers improve, resource shortages and population pressures will probably lead to deteriorating relations among many other societies. For example, in an era of growing water shortages and rising water requirements, 200 of the world's major river basins are shared by at least two different societies. Seventh, and finally, the decades immediately ahead will find increasing numbers of societies capable of initiating, or becoming active participants in, a nuclear war.

In summary, when we try to envision the social environment of virtually any society in the years ahead, we find it consists of a set of societies that are *more advanced technologically, more populous, more interdependent, less stable, more threatened and more threatening, and closer to one another* than the societies that constitute its social environment today.

It is abundantly clear that any social system with the potential for disaster that is inherent in the present world system of societies *requires some kind of regulation if chaos and collapse are to be avoided.* Yet there is still no mechanism to effect such regulation, because there is no world government. Anarchy (i.e., the absence of effective government) has, of course, always prevailed at the level of the world system. But this was unavoidable in the technologically less advanced world of the past. More important, anarchy mattered less in a world system in which the range of the possible, for good and for ill, was so much more limited than it is today.

No one can say with any assurance what the effect of a major nuclear war between the superpowers would be; the new weapons are so revolutionary that they render obsolete most of what we have learned of war from conflicts of the past. Experts have estimated, however, that even a very limited exchange of nuclear missiles between the United States and the Soviet Union, an exchange confined entirely to attacks on one another's missile installations, would cause between 3.4 and 21.7 million fatalities in the United States alone.*[38] In addition, many millions more would be crippled, burned, and incapacitated by radiation sickness, and large numbers of them would succumb later.

If a Soviet attack were directed at America's industrial facilities and population centers, the number of casualties would be far greater. For example, a 20-megaton attack on Boston could be expected to kill at least 2.2 million people from the initial blast and the subsequent firestorm.[39] People would be burned to death over a radius of twenty miles or more.[40] Not a single building would be left standing within four miles of the blast, and only the strongest reinforced concrete buildings would survive within the next two miles.[41] Bomb shelters would become ovens and pressure cookers. If comparable attacks were launched against other major American cities, most of the nation's medical facilities would be destroyed and the economy com-

---

*The variation in these estimates depended on the size of the warheads used, whether they were exploded in the air or on the ground, and how the winds were blowing.

pletely disrupted. Those who managed to survive the holocaust would find themselves in a desperate race to erect a new life-sustaining system before available supplies of food and other essential materials were exhausted.

What would be the long-run consequences of such a war? No one really knows. We cannot even say whether our species would survive. Some scientists believe that cockroaches and other insects, which can sustain far larger doses of radiation than either humans or the birds that keep insect populations in check, would inherit the earth. And many scientists now predict that a major nuclear exchange would be followed by a prolonged winter brought about by clouds of dust thrown up into the atmosphere. These clouds would cut off the rays of the sun, killing most plants, and condemning most animals, including humans, to death by starvation.

Perhaps the best outcome would be the permanent regression of societies to the horticultural or agrarian level of development, a return, perhaps, to the level of the Middle Ages, with scattered bands of people competing for scarce resources. The path to reindustrialization at a future date would probably be blocked forever, because, in order for industrialization to begin again, there would have to be substantial quantities of raw materials that could be obtained by people using only preindustrial tools and machines. Yet with every passing year, the quantity of fuels and minerals close to the surface of the earth, or otherwise easily accessible, is depleted further, and societies are forced to obtain these vital resources by methods that presuppose a high level of industrialization (e.g., setting up offshore oil rigs, smelting large quantities of low-grade ore).[42]

Faced as we are with such a threat, the obvious solution would seem to be the creation of a world government which would not interfere with the internal affairs of societies, but which would have the authority, the mechanisms, and the sanctions necessary to monitor the production of military weapons and control their use. Although it would be enormously difficult to develop such a polity, it would be possible if the governments of all or most industrial and industrializing societies want it badly enough.

One of the most difficult problems in such an endeavor stems from the great differences in economic development and standards of living between industrial and Third World societies. Recently, for example, per capita income in the United States was nearly $12,500 per year, while for the world as a whole it was only about $2,700 per year.[43] Efforts to include Third World societies in a world polity would almost certainly be met by demands for a significant redistribution of world wealth and income. In exchange for their cooperation (e.g., permission to monitor military installations), industrializing societies would probably insist upon substantial economic concessions. But this could easily kill the enthusiasm for world government by members of industrial societies. For if world income were distributed equally among the world's societies, per capita income would be reduced by nearly 80 percent in the United States, for example, causing a decline in living standards to *one-fifth* their current level.

Although this is hardly an attractive prospect, some less extreme version of income redistribution might eventually be agreed on. Even if it still seemed harsh to advanced societies, they might consider it preferable to the continuing threat of nuclear warfare and its aftermath. If there is to be a viable compromise in the years ahead, however, governments should begin soon to narrow the economic gap between societies. Incentives should be provided to industrializing societies to bring population growth to an end, so that standards of living can be improved, and industrial societies may have to sacrifice some of their own potential growth to provide these incentives and to reduce the gap between haves and have-nots. At present, however, the prospects for such action by the governments of industrial societies seem little better than the prospects for an end to population growth in the Third World.

Somewhat more likely in the next few decades is a gradual strengthening of the United Nations, the closest thing to a world polity that now exists. The greatest obstacle to the effectiveness of that organization is probably the system of representation in the General Assembly, which provides an equal vote for the People's Republic of China, with its population of more than a billion people, and for the Democratic Republic of São Tomé and Principe, which has only 90,000. The special powers vested in the Security Council, the veto power in particular, partly compensate for this, but the present organizational structure of the United Nations as a whole does not generate much confidence on the part of larger and more powerful nations.

Substantial changes will probably be needed if the United Nations is to become the basis of a future world polity. Until such a polity evolves, however, global anarchy will persist, and with it the ever-present threat of massive, irreversible destruction in a nuclear exchange.

Prospects: The Higher Goals

Early in this chapter, we reached the conclusion that sociocultural evolution has, more often than not, been accompanied by declining levels of freedom, justice, and happiness for the majority of people, but that the technological advances of the last 150 years have reversed this trend for the members of industrial societies. It would be gratifying to be able to predict that the increasing industrialization of the world system during the next quarter century would have a similar impact on the world as a whole. As our examination of population trends, the environment, war, and other matters has made clear, however, the prospects are dim for greater attainment of humanity's higher goals in the decades immediately ahead.

In the Third World, we can expect a decline in individual freedoms to accompany an increase in the number of authoritarian regimes. This could have the effect of alleviating some human misery, however, since such regimes would be better able to control birthrates and thus perhaps lower the number of severely malnourished individuals in these societies. But even if this happens, there is not likely to be any great gain in either happiness or justice, since so many people will still be doomed to lives of abject poverty in crowded slums and shantytowns. What is more, inflation, population growth, and shortages of vital resources will probably retard the pace of industrialization in many societies during the next few decades, greatly delaying the day when advances in productivity can begin to provide appreciable benefits for most of their members.

Although the prospects are brighter for industrial societies, continued improvement in terms of the higher goals is by no means inevitable. The members of some of these societies may well experience some decline in the level of freedom, although in most societies the likeliest prospect is that losses in some areas will be offset by gains in others. There is also the possibility that the level of suffering in some industrial societies will rise appreciably as a consequence of a growth in unemployment or other social problems (e.g., increasing numbers of elderly in nursing homes), or because of nuclear warfare.

Whatever difficulties human societies experience during the next few decades, however, they may suffer more later in the next century. The levels of freedom, justice, and happiness are almost certain to decline seriously for the world system as a whole during that period—unless humanity begins soon to address its most basic problems. Our potential for shaping a better world is still, at this point, excellent—far greater, in fact, than it has ever been before. But this situation will not last: *the range of attractive options will decline with every year we fail to act.* Thus, the larger the human population becomes before growth is halted, the more likely it is that future political regimes will be harshly authoritarian and individual freedoms severely limited. The further the biophysical environment deteriorates before that trend is reversed, the less likely it is that the human population as a whole will ever enjoy the enormous potential benefits of industrial productivity. And the longer sociocultural evolution continues to be shaped primarily by the blind force of intersocietal selection, the more likely it is that our future will be shaped by convulsive changes that are forced on us by developments beyond our control.

The latter is, in fact, precisely the outcome predicted for human societies by some who have considered the problem. For example, Robert Heilbroner, long noted for his insightful analyses, has written a book entitled *An Inquiry into the Human Prospect* in which he forecasts such events as nuclear war among societies that are experiencing severe population and environmental crises. He predicts, in effect, a future in which the forces of nature—including the irrational forces of our own genetic heritage—produce the answers to problems that *humanity failed to resolve with social and cultural resources.*

Heilbroner is not unaware of our species' remarkably adaptive capabilities. In fact, he believes that, in principle, we are capable of resolving our problems through social and cultural mechanisms. What he doubts, however, is our ability to do it *in time to avoid catastrophe.* He feels that it will require too long to alter certain dangerous behavior patterns—patterns that reflect our genetic tendencies toward individualism, self-centeredness, and expansiveness of needs, and which are reflected in our lack of cooperation, lack of concern for future generations and for members of other societies, and our disinclination to deny ourselves. Heilbroner points out the futility of pinning our hopes on what we believe it is possible for humanity eventually *to become.* Rather, he says, we must consider what people are likely *to be* during the period in question, and he notes that the socialization process tends to produce individuals who are a generation or more behind the times, people who, by tomorrow, will finally be prepared to respond to yesterday's problems.[44]

Even if one does not entirely agree with Heilbroner's pessimistic assessment, it is impossible to deny that certain aspects of our genetic heritage seriously handicap us in our efforts to solve our most urgent problems, or that the socialization process and other social and cultural mechanisms are often inadequate in helping societies adapt to the conditions created by a rapidly changing technology. But while there is nothing we can do to alter our genetic mechanisms, at least in the immediate future, *we can alter our social and cultural mechanisms.*

If we hope that humanity will be capable of handling the problems that confront it tomorrow, we must act *today* toward that end. Our decisions cannot be based on wishful thinking about the future; they must be based on cold, hard facts. We must recognize, for example, that the kinds of culturally derived needs and desires that develop in our children and grandchildren will have to differ in some ways from those that motivated our parents or that are central in our own lives. We cannot rely solely on traditional solutions in shaping our actions: if we are to be responsible, we must be innovative; if we are to be compassionate, we must be rational and analytical. In short, our values, ideals, and goals must become less and less unthinking responses to technological advance and more and more the product of deliberate and rational choices made with full awareness of all the alternatives.

Of all the species on this planet, ours is the only one that is not doomed to have its evolutionary course shaped entirely by forces beyond its control. Thanks to symbol systems and culture, we can not only comprehend the evolutionary process, *we can chart for ourselves an evolutionary course within the limits set by our genetic heritage on the one hand and the natural constraints of the biophysical environment on the other*—a course that can provide for most people a high degree of freedom, justice, and happiness.

We also have the option to ignore this possibility until it is too late.

Glossary

Adaptation   The process of adjusting to, or changing, environmental conditions; hence, broadly, problem solving.

Agrarian era   The period in history when there were no societies technologically more advanced than agrarian societies (about 3000 B.C. to 1800 A.D.).

Agrarian society   A society that depends primarily on agriculture for the material necessities of life. *Advanced* agrarian societies have iron tools and weapons; *simple* agrarian societies do not.

Agriculture   The cultivation of fields using the plow.

Archaeology   The study of cultures of the past, based on analysis of their physical remains.

Arithmetic mean   The value that results when the sum of a set of items is divided by the number of items; a measure of central tendency.

Artisan   A craftsman. The term is usually applied to a worker who uses hand tools and produces a complete product (unlike a modern factory worker).

Ascribed role   A role which is assigned an individual (e.g., age, sex, race, kinship position) and which the individual normally finds difficult or impossible to discard or alter.

Association   A formally organized secondary group that performs some relatively specialized function or set of functions.

Autocracy   Rule by one person (compare with *Democracy*, *Oligarchy*, and *Theocracy*).

Autonomous   Free from outside political control.

Band   A nomadic community at the hunting and gathering level.

Behavior   Any response by an organism to internal or external stimuli.

Biological evolution   The process of genetic change by which existing species of plants and animals have developed out of preexisting species.

Biophysical environment   The biological and physical components of the environment.

Biotic   Pertaining to life and living things.

Bureaucracy   (1) The administrative component of a government or other association; (2) an administrative system that is characterized by a highly formalized division of labor, a hierarchical system of authority, and action guided by a complex and formalized system of rules.

Capital goods   The goods in a society that are devoted to the production of other goods (e.g., factories, machinery, tools, etc.).

Capital-intensive industry   An industry in which the ratio of capital costs to other costs is high.

429

Capitalism An economic system in which the means of production are privately owned and the basic problems of production and distribution are settled by means of a market system, with minimal governmental regulation or control (see *Market economy*).

Civilization An advanced sociocultural system. The term is usually reserved for the cultures of societies with writing and urban communities.

Clan A kin group whose members claim descent from a common ancestor.

Class (1) An aggregation or group of people whose *overall* status is similar; (2) an aggregation or group of people who share a common resource that affects their access to power, privilege, or prestige.

Command economy An economy in which the basic questions of production and distribution are decided by political elites (contrast with *Market economy*).

Communication The exchange of information by means of signals or symbols.

Communism A future state of society hypothesized by Marx in which the distribution of goods and services would be based on need; a society in which there is no inequality.

Community An informally organized secondary group whose members are united by a common place of residence or by a common subculture (see *Geographical community* and *Cultural community*).

Continuity The persistence of cultural elements in a society.

Cooperation Interaction by two or more individuals for mutual benefit.

Correlation coefficient A measure of the degree of association between two variables. Correlation coefficients range from 0.0, when there is absolutely no relationship between the variables, to ±1.0, when there is a perfect relationship (i.e., one value is a perfect function of the other).

Cultural community A community whose members are united by ties of a common cultural tradition (e.g., a racial or ethnic group).

Culture Symbol systems and the information they convey.

Customs Informal norms that define normal or acceptable behavior in a society or a subgroup within society.

Democracy A political system in which sovereignty is vested in the people (contrast with *Autocracy*, *Oligarchy*, and *Theocracy*).

Demography The study of populations, their size, composition, and change.

Determinism The belief that a specific set of identifiable factors is sufficient to explain completely a given phenomenon.

Development, societal A process of change in which technological advance causes greater organizational complexity within a society or set of societies (compare with *Growth*.)

Diffusion Transmission of cultural elements from one society to another (contrast with *Invention*).

Discovery An innovation that results from a society's acquisition of new cultural information by means other than diffusion

DNA Deoxyribonucleic acid; the chemical molecule that embodies genetic information.

Ecological-evolutionary theory Theory concerning (1) the relationships within and among human societies, (2) the relationships between societies and their biophysical environments, and (3) the processes of sociocultural change and development.

Ecology The science of the interrelationships of living things to each other and to their environments.

Economic surplus Production that exceeds what is needed to keep the producers of essential goods and services alive and productive.

Energy The capacity for performing work.

Environment Everything external to an entity (organism, population, society, etc.) that affects it, or is affected by it, in any way.

Era A period of time during which a particular type of society is the most advanced in existence (e.g., the agrarian era).

Ethnography The description of contemporary sociocultural systems.

Evolution In general, a process of long-term, cumulative change in which later stages develop out of earlier stages (see *Biological evolution* and *Sociocultural evolution*).

Extended family A group of near relatives (e.g., cousins, aunts, uncles). More inclusive than the nuclear family, less inclusive than the clan.

Extinction, sociocultural The elimination of elements from a sociocultural system; also, the elimination of entire societies.

Family A group organized around ties of kinship; a major institutional system in every society (see also *Nuclear family* and *Extended family*).

Feedback A special type of causal relationship in which part of the effect of an initial cause or event reverts back to its source, modifying or reinforcing it (i.e., A influences B, thereby causing B to exert an influence back on A).

Fishing society A society dependent primarily on fishing, or fishing and gathering, to obtain the material necessities of life.

Fixed costs Costs of production that remain more or less constant regardless of the number of units produced (contrast with *Variable costs*).

Freedom The absence of constraints imposed by society or nature.

Frontier society An agrarian society that is expanding into territories which are uninhabited, or inhabited by preagrarian societies.

Function (1) A characteristic activity of a person, thing, or institution; (2) a consequence of, or purpose served by, that activity; (3) a relationship in which changes in the magnitude of one variable are associated in a definite and determined way with changes in the magnitude of another variable.

Functional requisites Conditions that must be met if a society is to survive.

Fundamental innovation An invention or discovery that either (1) opens the way for many other innovations or (2) alters the conditions of human life so that many other changes become either possible or necessary.

Gathering Foraging for wild fruits and vegetables.

Gene The basic unit of heredity; a conveyer of genetic information.

Gene pool The genes of all the members of a population considered collectively.

Genetic constants Genetic attributes that are the same in every population of a species.

Genetic variables Genetic attributes that vary among the populations of a species.

Geographical community A community whose members are united by ties of spatial proximity.

Governing class A largely hereditary class from which the political leaders of a society are recruited.

Gross domestic product Gross national product minus net income from other nations.

Gross national product The monetary value of the goods and services produced by a nation during a specified period (usually a year).

Group An aggregation whose members (1) act together to satisfy common, or complementary, needs, (2) have common norms, and (3) have a sense of common identity. The term is applicable to a society, an intersocietal aggregation, or an intrasocietal aggregation.

Growth An increase in size. For societies, the term may apply either to population size or to territorial size (compare with *Development, Societal*).

Guild A mutual aid association of merchants and artisans in the same trade (found in agrarian and maritime societies).

Headman The leader of a local community, usually in a preliterate society; one who leads rather than rules.

Herding society A society dependent primarily on herding to obtain the material necessities of life. *Advanced* herding societies are differentiated from *simple* by the use of horses or camels for transportation.

Hominid A member of the genus *Homo*, which in-

cludes our own species as well as an undetermined number of humanlike species that preceded us and are now extinct.

Homo sapiens sapiens Genetically modern humans.

Horticultural era The period in history when there were no societies technologically more advanced than horticultural societies (about 7000 to 3000 B.C.).

Horticultural society A society that depends primarily on horticulture to obtain the material necessities of life. *Advanced* horticultural societies are differentiated from *simple* by the manufacture of metal tools and weapons.

Horticulture The cultivation of small gardens using a hoe or digging stick as the chief tool. Horticulture is differentiated from agriculture by the absence of the plow.

Hunting and gathering era The period in history when there were no societies more advanced than hunting and gathering (to about 7000 B.C.).

Hunting and gathering society A society that depends primarily on hunting and gathering to obtain the material necessities of life.

Hybrid society A society that relies about equally on two or more of the basic modes of subsistence.

Hypothesis A proposition tentatively assumed to be valid until disproven.

Ideology Cultural information used to interpret human experience and order societal life. An ideology consists of a system of beliefs and related norms and values.

Industrial era The period in history when industrial societies have been dominant (from about 1800 A.D. to the present).

Industrialization Increasing reliance on inanimate sources of energy and the machines powered by them (compare with *Modernization*).

Industrial Revolution The revolution in technology that began in England in the eighteenth century, has since spread to most of the world, and is still continuing.

Industrial society A society that derives most of its wealth and income from productive activities dependent on machines powered by inanimate energy sources (i.e., coal, petroleum, natural gas, hydroelectric power, nuclear power).

Information A record of experience stored in the memory system of a plant, animal, or machine that influences its actions.

Innovation The process of introducing new cultural elements into a society; the new cultural element itself (see *Variations*).

Institution A system of social relationships and cultural elements that develops in a society in response to some set of basic and persistent needs.

Institutional system A system of interrelated institutions.

Intelligentsia   Well-educated persons; the upper part of the nonmanual class in East European societies.

Intersocietal selection   The process of selection *among* societies, whereby some survive while others become extinct; the basis of the primary trends in the world system of societies.

Intrasocietal selection   The process of selection *within* a society, whereby some of its cultural elements survive while others are eliminated.

Invention   An innovation that results from a useful new combination of information already possessed by a society (compare with *Discovery*).

Labor-intensive industry   An industry in which the ratio of labor costs to other costs is high.

Language   A system of symbols.

Laws   Norms sanctioned by the state.

Learning   The process by which an organism acquires, through experience, information with behavior-modifying potential.

Legitimate   That which is morally or legally justified by the norms or laws of a group.

Legitimize   To make legitimate; to provide an ideological or legal justification for a practice that might otherwise be regarded as objectionable.

Macroorganizational   Pertaining to the characteristics of large social systems, especially human societies and the world system of societies.

Macrosociology   The branch of sociology that studies large social systems, especially human societies and the world system of societies (contrast with *Microsociology*).

Maritime society   A society in which overseas commercial activity is the primary source of wealth and income.

Market economy   An economy in which the basic problems of production and distribution are settled by the forces of supply and demand (see *Capitalism,* and contrast with *Command economy*).

Marxist-Leninist society   A society governed by an elite that is committed to Marxist-Leninist ideology.

Mass media   Communications media developed in industrial and industrializing societies to reach the masses (i.e., TV, radio, newspapers, magazines, and movies).

Mean, arithmetic   See *Arithmetic mean.*

Median   The middle number in a series of numbers arranged in order from highest to lowest; a measure of central tendency.

Microsociology   The branch of sociology that studies individuals and small social units, such as families (contrast with *Macrosociology*).

Mixed economy   An economy that combines two or more basic principles of economic decision making, especially the market and command principles.

Mobility, vertical   See *Vertical mobility.*

Modernization   All the long-term changes associated with industrialization (compare with *Industrialization*).

Monogamy   Marriage with but one person at a time (compare with *Polygamy* and *Polygyny*).

Monopoly   A commodity market with only a single seller.

Nationalism   An ideology that emphasizes the importance of the nation-state.

Nation-State or Nation   A society governed by full-time officials (see also *State*).

Neophilia   The love of novelty or change for its own sake.

Nomad   A member of a group that has no permanent settlement and moves about periodically (usually in a well-defined territory) to obtain food and other necessities.

Nomenklatura   (1) A list of positions in Marxist-Leninist societies that can be filled only by Party approval; (2) the governing class in Marxist-Leninist societies.

Normative   Of, or pertaining to, norms; having a moral character.

Norms   Definitions of acceptable and unacceptable behaviors for the members of a society in their various roles; norms may be formal (e.g., laws) or informal (e.g., customs).

Nuclear family   A man, his wife or wives, and their unmarried children living with them.

Oligarchy   The rule of the few (contrast with *Autocracy*, *Democracy*, and *Theocracy*).

Oligopoly   A commodity market dominated by a few sellers.

Organism   A living entity; a plant or animal.

Peasant   An agricultural worker in an agrarian society.

Per capita income   National income divided by population.

Polity   The political system of a group, especially of a society.

Polygamy   A form of marriage in which an individual of either sex has two or more spouses at the same time (compare with *Polygyny*).

Polygyny   A form of marriage in which a man has two or more wives at the same time (compare with *Polygamy*).

Population   (1) Organisms of the same species that tend to interbreed because of geographical proximity; (2) the members of a society, or a subgroup within a society, considered collectively.

Positive-sum game   A contest in which the gains of one participant are not necessarily at the expense of others (contrast with *Zero-sum game*).

Priest   A religious functionary believed to have super-natural powers bestowed on him by an organized religious group; one who mediates between God, or a god, and humans (contrast with *Shaman*).

Primary group   A small group in which face-to-face relations of at least a fairly intimate and personal nature are maintained.

Primary industries   Industries that produce or extract raw materials (especially farming and mining).

Primates   An order of mammals that includes the prosimians (e.g., tarsiers and lemurs) and the anthropoids (e.g., monkeys, great apes, and humans).

Process   A series of related events with an identifiable outcome.

Race   A breeding population in which certain traits occur with a frequency that is appreciably different from that of other breeding populations of the species.

Religion   The basic ideological beliefs of a group of people and the practices associated with those beliefs. The term can refer to nontheistic ideologies, such as communism and humanism, but is more often applied to ideologies that involve theistic beliefs.

Republic   A nonmonarchical form of government.

Revolution   Change that is unusually sudden, rapid, or far-reaching.

Role   A position that can be filled by an individual and that has distinctive norms attached to it. The term may also be used to refer to the part a group, institution, or other social unit plays in the life of a society.

Sanction   A reward or punishment; also, the act of rewarding or punishing.

Secondary group   Any group that is larger and more impersonal than a primary group.

Secondary industries   Industries that process raw materials and turn out finished products.

Selection   The process that determines the fate of the variations in a gene pool, in a sociocultural system, or in the world system of societies (see *Intersocietal selection, Intrasocietal selection,* and *Variations*).

Serf   A peasant farmer who is bound to the land and subject to the owner of the land.

Shaman   A person believed to enjoy special powers because of a distinctive relationship he or she has established with the spirit world; a medicine man. Not to be equated with *Priest*.

Signal   An information conveyer whose form and related meaning are both determined genetically (contrast with *Symbol*).

Social   Having to do with relationships among the members of societies.

Social controls   Mechanisms that order societal life by regulating people's actions and relationships; norms and their related sanctions.

Social environment   The other social systems with which a given social system has contact.

Social institution   See *Institution*.

Socialism   An economic system in which there is little or no private ownership of the means of production (see *Capitalism*).

Socialist society   A society in which there is little or no private ownership of the means of production; alternatively, a society in which a socialist party governs.

Socialization   The process through which individuals learn to become functional members of their society.

Social movement   A loose-knit group that seeks to change society.

Social organization   The network of relationships among the members of a society or group.

Social structure   See *Social organization*.

Social system   A generic term that includes all kinds of social groups, from primary groups to societies and the world system of societies.

Societal   Of or pertaining to a society or societies.

Society, human   An autonomous group of people engaged in a broad range of cooperative activities.

Sociocultural   A combination of *social* and *cultural* elements.

Sociocultural evolution   The process of change and development in human societies that results from cumulative change in the store of cultural information available to them.

Sociocultural system   A system composed of a human population, its social organization, culture, material products, and social institutions; a human society.

Sociology   The branch of science that specializes in the study of human societies.

State   The government of a nation.

Status   The relative rank of a person, role, or group, according to culturally defined standards.

Stratification   Class or status differentiation within a population; hence, inequality.

Structural-functional theory   Theory concerning the structures of societies, and the functions of their various parts.

Structure   The organization of the parts of a system.

Subculture   The distinctive culture of a group within a society.

Subsistence   The material necessities of life; also, the process by which they are obtained.

Subsistence technology   The technology that is used by the members of a society to obtain the basic necessities of life.

Surplus   See *Economic surplus*.

Symbol   An information conveyer whose form is arbitrary and whose meaning is determined by those who use it (contrast with *Signal*).

System   An entity made up of interrelated parts.

Systemic   Having the qualities of a system.

Technology Cultural information about the ways in which the material resources of the environment may be used to satisfy human needs and desires.

Tertiary industries Industries that perform services (e.g., retail trade, government).

Theocracy A society ruled by a priesthood in the name of some deity or by a ruler believed to be divine.

Theory An explanation of some aspect of the natural world; a coherent set of principles that form the basic frame of reference for a field of inquiry.

Third World Industrializing societies of the contemporary world; hence, less developed societies.

Tribe A preliterate group whose members speak a common language or dialect, possess a common culture that distinguishes them from other peoples, and know themselves, or are known, by a distinctive name.

Unilinear theory of evolution A theory which assumes that all societies follow the same path of evolutionary development.

Urban community A community whose inhabitants are wholly or largely freed from the necessity of producing their own food, fibers, and other raw materials.

Values Moral beliefs to which the members of a group subscribe.

Variable Any property of an entity that is capable of varying in degree.

Variable costs Costs of production that tend to vary in proportion to the number of units produced (contrast with *Fixed costs*).

Variations Products of the process of innovation (see *Innovation* and *Selection*).

Vertical mobility Change of status, either upward or downward.

Working class Members of modern industrial societies belonging to families headed by manual workers.

World system The totality of human societies and their interrelationships.

Zero-Sum Game A contest in which the gains of any participant are necessarily at the expense of other participants. This concept is applicable to societies in which economic growth is absent and contrasts with the positive-sum game concept, which assumes economic growth.

Notes

Chapter 1

1. René Dubos, *So Human an Animal* (New York: Scribner's, 1968), p. 270.
2. William R. Catton, Jr., *From Animistic to Naturalistic Sociology* (New York: McGraw-Hill, 1966).
3. Kingsley Davis, *Human Society* (New York: Macmillan, 1949), p. 27. See also Alfred E. Emerson, "Human Cultural Evolution and Its Relation to Organic Evolution of Insect Societies," in Herbert Barringer et al. (eds.), *Social Change in Developing Areas: A Reinterpretation of Evolutionary Theory* (Cambridge, Mass.: Schenkman, 1965), pp. 50–51.
4. Edward O. Wilson, *Sociobiology: The New Synthesis* (Cambridge, Mass.: Belknap, 1975), part III.
5. Ibid., p. 595.
6. George Gaylord Simpson, *The Meaning of Evolution* (New Haven, Conn.: Yale, 1951), pp. 283–284. Quoted by permission of Yale University Press.
7. This paragraph is based on Paul B. Weisz, *The Science of Biology*, 3d ed. (New York: McGraw-Hill, 1967), chap. 2.
8. Simpson, p. 281.
9. This is a simplified summary of the basic principles of biological evolution as they are presently understood. It is based on Sir Julian Huxley, *Evolution: The Modern Synthesis* (London: G. Allen, 1942); George Gaylord Simpson, *The Major Features of Evolution* (New York: Columbia, 1953); Ernst Mayr, *Animal Species and Evolution* (Cambridge, Mass.: Harvard, 1963): Sol Tax (ed.), *Evolution after Darwin: The University of Chicago Centennial* (Chicago: University of Chicago Press, 1960), vols. I and III; Weisz, op. cit.; G. G. Simpson and Anne Roe (eds.), *Behavior and Evolution* (New Haven: Yale, 1958); John Maynard Smith, *The Theory of Evolution* (Baltimore: Penguin, 1958); and Helena Curtis, *Biology*, 2d ed. (New York: Worth, 1976).

10. Curtis., p. 914.
11. J. Z. Young, *An Introduction to the Study of Man* (New York: Oxford University Press, 1971), pp. 470–472; and Curtis, pp. 914–916.
12. Curtis, p. 914.
13. This definition is a slightly modified version of that provided by W. H. Thorpe, *Learning and Instinct in Animals,* 2d ed. (Cambridge, Mass.: Harvard, 1963), p. 55.
14. Wilson, pp. 151–152.
15. Sherwood L. Washburn and David A. Hamburg, "The Implications of Primate Research," in Irven DeVore (ed.), *Primate Behavior: Field Studies of Monkeys and Apes* (New York: Holt, 1965), p. 613.
16. Sherwood Washburn, "The Evolution of Man," *Scientific American,* 239 (September 1978), p. 204; Dorothy Miller, "Evolution of the Primate Chromosomes," *Science,* 198 (Dec. 16, 1977), pp. 1116–1124. See also Mary-Claire King and A. C. Wilson, "Evolution at Two Levels in Humans and Chimpanzees," *Science,* 188 (Apr. 11, 1975), pp. 107–116.
17. Carl Sagan, *The Dragons of Eden: Speculations on the Evolution of Human Intelligence* (New York: Ballantine Books Inc., 1977), pp. 181–182; and John E. Pfeiffer, *The Emergence of Man,* 3d ed. (New York: Harper & Row, 1978), pp. 390–392.
18. Leslie White, "The Symbol: The Origin and Basis of Human Behavior," *Philosophy of Science,* 7 (1940), pp. 451–463.
19. Milton Singer, "Culture," in *International Encyclopedia of the Social Sciences* (New York: Macmillan and Free Press, 1968), vol. 3, p. 540.
20. This paragraph is based on Edward O. Wilson, pp. 176–185.
21. Karl von Frisch, "Dialect in the Language of the Bees," *Scientific American,* 167 (Aug. 1962), pp. 3–7.
22. Masukazu Konishi, "The Role of Auditory Feedback in the Control of Vocalization in the White-Crowned Sparrow," *Journal of Comparative Ethology,* 22 (1965), pp. 770–783.
23. See, for example, Francine Patterson, "Conversations with a Gorilla," *National Geographic,* 154 (October 1978), pp. 438–466, or Pfeiffer, pp. 373–381. For a more skeptical view of the ability of apes to use symbols, see Roger Brown, "Why Are Signal Languages Easier to Learn than Spoken Languages? Part Two," *Bulletin of the American Academy of Arts and Sciences,* 32 (December 1978), pp. 38–39.
24. Pfeiffer, p. 381, citing Jane van Lawick-Goodall as authority.
25. Helen Keller, *The Story of My Life* (New York: Doubleday, 1903).
26. Robert Lord, *Comparative Linguistics,* 2d ed. (London: English Universities Press, Ltd., 1974), pp. 288–289.
27. John Locke, *An Essay Concerning Human Understanding* (New York: Dover, 1959, first published 1690).
28. Reinhold Niebuhr, *The Nature and Destiny of Man* (New York: Scribner, 1943), vol. 1; Robert Heilbroner, *An Inquiry into the Human Prospect* (New York: Norton, 1974), chap. 4; and Jan Szczepanski, *Polish Society* (New York: Random House, 1970), p. 100 and chap. 9.
29. Theodosius Dobzhansky, *Mankind Evolving* (New York: Bantam, 1962), pp. 224–225, and Pfeiffer, chap. 18.
30. Pfeiffer, pp. 354ff.
31. Rene A. Spitz, "Hospitalism," *The Psychoanalytic Study of the Child,* 1 (1945), pp. 53–72, and "Hospitalism: A Follow-up Report," ibid., 2 (1946), pp. 113–117.
32. Pfeiffer, pp. 429–430, and Sagan, *The Dragons of Eden,* pp. 47–48.
33. Stephen Jay Gould, "Human Babies as Embryos," *Natural History,* 85 (February 1976), pp. 22ff.
34. Curtis, pp. 717–720.
35. Noam Chomsky, *Syntactic Structures* (The Hague: Mouton, 1957); *Aspects of the Theory of Syntax* (Cambridge, Mass.: MIT Press, 1965); and *Cartesian Linguistics* (New York: Harper & Row, 1966).
36. Pfeiffer, chap. 19.
37. Dobzhansky, p. 354. See also Pierre van den Berghe, "Evolution and Creativity," unpublished paper, University of Washington.

38. For a more detailed discussion of this subject, see Gerhard Lenski, *Power and Privilege* (New York: McGraw-Hill, 1966), pp. 25–32.

39. A. H. Maslow, *Motivation and Personality* (New York: Harper & Row, 1954), especially chap. 5. See also Edward O. Wilson, p. 143.

40. William Graham Sumner, *Folkways* (New York: Mentor, 1960, first published 1906), p. 32.

41. For a good summary of these developments, see Marvin Harris, *The Rise of Anthropological Theory* (New York: Cromwell, 1968), chap. 2.

42. For a good review of the early history of social research, see Bernard Lecuyer and Anthony R. Oberschall, "Sociology: The Early History of Social Research," in *International Encyclopedia of the Social Sciences,* vol. 15, pp. 36–53.

43. See, for example, Wlodzimierz Wesolowski, *Classes, Strata and Power* (London: Routledge, 1979); Eugene Pusić (ed.), *Participation and Self-Management* (Zagreb: First International Sociological Conference on Participation and Self-Management, 1972); Antal Böhm and Tamás Kolosi (eds.), *Structure and Stratification in Hungary* (Budapest: Institute for Social Sciences, 1982); or K. M. Slomczynski and T. Krauze (eds.), *Social Stratification in Poland* (White Plains, N.Y.: Sharpe, 1986).

44. For pioneering statements of the new ecological-evolutionary approach, see O. D. Duncan, "Social Organization and the Ecosystem," in R. E. L. Faris (ed.), *Handbook of Modern Sociology* (Chicago: Rand McNally, 1964), pp. 39–45; and Walter Goldschmidt, *Man's Way: A Preface to the Understanding of Human Society* (New York: Holt, 1959). See also Marvin Harris, *Cultural Materialism: The Struggle for a Science of Culture* (New York: Random House, 1979) for a more recent statement.

Chapter 2

1. See, for example, David F. Aberle et al., "The Functional Prerequisites of a Society," *Ethics,* 60 (1950), pp. 100–111; or Talcott Parsons, *The Social System* (Glencoe, Ill.: Free Press, 1951), pp. 26–36.

2. J. S. Weiner, *The Natural History of Man* (Garden City, N.Y.: Doubleday Anchor, 1973), p. 170.

3. Theodosius Dobzhansky, Francisco Ayala, G. Ledyard Stebbins, and James Valentine, *Evolution* (San Francisco: Freeman, 1977), chap. 5.

4. For brief but fascinating discussions of the relation between human physique and climate, see Theodosius Dobzhansky, *Mankind Evolving* (New York: Bantam, 1962), pp. 287ff; Weiner, *The Natural History of Man,* pp. 160ff.; and E. Adamson Hoebel, *Anthropology: The Study of Man,* 3d ed. (New York: McGraw-Hill, 1966), pp. 214ff.

5. Weiner, pp. 153 and 167.

6. Dobzhansky, Ayala, et al., p. 148.

7. Dobzhansky, pp. 158ff.

8. Paul R. Ehrlich and Richard W. Holm, *The Process of Evolution* (New York: McGraw-Hill, 1963), fig. 11.1, p. 253.

9. Fred Blumenthal, "The Man in the Middle of the Peace Talks," *Washington Post,* July 14, 1968.

10. Helene Curtis, *Biology,* 2d ed. (New York: Worth, 1975), p. 159.

11. Hoebel, p. 35.

12. Karl G. Heider, *The Dugum Dani: A Papuan Culture in the Highlands of West New Guinea* (New York: Wenner-Gren Foundation, 1970) pp. 32–33.

13. Hoebel, p. 35.

14. Robert Lord, *Comparative Linguistics,* 2d ed. (London: English Universities Press, 1974), p. 316. For other interesting examples of changes in the meanings of words, see Charlton Laird, *The Miracle of Language* (Greenwich, Conn.: Premier Books, 1953), pp. 54ff.

15. Edward Sapir, *Selected Writings in Language, Culture, and Personality,* David Mandelbaum (ed.), (Berkeley: University of California Press, 1949), p. 162.

16. See, for example, Dell Hymes, "Linguistics: The Field," *International Encyclopedia of the Social Sciences,* vol. 9., p. 22.

17. V. Gordon Childe, *Man Makes Himself* (New York: Mentor, 1951), pp. 144ff.

18. This view of ideology borrows from Talcott Parsons's thesis that the prime function of religion is making sense out of the totality of human experience. If the term "religion" is defined to include nontheistic faiths (as we do in this volume), religion and ideology become almost indistinguishable. See Parsons, *The Structure of Social Action* (New York: Free Press, 1968), vol. II, pp. 566–567, 667–668, and 717.

19. See, for example, Robert S. Merrill, "Technology: The Study of Technology," *International Encyclopedia of the Social Sciences,* vol. 15, p. 576.

20. Ralph H. Turner, "Role: Sociological Analysis," ibid., vol. 13, pp. 552–557.

21. For a more extended discussion of classes, see Gerhard Lenski, *Power and Privilege: A Theory of Social Stratification* (New York: McGraw-Hill, 1966), pp. 73–82.

22. See Reinhard Bendix and Seymour M. Lipset (eds.), *Class, Status, and Power* (New York: Free Press, 1966), pp. 47–72.

23. Lenski, op. cit.

24. James K. Feibleman, *The Institutions of Society* (London: G. Allen, 1956), p. 52.

25. Anatol Rapoport, "Systems Analysis: General Systems Theory," *International Encyclopedia of the Social Sciences* (New York: Macmillan and Free Press, 1968), vol. 15, p. 454.

26. From "The Mistress of Vision."

27. René Dubos, *So Human an Animal* (New York: Scribner, 1968), p. 242. Quoted by permission.

28. Ibid., p. 28. Quoted by permission.

Chapter 3

1. See, for example, Fekri Hassan, *Demographic Archaeology* (New York: Academic Press, 1981) and Don E. Dumond, "The Limitation of Human Population," *Science,* 187 (Feb. 28, 1975), p. 717.

2. This summary is based on Theodosius Dobzhansky, Francisco Ayala, G. Ledyard Stebbins, and James W. Valentine, *Evolution* (San Francisco: Freeman, 1977), chaps. 1 and 2; Helena Curtis, *Biology,* 2d ed. (New York: Worth, 1976), sec. 2, and Theodosius Dobzhansky, *Mankind Evolving* (New York: Bantam, 1962), chap. 2.

3. Patrick Malone, "Major Breakthroughs in Genetic Research," *The Washington Post,* Aug. 27, 1973, D3.

4. Edward O. Wilson, "An Introduction," *The Nature Conservancy News,* 33 (Nov./Dec., 1983), p. 4.

5. For an early statement of this distinction, see F. Stuart Chapin, *Cultural Change* (New York: Century, 1928), p. 345.

6. A. L. Kroeber, *Anthropology* (New York: Harcourt, Brace, 1948), pp. 353–355. For other examples, see Howard A. Rush, "Right Time and Place: Many Medical Discoveries Found to Result from Series of Accidents," *New York Times,* June 8, 1969; Irving Page, "A Sense of the History of Discovery," *Science,* Dec. 27, 1974, p. 1161; and Vern Riportella, "Fifty Years of Radio Astronomy," *Science News,* 123 (Apr. 30, 1983), p. 283.

7. William F. Ogburn and Dorothy S. Thomas, "Are Inventions Inevitable? A Note on Social Evolution," *Political Science Quarterly,* 37 (1922), pp. 93–98.

8. Glynn Isaac, "The Food-Sharing Behavior of Protohuman Hominids," *Scientific American,* 238 (April 1978), pp. 90–108.

9. For an early discussion of this point, see William F. Ogburn, *Social Change* (New York: Viking, 1922), chap. 6.

10. Ogburn mentioned this factor briefly, but did not stress it. (Ibid., 1950, p. 110).

11. Ralph Linton, *The Study of Man* (New York: Appleton-Century, 1936), pp. 326–327. Reprinted by permission of Prentice-Hall, Inc.

12. Basil Davidson with F. K. Buah, *A History of West Africa* (Garden City, N.Y.: Doubleday

Anchor, 1966), pp. 8–9; William H. McNeill, *Plagues and Peoples* (Garden City, N.Y.: Doubleday Anchor, 1976).

13. Ogburn, 1950, p. 107.
14. O. D. Duncan, "Social Organization and the Ecosystem," in R. E. L. Faris (ed.), *Handbook of Modern Sociology* (Chicago: Rand McNally, 1964), pp. 37–39.
15. See William F. Cottrell, *Energy and Society* (New York: McGraw-Hill, 1955), p. 2, for a somewhat similar assertion concerning energy's impact on human life.
16. Robert Carneiro, "On the Relationship between Size of Population and Complexity of Social Organization," *Southwestern Journal of Anthropology,* 23 (1967), pp. 234–243.
17. Max Weber, *The Sociology of Religion,* trans. Ephraim Fischoff (Boston: Beacon, 1963); Joachim Wach, *Sociology of Religion* (Chicago: University of Chicago Press, 1944), especially chap. 6.
18. Robert Carneiro, "Political Expansion as an Expression of the Principle of Competitive Exclusion," in Ronald Cohen and Elman Service (eds.), *Origins of the State* (Philadelphia: Institute for the Study of Human Issues, 1978), pp. 205–223.
19. F. G. Bailey, *Tribe, Caste, and Nation* (Manchester: Manchester University Press, 1960).
20. See, for example, Loren Eiseley, *Darwin's Century: Evolution and the Men Who Discovered It* (Garden City, N.Y.: Doubleday Anchor, 1961).
21. Thorstein Veblen, *Imperial Germany and the Industrial Revolution* (New York: Macmillan, 1915). See also Elman Service, "The Law of Evolutionary Potential," in Marshall Sahlins and Elman Service (eds.), *Evolution and Culture* (Ann Arbor: University of Michigan Press, 1960), pp. 93–122.

Chapter 4

1. See Marvin Harris, *The Rise of Anthropological Theory* (New York: Thomas Y. Crowell, 1968), chap. 2; and Robert Nisbet, *Social Change and History* (New York: Oxford, 1969), chap. 4.
2. This method of classification is an expansion and modification of one developed earlier by Walter Goldschmidt in *Man's Way: A Preface to the Understanding of Human Society* (New York: Holt, 1959), chap. 6, and also reflects the influence of V. Gordon Childe, *Man Makes Himself* (New York: Mentor Books, 1951).
3. See, for example, R. F. Watters, "The Nature of Shifting Cultivation: A Review of Recent Research," *Pacific Viewpoint,* 1 (1960), pp. 59–99.
4. Goldschmidt, p. 194.
5. See, for example, Frederic Pryor, "The Invention of the Plow," *Comparative Studies in Society and History,* 27 (1985), pp. 727–743.
6. Goldschmidt, p. 210.
7. See Jacquetta Hawkes, *Prehistory* (New York: Mentor Books, 1965), chap. 6, for a good summary of archaeological finds relating to fishing. See also Grahame Clark and Stuart Piggott, *Prehistoric Societies* (New York: Knopf, 1965), chap. 7.
8. Robert Braidwood, "The Earliest Village Communities of Southwest Asia Reconsidered," and Karl Butzer, "Agricultural Origins in the Near East as a Geographical Problem," in Stuart Struever (ed.), *Prehistoric Agriculture* (Garden City, N.Y.: Natural History Press, 1971), pp. 222 and 249.
9. James Mellaart, *Earliest Civilizations in the Near East* (London: Thames and Hudson, 1965), p. 105, and R. J. Forbes, *Studies in Ancient Technology* (Leiden: Brill, 1971–1972), vols. 8 and 9.
10. See, for example, Leslie Aitchison, *A History of Metals* (London: MacDonald, 1960), vol. 1, p. 41, and Forbes, op. cit.
11. E. Cecil Curwen and Gudmund Hatt, *Plough and Pasture: The Early History of Farming* (New York: Collier Books, 1961), p. 64.
12. Aitchison, pp. 102 and 111–113; and Forbes, vol. 9, chap. 3.
13. Mellaart, p. 20.

14. William H. McNeill, *The Rise of the West: A History of the Human Community* (New York: Mentor Books, 1965), p. 150.

15. The data which follow are, with two exceptions, based on Murdock's codes for the first 915 societies listed in the journal *Ethnology*, vols. 1–5. The classification of societies is explained in the Appendix to the 1970 edition of *Human Societies*, pp. 503–507. The first exception involves the data in Figure 4.6, which are based only on those societies included in both the *Human Societies* Appendix and the summary report in the April 1967 issue of *Ethnology*. The second exception is the data on industrial societies, which are our own estimates.

16. Goldschmidt, p. 115.

17. This method of classifying religious beliefs is based on work by G. E. Swanson in *The Birth of the Gods: The Origin of Primitive Beliefs* (Ann Arbor: University of Michigan Press, 1960), chap. 3.

18. Leslie White was the leading proponent of this point of view for many years. See, for example, his stimulating but extreme essay, "Energy and the Evolution of Culture," in *The Science of Culture* (New York: Grove Press, Inc., 1949), pp. 363–393.

19. Talcott Parsons is one of many who have consistently minimized the role of technology in the process of social change. Though not as extreme as some in his views, he has been very influential. See *Societies: Evolutionary and Comparative Perspectives* (Englewood Cliffs, N.J.: Prentice-Hall, 1966), especially pp. 113–114, for his views.

Chapter 5

1. For an example of the use of the term "analogous peoples," see Grahame Clark and Stuart Piggott, *Prehistoric Societies* (New York: Knopf, 1965), p. 133. On the value of inferences from ethnography, see Frank Hole and Robert Heizer, *An Introduction to Prehistoric Archeology* (New York: Holt, 1965), especially pp. 211–214 and chap. 16; or Grahame Clark, *Archeology and Society: Reconstructing the Historic Past*, 3d ed. (London: Methuen, 1957), pp. 172–174. In several instances, contemporary hunters and gatherers have provided explanations for previously unexplained archaeological findings. See, for example, John E. Pfeiffer, *The Emergence of Man*, 3d ed. (New York: Harper & Row, 1978), chap. 15. See also Colin Renfrew, *Before Civilization* (Cambridge: Cambridge University Press, 1979), p. 254.

2. For more conservative estimates based on recent work in immunology, see Vincent Sarich and Joseph Cronin, "Molecular Systematics of the Primates," in Morris Goodman et al. (eds.), *Molecular Anthropology* (New York: Plenum, 1976), pp. 141–170; or Allan Wilson et al. "Biochemical Evolution," in Esmond Snell et al. (eds.), *Annual Review of Biochemistry*, 46 (1977), pp. 573–640. For estimates of earlier dates of speciation based on evidence from archaeology and paleontology, see Pfeiffer, prologue and chap. 2; and Richard E. Leakey and Roger Lewin, *Origins* (New York: Dutton, 1977), p. 56.

3. Pfeiffer, chaps. 3 and 4; and Leakey and Lewin, chap. 5.

4. J. S. Weiner, *The Natural History of Man* (Garden City, N.Y.: Doubleday Anchor, 1973), pp. 50ff.

5. Glynn Isaac, "The Food-Sharing Behavior of Protohuman Hominids," *Scientific American*, 238 (April 1978), pp. 90–108.

6. Geza Teleki, *The Predatory Behavior of Wild Chimpanzees* (Lewisburg, Pa.: Bucknell University Press, 1973).

7. Jacquetta Hawkes, *Prehistory: UNESCO History of Mankind*, vol. 1, part 1 (New York: Mentor Books, 1965), p. 172. See also Clark and Piggott, p. 45, or Grahame Clark, *The Stone Age Hunters* (London: Thames and Hudson, 1967), p. 25.

8. William Laughlin, "Hunting: An Integrating Biobehavior System and Its Evolutionary Importance," in Richard Lee and Irven DeVore (eds.), *Man the Hunter*, (Chicago: Aldine, 1968).

9. Pfeiffer, chap. 8, and Leakey and Lewin, p. 122. See also the comments by Carleton S. Coon, Dean Falk, W. W. Howells, and others following Grover Krantz's paper, "Sapienization and Speech," *Current Anthropology,* 21 (1980), pp. 780ff.

10. H. V. Vallois, "The Social Life of Early Man: The Evidence of Skeletons," in Sherwood Washburn (ed.), *Social Life of Early Man* (Chicago: Aldine, 1961), pp. 214–235.

11. Pfeiffer, pp. 153ff.

12. Ibid., p. 158.

13. S. A. Semenov, *Prehistoric Technology,* trans. M. W. Thompson (New York: Barnes & Noble, 1964), pp. 202–203.

14. E. Adamson Hoebel, *Anthropology,* 3d ed. (New York: McGraw-Hill, 1966), pp. 176–177, and Hawkes, pp. 212–213.

15. This and the following statements concerning the bow and arrow are based on Semenov, pp. 202–204.

16. Hawkes, p. 212.

17. J. G. D. Clark, *Prehistoric Europe: The Economic Basis* (London: Methuen, 1952), pp. 132–133.

18. Hawkes, pp. 184–188, and Pfeiffer, p. 194.

19. Peter Ucko and Andreé Rosenfeld, *Paleolithic Cave Art* (New York: McGraw-Hill, 1967); or Grahame Clark, *The Stone Age Hunters,* chap. 4.

20. Clark and Piggott, pp. 93–95.

21. Hawkes, pp. 293–294, including fig. 35b.

22. Sherwood Washburn, "The Evolution of Man," *Scientific American,* 239 (Sept., 1978), p. 206.

23. L. J. Angel, "Paleoecology, Paleodemography and Health," in Steven Polgar (ed.), *Population, Ecology and Social Evolution* (The Hague: Mouton, 1975), table 1, pp. 182–183.

24. Fekri Hassan, *Demographic Archaeology* (New York: Academic Press, 1981), chap. 12.

25. For good reviews of work on hunters and gatherers, see Richard Lee and Irven DeVore (eds.), *Man The Hunter* (Chicago: Aldine, 1968); Carleton S. Coon, *The Hunting Peoples* (Boston: Little, Brown, 1971); and Elman Service, *The Hunters* (Englewood Cliffs, N.J.: Prentice-Hall, 1966).

26. This figure is based on Elkin's estimate that there were approximately 300,000 aborigines in Australia at the time of the first white settlement. This estimate was divided by 60, a very generous estimate for the average size of these societies. See A. P. Elkin, *The Australian Aborigines,* 3d ed. (Sydney: Angus and Robertson, 1954), p. 10.

27. See Martin Baumhoff, *Ecological Determinants of Aboriginal California Populations,* University of California *Publications in American Archaeology and Ethnology,* 49 (Berkeley, 1963), especially pp. 227 and 231. See also Elkin, op. cit., and his estimate of an aboriginal population of 300,000 prior to white settlement. Since Australia contains nearly 3 million square miles, this means an average density of only 1 person per 10 square miles. In Alaska, there was only 1 per 25 square miles at the time of its purchase by the United States (Hawkes, p. 183).

28. Joseph Birdsell, "Some Predictions for the Pleistocene Based on Equilibrium Systems among Recent Hunter-Gatherers," in Lee and DeVore, p. 235, and Table 5.3 of this volume.

29. Gertrude E. Dole, *The Development of Patterns of Kinship Nomenclature* (unpublished Ph.D. dissertation, University of Michigan, 1957), p. 26, found an average life expectancy at birth in very primitive societies of only 22 years and also found that individuals who live to age 50 are rare. Allan Holmberg, *Nomads of the Long Bow: The Siriono of Eastern Bolivia,* Smithsonian Institution, Institute of Social Anthropology, 10 (Washington, 1950), p. 85, reported that the average life span among the Siriono was only 35 to 40 years *even among those who survived infancy.*

30. Gini Bara Kolata, "!Kung Hunter-Gatherers: Feminism, Diet, and Birth Control," *Science,* 185 (Sept. 13, 1974). p. 934.

31. William Divale, "Systemic Population Control in the Middle and Upper Paleolithic:

Inferences Based on Contemporary Hunters and Gatherers," *World Archaeology*, 4 (1972), fig. 11, p. 230; and John Whiting, "Effects of Climate on Certain Cultural Practices," in Ward Goodenough (ed.), *Explorations in Cultural Anthropology: Essays in Honor of George Peter Murdock* (New York: McGraw-Hill, 1964), table 9, pp. 528–533.

32. Don Dumond, "The Limitations of Human Population: A Natural History," *Science*, 187 (Feb. 28, 1975), p. 715.

33. Kolata, op. cit.

34. See, for example, John Garvan, *The Negritos of the Philippines* (Vienna: Ferdinand Berger, 1964), p. 27; or Edwin Loeb, *Sumatra: Its History and People* (Vienna: Institut für Volkerkunde, 1935), p. 283, on the Kubu.

35. Only one of the fifteen nonnomadic hunting and gathering societies in Murdock's data set depended on hunting and gathering for as much as three-quarters of its subsistence, whereas more than half of the 136 nomadic hunting and gathering societies were in this category. The one exception among the nonnomadic societies (the Nomlaki) was located in the Sacramento Valley of northern California, a territory as favorable for a hunting and gathering people as any in the world (see Baumhoff, pp. 205–231).

36. Colin Turnbull, "The Mbuti Pygmies of the Congo," in James Gibbs (ed.), *Peoples of Africa* (New York: Holt, 1965), pp. 286–287.

37. James Woodburn, "Ecology, Nomadic Movement and the Composition of the Local Group among Hunters and Gatherers: An East African Example and Its Implications," in Peter J. Ucko, Ruth Tringham, and G. W. Dimbleby (eds.), *Man, Settlement and Urbanism* (London: Duckworth, 1972), pp. 201ff.

38. Richard B. Lee, "Work Effort, Group Structure and Land-Use in Contemporary Hunter-Gatherers," in Ucko et al., pp. 181–184.

39. A. R. Radcliffe-Brown, "The Social Organization of Australian Tribes," *Oceania*, 1 (1930), pp. 44–46.

40. Elkin, p. 56 (Doubleday Anchor edition).

41. Service, *The Hunters*, pp. 32ff. For some exceptions, see Colin Turnbull, *Wayward Servants, The Two Worlds of the African Pygmies* (Garden City, N.Y.: Natural History Press, 1965), pp. 109–112.

42. See, for example, Elkin, p. 50; Ivor Evans, *The Negritos of Malaya* (London: Cambridge, 1937), p. 254; and Garvan, p. 82.

43. Service, p. 42.

44. David Aberle, "Matrilineal Descent in Cross-Cultural Perspective," in D. Schneider and K. Gough (eds.), *Matrilineal Kinship* (Berkeley: University of California Press, 1961), p. 677, or Burton Pasternak, *Introduction to Kinship and Social Organization* (Englewood Cliffs, N.J.: Prentice-Hall, 1976), pp. 111–112.

45. Elman Service, *Primitive Social Organization: An Evolutionary Perspective* (New York: Random House, 1962), chap. 3, especially p. 61.

46. See, for example, Elkin, pp. 134–137.

47. Garvan, p. 29.

48. Lorna Marshall, "The !Kung Bushmen of the Kalahari Desert," in Gibbs, pp. 257–258. Quoted by permission of Holt, Rinehart and Winston, Inc. See also Charles Hose and William McDougall, *The Pagan Tribes of Borneo* (London: Macmillan, 1912), pp. 190–191; Holmberg, p. 11; or Loeb, p. 300.

49. See, for example, Walter Goldschmidt, *Nomlaki Ethnography,* University of California *Publications in American Archaeology and Ethnology,* 42 (Berkeley, 1951), pp. 333–335 and 417–428.

50. See, for example, Loeb, p. 294, or Holmberg, pp. 30 and 91.

51. Turnbull, pp. 287 and 297; Frederick McCarthy and Margaret McArthur, "The Food Quest and the Time Factor in Aboriginal Economic Life," in Charles Mountford (ed.), *Records of the American-Australian Expedition to Arnhem Land* (Melbourne: Melbourne University Press, 1960), pp. 190–191; Kenneth MacLeish, "The Tasadays: Stone Age Cavemen of Mindanao," *National Geographic,* 142 (August 1972), pp. 243–245; Richard B. Lee, "What Hunters Do for a Living, or How to Make Out on Scarce Resources," in Lee and DeVore, pp. 36–37.

52. See Service, p. 13, and Marshall Sahlins, "Notes on the Original Affluent Society," in Lee and DeVore, pp. 85–89.
53. Goldschmidt, p. 417. See also Asen Balicki, "The Netsilik Eskimos: Adaptive Responses" and the comments of Lorna Marshall and Colin Turnbull, in Lee and DeVore, pp. 78–82, 94, and 341, for challenges to the effort to portray life in hunting and gathering societies as idyllic and trouble-free.
54. Lee and DeVore, op. cit.
55. See, for example, Lee, p. 40.
56. Coon, *The Hunting Peoples*, p. 176.
57. In the hunting and gathering societies in Murdock's data set, hunting was entirely a male activity in 97 percent of the cases and predominantly a male activity in the rest. On the other hand, gathering was wholly or largely a female activity in 91 percent of the societies and predominantly a male activity in only 2 percent (in the remainder the activity was shared by both sexes).
58. Of the hunting and gathering societies in Murdock's data set, 57 percent defined this as a male responsibility, 25 percent as a female, and 18 percent regarded it as appropriate to both sexes.
59. I. Schapera, *Government and Politics in Tribal Societies* (London: Watts, 1956), p. 93. See also Holmberg's description of the Siriono headman quoted on p. 116 of this volume, and Hose and McDougall, p. 190, on the Punan shaman. Other specialists, much less common, may include part-time workers in certain arts and crafts and occasionally an assistant to the headman. Such individuals are most likely to be found in settled communities that depend less than totally on hunting and gathering or in those with especially favorable environments. See, for example, Goldschmidt, pp. 331–332, and Elkin, pp. 254ff.
60. See, for example, Turnbull, pp. 287–288; Evans, pp. 57 and 112–113; Garvan, p. 66; or Hose and McDougall, p. 191. Turnbull warns, however, that many scholars exaggerate the dependence of the Pygmies on the neighboring horticultural villagers. He maintains that they turn to the villagers only for luxuries and diversion. See *Wayward Servants*, pp. 33–37.
61. Gerhard Lenski, *Power and Privilege* (New York: McGraw-Hill, 1966), pp. 95–96.
62. Occasionally there might be a second official. See, for example, Kaj Birket-Smith, *The Eskimos*, rev. ed. (London: Methuen, 1959), p. 145; Goldschmidt, pp. 324–325; and Frank Speck, *Penobscot Man* (Philadelphia: University of Pennsylvania Press, 1940), pp. 239–240.
63. Holmberg, pp. 59–60. Quoted by permission of the Smithsonian Institution Press. Following an older usage, Holmberg referred to the leaders of Siriono bands as "chiefs." In current usage, such persons are usually referred to as "headmen," and the term "chief" is reserved for the leaders of multicommunity societies. For this reason, the term "headman" has been substituted.
64. See, for example, John Cooper, "The Ona," in Julian Steward (ed.), *Handbook of South American Indians*, Smithsonian Institution, Bureau of American Ethnology, Bulletin 143 (Washington, 1946), vol. 1, p. 117; A. R. Radcliffe-Brown, *The Andaman Islanders* (Glencoe, Ill.: Free Press, 1948), p. 47; Hose and McDougall, p. 182, on the Punan of Borneo; Speck, p. 239, on the Penobscot of Maine; I. Schapera, *The Khoisan Peoples of South Africa* (London: Routledge, 1930), p. 151; and Roland Dixon, "The Northern Maidu," in Carleton S. Coon (ed.), *A Reader in General Anthropology* (New York: Holt, 1948), p. 272.
65. Baldwin Spencer and F. J. Gillen, *The Arunta: A Study of a Stone Age People* (London: Macmillan, 1927), vol. 1, p. 10.
66. Schapera, *Government and Politics*, p. 117. Quoted by permission of C. A. Watts & Co., Ltd. See also A. H. Gayton, *Yokuts-Mono Chiefs and Shamans*, University of California *Publications in American Archaeology and Ethnology*, 24 (Berkeley, 1930), pp. 374–376.
67. See, for example, Colin Turnbull, *Wayward Servants*, chaps. 11 and 12, or *The Forest People* (New York: Simon & Schuster, 1961), on the Mbuti Pygmies. As he indicates, the office of headman is sometimes found among these people, but it has been more or

less forced on them by the Bantu villagers and is of little significance except in their contacts with these villagers.

68. See, for example, Schapera, *Government and Politics,* p. 193, or Turnbull, *Wayward Servants,* pp. 100–109.

69. See John Honigmann, *The Kaska Indians: An Ethnographic Reconstruction,* Yale University *Publications in Anthropology,* 51 (1954), pp. 90–92 and 96–97; Radcliffe-Brown, *The Andaman Islanders,* pp. 48–52; and Schapera, *The Khoisan Peoples,* pp. 151–155.

70. Schapera, *The Khoisan Peoples,* p. 152.

71. Radcliffe-Brown, *The Andaman Islanders,* p. 50.

72. Schapera, *The Khoisan Peoples,* p. 152.

73. See, for example, Evans, p. 21; Marshall, "!Kung Bushmen," p. 248; or Radcliffe-Brown, p. 29. For an exception, see Birket-Smith, pp. 145–146. For intermediate cases, see Honigmann, pp. 84, 88, and 96; Elkin, p. 45; and H. Ling Roth, *The Aborigines of Tasmania* (London: Kegan, Paul, Trench, Trubner, 1890), p. 71.

74. Sometimes certain trees become the private property of an individual who stakes a special claim to them, but this is uncommon and the number of trees involved is generally small. See, for example, Radcliffe-Brown, *The Andaman Islanders,* p. 41, or Goldschmidt, p. 333.

75. See, for example, McCarthy and McArthur, "Aboriginal Economic Life," pp. 179–180; Schapera, *The Khoisan Peoples,* pp. 100–101; Radcliffe-Brown, *The Andaman Islanders,* p. 43; Hose and McDougall, p. 187; or Speck, p. 47.

76. Radcliffe-Brown, *The Andaman Islanders,* pp. 44–48.

77. See, for example, Goldschmidt, pp. 324–326.

78. Among the sample of hunting and gathering societies in Murdock's data set, 54 percent had provision for the hereditary transmission of the office, usually to a son of the previous headman.

79. William D. Davis, *Societal Complexity and the Sources of Primitive Man's Conception of the Supernatural* (unpublished Ph.D. dissertation, University of North Carolina, Chapel Hill, 1971), chap. 5. Davis reports such beliefs in all but one of the eleven hunting and gathering societies he studied. See also Service, *The Hunters,* pp. 68–70.

80. See Service, *The Hunters,* p. 70.

81. For descriptions of shamans and their practices, see Evans, chaps. 19–20; Coon, *The Hunting Peoples,* chap. 16; Honigmann, pp. 104–108; Schapera, *The Khoisan Peoples,* pp. 195–201; Radcliffe-Brown, *The Andaman Islanders,* pp. 175–179; Elkin, chap. 11; or Gayton, pp. 392–398.

82. See, for example, Dixon, p. 282.

83. Ibid., p. 272.

84. Jacob Baegert, S. J., *Account of the Aboriginal Inhabitants of the California Peninsula,* in Coon, *A Reader in General Anthropology,* p. 79. See also Radcliffe-Brown, *The Andaman Islanders,* p. 177.

85. Turnbull, *The Forest People,* p. 130.

86. See, for example, Elkin, chap. 7; Marshall, "!Kung Bushmen," pp. 264–267; Turnbull, "The Mbuti Pygmies," pp. 306–307; or Coon, *The Hunting Peoples,* chap. 14.

87. Herbert Barry III, Irving L. Child, and Margaret K. Bacon, "Relation of Child Training to Subsistence Economy," *American Anthropologist,* 61 (1959), p. 263. See also Michael R. Welch, *Subsistence Economy and Sociological Patterns: An Examination of Selected Aspects of Child-Training Processes in Preindustrial Societies* (unpublished Ph.D. dissertation, University of North Carolina, 1980).

88. Some of the best evidence of religious motivation comes from Australia (see Elkin, pp. 191–192, or 232–234). For an example of art employed as an instrument of sympathetic magic, see Evans, pp. 130ff.

89. Turnbull, "The Mbuti Pygmies," pp. 308–312, *The Forest People,* chap. 4, and *Wayward Servants,* pp. 259–267.

90. See, for example, Hose and McDougall, p. 192, and Speck, pp. 270ff.

91. Turnbull, *The Forest People,* p. 135.

92. This definition is based on Hoebel, *Anthropology,* p. 572, and Elkin, *The Australian Aborigines,* p. 25.

93. Examples are provided by the Punan of Borneo (Hose and McDougall, p. 183) or the Mbuti Pygmies of Africa (Turnbull, *Wayward Servants,* pp. 100–109).

94. Schapera, *The Khoisan Peoples,* p. 76. Quoted by permission of Routledge & Kegan Paul, Ltd.

95. See, for example, Goldschmidt, p. 324.

96. For similar comparisons, see Grahame Clark, *The Stone Age Hunters,* op. cit., and Pfeiffer, op. cit.

97. See, for example, Clark and Piggott, *Prehistoric Societies,* pp. 130ff; or Hole and Heizer, *Introduction to Prehistoric Archeology,,* pp. 225–226.

98. Orlando Lizama, "Death of Woman Marked Tribe's End: First Seen by Magellan," *Washington Post,* Aug. 17, 1975. p. F3.

99. Marshall, p. 273.

100. Kolata, p. 932.

Chapter 6

1. Jack Harlan, "The Plants and Animals That Nourish Man," *Scientific American,* 235 (September 1976), pp. 89–97; Jack Harlan, *Crops and Man* (Madison, Wis.: American Society of Agronomy, 1975); or Stuart Streuver (ed.), *Prehistoric Agriculture* (Garden City, N.Y.: Natural History Press, 1971), parts II and IV.

2. Mark Cohen, *The Food Crisis in Prehistory* (New Haven: Yale University Press, 1977).

3. Marvin Harris, *Cannibals and Kings: The Origins of Cultures* (New York: Vintage Books, Inc., 1978), p. 31.

4. Ibid., p. 30.

5. Lawrence Guy Straus et al., "Ice-Age Subsistence in Northern Spain," *Scientific American,* 242 (June 1980), pp. 142–152.

6. See, for example, R. F. Watters, "The Nature of Shifting Cultivation," *Pacific Viewpoint,* 1 (1960), pp. 59–99, or B. H. Farmer, "Agriculture: Comparative Technology," in *International Encyclopedia of the Social Sciences,* vol. 1, pp. 202–208.

7. See, for example, Robert Braidwood and Bruce Howe, "Southwestern Asia beyond the Lands of the Mediterranean Littoral," in Robert Braidwood and Gordon Willey (eds.), *Courses toward Urban Life: Archeological Considerations of Some Cultural Alternatives* (Chicago: Aldine, 1962), pp. 137, 152–153, and 346; James Mellaart, *Earliest Civilizations of the Near East* (London: Thames and Hudson, 1965), pp. 12, 32–38, 47–50, and 81; or Barbara Bender, *Farming in Prehistory* (London: John Baker, 1975), chap. 6.

8. For a good description of the radiocarbon technique, see Frank Hole and Robert Heizer, *An Introduction to Prehistoric Archeology* (New York: Holt, 1965), pp. 145–150.

9. Braidwood and Howe, p. 140; Mellaart, chaps. 3ff.; V. Gordon Childe, "The New Stone Age," in Harry Shapiro (ed.), *Man, Culture, and Society* (New York: Oxford Galaxy, 1960), p. 103; E. Cecil Curwen and Gudmund Hatt, *Plough and Pasture: The Early History of Farming* (New York: Collier Books, 1961), p. 33.

10. Jacquetta Hawkes, *Prehistory, UNESCO History of Mankind,* vol. 1, part 1 (New York: Mentor Books, 1965), pp. 442–452; Mellaart, p. 42; Childe, "The New Stone Age," p. 107.

11. Childe, "The New Stone Age," pp. 100–101.

12. See, for example, Farmer, pp. 204–205; or Curwen and Hatt, p. 68 and chap. 16.

13. V. Gordon Childe, *What Happened in History,* rev. ed. (Baltimore: Penguin, 1964), pp. 64–65.

14. Mellaart, pp. 50–51, or Jean Perrot, "Palestine-Syria-Cilicia," in Braidwood and Willey, pp. 156–157.

15. Hawkes, pp. 384–395; Childe, "The New Stone Age," pp. 104–105; or Perrot, pp. 154–155.

16. Hawkes, pp. 395–401; and Mellaart, pp. 40–42.
17. Mellaart, p. 47; and Bender, pp. 148–149.
18. Childe, "The New Stone Age," p. 105. Elsewhere Childe speaks of twenty-five to thirty-five households as "a not uncommon number" in central Europe and southern Russia. *See What Happened in History,* p. 66.
19. Mellaart, p. 36; or Hawkes, p. 310.
20. Mellaart, pp. 81–101.
21. See, for example, Childe, "The New Stone Age," p. 106, or *What Happened in History,* pp. 67–68. See also Braidwood and Howe, p. 138.
22. Mellaart, p. 36. See also p. 84 for his views on Catal Hüyük.
23. Childe, "The New Stone Age," p. 106.
24. Denise Schmandt-Bessert, "The Earliest Precursor of Writing," *Scientific American,* 238 (January, 1978), pp. 50–59.
25. Mellaart, pp. 43–44.
26. See Childe, *What Happened in History,* p. 67.
27. Childe, "The New Stone Age," p. 106, and *What Happened in History,* p. 67.
28. For a good review of these developments, see Hawkes, pp. 401–410 and 414–417; or V. Gordon Childe, *Man Makes Himself* (New York: Mentor, 1953), pp. 76–80.
29. Childe, "The New Stone Age," p. 107, or *What Happened in History,* p. 74.
30. Karl Heider, *The Dugum Dani: A Papuan Culture in the Highlands of West New Guinea* (New York: Wenner-Gren Foundation, 1970). See also the film "Dead Birds" based on the same society.
31. Childe, "The New Stone Age," p. 107.
32. For the ethnographic evidence, see Table 4.2, p. 87.
33. See Kwang-chih Chang, *The Archaeology of Ancient China* (New Haven, Conn.: Yale, 1963), pp. 130–131. See also Curwen and Hatt, pp. 16–18, on truths contained in ancient traditions.
34. The quotations in this paragraph are all from Chang. pp. 131–133, and are used by permission of the Yale University Press.
35. Mellaart, pp. 130–131, and V. Gordon Childe, *New Light on the Most Ancient East* (London: Routledge, 1952), pp. 118ff.
36. Childe, *New Light,* p. 115; and Hawkes, p. 425.
37. Childe, *New Light,* p. 115.
38. Mellaart, p. 130.
39. Colin Renfrew, *Before Civilization* (Cambridge: Cambridge University Press, 1979), p. 167.
40. R. J. Forbes, *Studies in Ancient Technology,* 2d ed. (Leiden, Netherlands: Brill, 1972), vol. 9, p. 30, or Leslie Aitchison, *A History of Metals* (London: MacDonald, 1960), vol. 1, p. 21.
41. Forbes, pp. 32–34; or Aitchison, p. 40.
42. Aitchison, ibid.; or Forbes, vol. 8, p. 26.
43. Childe, *Man Makes Himself,* p. 99.
44. V. Gordon Childe, *The Bronze Age,* (London: Cambridge, 1930), p. 11.
45. See, for example, Childe, *New Light,* p. 116. There is still some uncertainty about this point.
46. William Watson, *The Chinese Exhibition* (a guide to the exhibition of archaeological finds of the People's Republic, exhibited in Toronto, 1974), p. 14.
47. Some bronze seems to have been manufactured accidentally a few centuries earlier as a result of using copper derived from ores containing tin, but the deliberate and conscious alloying of metals did not begin until after 3000 B.C. See Forbes, vol. 9, pp. 151–152. Recent research by scholars at the University of Pennsylvania suggests that the invention of bronze may have occurred in Thailand prior to 3600 B.C., which would explain why bronze was an integral part of advanced horticultural societies in China, but not in the Middle East.
48. William Watson, *China: Before the Han Dynasty* (New York: Praeger, 1961), p. 57.
49. Te-k'un Cheng, *Archaeology in China: Shang China* (Cambridge, England: Heffer, 1960), pp. 206–207.

50. Shang kings, for example, mounted "many military expeditions with an army of between 3,000 and 5,000 men." Ibid., p. 210; and Cho-yun Hsu, *Ancient China in Transition* (Stanford, Calif.: Stanford, 1965), p. 67.
51. See note 46 above.
52. Cheng, pp. 200–206.
53. Ibid., pp. 200–215 and 248. For a more detailed picture of the system of stratification in the Chou era, see Hsu, op. cit. In reading this book one must keep in mind that the Chan Kuo period, the "period of the warring states," is included, and by then, north-central China seems to have reached the agrarian level of development.
54. Watson, *China: Before the Han Dynasty*, p. 141, and Chang, pp. 195ff.
55. Aitchison, p. 97.
56. Hsu, pp. 3–7 and chap. 4.
57. Chang, p. 150.
58. Watson, *China: Before the Han Dynasty*, p. 106. See also Hsu, pp. 15ff., on the interrelations between religion and politics in Chou China.
59. Chang, pp. 150 and 159.
60. Ibid., p. 171.
61. Jesse D. Jennings, "Origins," in Jesse D. Jennings (ed.), *Ancient Native Americans* (San Francisco: Freeman, 1978), pp. 1–41.
62. For a valuable survey of these developments, see Marvin Harris, *Culture, People, Nature*, 2d ed. (New York: Crowell, 1975), pp. 212–228; for an extended survey of the three most highly developed cultures of the New World, the Aztecs, Mayas, and Incas, see Victor von Hagen, *The Ancient Sun Kingdoms of the Americas* (Cleveland: World, 1961).
63. For an alternative view, see Stephen C. Jett, "Precolumbian Transoceanic Contact," in Jennings, pp. 593–650.
64. Marvin Harris, *The Rise of Anthropological Theory* (New York: Crowell, 1968), p. 4.
65. Harris, ibid., p. 4. Emphasis added.
66. A careful comparison of societies in the two eras suggests that modern simple horticulturalists may be a bit less advanced than their prehistoric predecessors. For example, more than a third of those in Murdock's sample did not make pottery and more than half did not engage in weaving, both common practices in simple horticultural societies of prehistoric times.
67. Only 10 percent of the hunting and gathering societies in Murdock's data set maintained fairly permanent settlements, and virtually all of these relied on either fishing or horticulture as a secondary source of subsistence. By contrast, 87 percent of the simple horticultural societies maintained such settlements.
68. A number of simple horticultural societies have built structures 50 or more feet long. See Gunnar Landtman, *The Kiwai Papuans of British New Guinea* (London: Macmillan, 1927), p. 5, or Gerhard Lenski, *Power and Privilege* (New York: McGraw-Hill, 1966), p. 121.
69. Lenski, pp. 124–125.
70. Ibid., p. 122.
71. See, for example, Steward and Faron's statement p. 300, with reference to villagers who occupied most of the northern half of South America, that "kinship was the basis of society throughout most of this area." Many similar statements could be cited.
72. See E. Adamson Hoebel, *Anthropology*, 3d ed. (New York: McGraw-Hill, 1966), pp. 374–376, for a good brief summary of these functions.
73. For similar findings based on Murdock's earlier sample of 565 societies, see David Aberle, "Matrilineal Descent in Cross-cultural Perspective," in David Schneider and Kathleen Gough (eds.), *Matrilineal Kinship* (Berkeley: University of California Press, 1961), table 17.4, p. 677.
74. Aberle reached a similar conclusion, p. 725. He states that "in general, matriliny is associated with horticulture, in the absence of major activities carried on and coordinated by males. . . ." See also Janet Saltzman Chafetz, *Sex and Advantage* (Totowa, N.J.: Rowman & Allenheld, 1984), pp. 42–43.
75. Multicommunity societies constitute only 2 percent of all pure hunting and gathering

societies (i.e., those in which fishing and horticulture are not important secondary sources of subsistence) but comprise 23 percent of all simple horticultural societies.

76. Lenski, pp. 119–120.

77. For an early statement of this process, see Lewis Henry Morgan, *Ancient Society* (Cambridge, Mass.: Belknap Press, 1965, first published 1877), pp. 109ff.

78. This dual role seems to have been quite common in South America. See Julian Steward and Louis Faron, *Native Peoples of South America* (New York: McGraw-Hill, 1959), p. 301, on the Indians of eastern Brazil and the Amazon Basin; or Julian Steward, "The Tribes of the Montaña and Bolivian East Andes," in Julian Steward (ed.), *Handbook of South American Indians,* Smithsonian Institution, Bureau of American Ethnology, Bulletin 143 (Washington, 1948), vol. III, p. 528. For a slightly different pattern in North America, see Irving Goldman, "The Zuni Indians of New Mexico," in Margaret Mead (ed.), *Cooperation and Competition among Primitive Peoples,* rev. ed. (Boston: Beacon Press, 1961), p. 313.

79. Robert Lowie, "Social and Political Organization," in Steward, *Handbook,* vol. V, p. 345. For examples of this, see Steward, *Handbook,* vol. III, pp. 85, 355, 419, and 478. See also Steward and Faron, p. 244.

80. See, for example, Alfred Métraux, *Native Tribes of Eastern Bolivia and Western Matto Grosso,* Smithsonian Institution, Bureau of American Ethnology, Bulletin 134 (Washington, 1942), p. 39, on the Araona; or Leopold Pospisil, "Kaupauku Papuan Political Structure," in F. Ray (ed.), *Systems of Political Control and Bureaucracy in Human Societies, Proceedings of the 1958 Meetings of the American Ethnological Society* (Seattle), p. 18.

81. For a more detailed discussion of these bases of status, see Lenski, pp. 126–131.

82. See Steward and Faron, pp. 302–303, on the former, and pp. 213–214, 243, and 248–249, on the latter.

83. Marvin Harris, *Cows, Pigs, Wars, and Witches: The Riddles of Culture* (New York: Random House, 1974), pp. 75–80.

84. William Divale, "Systemic Population Control in the Middle and Upper Paleolithic," *World Archaeology,* 4 (1972), fig. 9, p. 228.

85. Data provided by Leo Simmons, *The Role of the Aged in Primitive Society* (New Haven, Conn.: Yale, 1945), show that scalp taking or headhunting was a frequent practice in only one of five hunting and gathering societies but in thirteen of fourteen horticultural societies.

86. Alfred Métraux, "Warfare-Cannibalism-Trophies," in Steward, *Handbook,* vol. V, pp. 400–401. Quoted by permission of the Bureau of American Ethnology,

87. Sonia Cole, *The Prehistory of East Africa* (New York: Mentor, 1965), pp. 46 and 299–301.

88. Meyer Fortes, in Meyer Fortes and E. E. Pritchard (eds.), *African Political Systems* (London: Oxford, 1940) p. 5.

89. In one study of twenty-two African horticultural societies, a correlation of 0.67 (Kendall's tau) was found between level of political development and level of social inequality (see Lenski, p. 163). See also Basil Davidson with F. K. Buah, *A History of West Africa: To the Nineteenth Century* (Garden City, N.Y.: Doubleday Anchor, 1966), p. 174.

90. See Lucy Mair, *Primitive Government* (Baltimore: Penguin, 1962), especially chap. 4. The discussion that follows is based largely on her work. See also Lenski, chaps. 6 and 7; Morton Fried, *The Evolution of Political Society* (New York: Random House, 1967); and Elman Service, *Origins of the State and Civilizations: The Process of Cultural Evolution* (New York: Norton, 1975).

91. Estimated from the map in Davidson, p. 68.

92. I. Schapera, *Government and Politics in Tribal Societies* (London: Watts, 1956), p. 169. See also the Swazi proverb that "nobles are the chief's murderers."

93. See, for example, Davidson, chap. 14.

94. See, for example, George Peter Murdock, *Africa: Its Peoples and Their Culture History* (New York: McGraw-Hill, 1959), p. 37.

95. See, for example, P. C. Lloyd, "The Yoruba of Nigeria," in James Gibbs (ed.), *Peoples of Africa* (New York: Holt, 1965), pp. 554–556.

96. For an example of a multicommunity society, see P. R. T. Gurdon, *The Khasis* (London: Macmillan, 1914). This author reports that these people were divided into fifteen small states averaging 15,000 in population and controlling about 400 square miles apiece (pp. 1 and 66).

97. Lenski, pp. 160–162. See also Davidson, pp. 76–77.

98. See, for example, the writings of Count Joseph A. deGobineau or Houston Stewart Chamberlain.

99. See, for example, Charles Singer, "Epilogue: East and West," in Charles Singer (ed.), *A History of Technology* (Oxford: Clarendon Press, 1956), vol. II, pp. 754–772, or William H. McNeill, *The Rise of the West* (Chicago: University of Chicago Press, 1963), Parts I and II.

100. Robert W. Steel, "Africa: Natural Resources," in *Encyclopaedia Britannica,* vol. 1, p. 258; Philip L. Wagner, "Tropical Agriculture," ibid., vol. 22, p. 255; Andrew Kamark, "The Resources of Tropical Africa," *Daedalus,* III (Spring, 1982). p. 159; Andrew Kamark, *The Tropics and Economic Development* (Baltimore: Johns Hopkins Press, 1976); and Frederic Pryor, "The Invention of the Plow," *Comparative Studies in Society and History,* 27 (1985), pp. 727–743.

101. William H. McNeill, *Plagues and Peoples* (Garden City, N.Y.: Doubleday Anchor, 1976); Kamark, "Resources," pp. 159–160; and Matt Clark, "Blight of the Tropics," *Newsweek,* June 26, 1978, pp. 83–84.

Chapter 7

1. V. Gordon Childe, *What Happened in History* (Baltimore: Penguin, 1964), p. 77.

2. Ibid., chap. 4.

3. This paragraph and the one that follows are based on B. H. Farmer, "Agriculture: Comparative Technology," in *International Encyclopedia of the Social Sciences* (New York: Macmillan and Free Press, 1968), vol. 1, pp. 204–205.

4. See Gudmund Hatt, "Farming of Non-European Peoples," in E. Cecil Curwen and Gudmund Hatt, *Plough and Pasture: The Early History of Farming* (New York: Collier Books, 1961), pp. 217–218.

5. Childe, p. 89.

6. V. Gordon Childe, *Man Makes Himself* (New York: Mentor Books, 1951), p. 100.

7. Farmer, p. 205.

8. See Childe, *Man Makes Himself,* p. 100.

9. E. Cecil Curwen, "Prehistoric Farming of Europe and the Near East," in Curwen and Hatt, pp. 64–65; or C. W. Bishop, "The Origin and Early Diffusion of the Traction Plow," *Antiquity,* 10 (1936), p. 261.

10. Some scholars have argued that Egypt had no cities at this time. See, for example, John A. Wilson, "Civilization without Cities," in Carl Kraeling and Robert Adams (eds.), *City Invincible: A Symposium on Urbanization and Cultural Development in the Ancient Near East* (Chicago: University of Chicago Press, 1960), pp.124–136; or William McNeill, *The Rise of the West: A History of the Human Community* (New York: Mentor Books, 1963), pp. 87–88. Although there were surely differences between Egyptian and Mesopotamian cities, it seems to be semantic gamesmanship to deny the existence of cities in Egypt (see Kraeling and Adams, pp. 136–162). Especially telling was the comment of one Mesopotamian specialist, who noted that when the Assyrians came to Egypt, they spoke of "hundreds of cities" (Kraeling and Adams, p. 140). See also Tertius Chandler and Gerald Fox, *3000 Years of Urban Growth* (New York: Academic Press, 1974), p. 362.

11. Samuel Noah Kramer, *The Sumerians* (Chicago: University of Chicago Press, 1963), p. 123.

12. Childe, *Man Makes Himself,* pp. 143–144.

13. See, for example, Sir Leonard Woolley, *The Beginnings of Civilization,* UNESCO History of Mankind, vol. 1, part 2 (New York: Mentor Books, 1965), pp. 116, 119, 198, and 449ff.

14. Sir Leonard Woolley, *Prehistory* (New York: Harper & Row, 1963), vol. 1, part 2, p. 127.

15. Margaret Murray, *The Splendour That Was Egypt* (London: Sidgwick & Jackson, 1949), p. 174.

16. On Mesopotamia, see Woolley, *Beginnings,* p. 356; or A. Leo Oppenheim, *Ancient Mesopotamia: Portrait of a Dead Civilization* (Chicago: University of Chicago Press, 1964), pp. 84–85. On Egypt, see Ralph Turner, *The Great Cultural Traditions: The Foundations of Civilization* (New York: McGraw-Hill, 1941), vol. 1, p. 187; or George Steindorff and Keith Seele, *When Egypt Ruled the East,* rev. ed. (Chicago: Phoenix Books, 1963), p. 83.

17. Robert Adams, "Factors Influencing the Rise of Civilization in the Alluvium: Illustrated by Mesopotamia," in Kraeling and Adams, p. 33.

18. See, for example, Kramer, pp. 88–89; Woolley, p. 125; or Kingsley Davis, "The Origin and Growth of World Urbanism," *American Journal of Sociology,* 60 (1955), p. 431. See also Oppenheim, p. 140, who, though declining to estimate size, reports Nineveh to have been larger than Ur (generally thought to have been over 100,000) and Uruk nearly as large; or Mason Hammond, *The City in the Ancient World* (Cambridge, Mass.: Harvard, 1972).

19. Woolley, *Beginnings,* pp. 185ff; or Steindorf and Seele, pp. 89–90.

20. Woolley, ibid., p. 188. Later armies were even larger.

21. Turner, p. 312.

22. McNeill, p. 68; Turner, pp. 310–311; Steindorff and Seele, chap. 9; Pierre Montet, *Everyday Life in Egypt: In the Days of Rameses the Great,* trans. A. R. Maxwell-Hyslop and Margaret Drower (London: E. Arnold, 1958), chap. 10; Oppenheim, pp. 70ff., 230ff., and 276–277.

23. Oppenheim, p. 276. As one writer reports, "Sumerian bureaucracy has left us a staggering number of texts; we are unable to venture a guess as to how many tablets beyond the far more than 100,000 now in museums may be buried in southern Mesopotamia."

24. Childe, *Man Makes Himself,* pp. 148–149, or Childe, *What Happened in History,* p. 144.

25. See especially Kramer, p. 231, or Samuel Noah Kramer, *It Happened at Sumer* (Garden City, N.Y.: Doubleday, 1959), p. 3.

26. See Turner, p. 263, or Childe, *What Happened in History,* p. 118.

27. Childe, *What Happened in History,* pp. 118–119.

28. See Turner's excellent treatment of this topic, pp. 317–323.

29. Adolf Erman, *Life in Ancient Egypt,* trans. H. M. Tirard (London: Macmillan, 1894), p. 128.

30. Childe, *Man Makes Himself,* p. 180, quoted by permission of C. A. Watts & Co., Ltd. See also McNeill, p. 53, or Childe, *What Happened in History,* pp. 183ff.

31. *Man Makes Himself,* p. 181. Elsewhere, Childe adds a third innovation (or a fifth to the total list), the invention of glass in Egypt. See *What Happened in History,* p. 183.

32. See Childe, *Man Makes Himself,* chap. 9, for a classic discussion of this subject. The analysis that follows is heavily indebted to Childe's provocative discussion but varies in some details and emphasis.

33. See Childe, *What Happened in History,* p. 184.

34. For a classic statement of this principle, see Gaetano Mosca, *The Ruling Class,* translated by Hannah Kahn (New York: McGraw-Hill, 1939), p. 53.

35. For a good summary of the early history of iron, see Leslie Aitchison, *A History of Metals* (London: MacDonald, 1960), vol. 1, pp. 97–110. The discussion that follows is based largely on Aitchison.

36. Ibid., p. 113.

37. See, for example, Charles Singer's comparison of the level of technology in the ancient empires of Egypt and Mesopotamia prior to 1000 B.C. and later in Greece and Rome, in "Epilogue: East and West in Retrospect," in Charles Singer (ed.), *A History of Technology* (Oxford: Clarendon Press, 1956), vol. II, pp. 754–755.

38. Ibid., pp. 754–772.

39. This estimate was based on the known boundaries of these societies and on the fact that the Roman Empire, which was much larger and contained a much smaller percentage of uninhabitable land, had a maximum population of only about 70 million. See *The Cambridge Ancient History* (London: Cambridge, 1939), vol. XII, pp. 267–268. It is also noteworthy that in Roman times Egypt had a population of only 6 to 7 million. Even if allowance is made for the greater size of the Egyptian empire in the days of Egypt's independence, it is difficult to imagine a total population much in excess of 15 million. See Charles Issawi, *Egypt in Revolution: An Economic Analysis* (New York: Oxford, 1963), p. 20.

40. Chung-li Chang, *The Chinese Gentry: Studies on Their Role in Nineteenth-Century Chinese Society* (Seattle: University of Washington Press, 1955), p. 102.

41. On India, see Kingsley Davis, *The Population of India and Pakistan* (Princeton, N.J.: Princeton University Press, 1951), pp. 24–25; on Rome, see *The Cambridge Ancient History*, pp. 267–268; on Russia, see Blum, p. 278.

42. See, for example, Chandler and Fox, op. cit.

43. Warren Thompson and David Lewis, *Population Problems*, 5th ed. (New York: McGraw-Hill, 1965), p. 386; O. Andrew Collver, *Birth Rates in Latin America: New Estimates of Historical Trends and Fluctuations* (Berkeley, Calif.: Institute of International Studies, 1965), pp. 26–30; D. V. Glass and D. E. C. Eversley, *Population in History* (Chicago: Aldine, 1965), pp. 467, 532, 555, and 614. One of the lowest rates for an agrarian society prior to the twentieth century was for eighteenth-century Sweden, and it was nearly 36 per 1,000 (Glass and Eversley, p. 532).

44. See for example, Horace Miner, *St. Denis: A French-Canadian Parish* (Chicago: Phoenix Books, The University of Chicago Press, 1963), p. 65; Coulton, *The Medieval Village*, p. 322; Manning Nash, *The Golden Road to Modernity: Village Life in Contemporary Burma* (New York: Wiley, 1965), pp. 265–266.

45. See, for example, John Noss, *Man's Religions*, rev. ed. (New York: Macmillan, 1956), pp. 227, 304ff., and 420–421; and Miner, pp. 65–66.

46. Miner, p. 170.

47. Harrison Brown, *The Challenge of Man's Future* (New York: Viking Compass, 1956), p. 75.

48. H. Hollingsworth, "A Demographic Study of the British Ducal Families," in Glass and Eversley, tables 2 and 5, pp. 358 and 360.

49. Brown, p. 75.

50. Warren Thompson, *Population Problems*, 3d ed. (New York: McGraw-Hill, 1942), p. 73.

51. M. C. Buer, *Health, Wealth, and Population in the Early Days of the Industrial Revolution, 1760–1815* (London: Routledge, 1926), pp. 77–78. Quoted by permission of Routledge & Kegan Paul, Ltd.

52. D. E. C. Eversley, "Population, Economy, and Society," in Glass and Eversley, p. 52.

53. Robert S. Gottfried, *The Black Death* (New York: Free Press, 1983), p. xiii.

54. K. F. Helleiner, "The Vital Revolution Reconsidered," in Glass and Eversley, p. 79.

55. Turner, p. 911.

56. F. R. Cowell, *Cicero and the Roman Republic* (London: Penguin, 1956), p. 79. Quoted by permission of Penguin Books.

57. See, for example, Jerome Blum, *Lord and Peasant in Russia from the Ninth to the Nineteenth Century* (Princeton, N.J.: Princeton University Press, 1961), pp. 126 and 394–395, on Russia; or Ralph Linton, *The Tree of Culture* (New York: Vintage Books, 1959), p. 231, on China.

58. S. B. Clough and C. W. Cole, *Economic History of Europe* (Boston: Heath, 1941), p. 25.

59. Ibid. See also Blum, pp. 16 and 126.

60. Marc Bloch, *Feudal Society*, trans. L. A. Manyon (Chicago: University of Chicago Press, 1962), p. 192. See also Robert Heilbroner, *The Making of Economic Society* (Englewood Cliffs, N.J.: Prentice-Hall, 1962), p. 27; H. R. Trevor-Roper, ''The Gentry 1540–1640,'' *The Economic History Review Supplements*, no. 1 (n.d.).

61. Heilbroner, pp. 9–44.

62. A. H. M. Jones, *The Later Roman Empire 284–602: A Social, Economic and Administrative Survey* (Oxford: Blackwell, 1964), vol. 1, p. 465.

63. See page 193 below on peasant revolts. See also G. G. Coulton, *The Medieval Village* (London: Cambridge, 1926), chaps. 11 and 24–25.

64. Gerhard Lenski and Jean Lenski, *Human Societies*, 4th ed. (New York: McGraw-Hill, 1982), table 7.2, p. 190.

65. Blum, pp. 356–357.

66. Gideon Sjoberg, *The Preindustrial City* (New York: Free Press, 1960), p. 215.

67. See, for example, Chung-li Chang, *Income of the Chinese Gentry* (Seattle: University of Washington Press, 1962), pp. 37–51.

68. For a survey of these obligations, see Gerhard Lenski, *Power and Privilege* (New York: McGraw-Hill, 1966), pp. 267–270.

69. Ibid., p. 228.

70. See for example, Blum, p. 232, or W. H. Moreland, *The Agrarian System of Moslem India* (Allahabad, India: Central Book Depot, n.d.), p. 207.

71. George Sansom, *A History of Japan* (Stanford, Calif.: Stanford Press, 1963), vol. III, p. 29.

72. H. S. Bennett, *Life on the English Manor: A Study of Peasant Conditions,* 1150–1400 (London: Cambridge, 1960), pp. 232–236.

73. Robert Darnton, *The Great Cat Massacre and Other Episodes in French Cultural History* (New York: Basic Books, 1984), p. 24. Quoted by permission of the publisher.

74. Ibid., p. 29.

75. Robert K. Douglas, *Society in China* (London: Innes, 1894), p. 354.

76. Blum. pp. 424 and 428, on Russia; and Gunnar Myrdal, *An American Dilemma* (New York: McGraw-Hill, 1964), p. 931, on the American South.

77. See Coulton, pp. 80 and 464–469; Blum, pp. 426–427; G. M. Carstairs, ''A Village in Rajasthan,'' in M. N. Srnivas (ed.), *India's Villages* (Calcutta: West Bengal Government Press, 1955), pp. 37–38.

78. Bennett, p. 196; Coulton, pp. 190–191, 248–250, and 437–440.

79. G. G. Coulton, *Medieval Panorama* (New York: Meridan Books, 1955), p. 77, or Thompson, p. 708.

80. William Stubbs, *The Constitutional History of England* (Oxford: Clarendon Press, 1891), vol. 1, p. 454n.; Wolfram Eberhard, *A History of China*, 2d ed. (Berkeley: University of California Press, 1960), p. 32; and Yosoburo Takekoshi, *The Economic Aspects of the History of the Civilization of Japan* (New York: Macmillan, 1930), vol. 1, pp. 60–63.

81. See Boak, *A History of Rome*, p. 127, or Cowell, *Cicero and the Roman Republic*, p. 64. For an example of the application of Cato's principle in medieval Europe, see Bennett, p. 283.

82. See, for example, Bloch, p. 337; or George Homans, *English Villagers of the 13th Century* (Cambridge, Mass.: Harvard, 1942), p. 229.

83. See, for example, Morton Fried, *The Fabric of Chinese Society: Study of the Social Life of a Chinese County Seat* (New York: Praeger, 1953), pp. 104–105; Moreland, pp. 168 and 207; and Bennett, pp. 100–101, 112–113, and 131ff.

84. See, for example, the franklins in thirteenth-century England (Homans, pp. 248–250).

85. May McKisack, *The Fourteenth Century* (Oxford: Clarendon Press, 1959), pp. 331–340; Philip Lindsay and Reg Groves, *The Peasants' Revolt, 1381* (London: Hutchinson, n.d.), pp. 30, 34, and 63; Charles Langlois, ''History,'' in Arthur Tilley (ed.), *Medieval France* (London: Cambridge, 1922), pp. 150–151; and Paul Murray Kendall, *The Yorkist Age* (Garden City, N.Y.: Doubleday, 1962), pp. 171ff.

86. Sjoberg, p. 83; Lynn White, *Medieval Technology and Social Change* (Oxford: Claren-

don Press, 1962), p. 39; Henri Pirenne, *Economic and Social History of Medieval Europe* (New York: Harvest Books, n.d., first published 1933), p. 58; J. C. Russell, *British Medieval Population* (Albuquerque: University of New Mexico Press, 1948), p. 305; Blum, pp. 268 and 281.

87. See Sjoberg, pp. 108–116; or Samuel G. Stoney, *Plantations of the Carolina Low Country* (Charleston: Carolina Art Association, 1938), p. 36.

88. Kendall, p. 157.

89. Jerome Carcopino, *Daily Life in Ancient Rome* (New Haven: Yale University Press, 1940, p. 70.

90. See, for example, Sjoberg, pp. 183ff. For an interesting example of the persistence of this pattern into the latter part of nineteenth-century England, see W. Somerset Maugham, *Cakes and Ale* (New York: Pocket Books, 1944), p. 29.

91. On acquisition by marriage, see Elinor Barber, *The Bourgeoisie in 18th Century France* (Princeton, N.J.: Princeton University Press, 1955), p. 89, or Sansom, vol. III, pp. 128–129. On confiscation, see B. B. Misra, *The Indian Middle Classes* (London: Oxford, 1961), pp. 25–27; Takekoshi, vol. II, pp. 251ff.; Kendall, p. 181; or Sir James Ramsay, *A History of the Revenues of the Kings of England: 1066–1399* (Oxford: Clarendon Press, 1925), vol. I. p. 58.

92. Clough and Cole, p. 442.

93. John Lossing Buck, *Secretariat Paper, No. 1, Tenth Conference of the Institute of Pacific Relations* (Stratford on Avon, 1947), reprinted in Irwin T. Sanders et al., *Societies around the World* (New York: Dryden Press, 1953), p. 65.

94. Clough and Cole, p. 445.

95. See, for example, John Nef, *The Conquest of the Material World* (Chicago: University of Chicago Press, 1964), p. 69.

96. Cowell, p. 80. See also William Woodruff, *Impact of Western Man: A Study of Europe's Role in the World Economy* (New York: St. Martin's, 1966), p. 254.

97. Sylvia Thrupp, *The Merchant Class of Medieval London* (Ann Arbor: Ann Arbor Paperbacks, University of Michigan Press, 1962), p. 9.

98. See, for example, Nef. p. 78.

99. Sidney Gamble, *Peking: A Social Survey* (New York: Doran, 1921), pp. 183–185.

100. Thrupp, pp. 19, 30, etc.

101. Ibid., pp. 23 and 29–31; James Westfall Thompson, *Economic and Social History of Europe in the Later Middle Ages, 1300–1530* (New York: Century, 1931), p. 398.

102. Gamble, p. 283.

103. In Asia many were sold into prostitution by their parents. See Gamble, p. 253. Many more, in every part of the world, were ignorant country girls seeking work in the city who were trapped by hired procurers, while still others were driven into prostitution by unemployment and lack of funds. See M. Dorothy George, *London Life in the XVIIIth Century* (London: Kegan Paul, Trench, Trubner, 1925), pp. 112–113.

104. See, for example, Frederick Nussbaum, *A History of the Economic Institutions of Modern Europe* (New York: Crofts, 1933); Frank Aydelotte, *Elizabethan Rogues and Vagabonds* (Oxford: Clarendon Press, 1913), p. 4, or A. L. Beier, *Masterless Men: The Vagrancy Problem in England 1560–1640* (London: Methuen, 1985), chap. 2.

105. Lenski, pp. 197–198.

106. For the effect of war on the forms of government, see Herbert Spencer, *The Principles of Sociology* (New York: Appleton, 1897), vol. II, part 5, chap. 17; Pitirim Sorokin, *Social and Cultural Dynamics* (New York: Bedminster Press, 1962), vol. III, pp. 196–198; or Stanislaw Andrzejewski, *Military Organization and Society* (London: Routledge, 1954), pp. 92–95.

107. These figures were calculated from A. E. R. Boak, *A History of Roman Imperial Civilization* (Garden City, N.Y.: Doubleday Anchor, 1959), using Mattingly's list of emperors, pp. 351–355.

108. For figures on several other societies, see Lenski, p. 235.

109. Wolfram Eberhard, *Conquerors and Rulers: Social Forces in Medieval China* (Leiden, Netherlands: Brill, 1952), p. 52; and Blum, p. 558.

110. For an interesting popular account of the former, see Lindsay and Groves, op. cit.

111. Sorokin, vol. II, chap. 10, especially p. 352.

112. See, among others, Lenski, pp. 210–242 and 266–284, for more detailed documentation.

113. Douglas, p. 104.

114. See Max Weber, *The Theory of Social and Economic Organization,* trans. A. M. Henderson and Talcott Parsons (New York: Free Press, 1947), pp. 341–348; and Max Weber, *Wirtschaft und Gesellschaft,* 2d ed. (Tübingen: Mohr, 1925), vol. II, pp. 679–723.

115. Mattingly, p. 137. See also Turner, vol. II, p. 620, or Michael Rostovtzeff, *The Social and Economic History of the Roman Empire,* rev. ed. (Oxford: Clarendon Press, 1957), p. 54.

116. Hans Rosenberg, *Bureaucracy, Aristocracy, and Autocracy: The Prussian Experience 1660–1815* (Cambridge, Mass.: Harvard, 1958), pp. 5–6. Quoted by permission of Harvard University Press.

117. Chang, *The Income of the Chinese Gentry,* Summary Remarks, supplement 2, and chap. 1.

118. On the king's income, see Ramsay, vol. I, pp. 227 and 261. For the income of the nobility, see Sidney Painter, *Studies in the History of the English Feudal Barony* (Baltimore: Johns Hopkins, 1943), pp. 170–171. For the income of field hands, see Bennett, p. 121.

119. Lenski, pp. 219 and 228.

120. See, for example, Albert Lybyer, *The Government of the Ottoman Empire in the Time of Suleiman the Magnificent* (Cambridge, Mass.: Harvard, 1913); or Moreland, op. cit.

121. F. Pelsaert, *Jahangir's India,* trans. W. H. Moreland and P. Geyl and quoted by Misra, p. 47. Quoted by permission of W. Heffer & Sons, Ltd.

122. Lybyer, pp. 47–58, and 115–117.

123. See, for example, James Westfall Thompson's statement that "the medieval state was a loose agglomeration of territories with rights of property and sovereignty everywhere shading into one another," in *Economic and Social History of the Middle Ages* (New York: Appleton-Century-Crofts, 1928), p. 699. See also Bloch, especially chaps. 14–24; Blum, chap. 2; or Sidney Painter, *The Rise of the Feudal Monarchies* (Ithaca, N.Y.: Cornell, 1951), and *Studies in the History of the English Feudal Barony,* op. cit.

124. See Kenneth Scott Latourette, *A History of Christianity* (New York: Harper, 1953), pp. 15–16.

125. See Robert Bellah, "Religious Evolution," *American Sociological Review,* 29 (1964), pp. 367–368.

126. See, for example, Lenski, pp. 7–9. See also Kendall, pp. 232ff.

127. Lenski, pp. 257–258.

128. Ibid., pp. 262–266, gives a more detailed treatment of this aspect of religion.

129. J. W. Thompson, *Economic and Social History of the Middle Ages,* p. 684.

130. See, for example, Carlo Levi, *Christ Stopped at Eboli* (New York: Farrar, Straus, 1947), chaps. 11ff., for a good description of the role of magic in one agrarian community. On fatalism, see, for example, Edward Banfield, *The Moral Basis of a Backward Society* (New York: Free Press, 1967), pp. 36–37, 41, and 107ff.

131. Sjoberg, *The Preindustrial City,* pp. 146ff.

132. Ibid., p. 155.

133. Ibid., pp. 163ff.; Henry Orenstein, *Gaon: Conflict and Cohesion in an Indian Village* (Princeton, N.J.: Princeton University Press, 1965), pp. 53–57; Kendall, chaps. 11 and 12; L. F. Salzman, *English Life in the Middle Ages* (London: Oxford University Press, 1927), pp. 254–256.

134. Bennett, p. 260. For other descriptions of the uses of leisure in agrarian societies, see Margaret Wade Labarge, *A Baronial Household of the Thirteenth Century* (New York: Barnes & Noble, 1966), chap. 10; Bennett, chap. 10; or Coulton, *Medieval Panorama,* chaps. 8 and 44.

135. F. R. Cowell, *Everyday Life in Ancient Rome* (New York: Putnam, 1961), p. 173.

136. The data in this paragraph are drawn from Lenski, p. 212.

137. For further details on the expendables, see ibid., pp. 281–284.
138. See, for example, H. van Werveke, "The Rise of the Towns," in *The Cambridge Economic History of Europe* (London: Cambridge Press, 1963), vol. 3. pp. 34–37; L. Halphen, "Industry and Commerce," in Tilley, pp. 190–192; or Pirenne, *Economic and Social History of Medieval Europe,* pp. 187–206.
139. Amos H. Hawley, *Human Ecology* (New York: Ronald, 1950).
140. For important new analyses of the origins of ancient Israel, see Marvin Chaney, "Ancient Palestinian Peasant Movements and the Formation of Premonarchic Israel," in David Freedman and David Grof (eds.), *Palestine in Transition: The Emergence of Ancient Israel* (Sheffield: Almond Press, 1983), pp. 39–90, and Norman K. Gottwald, *The Tribes of Yahweh* (New York: Orbis, 1979).
141. See, for example, Richard Tomasson, *Iceland: The First New Society* (Minneapolis: University of Minnesota Press, 1980), chaps. 1 and 8; and Philip Longworth, *The Cossacks* (New York: Holt, Rinehart, 1970).
142. For the classic statement of the effect of frontier life, see Frederick Jackson Turner, *The Frontier in American History* (New York: Holt, 1920).
143. On the Incan empire, see Victor Von Hagen, *The Ancient Sun Kingdoms of the Americas* (Cleveland: World, 1961), p. 537; on Songhay, see Basil Davidson with F. K. Buah, *A History of West Africa* (Garden City, N.Y.: Doubleday Anchor, 1966).
144. Chung-li Chang, *The Chinese Gentry* (Seattle: University of Washington Press, 1955), p. 102; *The Cambridge Ancient History,* pp. 267–268; and Blum, p. 278.

Chapter 8

1. According to Murdock's data, the Manus of New Guinea come as close to full dependence on fishing as any people in the world. See *Ethnology,* vol. 6, no. 2 (April 1967), pp. 170–230. Yet, as Margaret Mead indicates in her report, these people also depend heavily for their subsistence on garden products that they obtain through trade from neighboring peoples and to a lesser degree on pigs that they raise or obtain through trade. See Margaret Mead, *Growing Up in New Guinea* (New York: Mentor Books, 1953, first published 1930), especially pp. 173–174.
2. For an earlier discussion of this point, see Gordon Hewes's excellent paper, "The Rubric 'Fishing and Fisheries,' " *American Anthropologist,* 50 (1948), pp. 241–242.
3. See Gerhard Lenski and Jean Lenski, *Human Societies,* 4th ed. (New York: McGraw-Hill, 1982), Table 4.2, p. 91.
4. For a good illustration of this, see Philip Drucker's excellent description of the Indians of the Pacific Northwest, in *Cultures of the North Pacific Coast* (San Francisco: Chandler, 1965).
5. The averages are hunting and gathering, 40; fishing, 60; simple horticultural, 95.
6. The percentages are hunting and gathering, 10; fishing, 23; simple horticultural, 21.
7. The percentages for permanent settlements are hunting and gathering, 10; fishing, 49; simple horticultural, 87.
8. See Hewes, pp. 240–241.
9. For an interesting account of one such group, see Wilmond Menard, "The Sea Gypsies of China," *Natural History,* 64 (January 1965), pp. 13–21.
10. See, for example, Lawrence Krader, "Pastoralism," in *International Encyclopedia of the Social Sciences* (New York: Macmillan and Free Press, 1968), vol. II, pp. 456–457; or Carleton Coon, "The Nomads," in Sydney Fisher (ed.), *Social Forces in the Middle East* (Ithaca, N.Y.: Cornell, 1955), pp. 23–42.
11. John L. Myres, "Nomadism," *Journal of the Royal Anthropological Institute,* 71 (1941), p. 20.
12. Krader reports that the average density of population in Mongolia was less than 1 per square mile, and among the Tuareg of Africa it was even lower (op. cit., pp. 458–459).
13. The percentages of single-community societies were 90, 78, 77, and 13, respectively, in Murdock's data set.

14. Found in 62 percent of these societies as against 3 to 37 percent of the rest.
15. For example, class stratification, by Murdock's definition, is present in 51 percent of these societies.
16. This requirement is found in 93 percent of these societies, compared to 37 to 86 percent of other types.
17. This requirement occurs in 97 percent of herding societies, compared to only 49 to 79 percent of other types.
18. Among the rest, it is most common in advanced horticultural societies, but even there it occurs in only 16 percent of the cases; in other types, the frequency ranges from 2 to 10 percent.
19. See William McNeill, *The Rise of the West: A History of the Human Community* (New York: Mentor Books, 1965), pp. 126ff.; or Ralph Turner, *The Great Cultural Traditions* (New York: McGraw-Hill, 1941), p. 259.
20. For a good discussion of this important subject, see McNeill, pp. 256ff.
21. Ibid., p. 111.
22. Immanuel Wallerstein, *The Modern World-System* (New York: Academic Press, 1974), pp. 209ff.
23. On the less familiar Carthaginian empire, see Donald Harden, *The Phoenicians* (New York: Praeger, 1963), chaps. 5 and 6. The British empire, it might also be noted, was an *overseas* empire.
24. Compare, for example, the status of merchants and the rate of innovation for Europe during the sixteenth, seventeenth, and eighteenth centuries with the situation in India. Both were higher in Europe. Although this could have been coincidence, the evidence suggests a causal link.

Chapter 9

1. Charles Singer et al. (eds.), *A History of Technology* (Oxford: Clarendon Press, 1954–1956), vols. 1 and 2. See also Terry S. Reynolds, "Medieval Roots of the Industrial Revolution," *Scientific American*, 251 (July, 1984), pp. 123–130.
2. William H. McNeill, *The Rise of the West* (Chicago: University of Chicago Press, 1963), pp. 570–571.
3. S. B. Clough and C. W. Cole, *Economic History of Europe* (Boston: Heath, 1941), pp. 127–128.
4. Ibid.
5. R. H. Tawney, *Religion and the Rise of the West* (New York: Mentor Books, 1947), p. 117.
6. Immanuel Wallerstein, *The Modern World-System* (New York: Academic Press, 1974), especially chap. 2.
7. Tawney, p. 257.
8. Elizabeth Eisenstein, *The Printing Press as an Agent of Change* (Cambridge: Cambridge University Press, 1979), vols. I and II.
9. James M. Wells, "The History of Printing," *Encyclopaedia Britannica*, vol. 18, p. 541.
10. Wells, pp. 541–542; and N. F. Blake, *Caxton: England's First Publisher* (New York: Barnes & Noble, 1976), chap. 1.
11. Ann Stanford, "A Link with The Past," *Endeavors*, vol. 2, no. 2 (Spring 1985), p. 8; Michael Clapham, "Printing," in Singer, op. cit., vol. II, p. 27.
12. See, for example, Arthur G. Dickens, *Reformation and Society in 16th Century Europe* (New York: Harcourt, Brace, 1966).
13. See, especially, Max Weber, *The Protestant Ethic and the Spirit of Capitalism*, trans. Talcott Parsons (New York: Scribner, 1958), or Reinhard Bendix, *Max Weber: An Intellectual Portrait* (Garden City, N.Y.: Doubleday, 1960), chaps. 3–8.
14. Tawney, pp. 92–93.

15. Neil Smelser and S. M. Lipset (eds.), *Social Structure and Mobility in Economic Development* (Chicago: University of Chicago Press, 1967), pp. 29ff.
16. Clough and Cole, pp. 185–194.
17. Ibid., pp. 308–315.
18. See, for example, Robert Heilbroner, *The Making of Economic Society* (Englewood Cliffs, N.J.: Prentice-Hall, 1962), pp. 101–102.
19. See, for example, John Nef, *The Conquest of the Material World* (Chicago: University of Chicago Press, 1965), especially part 2.
20. Paul Mantoux, *The Industrial Revolution in the Eighteenth Century,* rev. ed. (London: Cape, 1961), pp. 243–244.
21. Reynolds, op. cit.
22. Mantoux, p. 312.
23. Earlier in the century, Thomas Savery and Thomas Newcomen invented the atmospheric engine, which laid the foundation for Watt's work. Its only practical use, however, was to pump water out of mines.
24. Phyllis Deane and W. A. Cole, *British Growth 1688–1959; Trends and Structure* (London: Cambridge, 1962), p. 212.
25. For 1788, see Clive Day, *Economic Development in Europe* (New York: Macmillan, 1942), p. 134; for 1840, see Deane and Cole, p. 225.
26. Deane and Cole, pp. 55 and 216.
27. W. S. Woytinsky and E. S. Woytinsky, *World Population and Production: Trends and Outlook* (New York: Twentieth Century Fund, 1953), p. 1147.
28. Ibid., tables 30 and 37.
29. U.S. Department of Commerce, Bureau of the Census, *Historical Statistics of the United States, Colonial Times to 1970,* series F238–239.
30. J. H. Clapham, *An Economic History of Modern Britain,* 2d ed. (London: Cambridge, 1930), vol. 1, pp. 391–392.
31. Clough and Cole, pp. 594–595.
32. Ibid., pp. 535–537.
33. Deane and Cole, p. 225.
34. Ibid., p. 216.
35. *Historical Statistics of the U.S.,* pp. 500–501.
36. Alfred D. Chandler, Jr., *The Visible Hand: The Managerial Revolution in America* (Cambridge, Mass.: Belknap Press, 1977), part II.
37. Ibid., p. 232.
38. Clough and Cole, p. 538.
39. Calculated from Woytinsky and Woytinsky, p. 1003.
40. Alfred D. Chandler, "Industrial Revolutions and Institutional Arrangements," *Bulletin of the American Academy of Arts and Sciences,* 33 (May, 1980), pp. 40–45.
41. This figure is an estimate based on Clough and Cole's report of French production in 1902 (p. 773) and Woytinsky and Woytinsky's report of American production in 1900 and 1902 (p. 1168). See also James M. Laux, *In First Gear: The French Automobile Industry to 1914* (Liverpool: Liverpool University Press, 1976), fig. 5.
42. Woytinsky and Woytinsky, pp. 1165–1166, including fig. 328.
43. Ibid., p. 1164.
44. Ibid., p. 966.
45. The 1900 figure is estimated from information provided by Woytinsky and Woytinsky, pp. 897–900; the 1940 figure is from fig. 257, p. 897.
46. J. Frederic Dewhurst and Associates, *America's Needs and Resources* (New York: Twentieth Century Fund, 1955), p. 317; and U.S. Department of Commerce, Bureau of the Census, *Statistical Abstract of the United States, 1963,* p. 516.
47. Woytinsky and Woytinsky, p. 1171.
48. *Statistical Abstract of the U.S., 1963,* p. 586, and *Statistical Abstract of the U.S., 1984,* p. 633.

49. The 1938 figure is from United Nations, *Statistical Yearbook, 1951,* p. 261; the 1979 figure is from *UN Statistical Yearbook, 1981,* table 154.

50. The figure for the late 1930s is based on Woytinsky and Woytinsky's statement about output in the United States and other countries in that period (p. 1201); the 1980 figure is from United Nations, *Statistical Yearbook, 1981,* table 151, but translated into short tons.

51. United Nations, *Statistical Yearbook, 1965,* p. 353.

52. U.S. Department of Commerce, Bureau of the Census, *Statistical Abstract of the U.S., 1985,* table 980.

53. *Wall Street Journal,* Feb. 12, 1985, p. 3.

54. Robert Cole, ''The Japanese Lesson in Quality,'' *Technology Review,* 83 (July, 1981), p. 30.

55. *Newsweek,* June 30, 1980, p. 55.

56. Figures for 1940 are from Woytinsky and Woytinsky, pp. 897, 966, and 1167; figures for 1980 are from *Statistical Abstract of the U.S., 1981,* p. 865.

57. *Historical Statistics of the U.S.,* series W-109; and *Statistical Abstract of the U.S., 1985,* table 990.

58. See the high percentage of all research and development expenditures coming from the U.S. Department of Defense, *Statistical Abstract of the U.S., 1985,* table 991.

59. W. Parker Frisbie and Clifford J. Clarke, ''Technology in Evolutionary and Ecological Perspective,'' *Social Forces,* 58 (1979), pp. 591–613.

60. J. L. Hammond and Barbara Hammond, *The Town Labourer: 1760–1830* (London: Guild Books, 1949, first published 1917), vol. 1, chap. 3.

61. Ibid., chaps. 2 and 6–9; or J. T. Ward (ed.), *The Factory System* (New York: Barnes & Noble, 1970), vols. I and II.

62. Hammond and Hammond, vol. I, pp. 32–33.

63. Compare and contrast the work of Hammond and Hammond, op. cit., or Eric Hobsbawm, ''The British Standard of Living, 1790–1850,'' *Economic History Review,* 2d series, 10 (1957), pp. 46–61, with Thomas Ashton, ''The Standard of Life of the Workers in England, 1790–1830,'' *Journal of Economic History,* 9 (1949), supplement, pp. 19–38.

Chapter 10

1. U.S. Department of Commerce, Bureau of the Census, *Historical Statistics of the United States: Colonial Times to 1970,* series D152–153; and U.S. Department of Commerce, Bureau of the Census, *Statistical Abstract of the United States, 1985,* table 673.

2. J. Frederic Dewhurst and associates, *America's Needs and Resources* (New York: Twentieth Century Fund, 1955), p. 1116; and *Statistical Abstract of the U.S., 1967,* table 752.

3. *Historical Statistics of the U.S.,* series S-1; and *Statistical Abstract of the U.S., 1985,* table 949.

4. The 1750 figure is from W. S. Woytinsky and E. S. Woytinsky, *World Population and Production: Trends and Outlooks* (New York: Twentieth Century Fund, 1953), p. 1100; the 1970 figure is from *United Nations, Statistical Yearbook, 1971,* tables 121 and 122, and is converted to short tons.

5. The 1820 figure is from Woytinsky and Woytinsky, p. 1101; the 1974 figure is from *The World Almanac, 1976,* p. 109.

6. Production figures are from the *Statistical Abstract of the U.S., 1984,* table 1268. Per capita calculations are our own.

7. *Historical Statistics of the U.S.,* series F-3; and *Statistical Abstract of the U.S., 1985,* table 715.

8. Phyllis Deane and W. A. Cole, *British Economic Growth, 1688–1959* (London: Cambridge Press, 1962), tables 79 and 90; *Statistical Abstract of the U.S., 1985,* table 1481.

9. Robert Heilbroner, *The Worldly Philosophers,* rev. ed. (New York: Time Books, 1961), chap. 3; and Jacob Viner, "Adam Smith," in *International Encyclopedia of the Social Sciences,* vol. 14, pp. 322–329.

10. Heilbroner, p. 47.

11. See, for example, Daniel Bell, "Socialism," in *International Encyclopedia of the Social Sciences,* vol. 14, pp. 506–532.

12. Maurice Duverger, *Political Parties: Their Organization and Activity in the Modern State,* trans. Barbara North and Robert North (London: Methuen, 1959), pp. 118–119. Quoted by permission of Methuen & Co., Ltd.

13. Hedrick Smith, *The Russians* (New York: Ballantine Books, 1984, rev. ed.), pp. 367–376. In Polish Party headquarters I have observed that Lenin's picture is displayed prominently in offices, but not Marx's.

14. Lewis Feuer (ed.), *Marx and Engels: Basic Writings on Politics and Philosophy* (Garden City, N.Y.: Doubleday, 1959), p. 127.

15. V. I. Lenin, *State and Revolution* (New York: International Publishers, 1932), p. 73. See also Basile Kerblay, *Modern Soviet Society,* trans. Rubert Swyer (New York: Pantheon, 1983), p. 242.

15a. See, for example, Andrzej Walicki's review of Alvin Gouldner's volume, *Against Fragmentation: The Origins of Marxism and the Society of Intellectuals, New York Review of Books,* 30 (Apr. 25, 1985), p. 43.

16. See, for example, Michael D. Kennedy, *Professionals and Power in Polish Society* (unpublished Ph.D. dissertation, University of North Carolina, 1985), chap. 3.

17. Hans Kohn, "Nationalism," *International Encyclopedia of the Social Sciences,* vol. II, pp. 63–70.

18. John H. Kautsky, *The Politics of Aristocratic Empires* (Chapel Hill, N.C.: University of North Carolina Press, 1982), part IV.

19. Robert Bellah, "Civil Religion in America," *Daedalus,* 96 (Winter), pp. 1–21. See also Will Herberg, *Protestant-Catholic-Jew* (Garden City, N.Y.: Doubleday, 1955).

20. Thomas McKeown, *The Modern Rise of Population* (New York, Academic Press, 1976), p. 2.

20a. Amity Shlaes, "West Germany Wants a Berlin Wall Against Third World," *Wall Street Journal,* Feb. 26, 1986, p. 25.

21. *The World Almanac, 1983,* p. 590.

22. *Statistical Abstract of the U.S., 1984,* table 1510.

23. Associated Press wire service story, August 7, 1972.

24. For statistical analysis of data from contemporary societies, see Erich Weede, "Beyond Misspecification in Sociological Analyses of Income Inequality," *American Sociological Review,* 45 (June 1980), pp. 497–501; for historical evidence, see Gerhard Lenski, *Power and Privilege* (New York: McGraw-Hill, 1966), chaps. 8–13.

25. *Forbes,* May 26, 1980, p. 137.

26. Dan Morgan, "New Farming Frontier," *The Washington Post,* Oct. 20, 1974, pp. A1 and A4.

27. *Wall Street Journal,* Aug. 17, 1976, p. 1, and Apr. 7, 1977, p. 1. Dollar values have been adjusted for inflation.

28. U.S. Bureau of the Census, *Historical Statistics of the U.S.: Colonial Times to 1970,* series D182-232, and *Statistical Abstract of the U.S., 1985,* table 676.

29. Ibid. A similar trend is reported in the Soviet Union. See T. Anthony Jones, "Work, Workers and Modernization in the USSR," *Research in the Sociology of Work,* 1 (1981), p. 251.

30. *Statistical Abstract of the U.S., 1985,* tables 547 and 557.

31. Ibid., tables 478 and 482.

32. U.S. Department of Labor, *Dictionary of Occupational Titles.* (Washington, D.C.: Government Printing Office, 1977).

33. *Newsweek,* Mar. 26, 1973, p. 79.

34. Pehr Gyllenhammar, "Volvo's Solution to Blue Collar Blues," *Business and Society* (Autumn 1973).

35. Timo Toivonen and Stanislaw Widerszpil, "Changes in Socio-Economic and Class Structure," in Erik Allardt and Wlodzimierz Wesolowski (eds.), *Social Structure and Social Change: Finland and Poland* (Warsaw: Polish Scientific Publishers, 1978), p. 113.

36. *Statistical Abstract of the U.S., 1985,* table 663.

37. S. B. Clough and C. W. Cole, *Economic History of Europe* (Boston: Heath, 1941), pp. 693–698.

38. G. D. H. Cole, *A Short History of the British Working Class Movement* (New York: Macmillan, 1927),vol. II, p. 202; and Carroll P. Daughterty, *Labor Problems in American Industry* (Boston: Houghton Mifflin, 1941), p. 405.

39. G. Warren Nutter, "Industrial Concentration," *International Encyclopedia of the Social Sciences* (New York: Macmillan and Free Press, 1968), vol. 7, p. 221.

40. Ben Bagdikian, "Why Newspapers Keep Dying," *Washington Post,* July 23, 1972, p. B-5.

41. John Kenneth Galbraith, *The New Industrial State* (New York: Signet, 1968), pp. 38–39.

42. Peter C. Dooley, "The Interlocking Directorates," *American Economic Review,* 59 (1969), pp. 314–323.

43. Paul Samuelson, *Economics,* 6th ed. (New York: McGraw-Hill, 1964), chaps. 8 and 9.

44. See also David R. Burton, "About That Fall in Business's Tax Share . . ." *Wall Street Journal,* May 2, 1985, p. 30. These figures include the employer's share of social security and federal unemployment taxes.

45. Our own computation based on data in *Historical Statistics of the U.S.: Colonial Times to 1970,* series F-1 and Y-533, and *Statistical Abstract of the U.S., 1984,* tables 449 and 735.

46. Clough and Cole, pp. 148ff., or Edward S. Mason, "Corporation," in *International Encyclopedia of the Social Sciences,* vol. 3, pp. 396–403.

47. Statistics based on data in *Statistical Abstract of the U.S., 1985,* table 869.

48. *Forbes,* May 12, 1980, pp. 214 and 236.

49. See Robert A. Gordon, *Business Leadership in the Large Corporation* (Berkeley: University of California Press, 1961); or Edward S. Mason (ed.), *The Corporation and Modern Society* (Cambridge: Harvard Press, 1959) on American corporations; and P. Sargant Florence, *Ownership, Control, and Success of Large Companies* (London: Street and Maxwell, 1961); or David Granick, *The European Executive* (Garden City, N.Y.: Doubleday Anchor, 1964) on European corporations.

50. David Lane, *Soviet Economy and Society* (New York: New York University Press, 1985), p. 5.

51. Ibid., pp. 169 and 54.

52. Jan Szczepanski, *Polish Society* (New York: Random House, 1970), p. 79.

53. Galbraith, chap. 9.

54. Smith, chap. 9, or Elrad Parkhomousky, "Can't Anybody Here Make Shoes?," *Izvestia,* reprinted in *World Press Review,* July, 1982, p. 36.

55. Smith, p. 317.

56. Ibid., chap. 9.

57. Robert J. Osborn, *Soviet Social Policies* (Homewood, Ill.: Dorsey, 1970), pp. 137–139; or Osborn, *The Evolution of Soviet Politics* (Homewood, Ill.: Dorsey, 1974), pp. 381–382.

58. Szczepanski, p. 125. Quoted by permission.

59. Jones, pp. 272–275, and Lane, pp. 40–42.

60. Lane, p. 5.

61. Joseph Alsop, "Matter of Fact," *Washington Post,* Jan. 13, 1964, op-ed page.

62. Alec Nove, *The Soviet Economic System* (London: Allen and Unwin, 1977), chap. 11.

63. Richard Easterlin, "Economic Growth," in *Encyclopedia of the Social Sciences,* vol. 4, p. 405.

64. Calculations based on United Nations, *Statistical Yearbook, 1965,* table 148, and *Statistical Abstract of the U.S., 1979,* table 1539.

65. Stephen Moore, "Sweden, In Ideological About-Face," *Wall Street Journal,* Mar. 20, 1984, p. 37.

1. W. L. Guttsman, *The British Political Elite* (London: Macgibbon & Kee, 1963), pp. 18 and 41.

2. A. Todd, *On Parliamentary Government* (London: Longmans, 1887), p. 622, and W. L. Guttsman (ed.), *The English Ruling Class* (London: Weidenfeld and Nicolson, 1969), p. 154.

3. U.S. Department of Commerce, Bureau of the Census, *Historical Statistics of the U.S.: Colonial Times to 1970,* series Y-83.

4. U.S. Department of Commerce, Bureau of the Census, *Statistical Abstract of the U.S., 1985,* table 590.

5. Judith Ryder and Harold Silver, *Modern English Society* (London: Methuen, 1970), p. 74; Dankwort Rustow, *The Politics of Compromise: A Study of Parties and Cabinet Government in Sweden* (Princeton: Princeton University Press, 1955), pp. 84–85.

6. Rosa Luxembourg, *The Russian Revolution and Marxism or Leninism?* (Ann Arbor: University of Michigan Press, 1961), p. 62.

7. Ibid., p. 71.

8. Kenneth A. Bollen, "Political Democracy and the Timing of Development," *American Sociological Review,* 44 (August 1979), pp. 572–587.

9. Many recent studies have documented the relationship between high rates of literacy and education on the one hand and democratic government on the other. See, for example, Daniel Lerner, *The Passing of Traditional Society: Modernizing the Middle East* (New York: Free Press, 1958), especially pp. 63–64 and 86–89; or S. M. Lipset, *Political Man* (Garden City, N.Y.: Doubleday, 1960), pp. 53–58.

10. On the relationship between democracy and the development of the mass media, see Lerner, op. cit., and Lipset, pp. 51–52.

11. See, for example, Kurt Shell, *The Transformation of Austrian Socialism* (New York: University Publishers, 1962), especially chaps. 6 and 7; Rustow, chap. 8; Albert Parry, *The New Class Divided: Science and Technology vs. Communism* (New York: Macmillan, 1966), chap. 7; and John Reshetar, *The Soviet Polity* (New York: Dodd, Mead, 1971), pp. 218–225.

12. Ivo Feierabend and Rosalind Feierabend, "Aggressive Behaviors within Polities, 1948–1962: A Cross-National Study," *Journal of Conflict Resolution,* 10 (1966), table 3. Results of this study suggest that rates of political instability are greatest in societies making the transition from agrarian to industrial, though results were not statistically significant.

13. The figures shown in Table 11.3 are based on our own calculations, using the following sources: Robert Alford, *Party and Society* (Chicago: Rand McNally, 1963), pp. 136, 202–203, 234–235, and 274–275; Richard Rose (ed.), *Electoral Behavior: A Comparative Handbook* (New York: Free Press, 1974), pp. 147, 294, 334 and 398; Hannu Uusitalo, "Class Structure and Party Choice: A Scandinavian Comparison," Research Report No. 10 (1975), Research Group for Comparative Sociology, University of Helsinki, p. 21; Roy Pierce, *French Politics and Political Institutions* (New York: Harper & Row, 1968), table 10; Richard Rose, "Class and Party Divisions: Britain as a Test Case," *Sociology,* 2 (1968), pp. 129–162; Erik Allardt and Yrjö Littunen (eds.), *Cleavages, Ideologies and Party Systems: Contributions to Comparative Political Sociology,* in a series entitled *Transactions of the Westermarck Society* (Helsinki: The Academic Bookstore, 1964), vol. 10, pp. 102 and 212; S. M. Lipset, *Political Man* (Garden City, N.Y.: Doubleday, 1960), pp. 225 and 227; *Gallup Political Index,* Report No. 17 (October 1966), p. 15 and inside back cover; S. M. Lipset, "Industrial Proletariat in Comparative Perspective," in Jan Triska and C. Gati (eds.), *Blue Collar Workers in Eastern Europe* (London: Allen & Unwin, 1981), Figure 1.1; and Walter Korpi, *The Democratic Class Struggle* (London: Routledge & Kegan Paul, 1983), figure 5.3.

14. See, for example, Lipset, chaps. 2 and 4.

15. *Statistical Abstract of the U.S., 1985,* table 472; and *Historical Statistics of the United States: Colonial Times to 1970,* series Y308. Similar trends are reported in other countries. In France, for example, civil servants increased from 3.7 percent of the labor

force in 1866 to 16.7 percent in 1962. See Jacques Lecaillon, "Changes in the Distribution of Income in the French Economy," in Jean Marchal and Bernard Ducros (eds.), *The Distribution of National Income* (London: Macmillan, 1968), pp. 45 and 47.

16. *Statistical Abstract of the U.S., 1985,* table 472; and *Historical Statistics of the United States: Colonial Times to 1970,* series Y332.

17. Gallup poll published July 14, 1983.

18. See, for example, the statements of Lenin and Trotsky, quoted by David Lane, *The End of Inequality?: Stratification under State Socialism* (Baltimore: Penguin, 1971), p. 41; and Robert Osborn, *The Evolution of Soviet Politics* (Homewood, Ill.: Dorsey, 1974), p. 281.

19. *Encyclopaedia Britannica,* 23, pp. 716 and 800.

20. *Washington Post,* Nov. 9, 1976, p. 1.

21. See, for example, Harrison Brown, *The Challenge of Man's Future* (New York: Viking Press, 1954), pp. 222–228.

22. Michael Voslensky, *Nomenklatura: The Soviet Ruling Class,* trans. Eric Mossbacher (Garden City, N.Y.: Doubleday, 1984).

23. Ibid., p. 95.

24. Aleksander Smolar, "The Rich and the Powerful," in Abraham Brumberg (ed.), *Poland: Genesis of a Revolution* (New York: Random House, 1983), p. 43.

25. Voslensky, chap. 5, or Mervyn Matthews, *Privilege in the Soviet Union* (London: Allen & Unwin, 1978).

26. Daniel Singer, *The Road to Gdansk* (New York: Monthly Review, 1981), p. 212.

27. Ireneusz Bialecki and Michael Kennedy, "Power and the Logic of Distribution in Actually Existing Socialism: The Case of Poland," unpublished paper, Aug. 11, 1985, p. 24.

28. On American corporations, see, for example, A. A. Berle, Jr., and Gardner Means, *The Modern Corporation and Private Property* (New York: Macmillan, 1932). See also the sources cited in Note 49, chapter 10 above.

29. C. Wright Mills, *The Power Elite* (Fair Lawn, N.J.: Oxford University Press, 1956).

30. Ivan Szelenyi, *Urban Inequalities under State Socialism* (London: Oxford University Press, 1983).

31. Gerhard Lenski, "Income Stratification in the United States," *Research in Social Stratification and Mobility,* 3 (1984), table 1; and The World Bank, *World Development Report, 1982,* table 25.

32. Basile Kerblay, *Modern Soviet Society,* trans. Rupert Swyer (New York: Pantheon, 1983), p. 218.

33. Voslensky, chap. 5. See, also, Lenski, pp. 198–203, on the Polish-American comparison.

34. Greg J. Duncan et al., *Years of Poverty, Years of Plenty* (Ann Arbor: Institute for Social Research, University of Michigan, 1984), table 2.1.

35. Osborn, pp. 382ff.

36. Alex Inkeles, "Social Stratification and Mobility in the Soviet Union," *American Sociological Review,* 15 (1950), p. 476n. A recent sociological study of savings in a single unidentified region of the Soviet Union found that 3 percent of the accounts held more than 50 percent of the savings (London Observer news service, August 14, 1985).

37. *Statistical Abstract of the U.S., 1985,* table. 775.

38. One-third of the equity capital of the publicly owned companies in the United States is owned by employee pension funds. See Peter Drucker, "American Business's New Owners," *Wall Street Journal,* May 27, 1976.

39. Lenski, p. 202.

40. Personal communication by informed Eastern European social scientists.

41. On the reversal in Soviet society, see Kerblay, table 38; on the United States, see *Historical Statistics of the U.S.: Colonial Times to 1957* (1960), Series G169–190.

42. See, for example, Christopher Jencks et al., "The Wisconsin Model of Status Attainment," *Sociology of Education,* 56 (1983), pp. 3–19.

43. *Statistical Abstract of the U.S., 1985,* table 756. The figures cited assume a discount rate of 3 percent and a 2 percent average annual growth in productivity.

44. Ibid., table 746.
45. Members of minority groups usually adopt the dominant group's prestige evaluations for groups other than their own. Sometimes they even adopt its evaluation of their own group. See, for example, Emory Bogardus, *Social Distance* (Yellow Springs, Ohio: Antioch Press, 1959), pp. 26–29.
46. See, for example, Everett C. Hughes, *French Canada in Transition* (Chicago: University of Chicago Press, 1943), especially chap. 7. See also John Porter, *An Analysis of Social Class and Power in Canada* (Toronto: University of Toronto Press, 1965), *The Vertical Mosaic* chap. 3.
47. Calculated from Donald Matthews, *U.S. Senators and Their World* (Chapel Hill: University of North Carolina Press, 1960), fig. 1.
48. Our own calculations based on a listing in *Forbes*, June 8, 1981, pp. 114–116.
49. Calculated from Morris Janowitz, *The Professional Soldier* (New York: Free Press, 1960), p. 63.
50. David Lane, *State and Politics in the USSR* (New York: New York University Press, 1985), p. 165. On China, see *Newsweek*, July 15, 1985, p. 32.
51. New York Times News Service release, Sept. 2, 1979.
52. Janet Schwartz, "Women Under Socialism," *Social Forces,* 58 (1979), p. 83.
53. This is also true in the Soviet Union. See Kerblay, pp. 127–128.
54. *Historical Statistics of the U.S.: Colonial Times to 1970,* service 394 and 395, and *Statistical Abstract of the U.S., 1985,* table 755.
55. Hilary Land, "The Changing Place of Women in Europe," *Daedalus,* 108 (Spring 1979), p. 84.
56. *Statistical Abstract of the U.S., 1979,* table 772.
57. William J. Goode, *World Revolution and Family Patterns* (New York: Free Press, 1963), p. 55.
58. Gerhard Lenski, *Power and Privilege: A Theory of Social Stratification* (New York: McGraw-Hill, 1966), p. 412, and Akszentievics, p. 410.
59. Lenski, p. 228.
60. See ibid., pp. 313–318, for a more thorough discussion of this subject.
61. L. J. Zimmerman, *Poor Lands, Rich Lands: The Widening Gap* (New York: Random House, 1965), table 2.8, p. 38, and *World Development Report, 1982* Washington, D.C.: World Bank, 1982), table 3.2.

Chapter 12

1. U.S. Department of Commerce, Bureau of the Census, *Statistical Abstract of the U.S., 1985,* tables 31 and 71.
2. Urie Bronfenbrenner, "The Disturbing Changes in the American Family," *Search* (Fall 1976), pp. 11–14.
3. U.S. Department of Commerce, Bureau of the Census, *Historical Statistics of the United States: Colonial Times to 1970,* p. 53.
4. This is our own calculation based on 603 hunting and gathering, horticultural, fishing, and herding societies in Murdock's data set of 915 societies (see p. 86). We have omitted 104 hybrid societies, most of which were preagrarian. If these were included, the figure would rise to 15 percent.
5. *Statistical Abstract of the U.S., 1985,* table 80.
6. Calculations based on Warren Thompson and David Lewis, *Population Problems,* 5th ed. (New York: McGraw-Hill, 1965), p. 374; J. Bourgeois-Pichat, "The General Development of the Population of France Since the Eighteenth Century," in D. V. Glass and D. E. C. Eversley (eds.), *Population in History* (Chicago: Aldine, 1965), p. 498; and W. S. Woytinsky and E. S. Woytinsky, *World Population and Production: Trends and Outlooks* (New York: Twentieth Century Fund, 1953), p. 181.
7. Mary Jo Bane, *Here to Stay* (New York: Basic Books, 1976), table 2-2.
8. *Statistical Abstract of the U.S., 1985,* table 65.

9. Ibid.

10. In this section we have drawn heavily on suggestions provided by Joan Huber in two of her papers, "Toward a Socio-Technological Theory of the Women's Movement," *Social Problems,* 23 (1976), and "The Future of Parenthood: Implications of Declining Fertility," in Dana Hiller and Robin Sheets (eds.), *Women and Men* (Cincinnati: University of Cincinnati Press, 1976), pp. 333–351.

11. *Statistical Abstract of the U.S., 1985,* table 669.

12. Hilary Land, "The Changing Place of Women in Europe," *Daedalus,* 108 (Spring, 1979), p. 83.

13. Hedrick Smith, *The Russians* (New York: Ballantine, 1984), chap. 5.

14. Lisa Collins, "More Firms Giving Fathers Time Off . . ." *Wall Street Journal,* July 5, 1985, p. 9.

15. United Press International news release, June 1, 1980, and Robin Morgan, "The First Feminist Exiles from the U.S.S.R." *Ms.* (November, 1980), pp. 49–108.

16. Michael Getler, "Emancipation for E. German Women," *Washington Post,* Apr. 24, 1979, p. A-13.

17. Ibid.

18. Joann Lublin, "As Women's Roles Grow More Like Men's, So Do Their Problems," *Wall Street Journal,* Jan. 14, 1980, pp. 1 and 29.

19. Ibid.

20. *Historical Statistics of the U.S.: Colonial Times to 1970,* series H1004 and H1005; and *Statistical Abstract of the U.S., 1985,* table 292.

21. Calculation based on *Statistical Abstract of the U.S., 1985,* table 211.

22. See, for example, Randall Collins, "Functional and Conflict Theories of Educational Stratification," *American Sociological Review,* 36 (1971), pp. 1002–1019.

23. In 1981, there were 267,000 babies born to unmarried teenaged mothers in the United States (*Statistical Abstract of the U.S., 1985*), table 94. In addition, many more pregnancies were terminated by abortion.

24. *Statistical Abstract of the U.S., 1985,* table 65.

25. Lynn Langway and William Schmidt, "A Youthquake in Russia," *Newsweek,* July 7, 1980, p. 46. See, also, Smith, chap. 7.

26. Walter Connor, *Deviance in Soviet Society: Crime, Delinquency, and Alcoholism* (New York: Columbia, 1972), p. 153.

27. *Statistical Abstract of the U.S., 1985,* table 293.

28. See, for example, Richard Quinney, *The Social Reality of Crime* (Boston: Little, Brown, 1970).

29. Connor, pp. 93ff.

30. Ibid.

31. Bronfenbrenner, op. cit.

32. On Japan, see New York Times wire service story dated July 25, 1982; on the U.S., see UPI wire service story dated May 2, 1985.

33. Erik Barnouw, *A History of Broadcasting in the United States,* vol. 3, *The Image Empire: From 1950* (New York: Oxford University Press, 1970), p. 3.

34. Thomas E. Patterson, *The Mass Media Election: How Americans Choose Their President* (New York: Praeger, 1980).

34a. Personal observation.

35. David Halberstam, "The Media: The Powers That Be," public lecture, University of North Carolina at Chapel Hill, April 5, 1982.

36. See, for example, Walter Laqueur, *Terrorism* (Boston: Little, Brown, 1977), pp. 109ff.

37. Michael J. O'Neill, "A Newspaper Editor Looks at the Press," *Wall Street Journal,* May 6, 1982, editorial page, quoted by permission of the author and publisher. This article was adapted from a speech given to the American Society of Newspaper Editors, May 5, 1982.

38. Results of the Los Angeles Times poll were summarized by columnist James Kilpatrick on August 19, 1985; the national news media study results were reported by S. Robert Lichter and Stanley Rothman in "Media and Business Elites," *Public Opinion,* Oct./Nov., 1981, table 2.

39. *Historical Statistics of the U.S.: Colonial Times to 1970,* series H953, and *Statistical Abstract of the U.S., 1985,* table 275.

40. See, for example, David Phillips, "Natural Experiments in the Effects of Mass Media Violence on Fatal Aggression," *Advances in Experimental Social Psychology,* 19, forthcoming; L. Rowell Huesmann et al., "Intervening Variables in the TV Violence-Aggression Relation: Evidence from Two Countries," *Developmental Psychology,* 20 (1984), pp. 746–775; National Institute of Mental Health, *Television and Behavior* (Washington, D.C.: U.S. Government Printing Office, 1982), or newsletter of the National Coalition on Television Violence, *NCTV News.*

41. Robert Kalaski, "TV's Unreal World of Work," *American Federationist,* December, 1980.

42. Harry Waters, "Brave New Documentary," *Newsweek,* June 10, 1985, p. 71.

43. For a more detailed discussion of this subject, see Gerhard Lenski, "Marxist Experiments in Destratification: An Appraisal," *Social Forces,* 57 (1978), pp. 364–385.

44. Ireneusz Bialecki and Michael Kennedy, "Power and the Logic of Distribution in Actually Existing Socialism: The Case of Poland," unpublished paper, Aug. 11, 1985.

45. For an earlier prediction of this, see Gaetano Mosca, *The Ruling Class,* trans. Hannah Kahn (New York: McGraw-Hill, 1939), especially pp. 281ff.

Chapter 13

1. These figures are medians. The calculations are based on United Nations, *Yearbook of National Account Statistics, 1969,* table 3; and Food and Agriculture Organization of the United Nations, *Production Yearbook,* 1970, table 5. Here, as elsewhere in this chapter, we have ignored the new microstates such as Kuwait, Gabon, and Mauritania.

2. U.S. Department of Commerce, Bureau of the Census, *Statistical Abstract of the U.S., 1985,* table 1481.

3. Manfred Halpern, *The Politics of Social Change in the Middle East and North Africa* (Princeton, N.J.: Princeton, 1963), p. 80.

4. Ibid.

5. Bruce Russett et al., *World Handbook of Political and Social Indicators* (New Haven, Conn.: Yale, 1964), p. 277.

6. Gladwin Hill, "View of the World's Shantytowns Less Grim," *New York Times,* June 9, 1976, p. 4.

7. Olga Tellis, "India Proposes Sterilization," *Washington Post,* Mar. 31, 1976, p. A-1.

8. Barry Kramer, "The Politics of Birth Control," *Wall Street Journal,* May 8, 1978, editorial page. See also Stuart Auerbach, "Family Planning—India's New Orphan," *The Washington Post,* Aug. 7, 1980, p. A-26.

9. Jay Matthews, "China Pressures Couples to Have Only One Child," *The Washington Post,* Feb. 28, 1980, p. A-20.

10. Ibid. See also Chen Muhua, "Birth Planning in China," *Family Planning Perspectives,* 11 (Nov/Dec., 1979), pp. 348–354.

11. June Shaplen and Robert Shaplen, "Taking on the Tide," *New York Times Magazine,* Aug. 27, 1976, p. 62.

12. Alex Inkles and David Smith, *Becoming Modern: Change in Six Developing Countries* (Cambridge, Mass.: Harvard, 1974); or Alex Inkeles, "Making Men Modern," *American Journal of Sociology,* 75 (1969), pp. 208–225.

13. Ray Vicker, "Arab Industrialization Adds to the Problems of Western Producers," *Wall Street Journal,* July 9, 1980, p. 1.

14. United Nations, *Yearbook of International Trade Statistics, 1982,* vol. 1, Cuba, table 5; and Roger Lowenstein, "Sugar is Cuba's Triumph and Failure," *Wall Street Journal,* Aug. 3, 1984, p. 20.

14a. John F. Burns, "Let a Million Businesses Bloom, The Chinese Cry," *New York Times,* Oct. 3, 1985, p. A2.

14b. "Deng's Quiet Revolution," *Newsweek,* Apr. 30, 1984, pp. 40–55; Victor Fung, "China

Allows Rebirth of Some Private Corporations," *Wall Street Journal,* Aug. 10, 1984, p. 28; or Christopher Wren, "China's Cities to Get More Capitalism," *New York Times,* Oct. 14, 1984, p. 3.

15. See, for example, the unsigned editorial in Peking's *People Daily,* Dec. 7, 1984, p. 1.

16. See, for example, A. H. Hanson, *The Process of Planning: A Study of India's Five-Year Plans, 1950–1964* (London: Oxford University Press, 1966), part II, especially chap. 8; Peter Franck, "Economic Planners," in Sydney Fisher (ed.), *Social Forces in the Middle East* (Ithaca, N.Y.: Cornell, 1955), pp. 137–161; Louis Walinsky, *Economic Development in Burma, 1951–1960* (New York: Twentieth Century Fund, 1962), part V, especially chap. 29; or Lennox A. Mills, *Southeast Asia* (Minneapolis: University of Minnesota Press, 1964), chap. 11.

17. Paul Hollander, *Political Pilgrims: Travels of Western Intellectuals to the Soviet Union, China, and Cuba* (Oxford: Oxford University Press, 1981).

18. See note 15 above and Martin K. Whyte, "Destratification and Restratification in China," *Amsterdams Sociologisch Tijdschrift,* 5 (October 1978), pp. 242–243; Jay Mathews, "China Propagandizes in Favor of Material Incentives," *The Washington Post,* Dec. 30, 1977, p. A-13.

19. Elizabeth Becker, "Renewed Fighting Pushes Vietnam Deeper into Poverty," *The Washington Post,* Sept. 26, 1979, pp. A-1 and A-16.

20. U.S. Department of Commerce, Bureau of the Census, *Statistical Abstract of the United States, 1979,* p. 895; also personal communication from Cuban-American sociologist following return visit to Cuba.

21. World Bank, *World Development Report, 1982* (New York: Oxford University Press, 1982), table 19.

22. See, for example, Myron Weiner, *Party Building in a New Nation: The Indian National Congress* (Chicago: University of Chicago Press, 1967).

23. Neil Smelser and S. M. Lipset (eds.), *Social Structure and Mobility in Economic Development* (Chicago: Aldine, 1966), pp. 29ff. Statistics cited elsewhere in this paragraph are from the same source.

24. John Meyer et al., "National Economic Development, 1950–70," in John Meyer and Michael Hannan (eds.), *National Development and the World System* (Chicago: University of Chicago Press, 1979), chap. 6; or Russett et al., p. 277.

25. Smelser and Lipset, p. 37, and Jan Szczepanski, *Polish Society* (New York: Random House, 1970), table 15, p. 115.

26. Smelser and Lipset, p. 37. See also June Kronholz, "In Third-World India College Students Study Humanities, Not Skills," *Wall Street Journal,* May 7, 1982, pp. 1 and 15.

27. Halpern, p. 122.

28. Henry A. Landsberger (ed.), *Latin American Peasant Movements* (Ithaca, N.Y.: Cornell University Press, 1969).

29. For Latin America, see Robert E. Scott, "Political Elites and Political Modernization: The Crisis of Transition," in S. M. Lipset and Aldo Solari (eds.), *Elites in Latin America* (New York: Oxford University Press, 1967), p. 133.

30. See, for example, F. G. Bailey, *Tribe, Caste, and Nation* (Manchester, England: Manchester University Press, 1960), on the assimilation of hill tribes in India.

31. Gerhard Lenski and Patrick Nolan, "Trajectories of Development: A Test of Ecological-Evolutionary Theory," *Social Forces,* 63 (1984), table 1.

32. Ibid.

33. *Statistical Abstract of the U.S., 1985,* table 1481.

34. Lenski and Nolan, table 3.

35. See, for example, Es'kia Mphahlele, "Africa in Exile," *Daedalus,* III (Spring 1982), pp. 29–48; Jonathan Spivak, "In Nigeria, Payoffs are a Way of Life," *Wall Street Journal,* July 12, 1982, p. 23; Lee Lescaze and Steve Mufson, "Angry New Leaders in Africa Are Trying to Right Past Wrongs," ibid., July 18, 1985, pp. 1 and 15; David Ottaway, "Ghana's Prosperity Feeds Corruption," *The Washington Post,"* Jan. 29, 1978, p. A-27; or Leon Dash, "IMF Seeks to Aid Ruined Economy," *ibid.,* Jan. 1, 1980, p. A-1.

36. Lenski and Nolan, op. cit.

37. See, for example, Steve Mufson, "Little is Being Done to Control Explosive Growth of Africa's Population," *Wall Street Journal,* July 31, 1985, p. 22.

38. Lenski and Nolan, table 5.

39. Daniel Bell, "Socialism," *International Encyclopedia of the Social Sciences* (New York: Macmillan and Free Press, 1968), vol. 14, p. 529.

40. David Ottaway, "Tanzania Struggles in Vain to Meet the Needs of Its Poor," *Washington Post,* Feb. 3, 1979, p. A-10.

41. See, for example, Gwendolen Carter (ed.), *African One-Party States* (Ithaca, N.Y.: Cornell, 1962), pp. 371ff, and 461ff; Guy Hunter, *The New Societies of Africa* (New York: Oxford University Press, 1964), chap. 9, especially pp. 223ff.; International Bank for Reconstruction and Development, *The Economic Development of Uganda* (Baltimore: Johns Hopkins, 1962), pp. 23–24; or Ken Post, *The New States of West Africa* (Baltimore: Penguin, 1964), chap. 6.

42. Calculations based on *Statistical Abstract of the U.S., 1985,* table 1480.

43. Based on Inter-African Labour Institute, *The Human Factors of Productivity in Africa,* as summarized in William H. Lewis (ed.), *French-speaking Africa: The Search for Identity* (New York: Walker, 1965), p. 168. Many of these propositions were supported in papers presented to a subsequent conference on competing demands for labor in traditional African societies, cosponsored by the Joint Committee on African Studies of the Social Science Research Council, the American Council of Learned Societies, and the Agricultural Development Council. See William O. Jones, "Labor and Leisure in Traditional African Societies," *Social Science Research Council Items,* 22 (March 1968), pp. 1–6.

44. See, for example, J. L. Hammond and Barbara Hammond, *The Town Labourer, 1760–1832* (London: Guild Books, 1949, first published 1917), especially chap. 2.

45. On the latter, see, for example, J. A. K. Leslie's fascinating study, *A Survey of Dar es Salaam* (New York: Oxford University Press, 1963).

46. Hunter, p. 85.

47. Ibid., p. 94.

48. See, for example, June Kronholz, "In Africa Tribal Power Wanes, But Still Rivals Governments'," *Wall Street Journal,* June 15, 1981, pp. 1 and 14.

49. See Leslie, p. 32; or Merran Fraenkel, *Tribe and Class in Monrovia* (London: Oxford University Press, 1964), especially chap. 3.

50. Kronholz, p. 1.

51. Lucy Mair, *New Nations* (Chicago: University of Chicago Press, 1963), pp. 122ff.

52. David Lamb, "Africans Find Independence a Hard Road," *Los Angeles Times,* story reprinted in *Wall Street Journal,* Feb. 15, 1979, p. 15.

53. Ibid. See also Ray Vicker, "Arab Nations Growing More Cautious About Dispensing Aid to Third World," *Wall Street Journal,* Sept. 4, 1980, p. 30.

54. *World Development Report, 1982,* table 25.

55. John Paxton (ed.), *The Statesman's Yearbook, 1980–81* (New York: St. Martin's Press, 1980).

56. The figure for Dar es Salaam is from Leslie, p. 210, and that for Tanzania from Russett et al., tables 74 and 75.

57. Fraenkel, p. 154; and Russett et al., tables 74 and 75.

58. From *A Survey of Dar es Salaam,* p. 211, by J. A. K. Leslie, published by Oxford University Press, 1963. By permission of the Oxford University Press.

59. Ibid., pp. 210–211.

60. Fraenkel, pp. 158 and 162.

61. Hunter, p. 74, provides numerous examples.

62. Carter, pp. 433–434. Copyright 1962 by Cornell University. Used by permission of Cornell University Press.

63. See, for example, Vittorio Lanternari, *The Religions of the Oppressed: A Study of Modern Messianic Cults,* trans. Lisa Sergio (New York: Knopf, 1963), chap. 1; or Mair, pp. 171ff.

64. The same was true of Sekou Touré's Democratic Party in Guinea. See, for example, David Apter, *The Politics of Modernization* (Chicago: University of Chicago Press, 1965), p. 299, note 36.

65. L. A. Fallers (ed.), *The King's Men: Leadership and Status in Buganda on the Eve of Independence* (New York: Oxford University Press, 1964), p. 99.
66. Leslie, pp. 27–29.
67. Ibid., pp. 60–61; or Fraenkel, pp. 127ff.
68. See, for example, June Kronholz, "Kenyans Say Missionaries Who Tried to Stop Polygamy Caused Baby Boom," *Wall Street Journal,* Apr. 11, 1983, p. 24.
69. See, for example, Andre Gunder Frank, *Capitalism and Underdevelopment in Latin America* (New York: Monthly Review Press, 1969); Theotonio Dos Santos, "The Structure of Dependence," *American Economic Review* 60 (1970), pp. 231–236; or Celso Furtado, *Economic Development of Latin America* (Cambridge: Cambridge University Press, 1970).
70. Compare, for example, Frank, op. cit., with Johan Galtung, "A Structural Theory of Imperialism," *Journal of Peace Research,* 8 (1971), pp. 81–117.
71. See, for example, W. W. Rostow, *The Process of Economic Growth* (New York: Norton, 1962); Wilbert Moore and David Feldman, *Labor Commitment and Social Change in Developing Areas* (New York: Social Science Research Council, 1960); S. N. Eisenstadt, *Modernization* (Englewood Cliffs, N.J.: Prentice-Hall, 1966); Talcott Parsons, *The System of Modern Societies* (Englewood Cliffs, N.J.: Prentice-Hall, 1971); or Inkeles and Smith, op. cit.

Chapter 14

1. See, for example, Jacques Ellul, *The Technological Society,* trans. John Wilkinson (New York: Vintage Books, 1967).
2. George R. Scott, *The History of Capital Punishment* (London: Torchstream Books, 1950), pp. 39–40.
3. Dover Wilson, *The Essential Shakespeare,* as quoted by Ivor Brown, *Shakespeare* (New York: Time Books, 1962), p. 112.
4. See, for example, Colin Turnbull, *The Forest People* (New York: Simon and Schuster, 1961); John Garvan, *The Negritos of the Philippines* (Vienna: Ferdinand Berger, 1964); or Kenneth MacLeish, "The Tasadays: Stone Age Men of the Philippines," *National Geographic,* 142 (1972), pp. 218–249.
5. Friedrich Engels, *Herr Eugen Dühring's Revolution in Science (Anti-Dühring)* (New York: International Publishers, 1939, first published 1878), as quoted by D. G. Brennan in Foreign Policy Association (ed.), *Toward the Year 2018* (New York: Cowles, 1958), p. 2.
6. United States, Council on Environmental Quality and the Department of State, *The Global 2000 Report to the President* (Washington, D.C.: GPO, 1980), vol. 2, p. 190.
7. Ibid., pp. 192–193.
8. Ibid., pp. 259–262 and 355; see also Duncan Spencer, "Oceans' Pollution Prompting Weather Surprises," *Washington Star News Service,* Sept. 17, 1979, and Arlen J. Large, "Weather Report: More Heat," *Wall Street Journal,* Aug. 1, 1980, p. 12.
9. Elias P. Gyftopoulous, "Energy: Everybody's Business," *Forbes,* October 27, 1980, p. 86.
10. Ibid., p. 88.
11. *Newsweek,* Sept. 22, 1980, p. 90.
12. Harrison Brown, *The Challenge of Man's Future* (New York: Viking, 1954), p. 114.
13. Jean Mayer, "The Dimensions of Human Hunger," *Scientific American,* 235 (September 1976), pp. 46–47, and Nevin Scrimshaw, as quoted by Anthony Lewis, New York Times News Service, Oct. 2. 1973.
14. John Saar; "Japan Looks to Future of Fish Farms," *Washington Post,* June 1, 1977, p. A-18; and *The Global 2000 Report,* vol. 2, p. 112.
15. Nevin Scrimshaw and Lance Taylor, "Food," in *Scientific American,* 243 (September 1980), p. 85.

16. Doug McInnis, "How Technology Altered NCR and Dayton," *Washington Post,* Jan. 8, 1978, p. F-2.
17. Jessica Tuchman Mathews, "Factories Too Tiny to See," ibid., Jan. 23, 1980, p. A-23.
18. Associated Press, July 22, 1980.
19. Mathews, op. cit.
20. Thomas O'Toole, "In the Lab: Bugs to Grow Wheat, Eat Metal," *Washington Post,* June 18, 1980, p. A-1.
21. See, for example, the official paper of the Chinese Communist Party, *People's Daily,* Dec. 7, 1984; see also Amanda Bennett, "China's Leaders Reject Parts of Marxism," *Wall Street Journal,* Dec. 10, 1984, p. 31.
22. See, for example, Marlise Simons, "Cuba Reviving Market Forces to Lift Economy," ibid., May 29, 1980, p. A-15.
23. *The Global 2000 Report to the President,* vol. 2, p. 417.
24. Without some decline in the current rate of growth, human population will increase by 2 billion in just *21* years.
25. Spencer, op. cit.; Large, op. cit.
26. Spencer, op. cit.
27. *The Global 2000 Report to the President,* vol. 2, table 8-9.
28. Ibid., table 9-5.
29. Clifford P. Case, III, "Why Do We Refuse to Recycle?" *Washington Post,* Apr. 12. 1980, p. A-19.
30. Jay Mathews, "China Opts for Progress," ibid., Jan. 26, 1980, p. A-10, and "Chinese Metals Plant Is Fined $1.3 Million for Water Pollution," *Wall Street Journal,* Mar. 18, 1980, p. 13.
31. *ZPG Reporter,* 12 (Sept. 1980), p. 1.
32. Ibid. Italics added.
33. *The Global 2000 Report to the President,* vol. 2. table 6-12.
34. *ZPG Reporter,* 12 (Sept. 1980), p. 2.
35. Ibid.
36. Our own calculation based on the age distribution and life expectancy of the Mexican population, as reported in U.S. Department of Commerce, Bureau of the Census, *Statistical Abstract of the U.S., 1979,* tables 1585 and 1586, and population estimate and growth rate as reported in *Statistical Abstract of the U.S., 1985,* table 1475.
37. United Press International news release, Sept. 11, 1977.
38. Murray Marder, "A-War Estimate Held Too Low," *Washington Post,* Sept. 17, 1975, p. A-5.
39. Lee Lescaze, "Nuclear War Worse than People Imagine," ibid., Feb. 11, 1980, p. A-20.
40. Robert Heilbroner, *An Inquiry into the Human Prospect* (New York: Norton, 1974), p. 41.
41. Lescaze, op. cit.
42. Brown, p. 223.
43. Calculations based on *Statistical Abstract of the U.S., 1985,* table 1481.
44. Heilbroner, pp. 121–122.

Picture Credits

1.2 George Rodger/Magnum Photos, Inc.

1.3 Courtesy of Department of Library Services, American Museum of Natural History, Neg. #33052

1.4 Drawing by Edward Koren; copyright 1969, The New Yorker Magazine, Inc.

1.5 Photograph by Baron Hugo Van Lawick; copyright National Geographic Society.

2.1 Courtesy of Richard Lenski.

2.2 Courtesy of Department of Antiquities, Ashmolean Museum, Oxford.

2.3 Henri Cartier-Bresson/Magnum Photos, Inc.

2.4 United Nations.

3.1 John Nance, Magnum Photos, Inc.

3.2 Fundamental Photographs, New York.

3.5 Ed Fisher, by permission of the artist.

3.7 Courtesy of The Bettman Archive, Inc.

4.1 By permission of John Marshall, Peabody Museum, Harvard University.

4.2 United Nations.

5.1 The Spectator.

5.2 From Grahame Clark, *The Stone Age Hunters*; copyright 1967 by Thames and Hudson Ltd., London.

5.4 American Museum of Natural History.

5.5a From Hugo Obermaier, *Fossil Man in Spain*, plate XIV.

5.5b Copyright Prehistoric Division, Museum of Natural History, Vienna.

5.5c With permission from *Paleolithic Cave Art*, © Peter J. Ucko and Andrea Rojenfeld, 1967, Weidenfeld Publishers.

5.6 By permission of John Marshall, Peabody Museum, Harvard University.

5.7 National Anthropological Archive, Smithsonian Institution.

5.8 By permission of John Marshall, Peabody Museum, Harvard University.

5.9 By permission of John Marshall, Peabody Museum, Harvard University.

5.10 Neg. #38750, Courtesy of Department of Library Services, American Museum of Natural History.

5.12 Colonel Charles W. Furlong.

6.1 Neg. #326405, Courtesy of Department of Library Services, American Museum of Natural History.

6.2 Neg. #319379, Courtesy of Department of

Library Services, American Museum of Natural History.

6.3 Neg. #337036, Courtesy of Department of Library Services, American Museum of Natural History.

6.5 From W. Watson, *Early Civilization in China*; copyright 1970, Thames & Hudson, Ltd., London.

6.6 United Nations.

6.7 Courtesy of The University Museum, University of Pennsylvania, Philadelphia.

6.9 From *Yanamamö: The Fierce People* by Napoleon A. Chagnon. Copyright 1968 by Holt, Rinehart & Winston, Inc. Reprinted by permission of CBS College Publishing.

6.10 Neg. #333678, Courtesy of Department of Library Services, American Museum of Natural History.

6.11 United Nations.

6.12 Neg. #115758, Courtesy of Department of Library Services, American Museum of Natural History.

6.13 From Jacques Maquet, *Africanity, The Cultural Unity of Black Africa*; Oxford University Press, 1972, p. 112.

6.15 Courtesy of Stanford University Press, copyright 1946, 1947, 1956, and 1983, Reprinted from *The Ancient Maya*, 4/e by Sylvanus Griswold Morley and George W. Brainerd; revised by Robert J. Sharer.

7.1 Courtesy of The Metropolitan Museum of Art.

7.2 Evans, Three Lion Photos, Inc.

7.3 Courtesy of The Metropolitan Museum of Art.

7.4 Courtesy of The Metropolitan Museum of Art, Museum Excavations, 1919–1920; Rogers Fund, supplemented by contribution of Edward S. Harkness.

7.6 Courtesy of The Metropolitan Museum of Art, Museum Excavations, 1919–1920; Rogers Fund, supplemented by contribution of Edward S. Harkness.

7.7 United Nations.

7.9 Courtesy of Exxon Corporation.

7.10 Courtesy of Exxon Corporation.

7.12 United Nations.

7.13 From F. R. Crowell, *Everyday Life in Ancient Rome*, G. P. Putnam's Sons, copyright © 1961. By permission of B. T. Batsford, Ltd., London.

7.14 United Nations.

7.15 United Nations.

7.16 Courtesy of The Metropolitan Museum of Art, Bashford Dean Memorial Collection, Funds from various donors, 1929.

7.17 United Nations.

7.18 Lauros-Giraudon Photographie.

7.19 From F. R. Crowell, *Everyday Life in Ancient Rome*, G. P. Putnam's Sons, copyright © 1961. By permission of B. T. Batsford, Ltd., London.

8.1 United Nations.

8.2 Pietro F. Mele, Photo Researchers, Inc.

8.3 Courtesy of Monkmeyer Press Photo Service, Inc.

8.4 By permission of Institut Français d' Archéologie, Beirut, Lebanon.

8.5 Courtesy of The Metropolitan Museum of Art, Rogers Fund, 1906.

9.1 The Granger Collection.

9.2 From Fritz Rorig, *The Medieval Town*. Courtesy of The University of California Press.

9.4 The Smithsonian Institution, Photo No. 56012A

9.5 Courtesy of Historical Picture Service.

9.6 National Anthropological Archives, The Smithsonian Institution.

9.7 Courtesy of The Bettman Archive, Inc.

9.8 Cary Wolinsky/Stock, Boston.

9.9 Bob Adelman, Magnum Photos, Inc.

9.10 Courtesy of *The Times,* London.

9.11 The Edward L. Bafford Photography Collection, Albin O. Kuhn Library and Gallery, University of Maryland, Baltimore County.

10.1 Joe Munroe, Photo Researchers, Inc.

10.2 Rene Burri, Magnum Photos, Inc.

10.3 Courtesy of The Bettman Archive, Inc.

10.4 Courtesy of The New York Public Library—Astor, Lenox, and Tilden Foundations.

10.5 The Granger Collection.

10.7 German Information Center.

10.8 United Nations.

10.9 United Nations.

10.10 D. Kharachun, Tass from Sovfoto.

10.11 Cary Wolinsky/Stock, Boston.

10.12 Courtesy of the New York Public Library—Astor, Lenox, and Tilden Foundations.

10.13 E. Logvinov, Tass from Sovfoto.

11.1 Independence National Historical Park Collection.

11.2 Courtesy of The New York Public Library—

Author Index

473

474

476

478

SUBJECT INDEX

Page numbers in **boldface** indicate the most basic references. Cross references to a particular subject "under basic societal types" refer to Agrarian societies; Horticultural societies; Hunting and gathering societies; Industrial societies; Industrializing agrarian societies; Industrializing horticultural societies.

486

489

Property, private (*Cont.*):
  in Marxist-Leninist societies, 292ff., 297, 320, 358, 375
  offices as, 193–194, 199
  religious ownership of, 199
  women as, 156
  women's ownership of, 340
  (*See also* Capitalism; Elites, economic; Slaves and slavery; Wealth)
Proprietary theory of the state, 193–194, 298
Prostitution, 192, 330, 377
Protestant Reformation and Protestantism, 72, 205, 304, 380, 415, 422
  and democratic trend, 302–303
  and Industrial Revolution, 229–232

Quality of life (*see* Higher goals; Standards of living)

Races, 32–33
  theories regarding, 162–163
  (*See Also* Ethnic groups; Minorities)
Railroads, 191, 233–234, 237–238, 241
Rationality, 228, 230, 232, 356, 371, 414, 428
Reductionism, 50
Religion, 48–49, 58–59, 90
  animism, 120
  and art, 103–105, 122–123
  and cities, 183, 185, 189
  civil, 267
  and conflict, 308, 378
  cults, 347
  and economic surplus, 166–168
  and family size, 178
  and government, 197–199, 309
  and industrialization, 260ff.
  and Marxism-Leninism, 266, 381
  and politics, 302–303, 306, 316
  and population control, 178
  prehistoric, 101
  secular, **261ff.**
    (*See also* Communism; Marxism-Leninism)
  and societal type, 90
  and societal variation, 204–205
  trends in, 168, 197–198, 214–215, 260ff., 354
  tribal, 197
  universal faiths, 195–197, 207–208
    absence of, 393

Religion (*Cont.*):
  (*See also specific religions, for example:* Ancestor worship; Fertility cults; Hinduism; *religion under basic societal types*)
Reproduction, 10–12, 28, 53, 57, 76–77, 114, 211, 335ff., 346–347, 356, 420
  (*See also* Population, growth)
Republicanism and republican government, 193
  democratic, 261–262, 298–311
  oligarchical, 217–218, 261–262, 298–301
Resources:
  individual, 21–22
    (*See also* Brain; Genetic heritage of humans; Education)
  informational (*see* Education; Information, societal store of)
  natural, 39, 42, 74, 82, 97, 100, 124, 140, 211, 216, 228, 230, 248, 355, 364, 399, 408ff., 415–418, 424–426
  (*See also* Capital)
Retainers, 156–157, 160, 174, 188, 194, 202–203
Revolutionary socialism (*see* Marxism-Leninism)
Revolutions:
  peasant revolts, 185, 193, 203–204, 331
  political, 26, 158, 266, 290, 294, 303–303, 307, 331, 376–377, 379, 381, 414
  social, 135ff., 250ff.
  (*See also* Horticultural revolution; Industrial Revolution)
Ritual and festivals, 105, 115, 122, 150, 152–154, 160, 200, 254, 269, 388, 389
Roles, 29, **44–45,** 403
  (*See also specific roles, for example:* Merchants; Peasants; Shamans)
Roman society, 84, 149, 163, 178–179, 188–191, 193, 201, 208
Rulers (*see* Elites, political)
Russia (*see* U.S.S.R.)

Sanctions, 31, 41, 44, 400–401, 403
  (*See also* Social controls)
Sanitation:
  agrarian societies, 179–180, 270, 404
  industrializing societies, 363, 387, 397
  (*See also* Disease; Health)
Science, 3–4, 19, 38, 172, 220
  basic aim, 3, 78
  classification in, 78–80
  comparison, basis of, 3–4, 78
  different from technology, 247

496

497

500